Bargaining
with Baseball

Bargaining with Baseball

Labor Relations in an Age of Prosperous Turmoil

William B. Gould IV

McFarland & Company, Inc., Publishers

Jefferson, North Carolina, and London

LIBRARY OF CONGRESS CATALOGUING-IN-PUBLICATION DATA

Gould, William B.
Bargaining with baseball : labor relations in an age
of prosperous turmoil / William B. Gould IV.
p.   cm.
Includes bibliographical references and index.

ISBN 978-0-7864-6515-6
softcover : 50# alkaline paper ∞

1. Baseball — Economic aspects — United States.   2. Discrimination in sports —
United States — History.   3. Baseball players — Salaries, etc.— United States.
4. Free agents (Sports)— United States.   5. Professional sports contracts —
United States.   6. Professional sports — Law and legislation — United States.
7. Collective bargaining — Sports — United States.   I. Title.
GV880.G68   2011   796.357'64 — dc23   2011018158

BRITISH LIBRARY CATALOGUING DATA ARE AVAILABLE

Cover images © 2011 Shutterstock
Front cover design by David Landis (Shake It Loose Graphics)

Manufactured in the United States of America

*McFarland & Company, Inc., Publishers
Box 611, Jefferson, North Carolina 28640
www.mcfarlandpub.com*

Looking to the past, to the Station Field Gang —
the late Harry Bowie, Joe Asch, Richie Haunton, Bill Green,
and so many others who were part
of that scene long ago in the 1940s.
I developed my love for the game
playing with them on a daily basis.

Looking to the future, to Timothy Jr., Joey,
Alina, and William Benjamin VI —
baseball players and fans, all.

Table of Contents

"Van Lingle Mungo"
Words and music by Dave Frishberg

Heenie Majeski, Johnny Gee
Eddie Joost, Johnny Pesky, Thornton Lee
Danny Gardella
Van Lingle Mungo

Whitey Kurowski, Max Lanier
Eddie Waitkus and Johnny Vandermeer
Bob Estalella
Van Lingle Mungo

Augie Bergamo, Sigmund Jakucki
Big Johnny Mize and Barney McCosky
Hal Trosky

Augie Galan and Pinky May
Stan Hack and Frenchy Bordagaray
Phil Cavaretta, George McQuinn
Howie Pollett and Early Wynn
Art Passarella
Van Lingle Mungo

John Antonelli, Ferris Fain
Frankie Crosetti, Johnny Sain
Harry Brecheen and Lou Boudreau
Frankie Gustine and Claude Passeau
Eddie Basinski
Ernie Lombardi
Hughie Mulcahy
Van Lingle ... Van Lingle Mungo

Preface

I came into the world of baseball at what is now roughly the halfway mark of professional competition. My involvement began in 1946,[1] a little more than three-quarters of a century after the first openly professional team, the Cincinnati Red Stockings, appeared on the scene. Now, another 65 years have gone by since the days of sandlot baseball and my eternally passionate support of the Boston Red Sox in Long Branch, New Jersey.

Around 1948, in the midst of one of those well-heated pennant races down the stretch, John Brockriede (who later became an outstanding center with the Long Branch football team) threw me a fastball over the middle of the plate with which I somehow connected and tagged it over the creek in center field — the home-run boundary up against which outfielders were afraid to retreat for fear that they would fall in — onto Third Avenue. (In truth, I think that the distance was much shorter than the Memorial Day 2010 homer hit by one of my grandsons, Joey Gould, in Southern California.) I could scarcely believe what had happened as I hurriedly circled the bases, ever fearful that it was somehow all a mistake — Brockriede with his great velocity having supplied most of the power.

Then, a couple of years later at the age of 14, when I had hoped to play first base or second, I had my big chance. Subsequent to what seemed to be a solid batting practice session prior to a high school baseball scrimmage in my sophomore year, I had come to the plate and worked the count of three and two on a left-handed pitcher who had a sharp slider with some bite to it. He had caught the outside corner twice with pitches that I thought were off the plate outside — but the umpire had called them strikes, and I was convinced that the pitcher thought that I did not know the strike zone. On the next pitch, the "payoff pitch," as it is called, I thought that I would swing, expecting another pitch on that same outside corner in an area which had confounded me. But instead the pitch came in as a fastball almost entirely over my head, and I swung and missed wildly, looking very bad in the process. Coach John Hubley (who had seen me earlier in football) cut me from the team almost immediately and thus, except for shagging fly balls with my Stanford law students and my sons in the '70s and '80s, that was the end of my on-the-field baseball career.

But now my involvement with baseball and sports took on a different dimension. My former colleague at Wayne State Law School in Detroit, Professor Bob Berry, and I began to collaborate on and converse about the subject in the late '60s and '70s and to write scholarly articles on emerging baseball labor-management relations of the '80s. After each of us departed Detroit, we shuttled between San Francisco and Boston, producing a lengthy law review article[2] — a piece which was relied upon by some of the courts, particularly the Court of Appeals for the Eighth Circuit in the football cases[3] — and an article in the *New York Times*.[4] Ultimately a co-authored book on professional sports and labor was forthcoming.

1

Then in the late 1980s I began to teach a Sports Law seminar at Stanford Law School with the late Leonard Koppett, the renowned baseball journalist, and Alvin Attles, the former player, coach and general manager of the NBA's Golden State Warriors in Oakland.

With Leonard's encouragement and advice, I began to write newspaper articles for daily papers like the *Boston Globe*, *San Francisco Chronicle*, *San Jose Mercury News* and others in the late '80s and '90s. This work brought me firsthand contact with major league players and officials. The late Larry Whiteside, a *Boston Globe* writer whom I met in the Red Sox dugout in Anaheim in 1986, opened a lot of doors for me, with the Red Sox and elsewhere. A series of interviews was undertaken, principally with former players in the late 1980s, and the interviews continued throughout this past decade. I served as a baseball salary arbitrator and then embarked upon what was in retrospect my most important baseball experience — my service as chairman of the National Labor Relations Board (NLRB) in the '90s.

When I was first approached about the NLRB position in November and December of 1992, I had no idea that I would become deeply ensnarled in the labor law of the baseball world. But that happened soon, in less than a year after my arrival at the NLRB's Washington, D.C., headquarters. As chairman of the NLRB, I and the other board members were at the center of the storm — the mother of all strikes, in 1994-95. Ultimately, we decided, by a 3–2 vote, to petition then–Judge Sonia Sotomayor (President Clinton was later to promote her to the Court of Appeals for the Second Circuit, and President Obama named her to the United States Supreme Court in 2009) for an injunction. In ringing language, she endorsed our judgment that there was reasonable cause to believe that the owners had engaged in unfair labor practice conduct. Because she granted our injunction, the players returned to the field and the owners accepted them, and as I describe in Chapter 4,

Joey Gould, crossing home plate at age 8 on his first homer — and the first homer hit by his team, the Torrance Tarheels, Memorial Day, 2010 (courtesy the Diederich Family and Timothy Gould, Sr. Photograph editing by Jason Watson, Chief Technology Officer, Stanford Law School).

a comprehensive collective bargaining agreement was ultimately negotiated the following year. In the wake of both our injunction and the new contract, baseball labor and management have peaceably resolved their differences ever since. In some respects, this work in the baseball strike was an hour of trial in which the public could see that our labor law system, albeit flawed and imperfect, could under some circumstances work for labor and management.

Thus, my limited involvement in the game on the field, my reading of baseball newspaper articles and box scores and books, my subsequent academic work in the form of teaching and writing and my role as a government official appointed by President Clinton all contributed to this book about baseball on and off the field. In Chapter 1, "The State of the Game," I have attempted to outline an overview of the major issues and themes which permeate the book, against the backdrop of my passion for the game itself. Make no mistake about it: it is a love of the game, as well as for labor law and my abiding interest in the business of the game itself, which has prompted me to write this book.

The love of the game — shared by so many in this country and throughout the world — is set forth in Chapters 1 and 2. Chapter 2 describes my involvement as a child and how we played, read about and observed the game. But the backdrop that became ever so important for me in my professional life was the business of the game, which receives more detailed attention beginning in Chapter 3. This chapter opens with a discussion of baseball as a business and then considers the numerous baseball labor-management conflicts, which focused principally on the issue of free agency.

Chapter 4 is about the NLRB's involvement in the 1994-95 strike itself. Here I have emphasized the problems of NLRB governance and the response of the owners during the last of a series of disputes before the parties were able to peaceably resolve their differences at the bargaining table in 2002 and 2006.

Chapter 5 examines the business of the game as it has evolved during these past 16 years subsequent to the conclusion of the strike in 1995. It focuses upon finance and labor issues relating principally to player mobility and bargaining power.

In Chapter 6, I present the comments of many of the former players themselves, exploring how they have seen the game evolve in its business as labor has become more important. Here the principal focus is on the way in which the game has evolved in the post–World War II era, as experienced by players who were active between the 1940s and 1970s. The remaining chapters focus on some of the major challenges confronting baseball today. First, the scourge of drugs which has plagued baseball throughout much of these past 40 years, for the last two decades in the form of performance-enhancing drugs, is examined. In Chapter 8, I have addressed the problem of race manifested through the absence of blacks and other minorities in baseball's higher echelon of positions as well as on the field itself. The reasons for this are numerous, and in the case of the absence of black players from the field itself, complex.

Chapter 9 deals with one of the other problems and opportunities of our time, the globalization of baseball, as the sport becomes more international and players and even owners (see the experience of the Seattle Mariners) now cross national frontiers.

This book, like much of my work, attempts to bring together the law and the academically theoretical as well as demonstrate the practical impact of these factors on the lives of those who are deeply involved in the game. The conclusion attempts to sum much of this up and to speculate about the future of the game and what it all means for collective bargaining in 2011 and beyond as baseball renegotiates its collective bargaining agreement now and in the years to come.

The present work has been a long time in the making. I was able to develop my thinking through a series of lectures and presentations. One of the first was at the University of Iowa in April 1992, when I was invited to talk on this subject by two of my former students, Adrien Wing and Peter Blanck. Soon thereafter Dean Eric Schmertz of Hofstra Law School invited me to speak at a conference at that university commemorating the 100th anniversary of Babe Ruth's birth, and titled "Baseball and The 'Sultan of Swat.'" The following year another former student, Bob Percival, invited me as inaugural speaker to give the Annual Hughie Jennings Memorial Lecture at the University of Maryland Law School in April 1996. Subsequently I participated in a conference held at the Indiana University School of Law, Bloomington, Indiana, where I delivered a paper on baseball and globalization on February 25, 2000. That conference was titled "Baseball in the Global Era: Economic, Legal and Cultural Perspectives."

A few years later, I was honored to throw out the ceremonial first pitch at Fenway Park on April 15, 2006, when the Red Sox celebrated both Jackie Robinson and simultaneously honored my great-grandfather, William B. Gould. Shortly afterward, I was privileged to deliver another lecture in San Francisco on May 25 under the auspices of the Performing Arts/Theatre Interest Group. That speech was titled "The Drama of Baseball: Almost Off the Precipice a Decade Ago — Where Will It Go in 2007 and Beyond?" All of these speeches, lectures and presentations were important building blocks in assembling this book.

There are many individuals who have provided considerable help along the way. Stanford Law Library has been a particularly vital resource, with Erika Wayne at its nerve center, along with librarian Paul Lomio, as well as George Wilson and Alba Holgado. They have always responded to my many requests with alacrity and enthusiasm. The same is true of Kate Wilko, who has now departed for the United States Supreme Court Library. I am of the view that the Stanford Law Library is the best in the United States, and most probably in the world.

Robert J. Kheel of Willkie Farr & Gallagher LLP in New York city provided me with a substantial number of court documents and pleadings relating to the Mexican League litigation. Andrew Kramer of Jones, Day in Washington, D.C., provided me with memoranda and stimulated my thinking on the relationship between leagues and clubs.

Marty Lurie, Steve Treder, and David Koppett read earlier drafts of this book and I am grateful to them for their comments. In particular, Steve Treder's thorough fact-checking and spell-checking was invaluable.

Many students acting as research assistants were of critical importance. The ever-resourceful and extremely able William Adams (Stanford Law School 2004) was at the forefront. Others who provided particularly valuable service to me were David Zizmor (Golden Gate Law School 2007), as well as Mike Scanlon (Stanford Law School 2010), Zac Cox (Stanford Law School 2011) and Erik Christensen (Stanford Law School 2008). Messrs. Scanlon and Cox proposed and devised a number of important charts and graphs. I am also grateful to Daniel Muto (Stanford Law School 2009), Adriana Maestas (Stanford Law School 2005), Ashley Conrad Walter (Stanford Law School 2009), Ashlie Jensen Walter (Cornell Industrial and Labor Relations School, 2006), and Glen Truitt (Stanford Law School 2005). Down the stretch at the book's conclusion, Ben Roxborough (Stanford Law School 2010, LL.M.) provided valuable assistance as well.

I am particularly grateful to Stanford undergraduates like Alexandra Fox (Stanford University BA '09) and Carey Schwartz (Stanford University BA '12), who transcribed many of the interviews. Ms. Fox put in long hours on many of the interviews over a number of years. Suzanne Peterson and Shirley Cistrunk typed the manuscript, a very formidable assignment, and I am most grateful for their fine work. Patricia Adan assisted me on many tasks in connection with this and she and Linda Wilson helped me put the photographs together.

Similarly, the computer support people, particularly David Conand, Jeff Wilcox and Sandra Schuil, were cheerful and able in their willingness to help. Jason Watson and Joe Neto provided great help with the photographs. I am grateful to all of these able and extremely smart people who worked with me.

Of greatest importance, numerous people in baseball cooperated with me and with my work, and many of them participated in long interviews, in person and by telephone. There are so many of them that I have catalogued their names on a separate page.

I benefited from conversations with Larry Whiteside and Nick Cafardo of the *Boston Globe*, as well as Joe Castiglione, "Voice of the Red Sox." There are many others who were helpful as well, and the most prominent are Dick Bresciani, Debbie Matson, John Blake, Dave O'Brien, Pam Ganley, and Leah Tobin, all of the Red Sox. Bob Rose, who served both with the Giants and the Oakland A's during the period involved in writing this book, as well as Debbie Gallas of the A's and Maria Jacinto of the Giants, helped me with arrangements at their ballparks.

I also benefited from the participation of many in my Stanford Sports Law seminar. Larry Whiteside was one of them when he was a Knight Fellow at Stanford University in 1987. Gene Orza and David Prouty of the Major League Baseball Players Association; Chuck Armstrong, CEO of the Seattle Mariners; Jack Baer, general counsel of the San Francisco Giants; and Mike Port of Major League Baseball were helpful as well. Numerous discussions with Sparky Anderson of the Detroit Tigers, Walt Jocketty, now of the Cincinnati Reds, and Roy Eisenhardt when he was President of the Oakland A's, improved my understanding. I shall never forget the frequent after-the-game clubhouse discussions with Dusty Baker when he was the manager of the San Francisco Giants and the insightful comments that he provided to both Leonard Koppett and me during our many post-mortems after the reporters had departed.

I want to acknowledge the friendship and valuable perspectives that I have been able to obtain from Stanford baseball—particularly from discussions, interviews and contact with coach Mark Marquess, third base coach Dean Stotz and former pitching coach Tom Dunton—all of them great teachers as well as athletes and leaders. I also benefited from interviews and conversations with a trio who have cemented the Stanford–Red Sox connection—"Gentleman" Jim Lonborg, Dave McCarty and Jed Lowrie—and also another non–Red Sox Stanford alumnus, Bob Boone. Jim Beattie and Jim Kaat gave me two of my most detailed and comprehensive interviews and I am grateful to them for their patience.

Part of my Stanford baseball experience is bound up with Stanford baseball broadcasts that I was able to do in the late 1980s at the invitation of my former student, John Platz, Stanford Law School (1989). I am grateful to John for his invitation to be on the air during that period of time.

Finally, I wish to acknowledge permission to use portions of some of my previously published articles and books: "Globalization in Collective Bargaining, Baseball and Matsuzaka: Labor and Antitrust Law on the Diamond," 28 *Comparative Labor Law & Policy Journal* 283 (Winter 2007); "Labor Issues in Professional Sports: Reflections on Baseball, Labor and Antitrust Law Sports and the Law," 15 *Stanford Law and Policy Review* 61–98 (2004); "A Long Deep Drive to Collective Bargaining: Of Players, Owners, Brawls, and

Strikes," 31 *Case Western Law Review* 685–813 (1981); "Baseball and Globalization: The Game Played and Heard and Watched 'Round the World (With Apologies to Soccer and Bobby Thompson)," 8 *Indiana Journal of Global Legal Studies* 85 (2000); "The 1994–'95 Baseball Strike and National Labor Relations Board: To the Precipice and Back Again" 110 *West Virginia Law Review* 983 (2008) and in André Douglas Pond Cummings and Anne Marie Lofaso, editors, *Reversing Field: Examining Commercialization, Labor, Gender, and Race in 21st Century Sports Law*, West Virginia University Press, 2010; "Always Forever, a Red Sox Devotee," published in *Red Sox Nation*, June 1, 2008; *Labored Relations: Law, Politics and the NLRB—A Memoir*, Cambridge: MIT Press, 2000.

My 65 years of involvement in baseball in one form or another have given me a great opportunity to see enormous changes in the business of the game and the way the game itself is played, notwithstanding the fact that the rules governing what happens on the field are, in essence, the same as they were when I first learned the game in the 1940s.

Interviews Conducted by the Author with Players and Baseball Officials (1986–2010)

Alou, Felipe — September 1, 2004
Anderson, Sparky —1992
Armstrong, Chuck — September 10, 2004
Baker, Dusty — June 1, 2003
Bavasi, Bill — September 10, 2004
Baylor, Don — May 1986 and May 1, 2005
Beattie, Jim — August 25, 2004
Black, Bud — June 20, 2006
Blyleven, Bert — May 8, 2004
Boone, Bob — June 2002
Brown, Bobby — December 15, 1988
Burks, Ellis — March 1987 and September 8, 2004
Campanis, Al — May 1986
Cepero, Carlos — March 18, 2006
Chambliss, Chris — September 28, 2004
Coleman, Jerry — September 7, 2003
Cox, Bobby — April 2010
DiMaggio, Dom — 2005
Doby, Larry — June 1986
Doerr, Bobby — October 14, 2009
Evans, Darrell —1986
Evans, Dwight —1988 and 1989
Gorman, Lou — May 19, 1989
Gallego, Mike — August 9, 2009
Hale, De Marlo — June 3, 2009
Henderson, Dave — May 1, 2005
Hendricks, Elrod — *circa* July 1989
Hobson, Butch — June 13, 1992
Hooton, Burt — May 30, 2003
Hurdle, Clint — September 1, 2004
Jackson, Ron — September 10, 2004
Jones, Lynn — September 10–11, 2004

Kaat, Jim — September 25, 2004
Lachemann, Marcel — July 18, 2003
Lampe, Chris — August 10, 2004
LaRussa, Tony — October 9, 1988
Leyland, Jim — August 1, 2007
Lonborg, Jim — October 25 and November 3, 2009
Macha, Ken — June 29, 2005
Magowan, Peter —*circa* 2002
Marquess, Mark — December 7, 2004
McCarty, Dave — August 13, 2003
Melgretty, Ray — September 25, 2003
Miller, Jon — August 3, 2004
Mussina, Mike — June 1992
Nelson, Dave — April 23, 2005
Palmer, Jim — June 1992
Pesky, Johnny — September 2, 1988
Pinson, Vada —1987 and 1988
Port, Mike — December 24, 2009
Price, Jim — May 18, 2004
Remy, Jerry — September 8, 2004
Rigney, Bill — May 19, 1989
Robinson, Eddie —*circa* 2005
Santo, Ron — May 30, 2003
Silvera, Charlie — August 21, 2003
Scott, Dale — June 24, 2005
Stotz, Dean — December 8, 2009
Suppan, Jeff— 2003
Virgil, Ozzie —1987
Wagner, Charlie — March 23, 2004
Wakefield, Tim — June 4, 2003
Williams, Billy — May 30, 2003
Wilson, Earl — January 27, 1989

CHAPTER 1

The State of the Game

Opening Day 1975 at Fenway Park in Boston. More than even the autumn classic, the World Series itself, it is a day filled with anticipation and hope, whatever the year and circumstance. The bullpen gate swings open, and my father and I are on our feet as Luis Tiant, "El Maestro," the man of many deceptive deliveries, makes his majestic entrance. We join the capacity crowd's roar in appreciation of El Tiante's work done in the previous three seasons (57 victories *in toto*)—and again a few hours later, as he induces the great Hank Aaron to pop up with two men on and thus hold the Red Sox lead on this special day.

Filled with pageantry, grace, grit and drama, it is the quintessentially beautiful game. It is a beautiful game both to see and to play. Some call it God's game, in an attempt to sum up a contest which combines both the ballerina-like athleticism displayed so frequently in the field and that which is cerebral in its test of both strategy and intellectual complexity. Beyond the American League substitution of the designated hitter for the pitcher in the batting order, its basic rules have not changed for more than a century—the distances between the bases and pitcher's mound to home plate, as well as the number of innings and outs, are enduring and remain in perfect harmony.

There is nothing like the sound of the wooden bat striking the ball, the crack of the bat ... Red Sox left fielder Mike Greenwell lines a clothesline single to right field at the Texas Rangers' Port Arthur spring training facility in March 1993, and the ball carries authoritatively as it cuts through the humid Florida air. Nothing can be so authentic for the auditory sense.... And there is nothing which compares to the feel that the batter has as the ball hits that special sweet spot of the bat as the stitched horsehide takes off in a high blur of whiteness.

Though most frequently played at night now at the professional and college level, there is something very special about this game in a sun-drenched stadium afternoon, whether the ball is cracking in the catcher's mitt in a way which gives the outside observer a sense of the fastball's velocity (long before stadium speed gun announcement signs) the confusing mixture of the off speed with hard fastballs emanating from El Tiante or, alternately, the slow, tantalizing breaking pitches that lefty John Tudor served up in the Oakland Coliseum one lovely sun-filled afternoon in the early '80s before his departure to the St. Louis Cardinals.

Baseball, like other sports, is a team game, calling upon some batters to "sacrifice" themselves through the bunt so that a runner can advance and more easily score. Over the past half century the batter is given credit for a "sacrifice fly" when a runner from third may advance homeward after the ball is caught, even though, paradoxically, the batter may not have intended to give himself up for another with such a "sacrifice." And in contrast to the fast-paced up-and-down-the-court game of basketball, or football, which contains at least three or four games simultaneously within each game, baseball is relatively easy to observe.

The game's nuances make any observation a multi-layered one. The ball and strike count on a particular batter may determine the kind of pitch that is delivered, and that, along with the comparative strength of hitter and pitcher, will have a great deal to do with where the players position themselves in the field. The game's situation may dictate whether fielders look for a sacrifice bunt as opposed to anticipating that the batter will be swinging for a hit. So also will the fielders likely anticipate that a batter will try to hit the ball to the right side of the infield with a man on second base and less than two outs (the rules paradoxically provide for no sacrifice there, even though the batter intends to sacrifice himself). The configuration of the ballpark may influence a decision made by an outfielder to play deep or shallow. The hitter, like a knowledgeable fan, is always involved in a guessing game with the pitcher about the type of pitch which will be thrown and where it will go.

The seemingly transparent aspect of the game is that which puts great stress, however, upon individuality — particularly the individual confrontation between batter and pitcher, where competition of both ability and intelligence is raw and in the open. My recollections of the great Ted Williams when I first saw him in 1947 and '50 were those of a player who stood in left field shagging fly balls before the game's start and occasionally turning towards

the catcalls of the Yankee Stadium crowd, contemptuously spitting in the direction of the stands with his hands on his hips. It is hard to imagine a game which is more conducive to the John Wayne–type characteristics that Williams and others like him have displayed, rais-

Two-time triple crown winner Ted Williams of the Boston Red Sox, the last man to hit .400. In the author's estimation, he was baseball's greatest player during the past 65 years of the author's involvement with the game (courtesy Boston Red Sox).

ing the anticipation of the *High Noon* drama which is about to unfold. As he digs in at home plate amidst the cacophony of boos and cheers, a great cloud of dust ascends around the skinny "Splendid Splinter."

The game's beauty and drama make it difficult for some to see players as employees. Indeed, baseball's owners insisted that the players were not employees within the meaning of the National Labor Relations Act, the principal labor relations statute in the United States, which has been at the center of so many controversies between the players and owners since the 1960s. Hitting, running, the long run that is necessary to corral a long fly or line drive — these are all joyful experiences, the memories of which are enhanced with each passing year. But the relevant quasi-judicial administrative agency, the National Labor Relations Board, nonetheless concluded that players in all the major sports, as well as umpires, were employees affected by issues of compensation and working conditions at the dawn of a wide variety of sports-related labor disputes.

This was the first of many of legal interventions which established rights for players, made the business of the game more transparent for the public, and put both sides in the position of courting public opinion over issues that had been previously suppressed. These decisions ushered in a New World, where arbitrators, administrative agencies and courts were involved far more frequently than in the past. But the issues and problems were always there. As we shall see, they were in the forefront when our Station Field gang first took the field in 1946. Employees then and now addressed working conditions; notwithstanding compensation and club facilities available to players, the game is intrinsically difficult and physically punishing to play — particularly in an era of coast-to-coast jet travel with changing time zones. The extraordinarily talented St. Louis Cardinal center fielder Curt Flood threw underhanded from center field in the 1968 World Series rather than concede to injuries, a demonstration of perseverance not normally seen — particularly in an age of frequently swollen disabled lists when owners are sometimes cautious in the protection of their investments. And it was Flood, one of the early black American players when the informal quota system restricting blacks was particularly rampant, who spoke of himself as a slave, albeit a well-paid slave.[1]

Flood tried, but could not break down the barriers of the reserve clause, which held a player to one team for life at the team's own option, already at that time almost a century old. But his litigation against it, which culminated in a 1972 Supreme Court ruling against him, inspired others to file grievances protesting their status. James "Catfish" Hunter of the Oakland A's was one of the first to challenge owner control in the wake of the *Flood* decision, and out of that event came the guaranteed contract negotiated with the New York Yankees, ensuring payment even if the player was unable to play. In sharp contrast to football, the guaranteed contract became a baseball industry model — so much so that Red Sox lefty Hideki Okajima's 2010 non-guaranteed status attracted raised-eyebrow attention. Even more dramatic and against the contemporary grain was the attempt by the New York Mets to convert the contract of Francisco Rodriguez, one of the game's top closers, from a guaranteed to a non-guaranteed pact on the grounds that he had failed to maintain first-class condition by injuring his thumb in a fight with his girlfriend's father.[2]

The Hunter controversy resulted in his arbitral victory, leading to a sweeping arbitration award in 1975. In its wake came a series of strikes and lockouts as the owners attempted to recapture the player gains of the 1970s. But since that decade a number of collective bargaining agreements have preserved some form of free agency.

Though baseball's on-the-field rules remain constant and most runners (save the Seattle

Mariners' Ichiro) are out by one or two steps or more on every ground ball, the game has never been the same. New stadiums replaced the ugly concrete "cookie cutter" kind that were built in the '60s and '70s, beginning with the innovative and attractive 1992 Baltimore Orioles Park at Camden Yards. Rich and escalating television and cable contracts were negotiated. The Internet became a marketing force — and so did the licensing of baseball products and gear like caps and shirts, both in the United States and abroad. One can visit Turkey or Indonesia, for instance, as I did a few years ago, and see people of all ages wearing Yankee baseball caps,[3] even though the game is played there so infrequently as to be unknown to almost all who adopt such attire.

Baseball, though relatively tardy in comparison to National Basketball Association Commissioner David Stern's initiatives on behalf of basketball, has taken considerable advantage of the globalization phenomenon. The last few decades have seen a whole host of Latin American and Asian stars, and the game is spreading to and being advertised in other countries as well.

Meanwhile, the sense of the sublime has affected baseball in many ways. In 2007 superstar third baseman Alex Rodriguez, after socking 54 homers which kept his New York Yankees in the pennant race, opted out of his quarter-billion-dollar contract, prompting *The New Yorker* to characterize his *über* agent, Scott Boras, as "the extortionist."[4] One cannot begrudge baseball's millionaires in their attempt to become billionaires like the owners. Indeed, by the standards of other entertainers, or the obscene income provided to American CEOs present and past, such demands are quite modest and reasonable and, on balance, their performance more praiseworthy than the latter group.[5] Yet with no limit on salaries or an obligation on the part of the low-revenue teams to spend money on payroll, let alone any aspect of baseball itself, there is a sense of uncertainty and unease about where this process will go. As a dissatisfied Chicago Cubs fan said to me when I pointed out to him that Carlos Zambrano was tired because he had thrown more than 100 pitches in the midst of the sixth inning in a game in San Francisco: "He doesn't need to be tired. He's making zillions of dollars not to be tired!"

Perhaps equally unsettling to some is the way in which the game of baseball's appeal to the public has undercut the basic integrity of the system. Interleague competition long dreamed of by the players like Williams, who strode across the great stage of baseball history in the 1940s and '50s when there was none, affects the fairness of competition. This is so because all of the teams do not play the same teams and some teams must play in another team's park more frequently than they play them in their own facilities. And baseball, which is often thought to be the mirror image of a lifelong struggle with adversity by virtue of its lengthy schedule, including the exhausting "dog days" of August, has exacerbated the problem of championships won by chance through short series with the ever-more-profitable expanded postseason play. Integrity of competition — the watchword of any of any sport — is subordinated by these and other innovations as the award of the World Series' home field advantage depends upon whose league has prevailed in the summer All-Star game, uniformly regarded by the players as an exhibition contest! Because of this arbitrary rule, for instance, 2009 World Series MVP Hideki Matsui was able to be listed as the Yankee designated hitter in the fall classic more frequently than not because the Yankees could play more games in their park based on the American League triumph in the All-Star game.

And then there is the matter of race. Black Americans were excluded from the game altogether for almost half of the twentieth century, and subsequently were victimized by informal or *de facto* quotas in the age of Giants great Willie Mays and Yankee catcher Elston

Howard.[6] Today there is a sharp decline in the number of black American players on the field, a decline that is made particularly graphic when juxtaposed against the number of black athletes who play in other sports like football and basketball. Red Sox center fielder Coco Crisp, who made a spectacular over-the-head back-to-the plate Willie Mays–type basket catch one day in June '07 in the Oakland Coliseum when Curt Schilling had a no-hitter until the last batter (he had made two grabs like it earlier in that 4-game series), was the only black American player on the 2007 World Championship team.

Where are the black players in baseball at a time when 80 percent of the National Basketball Association is black and a growing number dominate the National Football League? Notwithstanding the increasing number of black Latino players, this is a perplexing and growing problem which baseball ignores at its peril in a multiracial society.

And finally there is the issue of performance-enhancing drugs with which superstar San Francisco Giant left fielder Barry Bonds, and later Yankee third baseman Alex Rodriguez and St. Louis Cardinal first baseman Mark McGwire, are most notoriously associated. It is Bonds who was dogged by not only his unconvincing Grand Jury testimony denials of drug taking but also the compelling evidence compiled by *San Francisco Chronicle* reporters in their landmark book *A Game of Shadows*, ultimately producing the above-mentioned indictment for perjury and obstruction of justice. The perjury indictment of fireballing and multi–Cy Young award winner Roger Clemens in 2010 is yet another baseball blemish.

One step in the process is the December 2007 Mitchell Report[7] authored by former Senator George Mitchell (D-Maine) without cooperation from virtually any players or the union, the Major League Baseball Players Association (MLBPA). Though baseball has long said that it has an impeccable state-of-the-art drug testing system in place, with each passing day its credibility sinks as the number of names involved in this scandal grows larger. Until Congress demonstrated an interest in the subject and its members preened before television cameras, the unity between players and owners in denying that a problem existed was completely intact. Baseball Commissioner Bud Selig then placed a distance between himself and the players union, and this resulted in the hammer of possible legislation, which led to a new mid-term agreement in 2006.[8] The television advertisements in which the Atlanta Braves pitchers complained enviously about the fact that the chicks loved the long ball became part of history.[9]

Some bemoan what *Sports Illustrated* called the "perfect storm of malfeasance" of the off-the-field activity, which has always been there and is just more commented on today. The same article stated that fans and taxpayers "watch their favorite players come and go through free agency and trades, and see their managers and their coaches get shuffled like playing cards. They cringe as the news crawl on their screen reports a heinous transgression committed by their son's hero whose replica jersey just lightened their wallet considerably. But they come back because the games matter to them and because sports fosters a sense of hope."[10]

Yet baseball was at the precipice of labor-management disaster until my National Labor Relations Board intervened in the mother of all labor disputes between the players and the owners in the 1990s, thus producing an era of peace through at least 2011. It is at the precipice again, though the problems are different from those of the '90s.

The game is the same and yet it is not the same. It is driven by substantial off-the-field developments, thus warranting asterisks and perhaps even record erasures due to the drug-enhancement scandal. Even prior to his indictment, the Hall of Fame had agreed to accept the ball which was hit as Bonds's 756th homer, breaking Hank Aaron's all-time home run record. The ball had an asterisk inscribed on it by the ball's donor.

It was and is the excessive and indeed hubris-fueled genuflections to commerce which created the drug problem. Other challenges to the integrity of the game pose substantial difficulties for the "national pastime" now.

*   *   *

The fundamental issues have not changed since the 1870s and the advent of professional baseball, first represented by the 1869 Cincinnati Red Stockings, the first team to be paid openly rather than under the table. But, again, in 1994 and '95, baseball was truly at the precipice, gazing into an abyss filled with both uncertainty and potential disaster. Nineteen ninety-four witnessed the first cancellation of the World Series since the 1904 New York Giants' refusal to play a second "champion of champions" series against the repeating American League Boston Pilgrims (known in the modern era as the Boston Red Sox). Just as there was money to be made by both players and owners in the fall of '94 which was forever lost to both sides, so also all could have profited in 1904 if only the games had been played. Nonetheless, said New York Giants owner John Brush that fall, the team "was content to rest on its laurels."[11] Said Brush about the Red Sox in their newly minted American League, "They are no more than winners in a minor league."[12]

Baseball was again content to rest on its laurels in '94 and '95. But the new *status quo* of that era was uninterrupted economic warfare between players and owners, in the form of both strikes and lockouts, beginning with a strike over pensions which delayed the opening of the 1972 season, and continuing for more than two decades. A thirty-year war between millionaires and billionaires ensued, threatening a self-defeating devastation through the injury inflicted upon the fans of the game. Neither party seemed able to come to grips with the new free agency which had emerged through Arbitrator Peter Seitz's sweeping 1975 award that made all baseball players free agents able to bargain a new agreement with any team subsequent to playing out the so-called option year after their contract of employment with a team had expired. (Less than a year after the Seitz award, a modified form of free agency was to be bargained between the players union and the owners.)

As numerous arbitration proceedings involving "collusion" awards against the owners made manifest in the late 1980s, the owners simply refused to accept free agency, initially claiming that it would mean the end of baseball "as we knew it."[13] And the players, through their union first created in 1954, utilized the collective bargaining process from the mid–'60s onward, resisting mightily any attempt to modify or eliminate the gains obtained through the Seitz arbitration award of '75 and numerous collective bargaining agreements negotiated in its wake.

The struggle and controversies between players and owners have been going on for some period of time. Baseball, whose origins are so clouded that some have even argued that the Russians brought it to California[14] (it seems to stem from the 18th-century English game of rounders), subordinated and substantially supplanted the amateur system beginning in 1869 with the appearance of the above-referenced Cincinnati Red Stockings. Coincidentally, the first amateur college football game was played the same year between Princeton and Rutgers. Attacked as the "brutal sport" at the turn of the previous century and viewed with some measure of skepticism even by manly Teddy Roosevelt, the game of pads and leather helmets (as it was at that time and throughout the 1940s) was still years away from the cataclysmically violent "hits" for which the public displays an insatiable appetite today at both the college and professional level.

Basketball was not even invented until more than two decades later. No professional league emerged in football or basketball until after the turn of the century, with the National Football League appearing on the scene in 1920 and the modern professional basketball league emerging in the form of the National Basketball League and the Basketball Association of America created immediately before and after World War II, respectively. (The National Basketball Association was the product of their merger in 1950.)

In football and basketball the amateur system thus antedated the development of professional leagues. The result has been a symbiotic relationship between the colleges and the leagues: the former have served as a kind of minor league system in which the latter rely upon an infinitesimally small slice of draftees as new recruits who will immediately come into the game. This never happened in baseball: the early development of professionalism—the first commercial leagues to exist anywhere in the world—sucked all the oxygen out of the college system which, notwithstanding the rise of college baseball during these past two or three decades, has never rivaled in stature the college game in football and basketball.

Baseball is a game which is played every day, and training for its highest level requires day-to-day involvement. This is not possible at the amateur or even semi-pro level, where most of the games are on the weekend with only the occasional weekday contest creating the potential for direct interference with scheduled classes in the colleges and high schools or, in the world of semi-pro, one's regular job during the week. Thus the training is generally not the prerequisite to immediate graduation to the professional ranks that it is in football and basketball.

Accordingly, beyond the historical chronology, the nature of the game does not lend itself to amateur prominence in the way that football and basketball do. Football takes place once a week, after which players nurse their wounds before beginning serious scrimmages on Wednesday or Thursday. Basketball's day-to-day games are much too exhausting for daily amateur competition, given the up-and-down-the-court pressure imposed upon the players. Though baseball is a physically demanding game at all positions in the field, its relatively sparsely attended games do not have the same prominence at the amateur level.

Again, in contrast to "King" football (so named because of its enormous revenues and athletic scholarships) and basketball, only at the professional level of baseball is the desired training provided, though a few—first baseman John Olerud of Washington State and Cincinnati twirler Mike Leake of Arizona State are prominent recent examples—have made the jump from the colleges directly to the majors.[15] From 1883 onward, minor-league experience became the tried and tested apprenticeship program for the majors, albeit a far more abbreviated period in recent years.

Professional baseball, initially through the National Association of Players in 1871 and later the more stable National League in 1876, constituted the first example of any closed professional league system anywhere in the world! And in its wake came rules which bound players to clubs, the first "reserve system" binding players to teams starting in 1879, in order to combat jumping from one team to another in mid-season, and limited the location of franchises to cities with at least 75,000 people. The National League, appropriately characterized today as the "senior circuit," initially prohibited Sunday play, as well as the sale of alcohol at the ballpark. Paid umpires became part of the system.

In 1877 came the first involvement of players in bribery, in the Louisville Grays' scandal. League President William Hulbert responded with expulsion. Gambling in the ballpark, as well as interaction between players and gamblers, was rampant in the early 20th century, most prominently during the 1918 pennant race.[16] This problem reared its ugly head again at the time of the 1919 World Series, when some members of the Chicago White Sox were involved with gamblers and apparently threw the World Series — thus to be forever characterized as the "Black Sox." Pete Rose of the Cincinnati Reds, both an outstanding player and subsequently a manager of the Cincinnati Reds, bet on baseball games played by his team and thus was banned for life.[17] Though the Rose incident took place in 1989, the problem does not appear to be present among players in baseball today, though the discipline issues surrounding it are directly related to other problems which fall under the general rubric of "cheating." Foremost among them is the use of the above-referenced performance-enhancing drugs from the '90s onward! The refusal of players and owners to address this issue harks back to their refusal to face the gambling incidents of yesteryear.

In the nineteenth century, players, who believed that they should be involved in the management of baseball since they constituted the product itself, formed a new league, the International Association of Professional Baseball Players. This coincided with ideas throughout American industry that workers should have a measure of involvement or control in the business itself. This new league, which did not limit the number of teams or require a minimum size of a city in which a franchise was to be located, soon became a rival to the National League. But "[t]he loose organization of the IL [International League], the effective competition from the NL, and the country's severe depression of the 1870s, following the banking crisis of 1873, were sufficient to doom the IL by 1880."[18]

The next rival to emerge was the American Association, which promoted the selling of beer. Like player management controversy and cheating, beer remains a significant part of the twenty-first century scene. Beer, along with the excitement of competition and the intrigue inherent in the uncertainty of outcome, seems to be an abiding feature of the game. Until recent concerns about the impact of drugs upon both the outcome of games and aspiring youths, beer was a prominent part of the baseball advertising world.

A new players league came into existence in 1890 and lasted a year, causing a bidding war for talent with the National League and the American Association. Starting in 1893, the National League and American Association brought its teams in by allowing them to buy existing franchises. A year later the National League and American Association merged to a single twelve-team circuit called the National League. A subsequent challenge was posed by the Western League, initially a minor league which would ultimately be transformed into the American League.

Once competition between teams for players was eliminated through an agreement between the American and National leagues, the Red Sox and Pirates played a colorful first World Series in 1903, with fans shooting revolvers into the air in order to show their pleasure with a particular play or result![19] Then, in the winter of 1904-05, not having played a 1904 World Series, baseball vowed to not repeat this mistake in the 1905 season. Public outrage against perceived petulance prompted New York Giants owner Brush to enter into a new agreement between the leagues which remained intact and annually produced what came to be called a World Series without interruption through 1994.

The scenario was entirely different during the '94-'95 winter in the wake of that World Series' cancellation. Instead, the parties engaged in unsuccessful bargaining, litigation about whether the bargaining had been conducted in good faith, to the point of "impasse" or deadlock, triggering the right of baseball to unilaterally change rules relating to both free agency and the salary arbitration system. And subsequent to an unsuccessful attempt to legislate both at the White House and Congress and an attempt to mediate the matter, it was left to the National Labor Relations Board to intervene and obtain an injunction which brought an end to the strike and a return of the players to the field in the spring of '95.[20] Ultimately, in the fall of 1996, both the players and owners were able to negotiate a comprehensive collective bargaining agreement which ushered in a new environment of labor peace amid financial plenty destined to endure through 2011 at the very least.

No sooner was the ink dry on the paper that fall of '96 than a year later the Boston Red Sox signed the exquisitely talented Pedro Martinez, obtained from the talent-rich but cash-poor Montreal Expos for the then-unprecedented salary of more than $12 million per annum in a six-year contract. Even prior to the execution of the contract, Chicago White Sox owner Jerry Reinsdorf, a "hawk" in the player-owner negotiations, enraged his fellow owners by signing Cleveland Indian slugger extraordinaire Albert Belle to a $55 million deal. A new round of handwringing ensued, and it is generally thought that the owners ratified the '96 collective bargaining agreement because they chafed at being told that they should do as Reinsdorf said and not as he did!

A decade later the same Red Sox, having left Martinez to escape to free agency and the New York Mets in 2005, paid $51 million to Japan's Seibu Lions to obtain negotiating rights to yet another ace right-hander residing outside of American territory, Daisuke Matsuzaka. ("Pedro Perfecto," after all, hailed from the Dominican Republic.) A negotiated six-year $62 million contract was to follow a month later.

Both deals were shockers in their own decades. But whereas the Martinez contract startled the world, the Matzusaka arrangement was viewed by some to be a bargain, notwithstanding the fact that the sum provided to Seibu was compensation to be paid if the contract negotiations with the pitcher were successful — an amount which inevitably diminished the player's market value. After all, Oakland A's lefty Barry Zito, not part of the top echelon of major league pitchers, was awarded $125 million over seven years in '07 by the allegedly parsimonious San Francisco Giants. Simultaneous with the Matzusaka agreement, ex–Seattle Mariner pitcher Gil Meche was signed by the lowly Kansas City Royals for five years, entitling Meche to the princely sum of $55 million. San Francisco Giant ace Jason Schmidt, considered to have his best years behind him (he soon developed a debilitating sore arm), was picked up by the Los Angeles Dodgers for more than $15 million per year over a three-year period. And Ted Lilly, considered by *Sports Illustrated* to possess statistics which are "the very definitions of average," negotiated a four-year, $40 million package with the Chicago Cubs. (And, in contrast to the sore-armed Schmidt, his '07 performance surprised the skeptics!)

These agreements, while hardly exceeding the quarter-billion-dollar package negotiated by Alex Rodriguez of the Texas Rangers (later dealt to the New York Yankees) at the turn of this century, as well as the agreement of former Cleveland Indian outfielder Manny Ramirez with the Boston Red Sox, placed in perspective and potentially set the stage for the more startling developments of '06 and '07. The Rodriguez deal was considered to be an inflated contract beyond what players could properly reference in their contract bargaining, but five years later, Rodriguez hit an astounding 54 home runs in '07 — and was able to negotiate a contract in considerable excess of the $27 million per year owed in 2008, '09 and '10 under his initial agreement with the Texas Rangers, in both amount and contract duration!

And then, to paraphrase the musical *Oklahoma*, in the winter of '08–'09, the New York Yankees were to go about as far as they could go! Denied a World Championship in the 21st century and excluded from the playoffs for the first time in almost two decades, the Bronx Bombers proceeded to go on a spending spree of $423.5 million during the Great

Recession, signing hard-throwing lefty CC Sabathia to a seven-year, $151 million contract; right-hander A.J. Burnett of Toronto to a five-year, $82.5 million deal; and premium power hitter Mark Teixeira to an eight-year, $180 million contract. The Yankees would now "rule the world"![21] And as Stefan Fatsis said the following year: "It's been said that there's no crying in baseball. It seems as if there's no recession either."[22] Initially, in the wake of the steroids scandal, it appeared that baseball owners and general managers were reticent and careful about signing the over–30 crowd to big contracts[23]—but in 2010-11 that caution seems to have been discarded.[24] (Indeed, when the oft-injured Edgar Renteria was offered $1 million to re-sign with the Giants for 2011, he claimed to be insulted.[25])

Baseball, in the intervening decade-plus, had indeed stepped back from the precipice of '94-'95. As in 1904, it did not like the alternatives. In 2006, when the collective bargaining agreement negotiated four years earlier had expired, awash with cash attributable to increased attendance, radio and television agreements, Internet profits, licensing of products and globalization, labor and management resolved their differences at the bargaining table without the imminent threat of either a strike or lockout for the first time in more than three decades.

The previous time around, in 2002, building upon the 1996 framework emerging out of the '94-'95 strike and NLRB intervention, the owners and players negotiated a revenue-sharing arrangement through which the rich teams would shift finances to the low-revenue and supposedly small-market clubs so as to enhance the latter's ability to be competitive and thus promote greater public interest in the outcome of games. The '94-'95 strike had been fought out over the owners' insistence upon a "salary cap" of the kind which football and basketball players had already accepted. Throughout the '80s and '90s, the players association (often referred to as the union) had been adamant in its resistance to any and all such proposals—and in '94 and '95 the divide on this and related issues re-emerged, leaving the players and owners entangled in bitter acrimony.

Nonetheless, in 2002 a luxury tax was negotiated which set a threshold of total team payroll beyond which a tax would be paid, the object being to discourage teams like the wealthy and free-spending New York Yankees from going too far beyond the rest of the baseball world. But the Yankees went right on spending, even to the tune of well over $200 million for its payroll in 2007, continuing through its World Championship year 2009. (Even before the New York renaissance, their lavish spending did not matter, as they were bounced from the playoffs in the first round for the third year in a row, and were left without a world championship in the twenty-first century for their sins!) In the process they paid the aging righty Roger Clemens $3 million for each of his six victories in 2007.

And for the first time, in the 2002 agreement, a prohibition against performance-enhancing anabolic steroids was not only incorporated in the collective bargaining agreement—possession of such drugs without a doctor's prescription had already been unlawful for baseball players and anyone else since at least 1991—but also a drug-testing program was expanded into something more comprehensive in response to congressional pressure. As we'll see in Chapter 7, the players had fiercely resisted the process for years, and the owners, complicit because performance enhancement appeared to make the game more attractive to the public and thus more financially profitable for the owners, possessed little enthusiasm for self-monitoring.

In 2002 had come the first peaceable settlement in three decades. In 2006, acting as mature labor and management representatives had done much of the time since the Great Depression of the 1930s in industries like manufacturing, construction and maritime in the private sector, the parties negotiated an agreement under the radar of press releases and publicity and far in advance of the expiration of the '02 agreement. In neither instance — '02 or '06 — was it necessary to involve the National Labor Relations Board or the courts again — and the court order providing for an injunction fashioned by a federal judge in April '95 requiring NLRB notification of the bargaining procedures was invoked only just as the parties were ready to sign off on the complete deal! The practical significance was that NLRB intervention, which was so vital in the '94–'95 dispute resolution, was now completely unnecessary.

In '06, there was genuine give and take on both sides, enhancing the dialogue properly promoted by federal labor policy. But the remarkable feature of this agreement was that, if anything, the much-excoriated free agency at the heart of prior discord was expanded, with less amateur draft compensation provided to teams which lost players through free agency (though not for the loss of the particularly valuable so-called "type A" and "type B" players, so ranked because of their statistical performance).

The baseball landscape was now fundamentally altered. Not only had the parties found that they could live well and prosper with free agency, but also they could actually expand their prosperity and use the free agency process in so doing! "Break up the Yankees" had been the clarion call of generations prior to free agency, and in its wake the vast resources of the Bronx Bombers seemed to damage all competition.

But at the turn of this century the Yankees, whose recruitment efforts were mildly diminished at best by the luxury tax, went for years without a world championship after 2000, though they were able to reach the postseason for twelve consecutive years from '96 through '07, and finally established themselves as World Champions for the first time in the 21st century in '09. And other teams like the Chicago Cubs, which spent more than $300 million in the winter of '06–'07, as well as the Boston Red Sox, the Los Angeles Dodgers, and even the tail-ending Kansas City Royals, now jumped into the financial fray. Said the *Boston Herald*:

> They have laid out $70 million for a right fielder, $36 million for a shortstop and more than $51 million just for the right to negotiate with a pitcher. Maybe the Red Sox are crazy, but they're certainly not cheap.[26]

All of this is quite different and distant from 1904, when the New York Giants players could not dissuade their superiors from declining the invitation to play the Boston Americans. (Manager John McGraw's role as to which side he was on is somewhat unclear.[27]) Similarly, the scope and dimension of money — and money received by players as well as owners — contrasts with the 1940s, a period of time examined by this book, both on and off the field. Yet money is an abiding characteristic that has stayed with baseball during its entire 140-year existence as a professional game: baseball is a business, and baseball exists fundamentally for money. Today there is exponentially more money — and more avenues to obtain it!

So, whatever the rhetoric engaged in by owners, it is the *amount* of money which has changed. Again, the amounts are enormous. But, after all, this historically rooted commercialism is hardly surprising in a nation where the Eisenhower administration's secretary of defense said: "What's good for General Motors, is good for the country." Money has always been the driving factor in the game. But some part of the contemporary sense of unease exists because of the concern that both drugs and salaries have been pushed to their logical extremes of absurdity.

Next to drugs, which have become a kind of surrogate for the gambling problems of yesteryear, and the amount of money involved, the biggest change relates to race. When I asked him what the biggest change in baseball had been since he first played in the 1930s, Red Sox Hall of Famer Bobby Doerr said: "Well, the big change, of course, was when the black player came in. And that changed the game around — they could run, and it changed the game into a more running game; it made the pitcher concentrate on the man on first a little more so it took his concentration away from the hitter a little bit, and there was a big change."[28] This post–World War II development brought back the stolen base so diminished by Babe Ruth's dominance from the 1920s onward. And in the process, baseball was a mirror image of societal change and a leader in the United States after the defeat of Germany and Japan in 1945 — indeed, the game had emerged as a leader in the race revolution which began to take place in the United States.

Forty years earlier, in 1904, the bar against black players had been complete. Fleetwood Walker, an outstanding catcher from the 1880s, and a few other black stars had been purged from the national pastime. In the aftermath, the only contact that existed between blacks and whites in baseball was through the Negro Leagues, where black teams engaged in exhibitions and sometimes barnstorming tours with the white stars of organized baseball. The "Sultan of Swat," the "Bambino," Babe Ruth, whose prodigious home runs in the 1920s put baseball on the map, is said not to have fared well against one of his outstanding near-contemporaries, the hard-throwing and deceptive pitcher Satchel Paige.[29] (Nonetheless, "there's no box score or game account to verify the claim [that Ruth had ever faced Paige]."[30])

In 1947, it was Jackie Robinson who first broke the major league color bar as a rookie with the Brooklyn Dodgers. Within a matter of months, Larry Doby, proceeding directly from the Negro League, followed suit in the American League as an outfielder with the Cleveland Indians. He was to become prominent in the Indians' World Championship year of '48, just as had Robinson when the Dodgers took the National League Pennant in '47.

All of this was a precursor to President Harry Truman's desegregation of the armed forces in 1948 and presaged the Supreme Court's landmark pronouncement in *Brown v. Board of Education*[31] declaring "separate but equal" in public education to be unconstitutional, and the civil rights legislation of the 1960s.

It seems obvious in retrospect that the breakthrough in race engineered by Branch Rickey of the Brooklyn Dodgers — the "Mahatma," as he was called — was an attempt to tap into previously unused talent and to expand the audience for baseball games. Again, the bottom line was money and finance, always a constant in baseball. Yet, the fact that motives were undoubtedly skewed to those things financial cannot detract from the role that baseball played in facilitating the change in race relations in the previous century.

Another form of player rights, fostered both in the courts and administrative agencies, produced the collective bargaining process. The rise of player rights and the collective bargaining process in baseball was brought about by the Major League Baseball Players Association or union, first formed in 1954, and subsequent to the 1966 appointment of Marvin Miller, its executive director, through the negotiation of comprehensive collective bargaining agreements. It was a unique brand of labor union unaffiliated with the AFL-CIO — or any other federation of the unions. The baseball union, like its counterparts in football, basketball and hockey, was a protest movement similar to the grievance-fueled litigation of blacks and women in the '60s and '70s — a phenomenon in which I participated as lead counsel in class actions on behalf of blacks and Latinos in racial and national-origin discrimination litigation during this period. In baseball the collective bargaining process produced money for both players and owners in the wake of the 1975 Seitz award on free agency, as well as the agreements negotiated afterward, which were ratified emphatically in the agreements of '02 and '06. Beyond its obvious and important financial implications, the baseball collective bargaining process was an important part of the rights movement of the '70s which, in the case of sports, gave players a say in where they would play and the conditions affecting such.

Collective bargaining has now become the forum for differences between the parties in baseball. Previously it was the courts which had been involved with disputes between players and owners every time a rival league emerged, particularly at the turn of the century before the establishment of organized baseball in 1901,[32] and again at the time of its rival's establishment, the Federal Baseball League in 1914. Players sought to "jump" from one league to another to enhance their earnings, and for the same reasons, owners sought to restrain them through contract and the reserve clause, which obligated a player to stay with a team beyond the contract expiration date.[33] In the post–World War II era the courts became involved again as the new Mexican League was formed and a number of name players were lured by a mirage of financial riches "south of the border." The year of the Mexican League, 1946, when dissatisfied players jumped ship from their American clubs in pursuit of the seemingly delectable financial bait provided by the Pasquel brothers, was a year when the boys came back from World War II in newfound competition with wartime players who had replaced them. Only 300 of approximately 1,000 World War II returning players were able to find continued employment in the majors.[34] It was a year of uncertainty and potential dislocation.

This took place alongside another development which was to prove unsuccessful in the short run (but, as noted, most successful in the long run): the attempt to form a union under the leadership of ex–National Labor Relations Board lawyer Robert Murphy. The effort fell by the wayside in the summer of 1946 when the Pittsburgh Pirates, at the urging of "blooper" pitch specialist "Rip" Sewell, refused to support the union and facilitated his teammates' ballot rejection of a strike. The owners instituted a pension fund soon thereafter, co-opting some of the leading players in the process. An attack upon the reserve system in baseball, let alone the idea that a union could properly represent the players, was at this point beyond the wildest stretch of anyone's imagination.

Fast forward now to the turn of this century. The extraordinary free-agent contracts of 2001 and '07 signed by Rodriguez, and in '09 by Sabathia and Teixeira, resulted from an environment created by the strong players union, beginning in the late '60s and '70s, and the legal machinery supporting it. As we shall see in Chapters 3 and 4, the success of the union lay in not simply its hardnosed bargaining tactics but also in the utilization of the negotiated arbitration machinery contained in its collective bargaining agreement. It was successful in preserving the fruits of free agency obtained through this process in a series of disputes in the '70s, '80s, and '90s — the "thirty years' war" of player-owner labor disputes which came to a conclusion in 1995.

These developments have affected virtually everything in baseball, the most immediate and obvious illustration being not only the player salaries but their conditions of employment, both at home ballparks and during travel on the road. Players in the post–World War II period, and for a substantial period thereafter, roomed with one another, something that never happens today! It has affected the relationship between managers and players as the former group's salaries have been dwarfed by the players' in most instances. And it has affected the way in which player performances are measured, the use of statistical data to determine what salary should be provided to a player, either through free-agency negotiations or through the salary arbitration process which is rooted in comparisons to others — and which in turn is used as evidence in free agency negotiations. The labor component has made owners more interested in competing for available dollars with the other major sports, raising revenues through ticket prices, radio and television contracts, and the sale of licensed products both home and abroad.

It may be that the most important development of all is globalization, something which was well under the radar screen until the beginning of the 1980s and the emergence of Los Angeles Dodger ace Fernando Valenzuela, a talented and colorful personality looking skyward in the midst of his dramatically long wind-up. He made the Dodgers realize that the "Valenzuela fever" or "Fernando mania" brought to them the loyalty and attendance of Mexican immigrants in southern California. A decade and a half later the Dodgers were to do it again with Hideo Nomo, who exploited available Japanese contract loopholes to bring his hands-high-over-the-head-in-hesitation pitching delivery to Los Angeles.[35]

Of course, traditionally a number of American players came from Latin America, particularly countries like Cuba[36] (where the game is truly the national pastime) and Venezuela at mid-century. Even the racially bigoted Washington Senators went after light-skinned Latin American players while they closed their doors to black Americans. But the numbers of foreigners have now increased to almost a third of all major league players, coming from the Dominican Republic, Mexico, South Africa, Japan, Korea, Taiwan and Australia — with Europe, mainland China, and Africa appearing to be part of baseball's twenty-first century future.

This has meant new venues for radio and television contracts abroad, as well as markets for shirts, caps, and a wide variety of other products licensed by Major League Baseball, revenues from which the MLB franchises share equally. It has meant, in the case of Japan and Korea, agreements between Major League Baseball and those countries which regulate the process through which players move back and forth across national boundaries. And it has meant large fees paid to American teams by Japanese companies anxious to advertise their product in Japan, where a nation watches raptly the performance of Japanese players abroad.

In Latin America it has meant the establishment of baseball academies in countries like the Dominican Republic, which, along with Venezuela, supplies a plurality of the Major League Baseball talent. As noted above, this has made discussions about race more hazy, with the advent of black Latino players and a large number of recruits who are perceived as black by traditional North American standards by virtue of their African ancestry.

And in 2006 the landmark World Baseball Classic — the first of its kind — was played in the United States, Latin America and the Far East. Another one was played in 2009! This enhanced the prospect of a true World Series and true World Championship at some point in the twenty-first century, as well as possible expansion of baseball to other countries and the internationalization of norms and standards to apply to relationships between players and owners across national boundaries. Notwithstanding the fact that jet travel has not progressed substantially beyond what it was in the 1950s and '60s, thus making a genuine international league with head-to-head competition at this point fanciful, future institutional international arrangements or leagues are nonetheless possible. They can and should happen.[37]

Expansion of sports coverage, and baseball coverage in particular, in cities like Boston and New York and on the West Coast, has made more fans knowledgeable. As the slow-curveballing ace of the '70s and '80s, Bert Blyleven, said to me: "Back in the early '70s and maybe even before that, you have only one or two beat writers that followed a ballclub.

Now you have, my goodness, the Internet, all these publications that follow the teams and everyone is looking for a story."[38]

With all of this, the information age has spawned more statistical data and more information about the games themselves — and, perhaps even more important, the speed through which one can learn about the day's events, no matter the country in which one resides or travels or visits. When I was a student at the London School of Economics, my father mailed me the baseball clippings that provided me with both the standings and articles about the developments relating to the Boston Red Sox in the spring of 1963. This didn't diminish my sense of excitement as the Carmine Hose soared to the top ever so briefly under the leadership of ex-shortstop-third baseman Johnny Pesky. Four years later, when I visited Britain during the "Impossible Dream" pennant race of 1967, I raced to Charing Cross station in downtown London to get the day-old reports in the *International Herald Tribune* during that fateful September, and when that was not available, the raw scores of the games (no more detail was provided than that!) in the British newspapers. In 2005, while teaching in London, I could not only know the previous day's events through computer but also attend a "game of the week" at a London sports bar as well.

But then again, there is the omnipresent bad news to which we have alluded. In recent years the business of drug-taking by baseball players has raised its ugly head. In the 1980s it was recreational drugs, and it was during this period that arbitral precedent in the baseball drug arena was established. But in the '90s and the following decade, performance-enhancing drugs became the scandal *du jour* of baseball. Both the above-referenced landmark book by *San Francisco Chronicle* reporters, *Game of Shadows*,[39] an expose on San Francisco slugger Barry Bonds that emerged from grand jury proceedings involving BALCO and numerous baseball stars, and the well-publicized congressional hearings in Washington on the question of whether baseball players had been taking steroids, forced the owners and the union to begin to come to grips with the issue, if ever so tentatively.

In the wake of these developments they negotiated twice about revising drug-testing mechanisms established for the first time in the 2002 collective bargaining agreement. As noted above, Commissioner Bud Selig in '06 appointed former senator and present-day Boston Red Sox owner George Mitchell to conduct an inquiry into this subject subsequent to the above-noted events. A comprehensive report (discussed in Chapter 7) was rendered in December 2007 and new contract provisions were put in place in '08. But new revelations in its wake made it clear that the Mitchell Report would be no more lasting in its attempt to make baseball transparent than was Judge Landis's supposed effort to do the same with gambling in 1920. In retrospect, the Mitchell Report is a tentative first draft.

The BALCO matter has had broad radiations and led to an examination of the question of whether Bonds had committed perjury so as to avoid a finding that he had taken steroids. Subsequently federal authorities have attempted to crack down on the distributors as well as recipients of performance-enhancing drugs.[40] (Indeed, the focus on the recipients has been used to sort out the identity of the distributors; this is what prompted the interest in Bonds.) Scandal has begun to spread to other preeminent players like Roger Clemens and Alex Rodriguez — as well as other, lesser-known major leaguers such as Cleveland, Los Angeles and Boston pitcher Paul Byrd,[41] and more recently, another San Francisco Giant hero, Matt Williams.[42] It is said that one player, 2010 Giants outfielder Jose Guillen, actually had the drugs shipped right to the Oakland Coliseum when he was a member of the A's[43]— a pattern he allegedly renewed with the Giants.[44]

It is this part of the story which is most ominous and which threatens baseball as no scandal has since the so-called Black Sox scandal of 1919, in which "Shoeless" Joe Jackson and other members of the Chicago White Sox were banned from baseball for consorting with gamblers and allegedly fixing the outcome of the World Series with the Cincinnati Reds. It taints any statistical comparison between both Bonds and McGwire and the all-time home run champion, Hank Aaron, as well as Babe Ruth, Roger Maris (who broke the Babe's record in 1961) and Willie Mays, all of whom Bonds has also surpassed, notwithstanding his protestation that his record is not "tainted." Baseball has been tardy in coming to grips with this problem, which flowered in the home-run-happy '90s, promoting a marriage of convenience and avoidance of the issue on both sides of the bargaining table.

But the issue would not go away — and it should not! Bonds's prominence alone made that impossible. Said *San Jose Mercury News* columnist Ann Killion when Bonds, prior to his indictment, hit his 756th homer to go beyond Hank Aaron, whereupon the Giants devised an elaborate ceremony to commemorate it:

> Still, for many longtime fans it is at best uncomfortable, at worst unforgivable, that Bonds has supplanted Mays as the ultimate Giant. That he [Bonds] sullied a legacy and a legend with his single-minded pursuit of glory, almost certainly aided by performance-enhancing drugs. That he put a franchise his godfather [Willie Mays] bathed in glory in a compromising position, making the Giants the laughingstock of much of baseball.[45]

HGH (human growth hormone), belatedly prohibited by baseball, could not be tested for as late as 2011. Meanwhile ex–Yankee pitcher Jason Grimsley purportedly implicated Yankee pitchers Roger Clemens and Andy Pettite in taking HGH, Clemens's physical appearance having changed dramatically over the years — as dramatically as that of Bonds and McGwire — and Pettite, in turn, implicated Clemens despite his continued denials. (It is said that Pettite's testimony was particularly critical in the indictment of Clemens in August 2010.[46]) Other prominent players, such as Troy Glaus of Toronto, Gary Matthews Jr. of Los Angeles, and Jay Gibbons of Baltimore, as well as Rick Ankiel, an ex-pitcher whose career had been revived with the St. Louis Cardinals as a slugger, were said by authorities to have received HGH in the mail. And in 2009, in the greatest 1-2 punch since Ruth and Gehrig, Manny Ramirez (suspended for testing positive in '09) and David Ortiz were revealed to have tested positive for forbidden drugs in 2003!

Perhaps Tom Boswell[47] of the *Washington Post* was correct to say that the "steroids era is over" as he noted that "[o]nly four men are on pace to hit 40 home runs this season [of '07], the first time it had happened since 1995, a season shortened because of the strike." Perhaps ... but all players except Yankee slugger Jason Giambi, who admitted to drug-taking in an interview and was warned by Yankee owner George Steinbrenner to "shut up," refused to talk to Senator Mitchell. And in any event, *Sporting News* noted, "the great power outage of '07" seemed to be attributable to injuries to sluggers as much as anything.[48]

During a Sunday Night Baseball telecast on ESPN, Peter Gammons said that he was "not sure what we need to know from years past," apparently assuming that in years past the players who had taken performance-enhancing drugs did not engage in conduct which was unlawful because drug testing has been introduced so recently. Former Houston and Cincinnati Hall of Famer second baseman Joe Morgan said:

> The fans are coming out more and more before. The game is growing so I guess the question is: do the fans really care about what happened four or five years ago? I guess that would be my question. Is it more that we care or more that the fans care? I mean, that's where it is. The fans do not seem to care. They come out and watch a baseball game.[49]

San Francisco Giant fans enthusiastically supported Bonds, notwithstanding the boos that he received in other ballparks. Within days of his tearful confession, McGwire was greeted enthusiastically by Cardinal fans! Boston Red Sox supporters applaud David Ortiz, who turned up as positive in the testing first done by baseball in 2003 — though "Big Papi" admittedly is far more loveable than any of the other strange and sullen characters involved in this ongoing controversy, most of them constituting the baseball mirror image of the bratty ex–Los Angeles Laker Sasha Vujacic.

This reaction highlights a basic disconnect on the drug issue: the apparent fact that fandom cares less about drug usage than it wants to preserve the pristine memories of long, frequently dramatic Bonds home runs landing in the San Francisco Bay. Said one letter writer in response to the Killion *San Jose Mercury News* column quoted above:

> What the heck is wrong with you? Here you had a chance to write about history, the swing, the crowd, anything that someone could keep the newspaper for years to come for their grandchildren. But no! You had to write about steroid scandals, and people in jail, and what that stupid commissioner was doing. You don't even know if Barry is guilty of steroid use....
> I'm not even a baseball fan, but I know this is not a newspaper article I will keep for all time.[50]

Some of my students in my Stanford Law School Sports Law seminar have suggested that the crackdown on National Football League players by NFL Commissioner Roger Goodell for involvement in criminal matters, including violence and crimes against women, is misguided because it has not affected football attendance. This is akin to the concerns expressed by Joe Morgan. Similar questions have been raised about the ban and criminal prosecution of ex–Atlanta quarterback Michael Vick, who tortured and executed dogs at his home. Many baseball fans are similarly numbed by the performance issue, suggesting that it is comparable to other forms of cheating, despite the public health problems with these drugs.

The 2007 controversy arising out of the filming of the New York Jets signals by the New England Patriots, in contravention of NFL rules, highlights the problem well. *The Sporting News* says: "Caught ya!: Everybody does it, but it's *cheating* only when you've been nabbed."[51] Signs are stolen in baseball too — the analog to *The Sporting News* commentary on the New England Patriots is binoculars or artificial devices. Ongoing controversy has now emerged from the New York Giants' spectacular mid–August comeback after trailing the Brooklyn Dodgers by thirteen and a half games and revelations that the Giants had someone in the bullpen examining signs through binoculars. This has even created controversy for Bobby Thomson's "shot heard 'round the world" off Ralph Branca, since it is possible that that pitch itself may have been tipped. Sign-stealing controversy has emerged anew — more recently through revelations about the Philadelphia Phillies and their behavior, particularly in the '09 World Series with the Yankees.[52] The prevailing mores are articulated by Cincinnati Reds Manager Dusty Baker: "If you steal signs it's okay. If you get caught sign stealing and are warned about it it's not okay."

Baker, when leading the Giants, himself was involved in a fracas with Felipe Alou, then managing the Montreal Expos, when Alou took offense to the idea that he, Baker, was ordering sign stealing. Compounding the complexities involved in this matter, even baseball's television audience know that every base runner on second base is looking in to take the sign from the catcher, which induces them to change the "indicator," i.e., which part of the body they touch before giving a series of finger signs.

Again, implicit in the remarks quoted above on Sunday Night Baseball is that the drug situation is in some respects comparable to these other forms of cheating — which are permissible if the player is not caught, but improper if the player is warned and caught. Thus it is clear that the drug culture which emerged in the wake of the '94–'95 baseball strike will take some time to eradicate even if the "steroid era" is truly over.

This is where baseball finds itself in 2011 and beyond, when the game has pulled itself back from the precipice of conflict and contentiousness which sorely tested the patience of the public. This book examines the enormous changes that have taken place in the game of baseball on and off the field since 1945, the conclusion of World War II. I conclude that many of those who run and own the game have frequently debased it in the name of commerce — a development which is not new to the game and one which is not brought about primarily by free agency, as some seem to believe. Labor conflicts and the handling of drugs present two facets of the continuum. Equally troubling but considerably less dramatic are the erosion of the game's integrity through such innovations as the bulk of the interleague schedule, which does not permit competitive teams to play the same teams in the same locale as one's competitor, and thus reduces the pennant chase to something arguably akin to hap — particularly when the contest is close. All of these problems are exacerbated by the endless chase for the dollar.

Paradoxically, in fundamental respects the game on the field is the same as ever — full of beauty and grace, with the bar of athletic excellence raised even higher than it was in the '40s. By all standards, notwithstanding the fact that the period of time in which a game is played has expanded, the game is a success on and off the field, with unprecedented revenues benefitting players and owners, though imposing economic hardships upon less affluent fans. The game has succeeded in spite of those who run it. In order to assess these issues in more detail, it is important to begin in the post–World War II era which I observed as a child — and which has influenced all of these matters so deeply. It is to this period that we now turn.

CHAPTER 2

The Post–World War II Era: Remembrances of Baseball Past

The subway train emerges from a darkened tunnel at the Bronx Grand Concourse station in New York City, 50 miles north of my home in New Jersey. It all happens so quickly that one is surprised by the brilliant sunshine — and left absolutely breathless by the suddenness of the view into Yankee Stadium, its grand field seen far below the train and platform, and thousands of spectator seats partially filled in with the arriving throng.

The date is August 21, 1946. This has been a sweet summer of sandlot baseball, virtually every day at the Long Branch, New Jersey, "Station Field" proximate to the New York–Long Branch railroad tracks in New Jersey on the "Jersey Shore." Every day after fourth grade had let out that June, our mothers packed our lunches for us before we jumped on our bikes to pedal towards the field. No uniforms, no umpires or adult supervision, sometimes the catcher — always without equipment — was on one's own team, standing far behind home plate as he took the pitch on one bounce. Sometimes we played with our pants half rolled up, as they were in order to avoid getting caught in the bicycle chains.

Only baseball, all morning and afternoon, with makeshift bases established where the grass had worn thin, without any exact rule of measurement from base to base or from an unelevated pitching mound and home plate. We knew nothing about the proper pitching distance of 60' and 6" that had been designated ever since 1893. And with no umpires, like the 19th century rules, which at one time did not contemplate called strikes and even allowed a batter to call for a high or low pitch (we didn't follow that rule), only peer pressure could induce one to swing at a pitch that was not precisely to a young hitter's liking. Under these circumstances, the pitcher would frequently groove one to tempt an otherwise reticent hitter who was waiting for that perfect pitch. Batting averages could thus soar well above .700 — and mine did — more than double what a good batter could hit in a properly organized game. With only one or two balls between all of us, it was imperative that it or they not be lost and that black tape be available so that the ball would not come apart at the seams — literally! Today it seems unimaginable that at both the professional and amateur levels before 1920, in the so-called dead ball era prior to Babe Ruth, the same ball would be kept in play for much of the game.[1] Under the circumstances of our sandlot ball, it goes without saying that the guy who owned the ball was particularly powerful and popular!

I loved to hit. The hotter the weather became as July turned to August, the better I thought I could hit and the more I felt relaxed at the plate.

On the other hand, my Louisville Slugger would often break on inside pitches on the hands — particularly in the cold March and April, when I did not like to hit — and the black tape came in handy there too, thus temporarily rescuing a good piece of lumber from the fire-place. As with the balls, the surgically repaired bats were never quite as good, but they had to do.

Fielding was a less-developed art. Gloves were positively primitive by today's standards, without deep pockets and elaborate webbing. We were always advised to catch the ball with two hands — not only because that approach was regarded as intrinsically sensible, but also because the gloves made one-handed catches unrealistic unless they were absolutely necessary!

Four seasons at the Station Field, grabbing line drives hit by other .700 hitters, wore my mitt to a frazzle, without even the remnants of the padding of the day. There was no webbing of which to speak. (When Willie Mays came to my office at Stanford Law School a few years ago before he was to speak in one of my seminars, he looked in horror at my Bobby Bonds glove from the '70s and said, "I'll send you a proper glove!" And its perfect complexity and beauty so exceeded my imagination that I have never dared use it!) In 1949 my parents bought me a new one, which was soon to wear out also, notwithstanding more infrequent use during the coming years.

Perhaps the gloves suffered as well from our practice of leaving them on the field when we departed to bat in our half of the inning. This was the practice in the major leagues as well until 1953, when Major League Baseball, through Rule 3.14, prohibited leaving "equipment" on the field when a team vacated it to come up to bat because of safety concerns. (In fact, the safety problems were much less considerable than in today's parks, where bullpens and high pitching mounds and photographic gear create a real hazard for hard-running outfielders and infielders as well.)

I think that all of us Station Field players saw something that was more inexact and uncertain about fielding that wasn't affected by arm and glove. Simply this: where you were positioned affected whether you might get to the ball, and when you put a glove on the ball you might be more easily charged with an error. In an age when defensive statistics based upon a player's ability to get to a ball hit to a particular "zone" were unknown, we Station Field kids knew that Yankee shortstop Phil Rizzuto's mobility did not translate into the best fielding average. Red Sox left fielder Bill Hall's September 2010 fumbled grounder on a base hit not only allowed the run to score but also a poor throw on the same play permitted the A's hitter to advance where he could score and tie the game. Neither event was ever recorded on the scorecard. My colleague, the late Leonard Koppett, said great statistics (always unrecorded, of course) are the mistakes that you didn't make that you could have made. Speaking of the obverse, jazz composer and pianist Dave Frishberg wrote:

> I see where Reggie Jackson made an error
> Now, how could they report that any fairer?
> The sun must have got in his eyes.*

But whether it was the more satisfying art of hitting or pitching where the confrontation was direct and someone won or lost, we would practice our swings, throws and set stretch positions as we held an imaginary runner on first — all of this without bat or ball, in our living rooms at home. Through most of my adult life, I have only seen those imaginary gestures engaged in by young children in the Tokyo subways — though more recently my grandson Joey never ceases to impress me with the way in which he practices his bat-cocked-high "corkscrew" Kevin Youkilis batting style and throwing motions as well, in anticipation of his next Little League game.

Watching the 1972 Oakland–Cincinnati World Series on the television years later, I

From "The Sports Page" by Dave Frishberg © Funny Side Music and Swiftwater Music. Used by permission.

was intrigued with "Blue Moon" Odom pitching out of the stretch, holding and watching the runner at first base out of the corner of his eye. This is what we would do when we were away from the field in our living rooms or at the bus stop.

When my father would come home from work, I would hold out my right hand to him, asking him to "check in" on his home run as he crossed the plate with what would be called a "low five" today. Only in the late '60s did Dusty Baker devise the "high five," and all of this antedated the ostentatious religiosity that emerged at the turn of this century when players began to point skyward — as if gesturing to God or a deceased family member — as they crossed the plate after a homer. Some even began to do this after a single! And in the past decade or so, teams took to celebrating game-changing or -winning home runs so violently that one player on the Los Angeles Angels was disabled by the celebration for the entire year!

In any event, in 1946 an understated game truly consumed us. And it consumed the entire country as well. For this was the year the boys came home from World War II.[2] FDR had insisted that the game continue during the war so as to promote morale among the population. Most of the great stars like Ted Williams, Joe DiMaggio, Bob Feller, Stan Musial, Bobby Doerr and Johnny Pesky had departed to take up their wartime duties in uniform (as Williams did once again during the Korean War in the early '50s). Now attendance soared mightily and the Red Sox–Yankee and Dodger–Cardinal rivalries only fostered excitement and pennant fever.

Meanwhile, back in Long Branch, amidst all the almost daily baseball playing, there was baseball talk as well. We discussed what we had read in the *New York Times'* detailed and gracefully written daily column descriptions which appeared on all games played outside of New York, as well as those involving the Dodgers, Giants, and Yankees. These articles consisted of pure descriptive and analytic commentary, in sharp contrast to today's quotation-laden inane player "remarks," e.g., "I was seeing the ball really good," in response to a question asking a player what he thought or felt at the time he hit a homer.

When we were not on the field, we could imbibe the radio-shaped images presented through that medium — Mel Allen and Red Barber were the two best in those days, and their personalities permitted them to make the transfer to television in the '50s. The mellifluous Allen was charming and folksy. During one of the Red Sox–Yankee contests that special summer as Sox reliever Mike Ryba entered the fray, Allen sang the hit tune of that time, "Hey Ba Ba Re Bop."[3] Mirthfully, Allen would boom in his melodic baritone, substituting Ryba for "Re Bop."

I enjoyed hearing the big league games on the radio almost as much as I loved to play and watch the game itself. No one had television in 1946 (though the Yankees' first televised broadcasts began that year), and in 1947 only a few wealthy people had it. (Only one family on our block had it, and I think that I saw my first televised game at that house in '47.) In the 1940s radio was dominant — though, because it competed with newspapers and magazines and the like for a literate public, it was not as supreme as television became.

All of this quickly changed in the 1950s. Jazz and blues singer Dinah Washington would sing that television was "the thing," and that radio, despite its greatness, was "out of date" in the era before the advent of Jon Miller and Joe Castiglione. Americans possessed 400,000 sets in 1948, 10 million by 1950, and 42 million in 1957. As James S. Hirsch has written: "[By the 1950s] the sport itself, as national televised entertainment, had arrived ... television showcased players in all corners of the country, forged connections with distant fans, and elevated stars to heroic status."[4]

In the 1950s, Yankee hegemony made baseball background music for me. But in the '40s I could not wait for 6:45 P.M. to hear Stan Lomax as he set forth the "day's doings in the world of sports" on New York's WOR, 710 on the dial. "Good evening," Lomax would

Stan Lomax, sports broadcaster for WOR, New York, to whom the author listened daily as a child (courtesy Stan Lomax, Jr. Photograph editing by Joe Neto, Creative Services Specialist Stanford Law School).

intone, "This is Stan Lomax with the day's doings in the world of sports and today those Boston Red Sox continued to rare and tear...." His next words would be drowned out by one boy's exultations at 458 Bath Avenue in Long Branch.

Those Boston Red Sox.... By the time that we started playing at the Station Field in June 1946, the Red Sox had an insurmountable lead against all comers. Thus, when we began to choose the team that each of us would support, I immediately identified with the Red Sox, who had their backs to the wind the entire summer, leaving the Detroit Tigers and the New York Yankees buried in the dust. (The Sox were to finish 12 ahead of the Bengals and 17 up on the Yanks.) As early as May that year the baseball cartoonist Willard Mullin wrote "break up the Red Sox," a humorous mimic of the "break up the Yankees" theme that had emerged in the midst of their success from the '20s through the '40s. The *New York World Telegram* ran an item which contained the pictures of Johnny Pesky, Dom DiMaggio and Red Sox catcher Hal Wagner stating: "Stop These Men: dangerous characters — headed this way, ... armed with powerful clubs ... a menace to our fair city."[5] (See charts).[6]

I took account of the fact that I had been born in Boston, Massachusetts; we moved to New Jersey when I was 4, but we would return at every opportunity to visit with my great-uncles and great-aunt in Dedham, Massa-

After the Red Sox had won the May 10–12 series against the Yankees in the Stadium, *The Sporting News* ran this front-page Willard Mullin cartoon in its May 16 issue (courtesy Shirley Mullin Rhodes and *The Sporting News*; reproduced from *When the Boys Came Back*).

chusetts, just south of Boston. All my life I had a solid identification with Boston, based upon our frequent visits there (my parents always thought that they would return to "the Hub" ultimately) and the accounts of that area which I heard in our New Jersey home. The visits to so many portions of the Bay State, including Cape Cod, the memories of my father pointing to his former boss's shamrock-laced mansion (it was still owned by beloved Mayor James Michael Curley), and my father's accounts of Boston's Abolitionist tradition and William Lloyd Garrison strengthened my alliance with Boston and some things Bostonian throughout my life. (At the same time, I was anxious to rid myself of my Massachusetts accent because it produced howls of laughter among my Jersey playmates.)

And there was yet another factor: my next-door neighbors, the Hessleins. Their family consisted of two boys and a girl (Robbie, Nate, and Joyce), and mainly due to the boys, the radio blared Yankee games from their porch. I would listen to their constant references and fanatical devotion to Joe DiMaggio and Phil Rizzuto during that summer of '46.

Robbie, the youngest and about 3 or 4 years my senior, was the patient and more sympathetic youngster, and his patience with me prompted him to build miniature World War II battleships for me, with nails representing the guns, which I could float in the bathtub as

STOP THESE MEN

— Dangerous Characters —

HEADED THIS WAY

Armed with Powerful Clubs

A Menace to Our Fair City

Johnny Pesky — .430

Dom DiMaggio — .391   Hal Wagner — .390

With the red-hot Red Sox headed to New York for what the writers were calling the "World Series in May," the *New York World-Telegram* ran this item (*The Sporting News*, May 16, 1946; reproduced from *When the Boys Came Back*).

I fantasized about our struggle with Germany and Japan during the war years. But their unqualified support for the Yanks put me off a bit (so did Mrs. Hesslein's admission that she wanted to see Billy Conn triumph over Joe Louis that summer because "we need a white champion"—Louis proceeded to knock him out in the eighth round). And besides, I was from Boston—I should be a Red Sox fan! That is how it all began—and that part of the baseball story was to unfold over many years.

Never again after 1946 would the Red Sox be quite so supreme. Even in the most triumphant year of 2004, when the Red Sox obtained their first World Championship in 86 years, the club could never catch the Yankees in the regular season Eastern Division race to the wire and thus replicate that sweet summer fifty-eight years earlier. Even then it was not quite the same as in '46!—though the heroics of David Ortiz and Dave Roberts made me think back to that third Dave: Dave Henderson, whose dramatic 1986 home run against the Angels rescued the Red Sox from playoff oblivion. They went on to a fourth post–World War II American League Championship, only to be denied at the altar again in the most excruciating of last-moment snatches of defeat from the jaws of victory.

Only in 2007, when the Red Sox would achieve yet another World Series sweep (I was able to be at the final games in both St. Louis and Denver in '04 and '07 respectively) was the Red Sox triumph truly perfect, given the Eastern Division championship as well as postseason success. Then the "Red Sox Nation," as it had come to be called in the past decade or so, could revel in newfound dominance which in some measure replicated the 5 out of 14 world championships obtained by the Red Sox in the early part of the twentieth century! Indeed, the club came close to repeating, losing in a hard-fought 7-game American League championship series with Tampa Bay, which went on to defeat in the '08 World Series.

But before then there would be many exciting pennant races in which the Red Sox would participate, particularly in '48, '49, '50 and '67 then in the '70s and the '80s, and again at the turn of this new century. In August '74 I watched the Red Sox take 2 of 3 in Oakland from the defending champion A's, with aging star Juan Marichal pitching eight innings of shutout ball, only to see a 7-game lead over the Baltimore Orioles quickly dissipated thereafter. This "left at the altar" experience was to be repeated many times!

Only in 1978 and in 2007 did they possess a lead comparable to that which they enjoyed in '46. In '78, that was to be frittered away in an injury-riddled September collapse from which the Sox revived 31/2 games back in the middle of the month, only to be beaten by the homers of Bucky Dent and Reggie Jackson in the second-ever American League regular season playoff game. The first was played also by the Sox 30 years earlier to the very day! (That time the result was also a defeat, which I listened to on the radio in the grammar school locker room: a one-sided 8–3 loss at the hands of the Cleveland Indians, led by manager-player Lou Boudreau, who homered twice in the game!)

Leaning against the back of a batting cage in Candlestick Park, bedecked then in a Chicago Cubs uniform, Don Zimmer, Boston Red Sox skipper in the 1970s, summed up my view well with regard to '77–'79 (as well as the '40s) when he said to me, "There were many more good days than bad ones." Indeed, this was to become my view in most of the 60-plus seasons with the Red Sox.

There was to be another aspect of this relationship as well: race. There were no black players in organized baseball in 1946. I was light-skinned as a youth, and my mother fretted about the dark tan that I was acquiring as I played baseball all day — but my father, in his perennially understated and gentle manner, told her not to worry about it.

When I first started playing baseball that summer still shy of my 10th birthday, I do not think that I knew that I was black, even though I had imbibed my parents' message of racial equality as a small child. But I was immediately confronted with racial epithets when other players at the Station Field would be angry with me, like "nigger," and "you are a lot of mulatto," which left me at that point puzzled as well as hurt. Only gradually did the true picture emerge for me personally — and only even later did I begin to understand the racially exclusionary policies of baseball generally as well as the Red Sox in particular. Every single player on the major league fields that summer of 1946 was white!

The Red Sox were to be the last team that would break the color bar, not hiring infielder Pumpsie Green until I was a student at Cornell Law School in 1959. Like all the other teams in baseball during that fateful summer of 1946, they had no black players. The difference for them was that they were to remain lily-white until even after teams like the racially exclusionary Detroit Tigers and the Washington Senators broke the color bar.

I did not know that when Tommy Harper, the fine outfielder and greatest base stealer in Red Sox history (until Jacoby Ellsbury in this century) came to the Carmine Hose in 1972 (subsequently he stayed on as coach in the 1980s, and again at the turn of the century)—he blew the whistle because of Red Sox complicity in the exclusion of black Sox players from a lily-white Winter Haven, Florida, social club. Later I learned through Red Sox Cy Young winner Jim Lonborg and his teammate Earl Wilson that this practice had existed in the 1960s. (When I wrote an op-ed piece in the *Boston Globe* on Opening Day in 1986 attacking Red Sox management I, in turn, was attacked in the *Globe* by the late Will McDonough. He said I knew nothing about the Red Sox and that he had spoken with Red Sox management who assured him that their predecessors had not been racists![7])

I did not know that Jackie Robinson—who would be such an important part of our household discussions in 1947—had already had a tryout in '45 with the Red Sox in Fenway. By all accounts he tattooed the left-field wall that day. The Red Sox had not contacted him thereafter, and only later did I learn that Pinky Higgins, the third baseman with the pennant winners and one of owner Tom Yawkey's favorites, whom he twice served as manager in the '50s, was an avowed racist. The unvarnished truth would emerge on the basis of more complete information years later (as described in Chapter 8).

Meanwhile, there were other things relating to the game in my life besides Major League Baseball in 1946. With friends and sometimes my parents, I frequently attended so-called City League games on weekday evenings and became a supporter of Cammarano's Bar, a team composed of the Long Branch Acerra Brothers. These Acerra Brothers were a mainstay in the Long Branch tradition and lore, and even when my parents were elderly, one of them delivered mail to their residence. The weekends often saw our family go on driving excursions into the countryside in our 1937 Plymouth, which my parents had bought second-hand just before World War II. The purpose of those trips was often bird watching, my parents being avid ornithologists. But as we drove through rolling hills in Jersey rural areas I could only imagine chasing fly balls up the near-mountainous terrain—an image which was reawakened for me in Vero Beach, Florida, in 1987. The outfield was not fenced off from the hill behind it where spectators sat, and I saw young then-rookie Ellis Burks race up the hill to grab a long drive by Dodger catcher Alex Trevino, scattering the sun-bathing spectators in his wake.

The Sundays of those weekends were very special baseball days after attendance at St. James Episcopal Church, where I was a choirboy from 1943 to 1949. Sunday was the Jersey Shore League, a group of semi-professional players who were a cut above our Long Branch City League. On most Sundays I was able to see the Long Branch Green Sox play their local rivals from Red Bank and Fair Haven and watch Joe Magill with his big roundhouse, over-hand, over-the-top fastball stride toward the plate with an ominous straight-legged kick forward which made most of us perceive him to be unhittable. Frequently I would bike over to Fort Monmouth, where my father worked, and watch black first baseman "Chief" Crump play for a fine military team that knew how to play the game well. (Korean War draftee and Yankee ace "Whitey" Ford was on the team briefly—and they played well in competition with the Philadelphia Athletics and Pittsburgh Pirates in that time period.)

My father had little interest in baseball, but took an interest in my involvement because of his interest in me. Occasionally we would have a catch together, and when Father Robert Anderson, the curate of our parish, would visit our home he would don a glove and short-hop bad throws in the dirt gracefully, prompting much applause from my father and neighborhood kids like Harry Levin, who lived across the street and would always wander to our home when he heard that Father Anderson was in the neighborhood. Years later in the Oakland Coliseum I would think anew of Father Anderson as I watched A's third sacker Eric Chavez gracefully short-hop difficult grounders which came in his direction.

One time, listening to Ted Williams strike out with the bases loaded against the Yankees on the radio, my father consoled me by recalling his memories of Babe Ruth. He said, "It happened to the Babe also." Though my father grew concerned because of my fanatical and almost obsessive devotion to baseball, in 1947 he hooked up a shortwave radio for me in our cellar so that I could listen to Jim Britt broadcast the Red Sox games and hear those of the National League's Boston Braves as well! Many of the Braves' road games were by tele-graph recreations where the clickety-clack could be heard in the background.

Based upon my reading of the *New York Times* and various baseball magazines (I was forbidden to read the sports section of scandal-filled tabloids like the *New York Daily News*, although I caught a quick read of it when I went to the barbershop, where it was available to all who dared pick it up), I knew all the hitting and pitching statistics for all twenty-five players on all sixteen clubs. My father confided in Father Anderson that this kind of pursuit of any subject seemed to him to be out of balance — and it probably was!

In the 1950s I was to reverse course because of both a determined effort to catch up on the reading of history, politics, and literature that I had missed earlier, and boredom and bitterness over New York Yankee hegemony. Then, my father reversed course as well, and asked me on more than one occasion: "Whatever became of baseball?" In the 1960s both the decline of the Yankees and the rise of the Red Sox were to revive my interest. The 1967 "Impossible Dream" season, in which Carl Yastrzemski, with his late-inning dramatic and late inning home runs, seemed to singlehandedly take the Red Sox to the pennant that Sep-tember, was a real turning point for me. Yastrzemski, like Williams before him in 1942 and '47, was to be a Triple Crown winner (leading the league in batting average, home runs and runs batted in), and the last hitter to do this in baseball. As much as anything, that great four-way pennant race of 1967 brought me back to those days in the 1940s when my father cautiously indulged my baseball passion.

Though he had not played baseball in his youth, he had been more of a competitive athlete than I, having been a half back for Hyde Park High School and Worcester Polytechnic Institute in Massachusetts. Like his son, he was not fast and would often tell me stories deprecating his skills. One that I remember in particular is about a game played against Fitchburg: he said the line opened a hole "big enough to drive a Mack truck through." Toward the end of the game, he received the handoff and would have scored the game-win-ning touchdown if he had only held onto the ball, but he fumbled it away. He said that years later he went to a dance and made a great impression upon a girl from Fitchburg until, he said, she stood back and looked at him with dawning recognition: "Oh, you're the guy who fumbled at Fitchburg!" My father claimed that the evening went downhill from that moment onward!

That summer of 1946, notwithstanding his lack of baseball interest, he agreed to take me to my first game in Yankee Stadium. This was no small undertaking, for New York City was 50 miles to the north, and the train ride, tickets, and other incidentals were quite a financial investment for a family of modest means. August 21 was that big day. It was a dou-ble-header between the Yankees and the Chicago White Sox in "The Stadium."

The first game was relatively straightforward and one-sided, with the Yankees routing the White Sox 10–1. Joe DiMaggio hit a long home run to left field and outfielder Charlie "King Kong" Keller hit a towering shot to deep right. Nonetheless, Mike Tresh, the White Sox backstop, made a great impression on me as he seemed so stolid behind the plate in the second game or "nightcap," as it was called. Chicago White Sox manager Ted Lyons disputed a call when one of his players had been thrown out. Lyons just jumped up and down and gesticulated and even kicked some dirt. My father laughed aloud and noted the similarity between the game of baseball and grand theater. I am not sure that he would have concurred with the MLB Vice President for Umpiring Mike Port's views when Port said: "This [theatrical behavior] is part of the fabric of the game ... perhaps what leads to arguments and ejections might relate to the number of decisions made by those officials and those competing within the rules."[8]

The second game went 12 innings, with the Yankees prevailing again — this time in the bottom of the 12th, 5–4. Joe D. hit another one. Yankee Johnny Murphy was on the mound in relief and got the victory. (He would be acquired by the Red Sox in the following year in their vain attempt to catch the Yanks in '47.) My father called my attention to some of Murphy's mannerisms: a deep bow before he would begin his wind-up, although my father was quick to say that perhaps other pitchers did this in the same way. This, along with a profound swing of the arms backward and forward during the windup prior to the ball's delivery, was a mannerism peculiar to the pitchers of the '40s and '50s. (This was the precise motion displayed by Cleveland's Paul Byrd, who exercised such mastery over both the Red Sox and the Yankees in the 2007 playoffs.) The two of us were getting our first look at big league pitchers together, for it was my father's first game too.

This first game was emblazoned in my consciousness all throughout my life. Though I was grateful to my father for taking the time to go with me to New York, I am not sure that I was adequately appreciative of the fact that he got far more than he bargained for — not only a double-header, but extra innings as well! This was a very long excursion, particularly for a man who had very little interest in baseball at that time.

There are features of that double-header that will always be with me. The reaction of the cognoscenti when a particular pitcher would appear from the bullpen — so many knew him by his appearance in the distance, through the way in which he walked in from the bullpen. (No relief pitchers ran in from the bullpen to speed the game up in those days; they walked in a stately, measured and dignified manner.) The crack of the catcher's mitt as he was receiving the pitcher's warm-up in the bullpen and the echo that resonated from the concrete walls of the bullpen. Years later the sounds that I would hear in Anaheim Stadium before its 21st century renovation, the home of the expansion California Angels (now called the Los Angeles Angels of Anaheim), reminded me of that early auditory experience.

The 1946 season moved on. Everything that sweet summer was so perfect as the Red Sox held their insurmountable margin. Ted Williams belted two homers at the All Star game played in Fenway Park, one off Pittsburgh Pirate veteran (and anti-union) pitcher "Rip" Sewell's so-called Euphus pitch, which was a soft "blooper" rising high in the air and descending just as it moved plateward. The American League won the game in an unforgettable rout, 12–0, to which I listened on the radio in a Station Field teammate's house on Bath Avenue.

Subsequently, Stan Lomax described the difficulties that the Red Sox had in clinching the pennant notwithstanding their runaway lead. The champagne was being kept on ice, he said, for a number of September days during a six-game losing streak which took the Sox from Washington to Philadelphia to Detroit and then to Cleveland, where they were beaten by Bob Feller in the first game of the series. And then came that special day in Cleveland when Tex Hughson outdueled Red Embree. Lomax described Williams's unusual opposite-field inside-the-park home run in Cleveland's Municipal Stadium — he was up against the Boudreau Shift that year, where the shortstop was on the right-field side of second base (similar to that employed against Jason Giambi, Barry Bonds and David Ortiz in recent years)—and he generally refused to do anything but pull. He would not give in. But that day was different. Williams sliced one to left, thus producing one of two Red Sox hits, which was enough to give the team a 1–0 victory and to put the Red Sox in the World Series for the first time since 1918.

Joyfully, I heard Stan Lomax's recapitulation of it all. Said Frederick Turner later:

> The ball rolled all the way to the wall and into a drain before Mankiewicz [the Cleveland center fielder] could get to it, and even then he had trouble fishing it out. Meanwhile, Williams with his long, loping gait had gotten into high gear and Cronin coaching at third gave him the sign to go home. Williams did, scoring well ahead of the throw on the first, and only, inside-the-park home run he ever hit.[9]

The Red Sox were now American League champions the first time in almost thirty years. But the 1946 World Series itself was to be a different matter. I was to learn a good deal about it because of home confinement due to illness.

Notwithstanding my deep involvement with baseball and then football, I was a very sickly, asthmatic child, out of school more than I was in, with a number of bouts of pneumonia before the days of penicillin. During these illnesses, my father would make me laugh by imitating the facial expressions and the dance routine of a young man who had competed with him for my mother's affections before they were married. He would make me giggle with laughter no matter how badly I felt. And he would raise my spirits by singing the songs of World War I that his uncles had brought home, along with the "Battle Hymn of the Republic" and "Marching Through Georgia," both of which he had heard so frequently at the knee of my great-grandfather, a Civil War naval veteran. "Left, left," he would intone the World War I American Army chant, "I had a good job when I left. I left my wife and two fat babies. Left, left...."

I had one of those sick bouts, home ill from grammar school, during portions of the 1946 World Series. I was able to listen to three or four of the games on the radio and was mildly surprised by manager Joe Cronin's selection of Tex Hughson to pitch the opener. Still exclusively dependent upon Yankee broadcasts, I thought that that role belonged to Mississippian Dave Ferriss, who had been invincible against the Yankees and had won five more games than Hughson (25–6 for Ferriss and 20–11 for Hughson). The pitching rotation could be established exactly as the Red Sox wanted it because they had waited while the Cardinals and Dodgers, having finished in a flat-footed tie in the 154-game pennant race, played a two-out-of-three-game playoff series (which the Cardinals won in 2) to determine who would be the National League Champion. In order to keep sharp, the Red Sox had played a group of collected All Stars, and Stan Lomax had advised us in his WOR broadcast that Ted Williams had been hit on the elbow in that game by Washington Senator lefty Mickey Haefner's errant pitch inside. This development was to have an impact on the Series itself, and it highlights the 2007 dilemma confronting the Colorado Rockies, who had prevailed in their unforgettable "Roctober." They too had no team to play as they waited in the snow for the outcome of the Red Sox–Indians American League Championship Series that year.

That day in 1946, I listened to the radio on Sunday afternoon when the Series opened, as first baseman Rudy York, the Red Sox hero of the Series, tagged a 10th-inning home run to give the team the 3–2 victory. My exultation subsided, however, in the second game as Harry "The Cat" Breechen (of whom both its composer, Dave Frishberg, and Blossom Dearie had sung in the song "Van Lingle Mungo") bested Red Sox lefty Mickey Harris to tie the Series up.

But then it was back to Fenway Park for the third game as I still lay in bed home from grammar school. The seemingly invincible Dave Ferriss took the mound and shut out the Cardinals, only faltering slightly in the 9th when Stan Musial, the outstanding Cardinal hitter, tripled with two outs. But Ferriss was equal to the task, striking out Enos Slaughter to end it all. Rudy York had homered again to put the Sox in front. Meanwhile, the bat of the great Ted Williams was silent and he was to hit only .200 in the Series. I listened in shock when he laid down a bunt on the third base line which was a sure base hit against the "Boudreau shift" (named for the Indian player-manager who had devised it to cope with Williams's pull-hitting tendencies), which Cardinal manager Eddie Dyer substantially adopted so as to deprive Williams of hits on most things hit inside the park on the right field side.

I was able to hear at least one other game in its entirety on radio, but I have always tried to suppress the memory of that Cardinals 12–3 rout of the Sox to even it up. By the 7th and deciding game my parents had decided that my health had recovered sufficiently and I had to go to school that day.

When I returned home after school to turn on the radio I was stunned to hear the Cardinals pounding Red Sox pitcher Ferriss and astounded by Enos Slaughter's dash to the plate, coming all the way from first base on a Harry "the Hat" Walker double to center. That night Stan Lomax characterized Red Sox shortstop Johnny Pesky as "the goat" of the Series because he maintained that Pesky, the recipient of the relay throw from the outfield,

Enos Slaughter's mad dash to the plate ruins the author's blissful summer of 1946. Scoring from first base, Slaughter gives the Cardinals victory over the Red Sox for the World Championship, October 1946. Umpire Al Barlick calls him safe, as catcher Ray Partee awaits the throw to the plate. Marty Marion, up next for the Cardinals, looks on (courtesy Roy Partee).

The greatest "shot heard 'round the world" since Bobby Thomson in 1951, Bill Mazerowski in 1960 and Carlton Fisk in 1975. Dave Henderson revives the Red Sox from postseason oblivion in October 1986. The author and his eldest son are sitting down the left field line in this photograph celebrating. The inscription, written by Henderson, says: "This is the game all of Boston remembers and a pretty good day for me" (courtesy Dave Henderson).

had hesitated in throwing the ball to the plate, thus allowing Slaughter to score the winning run. As time went on, however, more attention focused on the fact that Leon Culberson, called in to substitute for ailing Red Sox centerfielder Dominic DiMaggio,[10] had been slow to retrieve the hit. And the movies of the game — there were no TV tapes or videos then — were inconclusive on Pesky's responsibility.

Said Bobby Doerr years later:

> [I] did call out that play.... I'm on second base, thinking the play might come in there, and Pesky's on the grass out in back of shortshop, and I looked over and I saw Gonzalez [Cardinals third base coach] holding up his hands up in the air trying to hold Slaughter up. And I saw that so I'm sure that I had to yell out home, and actually I've seen replays and Pesky turned about as good on that as if he would have got the call — he made a pretty good play on that ... Culberson went out there he was playing very conservative as he played the ball — when Dom [DiMaggio] would have charged it, because of [being] used to playing out there. And I think that that probably cost the play there, that he didn't come in and charge the play....

That was just before the end of the 7th game in the Red Sox' ninth inning in St. Louis. (Under today's rules it would have been played in Boston — but more about that later!) Then, in the bottom of the inning, Tom McBride grounded out to second base for the final out and the unthinkable had happened: the Sox had lost the Series.

Baseball in 1946 was over. A lot of baseball had taken place off the field, which, at least for awhile, was barely in the subconscious of our Station Field gang, if at all. There was much player dissatisfaction. A few months before we had taken the field, many prominent players had departed for the Mexican League to chase an illusory promise of improved pay and conditions, and the owners had been alarmed by an unsuccessful attempt to organize the players into a union. But now, in my world, there was next year — and after winter's long months, 1947 played out. This time the pundits had it wrong again. In 1946 they had assumed that the Yankees would regain their prewar preeminence. That year one of the vestrymen at St. James Church had been at spring training and reiterated what all the prognosticators were saying: that the Yankees would win in a romp. Now, in '47, the Red Sox, having left Detroit and New York in their wake the previous year, were established as the same prohibitive favorites, and this time around the soothsayers were as wrong as they had been in '46. But as the 1947 season began, an event much more important than predictions about the Red Sox took place — the promotion of Jackie Robinson to the Major Leagues as the first black American in Major League Baseball in the twentieth century.

I had been hardly aware of Robinson's 1946 successes with the Montreal Royals, the Dodgers' farm team, even though the Royals played some of their games to the north of us, in Jersey City and Newark. But his '47 debut created drama and excitement in our Long Branch home. When the Dodgers came north from spring training, my father — who had had so little interest in baseball — began the pre-dinner conversation by discussing the Yankee–Dodger Subway Series in which Robinson played. "I hear that Robinson knocked one in today," he said. The eyes of the world were on Brooklyn when he started for them on April 15, 1947. His fine hitting, defensive play (he was placed at an entirely new position which he had not played, first base), and dramatic base-running skills and intelligence made his appearance the greatest development in modern U.S. race relations. Seven years before *Brown v. the Board of Education*, the Supreme Court's landmark decision declaring segregation of the races in public education to be unconstitutional, his courage and success inspired people of all races.

I did not see Robinson until a double-header against the Cubs in 1949 when he was established clearly as a .300 hitter — and afterward my sharpest recollection was of another black pioneer, his teammate Roy Campanella's snappy pickoff throws to first base, which he made while he appeared to be looking directly at the pitcher. Notwithstanding the passions that I felt for Robinson in 1947, the passion for the Red Sox was now equally strong. Accordingly, in May of that year my father and I were to travel to Yankee Stadium by train as the rain and clouds threatened to cancel our attendance of that Red Sox–Yankee matchup — my first Red Sox game in my life.

James F. Dawson, of the *New York Times*, in a column which appeared adjacent to a classy advertisement about the Red Sox and a portrait of center fielder Dom DiMaggio, summed it up well:

> Dave (Boo) Ferriss was the victim in this latest abuse of American League royalty. The giant from Shaw, Miss. was buried under the driving power of the Yankee squad which clubbed him for eight solid hits, ran the bases with what appeared reckless abandon and thrilled onlookers with defensive display that sparkled in harmony with the superlative pitching of [Spud] Chandler.[11]

Chandler was perfect that day, going the distance and throwing a two-hitter at the Red Sox, one of them collected by good hitting pitcher Ferriss himself. In the first of a number of games in which I was to see the same thing, Williams was hitless. George (Snuffy) Stirnweiss (the last wartime batting champion with a .309 average) made a beautiful backhanded catch behind second base in shallow center on a line drive hit by veteran Wally Moses, who pinch-hit for the catcher. Billy Goodman, the much-heralded rookie from Louisville who was to be sent back before returning for a number of distinguished years with the Sox, struck out as a pinch hitter in the 8th.

The Red Sox were not to seriously challenge the Yanks that summer. They were doomed to a third-place finish far off the pace in a role reversal with the '46 Bronx Bombers, notwithstanding Ted Williams's Triple Crown achievement. Three of the four-man starting rotation (Ferriss, Hughson, and Harris) came up with sore arms prior to a new age of modern surgery. None of them would ever be the same pitcher again.

That summer of 1947, I listened to the shortwave radio which my father, employed in the Signal Corps at Fort Monmouth, set up for me in our cellar. Thus before television, satellite hook-ups and Major Baseball League Cable, I was able to hear Red Sox games home and away (and, when the Red Sox were not playing, listen to the Boston Braves as well). From the beginning I was intrigued with the "whoop" sound that the fans would make when a foul ball rolled off the screen behind the plate. (That Fenway tradition seems to have been forgotten in this century.) Utility infielder Eddie Pellagrini hit thirteen of those fouls in one at-bat that summer.

In both these shortwave broadcasts, and in the regular ones of the Yankees in which our favorite broadcaster, Mel Allen, produced enjoyment with his mellifluous voice, I was continuously intrigued by enigmatic references such as "double-barreled activity in the bullpen." What was double-barreled? I wondered before discovering that it was two pitchers warming up, most frequently righty and lefty. What was this thing called a "bullpen"?, I thought, not knowing its apparent derivation from Indian fighting days where "the bullpen" was a square log military enclosure used to contain captured Indians.[12] This came to mean any area of confinement — in baseball, the area where the pitchers warmed up.

And the trades in that year of 1947 were so stunning ... as the Red Sox played the Chicago White Sox in an early spring series, Rudy York was traded straight up for "Jake" Jones and the two of them were playing for their new teams against their old teams the very next day. Hal Wagner, who had caught the Red Sox starting rotation in '46, was traded to Detroit for Birdie Tebbetts in a deal that I thought worked much to the Sox' advantage. Yet Birdie, in a critical Red Sox–Yankee night game which I listened to on the radio, uncorked an errant pickoff throw to second base which rolled into center field and seemed to turn the tide forever against the Sox in the game itself and the entire season.

And then for a couple of years in the late '40s I was not to see the Sox in person — only to listen on the radio which my father had put together for me. On one of our trips to Boston in 1949 the Boston Braves were home, and along with 3,000 other fans after the Braves' hopes of repeating their '48 National League championship had disappeared, I watched high-kicking Warren Spahn defeat the Chicago Cubs there. Meanwhile, my mother and I went to a 1948 double-header between the '48 World Champion Cleveland Indians and the Yankees. I never saw anyone swing as hard as Cleveland outfielder Larry Doby, who came up the same year as Robinson and was the first black American League player. Frequently, when he swung and missed a pitch, he would fall down from the force of his hard cut. His intensity made me a Larry Doby fan immediately. And just beyond our seats down the left field line that day, ex–Negro League pitcher Satchel Paige (supposedly then 40!) would amble in and get the Yankees out in the wicked humidity of a Bronx summer.

Paige, the veteran black hurler who had been barred by baseball's color bar for so many years, walked past our seats down the left field line as he sauntered in from the bullpen to retire three Yankees consecutively in the last half of the 8th inning of the second game. His famed "hesitation pitch" seemed to baffle the opposition. And the right note was struck

Bobby Doerr, All-Star second sacker for the Red Sox in the 1940s. The author attempted unsuccessfully to follow in his footsteps (courtesy the Boston Red Sox).

for us when Doby collected three hits that day.

Player-manager Lou Boudreau moved far to his right and fielded a ground ball that was hit in foul territory beyond third base. The fans shouted desperately, "Lou, Lou!" pleading with him to toss the ball to them in the stands. He would not do so since all players would be fined for such an infraction — a sharp contrast to the post-'94-'95 strike era when the owners encouraged the players to toss foul balls into the stands so as to win back those who had been disillusioned by baseball's long strife.

Still, I followed the Red Sox from the beginning to the end of those madcap 1948 and '49 pennant races in which the Red Sox, in both seasons, fumbled at the outset and started far behind, only to relentlessly march to the top — just losing the pennant in both instances in the last game played, in the first of a number of those "left at the altar" scenarios. In '48 the Red Sox had spent the prior '47-'48 winter (a memorable one in which I dug my parents out of five feet of snow just before Christmas) stocking up with the St. Louis Browns' stars, like slugging Vern Stephens, ace right-handers "Handsome" Jack Kramer and Ellis Kinder, and utility infielder Billy Hitchcock, who was to successfully fill in for Bobby Doerr when Doerr was injured in the summer of '48. It was a veritable fire sale, costing the Sox $375,000 and utility players.

The Sox also had obtained the Washington Senators' outstanding hitter Stan Spence, who never really panned out in a Red Sox uniform — at least at the level comparable to his performance as a Senator. (These acquisitions were subsequently rivaled only by those that occurred in the winter of 2003-04 when the club obtained premier starting pitcher Curt Schilling and ace reliever Keith Foulke, a free agent coming over from the Oakland A's and, again, in 2010-11 when they picked up Adrian Gonzales and Carl Crawford.)

In the winter of '47-'48, as Czechoslovakia fell behind the Iron Curtain, Manager Joe Cronin was kicked upstairs to the general manager slot and replaced by "Marse" Joe McCarthy, who wore a uniform without a uniform number. Though he wore a uniform, he, like Philadelphia A's Manager Connie Mack, could not come on the field of play itself because the uniform was unnumbered. (Mack himself wore a stylish and well-tailored suit in the dugout.)

"Marse" was the plantation term for "Master," which resulted from his harsh disciplinarian ways when he was the successful New York Yankee manager, and was a term that seemed to offend no one in the still nearly all-white world of baseball at the time. McCarthy, characterized as a "push-button" manager in his Yankee days, always had a set lineup[13] with the Red Sox (in contrast to Casey Stengel's two platooning lineups with the Yankees), and he came to be regarded by Red Sox players like Doerr and Johnny Pesky as remote and distant (though Pesky found him to be appreciative of good work nonetheless).

In sharp contrast to '46 and '47, when the Red Sox and Yankees had pulled far in front of the rest of the League, '48 was a dogfight — a three-way contest with the Detroit Tigers fading earlier and the Red Sox, Yankees, and Indians in contention until the last weekend, when the Yankees were forced out.

As in '47, however, the Red Sox trailed early — and this time came on and got themselves into contention as the weather grew hotter. This was another great year for Williams, though his batting average rising to .369, about 20 points higher than where he had been the previous two years, seemed to provide something of a trade-off in the home run area when he hit only 25. The 1948 season marked the rise of the rookie Mel Parnell, who had been sent down earlier in '47 (along with Harry Dorish), and who was somehow mysteriously unavailable in the first playoff game ever played in the history of the American League — it was necessitated by a flat-footed tie between the Indians and the Red Sox on the last day. At grammar school at the end of a P.E. class, I heard the bits of the broadcast providing the sad news that the Indians had triumphed 8–3 with only Bobby Doerr homering for the Sox and Williams's bat again silent as it had been in the '46 World Series, this time throttled by lefty Gene Bearden.

Winter was again filled with what might have been and the focus was on McCarthy's questionable choice to pitch another erstwhile St. Louis Brownie, Denny Galehouse, rather than 15-game-winner rookie Parnell. (McCarthy was also second-guessed, Yankee announcer Mel Allen told us, for placing defensively limited Vern Stephens at short, moving Johnny Pesky from that position to third.)

The 1949 season produced yet another torrid pennant race, this time one in which Cleveland and Detroit were pushed to the background as the Red Sox and the Yankees fought it out in a 154-game season which was described so vividly by the late David Halberstam in *Summer of '49*. This represented yet another poor start from the gate by the Red Sox, who possessed virtually all the key personnel that they had relied upon in '48. The big difference this season was the acquisition of Al "Zeke" Zarilla, again from the hapless Browns, who periodically dealt their best players away — just as the more successful Oakland A's today have allowed the escape of Mark McGwire, Jason Giambi, Miguel Tejada, Keith Foulke, Tim Hudson, Mark Mulder, Rich Harden and Don Haren to other, more prosperous teams through the free agent process, as well as countless trades of those who were about to become free agents. Moreover, the Red Sox pitching was much stronger this time around with the true blossoming of Parnell (25–7), who, along with ex–Brownie Ellis Kinder (23–6), provided the team with a 1–2 pitching combination similar to that of Johnny Sain and Warren Spahn of the Boston Braves (remember the adage "Spahn and Sain and two days of rain"?[14]) and 2004's Curt Schilling–Pedro Martinez combo for the World Championship Red Sox. As in '48, the '49 pennant race seemed to have an ebb and flow to it.

Again the Bosox stumbled badly at the beginning and then in June seemed to be making a move towards the top. While I was playing softball and boxing at New Jersey's Camp Ockanickon during the summer of '49, the word filtered back to us as to how the Yankees, having missed Joe DiMaggio for the first part of the season (because of a bone spur in his heel), swept the Red Sox in Fenway, Joe D winning it all with a startling display of home run power. But as in '04, when the Red Sox recovered from a mid-season setback at Yankee hands in Fenway, Joe McCarthy's crew was not to be counted out. As in '48, the club regrouped and began a steady march back towards the top of the pile.

With a week to go in the September race I listened on the radio to a game played in

Yankee Stadium (after the Red Sox had won two in Fenway) to hear the Sox prevail on a circus-like leaping catch by Zeke Zarilla in right field, robbing the Yankees of a homer, and Johnny Pesky's slide to the plate under Ralph Houk's tag with a go-ahead run. (Yankee broadcaster Mel Allen was beside himself in describing this — he had already called Pesky out from the radio booth when the ball arrived before Pesky did!)

And then it was on to the season's last week, when the Red Sox lost some of their advantage as Ray Scarborough of the Washington Senators beat them in the mud in that town. But on the final weekend the Sox were still ahead by one game as they arrived in Yankee Stadium with two to go, needing only one to clinch the pennant. This, then, was the culmination of two seasons filled with exultation and despair where spring, the long summer and now fall, were the mirror image of life's valleys and mountains.

I *had* to see this on television — a medium which my family did not possess — and my father arranged with one of his friends, a Red Sox fan named Dan Kelly who hailed from Massachusetts, to have me come over and witness history with him, the two biggest games of the season. I knew the route well because Kelly lived around the corner from St. James Church, and I jumped on my bike and arrived at his house on the Saturday of the first one with some time to spare.

The game, pitched by Parnell, the first of the above-mentioned 1–2 rotation, saw the Sox give him the lead. But Johnny Lindell's home run turned the tide for the Yankees and it was now a flatfooted tie between the two clubs for first. Sunday would decide it all.

That second game, which I biked back for again, was an even more dramatic one. This time it was Ellis Kinder on the hill against Yankee ace Vic Raschi. In the first inning a line drive hit down the left field line by Phil Rizzuto was kicked around by Ted Williams against the bullpen, bouncing away from him to his right. (That memory was renewed when, during the '86 playoffs which I witnessed between the Red Sox and the California Angels, a ground ball inexplicably went through Red Sox slugger Jim Rice's legs, rolling to deep left field! He threw his arms up in horror as soon as it happened!) That liner and fielding miscue produced a triple. Rizzuto then scored on a ground ball and the 1–0 lead held up until the fateful 8th inning.

In the 8th, the pitcher, Kinder, was scheduled to hit; no designated hitter rule existed until 1973. The one major weakness of the '49 Red Sox was a thin bench and manager McCarthy elected to pinch-hit for Kinder with a relatively untried and untested rookie who was the batting champion in the American Association, Tom Wright. Wright grounded out in his pinch hitting role.[15]

In the Yankee 8th, the home team unloaded on a series of Red Sox relievers, prominent among them being the erstwhile greats of the '46 team, Ferriss and Hughson, who never reclaimed their former abilities and certainly did not do so that day. The Yankees scored four runs, which gave them a 5–0 cushion. In the 9th the long-silenced Red Sox artillery opened up and scored on a long drive going over Joe DiMaggio's head, and the score was now to 5–3.

But then, just as radio had brought the news of McBride's groundout to second in 1946, Birdie Tebbetts was to foul out to Tommy Henrich near the dugout for the third out and another defeat, this time brought to me on this new medium called television. The Red Sox had not won either of those last two games. Williams's bat was again silent and I would go through life forever second-guessing McCarthy's decision to pinch-hit Wright for Kinder.

This was the beginning of perhaps the most formidable Yankee dynasty of all, which produced five straight world championships between 1949 and 1953, an ugly period of New York dominance more complete than that between 1998 and 2000! (The latter, we now know, was steroid assisted!) The '50s became a period of history which helped drive me as far away from baseball as I could be. And dwindling attendance figures showed that others were driven away through boredom as well.

Now, to make matters worse, Ernest Hemingway could have the old man in *The Old Man and the Sea*, the Yankee fan from Cuba, speak of the powerful-pitching Cleveland Indians as the Yankees' archrival. He would say continuously, "I fear the Indians of Cleveland." The Sox were hardly even an afterthought for the old man — but their decline through this period still saw some good teams as well, at least through 1952. Then Williams left to serve in the Korean War, though not before clubbing a dramatic two-run homer in his last game on April 30, 1952, to give the Red Sox a 5–3 victory duly chronicled that evening by Stan Lomax. Williams's plane, later shot up over North Korea, was forced to make a landing on a "wing and a prayer." Then Dom DiMaggio, "The Little Professor" — so named because he was one of the few players to wear glasses — retired prematurely after then Sox Manager Lou Boudreau benched him. Johnny Pesky left in a blockbuster trade with the Detroit Tigers and Vern Stephens would be dealt away as well. Suddenly, now a teenager, I watched the young men grow old as I reflected upon mortality for the first time!

But before this could happen, 1950 — a year in which I would unsuccessfully attempt to establish my football bona fides with Coach Mazzaco, and one in which the North Koreans crossed the 38th parallel in June — would provide a new round of drama. On Opening Day 1950, hopes were high yet again and the Red Sox, facing the Yankees that day with Parnell on the hill, moved out to a 9–0 lead in the 4th inning. It seemed insurmountable. But, like the 1978 season itself, it was not. In one of the most demoralizing games I have ever listened to on the radio, the Yankees chipped away at that lead, ultimately going ahead 10–9 and winning the game, 15–10. Again, as had been done on the last day of the '49 season, the Red Sox emptied the bullpen with Ferriss making the long trek in a futile quest to quell the Yankee bats.

Yet again, the Red Sox seemed to pick themselves up and march forward in the month of May, and when they arrived in Yankee Stadium on Memorial Day in 1950 it seemed as though everyone, or virtually everyone, was hitting .300 in the Red Sox lineup. My mother and I jumped on the train to head to Yankee Stadium yet again in the hope that the Red Sox would continue their now improved season.

Memorial Day 1950 was memorable not simply because of the two games played that day, as well as the intensely hot weather that was reminiscent of earlier stadium games that we had seen, but also because my mother's pocketbook was picked as we proceeded down the Yankee Stadium walkway at the double-header's completion. In some respects that event was emblematic of what we had witnessed on the field that day.

In the first game, Mel Parnell, not nearly as successful in 1950 as he was in '49, could not get out of the first inning. Eleven Yankees batted during that frame and the first five crossed the plate. A throng of 73,728 (the fire regulations were less strict then for standing room) watched Yankee pitcher Tommy Byrne's single send Parnell to the showers. Walt Masterson, another Sox acquisition from the doldrum-dwelling Washington Senators (first in the country and last in the American League, said the wags), relieved Parnell, and his slow junk made Yankee lefty "Steady" Eddie Lopat, who pitched the second game, look positively fast, though Lopat was regarded as a junk pitcher himself.

The Sox threatened seriously once when, as they trailed by an 11–7 score, Vern Stephens launched a long bases-loaded drive which disappeared into the left field seats just on the wrong side of the foul pole. Baseball is a game of inches.

The second game was equally depressing. This one belonged to Ellis Kinder, who had been given a 3–2 lead until the 6th. Joe Collins tagged two into the short right field porch of 296 feet from home plate, which had been built for Ruth in Yankee Stadium (it looked even shorter that day), to give the Yankees a second-game victory over the Sox in what John Drebinger of the *Times* called the "after piece." This time Williams, "The Thumper" as we called him in those days, had a hit in each game, although I can scarcely recall them. No home run was produced by Williams, though Stephens, his RBI partner in those years (much like David Ortiz was to Sox slugger Manny Ramirez), socked one in the first contest prior to his long foul ball. (In fact, the Williams–Stephens and Ortiz–Ramirez combinations are the two greatest run-producing combinations in baseball since Babe Ruth and Lou Gehrig of the Yankees!)

It was a long, hot Memorial Day. The fall of that year would bring me back to the stadium once more with my 9th-grade classmate Harvey Stein in the cool air of September. The result was regrettably the same: a defeat at the hands of Casey Stengel's Yankees and consequent daydreams about 1951. That day I passed a disconsolate-looking Johnny Pesky (now switched back to shortstop by new Sox manager Steve O'Neill) as he walked down the sidewalk next to Yankee Stadium.

*   *   *

So much has changed on the field as well as off it, from my period in the 1940s through 2011. Double-headers — those that I saw in '46, '48–'49, and '50 — were a part of my basic baseball consciousness. In those days there were always a number of scheduled double-headers — particularly on the major holidays like Memorial Day, July 4th and Labor Day. These "twin sets" added to the game's peculiar and unique characteristic of timelessness, in which the clock stands still forever, exaggerated by two games which can be played from early afternoon sometimes through early evening.

The '40s and '50s were in advance of the day of the twilight double-header, and most certainly before the more common twilight or "twinight" double-headers, in which the fans must leave so as to empty their seats for a new crowd which is to see the second game at a separately scheduled time. But, as late as 1964, while working as a junior lawyer for the National Labor Relations Board in Washington, I went to Sunday batting practice at D.C. Stadium before a more traditional Sox–Washington Senator twin bill and probably spent about 9 hours there! Three years later, in a dramatic four-way pennant race involving the Red Sox (a 100-1 underdog at the season's commencement), the Sox came to Yankee Stadium for a big four-game set at the end of August. When the club in the dignified Boston gray lost the second game of a twinighter after 20 innings, it was about 2:00 A.M., and I did not return to my West Side apartment until an hour later at 3 A.M.! Today the traditional double-headers are rarely scheduled, if at all, because of the increased cost, triggered in substantial part by player salaries. The owners are now reluctant to allow fans to get double their money. Generally, when double-headers are scheduled today it is because a rainout has made it necessary to reschedule games. So anxious are the owners to avoid the cost problems associated with double-headers, that in 2004 a Red Sox–Oriole rainout was rescheduled for one game in between two series and just before the Red Sox were to depart for the West Coast. Until the end of the 1970s, the double-header was regarded as something which would attract fans and make more money for the owners. Sadly, this is no longer the case!

The joy of double-headers is inevitably tied into one of the game's most important characteristics. Timelessly, baseball has no clock. It must continue to conclusion — as indeed the duel between pitcher and hitter must continue until the conflict is resolved definitively. In June 2004, Pedro Martinez stared icily at California Angel first baseman Casey Kotchman as he fouled off pitch after pitch only to be retired at the end of his fifteenth pitch at bat, in complete disapproval of the rookie's youthful audacity in Anaheim that night. There had to be strike three, or ball four, or the ball would be put in play — and strike three it was, as the veteran Pedro prevailed.

Again, that 1946 Yankee–White Sox double-header in which my father and I saw our first games together was one in which the Yankees would prevail in a nightcap constituting twelve innings. But the August 1967 double-header was particularly like a Kinsella novel[16] in which the game seems to go on forever — even day after day — when the second of the twilight double-header lasted six hours and nine minutes. The first had been quite different as I had witnessed "Gentleman" Jim Lonborg's victory over the Yankees 2–1. The first game was one of those contests in which there seems to be no question of going to the bullpen (no pitch count appeared in the *New York Times* the following day), and indeed Ellie Howard's catcher's mitt cracked with Lonborg's fastballs in the ninth as he struck out the first two batters and induced the last to ground out to shortstop Rico Petrocelli.

But the second game took an entirely different form — one which went so long that Sox third baseman Joe Foy had 9 at bats. The seventh pitcher of the night, Jose Santiago, surrendered that single in the 20th, which allowed the winning run to score. First baseman George Scott was so exhausted that an earlier throw across the infield had hit his shoe and bounced into the outfield. The game had to be completed no matter how long it took or how exhausted the players were! After all, the song, "Take Me Out to the Ball Game" has as a refrain: "I don't care if I never get back."

An equally abiding feature, and one that also adds to the game's undying attractiveness, is that baseball is peculiarly well suited to observe through attendance rather than television. Television has been particularly important for football and, to a lesser degree, basketball because there are so many things going on at one time that the isolated camera and the replay give one a more profound understanding of the game. In football there are at least three or four games and centers of action going on simultaneously. Basketball moves quickly, and since the observer is watching the player with the ball he cannot see, for instance, player positioning or a foul away from the ball in many or most instances.

In baseball too there is action away from the pitcher and the catcher and wherever the ball goes. The positioning of the fielders tells the observer much about what the defending team perceives the hitter's tendencies to be and the diet of pitches that are being served to him. True, relatively speaking, baseball is transparent — though it too is sometimes dependent upon television to clarify matters. This is particularly true of close plays where the TV can expose umpire errors on whether a runner is safe or out.

The classic illustration is the 1985 World Series, when First Base Umpire Don Denkinger made a call against the St. Louis Cardinals as they appeared to be in a position to beat the Kansas City Royals, concluding that Jorge Orta had beaten out a ground ball for a base hit. Instant replay showed Denkinger's call to be clearly erroneous, and the Royals took advantage of it to tie the Series and eventually beat the Cardinals in the seventh game. Another one initially called wrong was in the sixth game of the ALCS in 2004 between the Red Sox and the Yankees, when a Mark Bellhorn home run which I witnessed at the Stadium clearly made it into the left field seats but was called a ground rule double. Fortunately, the call was reversed, and many have said that, particularly in the postseason when there are outfield umpires, they should be playing further down the line to make these calls correctly. Sometimes, in the postseason when there are additional umpires in the outfield, it is thought that responsibilities are frequently confused and that because umpires are out of their natural position they are thus less properly equipped to make the right judgment.[17]

Bruce Weber reports that some of the most distinguished umpires have had no objection to instant replay: "'I have no problem with it,' the veteran Tim McClelland said to me when I asked if he would object to instant replay on home run calls, 'it takes the pressure *off* us.'"[18] But it is generally thought that replay reviews of the kind which exist in professional football would undermine baseball's ambience and create further delay at a time when baseball wants to expedite its games. Nonetheless, Commissioner Bud Selig had heard so much controversy that in 2007 he was determined to poll all the clubs' general managers.

In the fall they voted to institute instant replay by a vote of 25–5, limiting the replay to "calls involving home runs — whether balls go over foul poles or to the fair side or the foul side, whether balls clear fences and carom back onto the field, whether they go over painted lines at the top of outfield fences, whether fans interfere with balls that appear to clear the fences."[19] This position was subsequently ratified by the owners, players and umpires at some point — and now Selig's new Rules Committee is considering the entire replay issue anew.[20] Squarely at issue in any study of this matter is Rule 9.02(a), which precludes any team from questioning a judgment decision, and Rule 9.02(c), which states: "No umpire shall criticize, seek to reverse or interfere with another umpire's decision unless asked to do so by the umpire making it."

A towering foul home run as high as it was deep in Comerica Park in June 2009 by Micky Cabrera off Tim Wakefield was called foul — and when Tim Tschida led his umpiring crew under the stands to review it, it was confirmed as they emerged on the field. Technology's revelation that umpires had botched a substantial number of calls in the 2009 postseason renewed a debate about whether the instant replay rule should be extended beyond disputes about home runs and home run fences. Incredibly, with two Yankees tagged off base in the ALCS, only one was called out, a product more of brainlock than technology — by the distinguished Tim McClelland, of all people! At the same time, it is important to note that that situation had rarely if ever been seen by anyone.

Said MLB's Mike Port: "The umpires are in a bit of a slump. But there are no excuses. I understand the frustration, I understand the emotion, it's officiating. You aspire to perfection but it's not perfection."[21] The 2010 collective bargaining agreement between MLB and the umpires allows the umpires to be assigned to the postseason in consecutive years, thus avoiding a strict seniority or strict rotation selection so as to assign the very best people. In 2009 it was thought that, for a variety of reasons, the best were not available. In 2010 some of the '09 poor performers did not reappear in the postseason.[22] To complicate matters, as the '10–'11 conclave between players, umpires and owners testifies to, these matters involve the conditions of employment and the collective bargaining process for all parties affected.

The conundrum of the replay debate is between the peril of the game's disruption and the undermining of its ambience on the one hand, and on the other hand, the need to get things right. A difficulty here is that, as in all areas outside hard science, it is sometimes hard to determine the actual truth, as Alex Rodriguez's home run into the new Yankee Stadium's right field short porch in the '09 World Series demonstrated — it was yet another call which was reversed upon review, and yet one could not be certain of the right call at the time of review! Highlighting the subjectivity of calls, "umpire Marty Foster called the Yankee's Derek Jeter out on a steal of third, and though it appeared he was never tagged, Mr. Jeter said Mr. Foster explained that he didn't need to be tagged to be called out because the ball beat him to the bag. Talk about judicial activism! An uproar arose over this, ... [but Mr. Foster may have simply] ... been ... expressing [unwisely] aloud a generally unspoken umpire tenet that allows for some discretion on close plays to keep managers and fans, who can clearly see throws but not tags from the dugout or the stands, from causing a ruckus."[23] Mike Port quotes the old maxim: "What the eye sees, the mind anticipates."

Two points raised by Port highlight the problem. He notes that when Joe West missed a tag he reviewed the video and said that he "would have gotten the call right if I had been standing on the right field roof like that camera was." Similarly Port points that in the 2009 World Series, Philadelphia Phillies second sacker Chase Utley was called out when in fact the ball was six inches away from Mark Teixeira's glove — the time measurement involved between where Utley was when he crossed the bag and the ball's arrival in Teixeira's glove? Four thousandths of one second! Probably baseball would not benefit from reversal of these close calls, which can hardly ever be seen by a human being. Moreover, when players have acted upon a call already made, difficulties are created where replay reverses it. Numerous problems arise.[24]

The Rodriguez home run makes clear the limitations of technology. The steal of home plate by Jackie Robinson as Yogi Berra tagged him in the 1955 World Series, in which the camera indicates that the call was wrong, is a classic. On the other hand, there is the most egregious and unfortunate error of all — the 2010 clearly erroneous call by Jim Joyce with two outs in the 9th, depriving Armando Galarraga of the Detroit Tigers of a perfect game.[25] Perhaps, as lawyers and judges say, hard cases make bad law. But some further incursions upon judgment calls by technology overrides seem inevitable. And beyond this have come calls for more training around the year by umpires.[26]

And then there is the matter of scoring, and a perennial quest to get things right there. Here one can see that the difficulty of determining truth transcends the calls of umpires. Notwithstanding the jazz singer Dave Frishberg's idea that a hit is a hit and a run is a run, in fact, as all scorers and Frishberg know, there is the never-ending debate about what is a hit and what is an error. There seems to be a tendency among scorers (though they are now retained by the League rather than the home team club as was the case in the past) to call hits rather than errors. Only the pitcher is upset with such a call because it can inflate his earned run average if the runner scores, and in any event can increase the number of hits against him — whereas the hitter increases his average and the fielder's deficiencies are not exposed if the scorer rules in favor of a hit.

Beyond the considerations of transparency and the perennial quest for the Holy Grail of truth in determining what actually happened on the field, along with rules and endless debates about such, another attraction of the game is the gracefulness of the play on the diamond. This has not changed — as Joe DiMaggio's seemingly effortless retreat into the old Yankees Stadium's "Death Valley" to grab a fly ball comes to mind.

In the 1994-'95 baseball strike, almost a half century after my love affair with baseball began on the "Station Field," I cast the deciding vote as chairman of National Labor Relations Board to seek an injunction, which successfully brought the longest strike in baseball's history to a conclusion. The then District Judge Sonia Sotomayor (now Justice Sotomayor of the United States Supreme Court), in granting our request for an injunction against unfair labor practices, said the following:

The often leisurely game of baseball is filled with many small moments which catch a fan's breath. There is, for example, that wonderful second when you see an outfielder backpedaling and jumping up to the wall, and time stops for an instant as he jumps up and you finally figure out whether it is a home run, a double or a single off the wall, or an out.[27]

More than a quarter of a century before that 1995 baseball case, on a typically warm and humid night in Washington's D.C. Stadium (later RFK Stadium), Red Sox lefty Dick Ellsworth was on the hill against the hometown Washington Senators and was clearly tiring in the late innings of that 1968 summer night. But Manager Dick Williams had no one in the bullpen effective enough to relieve Ellsworth and thus stayed with him as Hank Allen stepped in at the plate with the Senators trailing 2–1 with two on and two out in the bottom of the ninth. Allen hit a prodigiously long shot to deep left center which Reggie Smith, the then Sox centerfielder, somehow beautifully tracked down and raced to the wall for — and leaped high against the fence.

As he descended to the centerfield grass, there was that precious moment of which Justice Sotomayor spoke. It was similar to Manny Ramirez's spectacular grab in the September 2004 Yankee Stadium Series of a ball which he plucked out of the left field stands after it had been hit off the bat of the Yankee second baseman who circled the bases, thinking he had hit the home run. But in Reggie Smith's descent to *terra firma*, if the ball was over the fence, the Senators had won the game by two runs on a "walkoff," or what the Japanese called a *sayonara* home run. And if it was caught, the game was also over with, the Red Sox the victors.

Only when the Sox bullpen erupted, racing down the left field line and onto the field to greet Smith as he held the ball high, was the result apparent. Smith had made a spectacular grab. This was then that breathless, inescapable moment.

On a brisk evening in Oakland, California, twenty years later, a ground ball is hit into the hole between short and third, for which shortstop Alfredo Griffin ranges far to his right. Griffin turns, as if to throw to first base — and the runner from second base advances off the bag, anticipating an effortless capture of the third sack on the throw to first. And then in mid-air, with the skill of a ballet dancer, Griffin gracefully twirls and throws to second, eliminating the lead runner from the base path.

Even more than its gracefulness — after all, the more athletic basketball players fly through the air with the greatest of ease — the pace of baseball makes it both special and indeed unique. Yet, at the same time, baseball is a contemplative game which induces both reflection and a sense of peacefulness.

The game moves slowly. My sons and I would often stay in the seats of the Oakland Coliseum after the players had long left the field, daydreaming about what we had seen and imagining that it could continue in front of our eyes. Sometimes we stayed so long that the ushers would have to shoo us out. In the '80s, after my sons had departed the household, sometimes I would jump in the car by myself and sit in the bleachers where I could muse in solitary uninterruption.

In June 1951, when my family was visiting my great-uncles in Dedham, Massachusetts, I was able to go to my first game at Fenway Park with my childhood friend Allen Bowser. We watched the Red Sox play the Philadelphia Athletics. Ray Scarborough (now belatedly acquired by the Sox after his Red Sox–killing tours of duty with both the Senators and the White Sox) was the starting pitcher and singled against A's right-hander Carl Scheib in the third inning. Scarborough led off first base. Scheib turned and fired to the base to keep Scarborough close. Scarborough returned to the bag quickly.

The only problem was that A's first baseman Ferris Fain *did not*. Like fans do sometimes when observing the game, he was daydreaming about something else. The pickoff throw hit Scarborough directly in the back of the head providing a sickening crack of his skull which echoed throughout Fenway. Later, notwithstanding a blast to centerfield by A's slugger Gus Zernial for which Red Sox centerfielder Dom DiMaggio stood motionless, not twitching a muscle in his body as the ball sailed beyond him, the Sox prevailed that day 6–5. But I shall never forget Scarborough's departure to the hospital, the victim of a daydream of the sort frequently associated with outfielders and spectators whose attention spans inevitably falter.

Many of the 1940s stadiums — and the same is true of those built in the '90s — possess characteristics which are charmingly idiosyncratic. The nooks and crannies of a field like Camden Yards in Baltimore, which pioneered the so-called "retro" look, with O's outfielder Brady Anderson racing around second as one of his shots ricochets upward from the ledge in right field, is forever emblazoned in one's mind. These features have been emulated in new parks like Safeco Field in Seattle, Jacobs Field in Cleveland, PacBell (now AT&T) in San Francisco, Pittsburgh's PNC Park, and more pitcher-friendly Petco Park in San Diego.

In contrast to the uniformity of basketball and football playing surfaces, the contours of baseball stadiums differ appreciably, making it important for the Red Sox, for instance, to have right-handed power hitters who can reach the left field "Green Monster," and for the Yankees to have left-handed power hitters who can get to the short porch in right field — an advantage initially enhanced in the new 2009 stadium not only by distance but by an apparent wind tunnel which helps propel the ball in flight. Oakland Coliseum gives tremendous advantages to pitching: the A's stellar trio of Tim Hudson, Mark Mulder, and Barry Zito, and the group which succeeded them headed by Joe Blanton and Don Haren, have all benefited from the spacious foul territory in that park, where balls are caught for outs rather than falling harmlessly into the box seats in the stands. They all have since departed through trades or free agency and none have ever recaptured fully the glory obtained in the East Bay of northern California during the early part of this past decade.

The new parks possess dimensions designed to enhance offense as well as charm. At the same time, it is said that Alex Rodriguez was convinced to leave Seattle for Texas because of his complaints about the distant fences in Safeco Field, created in 1999. Yet in this pitcher-friendly terrain, which arguably diminishes the excitement that offense holds for the uninitiated (San Diego's 2004 Petco Field is another), the non-baseball *aficionado* public in Seattle is properly enchanted with the tasteful and romantic train whistle in gentle coexistence with the game beyond its outfield fences.

Though it is said that most of his homers were not pulled sharply to the short porch and that many or most were majestic clouts to right-center, Yankee Stadium was built for Ruth (and indeed *by* Ruth, given his production of spectators after the low-home run "dead ball" era preceding the 1920s), and many of those 714 homers a total unsurpassed until Hank Aaron and Barry Bonds) must be understood in that context. Left-hander Roger Maris had the same advantage as did Mickey Mantle when batting from that side of the plate against right-handed pitchers. Aside from the fact that the swelling crowds were drawn to see the Yankees by the Babe's home run hitting capacity, "the house that Ruth built," having been built for Ruth with dimensions even shorter than those today, constituted one of the first true enhancements long before the days of steroids and the debates and litigation which follow in their wake.

Today the upsurge in home runs and extra base hits, if not batting percentages, is in part attributable to the smaller baseball stadiums which have been constructed beginning in the '90s. They are a response to the ugly concrete jungles or "cookie cutters" with symmetrical and uniform distances built in cities like Pittsburgh, Cincinnati, and Philadelphia in the '70s, and frequently covered by dangerous artificial turf, which caused unnecessary injuries.

This can be seen graphically when one compares the average ballpark dimensions of the 1940s with the first decade of this century. Then the average left field fence was 340 feet; today it is 331. Then to center field, where the average was 424 feet; today it is 405. The comparable figures for right field, paradoxically, are 313 then and 328 now. But the contrast between the average deepest part of the park is instructive: 432 then and 409 now.

Because of these stadium dimensions and a host of other factors like equipment, the height of the pitching mound, the dilution of pitching attributable to the expansion of the 1990s, a widening pool of Latin American players — a factor relevant to all discussions about competitive balance — and even the ball itself, as well as drugs (discussed in Chapter 7), there has been an enormous upsurge in home runs. Sixteen of the seventeen biggest home run seasons have taken place since the 1994 strike — and the other one, 1987, seems to be an outlier and perhaps attributable to the quality of the ball alone. As Joe Posnanski has written, the 2009 Yankee team, operating in what he calls a "pinball machine" — I call it a right field wind tunnel — hit more homers than any other Yankee team in history, including the 1927 "Murderers' Row," the 1998–2000 steroid-fueled gang, and the great Yankees teams of the '50s and the '60s, among which was the Maris and Mantle 1–2 punch of 1961![28]

Stadium dimensions and configurations have always been important, though not as much so as in this century. Fenway Park, which I first saw in '51 at that Red Sox–A's game, receives a lot of attention for its 315-foot left field "Green Monster," which can produce fly ball home runs (until '03 those homers were captured in the net above the wall unless they cleared the screen altogether) and doubles that would be caught for outs in other parks — and simultaneously, as sluggers like Red Sox left fielder Jim Rice know, hard-rising line drives off the wall which would be home runs in other parks but which ricochet into the hands of a left fielder who is able to hold the hitter to a mere single. Indeed, as Rice saw, the wall taketh away as well as giveth. For high fly ball hitters like right fielder Tony Conigliaro and shortstop Vern Stephens, it giveth.

And the wall itself has produced memorable fielding events which were exploited effectively by both left fielders Williams and Carl Yastrzemski. In May 1974 my entire family and I took an East Coast trip and saw the Red Sox defeat the Yankees behind the tempestuous lefty Bill Lee and rookie shortstop Rick Burleson as he gave the Red Sox a lead by lining a double off the wall. Yastrzemski, with a man on first and confronted with a high fly ball, tapped his glove as though he was going to catch it — and then turned quickly at the last moment to gather it in as it came off the wall, throwing to second to force the runner, who much too belatedly made his advance from first for fear of being doubled off that base. (A new wall with the same dimensions was constructed in 1976 — and Yaz and Rice as well had to learn the new carom shots which came off it.) Fenway's right field dimensions are formidable when the ball is hit straight away (380 feet), as Ted Williams — and other renowned Sox left handed sluggers like "Mo" Vaughn and David Ortiz — regretfully discovered (the fence was actually brought in for Williams in 1940). But the cheapest home runs imaginable can shoot down the right field line in "Pesky Corner" (named for shortstop Pesky, who was not known for his power) just inside the foul pole (sometimes called "Pesky Pole") itself.

The vines on the outfield walls of the Chicago Cubs' Wrigley Field, baseball's second-oldest park (Fenway was built at the time of the *Titanic* in 1912, and Wrigley was constructed in 1914) always put me in mind of the Long Branch Station Field, where we had to look for line drives and fly balls in the hedge, trying to retrieve them so as to throw out the runner who was moving rapidly around the bases. Your teammates would scream at you with unforgiving reproach if you could not find and pick the ball out of the bushes quickly — the short distance to that hedge comparable to the dimensions of the Los Angeles Coliseum, in which the Red Sox and Dodgers played one wondrous and quixotic exhibition game in March 2008. This frantic search for the hidden ball lodged in vines is the plight of Wrigley outfielders who, as runners circle the bases, must attempt to find the ball which has been hit into the ivy.

Yankee Stadium ... the first major league ballpark I ever saw, with its majestic stanchions into which I witnessed Mickey Mantle's homers disappear. In the 1940s more than 70,000 fans were present for the capacity games between the Yankees and teams like the Red Sox and the Cleveland Indians. In a 1955 night game between the Red Sox and the Yankees in which Willard Nixon stopped the Bronx Bombers, 4–1, Eddie Robinson blasted a long shot to right center that brought the Yankee crowd to its feet just as the subway was coming into the Bronx Concourse Station. The confluence of the noise of the crowd and the sound of the subway together was deafeningly dramatic — I have never heard anything like it in my life before or since. My heart did not slow down again until the ball was safely caught.

The flip side of this was Tiger Stadium, where I saw my first Red Sox–Tigers game in the summer of 1960. Frank Malzone singled in that game with the bases loaded and the crowd was so silent that one could hear the footsteps of the Red Sox runners circling the bases. This was long before the days when the recently minted Red Sox Nation traveled with the club to other cities. The only noise in the ballpark at that point came from me as I leapt to my feet shouting solitary support for Malzone and the Sox!

Like the loud Red Sox footsteps that 1960 Detroit afternoon, I can recall another sound, this time as a thirteen-year-old in that Cubs–Dodgers double-header in Ebbetts Field, when Frankie Baumholtz lined a double off the right center field wall in that venerable park. I jumped as I heard the tinny sound of the ball pounding off the wall's aluminum padding on that line shot!

At the other extreme from the Yankee Stadium subway train-crowd deafening-roar phenomenon is the sound of the near-empty ballpark. Even Fenway Park in that '51 Red Sox game had only a little more than 5,000 fans present that summer day — something unimaginable for the Red Sox in the '40s and during these past four decades in the wake of the "Impossible Dream" pennant race of 1967 — an unbelievable phenomenon during the continuous sellout crowds in Fenway at the beginning of the new century. The photo finishes and the retirement of the veterans had discouraged even the more loyal elements of the Boston baseball crowd.

Even before the early '50s, the Sox' city rivals, the Boston Braves, had fallen on hard times in 1949. I watched the high kick of left-hander Warren Spahn — and obtained an autograph of No. 96, pitcher Bill Voiselle — as the former subdued the Chicago Cubs 8–4 before 3,363. The near silence of the small scattered crowd in old Braves Field could be matched only by the hundreds who were present in a mid-'80s Red Sox–Toronto game in old Exhibition Field, when all except myself and a few other hardy souls were literally sent to the Canadian showers by a three-hour rain delay, after which the game resumed. Just like Stanford's Sunken Diamond, with its laid-back student body sunbathing on the grass beyond the visiting team dugout, or the Long Branch High School diamond when the City League or the Jersey Shore League played there, one could hear the chatter and whistles of the players.

Even with big crowds, like that in Anaheim Stadium on Opening Day 1984, the piercing whistle of Red Sox shortstop Jackie Gutierrez could be heard above the noise and din. The sounds of the game are often connected not only to the ballpark's idiosyncrasies but also to the crowd itself. Though New York Yankee games played in Oakland have sold out on a number of occasions, the overriding constant for most of my California years has been crowds of 5,000 to 10,000, in which spectator passions and knowledge — or the lack thereof — are more easily exhibited. This problem has grown worse in recent years — indeed, the A's attendance is the worst in baseball as of 2010 — as the Oakland club has threatened to move to San Jose.[29]

The fans, of course, matter and baseball announcers, at least, frequently speak of "taking the crowd out of the game," just as they do in basketball and football. This is particularly true in the traditional parks like Yankee Stadium, Fenway Park, and Wrigley Field, where passions run more deeply.

Meanwhile, on the West Coast, both in northern and southern California and in Seattle, a substantial number of transplanted Red Sox and Yankee fans — even Detroit Tiger fans — are at the ballpark in such numbers that there sometimes seem to be as many fans rooting for the opposition in Anaheim, Oakland and Seattle's Safeco Field as there are supporting the home team. Indeed, both the Red Sox and the Yankees have seen large groups of fans who travel from coast to coast in the past few decades and thus, coupled with the transplants, drown out support for the home team. Because of the rising cost and unavailability of tickets in places like Boston, more fans have been induced to obtain cheap flights to Baltimore, Montreal, Philadelphia (where interleague games have been played with the Phillies and late Expos), and even Tampa Bay. Until recent years this phenomenon seemed to be exclusively associated with European "football" or soccer teams and the unruly hooliganism which followed in their fans' wake.

Though there had been instances of fan violence in recent years, even fighting between fans and players in the early part of this century, and most recently a chair-throwing incident arising out of the taunting of Texas pitchers in Oakland (discussed in Chapter 7), fan presence is not as important as in Japan, where there is a flag-waving and truly inspirational song-singing audience. In the very fine minor league park of the Buffalo Bisons, the understated chants of "Let's go Buffalo" provide a welcome contrast to the attempt to rattle an opposing player by shouting his name in a mockingly melodic manner — Daryl Strawberry was the classic example in the 1986 World Series games played in Fenway Park.

As noted, the 1970s and '80s witnessed the new "cookie cutter" characterless concrete stadiums which were boringly symmetrical. Regrettably these ballparks, whether they were of the outdoor variety or the domed gymnasium types like the old Kingdome Stadium in Seattle and the Metrodome in Minneapolis, frequently possessed Astroturf, which threatened to destroy one of the basic aspects of the game: that it should be played on grass. Even Candlestick, for a period in the '70s, went with Astroturf, and the bounce of the ball was so enormous as to provide an extraordinary advantage to teams like the St. Louis Cardinals. The Cards' speedy hitters benefited from countless balls hit down on the infield; by the time they descended to earth, the hitter was comfortably resting at the first base. The prototype of this was the much-traveled Willie McGee, who spent a considerable amount of time with both the Cardinals and Giants, as well as other teams. The new parks of the '90s and this century have consisted uniformly of grass and not turf. This is the way baseball was intended to be played.

But Astroturf remains in Toronto and was used until recently St. Louis. The consequences are not simply aesthetic. A Red Sox–Blue Jays series in an old Toronto exhibition field saw Ellis Burks diving to make a beautiful stretched-out catch in the outfield. At the end of the game he had an abrasion covering his entire left arm where it had been exposed to the turf. The health consequences are even more difficult for football players, who are jarred upon impact as they go down during a play, but the problem for baseball players is formidable as well.

Baseball is an outdoor game. Among the other major sports, only football is as affected by the weather as baseball is. Along with the peculiar contours of the stadium itself, this is one of the fundamental variables in the game. The wind and the sun, of course, affect baseball, and the fielders must make adjustments through constant examination of the way the flags are blowing in order to determine how to play the ball best.

Again, "The sun was in my eyes" is the traditional baseball excuse ascribed to Reggie Jackson by Dave Frishberg. But sometimes it is valid, just as the lights at night can blind a player temporarily, allowing an easy fly ball to fall harmlessly. Matt Holliday of the St. Louis Cardinals was apparently victimized through night lights at a key moment in a postseason Cardinals–Dodgers game in '09.

The heat can be unbearable, particularly in the East and the Midwest, and — with the arrival of baseball in Atlanta in 1966, and then in Texas — in the South as well. But the West Coast can have its share of this weather too. A three-game series between the Red Sox and the Angels in August 1988 was one which took place in such intense heat that one could not sit in the seats without fear of being burned — as Red Sox closer Lee Smith ambled in from the bullpen to hot-foot the Angels. The same seemed to be true in Yankee Stadium when my mother and I saw Satchel Paige in 1948.

But I, along with every other California-based Bay Area resident exposed to baseball, well know that heat is not the only problem. I have often remarked that my first game at Candlestick Park, the predecessor of the Giants' PacBell or AT&T, was colder than Detroit in January.

In Candlestick there was often brilliant sunshine after the fog had been blown away in the afternoon — though in an almost clock-like fashion, the hot dog wrappers began to swirl around the outfield as the wind gusts and the sea gulls arrived at about 3:00 P.M., much as they do in today's AT&T Park by the China Basin in San Francisco. But Hank Greenwald, the former Giants announcer who subsequently covered the Oakland A's, summed it up well when he said in describing one of his Giant broadcasts at Candlestick: "I was fighting my usual losing battle with the elements when I happened to glance to my right. A couple of booths over, there sat [Dodger announcer] Vin Scully, unruffled, unflustered and with the window closed.... From that moment on, I decided that if the closed window at Candlestick was good enough for Vin, it was good enough for Hank."[30]

Some of the night games were absolutely intolerable! Tim, my second oldest son and a lifelong Giants fan, and I went to Candlestick with the same understanding that existed for us in all other ballparks — we would stay until the very end no matter the score. In 1998 we were rewarded by a Sammy Sosa blast to straightaway centerfield that was hit so hard and deep that one felt that it was still going long after it descended beyond the park's contours. But, a number of years before, on one bitter cold night as the blustery fog and winds rolled in on Hunter's Point from the Bay, I turned to Tim and said: "Do you think that we should go?" His answer was quick and to the point, "Yes." And uncharacteristically, we did so in short order.

CHAPTER 3

The Early Years: The Game and the Law

June is that special month when baseball pennant races often take some form. In this near-solstice 1976, the Boston Red Sox, having obtained their third post–World War II American League Championship, are fading as they did in all those postwar seasons after 1947, in 1968, now in '76, and as they would on the fourth, fifth and sixth occasions yet to come in 1987, 2005 and 2008. As in the winter of '04-'05, the Red Sox and their now newly revived New York Yankee rivals are competing for a passel of star players which, in yet another fire sale reminiscent of the St. Louis Browns in the '40s, now in '75-'76, Charlie Finley's Oakland A's are unloading.

A new era of free agency for baseball players has just dawned as arbitrator Peter Seitz in December 1975 has held that once a player plays out his one-year contract option subsequent to the expiration of his contract under the collective bargaining agreement between the Players Association and the owners, he becomes a free agent.[1] Finley, irascible, overbearing and unpopular with his fellow owners, believes that the best answer to the actual free agency and salary arbitration awards is to allow all players to become free agents and thus diminish the price that they can command in light of the increased supply of those available. As the prospect of free agency became imminent and along with it the unavailability of compensation for star players who would be lost, Finley dismantled one of baseball's last dynasties. The A's had won three consecutive world championships from '72 to '74 and had prevailed in the west with two bookend Western Division championships in '71 and '75.

On June 14 and 15, 1976, the A's, for the then princely grand total sum of $2 million, sold outfielder Joe Rudi and ace reliever Rollie Fingers to the Boston Red Sox, who hoped to jump back into contention for the Eastern Division race after a wild fist fight in Yankee Stadium that both injured lefty Bill Lee and also erupted into a melee. Popular left-handed starter Vida Blue was dealt to the first-place Yankees for $1.5 million. Both deals took place just before the then baseball trading deadline at midnight on June 15.

Again, this arranged blockbuster deal could have pushed World War III off the front-page headlines in Boston, New York, and the Bay Area. Though the trade replicated the one-sided player-for-cash kinds of deals that reflected the very same market disparities between the clubs in the '40s, '50s, and '60s, baseball was not amused. And the reason was that the cash provided would be exhibit #1 in future negotiations and salary arbitrations between the players and the Red Sox or Yankees, or whatever club entered into a subsequent agreement with them in the brave new world of free agency. Commissioner Bowie Kuhn thus declared that Finley's actions were "not in the best interest of baseball" under authority purportedly given to the commissioner. He then disapproved the player assignments which had been negotiated between the clubs. Commissioner Kuhn declared Finley's transactions to be against the integrity of the game and public confidence in it by virtue of the fact that (1) it diminished the Oakland Club; (2) it lessened competitive balance through which success could be bought; (3) it worsened "the present unsettled circumstances of baseball's reserve system." Finley's challenge led directly to the federal courts in Chicago.

A district court in Chicago held for the Commissioner on the ground that baseball was beyond the scope of antitrust and that a covenant not to sue in the major league agreement was valid and enforceable. The Court of Appeals for the Seventh Circuit, speaking through Judge Sprecher, affirmed — but on different grounds.[2]

The owners, who had begrudged the success of the Commissioner's authority since the days of Judge Kenesaw Landis, who was given plenary power to deal with the "Black Sox" gambling scandal in 1919, allowed their hostility to Finley, and what his deal meant for the prices that they would have to pay in the free agent market, to trump any anti-commissioner instincts that they possessed then — and would soon possess again in the years to come, in controversies with Fay Vincent after Finley had been beaten down. Said the court in considering the challenge to the Commissioner's authority:

> In no other sport or business is there quite the same system, created for quite the same reasons and with quite the same underlying policies. Standards such as the best interest of baseball, the interest of the morale of the players and the honor of the game, or "sportsmanship" which accepts the umpire's decision without complaint are not necessarily familiar to courts and obviously require some expertise in the application. While it is true that professional baseball selected as its first Commissioner a federal judge, it intended only him and not the judiciary as a whole to be its umpire and governor.[3]

The court found persuasive the Commissioner's testimony that the Red Sox and Yankees were bypassing the "usual methods of player development and acquisition which have been traditionally used in professional baseball."[4] This surely surprised not only the Red Sox, who had both purchased players and traded them, but particularly the Yankees, who in 3 successive years had purchased the 3 Johnnies toward the season's end so as to put them across the pennant line — Johnny Mize (the "Big Cat" of New York Giant fame), Johnny Hopp (the line drive-hitting first baseman from the Boston Braves), and Johnny Sain of "Spahn and Sain" fame. No player development there for those veterans — and no "traditional" acquisitions. With the exception of the Sain deal, in which the Yankees gave up then prospect Lew Burdette as well as $50,000, it was just cold, hard cash!

Nonetheless, the Commissioner maintained that the transactions in *Finley* were "unparalleled" — but, as we have seen, there were many trades as well as purchases of similar scope and dimensions. But the district court concluded that these deals in dispute were "at a time and under circumstances making them unique in the history of baseball." Again, however, what was waiting in the wings in 1976 and completely inapplicable to the Stephens, Kinder, Kramer and Lopat era was the prospect of free agency and the impact that the sale would have upon the kind of compensation the players would receive for their own worth.

Those deals were of another time. They took place when there was no such thing as the "major league double play," as it is called today in both the professional and college level, when the second baseman or shortstop had already left the bag when he received the throw[5]; when players had to "break their wrists" in order to be charged with a strike, as opposed to today's more nebulous and elusive umpire call that the player has "gone around"; when batters were charged with an at bat for producing a sacrifice fly run while batting in the run (RBI) — Ted Williams, the last batter to hit .400 with an average of .406 in 1941, would have had an average of .411 under the new rules; when outfielders stood in stony isolation as infielders whipped the ball around the infield, perhaps concerned that similar warmups on their part might erode the dignity that was theirs; when players traveled by rail in the East and Midwest before baseball's westward expansion in the 1950s was unleashed by the relocation of the Braves to Milwaukee and the transcontinental migration of the Giants and Dodgers to San Francisco and Los Angeles respectively; when the cost of rehabilitation for an injured player — even Eddie Waitkus, shot in a hotel room by a love-crazed would-be murderess — had to be borne by the player himself; when few players had their salaries stretched through twelve months as sidearming Ewell ("The Whip") Blackwell did, and a second job during the winter was necessary and much sought after, given the low player salaries. As Yankee ace Floyd "Bill" Bevens said, "Even if we win the World Series, you will find me back on the delivery truck at Salem, Oregon, in the winter."[6] Free agency and collective bargaining were still considerably down the road. The times were dramatically different, and it is important to understand how we got from there to here.

Baseball's Origins

Long before professionalism, the game's origins, as chronicled by Harold Seymour and Dorothy Seymour Mills, lay not in Cooperstown, where the Doubleday "myth"[7] has promoted the idea that the game was invented by General Abner Doubleday in 1839, but rather stemmed "directly from the English game of rounders, and it was known by that name and played in America before 1839," as early as 1744.[8] States Seymour about the game as played in the late eighteenth or early nineteenth century:

The ball games of the period were admirably suited to a young, essentially rural America. Few people had great wealth, or leisure. Playing sites were plentiful and convenient. Only the rudest preparation was necessary — laying "goals" or bases by driving sticks into the ground or placing flat rocks at appropriate distances. Equipment was cheap and easy to come by. Any stout stick, wagon tongue, ax or rake handle made a capital bat, and a serviceable ball could be made by winding yarn around a buckshot or chunk of india rubber and then sewing on a leather cover, perhaps cut to size by the local shoemaker, to prevent unwinding. No other paraphernalia were needed. Projecting one's power by swatting and throwing an object hard and far, and experiencing the excitement of the race to reach base ahead of the ball, satisfied elementary human urges. All these factors made for popularity and wide participation.[9]

Until substantial urban growth there were no spectators for the game, horse racing being the only organized sport of interest in the 1820s and '30s, the foremost team sport of the period being the English game of cricket. As baseball became popular in urban areas many clubs played both games interchangeably. Initially, before New York rules became dominant at the eve of the Civil War, baseballists, as they were called, followed the "impractical retention of 'soaking' (recording an out by hitting a runner with a thrown ball), ten-to-fourteen-man squads, stakes instead of bases, and one-hundred-run requirements for victory."[10]

Soon, however, "baseball was growing steadily in popularity, and after the Civil War left cricket far behind."[11] The first organized baseball club appears to be the Knickerbocker Base Ball Club of New York, a social or "exclusive" club. "The Knickerbockers blazed a path others were to follow."[12] Theirs was a game which placed baseball on the track to become an important entertainment business which would be commercialized in a matter of decades. As Seymour and Mills wrote:

> [A]s the game started slipping from the polite fingers of teams such as the Knickerbockers into the more lusty embrace of the masses, its complexion began to change perceptibly. Rooting grew more vehement as spectators became noisy partisans. Betting began to creep in. At the Fashion Race Course all-star series, even women were observed exchanging small wagers. Rowdyism and occasional riots also marred the scene. One reporter complained acidly that the crowd seemed to think that games were got up for their special entertainment and that they were conferring a favor on the players by their presence. These new elements heralded baseball's march toward professionalism and commercialism.[13]

The game's appeal, of course, lay in the fact that there was an equal chance for both sides to score and the absence of time restrictions. The game could always be more easily observed than comparable team sports and thus was more exciting to watch. In the 1850s it began to be called the "National Game," basketball not being invented until 1892 and football subsequently stigmatized for its "excessive brutality."[14] Again, by the time of the Civil War, it had taken root in American soil, newspapers and their sporting page promoting baseball as early as the 1850s.

The game, though recognizably baseball, looked quite different. For instance, each player — the first baseman, second baseman and third baseman — would stand on the base and the catcher would be without equipment thirty feet back of the batter, much along the lines of the way we kids played the game in the 1940s at the Station Field. And like our sandlot ball in the '40s, the batter could wait until he got a pitch to his liking before he would swing.

After the Civil War the game began to take off, the river towns of Cincinnati and St. Louis becoming particularly important. By 1867 there were nine clubs in Des Moines, Iowa, and Marshalltown, Iowa, was to produce an individual, Adrian "Cap" Anson, who was to be important as a player and manager — and also one who worked to exclude black players from the game before the turn of the century! The precursor to his role existed by virtue of the National Association of Base Ball Players' instituted ban. Write Seymour and Mills:

> But baseball's democratic trend did not include the Negro. It is generally known that professional baseball had an unwritten rule against colored players for many decades. What has not been revealed before this is that as far back as 1867 there was a written ban against them. The faded official records of the National Association's 1867 convention prove that Negro players and clubs were barred from membership.[15]

As baseball became more accessible, players began to receive payments or so-called gifts which were designed to lure them to particular clubs. The 19th century Washington Nationals, who played before Andrew Johnson became the first president of the United States to attend a game, barnstormed through the country. Soon thereafter prominent New York and Brooklyn clubs began playing for a share of the gate money as they charged admission to their games. Soon there emerged a so-called "twilight zone between amateurism and professionalism, a semi-professional period in which hypocrisy reigned."[16] This led to a practice called "revolving," whereby players moved from team to team in response to better offers. Soon gambling became a problem, leading to fixes of some of the contests, reflecting the mores, it was said, of elements in the Grant administration at that time.

Initially, the protest against such conduct took the form of attack upon professionalism — but ultimately, with so many players paid under the table, the concern became hypocrisy. The first avowedly professional club was the Cincinnati Red Stockings, the precursor of the modern Cincinnati Reds, in 1869. The following year a new professional association was created which had at one time or another twenty-five or more teams — the enduring ones who competed every year being the Philadelphia Athletes, the Boston Red Stockings, and the New York Mutuals. A fourth club member, the Chicago White Stockings, missed the seasons of 1872 and 1873 due to the Chicago fire. Now baseball began to move more towards being a genuine business. The difficulty was that the problems with gambling, "revolving" and one-sided competition, and the disappearance of many clubs, were difficult to deal with (the Boston franchise, four-time pennant winners in a row during this period, won 71 and lost only 8 games in 1875!).

The result: the formation of the National League of Professional Baseball Clubs, a league of teams rather than an association or a player association. This meant that the clubs were now dominant and the players were relegated to secondary status and, most important, the concept of territorial rights for the clubs emerged, which was to promote the monopolistic concept which exists to this very day. Write Seymour and Mills: "Like so many tycoons of the time, they gave lip service to competition while working overtime to eliminate it."[17]

The development of the National League is of critical importance in the history of baseball. As noted, it established a framework for limiting competition which endures to this day, albeit operating under a loose confederation playing an even looser schedule. The Cincinnati Red Stockings, along with the Chicago Cubs, were particularly important as the first league moved towards establishing sufficient control over member clubs to survive the rebelliousness of individual owners. The 1876 constitution of the League allowed players to enter into contracts with other teams for future services — but this was reversed quickly in 1879, barely three years after the League's founding.[18] This then was the beginning of the so-called reserve clause, which was to be a matter of dispute in Arbitrator Peter Seitz's 1975 arbitration award and the disputes and litigation which followed it into the twenty-first century.

The rules of this new 1876 league have established a framework for today, though a number of them have changed markedly. For instance, under the original rules, if the pitcher did not pitch in a motion where the arm stayed below hip level, a "foul balk" would be called. The batter who struck out also had to be thrown out at first base — whereas today that would only be the case if the catcher dropped the ball and there was no runner on first. A batter could call for a high, low, or fair pitch, a fair pitch being a combination of a high or low pitch. The umpire, a solitary soul in those days, was prohibited from venturing into fair territory. And going far beyond the only modern analog — Japanese umpires, who seek to explain their decisions to the crowd — the umpire in 1876 could enlist the spectators' aid in making difficult calls, relying presumably on the best testimony available. Imagine the late Yankee owner George Steinbrenner, or, should he venture into baseball as he apparently desires, Mark Cuban of the NBA Dallas Mavericks, in such a milieu!

One feature of the new National League's constitution provided for the expulsion of miscreant clubs — and that occurred in 1879, the culprit being none other than the original professional team of the Cincinnati Red Stockings. Their offenses were playing games on Sunday and allowing liquor to be consumed in the stands. The Red Stockings were expelled, but this quickly backfired inasmuch as Cincinnati was a primary force in bringing about the American Association's creation in 1882. In the first in a long line of challenges to the National League's monopoly, the emergence of the American Association ignited the first legal disputes in sports about player contract breaches, establishing a litigation pattern which was bound up with the subsequent establishment of new rival leagues such as the Union

Association, the Players' League, and eventually the American League, the Federal League and the Mexican League. Accordingly, the new leagues and subsequent mergers produced conflict between players and owners in which the balance of power shifted depending upon supply and demand of both players and leagues and the rulings of the courts.

The 19th century produced wars between various leagues, and as part of a recurring theme in all sports, a merger in the 1880s on the part of three leagues to respect the reserve "list" of each league so as to suppress competition and diminish player strength. Again, the concept had been devised by the owners in 1879.

A new Union Association emerged in 1884 to challenge this. But it was soon devoured by the National League and the American Association, which had agreed to stop raiding each other's players and to form a united front against such unwelcome interlopers as the Union Association and, a few years later, the Players' League. The Union Association lasted less than a year. And litigation about player contracts emerged from this.[19]

The Players' League was created at the end of the 1889 season, and here contract jumping was done by such stars as John Montgomery Ward and Buck Ewing. The Players' League resulted from a sense that player demands were not being met by obdurate owners and that only the players themselves could successfully reach their goals. Judging by attendance figures the Players' League seemingly was a successful one — but it failed because the players sought to place control of each club in the hands of the players themselves rather than managerial specialists, and at the end of one year all the clubs had lost money.

Accordingly the players disbanded and returned through readmittance to their old clubs or joined new ones. So rapacious was one club in going after the returning players that it earned a new nickname — the Pittsburgh Pirates. The Philadelphia Athletics "failed to reserve 'two of its players, who jumped to National League teams. One of them signed with Pittsburgh, which had gone by the name Alleghenys. In response to the perceived raid, the Athletics angrily condemned the Pittsburgh club as Pirates, and the nickname stuck in a city hundreds of miles from the sea.'"[20]

Now, the American Association withdrew from its agreement with the National League. Shortly after the demise of the Players' League, the American Association collapsed. And this led to a new challenger to the National League which was to have more staying power.

This was the American League, which was officially born in 1900, though it evolved from a predecessor minor league, the Western League. This new league was to provide the most serious of all of the sustained challenges to the National League and ultimately to merge with the National League in 1903, constituting the beginning of organized baseball or, in contemporary parlance, Major League Baseball. The leagues merged so as to put a stop to this trend.

This merger, like subsequent ones both in baseball and more recently in football, basketball and hockey, was triggered by the raiding between the leagues and the escalation of salaries and conditions that this meant for the players.

The Beginnings of Baseball Law

Prior to the emergence of the American League a number of the disputes about so-called jumping to new leagues had gone to the courts. The existence of reserve clauses in the players' contracts — again, first created in 1879 — raised basic issues not confronted in entertainment cases, such as an earlier one involving a young opera singer who had left for more lucrative engagement. In that case, *Lumley v. Wagner*,[21] the court, while conceding that it could not order the singer to perform for her first employer, held that she was prevented from performing elsewhere in the immediate geographical area, an order which came to be called a negative injunction.

The first player disputes generally constituted contract litigation which emerged from the above-mentioned Players' League. Controversies in both a federal and a state court resulted in victories for the players. Buck Ewing, an established National League star who was to become player/manager of the New York entry in the Players' League, was the first to test the waters. In *Metropolitan Exhibition Co. v. Ewing*,[22] a U.S. district court found that the reserve clause in his contract did not adequately define what would appear in a new contract if that clause was invoked by the club. The court held that reference to trade custom and usage did not resolve the indefiniteness. It refused to grant injunctive relief against the player and held that damages would be inappropriate as well.

In a companion case in the state court of New York, *Metropolitan Exhibition Co. v. Ward*,[23] one of the Brotherhood organizers, again John Montgomery Ward, successfully defeated his National League club's request for an injunction on the grounds that the contract clause was indefinite, and in addition, that the contract lacked mutuality in that Ward could be let go on ten days' notice but be bound, at the club's option, for an indefinite period. After its loss in *Ewing*, the club in *Ward* tried to argue that the reserve clause was the club's right to reserve the ballplayer for only the ensuing season at not less than the present season's salary. The court, however, found that the clause did not explain or define any of the terms of the subsequent contract and thus rejected the club's attempts to explain away the ambiguities. As to the mutuality issue, the court said that the concentration of power in one party to a contract — in which, as here, a club could either bind a player in perpetuity or release him on ten days' notice — could lead to great inequities. The club, for example, might hold the player until the time had passed when he reasonably could gain employment with another club, then release him with no further obligations. This imbalance in the positions of the parties was sufficient, in equity at least, to constitute a lack of mutuality and be fatal to a claim for injunctive relief.

For Ewing and Ward and the other Players' League defectors, these substantial victories in court were hollow ones. By the time the legal dust had cleared, the Players' League was itself in ashes. As so often happens, developments on the ground overran the decrees of the courts. The league lasted a year, undermined in large measure by the new group of owners brought in by the players to help finance the operation. This new group found that they had more in common with the National League owners than they did with their own players. The tale is somewhat more complicated than that, but it underscores the fact that there is more to winning than having the law on one's side. Ewing and Ward returned to the National League, played out their careers in brilliant fashion, and are now in the Hall of Fame as two of the early stalwarts of the national pastime. But their great dream was defeated, not by the law but rather by business maneuverings.

The next round of litigation came ten years after *Ewing* and *Ward*. Much happened in the 1890s. After the Players' League folded, the two remaining leagues that had operated in relative harmony since 1884 under a national agreement fell into dispute. The American Association withdrew from the agreement and attempted to operate alone. This shortsighted move was compounded by a number of economic mistakes, perhaps fostered in part by National League actions that led to the American Association's demise in 1891.

In the American League–National League dispute one Napoleon Lajoie became the source of controversy. By 1900 Lajoie was a leading player in the National League, holding down second base for the Philadelphia Nationals. (That was the year in which they acquired the Phillies nickname.) At the same time, he was forced to labor under the $2,400 maximum salary imposed by National League rules. He was ripe for a move, and he moved all the way across town to the new Philadelphia club of the equally new American League. The National League club brought suit.

The first round of *Philadelphia Base-Ball Club v. Lajoie*[24] went to Lajoie. The trial court, relying heavily on English and U.S. precedent, found that Lajoie's work at second base and at the plate was not sufficiently unique to place his services in the category of an impossible-to-replace player. The court also dismissed the complaint on the grounds that the contract was unenforceable due to a lack of mutuality. As in *Ewing* and *Ward*, the court noted that the club could terminate the contract at any time after giving ten days' notice but that it could at the same time, if it chose, extend the agreement from time to time for a total of three years. In light of the earlier sports cases, albeit in other jurisdictions, the trial court's holdings were not particularly surprising. The case was appealed, nevertheless. In the interim, Lajoie played the 1901 season and batted .422, which is still the American League single-season high, comfortably beyond Ted Williams' formidable .406 average compiled in 1941 (as we have seen, it was really .411!) when he became the last man in baseball history to hit .400.

Lajoie's 1901 play was not noted by the Supreme Court of Pennsylvania, but it did regard the case in substantially different fashion than had the trial judge. The high court's opinion of April 21, 1902, established in its analysis a memorable precedent for the professional sports industry. The court thought that the trial judge regarded Lajoie's talents too lightly and that the evidence warranted a stronger finding as to his baseball acumen. The court concluded about Lajoie's ability: "He may not be the sun in the baseball firmament, but he is certainly a bright particular star."

The mutuality issue presented more difficulty; however, the court noted two points: (1) It is not necessary for both sides in a contract to have identical rights or remedies; and (2) Lajoie's "large salary" was in part consideration received for the ten-day termination powers given the club. Thus, the court neutralized the termination powers through the salary, leaving the length of the contract as not unreasonable. Since plaintiff had exercised its right of renewal of the contract for the 1902 season, the defendant was enjoined from playing for any other club for that season.

This time there was a hollow quality to the legal victory obtained by the league. Lajoie did not meekly return to the Nationals, nor did the American League roll over. Instead, Lajoie was traded to Cleveland, safe there from the impact of the Pennsylvania injunction because the Ohio courts refused to adhere to the Pennsylvania decree. Lajoie was inconvenienced only by not being able to travel with his club to Philadelphia, which lasted only until the two leagues came to a new national agreement a year later.

But in a substantial number of litigated cases baseball players have been viewed as "unique." For the most part the legal terrain began to change. The new challenge came about through an assault upon monopoly conditions which resulted from the establishment of the Federal Baseball League and organized baseball in the years leading up to and beyond World War I.

Enter Antitrust Law

Now the legal terrain shifted anew and focused upon not simply contract law but the Sherman Antitrust Act, enacted by Congress in 1890, aimed as it was at monopolies which threatened the public interest, sometimes through the suppression of competition. There was no legislative history suggesting that Congress had any concern with professional baseball and its monopolistic tendencies — and, of course, other leagues such as those involving football, basketball and hockey were yet to come on the scene. While 1890 antedated controversies involving the Players' League as well as the American Association and the American and National Leagues, there is no record of antitrust litigation involving any of this. It was not until 1914 — the very date of the formation of the Federal Baseball League — that Congress enacted legislation, in response to the concerns and demands of organized labor, which allowed for private parties as well as the United States government to institute antitrust suits, this time through the so-called Clayton Act of 1914. Now the courts became ensnarled with baseball through antitrust.

The first of the cases involving the Federal Baseball League involved the well-known first baseman Hal Chase, who signed with Buffalo of the new Federal League while under contract to Chicago of the American League. Although the court held in *American League Baseball Club of Chicago v. Chase*[25] that Chase's services were sufficiently unique to suggest, initially, the appropriateness of injunctive relief, the court further held that the contract evidenced an "absolute lack of mutuality" and would not be enforced. As in *Ward*, the court contrasted the ten-day termination clause that could end the player's contractual rights with the option clause that could extend them, both of which were exercisable only by the club. In this respect the case affirmed *Ward* and disagreed with *Lajoie*. But the court went further and examined both the federal and state antitrust implications of the system under which the established baseball leagues operate. While it concluded that there had been no violations of the Sherman and Clayton Acts — statutes which provided for treble damages, injunctive relief and criminal penalties — because it felt that baseball was not interstate commerce covered by the Act, the court did determine that "organized baseball" was an illegal combination "in contravention of the common law." It was "as complete a monopoly ... as any monopoly can be made," and invaded the right to labor as a property right and the right to contract as a property right, and was the result of a combination illegally restraining the rights to exercise one's profession.

This wedge, provided by the application of state concepts of restraint of trade, was nevertheless an inadequate one. It required each jurisdiction to interpret the common law aspects of trade restraints, and it directed itself mainly at the contracts of individual players. The Federal League lasted little longer than the Players' League had in 1890. But before it expired, it attacked the National Agreement entered into between the American League and National League in 1903 as an unlawful monopoly under the Sherman Antitrust Act. The complaint focused upon both the territorial monopoly which organized baseball established for itself by excluding clubs within 75 miles of a city which had a franchise and, in particular, the retaliation against players who ignored the reserve cause subsequent to the expiration of a contract and played for the Federal League.

A new league was established in March 1913 shortly after one of the most exciting World Series the previous fall, a faceoff between the Boston Red Sox and the New York Giants. The 1912 World Series[26] was between the two clubs which would have been involved in the 1904 World Series — the first of two not to happen — when the Giants backed out. The Sox had just moved into their new Fenway Park, just as a half dozen other teams had adopted new facilities. Boston had Smoky Joe Wood, one of the few players that my father recalled vividly from the time that he was a child. Wood had an extraordinary record that year of 34 wins and 5 losses with 10 shutouts and an ERA of 1.91. The Giants at that point had baseball's folk hero Christy Mathewson to face off against the Sox. In the deciding game a fly ball was dropped by Giants center fielder Snodgrass, who also made a sensational catch off Red Sox outfielder Harry Hooper. Tris Speaker fouled one that Giants infielder Merkle converged upon — and missed! It is to be recalled that it was Fred Merkle whose base-running miscue had been a decider in 1908. Speaker then promptly singled to right, setting up the winning run which was to give the Sox the World Championship.

A new league, the United States League, had attempted to get going in 1912; it did so again in '13, but quickly fell by the wayside. The Federal League of Baseball Clubs now invaded baseball's territory, establishing franchises in Chicago, Cleveland, Pittsburgh, St. Louis, Indianapolis, and across the river from Cincinnati in Kentucky. In 1914, the Federal League attempted to "go major" and to sign players who were on the reserve list of various American and National League clubs. It was able to sign up 81 of its 264 players from the majors. Now, like Chase before it in early 1915, the League soon sued organized baseball for antitrust violations because of baseball's insistence upon the reserve clause during the previous season and the consequent economic tribulations suffered. The judge assigned the case was Kenesaw Mountain Landis, with something of a reputation as a trust-buster because of his $29 million judgment (later reversed) against Standard Oil. But as Leonard Koppett said: "Landis, it turned out, was also a rabid Cubs fan, a bigot, a wild-eyed jingoist patriot and ... a whiz, not at jurisprudence, but at public relations."[27]

Landis, soon to become baseball's first Commissioner as the result of the "Black Sox" scandal involving the Chicago White Sox in the 1919 World Series, sat on the case without acting on it, and in the fall of 1915 the parties entered into an agreement settling their differences. But unlike that which would emerge in other sports in the post–World War II era, the settlement did not provide for admission of any of the clubs to the Major League, but rather simply the acquisition of the Chicago Cubs by Chicago Whales owner Charlie Weeghman and his right to bring the Cubs to his new ballpark on the North Side at Addison and Clark. There was an ownership right for the St. Louis franchise owner as well. The Baltimore Terrapins, now abandoned by their most successful owner and frozen out of organized baseball itself (as well as the International League), was one of the few franchises that refused to participate in the 1916 dissolution proceedings which ensued. They sued.

The Federal League had folded amid allegations that the established leagues engaged in activities that went beyond holding players to allegedly improper contracts. And Baltimore's owners felt they had been undermined in numerous ways, particularly by fellow owners who sold out to the established leagues. Baltimore was offered a relatively small amount of money — the city, which had seen its team depart in 1903 and become the New York Yankees (initially the Highlanders), was not regarded as attractive baseball terrain. Thus, Baltimore brought suit against each of the sixteen teams in the National and American Leagues, against the two league presidents and a third person who together constituted what was then called the National Commission, and against three former owners or persons having powers in the Federal League. The suit was filed against organized baseball, then called the National Commission, headed by Ban Johnson, who had blacklisted the players who had jumped to the Federal League; three of the former Federal League owners were also defendants. The complaint alleged that a conspiracy among the defendants, in violation of the Sherman Act, had severely damaged the plaintiff in its attempts to launch a viable baseball team.

Plaintiff prevailed at the trial level and won a verdict for $80,000, which was trebled under the provisions of the Clayton Act of 1914, which now amended the Sherman Antitrust

Act. On appeal, however, the court held that the activities of the defendants were not within the act. The United States Supreme Court then considered the matter.

In one of the most wrongheaded decisions ever rendered by the United States Supreme Court, the landmark *Federal Baseball*[28] opinion authored by Justice Oliver Wendell Holmes on behalf of the unanimous bench, the Court held that baseball was not a business within the meaning of the Commerce Clause of the Constitution and commerce in other contexts. Conceding that baseball was in fact a business, the Court reached the conclusion that it was not a business that involved the crossing of state lines sufficient to invoke commerce as a constitutional matter. The Court expressed its reasoning in this language:

> The business is giving exhibitions of baseball, which are purely state affairs. It is true that in order to attain for these exhibitions the great popularity that they have achieved, competition must be arranged between clubs from different cities and States. But the fact that in order to give the exhibitions the Leagues must induce free persons to cross state lines and must arrange and pay for their doing so is not enough to change the character of the business ... the transport is mere incident, not the essential thing. That to which it is incident, the exhibition, although made for money would not be called trade or commerce in the commonly accepted use of those words. As it is put by defendant, personal effort, not related to production, is not a subject of commerce.[29]

The reality was considerably more complicated than the picture drawn by Justice Holmes in *Federal Baseball*. To put matters charitably, Holmes, like most ballplayers (and some law professors!), had a very bad day when he wrote this opinion.[30] It consisted of an "astonishing inability" to grasp "the practical meaning of baseball's governing rules."[31]

This was to be the last of the baseball major league rivalries in the United States, though Major League Baseball was subsequently threatened by potential rivals with the so-called Continental League, which was waiting in the wings in the late 1950s prior to the second round of expansion of baseball teams. Expansion then bought off a number of the key people,[32] just as they had been bought off at the time of the Federal League's demise. (There were murmurings of a new league at the time of the labor disputes of the 1990s, particularly in the wake of the 1994-'95 strike, but they turned out to be nothing more than murmurings!) Meanwhile, rivalry, litigation and ultimate settlement with potential rivals came to be a *de facto* acceptance of expansion — a tactic employed against leagues already in existence in football and basketball by the National Football League and the National Basketball Association. For instance, the San Francisco 49ers and the Cleveland Browns left the dissolved All-American Conference to become part of the National Football League in 1950. Similarly the process was repeated by the new American Football League of the '60s. Twice — in 1950 and again in the '70s — the same process was followed in basketball.

Ironically, the judge-made exemption of baseball from antitrust law was not applied to other sports, including basketball,[33] football,[34] hockey[35] and boxing.[36] But, as we shall see, with relatively minor modifications toward the end of the twentieth century, the Court's *Federal Baseball* decision has remained intact, thus precluding baseball players and others from litigating against the anti-competitive reserve clause on antitrust theories and the like.

This did not mean that players were completely unprotected prior to collective bargaining. Though baseball ownership was successful in fighting off claims of competitors and players through antitrust litigation, the rise of an all-powerful commissioner, Judge Landis, who was given plenary authority in the wake of the so-called Black Sox scandal arising out of the 1919 World Series,[37] meant that the authority of the clubs themselves was hardly unqualified. Judge Landis had a peculiar aversion to the existence of farm teams in a "farm system" affiliated with major league teams, placing him on an uneasy collision course with the system's author, Branch Rickey. The Commissioner's hostility to the farm system meant that the authority of the clubs vis-à-vis players was subject to restrictions. Thus, for instance, when the owner of the St. Louis Cardinals — for whom Rickey first devised his farm system idea — which "completely controlled [the Milwaukee] club" by owning fifty percent of it, assigned a player to Milwaukee with the right to recall him, the Commissioner held that such conduct was "detrimental" to baseball. Federal courts affirmed the authority of the Commissioner to make the player in question a free agent.[38] Because of these rulings, for instance, "Old Reliable" Tommy Henrich of the Yankees was pried loose from the Cleveland Indians farm system. Leonard Koppett writes that nonetheless the Commissioner was "shoveling against the tide"[39] and was forced to back down in most instances through the collective insistence of the owners. (The Commissioner's authority was at its zenith under Landis, who could rule in the "best interest of baseball" a baseball rule which was modified subsequent to his death in 1944 and expanded anew in the 1960s.[40]) Thus for the most part, given the difficulties that Landis had with establishing free agency for minor league players, baseball players were stymied and unable to negotiate with clubs or to bargain in any sense of the word.

In the wake of *Federal Baseball*, the players were quiescent. Night baseball began to increase attendance by attracting fans during non-working hours, and radio became the accepted medium by which to boost the game's popularity from 1920 onward. The Great Depression left players, along with many other employees, feeling fortunate to be employed at all. Hearing the roar of the Fenway Park crowd from their Boston apartment when first married in 1934, my parents frequently spoke of the fact that they felt lucky to have a nickel or dime in the house for the day's expenses during this severe period. Baseball was not immune from the hard times of the '30s.

Of course, in the '20s some players did well. Babe Ruth, the Sultan of Swat, when asked why he received a salary that was higher than that of President Herbert Hoover, is reputed to have said, "I had a better year than he did." Ruth's salary, $80,000, topped President Hoover's mere $75,000. In a series of contract disputes with both the Red Sox and the Yankees, the "Bambino" had been quite successful in renegotiating salary increases![41] Yet even he saw his salary reduced as his production diminished in the '30s — he went to $75,000 in 1932, $52,000 in '33, and down to $30,000 in '34. Lou Gehrig saw his salary cut by $4,000 in 1939, the year in which he was to suffer paralytic illness.[42] Multi-year guaranteed contracts were something in the distant future.

During the Depression, Joe DiMaggio, coming off a banner year in 1936, batting .322 with 21 homers and 125 runs batted in, was told that he must accept a salary freeze, and he did so, notwithstanding his performance and fan popularity.[43] Under the circumstances, the holdout by a player was an ineffective tactic. But there was no other. Then, after the "Yankee Clipper" set the still unchallenged record of 56 consecutive games with at least one hit, leading the American League in RBIs with 125 and being named MVP of the American League in 1941, in the 1942 season he was confronted with an offer of $5,000 less than he had been paid in '41.

With the end of World War II, when most of the established prewar veteran players returned from military service, there were new developments in the employment relationship. The first related to a rival baseball league beyond the borders of the United States, the Mexican League, which attempted to lure leading players "South of the Border" and succeeded with some. The most prominent of these players was Brooklyn Dodgers catcher Mickey

Owen, who had dropped Tommy Henrich's third strike in the 1941 World Series; New York Giants pitcher Sal "The Barber" Maglie, known for his effective inside and "brush-back pitches"; St. Louis Cardinals ace left-handed pitcher Max Lanier, along with his teammate, hurler Fred Martin; and the relatively light-hitting Danny Gardella of the New York Giants (though he did hit 24 homers in 542 at bats for the '44–'45 Giants), who would be a plaintiff in future antitrust litigation. Baseball "blacklisted" these and other players who left to go to Mexico by imposing a five-year suspension, a particularly severe penalty considering the abbreviated nature of baseball players' careers. Lanier summed up the players' perspective: "Of course, everybody who went to Mexico was suspended from the big leagues for five years. I thought that was a little stiff. Heck, we didn't go there to hurt anybody. We just didn't think we were making enough money."[44] But soon the promises of Mexico were not realized and a number of players were reduced to barnstorming. In 1948 many of them who stayed in Mexico were losing money. They wanted back into Major League Baseball. When rebuffed, they sued.

Billy Consolo of the Boston Red Sox, one of the first "bonus babies"—a technique designed to suppress player salaries after World War II (courtesy Boston Red Sox).

Gardella was to be successful in antitrust litigation, which reached the Court of Appeals for the Second Circuit in New York. Both Judge Frank and Judge Learned Hand concluded for a majority of the court that the advent of radio and television had created commerce or the potential for it — the statutory prerequisite for antitrust jurisdiction — which had been presumed by the Court in *Federal Baseball* to be absent. After all, television was not even in existence at the time of *Federal Baseball*, and radio, in its infancy, was not broadcasting baseball.

Accordingly, the case was remanded for trial and baseball, seeing the handwriting on the wall, quickly settled. Like the '20s in which it was decided, *Federal Baseball* now seemed to be distant history. As we youngsters (now about twelve and thirteen) played our sandlot ball at Long Branch's Station Field that summer of '49, we were suddenly confronted with names of returning players with whom we were totally unfamiliar because their 1946 departure occurred just as we were getting started.

Because Major League Baseball settled with the players, the *Gardella* decision did not go to the United States Supreme Court as the owners feared. But, as we shall see, its reasoning — in truth it had two sets of reasoning provided by the two judges in the majority — died aborning.

The two judges in the *Gardella* majority took different paths to their respective conclusions. Judge Learned Hand, noting his skepticism about any implied overruling of *Federal Baseball*, nonetheless voted to remand the case to the trial court because the complaint averred "enough to present an issue upon a trial."[45] Judge Hand explained:

> When the case goes back to trial — assuming that it does so upon our opinions — it will be necessary, as I view it, to determine whether all the interstate activities of the defendants — those which were thought insufficient before, in conjunction with broadcasting and television — together form a large enough part of the business to impress upon it an interstate character.... [Antitrust laws] certainly forbid all restraints of trade which were unlawful at common-law, and one of the oldest and best established of these is a contract which unreasonably forbids any one to practice his calling. I do not think that at this stage of the action we should pass upon the "reserve clause," and therefore I do not join in my brother Frank's present disposition of it, although I do not mean that I dissent from him....[46]

In a more ambitious and far-reaching opinion, Judge Frank directly questioned the underpinnings of *Federal Baseball*, noting that no one can "treat as frivolous the argument that the Supreme Court's recent decisions have completely destroyed [its] vitality."[47] Calling the decision an "impotent zombi,"[48] Judge Frank stated that the MLB monopoly, which affected "ball-players like the plaintiff,"[49] possessed characteristics which were:

> [s]hockingly repugnant to the moral principles that, at least since the War Between the States, have been basic in America, as shown by the Thirteenth Amendment to the Constitution condemning "involuntary servitude," and by subsequent Congressional enactments on that subject. For the "reserve clause" ... results in something resembling peonage of the baseball player.[50]

Noting that only the Supreme Court could reverse *Federal Baseball*, Judge Frank nonetheless found that precedent to be easily distinguishable from the *Gardella* case. In his view, the principal difference was the use of radio and television as opposed to telegraph, which provided "mere accounts of the games as told by others, while here [in *Gardella*] we have the very substantially different fact of instant and direct interstate transmission, via television, of the games as they are being played, so that audiences in other states have the experience of being virtually present at these games."[51]

Finally, Judge Frank discounted the claim by organized baseball that it would be unable to exist without the reserve clause. Baseball writers like Daniel M. Daniel had written that "not a single player doubted the absolute necessity of this [reserve clause] form of contract."[52] John Drebinger of the *New York Times* wrote that if the reserve clause were eliminated, a "few wealthy clubs quickly would corner all the stars.... [F]ew ... seem aware that the reserve clause actually protects rather than exploits the majority of average players."[53] And Branch Rickey warned that those who opposed the reserve clause were also proponents of the Communist system.[54]

Judge Frank concluded that there was no proof that the end of the reserve clause meant the end of the existing baseball system. Writing in a separate opinion he said: "[N]o court should strive ingeniously to legalize a private (even if benevolent) dictatorship."[55]

Meanwhile, another development in 1946 was to constitute the beginning of longer-lasting consequences for baseball. Industrial strife broke out throughout all major industries such as auto, steel, and electrical equipment as pent-up wage demands, previously suppressed by the controls existing during World War II, now broke out. The response of the Republican-controlled 80th Congress was passage of the Taft-Hartley Act, which imposed new restrictions upon organized labor—a bill which was vetoed by President Truman. But the "do-nothing" Republican Congress, as President Truman called it, overrode the veto.

Throughout the United States union agitation in the form of strikes and walkouts, as well as organizing initiatives, rose in the post–World War II period, and baseball did not prove to be an exception as the boys came home from the war. Insecurity was on the rise as the World War II veterans competed with those who had taken their place for the few spots available on the roster. Some of the players on the Pittsburgh Pirates' roster attempted to form a union in conjunction with efforts by ex–NLRB labor lawyer Robert Murphy. The union was called the American Baseball Guild. Murphy appeared to have focused upon the Pittsburgh Pirates because of the fact that Pittsburgh was such a highly unionized city. When a meeting between Murphy and the club went nowhere, the Guild threatened a strike which was opposed by Pittsburgh ace veteran "Rip" Sewell. As a result of his opposition, the players rejected the strike in a ballot conducted that summer. The union effort was stopped in its tracks.

Spring training in 1947 saw some of the passions reemerge. The Yankees obtained the guarantee of $30,000 for two weeks of exhibitions in Puerto Rico and another $35,000 for seven days in Caracas, Venezuela. This backfired badly on the club as players were "already beginning to organize themselves for a general revolt against a lot of evils that they held against the owners." Some of the players were reported to ask, "Where does a ball club get off ... to clear all that money through our efforts when we actually get none of it?" Said Drebinger: "[W]ith players jumping over the border into the Mexican league," there was the threat of "firebrands" to form a "vast and powerful player-union" which might panic the owners.[56]

Thus, notwithstanding their apparent triumph over the Guild, baseball owners were uneasy and set about the business of creating a "company union" which was and is illegal under the National Labor Relations Act of 1935. The result was the creation of what came to be called a joint major league committee, which emerged from owner meetings initiated by Yankee general manager Larry MacPhail. Veteran players represented the player side: the twenty-five men selected by the players had an average of 11.6 years of major league experience. Dixie Walker of the Dodgers (he left for the Pirates via a trade Branch Rickey organized because of his objections to playing with Jackie Robinson in 1947) and Johnny Murphy of the Yankees (and later the Red Sox) were to be among the leaders.

The league presidents along with some of the prominent owners were part of the Committee as well. The focus was the establishment of a uniform players' contract as well as other reforms, and the following were approved: a guaranteed $5,000 minimum salary; the extension of barnstorming after the season from ten to thirty days; permanent player representation; revisions in the uniform players' contract; and $25 per player per week for spring training costs over and above transportation, meals, and housing expenses.[57] (This came to be known—and still is known—as "Murphy money," named after Robert Murphy in his attempt to unionize the Pirates.)

But perhaps the most significant development was the establishment of a pension plan, comprising matching contributions from clubs and players. Initially it seemed as though the resolution of the pension issue had achieved its basic purpose of ending protest and stopping further organization. Said Daniel: "The 1947 hymnal of the Major League Baseball

Players opens with this significant line—'praise the club owners, from whom all blessings flow.'"[58] Not so long ago, said Daniel, there were complaints about abuses and "monopolies" and the phenomenon of disgruntled players "dashing into the Mexican League."[59] Now a different situation prevailed. Said Daniel: "But now all is harmony and serenity. Now there are reforms. Now the American Baseball Guild is gone. Murphy is forgotten. Application of national labor legislation to the diamond is recognized as impossible because baseball is a highly specialized profession, and not a trade like bricklaying or plumbing."[60] Thus, said Daniel, all of the talk of July 1946 to the effect that if baseball did not do "something radical the American Baseball Guild would capture a majority of the players, and the red-hots would throw the entire game into turmoil,"[61] had not panned out.

But the effect of what was done was to create the opportunity for future player action about working conditions, ultimately culminating in an independent union separate from the committee representation brought into existence in 1946. This took the form of the Major League Players Association (MLPA or Players Association, sometimes called the Union), which was formed in 1954. The Association had its origin in not only widespread player dissatisfaction with the administration of the '46 pension fund but also the ongoing dissatisfaction with salaries as a percentage of revenues.

In 1929 salaries had been 35.3 percent of revenues and in '39 it was 32.4 percent. The fact that salaries continued to decline as a percentage of revenues (by 1974 the percentage of salaries as a portion of revenue decreased even further, to 17.6 percent) led directly to a decision to hire Marvin Miller as executive director in 1966. (Previously he had served with the United Steelworkers as economist and bargainer.)

In the Association's first eight years under Miller's leadership, players' pensions more than tripled, the minimum salary rose from $6,000 to $16,000, and the average salary more than doubled to $40,956. A new energy and focus were to drive the collective bargaining process from the late '60s and early '70s onward. Meanwhile, however, the Association supported St. Louis Cardinal centerfielder Curt Flood (who had turned in stellar performances for that club in the '67 and '68 World Series; in the latter he was throwing effectively from centerfield underhanded because of an injury) in his unsuccessful bid to thwart his trade from the Cardinals to the Philadelphia Phillies through an attack on the "reserve clause" under antitrust law. Flood attempted to get the courts—ultimately the United States Supreme Court—to revisit *Federal Baseball* and thus expose organized baseball to the Sherman Antitrust Act so as to invalidate the reserve clause, which bound Flood and all other players to one team for life and which compelled him to play for no one else but the Phillies.

In a 5–3 decision issued in 1972, the Court adhered to what lawyers call *stare decisis*, a doctrine that means that courts will adhere to judicial precedent, in this case *Federal Baseball*, even if they might

No man is more responsible for changing the face of baseball in the twentieth century than Marvin Miller, leader of the players' union from 1966 through the '80s (courtesy Terry Cannon of The Baseball Reliquary).

have decided differently when writing on a fresh slate. Curiously, the Court concluded that *Federal Baseball* was mistaken in not regarding baseball as an industry within the meaning of commerce. Antitrust law, it is to be recalled, covered businesses which were under Congressional authority to regulate pursuant to the Commerce Clause of the Constitution. Yet, nonetheless, *stare decisis* prevailed. Flood lost his case and subsequently played for the Washington Senators as well as developing other creative skills abroad, encountering numerous personal difficulties along the way.[62] But this was to prove to be the last setback for the players in what became a disputatious thirty years' war producing strikes, lockouts, litigation and substantial improvement in players' standards and protection.

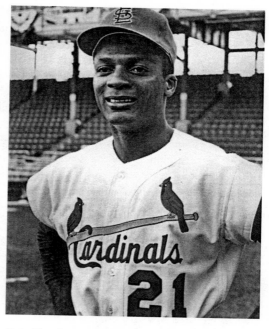

Curt Flood, center fielder for the St Louis Cardinals. He sued baseball under antitrust laws. Unsuccessful at the Supreme Court, he inspired other players to protest the "reserve clause" (courtesy National Baseball Hall of Fame and Library, Cooperstown, New York).

First, the players had already been successful in negotiating their first collective bargaining agreements in 1966 and 1968. Even though the Association was not called a union, from this point on it really did what most unions do: negotiate a contract. Previously the players had been led by individuals like Judge Cannon, who had a rather "romantic"[63] view of baseball that precluded any form of confrontation. Bob Feller, who struck out the 348 batters during that sweet summer of 1946 while toiling for the Cleveland Indians, had said: "You cannot carry collective bargaining into baseball." His successor, Bob Friend, a Pittsburgh Pirate pitcher, put it more bluntly: "I firmly believe a union in the fullest sense of the word, simply would not fit the situation in baseball."

But in '66 and '68 the Rubicon was crossed in that the Association was functioning as traditional unions had done, albeit on behalf of individuals who had very different employment relationships from those of auto and steelworkers and craftsmen traditionally represented by the labor movement. Most important, the players obtained grievance-arbitration machinery through which a wide variety of disputes could be resolved by an impartial arbitrator jointly selected by both the owners and the players. This process was to be important in some of the seminal cases involving player rights.

The Modern Labor Law

A second and related development that represented a big change and the enhancement of opportunities for the players was a decision by the National Labor Relations Board in 1969 involving the umpires. The Board interprets the National Labor Relations Act of 1935, which was passed during the Great Depression, signed into law by President Franklin D.

Roosevelt, at the urging of Senator Robert Wagner (D-NY) (the statute was initially called the Wagner Act, particularly before it was amended by the Taft-Hartley Act in 1947). It was enacted thirteen years after the Court's landmark *Federal Baseball* holding on antitrust law.

The statute provides both for unfair labor practice prohibitions — initially under the Wagner Act applicable only to employers, but now covering both sides — and for representation proceedings through which workers could choose to elect bargaining representatives through secret ballot box machinery or other methods.[64] The bargaining representative is to be the exclusive entity which bargains for employees over wages, hours and other conditions of employment. As we shall see, this principle of exclusivity, furthered by a series of Supreme Court decisions in the 1940s,[65] raises issues and problems which are peculiar to professional sports and baseball in particular.

In 1969 the Board took jurisdiction over organized baseball,[66] the owners arguing that the Supreme Court's *Federal Baseball* decision constituted precedent to the effect that baseball was not a business in interstate commerce under the Sherman Antitrust Act and that *Federal Baseball* had applicability to the National Labor Relations Act, which grants the NLRB jurisdiction over businesses which are in interstate commerce. But the Board rejected this reasoning, and this meant that baseball players, as well as their football, basketball and hockey counterparts, could go to the NLRB to complain of unfair labor practices (the owners could as well) and to file petitions for representation elections which would determine whether players wanted to be represented by a union. As noted, a representative union was viewed by the law as the exclusive bargaining entity.

The landmark ruling of the Supreme Court in 1944 in *J.I. Case Co. v. NLRB*,[67] had held that individual contracts of employment cannot be utilized by an employer as a basis for precluding negotiations with the union on the same subject matter. The Court held that an individual hiring contract was "subsidiary" to the terms of a collective bargaining agreement, and that therefore such a contract cannot waive any of the agreement's benefits "any more than a shipper can contract away the benefit of filed tariffs, the insurer the benefit of standard provisions, or the utility customer the benefit of legally established rates." Wherever there was no obligation to bargain with a union, an individual contract could be entered into or relied upon. But, said the Court:

> Individual contracts, no matter what the circumstances that justify their execution or what their terms, may not be availed of to defeat or delay the procedures prescribed by the National Labor Relations Act looking to collective bargaining, nor to exclude the contracting employee from a duly ascertained bargaining unit; nor may they be used to forestall bargaining or to limit or condition the terms of the collective bargaining agreement....
>
> The practice and philosophy of collective bargaining looks with suspicion on such advantages. Of course, where there is great variation in circumstances of employment or capacity of employees, it is possible for the collective bargain to prescribe only minimum rates or maximum hours or expressly to leave certain areas open to individual bargaining. But except as so provided, advantages to individuals may prove as disruptive of industrial peace as disadvantages....[68]

The last two sentences in the quoted language from *J.I. Case* have particular relevance to the business world of professional sports, where, as in entertainment, individual contracts of employment are important, notwithstanding the role of collective bargaining agreements in providing minimum salaries and other conditions of employment. Though football and hockey have flirted with the idea of collective representation for individual contracts, generally what has emerged has been minimum salaries and benefits which are applicable to the group *in toto* with the right and practice of individual contracts of employment between players and clubs. In baseball, potential for tension between the two has been addressed through collective bargaining agreements which have provided for both recognition of the union and the uniform players contract, i.e., the individual contract of employment. This leaves considerable scope for the role of the agents such as Scott Boras, who represents Alex Rodriguez, J.D. Drew and many other first-line players, to carry the ball in the individual contract negotiation process and to participate, along with the union, in representing the player in the contractually established salary arbitration procedures.

Unfair Labor Practices

Players and owners could take disputes about whether the other side had engaged in so-called unfair labor practices — prohibited by the National Labor Relations Act — directly to the Board, and this gave them a forum in addition to arbitration. The key unfair labor practice prohibitions contained in the National Labor Relations Act relate to discrimination on the account of membership and the obligation from both sides, labor and management, to bargain in good faith. The players were to invoke the Board's processes in the 1980s and '90s alleging unfair labor practices which consisted of owners' refusals to bargain in good faith as the NLRA requires. But this occurred when the parties' own negotiating procedures had broken down.

What is good-faith bargaining? What is bad-faith bargaining? When the Wagner Act (the original portions of the National Labor Relations Act) was being debated in 1935, Senator Walsh, the chairman of the Senate Labor Committee, stated that the question of how a party (at the time of the Wagner Act only an employer) would discharge its obligations to bargain under the statute was a relatively simple one. The National Labor Relations Board would take the parties by the hand to the conference room in which negotiations were to take place. It would see that the parties were properly seated and would close the door so that negotiations could commence. The difficulty is that this relatively simple picture painted by Senator Walsh in 1935 has become far more complicated. The Board has increasingly found itself pushing open the door to become involved in the discussions and the tactics of the parties while the process moves forward. Although the Board has been careful to state that a proposal by one side does not necessitate a counterproposal by the other, some response is required as a test of good faith. Neither side may engage in discussion that is simply "surface bargaining." At the same time, neither party is required to enter into a contract. Good-faith bargaining is an attempt to consummate an agreement. However, the other party may be so obstinate, or its demands may be so unacceptable, that it becomes impossible to negotiate a contract.

The Supreme Court, in the landmark *Borg-Warner*[69] case, held that there are three categories of subject matter that might be raised by the representatives of the union or the employer at the bargaining table: mandatory, nonmandatory, and illegal subjects of bargaining. Until an impasse is reached, the employer may not unilaterally change conditions of employment because this would preclude or limit both sides in negotiations about unresolved items, and thus it is inconsistent with the concept of good-faith bargaining. (It is generally the permanence of the change that precludes good-faith bargaining.) In order for the unilateral change to be unlawful, it must be "material, substantial, and significant."

With regard to mandatory subjects, both sides have an obligation to bargain to the point of impasse — but on some issues, such as the implementation of merit pay proposals, which would give the employer *carte blanche* over wage increases without regard to time, standards, and criteria, the obligation to bargain without making unilateral changes continues beyond impasse.[70] This does not mean that the parties must be deadlocked on all issues or items but rather that they must be deadlocked in the negotiations generally. If either negotiating party remains willing to move further toward an agreement, an impasse cannot exist: the parties' perception regarding the progress of the negotiations is of central importance to the Board's impasse inquiry.

Under the NLRA the party that refuses to bargain on mandatory subjects to the point of impasse is unlawfully refusing to bargain. The significance of such an unlawful refusal, in this context and others, is not merely that the Board will issue a "cease-and-desist" order aimed at remedying the parties' bargaining behavior. Rather it lies in the possibility that a strike ensuing as a result of such bargaining behavior would be an unfair-labor-practice strike and that therefore, in contrast to economic strikers who may be replaced, the workers would be entitled to reinstatement and possibly to back pay. Accordingly the *Borg-Warner* rule can alter considerably the balance of power in a strike deemed to have been caused by the employer's posture at the bargaining table.

A nonmandatory subject is "permissive." That is to say, either party may raise the subject at the bargaining table for the purpose of discussion. It is perfectly lawful to discuss such an issue. However, when a party insists upon a position in such an area to the point of impasse, an unlawful refusal takes place under the Act. The purpose of the rule — which is extremely difficult to implement — is to exclude frivolous subjects from the bargaining table and to infer bad faith on the part of the party that clogs the table with such subjects. (Illegal subjects may not be discussed at all.)

In a series of rulings which have considerable applicability to baseball and sports, the Supreme Court has attempted to define what constitutes mandatory bargaining. The Court has focused upon whether the subject matter involves the "literal definition" of "conditions of employment"; whether industrial peace is likely to be promoted through negotiation of the issue; and whether other unions and employers have negotiated similar subject matter.[71] Matters which involve the "scope of the enterprise" are not bargainable under these criteria.[72] Discussed below, issues such as the so-called designated hitter rule implemented in the American League since 1973, as well as the strike zone and its relationship to both umpires and players, present complex issues on the question of whether the subject matter is mandatory or a management prerogative. In the latter instance, one involving an issue which is a management prerogative, the subject is beyond that which either side can be compelled to bargain about to the point of impasse.

The World Umpires Association, the union representing major league umpires, has been concerned about MLB's use of automated equipment designed to track balls and strikes — a matter which appears to be a vital concern to players, owners and umpires. The question of whether the introduction of this system constitutes a mandatory subject of bargaining has not been resolved, though the umpires have lost unfair labor practice litigation on related matters.[73] This obviously affects the game directly, suggesting that it is a management prerogative beyond bargaining rights and obligations. But the implementation of such policies can affect conditions of work — and the law frequently requires bargaining over the effects of such decisions even if the decision itself is a management prerogative. From the players' perspective a wider strike zone should give an advantage to the pitcher portion of the bargaining unit represented by the union — though if it takes away low called strikes, pitchers who have difficulty throwing high hard fastballs beyond hard-swinging hitters may not feel advantaged.

Highlighting the sometimes synthetic demarcation line between bargaining and management prerogatives, the National Basketball Association Players Union has charged the NBA with unilateral changes in conditions of employment without bargaining lawfully to the point of impasse because the League has introduced a new synthetic composite basketball, which replaced the leather ball that had been used since the "onset" of the game, thus raising directly the mandatory bargaining issue. The NBA union charged a violation of the refusal-to-bargain provisions in the NLRA, alleging that the League had unlawfully "changed the basic working conditions for each and every player in the NBA" by introducing a ball which "due to its synthetic surface ... causes small cuts on the hands of players (similar to paper cuts) when they handle the ball." In the charge the players also alleged that "players overwhelmingly feel that the new ball also does not bounce as high, becomes extremely slick when wet and generally does not perform as well as the leather basketball used previously."[74] The matter was not resolved by the Board, as the NBA withdrew the new ball and the players withdrew their charges.

As collective bargaining emerged in baseball, the role of the right to strike by players and the right to lock out by owners became particularly important. Striking in itself is protected activity, meaning that employees may not be dismissed or disciplined for engaging in it. Though inapplicable to the kind of holdouts engaged in by Joe DiMaggio, and any other player like him who was seeking to affect only his individual contract terms, Section 13 of the labor law specifically states that nothing in the NLRA is intended to interfere with the right to strike. However, there are a number of limitations on the right, and some of them are set forth in the 1947 Taft-Hartley amendments' prohibition of strikes during emergencies affecting the nation's safety and health. (Despite its importance, no one has ever contended that baseball is such an industry, or should receive special treatment under any part of labor law.)

Sometimes the Supreme Court and the NLRB have limited the strike through statutory interpretation without any explicit provision in the law. A leading decision relating to strikes was rendered by the Supreme Court in 1938 in *NLRB v. Mackay Radio & Telegraph Company*,[75] in which it was held that, although striking is protected conduct, employers may permanently replace striking employees with strikebreakers. In other words, even though an employer may not discharge or discipline workers for engaging in a strike, the employer, in order to keep production going and the plant open, has a business justification for permanently ousting strikers by replacing them through the recruitment of strikebreakers, and thus may just as effectively deprive employees of their job security as would be the case if they were dismissed or disciplined for striking. Except in one instance — the 1994-'95 strike, when the owners contemplated using temporary replacements, as discussed in Chapter 4 — *Mackay* has had limited impact upon baseball, which has found it difficult and impractical to use strike replacements. This is different from the response of baseball to umpire strikes and that of basketball to referees, where replacements have become the order of the day,[76] and it is also in contrast to football, where fungibility and lack of identity for many players on the field, such as linemen, make the strike replacement a more feasible weapon. (As noted above, football used the replacement tactic with a great measure of success in the 1987 dispute between the players and the owners.) It is generally thought that the orders given to football players and the regular infliction of pain upon them in the process of the game have created more difficulty for the unions and a greater willingness on the part of the players to follow the voice of authority, in this case the owners.

What of other employer rights beyond the replacement of strikers? What may the employer do to utilize its own economic weaponry and protect its bargaining position aside from disputes relating to the duty to bargain and the replacement of strikers? In *American Ship Building Company v. NLRB*[77] (the company is owned by the Steinbrenners), the Supreme Court held that under certain circumstances lockouts by employers are lawful under the NLRA. Until the *American Ship Building* decision the lockout was thought to be verboten, and it had been generally assumed that a lockout was unlawful unless it was used defensively — where, for instance, the employer was protecting a perishable product or was part of an employer association and locked out its employees in response to an attempt by the union to divide and conquer the association by striking against one employer at a time (called "whipsawing").[78] For instance, if the players struck one team such as the Pittsburgh Pirates, where there was such an attempt in 1946, the rest of the teams could lock out the players in response to that tactic inasmuch as the Supreme Court has characterized professional sports leagues as multiemployer bargaining associations. (On the other hand, if only the Pirates were certified as in an appropriate bargaining unit for the purpose of collective bargaining, rather than in Major League Baseball itself as is presently the case, the right to lockout would be more complex. But even in this unlikely scenario the issues common to clubs, e.g., player mobility between teams, would provide a sufficient unity of interest for all clubs to act together in engaging in the lockout.)

In a way, *American Ship Building* is consistent with the same general theme expressed in these decisions. The employer there was confronted with a bargaining history in which the union had struck on a number of occasions in the past and appeared to be deliberately delaying negotiations during a slack period so that it could bring economic pressure to bear at a time when the employer needed to deliver goods and was thus weak and vulnerable. Said the Court:

> Although the unions had given assurances that there would be no strike, past bargaining history was thought to justify continuing apprehension that the unions would fail to make good their assurances. It was further found that the employer's primary purpose in locking out its employees was to avert peculiarly harmful economic consequences which would be imposed upon it and its customers if a strike were called either while a ship was in the yard during the shipping season or later when the yard was fully occupied.

Accordingly the, Court took the position that the lockout may be utilized by management to protect its collective bargaining position. In *American Ship Building* there was no evidence that the employer was hostile to the employees' interest in organizing for the purpose of collective bargaining or that the lockout was used to "discipline" them for engaging in the bargaining process. Thus the Court noted that it could not be said that the employer's intention was to "destroy or frustrate the process of collective bargaining" or that there was an indication that the union would be diminished in its capacity to represent the employees in the unit.

The Court, in *American Ship Building*, spoke of the lockout and the strike as "correlative" in terms of statutory usage. But it seems questionable whether *American Ship Building* and the right of employers to lock out can apply where the bargaining relationship is not so well-established as it was in that case, particularly in a first-contract situation where the parties are dealing with one another for the first time and the relationship is not as mature as the one in *American Ship Building*. Moreover, the employer had a legitimate apprehension based on the union's previous behavior. It would have been placed in a very difficult position if it had been confronted with a strike during its boom period. In effect it was transferring the economic burden of the dispute to the employees.

American Ship Building has had a great impact upon collective bargaining in sports. While lockouts can create legal liability where the collective bargaining relationship is fragile, generally sports owners are unlikely to seek the union's elimination because its existence is a prerequisite for any exemption to antitrust law. The impact of the lockout under *American Ship Building* has considerable relevance to sports because the players' leverage is greatest just before the postseason, when the owners obtain increased revenues through television and capacity attendance. This is so because the public's interest is greater during such a period. Therefore, threat of the strike and the strike itself is of much greater value during this period.

Conversely, the owners, relying upon *American Ship Building*, are encouraged to use the lockout and deprive the players of pay at a point where players do not have comparable leverage, i.e., at the beginning of the season or early in the season. This has been done in hockey a couple of times (though in the most recent instance the entire season was canceled), in basketball, and, as we shall see, in baseball itself in 1990, when the owners locked out during spring training. (Curiously, in 1990 the lockout was commenced during a time when the players were not paid and therefore did not suffer economic losses — though undoubtedly this was intended as a shot across the bow which would influence future union positions.)

Thus the lockout, the strike and the duty to bargain obligation, all part of American labor law terrain, establish the backdrop for relationships between players and owners in baseball.

The Modern Era

The National Labor Relations Act was soon to become a major part of labor-management relations in baseball. For a number of years before and after the enactment of the NLRA, most would have agreed with the view of Judge Landis when, in the *Federal Baseball* trial, he objected to the Federal League characterization of the work of baseball players as "labor." Said Judge Landis: "As a result of thirty years of observation ... I am shocked because you call playing baseball 'labor.'"[79] Labor law, collective bargaining and baseball soon became inextricable both in reality and in the public's mind. But throughout the thirty years' war of disputes discussed below, much of the public, like Judge Landis, found it difficult to think of baseball players as laborers.

At the beginning of baseball collective bargaining, as the players negotiated their agreements and assessed their newfound rights under the National Labor Relations Act, the focus was not so much upon the reserve clause. When Marvin Miller first sounded out players on their dissatisfaction or interest in reforms, he heard that the season was too long, that the travel and schedule were difficult and "brutal," and that playing conditions in certain parks were "terrible." And, of course, he heard about the need to improve pensions. Indeed, the *Curt Flood* litigation was regarded by many on both sides of the labor-management divide as unusual in that regard, inasmuch as many of the players had expressed no interest in changing it then, or in the landmark Congressional Cellar hearings held twenty years earlier.[80]

The issue of pensions was longstanding, well in advance of the 1946-47 developments discussed above, given the abbreviated length of a baseball player's career. It was pensions that were to provide the backdrop for the first strike in baseball since 1912, when Ty Cobb of the Detroit Tigers, the target of "profane and vulgar words" from a persistent and disabled heckler, jumped into the stands, knocking him unconscious with fists and feet. As the result of his violent behavior Cobb was suspended indefinitely and this induced his teammates to strike. Replacement players were recruited for a game against the Philadelphia Athletics:

> The sandlot strikebreakers lost 24–2; a ground ball knocked out two teeth of a third baseman; an outfielder had a fly ball land on his head; and the pickup team committed nine errors in the game—which was counted in the official standings. Thus sobered, Cobb urged his team mates to return to work. These players were fined $100 each, while Cobb got a $50 fine and a ten-day suspension.[81]

Thus the beginning of player strikes was not auspicious. But the pension issue was to produce a second strike in 1972, delaying my ability to witness the first in a series of Opening Days which I attended at Fenway Park. In contrast to 1912, this one was completely successful from the players' perspective.

The background was as follows: a three-year pension agreement had been reached between the players and owners in 1970, but in 1972 the pension and health benefit plans were open for negotiation—and a dispute had emerged in spring training of '72 over how the pensions were to be calculated. The owners did not believe that the players would strike for the first time in sixty years. But they did so. This was to be a continuous pattern: owner belief that players would not strike, and the players' willingness to strike. It would continue without abatement for the next thirty years.

The '72 pension strike caused the cancellation of eighty-six games at the start of the regular season, lasting for thirteen days and allowing me and Bob Berry, my colleague from Boston College Law School, to see our Opening Day at Fenway Park a couple of weeks late. Significantly, under the agreement that was finally reached, the owners capitulated to the players by adding $500,000 for health care benefits in agreeing to a cost of living increase in retirement benefits—though in yet another dispute regarding the pay for games missed, the games were not rescheduled and player salaries were docked.

This meant that not all teams played the same number of games—some clubs played 153 games and others played 156. This was considered to be at its time a remarkable interference with baseball's integrity, but it was far in advance of disputes about unbalanced schedules. Particularly, interleague competition was to result in a free fall into the land of unfair competition and away from baseball's integrity because different teams in competition with one another played different teams and not the same ones. Teams no longer play the same number of games at home against a particular team as opposed to those in the opponent's park. But all of this was to happen subsequent to the 1972 strike.

The uneven number of games played that year was to figure in the Eastern Division championship race (divisional playoffs had begun only in 1969). As Marvin Miller, the association's first leader, said: "That twist of fate may have cost the Red Sox the pennant—they finished behind Detroit by one-half a game."[82]

Ultimately, as Miller noted, the Red Sox finished one half of a game behind the Eastern Division champion Detroit Tigers. On a Carl Yastrzemski extra base hit, shortstop Luis Aparico slipped coming around third base, spoiling a rally for the Red Sox as they were eliminated from the race on baseball's penultimate day of the season. Just as I had possessed infinite faith in the ability of Red Sox twenty-five game winner Dave Ferriss in 1946 and was disbelieving when I heard the radio announcer tell me that the Cardinals were pounding

"El Maestro," Luis Tiant, whom the author and his father saw pitch more than once in the 1970s (courtesy Boston Red Sox).

him in the seventh game of the World Series, so also my oldest son Bill was beside himself when Luis Tiant (with a 1.91 ERA) was beaten that day. My wife telephoned me directly in Seattle, where I was in the midst of a speaking engagement, to see if I could console him in his tears.

The 1972 season, in which Red Sox fan favorite Dwight "Dewey" Evans came up from the minors as a rookie right fielder (he would remain until 1990) was thus a watershed. The players had struck, as the owners had never believed they would, and they had won! This was to be the first of a number of owner miscalculations about player resolve.

Now the developments were to proceed even more quickly. In the wake of the *Flood*, decision which highlighted the complete control that owners had over players, a new collective bargaining agreement was negotiated in 1973 which provided for a number of changes. First, the Players Association and Major League Baseball negotiated the so-called "10 and 5 Rule," which allowed players with ten years of seniority and five years of service with one club to veto a trade of which they disapproved. In a sense this was a direct reversal of the result obtained in *Flood* itself, because that veto power was what the Cardinals' centerfielder had sought from the courts when he had attempted to invalidate his trade to the Phillies on the ground that they had conspired to interfere with his ability to contract for his labor. Chicago Cub third baseman Ron Santo (later a Cubs broadcaster) was the first player to invoke these provisions and veto a trade to which he objected. Because of the player defeat in *Flood*, Santo had been able to win through the collective bargaining process what Flood could not obtain through antitrust law.

Second, a newly negotiated salary arbitration system in '73 now meant that there were now two forms of arbitration: (1) the grievance arbitration machinery, involving disputes relating to interpretations of the collective bargaining agreement, which had been put in place in '66; and (2) salary arbitration, which allowed either the club or player with a total two years' major league service in three seasons to submit a salary dispute to final and binding arbitration. (Subsequently eligibility was modified so as to provide in 1976 that

IN THE BLEACHERS By Steve Moore

"Not right now, Timmy. First we're going to work on fielding ground balls. Maybe later we can discuss collective bargaining."

Labor disputes became part of the sports pages beginning in the '70s, '80s and '90s (IN THE BLEACHERS © Steve Moore. Reprinted with permission of UNIVERSAL UCLICK. All rights reserved).

only players with less than six years and more than two years of service in the major leagues were eligible — and the minimum in '85 and '90 was to be three years and two years plus, respectively.[83])

The system was designed to encourage voluntary negotiations by precluding the arbitrator from compromising or from coming to some kind of middle ground. Thus this was characterized as so-called "final offer" arbitration, which had arisen in public employee disputes in the late '60s. In these cases, the unions were precluded from using the strike weapon in so-called interest disputes about new terms of collective bargaining agreements, including wages, hours, and working conditions. Whoever prevailed under this kind of arbitration obtained a windfall in baseball and elsewhere because the arbitrator, after identifying the ways in which the salary should be fixed (principally on the basis of comparison to other players with comparable seniority), was required to see which party was closest to the so-called midpoint between the two positions. Whichever party was closer would prevail and inevitably obtain a windfall. The system presumed that because both sides would fear that a windfall would be imposed upon it, they would thus negotiate a voluntary resolution of their differences without resort to arbitration. Generally this has proved to be the case, and the number of instances in which this process has been used has declined substantially. (Three arbitrators are now utilized[84] to hear each case so that a perceived inclination or tendency for a third party to split the differences between the two sides — i.e., resolve a balanced number of disputes in favor of players and owners — would be diminished since players and owners do not have access to the vote that is taken inside the panel and there are no dissenting opinions filed.)

TABLE 3.1. SALARY ARBITRATION RESULTS

	Cases Filed	Cases Settled	Cases Won by Player	Cases Won by Team
1974			13	16
1975			6	10
1976				
1977				
1978			2	7

	Cases Filed	Cases Settled	Cases Won by Player	Cases Won by Team
1979				
1980			8	5
1981			15	11
1982			11	10
1983			8	14
1984			13	17
1985			4	6
1986			6	7
1987			15	20
1988			10	16
1989			7	11
1990	164	138	7	5
1991	159	142	14	10
1992	157	137	6	11
1993	118	100	9	11
1994	91	75	6	12
1995	58	50	6	10
1996	76	66	2	6
1997	80	75	7	3
1998	81	73	1	4
1999	62	51	3	5
2000	91	81	2	9
2001	102*	87	4	6
2002	93	88	6	8
2003	72	65	1	4
2004	65	58	2	5
2005	89	86	3	4
2006	100	94	1	2
2007	106	99	2	4
2008	110	102	3	4
2009	111	108	2	6
TOTALS			207 (42.5%)	280 (57.5%)

*One player outrighted/elected free agency.
Data provided by Major League Baseball Players Association, current through cases heard in 2009 (prepared by Zac Cox based on data provided by Major League Baseball Players Association).

These provisions, along with free agency procedures negotiated in 1976 discussed below, produced enormous changes. Between 1969 and the early part of the twenty-first century, salaries in baseball increased more than one hundredfold! Salary arbitration did not anticipate free-agency developments that were to come within two years of the 1973 agreement, and it is fair to say that the two procedures have operated in tandem to ratchet up salaries in a manner that the parties — and certainly the owners — did not fully anticipate.

Subsequent to the 1973 collective bargaining agreement there were yet more developments in the free agency arena due to the utilization of the grievance-arbitration process. In 1974 Oakland Athletics pitcher Jim "Catfish" Hunter and Oakland owner Charlie Finley faced off against one another. This dispute was to have enormous implications for both salary negotiations and for the way in which the game was to be played on the field itself. We have encountered Mr. Finley at an earlier point (but chronologically later on, in 1976) as he was ensnarled with Commissioner Bowie Kuhn after attempting to engage in his own St. Louis Browns–type "fire sale" to move leading players to both the Red Sox and the Yankees.

Even the "Catfish" Hunter matter was not Charlie Finley's first altercation with a player. First baseman Ken "Hawk" Harrelson (now a Chicago White Sox broadcaster) was released by Finley in August 1967 after calling Finley a "menace to baseball." Finley did not want Harrelson's services in light of his comment and released him, improving the Hawk's fortunes dramatically. His salary went from $12,000 to $35,000. He signed with the Red Sox, who were engaged in that four-team pennant race discussed in Chapter 2, just after they had lost home run–hitting Tony Conigliaro, who was beaned and suffered a severe eye injury the same month of August in which Harrelson was released. The Hawk soon became a popular figure in baseball and in Boston, notwithstanding the heart flutters that many felt when he camped under a fly ball in right field (his natural position was first base). And when he was traded to the Cleveland Indians in the spring of 1969 (in a multiplayer deal that brought pitcher Sonny Siebert to the Red Sox along with others), the transaction produced Fenway Park picketing by Red Sox fans. Again, the Hawk was able to negotiate effectively in this context as well, obtaining additional monies from the Indians and even persuading them to draw in the distant fences in Municipal Stadium so that they were close enough for him to resume home run hitting comparable to that which he had been able to produce in Fenway. Harrelson had done it again.

But the Hunter case had more immediate and long-range implications. In the previous season with the A's, Hunter had obtained a 25–12 record; he had been a twenty-game winner for four consecutive seasons, compiling a total of 88 victories in his four years with the A's. The A's and Hunter agreed on a two-year contract which provided that $50,000 would be paid to a deferment plan of Hunter's choice — and the "Catfish" had specified a deferred payment provision that would enable him to avoid immediate tax liability for the $50,000. Finley, however, subsequently discovered that he would incur tax liability and insisted that the contract did not provide that he should assume this burden.

During the 1974 season "Catfish" Hunter routinely received the portion of his salary that was to be paid directly to him, but the deferred payments were not made to the designated investment company. When the season ended with the deferred payments still not made, "Catfish" claimed that Finley's failure to make payments constituted a material breach of contract, thus enabling the pitcher to exercise his right to terminate it. Therefore, in Hunter's view, he was a free agent. When Finley offered the $50,000 which was part of the deferment plan as a direct payment, Hunter rejected it as contrary to his contractual rights.

The matter went to arbitration under the grievance arbitration machinery which had been negotiated in 1966. Arbitrator Peter Seitz ruled in Hunter's favor, finding no ambiguity in the contract language outlining the club's obligations. The arbitrator held that since the club failed to perform its obligation, Hunter lawfully had the right to terminate the contract and therefore did not have a valid contract with the A's. Therefore, Hunter was a free agent and could entertain offers from any other major league club.

On December 31, 1974, the "Catfish" accepted an offer from the New York Yankees for what was at that time an unprecedented salary package. Hunter received a $1 million signing bonus, a $150,000 annual salary for five years, life insurance benefits worth $1,000,000, and a substantial amount of deferred compensation. Only later was it learned that the bidding for Hunter had actually exceeded the Yankees' offer, through evidence submitted at the *Joe Kapp*[85] football trial involving free agency. Hunter had rejected a $3.8 million offer from the Kansas City Royals, the evidence establishing how competition for players might affect salaries.

The Guaranteed Contract

But the greatest immediate significance of the Hunter contract was a special covenant which, though the word guaranteed was not used, nonetheless provided that salary payments "shall be the obligation of the Club, notwithstanding the inability of the Player to perform the services for under the contract." Salary payments were to be payable "as long as the inability to so perform said services is due solely and strictly to a medical condition."

In a baseball arbitration decided after the *Hunter* case it was noted that this guarantee represented a "substantial departure" from salary obligations assumed until then by clubs under typical player agreements. There was a presumed right on the part of the clubs to renew the contract from year to year indefinitely, and the Uniform Players Contract also gave the club the right to terminate the player if he failed, in the opinion of the club's management, "to exhibit sufficient skill and competitive ability to qualify and continue as a member of the team." Even where a disability arose out of an injury due to playing, the club was obligated to make only limited payments and the player received the balance of his salary for that year alone. If a player was terminated prior to spring training, he received no payment at all. If he was cut during spring training the player received thirty days' pay, and if during the championship season, sixty days' pay. Baseball arbitrator Raymond Goetz, a Kansas law professor, noted:

> Thus, even though Hunter's contract was for five years, without the special covenant it could have been terminated by the Club during the period in accordance with the usual terms thereof, and he would receive at most the balance of his salary for the year, or possibly nothing. With this covenant, he was assured the full five years' salary even though he might become unable to perform due to some physical disability.[86]

This new guaranteed contract is at least as important as the establishment of free agency in baseball. Arbitrator Goetz noted in the salary dispute involving hard-throwing Frank Tanana of the California Angels (only later in his career with the Boston Red Sox and the Texas Rangers did he rely upon guile and slow-moving "junk") that the first guarantees were provided in contracts for 1974-1975 between the Cleveland Indians and James Perry and Steven Kline.[87] As the opinion noted, they "did not happen to be free agents at the time that their contracts were negotiated," and thus Hunter was the first to negotiate one while a free agent. Said Professor Goetz:

> Salary guarantee provisions of one kind or another then became almost standard in the numerous long-term Player contracts entered into during the era of free agency ushered in [in 1975].... As free agents, these Players were in a position to negotiate and contract with any Club, instead of just the Club that had supposed it had an annual right to renew the existing contract.[88]

Guaranteed contracts have been the relatively rare exception in football — though substantial signing bonuses have become a surrogate for them[89] — and less frequent in basketball than in baseball. Terrell Owens, the talented and volatile pass receiver of both the San Francisco 49ers and Philadelphia Eagles before he wore out his welcome in those cities and moved on to the Dallas Cowboys, Buffalo Bills, and Cincinnati Bengals, complained bitterly about the fact that he was bound to football teams contractually when they, by virtue of the non-guaranteed tradition in football, were not bound to him![90] The *Hunter* case made baseball different.

In 1976, the first year of free agency in baseball, Red Sox noteworthies, like shortstop

Rick Burleson, whom we had seen line one off the Fenway wall as a rookie in May 1974, as well as 1975 Rookie of the Year centerfielder Fred Lynn and catcher Carlton Fisk — he of the 1975 fame for his home run that he willed fair in the World Series' sixth game — all negotiated guaranteed contracts with the Red Sox. Other notables were soon to follow, thus making this kind of agreement an industry practice. Moreover, these were to be multi-year contracts, extending for a period of somewhere between 2 to 5 years — and later as long as 10 years with deferred payments due thereafter!

The Reserve System Reconsidered

Beyond the emergence of the multi-year guaranteed contract, the other shoe to drop was baseball's reserve system itself, alluded to in the guaranteed contract arbitrations noted above. The procedure was attacked, again, through the very same grievance-arbitration procedures of which Hunter had availed himself. Bobby Tolan of the Cincinnati Reds and San Diego Padres, dissatisfied with the contract offered to him, had planned to play out his contract year, asserting that the limitation of a one-year option for renewal contained in the Uniform Players Contract was incorporated in the collective bargaining agreement. He would contend that he could enjoy free agent status at the end of the option year subsequent to the expiration of his contract.

Tolan was to settle, but similar grievances were filed by pitchers Andy Messersmith of the Los Angeles Dodgers and Dave McNally of the Montreal Expos. The leagues' position was that the reserve clause meant that the option year set forth in the individual contract of employment existed in perpetuity in the event that the player and the owner could not agree upon new contract terms. A contrary result, they contended, would be inconsistent with the historically well-established and accepted reserve clause. The owners maintained that not only did the grievances filed by Messersmith and McNally not have merit but that the arbitrator did not have jurisdiction, in part because of an agreement between the players and the owners about reserving the issue of the *Flood* dispute for the courts.

Arbitrator Peter Seitz — the same arbitrator who had handled "Catfish" Hunter's grievance — had some difficult issues before him. The collective bargaining agreements' grant of jurisdiction to the arbitrator stated that it did not "deal" with the reserve system. But this declaration had emerged from a standoff between the players and the owners over the *Flood* litigation, when the parties had awaited resolution of the free agent issue under antitrust law by the Supreme Court. The Association had attempted to immunize itself from damage liability in the event that the Court ruled for Flood. Now the Court had ruled in 1972 and the standoff was over. To confound the problem of contract interpretation, the collective bargaining agreement also incorporated the one-year option in the Uniform Player Contract, meaning that the club had an option to renew for one year after the contract had expired. The same contract incorporated the Major League Rules which set forth the reserve list and no-tampering regulations. Thus it appeared that both the reserve system and option clauses were within the arbitrator's jurisdiction inasmuch as the collective bargaining agreement addressed both.

In any event, Arbitrator Seitz concluded that the dispute was within his jurisdiction, and on the merits held that a contract could not be extended beyond the one year of renewal in the so-called option year. Said Seitz: "When that year comes to an end, the player no longer has contractual duties that bind them to the club."[91] Yet the opinion seemed to ignore the fact that the reserve rule system had been in effect for a full century, going back to the 1870s and '80s, when clubs attempted to restrain players from revolving from one team to another.

The arbitrator urged that the parties negotiate their differences with one another at the bargaining table, just as he had done prior to the issuance of his award. But the owners, encouraged by their 1972 victory in *Flood*, had not only declined a pre-award Seitz invitation to negotiate or mediate the issue, but also saw no need to negotiate on the reserve clause post-award — since, in their view, they could get the arbitrator's decision and award reversed on appeal.[92] What they failed to recognize was that the Supreme Court, in a series of cases going back to 1960, had made it very difficult to reverse an arbitral award[93] on either the arbitrability issue — that is to say, whether the arbitrator had jurisdiction — or the merits themselves. After 1960 notwithstanding, the fact that courts must determine whether an arbitrator has jurisdiction[94] had made it difficult. And in a result that most labor lawyers would have predicted in the baseball dispute, the Court of Appeals for the Eighth Circuit in St. Louis enforced the award, following the 1960 Supreme Court precedent.[95] This was to be but the second after *Catfish Hunter* in a long series of legal decisions which the owners would lose after their *Flood* victory! The frequency and gross error of their legal mistakes was to grow with each dispute.

Initially, the owners responded by shutting down the spring training camps in March 1976 as they faced the prospect of bargaining with players, many of whom would soon become free agents at the end of the option year. This lockout lasted seventeen days until then Commissioner Bowie Kuhn ordered the camps reopened "without further delay," and thus overrode the decision of the owners, employing his "best interests of baseball" authority.

Thus a new era began. The landscape consisted now of free agency established by Arbitrator Seitz, guaranteed and frequently multi-year contracts being negotiated for individual players along the lines of that obtained by Hunter, and the salary arbitration procedures which had been negotiated in 1973. But what would free agency provide? A vacuum emerged in which all players could become free to negotiate with any team that they wanted after their option year had been played out. The matter was resolved in August 1976, in a new round of collective bargaining, when the parties negotiated an agreement which remains the general framework for free agency today.

Under this agreement, free agency eligibility exists after six years of service and the salary arbitration final offer procedures negotiated in 1973 are applied to players with two, and since '90, two-plus to six years' seniority. This meant that the free agency and salary arbitration operated in tandem with one another and that, because the financial position of an individual club could not be taken into account in a salary arbitration, the free-spending practices of the wealthier big-market teams would eventually filter down to low-revenue teams through salary arbitration. And this in turn created new pressure for another round of bargaining — the first in a series of negotiations which would result in a strike or lockout in every single instance up until 2002 — and all which involved attempts by the owners to recapture the 1976 concessions that were made to the players in the free-agency arena because of Arbitrator Seitz's award.

In the Wake of Free Agency

Now the grievance-arbitration machinery would be invoked anew over the tension between collective representation and individual bargaining. The negotiated agreements have addressed this and numerous disputes about the interpretation of the contract to be provided by arbitrators. In Article II (as presently written) the reiteration of the Association as the "sole and exclusive bargaining agent" contains a proviso to the effect that "an individual Player shall be entitled to negotiate in accordance with the provisions set forth in this Agreement (1) an individual salary over and above the minimum requirements established by this Agreement and (2) Special Covenants to be included in an individual Uniform Player's Contract, which actually or potentially provide additional benefits to the Player." Again, in Article III the obligation not to enter into a Special Covenant which is "inconsistent" with the Agreement is set forth. Moreover, the collective bargaining agreement's applicability has no impact upon the rights and duties of the club and player in any individual contract and, specifically, the Agreement does not "impair, limit or terminate" these rights and duties. These provisions existed by virtue of the 1944 Supreme Court *J.I. Case* decision alluded to above, while enshrining the statutory command of exclusivity, allowed the parties to make modifications to that principle.

It is not surprising that this language has given rise to a series of disputes, given the unusual nature of baseball collective bargaining agreement language and the consequent lack of precedent. One of the first disputes arose out of so-called "right of first refusal" covenants, similar to those contained in football and basketball agreements, which allowed the club to be able to match an offer provided by another team and to retain a relationship with such a player rather than give him up through free agency. In the wake of the 1976 collective bargaining agreement and the new negotiated rules for free agency, the Red Sox executed such agreements with shortstop Rick Burleson and catcher Carlton Fisk, but the union grieved the contract provisions on the theory that the covenant provided no benefit to the player as the collective bargaining agreement requires. The contention of the Red Sox was that the player would benefit from his retention because of his presence in a big-market arena and the consequent ability to negotiate other commercial arrangements as well as to obtain postseason playoff and World Series payments. (The Red Sox had won the 1975 American League Championship and lost to the Cincinnati Reds in the World Series, subsequent to a dramatic Game 6 Carlton Fisk home run, in a seven-game series.) But, notwithstanding the willingness of unions to negotiate collective bargaining agreements which provide for the right of first refusal with the National Football League and the National Basketball Association, a baseball settlement emerging from the Red Sox dispute provided for the elimination of such provisions. The Red Sox retreated, the union prevailed, and the "right of first refusal" covenants became a matter of history completely inapplicable to baseball.

One of the earliest controversies involving free agency arose as the result of a contract between Alvin Moore and the Atlanta Braves in which a Special Covenant gave Moore the right to demand a trade which could not be consummated without his prior consent if he was dissatisfied with his playing time. In the event that a trade could not be consummated by the end of the 1977 championship season, Moore would become a free agent if he so desired.

The National League disapproved this Special Covenant and the Association filed a grievance on the ground that actual or potential additional benefits were provided for the player within the meaning of the collective agreement. The clubs maintained that the free agency provisions in the 1976 agreement were exclusive, providing the only basis upon which free agency rights could be exercised. But the union argued that there were still other avenues to free agency, such as an unconditional release by a club because the player was not sufficiently qualified. The arbitrator held, in this case, that the six-year service requirement through which a player could exercise free agency was for the individual club's benefit in the sense that it would want to retain the player for a particular period of time.[96] Thus, the benefit of "long-term title and reservation rights" could be waived by the club. On the other hand, the reentry mechanism through which other clubs would have an opportunity to negotiate with a player who becomes a free agent was a matter covered by all the collective bargaining agreement, so an attempt by club and player to evade such procedures would be "inconsistent" and thus prohibited. Said the Arbitrator:

> There is clear merit in the Association's argument that the words "additional benefits to the Player" should be liberally construed to support a wide variety of benefits to a Player over and above the benefits accorded to him by the Basic Agreement. Though covenants containing such benefits may be "inconsistent" with a particular provision of the Agreement dealing with the same subject matter, there is logic in the Association's argument that they are not, in fact, "inconsistent" because Article II authorizes such inconsistencies where they provide additional benefits to the Player.[97]

In a subsequent case involving Mike Marshall and the Minnesota Twins, an attempt to waive compensation — in this case an amateur draft free selection — that the club would receive was invalidated because the compensation provisions of the collective bargaining agreement are designed for all of the clubs and not the benefit of one particular team that loses the player through free agency. Said the Arbitrator:

> The benefit to the losing Club is not the sole factor in [the] compensation scheme.... Of equal importance, as League President MacPhail points out in his testimony herein, is the detriment or cost to the signing Club of being required to give up an amateur draft choice in return for signing a Player who became a free agent pursuant to [the collective bargaining agreement].[98]

One of the more important modern cases involved pitcher Richard Tidrow (now in the San Francisco Giants front office) and the Chicago Cubs after his trade to that team from the New York Yankees. Here Tidrow and the union sought to invalidate a covenant which allowed the club an option to renew and thus deny the player the right of free agency. The Cubs contended that under the additional benefit test, all special covenants which were part of an individual contract of employment had to be considered as a package. But the Arbitrator concluded that such a package approach would virtually nullify the inconsistency restriction since an "off-setting additional benefit in another special covenant" could always be provided. The key, said the Arbitrator, was whether the inconsistent covenant in question itself provided the actual potential benefit. The benefits were a $200,000 salary — at that time considerably above the minimum provided in the collective agreement — as well as the guaranteed nature of the contract. Said the Arbitrator:

> Whether these two factors *actually* would provide additional benefits of course could not be determined at the time Tidrow's contract was executed in the spring of 1978, since their operation was contingent upon future action by the Club in exercising the option and on other uncertainties. But as of the date of contract execution it would appear that they could *potentially* provide additional benefits, not only over the standard Uniform Player's Contract generally, but what is equally important, over the then indeterminate prospects of free agency for 1981 which they could supplant.[99]

Accordingly, the Arbitrator concluded that Tidrow was "contingently substituting for free agency an otherwise bona fide alternative which at that time he could realistically deem in itself to be potentially better."[100] Although Arbitrator Goetz stated in dicta (language which is unnecessary to the resolution of the dispute itself) that Tidrow's situation was different from that of a "hapless rookie," in a subsequent case the Arbitrator held that "buy-outs" of salary arbitration for young players at that time ineligible to invoke the Agreement's machinery was also permissible.[101] The Cleveland Indians built a powerful team in the '90s on the basis of such long-term agreements, as did some other so-called "small-market" clubs.

Finally, in another case that has implications for other contemporary issues, it was held that guaranteed contracts between the Cincinnati Reds with outfielder Ron Gant and relief pitcher Xavier Hernandez and that of the Florida Marlins with Terry Pendleton, which provided that Clubs could withhold payment for on-field misconduct suspensions by the League president, was in violation of the Agreement because in no sense did it provide a benefit to the player.[102] More recently, however, the Houston Astros' reliever Shawn Chacon had his contract terminated after he had a physical altercation with Houston General Manager Ed Wade. As a result of this, Chacon lost almost half of a $2 million contract. Both this case and a subsequent one involving Francisco Rodriguez, the New York Mets' closer, bring into play the Uniform Player Contract, incorporated as it is in the collective bargaining agreement, in which the player promises to "keep himself in first-class physical condition and to obey the Club's training rules, and pledges himself to the American public and to the Club to conform to high standards of personal conduct, fair play and good sportsmanship." Since about 2000, a number of clubs have negotiated special covenants with players like Rodriguez which allow them to convert a guaranteed contract to one which is non-guaranteed, and the question in cases like *Rodriguez* is whether a player has met these standards under paragraph 7(b)(1), which allows the Club to terminate a contract. Settlements have been reached in connection with Colorado and Denny Neagle, and with Baltimore when confronted with a series of alcohol-related incidents with Sidney Ponson. These cases might have been cited in connection with the Barry Bonds Covenant with the San Francisco Giants which reportedly stated that the contract can be voided in the event that he is indicted. And indicted he was, though Bonds was no longer under contract to play with the Giants at that time. The overriding questions in these cases are (1) whether in fact the player has engaged in the misconduct and (2) the materiality of the breach by the player. That is to say, is the conduct so inexcusable that the entire contract is void? (Recall that that was the result in the *Hunter* decision when the Oakland A's were guilty of such misconduct.)

More straightforward conflicts between the "benefits" clause in the collective bargaining agreement and special covenants relating to salaries have come into play, for instance, in connection with a controversy relating to "Mo" Vaughn, the Red Sox' and Angels' erstwhile slugger of the '90s, who was traded to the New York Mets from the Angels. Vaughn wished to leave the West Coast and to go to New York City, so as to play for the Mets. The arrangement between the Angels and Mets provided for deferred payments which would have cost Vaughn "millions,"[103] and the union, intervening under the "additional benefits clause," accepted an agreement which, while providing for a loss of $500,000, was made in exchange for the Mets' giving Vaughn "a much greater say in whether he could be traded and where." The *Tidrow* precedent had taken into account the salary received by the pitcher alongside of consideration of the option clause providing for renewal in lieu of free agency in that case.[104]

An antithetical result was provided in the better-publicized Texas Rangers–Boston Red Sox proposed deal involving Alex Rodriguez. Rodriguez, who came to be a beneficiary of a $252 million contract with the Yankees over ten years, was traded to Boston for outfielder Manny Ramirez and would have been required to take a more substantial multi-million-dollar decrease in connection with a trade to which he consented. This arrangement, vetoed by the union under the collective bargaining agreement,[105] resulted in the subsequent trade of Rodriguez to the New York Yankees. The spectacular grab of a player whom the Red Sox had coveted enhanced the Red Sox rivalry, creating more interest in fisticuffs between Captain Jason Varitek and Rodriguez in the midsummer heat of an '04 pennant race and the years to come. This was particularly true in 2007, when the Red Sox won the East for the first time since 1995, though not before a hard and failed charge by the Yankees in the second half of the season!

Finally, one of the most important arbitration rulings involved Alex Johnson of the California Angels. The team had suspended Johnson for "failure to give your best efforts" and the Commissioner had placed him on the "restrictive list," the practical effect being to keep him off the payroll for the balance of the season.[106] In this important case, Arbitrator Gill credited testimony to the effect that Johnson was suffering from "acute illness" and a "'severe reactive depression,' with the result that at this time 'Mr. Johnson is not able to resume function as a major league player.'"[107] Accordingly the Arbitrator held that Johnson should have been placed on the disabled list just as he would have been placed if he had been physically disabled. Said Arbitrator Gill, the *Johnson* ruling was not intended to excuse players who simply asserted that they were under "emotional stress" or "mental illness":

> All that is actually decided here is that where highly-qualified and respected psychiatrists retained by both sides have agreed that the player was and is unable to perform because of a mental condition, he should be placed on the disabled list rather than disciplined.[108]

Though the decision is nearly four decades old, it has had considerable practical effect in this century, allowing players such as Joey Votto, Zack Greinke, Dontrelle Willis, Milton Bradley and Justin Duchscherer all to take disability without loss of pay.[109]

The Strikes and Lockouts

Subsequent to the events of '75 and '76, the next chapter in the labor story unfolded in 1980 and '81, when the principal focus became the question of whether clubs which lost free agents should be compensated for their loss. This has been the principal part of the issue ever since, and the players, fearing that compensation would deter clubs from signing free agents, have always resisted it. In part their experience was based upon the compensation features in both football and basketball, particularly the so-called Rozelle Rule in football, which allowed the commissioner to determine whether a club which had lost a free agent could get compensation. This process is generally regarded as a major impediment to free agency because it would deter clubs from signing free agents. Even after the Rozelle Rule was struck down by the courts as a violation of the Sherman Antitrust Act,[110] the new compensation procedures which followed in the Rule's wake did not substantially enhance football player free agency status, in part, because of the deterrence of compensation which was retained in the new contract. Thus the baseball players were deeply suspicious of any such proposal.

Ultimately, after a joint study committee had been created in 1980 putting the issue over to 1981, the players struck. As our family took the train to Los Angeles from San Francisco to see the Red Sox play the Angels in Anaheim, we saw photos of Jim Rice leaving the dugout in what was presumed to be the last moment of play before the strike. We arrived nonetheless at Anaheim Stadium but were greeted by a sorrowful security guard who lamented the fact that the ballpark was indeed under lock and key and that the strike was on.

In this dispute the players, even before they struck, had made their first resort to the unfair labor practice provisions of the National Labor Relations Act and had attempted to convince the NLRB to seek an injunction against the owners in federal district court in New York on the ground that owners had unlawfully refused to open the books and disclose financial information.[111] The Board, in late May 1981, sided with the Players Association, and during a New York hearing caused consternation among the owners when NLRB administrative law judge Mel Welles, a New York Yankees fan, sought the autographs of a number of prominent players immediately upon conclusion of the hearing. When the Board sought a judicial decree to enforce its order, Judge Henry Werker held that statements about an inability to pay and consequent financial limitations had not been made by those with bargaining responsibility in the collective bargaining process, and thus dismissed the Board's request to obtain an injunction providing for financial disclosure with a call to "play ball!!!"[112]

The judge's statement, of course, was a call for the players not to strike, and my family, traveling to southern California in part to see the Red Sox play the Angels, remained cautiously optimistic notwithstanding photos of left fielder Rice leaving the dugout. But as we were to discover that day in Anaheim as Tim and I sought to watch the Red Sox and the Angels, no ball was to be played for a considerable time thereafter. The union was not going to heed the judge's exhortation unless he could control the behavior of the owners, which he could not!

Ultimately, subsequent to a stoppage lasting more than eighty days and shortly after the owners' strike insurance had run out, thus placing considerable financial pressure upon the owners, a compromise was reached. The agreement provided that each team would have to contribute to a "pool" of players which would compensate a club losing a free agent player to another team, the theory being that since the compensation was not necessarily required of the team that was signing the free agent it would not be deterred from doing so. This assumption that there would be no deterrent in signing free agents proved to be an accurate one. As Professor Andrew Zimbalist noted: "The final compromise did little to alter the course of signing a free agent."[113] Again, the owners gained nothing but acrimony and distrust. As noted, the strike, which lasted until August 1, was settled a week after the owners' strike insurance money ran out, and a split season playoff procedure in which the division winners in each half of the season would play a one-game playoff with one another was devised.

This dispute produced controversies relating to the tension between the right to strike and guaranteed contracts. Various players stated that their guaranteed contracts entitled them to be paid during the strike itself. In a series of arbitration decisions growing out of the 1981 strike, Arbitrator Goetz rejected this argument on the ground that employers generally do not finance strikes against themselves and that, in the absence of explicit contract language to the contrary, such an intent would not be presumed — particularly where the contract provided that an "arbitrary and capricious" refusal to provide services would be an exception to the guarantee.[114] Moreover, it was noted that even where the clubs unsuccessfully bargained for an exception in the case of the strike, given this reality, this bargaining posture could be deemed to accomplish clarification of an intent already in the individual contract. Said the Arbitrator with regard to lefty Frank Tanana:

The wording of the compensation provision in Tanana's contract cannot properly be extended to guarantee payment in the strike situation because that would be totally unrelated to the parties' clearly ascertainable purpose of protecting the player against loss of ability to play due to disability or similar circumstances beyond his control. This limited objective of the salary guarantee — unelaborated by any preliminary discussions — also buttresses the conclusion that in this case at least, the "arbitrarily refuse" proviso should not be interpreted so narrowly as to preclude it from providing the customary suspension of compensation during participation in a strike.[115]

The issue of whether the guarantee is entitled to be paid during a lockout when the employer initiates the dispute has yet to be resolved in baseball. But in a case arising out of the 1998-99 basketball lockout, Arbitrator John Feerick held that the owners were not obliged to pay the guarantee under those circumstances — and it is generally thought that this award brought the lockout to its conclusion on terms more favorable to the owners.[116] The Arbitrator in the basketball lockout noted that while the Supreme Court had not explicitly held that the strike and lockout are "correlative" (it had so said in dicta[117]), nonetheless "the right to lock out is now well established and firmly grounded in federal substantive labor law. There has been an increasingly solid presumption of its corollary relationship with the right to strike" — noting Supreme Court authority in *American Ship Building* as well as other decisions[118] to the effect that the use of economic pressure by labor and management is part and parcel of the system that the Wagner and Taft-Hartley Acts have recognized.[119]

In considering the relationship between the individual contract of employment and the collective bargaining agreement, the arbitrator noted that this was a "somewhat murky" area but that the Supreme Court had adumbrated guidelines in *J.I. Case* to the effect that the individual contract could not "forestall bargaining or ... limit or condition the term of the collective agreement."[120] Here the arbitrator relied upon contractual provisions in the collective bargaining agreement to the effect that player contracts could not "serve the purpose of defeating or circumventing the intention of the parties as reflected by all of the provisions of this [collective bargaining] Agreement."

Stare decisis, a legal doctrine providing strict adherence to precedent, is not applicable to arbitration but nonetheless can be employed. In the absence of an individual contract of employment to the contrary, it would seem that the basketball decision, while not binding upon baseball, will be persuasive and that guaranteed contracts may not be held to be payable in a future baseball lockout. This is especially true given the baseball agreement language to the effect that inconsistencies in the individual contract of employment are to bow to the collective agreement.

In the wake of the 1981 strike, more free agency signings commenced and salaries continued to climb upward. Naturally, this led to more owner dissatisfaction and another strike, albeit only for a two-day period, in 1985, under the reign of a new Commissioner, Peter Ueberroth. A tightening of the salary arbitration procedure ensued, triggering much discontent — especially on the part of Red Sox ace Roger Clemens, who, after a Cy Young and MVP year in 1986, was unable to go to arbitration and was required to accept what the Red Sox offered. Under the 1981 agreement Clemens would have been eligible for salary arbitration or free agency since he possessed two years of seniority, having come up from the minors during the San Francisco Democratic Party Convention in 1984. But the 1985 agreement required that a player could only be eligible for salary arbitration when he had three years of seniority. Thus, for the first time, the baseball union found itself on the receiving end of discontent by players who were denied rights under the change in the rules. Meanwhile, however, the pool concept was abandoned because the owners could see that it had little impact upon the salaries and free agency, and amateur draft choices were reinstated as the sole means of free agent compensation.

The Collusion Cases

But in the wake of the '85 agreement a new chapter was to unfold; it was called collusion. The players brought a series of grievances to arbitration based upon the anti-collusion language which had been incorporated in the collective bargaining agreement at the owners' insistence because of the collective holdout of the Los Angeles Dodgers' pitchers Sandy Koufax and Don Drysdale in the 1960s. Until this happened, the traditional holdout had been akin to the one that we have seen Joe DiMaggio employ — or attempt to employ. If anything, this demonstrated the relative weakness of even established and skilled players.

The owners had regarded this new tactic employed by Koufax and Drysdale as "improper concerted activity" action because of their superstar status. These two outstanding hurlers would have had extraordinary leverage over any team for which they played, let alone the Dodgers. With the advent of free agency, the owners feared that this collective tactic — a tactic perfectly permissible and ordinary in most collective bargaining, where individual negotiations are not particularly important — was so powerful that it should be prohibited. (A variation on this theme was evident in 2010, when LeBron James coordinated his bargaining with two other superstars so that they could all sign with the Miami Heat.) Thus in 1976 they sought and obtained anti-collusion protection under which more than one player could not band together for the purpose of salary.

But the players, though they accepted the owners' position on this matter, insisted upon and obtained similar anti-collusion language vis-à-vis the owners, and it was this that they employed successfully in a series of arbitrations involving free agency. These disputes arose after the 1985 agreement had been negotiated. The free agent market began to dry up, even though certain clubs such as the Atlanta Braves, the California Angels, the New York Yankees, the San Diego Padres and the Texas Rangers had been major players in the free agency market previously. In the first free agency negotiations during the winter of '85-'86, only catcher Carlton Fisk, at that time having played a number of years with the Chicago White Sox (he had escaped earlier from the Boston Red Sox through a relatively unusual free agency situation[121]) received an offer from a team other than his own team. Said Arbitrator George Nicolau in the first of these cases which proceeded to arbitration:

> Of the re-entry free agents, none, except for Carlton Fisk, had received a "bona fide" offer from another club until his former club announced that it did not desire to re-sign him. Except for Fisk, whose offer was a "private" one from Yankees owner George Steinbrenner, none of those who were offered salary arbitration received any offers from other clubs and all, including Fisk, signed with their former clubs by January 8.[122]

A pattern of inactivity continued beyond the first year into the second year of negotiations in '86-'87. Again, an essential theme in the players' position was that in practically every instance where a team wanted to retain an incumbent player on its payroll, no other team would bid for the player. Players complained that this was because of collusive activity on the part of the owners prohibited under the agreement since '76.

Two cases in '86-'87 illustrate the players' point well. The first was described dramatically by Murray Chass of the *New York Times* a number of years after:

The Yankees had finished in second place behind Boston, but Dennis Rasmussen, with 18 victories, was their only pitcher with double-digit victories. Morris, a 31-year-old free agent, was exactly what the baseball doctor ordered. This is what free agency was all about. Yet Morris walked out of Room 600 of the Bay Harbor Inn without a Yankee deal. He was a victim of the second year of the owners' conspiracy against free agents. Steinbrenner was not a victim, but he surely was an unwilling participant, given his penchant for lavishing free agents with money.[123]

The second involves Andre Dawson, who had played for the Montreal Expos and wanted to leave because of the impact that the Astroturf had upon his knees. His agent was successful in negotiating an agreement because, and only because, he allowed the Chicago Cubs to fill in the salary unilaterally in his contract. The Cubs would have looked silly had they refused Dawson's services under such circumstances.

The Association's position was accepted by two arbitrators in three separate awards.[124] As a result of these cases a settlement was reached which provided $280 million in collusion damages. All of this set the stage for a new round of collective bargaining in 1990 as the 1985 agreement expired.

Meanwhile, other problems were emerging. The owners, soon after the 1985 collective bargaining agreement, reduced their rosters from 25 to 24 players so as to reduce labor costs — much as they had done previously in the Great Depression, when the reduction was from 25 to 23.[125] Though this action was protested by the union through the filing of a grievance in a rare victory on a matter of consequence, the owners' position was upheld in arbitration.[126] But more formidable problems, in which the salary arbitration process was implicated and invoked, were on the horizon.

The 1990 Negotiations and Lockout

Thus a collision course for the 1990 negotiations was apparent, given the fact that the owners were dissatisfied with salary arbitration, seeing it as a "heads you win, tails I lose" process. As a Los Angeles radio announcer said about a salary arbitration that I arbitrated subsequent to the negotiation of the '90 agreement when I ruled against then California Angels outfielder Luis Polonia: "Luis has lost his arbitration before the arbitrator. But he won't be in need of food stamps."

As noted above, the 1973 agreement and all subsequent ones containing salary arbitration had required that the arbitrator choose between the final offer of each side, and this offer was frequently a handsome one from the players' perspective. The offers generally proceeded from comparisons with what players were obtaining on the free-agent market from the more financially secure and high-spending clubs. Through arbitration these patterns were made applicable to all of the teams, exacerbating the rich-poor, "them and us" divide between teams like the New York Yankees and the Montreal Expos.

Specifically, the salary arbitration contractual provisions have always focused fundamentally upon comparability.[127] But comparability to what? When I heard the salary dispute between Andy Benes and the San Diego Padres in 1993, the first thing that the Padres invoked was Benes' won and lost record. I said at the beginning of the hearing: "I think that the most deceptive statistic in baseball is a won and lost record. It does not take into account slow infielders, poor bullpens and sloppy outfielders." Immediately I saw frowns on the faces of the Padres executives. But other stats such as earned run averages are always in my view more relevant. Even these data, however, suffer from the same limitations — and today a whole new realm of statistics have come into play in salary arbitrations which have influenced, for instance, Cy Young Awards given to both Tim Lincecum, Zack Greinke in 2009 and Felix Hernandez in 2010. Hernandez won the Cy Young with only 13 victories, "the fewest victories ever by a starter who won the award in a nonstrike season."[128] All of these awards were provided substantially after my ruling for Andy Benes in his case with the Padres.

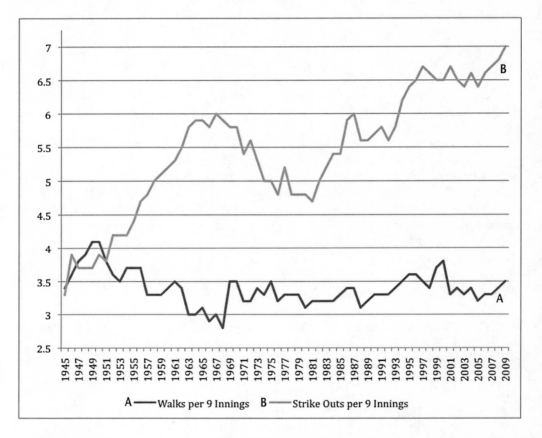

Walks accelerated and strikeouts diminished in the post–World War II period (prepared by Mike Scanlon based on the data presented in the Baseball Reference website. See http://www.baseball-ref erence.com/).

A new focus upon strikeout to base-on-ball ratio made the value of Pedro Martinez all the more clear in the '90s. In the offensive arena, just as Padres management was unhappy with the scope of my inquiry, so also did the agent for Luis Polonia, in his salary dispute with the California Angels, recoil upon my reliance on the number of instances in which Luis had been caught stealing when they had relied upon stolen bases. Nothing takes a team out of an inning more quickly than being caught stealing. (More about this later.)

Much of the new statistical data stem from Bill James and others who have followed in his wake. *Moneyball*, the purported examination of Billy Beane and the Oakland A's, and the evaluation of their methodology in choosing players, popularized this. The public was

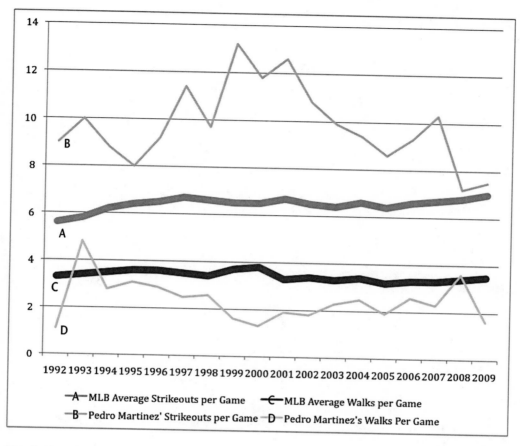

The Genius of Pedro Martinez (prepared by Mike Scanlon based on the data presented in the Baseball Reference website. See http://www.baseball-reference.com/).

left with the impression that on-base percentage was a new approach, though it was well known that the great hitters like Williams and Cobb had flourished because of their ability to get on a base through walks as much as their extraordinary hitting talent — and their on-base percentage had been referenced in numerous broadcasts and discussions. But the new frontier of baseball's statistics downplays RBIs (runs batted in) — because they are predicated upon having good players who can get on base and "set the table." These data emphasize a combination of slugging percentage (a division of total bases by at-bats) with on-base percentage to show a player's productive value. Both in terms of offense and defense, the statistical plot has thickened as the years have gone on.

The new frontier of statistics which pose a challenge for salary arbitration are the defensive statistics. These data purport to address both (1) the subjectivity inherent in the Rule 10.05 standard to define a base hit as a ball which could not be fielded with "ordinary effort"; and (2) difficulty in determining "range factor," the superficially boring way in which the Yankee Clipper, Joe DiMaggio, made long drives hit to Death Valley in deep left-center field in Yankee Stadium look easy. The difficulties in the range factor area are numerous and obvious — though it is determined by the number of balls fielded by a particular player, it does not take into account the fact that other factors can diminish those balls, e.g., Ted

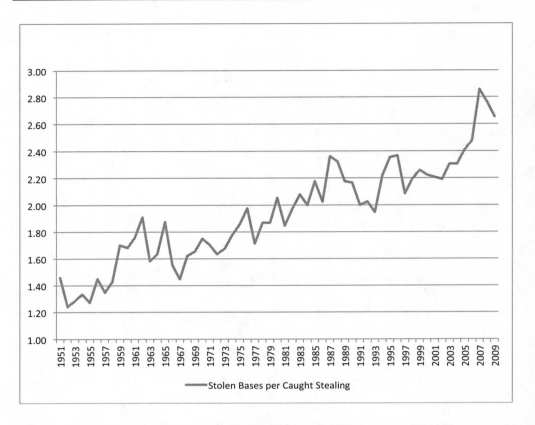

The success rate for base stealing (prepared by Mike Scanlon based on the data presented in the Baseball Reference website. See http://www.baseball-reference.com/).

Williams frequently allowed Dominic DiMaggio to drift far over into left center to take fly balls that otherwise might go to Williams — Dominic DiMaggio, like his brother Joe, was a particularly proficient centerfielder and thus able to range far out of center field. Should this be computed as a phenomenon attributable to Dominic's defensive ability or Williams's lack thereof? Moreover, the ballpark in which a player plays must be assessed for its unique characteristics as well as the pitching staff's tendency to strike hitters out, thus diminishing balls in play, and to induce ground balls which will inflate the infielders' balls in play, or fly balls which will do the same for outfielders.[129] Both the Seattle Mariners and the Boston Red Sox appear to have invested heavily in this approach, which owes its origins to the thinking of Bill James — but the jury is out on the result.[130]

In the salary arbitration system the arbitrator has always been precluded by the collective bargaining agreement from considering the financial circumstances of each team. This appeals to both sides: the union, because it pulled salaries upward to the more wealthy teams, thus bridging a large and potentially divisive chasm which would otherwise exist in its membership ranks; and the owners, because they did not want third parties of any kind to become involved in their finances. For, as the 1981 NLRB litigation over the owners' failure to disclose financial information demonstrated, the clubs did not want the arbitrators or the NLRB, for that matter, mucking around their books and financial records! So secretive are the owners that they do not want to even reveal the 1990s' negotiated revenue-sharing data: "[A]ccess to the teams' audited financial statements is usually limited to the commissioner's office [and] baseball's lead bankers."[131]

Nonetheless, the owners were concerned about salary arbitration because (1) they were frustrated by the tandem process through which arbitration and free agency ratcheted up salaries; (2) the "heads you win, tails I lose" nature of the process which rarely, if ever, produced decreases in salary as a result of the process; (3) their intuitive feeling that arbitrators, notwithstanding their inability to split the difference in a particular case, were splitting the difference in deciding groups of cases in the hope that they would remain acceptable to both sides. (As noted above, this was eventually addressed by creating arbitration panels of three so that arbitrators as individuals would not be identified with the result of a particular case.)

All of this created great pressure among the owners to eliminate the salary arbitration process, so they proposed in the 1990 negotiations that a pay-for-performance formula for players with two to five years' seniority be devised. But the players had an entirely different perspective, facing dissatisfaction from the likes of Roger Clemens, who not only wanted to preserve salary arbitration but also sought a return to the 1985 eligibility standard of two years.

Further, the owners now proposed a salary cap for the players which would constitute forty-eight percent of defined gross revenue. The players, of course, resisted this idea, and in contrast to football, basketball and ultimately hockey, have always resisted this entire concept as anathema. As we shall see, the salary cap became a critical issue in disputes to come.

The combination of these issues and the resolve of the owners led to a thirty-two-day spring training lockout imposed by management. The owners, demonstrating again a peculiar propensity to shoot themselves in the foot, did not profit from the lockout tactic and thus were not able to realize most of their proposals in the collective bargaining process. The reason is that most of the players who are reasonably established are not particularly excited about the idea of playing during spring training in any event, given the fact that they do not receive compensation until its near conclusion, and the fact that many of them train during the winter rather than driving trucks as Bill Bevens did in Salem, Oregon. Thus, a much greater number of them are in shape by virtue of off-season conditioning programs which did not exist in the '40s, '50s, and '60s, when low salary levels required them to take regular employment outside of baseball during the off-season late fall and winter months.

Accordingly, once again, this new agreement in '90 reflected player gains — this time because there was no real pressure on the Players Association to settle. No salary cap was contained in the contract and a compromise was arrived at on salary arbitration, which allowed seventeen percent of the players, those more than two years' but fewer than three years' service, to be eligible for salary arbitration. This moved the system back to something closer to what had existed in 1985, thus giving the union some gains. The irony here is that in a dispute which was triggered by the initiative of the owners through a lockout, the union wound up as winners again. The beat went on!

This new agreement, which lasted until December 31, 1993, also provided for an increase in the minimum salary from $68,000 to $100,000, an increase in the yearly pension fund contribution to $55 million and, most importantly, treble damages for any future owner collusion cases concerning the signing of free agents. Thus, notwithstanding the lockout tactic, the owners once again wound up with egg on their faces and another setback in the pursuit of their ambitions. But the owners were now more determined than ever in renewing their goals in the next round of negotiations. This set the stage for the mother of all disputes, the 1994-95 strike.

In a sense, of course, 1994-95 was to be more of the same. Either a strike or a lockout had occurred in 1972, '76, '81, '85, and '90. Negotiations in 1994 addressed the same or similar issues involved in the collective bargaining process over the past two decades: the problem of ever-escalating salaries for free agents — the increases fueled by the salary arbitration process operating in tandem with free agency — and the attempt by owners to impose a salary cap, or some variation on it, as a solution to this problem.

The position of the owners was that the increase in salaries provided by large-revenue clubs destroyed the competitive balance between those teams and others — though in fact in the late '70s, '80s, and early '90s it appeared that there was more parity between the teams than there had been in the pre–free agency era when, in the main, the New York Yankees were unquestionably preeminent. The Yankees' five straight World Championships from 1949 to 1953, and their continued dominance in the '50s through the mid–'60s, never again was to be repeated. The Yankees did not win a championship after the 1981 strike through the '94 negotiations, prevailing ultimately in 1996.

Nonetheless, the owners maintained that the public interest in baseball was undermined by the free agency system because so many fans and non-large revenue or small-market cities had no hope that their teams could compete effectively. This was a variation on the same theme that had been heard in the 1940s at the time of Mr. Murphy and the Baseball Guild: all the players would go to the few rich teams! The public, as it had in '49–'53 when the Yankees were supreme, would lose interest, and baseball would suffer through poor attendance and the inability to obtain advertisers so necessary to radio and television — or so ran the argument.

Thus, the parties moved inexorably towards the mother of all disputes, the strike which was to emerge in the summer of 1994.

CHAPTER 4

The 1994-95 Baseball Strike and the NLRB

In a series of strikes and lockouts commencing in 1972, baseball labor and management had engaged in what came to be regarded as a near thirty-year war![1] The relationship was hardly the average one. For, beginning with the 1972 pension strike and counting the 1994-95 strike which was to come, baseball players had struck or owners had locked them out twenty-five times as often as was the case in other industries! The game was truly strike and lockout happy!

In 1994, the National Labor Relations Board (NLRB) was at the center of what would become the mother of all Major League Baseball disputes. This did not constitute the first involvement of the Board, inasmuch as it had issued a complaint and unsuccessfully attempted to obtain an injunction against the owners in 1981. That petition had been rejected by a federal district court.[2] That time, the NLRB case went nowhere as the parties labored onward for more than eighty days until the owners' strike-insurance fund was exhausted. This time around the NLRB obtained the injunction, and in so doing, it brought the players back to the field and ultimately produced a collective bargaining agreement — the essential objective of the National Labor Relations Act, which the Board is charged to interpret.

This time around I was to be chairman of the NLRB, a five-member administrative agency which possesses quasi-judicial authority and responsibility. I had been nominated by President Bill Clinton on June 28, 1993, and after a nine-month delay I was confirmed by a Senate vote of 58–38 on March 2, 1994. In those nine months, my writings in support of the National Labor Relations Act were debated and attacked by many on the conservative side of politics. My confirmation obtained the greatest number of "no" votes of any Clinton nominee through that date, more than a year into the Clinton presidency. But the price of my confirmation was acceptance of a right-wing Republican conservative board member who was to be a thorn in my side during my NLRB tenure, and who was to cause me considerable problems in the resolution of the baseball dispute itself. Although they were still not in a majority — that was yet to come in the 1994 fall elections — Republicans in the Congress had considerable leverage. Senator Edward Kennedy wrote me the day after my confirmation, "It's a good thing the Republicans decided not to filibuster!"[3]

They had the votes to do it — to talk on endlessly in the absence of the sixty votes which are a prerequisite for cloture and thus shut off debate and have a vote! Previously utilized almost solely in connection with major issues, the filibuster had now come to be routinely used or threatened in connection with nominations — and the bluff of the filibusters is rarely or never called. Thus who threatened to filibuster in order to block a vote are not required to actually engage in the physically exhausting task of speaking continuously during a real live filibuster.

The 1990s were arguably the first instance in which the Board had been in the cockpit of public controversy, generated by the Republicans and some business elements. It had faced grueling and difficult hearings conducted by Congress in the late 1930s and the early '50s.[4] The Board had been created by the National Labor Relations Act of 1935 and is one of the small so-called alphabet administrative expert quasi-judicial administrative agencies which came out of the FDR New Deal of the Great Depression. The reason for these agencies — and the NLRB, as it is called, illustrates the point precisely — was that the courts of general jurisdiction had proved incapable and inexpert in resolving labor management controversies and other matters. It was therefore thought that specialized administrative tribunals could do a more effective job. The idea contained in the creation of these agencies was that they were to act independently, without instruction from the executive and legislative branches, and remain committed to the rule of law. On the law itself, the Board can be reversed by the Supreme Court alone — or by Congress if it enacts new legislation. (Intermediate courts may nonetheless refuse to enforce some of the NLRB's decisions.)

The Act protects the rights of employees to protest working conditions that they deem to be unfair, to organize into unions, and to select representatives of their own choosing normally through a secret ballot-box election. The statute obliges both management and labor to bargain in good faith when the union represents a majority of employees. The policy assumption is that an unregulated labor market produces an unacceptable degree of inequality between capital and labor.

Amendments to the law, enacted in 1947 and 1959, protect employees in their right to refrain from union activity, and thus put the Board in the position of not only promoting freedom of association for employees as well as the collective bargaining process, but also acting as a kind of impartial referee between labor and management. I was proud that the Board remained faithful to this objective during most of my tenure in Washington, within the limitations of the law that have produced proposals for reform.[5]

Traditionally the Board, which operates in Washington, D.C., but has thirty-six regional offices throughout the country, consists of three members of the president's own party and two members of the opposition. All such individuals, as well as an independent General Counsel who acts as a prosecutor, are appointed by the president and confirmed with the advice and consent of the United States Senate. Cases which come before the Board are triggered by charges alleging so-called "unfair labor practices" on the part of either unions or employers and petitions for representation. Most of these controversies arise in connection with the attempt by unions to organize and recruit employees in the workplace, but some can occur within established relationships — as they did with the dispute between the players and the owners.

The basic structure of the National Labor Relations Act, notwithstanding some important amendments, has remained intact now for more than seventy-five years — considerably longer than any comparable legal or regulatory framework relating to labor-management practices in other industrialized countries like Great Britain, Germany, France, Italy or Japan. But over the past thirty years or so there have been many important changes in the ways in which the NLRB is able to function — principally due to the exploitation of "loopholes" in the law by some employers. The unions have declined in membership for numerous reasons, a subordinate one consisting of the ineffectiveness of the legal framework. And except for my chairmanship in the 1990s, the caseload has diminished — during the presidencies of Ronald Reagan and George W. Bush in particular. In the latter period, in the early part of this century, the caseload had diminished to an almost minuscule level.[6] This is because the unions lost confidence in the Board during these periods, and because the Act, while it remains supportive of the collective bargaining process as written, has nonetheless been administered by NLRB members who frequently do not subscribe to its principles.

All of this is bound up with a second factor. This is the increased partisan divide which has emerged during the same period of time. True, in both the late 1930s and in the first two years of the Eisenhower administration in the 1950s, Congress scrutinized the Board with a good measure of hostility. But all of this was to reach new heights during the Clinton presidency in the '90s, particularly after the Republicans seized control of the Congress in 1995 and the party's moderate wing became virtually non-existent. Even in the 1980s,[7] before the Gingrich revolution and its Contract with America (we have always called it a contract *on* America), the appointments to the Board had fueled considerable controversy. This developed in advance of and ultimately in the shadow of the highly confrontational and contentious battles that arose out of the nominations of both Robert Bork and Clarence Thomas to the Supreme Court. Future nominees of both President Clinton and President Obama who had difficulty with the Senate — and there were many of them — sometimes were said to be "Borked" in the wake of the Senate's refusal to confirm him to the Court.

There have been a number of distinguished appointments to the National Labor Relations Board. President Franklin D. Roosevelt's first chairman was James Warren Madden, a University of Pittsburgh law professor; the second was Harry Millis, who was a labor economics professor at the University of Chicago as well as an arbitrator. Madden was appointed as the result of a friendship that he had with Lloyd Garrison, a friend of President Roosevelt — a friendship which emerged from his teaching during the summer of 1933 at Stanford Law School. Some career NLRB civil servants have been appointed as well — one of them being Gerald Brown, appointed by President Kennedy in 1961, with whom I had contact when I was a junior lawyer at the NLRB in the early '60s. Frank W. McCulloch, my boss when he was President Kennedy's appointee as chairman in the '60s, was another example of a distinguished figure in the tradition of Madden and Millis.

But by the time that the 1990s unfolded, coinciding with President Clinton's nomination of me straight from my professorship at Stanford Law School, a more divisive pattern had begun to emerge from partisan gridlock between not only Democrats and Republicans, but also labor and management. The appointments began to take on a different flavor and bargaining with packages or "batching" of groups of nominees emerged — so much so that this new development, which has only come into existence during the past fifteen years, is now referred to by some as a tradition. Under this "tradition" one nominee could not be voted upon by the Senate on his own merits, as President Clinton attempted to do with my nomination.

And there is more to the story. Colby College political science Professor G. Calvin Mackenzie has addressed this in his writings — and he is right on target. Said Professor Mackenzie:

> What is most distressing ultimately is the transcendent loss of purpose in the appointment process. The American model did not always work perfectly, but it was informed by a grand notion. The business of the people would be managed by leaders drawn from the people, Cincinnatus, in-and-outers, noncareer managers — with every election would come a new sweep of the country for high energy and new ideas and fresh visions. The president's team

would assume its place and impose the people's wishes on the great agencies of government. Not infrequently, it actually worked that way.

But these days, the model fails on nearly all counts. Most appointees do not come from the countryside, brimming with new energy and ideas. Much more often they come from congressional staffs or think tanks or interest groups — not from across the country but from across the street: interchangeable public elites, engaged in an insider's game.[8]

This phenomenon, attributable to polarization between Democrats and Republicans as well as labor and management (the latter enhanced by organized labor's precipitous decline in membership), made the Board a difficult and contentious agency, divided deeply on ideological grounds. This phenomenon affected many cases and the baseball strike constituted one of the most prominent illustrations: a dispute involving a union, the Major League Players Association, now as or more powerful than the previous "barons" of labor had become in the 1950s and '60s — the pattern makers and pacesetters like the United Auto Workers, the United Steelworkers, the International Brotherhood of Teamsters and the construction unions which were formidable adversaries in their time for the employers with whom they bargained.

Now, in the summer of 1993, subsequent to President Clinton's election, once nominated, I faced relentless interrogation by the Republicans in Congress and some of the press. Often, it was to be a lonely fight. At that point, I had no knowledge about Professor Mackenzie's writing nor a real sense of how the composition of the Board which emerged from congressional stalemate would play out in future labor disputes as well as baseball itself.

Meanwhile, Senator Nancy Kassebaum, the ranking Republican minority leader on the Senate Labor and Public Welfare Committee, had interviewed all potential Republican nominees by asking them this question: "If Chairman Gould is in the majority in a policy case of consequence, will you dissent from his position?" A number of individuals could not give that guarantee because, quite obviously, they could not foresee the cases that would come before us and what our respective positions would be in advance of their resolution. Those who regarded this kind of pledge as inconsistent with the independence that is inherent in the NLRB's quasi-judicial process did not make the cut. Only those aspirants who answered the question affirmatively could be supported by the Republicans, most of whose representatives in Congress would not have voted for the National Labor Relations Act and its promotion of collective bargaining itself! This was then the environment for the baseball dispute which was to emerge during my tenure as NLRB Chairman, and it helps explain the sharp and vigorous dissents rendered against our majority opinion in that case (as well as numerous other policy cases). These dissents were frequently cited by both the Republicans in the Congress and, in this case, the baseball owners, as evidence for the proposition that the NLRB was not impartial or had not properly interpreted the statute in the baseball dispute.

Again, the Board was immediately involved in a number of policy issues, and baseball was only one of them, albeit the most visible dispute that we handled while I was in Washington! Before departing from Stanford for the nation's capitol, I had told the late Leonard Koppett, my good friend and co-teacher at Stanford Law School, that my deepest regret in taking the NLRB job was giving up my baseball salary arbitrations. In '92-'93 I had arbitrated a series of cases (some of them noted in the previous chapter) involving then California Angels outfielder Luis Polonia, as well as Oakland A's utility infielder Jerry Browne (often referred to as the Governor), Dale Sveum, utility infielder of the Philadelphia Phillies, and the San Diego Padres' ace starter Andy Benes.

My answering machine told me that my hearing involving Atlanta Braves pitcher John Smoltz was canceled as my plane came to a halt on the runway at Chicago's O'Hare Airport just as the parties reached a settlement. Benes was the only one of the above-mentioned foursome whose position I favored. But this award had radiations beyond Benes and the Padres, and appeared to affect the Smoltz settlement as well as that of Kevin Tapani of the Minnesota Twins. Some of the owners pilloried the Benes award. For instance, the Los Angeles Dodgers maintained that they had to enter into a similar settlement with their then ace Ramon Martinez because he had a better "won and lost" record than Benes, ignoring my view expressed at the Benes hearing that "won and lost" records are frequently deceptive as a measure of a pitcher's worth because of the poor hitting, fielding, and bullpen which may surround the pitcher. (Benes had not pitched for many winning Padres teams at that time and, in my opinion, was a classic illustration of this point.)

But I had enjoyed these cases and thus expressed to Koppett my deepest regret that I would be giving them up for the NLRB. But, replied Leonard, "You'll be more involved now than you ever were in the past. A big conflict is coming between the parties, and the National Labor Relations Board will be right in the middle of it. You'll see." Truer words were never spoken.

I was confirmed by the Senate as baseball negotiations for a new collective bargaining agreement were proceeding. As late as June of 1994 there was little talk of a strike, although Murray Chass of the *New York Times* reported that a strike threat for August was materializing. Chass noted, "In ownership circles there is talk of gloom and doom but not because of the threat of a strike. The atmosphere is bleak because owners of a sizable number of teams believe they face financial doom if they don't get the salary cap they covet."[9]

As in '81, '85, and '90, when labor disputes followed the 1976 agreement which had provided abiding standards for free agency in the wake of Peter Seitz's 1975 award, the owners expressed a firm intention to change the status quo by altering the mechanisms that allowed players to obtain substantial salary increases. It seemed clear that the owners' advocacy of a salary cap would be the major issue in the 1994 negotiations. Some of the owners believed that the players would not strike because they would not want to relinquish their very large salaries. (This view had been manifested earlier at the time of the '72 strike and again in '81 and thereafter!) Directly related to this was the view, held by many, that if there was a strike and the strikers saw replacement players taking the field, the picket lines would quickly dissolve and the players would return on the owners' terms. In the previous negotiations, the lawful replacement tactic — the United States Supreme Court had said in 1938 that strikers may be permanently replaced[10] (apparently, the owners were only thinking of temporary replacements, which are also lawful[11]) — had not been utilized. This time, reasoned the owners, it would be different. This time around they were unified!

Thus, in the earlier disputes the owners had conceded that the strike brought baseball to an end and that the game could not continue until the issues were resolved — a position which provided vivid contrast to that prevailing in football, where the owners successfully attempted to replace strikers in the 1980s. The previous baseball position up until 1994 was similar to that which has prevailed in the automobile industry, that a strike meant that the enterprise would not operate. This was not to be the case in 1994 and 1995. Again, the owners' view was that the players would not be able to resist the temptation to return once they saw replacements playing in their positions. (This view of the situation in '94-'95 — that is, that the strike would crumble when the players saw their positions filled by replacements — appears to be held by a substantial number of owners to this very day!)

A peculiar element in the owners' position, however, was that they did not intend to use their very best minor league players as replacements — those at the Triple A level — but rather would plan to bring in those below them. This was predicated upon the view that eventually the players would return and find it difficult to play with the replacements. Thus, the owners did not want to bring in those players as replacements who would likely play with the incumbent team members at some future date because of concern that this would disrupt team harmony and effort. Moreover, there could be no pretense in providing some kind of substitute for the real thing. Clearly only in theory would the players be on the field.

The sultry and humid summer of 1994 in Washington, D.C., moved on, and telephone calls that I received in my NLRB office from Secretary of Labor Robert Reich and others in the Department of Labor reflected their concern that a strike might be imminent. I was queried about both the practice of collective bargaining in baseball and the state of the law under the National Labor Relations Act as written. The Clinton Administration wanted to do something, but it did not know what to do — and the NLRB, in the absence of a charge by one side or the other that the statute was being violated, could not become directly involved. The agency is not charged with the power and responsibilities of a mediator or arbitrator.

The players set an August strike deadline and desultory negotiations moved forward intermittently, but they languished right up until the eve of the deadline. The dynamics between the parties and the *American Ship Building v. NLRB*[12] holding (in which the Supreme Court held that, when motivated by an attempt to time the stoppage at a point which will give the employer a bargaining advantage, lockouts are lawful under the NLRA) made the players feel that if they did not strike well in advance of the season's end, the owners would unilaterally institute their own position on free agency during the winter months and open the camps the following spring without them, relying, if necessary, on the temporary replacements. This tactic is also lawful and was very much a part of the 2004-05 hockey lockout dynamics.[13]

The players felt that threatening a stoppage near or during the postseason playoffs, which brings owners most of their revenues, would give the union the maximum amount of leverage. (This is why employers are able to use the lockout to their bargaining advantage under *American Ship Building* by producing a stoppage at a time when employee earnings will diminish, meaning there is no employer incentive to settle.) For this reason, they viewed as misguided the proposal that Secretary Reich made at Fenway Park in Boston during a game; he wanted the parties to continue talking without resorting to warfare. On August 12, while I was en route to speaking engagements in Vancouver, British Colombia, and Seattle and Spokane, Washington, the players struck.

In fact, at least in the short run, this aspect of the players' strategy misfired. The owners did not back away from their positions, and the remainder of the 1994 season and the World Series were canceled — a result that the players did not seem to anticipate. This was the first time that the World Series had been canceled since the obduracy of John Brush of the Giants in 1904, and it seemed unimaginable and unthinkable. But nonetheless, it was the reality! The Federal Mediation and Conciliation Service — the principal mediation office in the United States Government and entirely separate from the National Labor Relations Board — viewed it as a victory when, in early September, they were able to get the players and the owners to simply go through the motions of having a meeting together. The Service was able to get the parties to return to the bargaining table, the talks having been in recess since late August. But that was about all that they were able to do. They were not able to get the parties to discuss the issues, let alone agree on anything.

The season's end without resolution of the dispute and no World Series was ominous for the Union because unions almost always lose long strikes: members can never recoup what would have been obtained had the employees continued to work during the dispute. Nonetheless, Professor Roger Noll at Stanford wrote: "The owners' efforts to limit the growth in player salaries would have cost the players $1.5 billion over the life of the proposed agreement. The strike only cost the players $300 million. Given these numbers, it is easy to see why the players didn't come out and play."[14] But the difficulty with a long strike such as that which the players faced throughout '94 and into the spring of '95 is that many of the players in the bargaining unit did not continue to play after the strike — or played for a very short period — and thus were unable to enjoy the increased benefits. Though the principle that labor loses a long strike applies to disputes elsewhere, usually such employees will be able to work and obtain benefits through their 60s when they retire. Even under such circumstances, the ability to recoup lost income can be problematic. But in baseball the abbreviated nature of the players' careers makes it less likely that many of the players involved in the dispute would enjoy the benefits of which Noll wrote.

In any event, after the season's collapse, negotiations continued but with little impetus until December, when the owners sought to change the negotiating environment. Under American labor law, when labor and management have bargained to the point of impasse or deadlock, employers may unilaterally institute either the last offer or a package which is substantially equivalent to it when they have bargained in good faith on so-called "mandatory subjects" relating directly to wages, hours, and conditions of employment.

On December 20, Jerry McMorris, owner of the Colorado Rockies, had an evening meeting with Don Fehr, the executive director of the Players Association, and advised him that the owners needed a "significant drag" on players' salaries — considerably more than what the union was offering. McMorris told the mediator that he did see any way to reach agreement. Fehr stated that he did not agree with McMorris's assessment.

Two days later, on December 22, the owners unilaterally implemented their salary cap proposals and eliminated salary arbitration for certain players. However, the owners' argument that there was deadlock or impasse was somewhat undermined by the fact that a series of union and owners' proposals had been passed back and forth on both salary arbitration and free agency during the previous week. Subsequently, the owners were to take the position that, though clearly they had not bargained to impasse on salary arbitration, this was irrelevant because salary arbitration was not a mandatory subject affecting conditions of employment within the meaning of the National Labor Relations Act on which they were obliged to bargain to impasse. (Grievance arbitration involving the interpretation of terms of the collective bargaining agreement is a mandatory subject of bargaining,[15] while interest arbitration, relating to new terms of the collective agreement, is not.[16] The owners apparently viewed salary arbitration as more akin to the latter.).

On that fateful day of December 22, the union, for the first time, presented a revised proposal that included a marginal tax plan that would address profligate owners through taxation rather than a cap. The negotiations resumed. Five hours later, however, the owners rejected the players' proposal, noting that, while the new position represented a major philosophical shift for the union, a more stringent tax was needed to alter salary patterns. When the players asked for a counterproposal, the owners replied that they saw no reason to believe that a counterproposal, within the same framework, would significantly lower the salary brackets or that increasing the tax rates would help. They announced that, in their view, the negotiations had reached an impasse. Accordingly, the owners then unilaterally instituted or put into effect their position on both free agency and salary arbitration.

The Major League Players Association filed unfair labor practices with our regional office of the NLRB in New York City, alleging that the unilateral declaration of an impasse and change in employment conditions by the owners was a refusal to bargain in good faith and that impasse or deadlock had not in fact been reached. Subsequently, the owners stated in proceedings before the New York City office that they had changed the method of free agent negotiation so that it would proceed on a centralized basis rather than club by club. But again, the issue was whether the system of free agent compensation could be altered under these circumstances. If the clubs had been successful in centralizing the negotiations as they intended to do subsequent to their unilateral change in working conditions, the response of the union might have been to dissolve what the Supreme Court came to characterize in *Brown v. Pro Football, Inc.*[17] as multi-employer association bargaining. Though a union effort to organize the players in 1946 was aimed at a club, the Pittsburgh Pirates, it is difficult to imagine bargaining between the union and individual clubs given the mutual dependency of all of them in a league situation, scheduling problems, etc. But since the union could always assert its role to bargain on all matters as the exclusive bargaining representative under *J.I. Case Co. v. NLRB*,[18] it could withdraw its delegation to individual players and ultimately withdraw from multi-employer bargaining—though not in the midst of collective bargaining itself.[19] In any event, as we shall see below, none of this nor the legal issues associated with it came to pass.

Thus, the issue that was to come before the Board was whether proper procedures had been followed. The popular perception, that the NLRB had substantively sided with the players, was different. As a Stanford baseball aide said to me at an exhibition game at Sunken Diamond in late 2007 as we were discussing the Stanford slugger Joe Borchard's $5 million-plus bonus when he signed with the Chicago White Sox, "He has you to thank!" I was taken aback—and after reflecting for a moment I then replied to her, "Oh, because of the NLRB injunction?" She nodded affirmatively.

Of course, in a vague and generalized way, one could say that this was the result of our injunction—that the parties were able to bargain a series of collective bargaining agreements which expanded free agency and may be said to have created prosperity for draftees as well. But we were never to be involved in the rights or wrongs or efficacy of the players' and owners' substantive positions—under the American system of collective bargaining and labor law, that is for the parties themselves and not for any government agency. Again, the question was whether the parties had followed the proper procedures.

Another issue, which troubled many outside observers, was the law relating to bargaining itself. I was interviewed by radio stations which wondered why, if the owners were prohibited from unilaterally changing terms and conditions of employment without bargaining to impasse, there was not a similar obligation to be imposed upon the players before striking. Of course, we followed the law as Congress had written it, and this is what it provided. Moreover, these commentators failed to note that the owners had many weapons at their disposal, including the right to lock out,[20] to replace strikers[21] and perhaps even the players who were locked out,[22] and to unilaterally change conditions subsequent to impasse.[23] Essentially, the strike is all that labor possesses and one of its major limitations lies in the fact that strikers may be replaced. In any event, the Board had to follow the law as it was written and interpret it as best we could on the basis of the facts of the baseball dispute.

Now, in the wake of December 22, two fronts of negotiations began to open. One was the litigation before the Board, which was investigated by our regional offices acting by the authority of the General Counsel under a bifurcated arrangement which exists in the agency. The General Counsel, like Board membership, is also a presidential appointee, and is the prosecuting and investigative independent arm of the Board. Though some of the newspapers tended to confuse this — and the then incumbent General Counsel sought to confuse it as well — his office does not speak for the Board, which retains final authority over all issues. The General Counsel makes argument and recommendations to the Board members. The matter could not go to the courts without the Board's approval in one way or another. Again, the Board had the final say — a say that was not to be provided until a number of months down the road in the spring of 1995!

The second front became Congress and President Clinton's attempts to resolve the matter. The previous August 2, while at the White House for a social function involving California Democrats, I chatted with President Clinton in a receiving line. I remarked that Secretary of Labor Bob Reich and I had been discussing the baseball negotiations. The President expressed dismay at the prospect of a strike and said, "This is the best year in a long time," referring to the home run records that might be set by such sluggers as Ken Griffey, Mark McGwire, Matt Williams and others. He remarked that it was hard to have sympathy for either side, given their wealth and "greed." As we parted he said to me, "If you guys could resolve this, they would elect me president for life!" (Subsequently, when we did intervene effectively, some of the regional directors advised me that Secretary Reich had said that President Clinton was "jealous" of us in that he wished that he had settled the matter himself!)

Now as the new year of '95 unfolded, some members of Congress began to focus on the question of whether the antitrust exemption provided by the Supreme Court's holding in *Federal Baseball Club of Baltimore v. National League of Professional Baseball Clubs*[24] should be eliminated or revised, thus arguably allowing players to sue the owners in federal district court for any restrictions placed upon free agency. The White House flirted with the possibility of compulsory arbitration or some other third-party mechanism to resolve the labor dispute, but the new Republican-controlled Congress was against it.

In January, the White House appointed special mediator W.J. Usery, the former Secretary of Labor in the Ford administration. As he saw it, part of his job was to recommend terms for an agreement. President Clinton announced that the administration was "turning up the heat" on the parties and was setting a February 6 deadline for them to resolve matters themselves before government intervention. Stating "I want this thing settled," President Clinton summoned the players and owners to the White House a few days later.

Soon thereafter, it appeared as though mediator Usery might provide recommendations that would take the form of legislation. But the newly arrived Republican majority in Congress — this was the first few months of the heady "Gingrich revolution" — pulled the rug from under the White House and refused to support legislation through which Usery's recommendations could be implemented.

Now the White House, faced with Republican reticence, went into retreat. Thus, both negotiations and government intervention in the form of legislation seemed to dissipate. Prospects for settlement were becoming far less promising. Meanwhile, the Players Association had begun to display dissatisfaction with mediator Usery. This feeling arose out of distrust when Usery had expressed displeasure with their position while at the White House. The Players Association thought that Usery was siding with the owners.

As spring training was about to commence, the owners were ready to do the unthinkable — to use replacement players — and Congress was signaling that it would not intervene in any way, shape, or form. Into this vacuum stepped the NLRB.

The players were attempting to obtain support from the Board for an injunction against the unilateral changes made on December 22. This was the very legal tactic that had failed in the 1981 strike, albeit in a different context which this time around did not present any issue relating to an employer obligation to open their books or to disclose financial information, as was the case in that dispute. This question of whether the Board could go to federal district court, under a special procedure placed in the law in 1947, to obtain an injunction against the changes in free agency and salary arbitration, became the key issue before us in March.[25]

I had a number of speaking engagements in the West and was in Los Angeles on March 17, 1995, when the matter was submitted to the Board. By the time I returned on March 22, two of the Board members, both Democrats, had voted for an injunction and two of the others, both Republicans, had voted against it. I was the man in the middle — a position not dissimilar to the one which I occupied on a number of policy issues during my tenure where the two Democrats and two Republicans were almost invariably aligned with labor and management respectively.

I had not expressed a view on the question of whether the facts and law authorized us to say that there was reasonable cause to believe that the owners had not bargained in good faith and whether it was necessary to proceed into federal district court without delay. These considerations were acknowledged to be the applicable statutory prerequisites for an injunction of this kind. (My Board, particularly during my first two years — but also throughout my entire four-and-a-half-year tenure as chairman — had issued the greatest number of these injunctions in the history of the NLRB! From March of 1994 to March of 1998, the Board authorized 292 injunctions, an average of 73 per year.[26] From March 1998 to January 2001, the Board only authorized an average of 58 per year.[27] This was a matter that quickly caught the attention of a hostile Republican Congress, which frequently tried to come to the rescue of the defendant employers.)

When I returned to my Washington office early in the evening of March 22, my chief counsel, Bill Stewart (later to receive the most prestigious award that a career employee can have from the White House[28]), had left a note for me that Usery had left a message that he would like the Board to delay its decision in the baseball case and he would like me to call him. I did so between 8:00 and 8:30 that night.[29]

Usery told me that he had had two "constructive days" with the parties on a "confidential and fairly quiet" basis. He said that he was trying to establish a meeting between then Acting Commissioner Bud Selig and Players Association Executive Director Donald Fehr for the following Saturday and Sunday, and that these meetings might possibly run into Monday. Usery expressed concern to me that if we issued an authorization for an injunction in federal district court we would run the risk of impeding negotiations and inflaming the relationship between the parties. Usery also said that he had spoken with fourteen owners and that there was a group that would meet with the Union to discuss a framework or approach that he was recommending. He also told me that Gene Orza, then general counsel of the Players Association, had asked him not to interfere with the unfair labor practice aspects of the case — though that is exactly what he was doing through the phone call.

I then called President Clinton's counsel, Ab Mikva, previously on the Circuit Court of Appeals for the District of Columbia. Mikva, after checking with his sources, said that, while Usery is "technically still our mediator," nobody thought he could reach the players. "He has lost his influence," said Mikva. I then advised the Democrats on the Board of this conversation, but only told the Republicans about the Usery conversation and recommended to both that we address Usery's recommendation, though I was personally disquieted by Mikva's assessment of the negotiations. The Board followed my recommendations.

But Usery's communication to us was soon revealed in the press, and the Players Association was immediately critical of him. He turned around and told the Association that I had called him and that he had not called me. Welcome to the world of Washington *realpolitik*!

I called Usery back about this and he agreed that, of course, he had called me but did not deny his characterization of our conversation. Now the weekend was coming and *New York Times'* baseball columnist, Murray Chass, reported that no negotiations had been scheduled for the weekend, and that the future of the talks did not "appear promising."[30]

On Friday afternoon, March 24, I went to both the general counsel and the other Board members, recommending that we meet on Sunday or Monday morning and resolve this matter at that time so that the Board could proceed to court expeditiously. Ultimately, notwithstanding the protestations of some Board members, a meeting was set for Sunday afternoon on March 26, and after a very sleepless night, I walked from my condominium on Pennsylvania Avenue to the Board's offices on L and 14th. As I arrived at the office, television cameras were staked out in front of our building, and they remained there as we deliberated on this matter. Indeed, so visible was the Board at that time that television anchor David Brinkley commented on how unusual it was for government employees to work on the weekend (I had actually worked not only a large number of weekends but also the day of President Nixon's funeral earlier in the year, when all the air conditioning was cut off!). A nationally published cartoon had one character asking the other to refresh his recollection about baseball abbreviations (e.g., RBI) and the abbreviations included NLRB as well![31]

That day the Board voted on the question of whether we should seek an injunction in the baseball dispute, and I cast the deciding vote to authorize an injunction, 3–2. I decided, as a matter of law, that the injunction was appropriate. But this did not happen until countless and difficult controversies about contacts with journalists and the question of whether the vote should be revealed. Most of the Board members did not want to reveal anything or have any contact with journalists — but I said that, in my capacity as chairman, I would not be muzzled. When I said this, one of the dissenting Republicans said that he would reveal his opinion. When criticized (improperly in my view) for doing this, he said that I was responsible because I was against secrecy!

One Board member, John Truesdale, a perennial favorite of many Washington insiders who always kept a wet finger in the air to determine which way the wind was blowing, said that if the vote was revealed this would be the "worst thing that could happen." These were the words of a career Washington bureaucrat which I found difficult to believe or accept because, in my view, the votes and opinions of Board members should always be made known to the public notwithstanding any traditional custom that Truesdale had relied upon to the contrary. After all, this was the public's business, and in my view, it should be revealed to the public! Indeed, after we made a decision to publicize our views, the President's counsel, Judge Mikva, commended us. For, as he said, it is always a good idea in "high visibility or important cases" for the Board to make its views and reasoning known.

Continuing, however, in the opposite vein, Truesdale excoriated me for speaking with the press about our activities on the injunction, and at times shouted in such a loud voice that he frightened the secretaries who were sitting in the anteroom near my office. (Subsequent to my departure as chairman in 1998, Truesdale became chairman as a result of support provided by a supporter of white supremacist organizations, Senator Trent Lott of Mississippi!)

There was yet another controversy relating to publicity. A television crew had asked us if they could bring television cameras into our agenda room and do some filming, preferably while Board members were present at the time of the weekend vote. A majority eventually rejected the request. But before the vote, Republican Board member Cohen told my chief counsel that he could not make up his mind on the camera question until he knew whether, if the television cameras didn't have access to our headquarters, they would come to the chairman's office. He said to my chief, "I can't vote on this issue until I know what the answer is."

My chief counsel, Bill Stewart, replied that he had no idea what the television people intended — and I didn't either. He gained the very distinct impression that Cohen's overriding concern was ensuring that no attention be given to the Chairman's role in the dispute. If anyone was to receive attention, he appeared to reason, it should be either him or the Board as a whole. This almost puerile obsession and resentment of the press's focus on me as chairman manifested itself again and again!

After the Board authorized the injunction over the strong dissent of the two Republican members, our staff lawyers, as well as those of the Players Association, went before then Judge Sonia Sotomayor of the federal district court in New York City to request the injunction. Her opinion and order exceeded our expectations. Since, as she found in agreement with a majority of our Board, impasse had not been reached in the bargaining process and therefore the unilateral changes in work rules on free agency itself and salary arbitration were unlawful, the parties were required to return to her court prior to the implementation of any new set of working conditions. This was an additional bonus which made our victory complete in that it gave us considerable leverage should the owners attempt to make a new change in working conditions at some point down the road. The Board had been able to demonstrate to the public that the labor law of the nation, however hobbled and deficient, could operate effectively and expeditiously.

Appointed to the Supreme Court by President Obama, Justice Sonia Sotomayor granted the NRLB petition for an injunction in 1995 when the author, as chairman of the agency, cast the deciding vote to request it (courtesy Collection of the Supreme Court of the United States).

Back on the playing field itself, the owners, having already used temporary replacements in spring training, had planned to use them in the regular season itself. As Baltimore Orioles owner Peter Angelos stated, this would have deprived the team's shortstop Cal Ripken of his chance to break

DRABBLE/KEVIN FAGAN

During the NRLB's intervention in the 1994-95 strike, the NRLB itself became a well-known acronym in baseball (Drabble © Kevin Fagan/Dist. By United Feature Syndicate, Inc.).

Lou Gehrig's consecutive-game record. (Angelos became a great friend and ally of the NLRB during my Washington years.) Luckily because of the Board's decision to seek injunctive relief and Judge Sotomayor's grant of it, this did not happen. Later in the season, months after our successful injunction in New York, Ripken would break the record, and I was able to sit in Angelos' special box along with President Clinton, Vice-President Gore, and other dignitaries to celebrate this great event!

Meanwhile, in April, not long after Opening Day, I had traveled to Hofstra Law School in New York to speak at a conference celebrating the 100th anniversary of Babe Ruth's birth. New York City labor arbitrator Dean Eric Schmertz introduced me as the head of the agency that had brought about the resumption of baseball. Earlier in the evening I had met Phil Rizzuto, the Yankees' shortstop when I was growing up in New Jersey. When he heard Schmertz's introduction he exclaimed to me excitedly, "You didn't tell me that! You didn't tell me that!" That spring, the injunction which restored baseball received a good deal of attention, most of it laudatory.

But, meanwhile, the owners snarled angrily. They remained bitter with the injunction long after it was issued, because they thought that if they had been able to use replacements they would have been able to break the play-

Shortstop-third baseman, Cal Ripken of the Baltimore Orioles, pictured with the author in 1995. That year, Ripken's consecutive game record surpassed Lou Gehrig. This record was placed in jeopardy by the '94-'95 strike and the owners' plan to open the '95 season with replacement players (courtesy Baltimore Orioles and Maroon PR on behalf of Cal Ripken).

ers' resolve and dissipate their solidarity. Yet their forecast about player resolve was an old one and had proved erroneous in every single dispute from 1972 onward. This did not stop them from stating to me and others on a number of occasions after the strike was concluded and a collective bargaining agreement had been negotiated, that if we had not intervened, they could have imposed their terms on the players because the picket line would have disappeared once a large number of temporary replacements were going onto the field.

Indeed, the owners were so angry with me that, two years later, at the 50th anniversary of Jackie Robinson's rookie Brooklyn Dodger season, when they held a party at the New York Mets' Shea Stadium where I and an entourage of Clinton appointees arrived with the President, they sent word to a good friend that I was not invited! (Nonetheless, I was able to enjoy myself at this important function and to meet Robinson's widow, Rachel Robinson.)

The author with the late Phil Rizzuto, outstanding Yankee shortstop in the 1940s, who provided a defensive spark which the Red Sox lacked. At Hofstra University, April 1995, the 100th anniversary of Babe Ruth's birthday (courtesy Eric Schmertz).

In any event, on April 2, 1995, in the wake of Judge Sotomayor's approval of our decision, the owners decided not to lock the players out, the players agreed to return to the field, and the parties agreed to start the season on April 26. As it turned out, the Board's position was not only correct on the law, but also, as the law contemplates, enhanced the collective bargaining process and provided for a resumption of the baseball season itself. In the following September, just as Sparky Anderson's Detroit Tigers pulled into town to play the Orioles (Anderson had also been out of favor because of *his* opposition to the replacement strategy), the Court of Appeals for the Second Circuit enforced the district court's order.[32] Meanwhile, in the wake of the injunction, the 1995 season ran its course and the Boston Red Sox finished first in the Eastern Division — a championship not recaptured again until 2007, when the Red Sox became world champions for the second time in four years!

The Strike and NLRB Aftermath

That summer of 1995 I was invited by Baltimore's Peter Angelos to throw out the ceremonial first pitch when the Red Sox came to Camden Yards in Baltimore — the first of 5 ceremonial pitches which I was to throw. (The most recent was on Jackie Robinson Day in Fenway Park in April 2006.) The *Baltimore Sun* commented that the owners "despised" me more than they did Angelos, who had incurred their wrath because of his opposition to the owners' temporary replacement plan.[33] But Nick Cafardo of the *Boston Globe* also had this to say:

A cloud of smoke from Boog Powell's tasty barbecue stand hovered over right field in front of the brick warehouse. Last Aug. 11, the last time these two teams played here, the smoke was black and ominous, signaling the end of baseball because of a work stoppage. Last night it was like a breath of fresh air ... baseball was alive and well, at least here, where these two teams ended their seasons prematurely last year. There was a touch of irony to Bill Gould, chairman of the National Labor Relations Board whose decisions against the owners got the game back on the field, throwing out the first pitch. [Pitcher Roger] Clemens did the most effective throwing after that.[34]

Later in the year, I was able to avail myself of the peaceful relations created by our order and to get back to Fenway Park to see the Red Sox once again and one of Tim Wakefield's many 1995 gems that he twirled in his best season ever. Luis Alicea turned the most acrobatically beautiful double play that one can imagine, as the Red Sox marched toward an Eastern Division championship only to be knocked off by the World Series–bound (soon to be American League Champions) Cleveland Indians. Old friend, catcher Tony Peñas, hit a home run in Cleveland in the second game of the playoffs that truly sank our ship. I took it all in during the wee hours of the morning, watching my TV in my Washington condominium. But, forever hopeful, I nonetheless jumped on a plane to see the anticlimactic third game at Fenway in which Wakefield was beaten and the Sox were eliminated.

During the following year, we were able to see more directly the policy-relevant fruits of the NLRB's work. In late 1996, after the completion of the next season, the parties negotiated a comprehensive collective bargaining agreement that resolved many of their outstanding differences. But, important though it was, it was not simply the NLRB's restoration of the collective bargaining process that had produced the agreement. One of the owners who was an outspoken "hawk" arguing for player salary restraint, Jerry Reinsdorf of the Chicago White Sox, gave former Cleveland Indian slugger Albert Belle a record $55 million contract. He argued for a salary cap and decried the proposed collective bargaining agreement as inadequate![35] Reinsdorf's adherence to this double standard convinced a number of owners previously opposed to the agreement to switch their vote and to ratify it, notwithstanding the absence of a salary cap.

Almost a year to the date of the agreement in November, the Boston Red Sox obtained Pedro Martinez from the Montreal Expos for two promising pitchers. Martinez was to become one of the winningest pitchers for the Red Sox during the seven years of his contract, which brought him the then unprecedented amount of $92 million. I was to see him in the opening series with the Mariners in the spring of 1998 — the same one in which "Mo" Vaughn smashed a bases-loaded homer to right in the bottom of the ninth to defeat the M's on the Good Friday Fenway Opening Day itself. Pedro Perfecto, as I liked to call him, had a winning percentage higher than any Red Sox pitcher, with at least 100 decisions in the seven seasons with the Red Sox —.760 for a 117–37 won and lost record. When he was to bid the Red Sox farewell in late '04, bound for a $52 million, four-year contract with the New York Mets, it constituted perhaps the most traumatic of the free agent divorces that the Red Sox had had — including "Mo" Vaughn's departure to the California Angels, that of fireballing Roger Clemens to Toronto in '96, and the loss of "El Maestro" Luis Tiant in 1980 to the hated Yankees.

But it was in 1997 that the '96 agreement was to establish the framework for the Bosox acquisition of Pedro and the new free agent environment and to dim the unpleasant memories of the losses of Tiant and Clemens, and to assuage hurt from the one to come in 2000,

"Mo" Vaughn. And it was NLRB intervention that launched baseball on the road to uninterrupted peace between labor and management and unprecedented prosperity, along with ever-escalating salaries for the players and revenues for the owners!

The '94-'95 strike and the large number of players left without contracts in a kind of no-man's land in the spring of '95 seemed to produce unprecedented player mobility. Until the mid-'90s, however, there was no more player movement than there had been prior to the days of free agency. Prior to the advent of free agency in 1975, Dick O'Connell, the former Red Sox general manager, had said that a blockbuster trade would push World War III off the headlines in Boston! He made this comment around the time that the Red Sox sent Jim Lonborg and slugging first baseman George Scott to the Milwaukee Brewers for Marty Pattin, Lew Krause and Tommy Harper. Rudy York had been traded straight up for Jake Jones in the spring of '47 while the Red Sox and White Sox were playing one another and the players simply switched uniforms in the midst of the series.

In one of the most regretted deals, ace reliever "Sparky" Lyle had been dealt to the New York Yankees for first baseman Danny Cater — the Yankees also benefiting from an earlier deal through which they acquired starting pitcher Allie Reynolds for second baseman Joe Gordon, sent on to the Cleveland Indians. And nothing was more spectacular than the straight-up trade of Rocky Colavito, with his unorthodox batting stance, bat-waving techniques and prodigious home runs, from Cleveland to Detroit for batting champion Harvey Kuenn.

Baseball had always witnessed player mobility, though, as stated, after '95 the instability caused by the strike seemed to take it up a notch. In 2007 Royce Clayton joined the Red Sox and wore No. 11 to signify that this was the eleventh club of which he had been a member, tying the all-time record previously set a few years earlier by Tod Zeille.

Finally, even with regard to the roster turnover for the top teams, the differences are compelling. For instance, with the A's winning between '72–'74, 17 players were on all three teams; '88–'90, 20 players were on all three. Even when the Yankees won between '98 and '00, when they had three World Championships, 17 players were on all three clubs. But between '04 and '07, when the Red Sox won 2 out of 4, only eight players were on the second team who had been in on the first World Championship.

At the time of the NLRB intervention and the subsequent collective bargaining agreement, there were changes aplenty. No one could have anticipated that baseball would enjoy at least seventeen years of peaceable relations between labor and management. But that is what happened, though problems ahead were considerable.

CHAPTER 5

The Financial Aftermath of the Mother of All Strikes

Baseball is indeed a business, though much of the public commentary thinks that this involves some kind of change. Let us step back a few years. It is one of those hot, sweltering and humid summers for which Chicago is famous. I stand in the Chicago Cubs clubhouse alternately chatting with Dusty Baker, whom I had seen much more frequently when he was the manager of the San Francisco Giants, and Wendell Kim, the Cubs' new third base coach who, in earlier days, was guiding traffic at the same "hot corner" with the Boston Red Sox. It is the summer of 2003. Dusty steers me toward both Ron Santo and Billy Williams, two of the vintage Cubs from an earlier era when Eisenhower, JFK and LBJ were in the White House. Santo, commenting on the way the game has changed, says, "It is a business now — not a game as it was."

Yet as Virginia law professor G. Edward White notes about the game: "From its earliest modern decades, baseball was thought of as a business, a form of entertainment for profit, but implicitly presented as a much more engaging spectacle than a circus or an opera or a play. It conjured up idyllic rural and pastoral associations, of those staged in an urban setting."[1] Said historians Harold Seymour and Dorothy Seymour Mills:

> To be sure, the old-time owners were not engrossed in the intricacies of capital gains, tax deductions, and complex television contracts, but they were always intent on making money out of professional baseball. Perhaps, as is sometimes claimed, they had more affection for baseball than some of today's owners, but *Sporting News* stated in 1904 that their love of the game depended on the box office. "Don't for a minute think," the editor wrote, "there are any of the club owners in base ball for the sport." The early owners themselves freely admitted they were running a business and made no bones about their interest in money-making.[2]

And as for the players, Seymour and Mills wrote:

> Back in 1910 *Sporting News* sounded the same lugubrious note heard today: players do nothing but talk money on and off the field. The paper fondly recollected a former time when sportsmanship and competition were uppermost. Current fans might be less dismayed at players' dabbling in the stock market if they knew that many of the titans of old also were interested in Wall Street quotations as well as batting averages, and that John McGraw asserted that players of those days were primarily businessmen trying to sell their wares. The truth is that from the beginning of baseball's professional era, as readers of the first volume of this history may recall, players were always keenly interested in such unheroic matters as salaries and working conditions....[3]

Pastoral images of days gone by: as a small child on a drive through the countryside with my parents, viewing rolling hills in New England and imagining the effort that it would take to race up one of those hills after a long fly ball. Yes, baseball is business — and yet something more.

Fast forward a quarter of a century: it is now the summer of 1972 when my family and I have arrived in California's lovely Bay Area, and I make the trip with my sons to the Oakland Coliseum to see the A's and Tigers in the American League Championship Series. We arrive early, as we did so frequently, to watch batting practice, but the gates are locked. We hear the crack of the bat from the inside of the park and are aware that batting practice has begun. But A's owner Finley's employees tell us that we cannot enter and it is clear that the major reason for this is that the wages of the ballpark employees would have to be paid out for those extra hours inside the stadium. The 1970s are now the beginning of a different era when there are hardly any more double-headers for the same cost reasons. (Ironically, as Seymour and Mills have noted, the earlier generation of owners would call off games at the slightest hint of rain so as to schedule double-headers and thus obtain "bigger gate receipts."[4])

As noted, the A's irascible Charlie Finley, whose fan lockout of the Oakland Coliseum during batting practice caused such irritation for me and my sons, had done some damage to his franchises in both Kansas City and Oakland. My sons and I were nonetheless delighted that Finley's penny-pinching ways produced small crowds in Oakland, such as 5,000 fans on Friday nights, and that there were always walk-up tickets that we could buy on the day of the game to sit just a few rows behind the Red Sox dugout on the first base side of the park.

Though, as also noted above, Finley saw his dealings with the Red Sox and Yankees invalidated in the wake of free agency in 1976, Commissioner Bowie Kuhn subsequently announced that Finley's 1977 sale of relief pitcher Paul Lindblad to the Texas Rangers for $400,000 marked the maximum of what he, Kuhn, would allow. In 1947, $375,000 changed hands between the Red Sox and the Browns: $310,000 in the Stephens deal and $65,000 in the one involving Kinder. Surely players of that stature were worth far more than the Lindblad $400,000 thirty years later! But subsequently the Commissioner approved in 2004 the transfer by the Rangers of $67 million to the Yankees to facilitate the Alex Rodriguez trade to that club![5] The business aspect remained, but the dollars had obviously increased exponentially!

Finley's irascibility was shrewd and ahead of the curve in seeing the picture which his fellow owners were unable to glimpse. For instance, he seems to have foreseen the free-agent situation and devised approaches to it which were at once both clairvoyant and, at the same time, the source of considerable unpopularity among his fellow owners. As Professor Charles Korr has noted, Finley said that the players' demand for free agency should be answered by making all players free agents. The owners were horrified by this idea because it ran straight up against their contention that one of the reasons that free agency would hurt the game was that the public identified players with particular teams. They had forgotten about not only the numerous trades referenced above but also that the Detroit Tigers and the Philadelphia A's produced enormous excitement through the trade of batting champion third sacker George Kell for outfielder Barnie McCoskey (also of Blossom Dearie "Van Lingle Mungo" fame) in the early '50s.

Thus Finley was to break with the other owners, not only because of the precedent of player movement as demonstrated by those trades — a movement that remained constant fifteen years before and after the advent of free agency — but also because Finley foresaw that a large number of players on the market simultaneously would depress demand. The earlier financial success of both Ken Harrelson and "Catfish" Hunter, who had escaped Finley's clutches, was in part attributable to the fact that each was the only game in town, so to speak, the only player on the market. And, according to Professor Korr, Marvin Miller, the executive director of the Major League Baseball Players Association from 1966 through the early '80s, was "scared" of the Finley idea.[6] The restricted labor market, which was the product of compromise collective bargaining in 1976 through which players were available for free agency after six years in the majors, controlled supply and thus enhanced demand. Ultimately from the '90s onward, the owners seemed to have come around from the position earlier taken to Finley's thinking, placing ever-increasing numbers of players on the free market by refusing to tender contracts to players whose services they could retain at compensation lower than arbitration would provide. This helps account for the Tod Zeille and Royce Clayton club mobility phenomenon.

The 1976 collective bargaining agreement, which Finley anticipated through his proposed June fire sale, was finalized in August. As noted, it has provided that players could become free agents after six years. Free agents, and represented frequently by agents possessed of both skill and avarice.[7] As we have already seen this was to be the most cataclysmic change in the game. None of the labor disputes which were designed to change this basic framework accomplished their objective. The 1976 framework is with us today. Yet there are new changes.

Revenue Sharing

New features in the '96 agreement began to address the problems of competition anticipated by the Finley deal. What makes baseball so different from football, for instance, is that most revenues are local, e.g., television and attendance. Football, which had nationwide television contracts, found the revenue-sharing concept easier to accept. And telegenic football, which has a greater appeal to a television audience because of the fact that so many games within the game are going on simultaneously, fashioned a nationwide television contract at an earlier stage once it had cleared away the antitrust legislative underbrush.[8]

Because local revenues in baseball differ so sharply, the case for revenue sharing was more difficult to accept. Logically, this spelled out a greater need in baseball for revenue sharing. But as Justice Holmes said, a page of history is worth a volume of logic. Steinbrenner and the New York Yankees did not take kindly to handing over their revenues to their poor country cousins. Indeed, they were to threaten litigation grounded in the argument that revenue sharing was an unlawful and unconstitutional taking of their property.

The NFL Players Association emphasized revenue sharing as a vehicle toward competitive bidding between clubs for players. In baseball, the union sought to have the super-rich Yankees drive the market while utilizing a system of salary arbitration (not present in statistically impoverished football or basketball) as a vehicle to bring up the salaries of those employed by the have-nots. Thus, in baseball, revenue sharing was an objective of the owners, something which the players accepted with a measure of reluctance.

In the 1996 collective bargaining agreement, the parties adopted their first revenue-sharing procedure, which by 2001 taxed each team at twenty percent of its net local revenue, minus stadium expenses. Three-quarters of the revenue thus taxed was collected and distributed equally among the thirty teams (the so-called "straight-pool" system) and one-quarter was distributed only to clubs with below-average team revenue (on a co-called "split-pool" basis), with the amount allocated depending upon how far below the average they were.

Nonetheless, it seems possible that revenue sharing may have exacerbated rather than enhanced competitive imbalance, notwithstanding the fact that parity between the clubs seems better or as good as ever. Some owners, anticipating that their club would not make it to the postseason, would reduce payroll and thus team performance and consequent revenues. Because there is no requirement that clubs provide for a minimum payroll — something that the clubs were to propose in the 2002 negotiations — owners could simply pocket the monies transferred under the revenue-sharing programs. The players resisted the minimum payroll concept, apparently because they feared that it would set a precedent for a maximum payroll as well. Thus there was no requirement provided in the agreement that the monies be used for salaries, scouting, or strengthening of the minor league system. This was for the clubs to determine themselves, though clubs are obliged to use revenue sharing receipts under the collective bargaining agreement "in an effort to improve its performance on the field."

The Commissioner of Baseball is obliged to "enforce this obligation by requiring, among other things, each Payee Club, no later than April 1, to report on the performance-related uses to which it put its revenue sharing receipts in the preceding revenue sharing year." The Commissioner, "consistent" with his authority under the Major League constitution, may "impose penalties on any club that violates this obligation." The Commissioner has not done this in any reported instance. Though some owners speak of baseball as a "quasi-public trust," none of the reports have been made public! The same is true of the figures given regarding what is received and distributed by various teams under the revenue-sharing process itself.

Throughout the '94–'95 strike and in the '94–'96 round of bargaining prior to the negotiation of the '96 agreement, the players continued to successfully resist a salary cap, in contrast to their football, basketball and hockey brethren. Thereafter, the matter was never pursued by the owners in the '02 and '06 negotiations. It must be admitted by all that a salary cap, in contrast to those other sports, would do little to level the playing field unless revenues were divided equally — an impossibility, given the relative importance of local revenues in baseball and the history of the sport's finances. The salary cap would simply diminish the players' share of whatever was available. Another difference between sports is that the rich teams, if restrained from payroll spending, would simply funnel their resources into minor league scouting, and player development — a process which other sports are not engaged in, given their reliance upon college players who proceed directly to their professional ranks rather than serve at a further apprenticeship (except in the NBA's development league) in the professional league itself.

Like the hockey lockout of 2004-05, where the players ultimately accepted a cap, the cap was at the heart of the long '94–'95 baseball strike. But in place of the cap, a luxury tax on high team payrolls, a kind of surrogate for a cap aimed principally at the historically profligate New York Yankees, was negotiated. A threshold payroll figure was set at the midpoint between the payrolls of the fifth- and sixth-highest payroll teams. The five highest payroll teams were to pay a tax equal to 35 percent of the amount by which they exceeded the threshold. In the 2006 negotiations the parties revised the threshold upward. The Yankees, though spending madly in 2008-09 for a new group of free agents who helped them on to their first World Championship of the century, stayed just above the $200 million annual payroll mark, far in excess of any of their competitors. A luxury tax bite of 40 percent or so for them was not a deterrent, so vast were their resources.

What of the Great Recession of 2007—and beyond? It seems unlikely that baseball salaries will take the hit that we have already seen and observed in the Great Depression of the 1930s.[9] While some have predicted that these difficult economics will produce a kind of fan rebellion against corporate profits and sky-high salaries, there has not been an appreciable downturn of fan interest in baseball,[10] though some clubs are suffering in basketball.[11] Commentators have noted that "leagues and franchises are taking their financial lumps: canceled corporate sponsorships, lower season-ticket renewals, lagging merchandise sales. (Team owners aren't thrilled about their shrinking personal portfolios, either.) Since total player compensation in every major sport but baseball is allocated as a percentage of actual revenue, a decline in player pay is inevitable if such slowdowns continue. The decision for clubs will be where to inflict the relative pain."[12] But the trend is not entirely clear and perhaps best reflected by the comment of Manny Ramirez, whom the Red Sox finally traded after tiring of his antics. Said Ramirez after helping the Dodgers to the playoffs in 2008: "Gas is up and so am I."[13]

Sports has taken a hit.[14] Even the Red Sox have demonstrated ticket price restraint[15]—though that was quickly abandoned in 2009 for the '10 season. And, as noted above, the Yankees seem undeterred: their ticket prices for the new Yankee Stadium were obscenely high—and they drive the market![16]

Where does baseball stand today? And what should be the influences, if any, of the

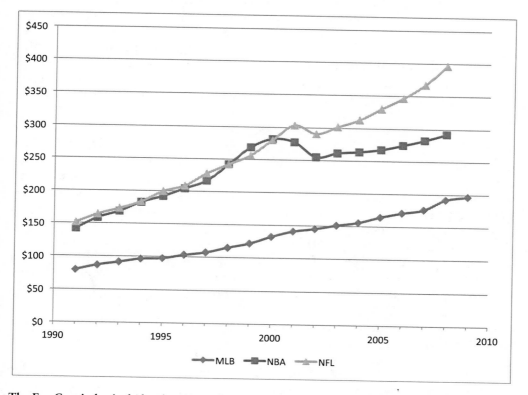

The Fan Cost index includes the prices of (1) two adult tickets, (2) two child tickets, (3) four small soft drinks, (4) two small beers, (5) four hot dogs, (6) two programs, (7) two baseball caps, and (8) parking. These data have been collected by Team Marketing Report since 1991 (graph prepared by Zac Cox).

other major sports on baseball? Before turning to these questions and examining parity, revenues, and payroll, it is important to understand the overlay that has emerged in baseball since the end of the '94-'95 strike and the '96 collective bargaining agreement.

The Curt Flood Act of 1998

Since 1922, *Federal Baseball* has received much criticism, as has its progeny, both *Toolson* and *Flood*, where the Court acknowledged that baseball was a business in interstate commerce and that the precedent extant was an "anomaly" given the antitrust coverage of other sports. The players, through the MLBA, had argued for a reversal of case law through congressional repeal, and during the strike various senators expressed an interest in changing or reversing *Federal Baseball*—though some, like the late Senator Ted Kennedy, who was an antitrust proponent, did not take this position, apparently due to his proximity to and love for the Boston Red Sox.

In the wake of the 1996 collective bargaining, the players and owners committed themselves to lobbying Congress for a partial repeal of the antitrust exemption. But the agreement, negotiated in November 1996, took a different form than might have been anticipated from the traditional debates about the *Federal Baseball* antitrust exemption. This was so, in part, by virtue of the Supreme Court's landmark antitrust ruling in *Brown v. Pro Football, Inc.*,[17] an 8–1 decision handed down earlier in the year. The Court's ruling in *Brown* was to have implications for baseball player-owner relations and, more than arguably, it helped set the stage for the more successful 2002 collective bargaining that was to follow because (1) generally speaking, it took the antitrust exemption issue out of the equation wherever unions were on the scene in sports, (2) in so doing it helped to provide an opportunity for, at that time, an unusual illustration of labor-management cooperation in baseball.

The backdrop to *Brown* was as follows. The coexistence of and tension between antitrust and labor law had been considerable in sports other than baseball, beginning in the 1970s with football, basketball, and hockey. The question in cases that arose in labor disputes generally involving owner-fashioned restrictions upon player mobility was whether and under what circumstances the so-called "nonstatutory labor exemption" to antitrust law, applicable to all other sports notwithstanding *Federal Baseball*, would shield parties to a labor-management relationship from the treble-damage verdicts (as well as criminal prosecutions and injunctive proceedings) that are part of antitrust law remedies where players were precluded by reserve systems from moving from team to team. Football, basketball, and hockey players took a very different road from their baseball counterparts, the latter governed, as they were, by *Federal Baseball* and its progeny.

In football, the "Rozelle Rule"—named for Commissioner Pete Rozelle, who pioneered a series of innovations through which football successfully challenged the preeminence of baseball in America in the '50s and '60s—was initiated by the National Football League (NFL) in 1963. It provided that when a player became a free agent and signed a contract with a different team, the Commissioner of the NFL was authorized to award to the club that had lost the players one or more players of the acquiring club as compensation. From 1963 to 1974, only four players moved from one club to another via free agency under the Rozelle Rule. Quarterback Joe Kapp litigated against the rule, which was found to be a violation of the Sherman Antitrust Act.[18] However, Kapp won the battle in establishing a statutory violation and lost the war, inasmuch as he could not obtain damages from the jury.[19]

In 1974, the NFL Players Association, which had not been on the scene when the Rozelle Rule was first devised, instituted a forty-two-day walkout in training camp. But when their strike was unsuccessful they, like Kapp, instituted an antitrust action attacking the Rozelle Rule and were successful.[20] However, they subsequently agreed to a right-of-first-refusal compensation system that proved to be similar to the Rozelle Rule in practice — and the union was now unable to attack the system because of the nonstatutory labor exemption in which they had become ensnarled as the result of this agreement.[21] The conundrum for non-baseball players in other sports who could avail themselves of antitrust law to attack the reserve system always was that the antitrust law was available to them as well as labor law. The unresolved question was which law was available to the parties, when, and under what circumstances.

The owners could be shielded against the formidable treble damage liability provided by antitrust law and could avail themselves of a more employer-friendly labor law so long as they entered into a collective bargaining agreement. Once a collective bargaining agreement was in place, football players could only obtain reforms of restrictions on player mobility through the strike — and the strike proved to be ineffective in 1982. (The strike-shortened season of '82 would be further shortened for the defending Super Bowl champion San Francisco '49ers when Ray Wershing, the place kicker of the reigning champions, who would touch his place-holder quarterback Joe Montana on the shoulder before positioning himself, missed a field goal which would have taken them to the playoffs!)

When the players struck again in 1987, the owners were able to continue the games with replacement players.[22] The Players Association, in retreat, was defeated through collective bargaining and labor law, which allowed for replacement of strikers. New antitrust litigation was commenced, and in 1989 the NFL implemented so-called "Plan B," which allowed the clubs to reserve thirty-seven players on their rosters, but allowed others to be unrestricted free agents. Meanwhile, the Court of Appeals for the Eighth Circuit ruled that the nonstatutory labor exemption survived both the expiration of the collective bargaining agreement and the impasse in labor negotiations,[23] a position advocated by Professor Bob Berry and myself.[24] The Court of Appeals relied upon our article on the matter. But this decision, notwithstanding the fact that it was the correct one, had the regrettable effect of undercutting some of the NFL Players Association strength.

Thus the football players, defeated by the use of inexpensive replacements during the 1987 strike, grew weary of the labor law model as a basis for resolving employee-employer differences and withdrew as bargaining representatives altogether so that they could remove the nonstatutory labor exemption from antitrust laws. Again, a labor-management relationship is a prerequisite for the exemption — that much was always clear, though much remained to be litigated in the future. The owners attempted to show that this process was a sham — which it was — because the union adopting such a strategy (the basketball players had threatened it on more than one occasion!) would always miraculously revive and bargain a collective agreement as part of the antitrust settlement. But the owners were ultimately unsuccessful.

In this way, antitrust became the principal lever in collective bargaining — but perversely and illogically, collective bargaining on the football field itself had to be destroyed in order to use it.[25] After decertification, in *McNeil v. National Football League*,[26] eight plaintiffs obtained $1,629,000 in the initial round of litigation; additional players prevailed in subsequent litigation as well.[27]

As a result of the players' legal successes, the relationship between the parties changed appreciably in 1993. They restored collective bargaining—*mirabile dictu*, the union and the bargaining relationship revived—and agreed to a revenue-sharing procedure with a salary cap, implementing a system where the players retained exactly 58 percent of the revenues. (Ironically, the owners had to insist upon the return of collective bargaining in order to obtain immunity from the strictures of antitrust law.) Other features of the agreements included complete free agency after five years of seniority, restricted free agency for others, and a "franchise" player system through which such players not eligible for free agency receive pay equal to the average of the top five players at the player's position. (The percentage of share of revenues for the players was revised upward in the important 2006 collective bargaining agreement.)

With all of this as a backdrop, a near-unanimous Supreme Court concluded in *Brown v. Pro Football*[28] that antitrust law could not be used in collective bargaining relationships by virtue of the nonstatutory labor exemption unless the negotiation process was eliminated or something akin to that had transpired. In other words, the Court made what had been a minimum requirement for the availability of antitrust law into a maximum, i.e., whether there was a collective bargaining relationship, and only with the absence of such would antitrust law trump labor law. The Court, noting that it was addressing professional sports as one that presented a multi-employer association bargaining relationship, held that only where the agreement between the owners and the players' union was "sufficiently distant in time and in circumstances from the collective-bargaining process [would] a rule permitting antitrust intervention ... not significantly interfere with the process."[29]

After *Brown*, football, basketball and hockey operated as if antitrust could only be utilized when the union had been decertified or was defunct, or where recognition had been properly withdrawn. Thus, after *Brown*, unions in all sports covered by antitrust law (this meant every sport except baseball) were deprived of the tactic of antitrust liability unless they were willing to decertify themselves or could produce evidence that would establish something akin to a moribund bargaining process. As a result, arena football owners ironically found themselves in a situation opposite to that in which most employers find themselves. Fearing antitrust liability, they threatened a lockout unless their employees *joined* a union! Most employers do the exact opposite![30] Because all sports industry owners have an interest in restricting mobility and instituting some constraint like a reserve clause, a union is the very thing that they need in order to shield themselves through the non-statutory labor exemption from a restraint of trade liability. Again, this is completely antithetical to the realities of most labor-management relations, in which employers, in the main, are attempting to avoid unions and collective bargaining agreements.

Brown came down before the Court adjourned in June 1996. Thus the decision influenced the position of the baseball parties as they considered the viability of *Federal Baseball*—particularly the owners in the collective bargaining agreement which was ultimately negotiated in November 1996. Because *Brown* had substantially diminished the impact of antitrust law in other sports, the baseball owners were willing to negotiate a promise to seek partial repeal of their antitrust exemption. The result of baseball's lobbying efforts was the Curt Flood Act of 1998,[31] which reversed *Federal Baseball* insofar as that decision had provided baseball owners with immunity from major league player litigation arising from their employment relationship. The consequence of the 1998 Act was that such actions could be maintained, but only where the union was decertified, defunct or moribund within the meaning of *Brown*. Thus the practical significance of a partial repeal of *Federal Baseball* was weakened considerably.

Meanwhile, there is what might be best described as a double-barreled attack on any antitrust gains obtained for players in football, and by virtue of the Curt Flood Act, perhaps baseball as well. In the first place, the National Football League has attempted to convince the courts that *Brown v. Pro Football*—in which the Court spoke of professional sports as consisting of a joint employer bargaining unit and in dicta referenced the fact that cooperation as well as competition is involved in such entities — has eliminated antitrust liability in labor disputes within a league. In *Reggie White v. National Football League*,[32] the Court of Appeals for the Eighth Circuit said that the Supreme Court's *Brown* holding was concerned with the potential for disruption of the collective bargaining process through antitrust litigation and that, to the contrary, the bargaining relationship between the parties in football had not been one in which the owners were restrained by fear of antitrust liability. The court viewed its rulings in football, in which antitrust liability has been imposed upon that professional sport as well as others, as consistent with the Supreme Court's *Brown* holding. In essence, although there is some tension with some of the Second Circuit post–*Brown* rulings in this respect,[33] the Court of Appeals for the Eighth Circuit was of the view that Brown was about *when* antitrust liability could be imposed, not *whether* it could be imposed.

The second attack is in some respects even more formidable, at least in terms of its radical approach. Antitrust liability has been imposed upon professional football because of the Supreme Court's holding in *Radovich v. the National Football League*,[34] in which the Court distinguished *Federal Baseball* and held that antitrust laws applied. All of the cases in football and other sports have been predicated upon *Radovich*, which found that owners acted as independent entities and conspired with one another to restrain trade in violation of the Sherman Antitrust Act through restraints upon player mobility and compensation such as the Rozelle Rule in football. But the National Football League took the position before the United States Supreme Court in the *American Needle* case that *Radovich* does not apply to internal disputes within the league which involve independent owners acting in concert with one another to conspire in violation of antitrust strictures, but can only be understood by looking at the facts of that case wherein the NFL attempted to retaliate against Radovich through an "agreement between the Pacific Coast League and the NFL not to hire him."[35] If *Radovich* is so read, the antitrust weapon would become inapplicable to football and to other professional sports including baseball, notwithstanding the fact that the Curt Flood Act of 1998 was passed based upon the assumption that labor-management controversies within a league could under some circumstances give rise to antitrust liability.[36] If the argument that professional sports leagues are one entity and that therefore there cannot be antitrust conspiracies between competing teams, notwithstanding the fact that they are separately owned and, and in some measure, separately operated, had prevailed, this would have had enormous implications for baseball.

During the oral argument in *American Needle* this interesting exchange took place between Justice Breyer and counsel:

> JUSTICE BREYER: ... The Red Sox — I know baseball better. You want the Red Sox to compete in selling T-shirts with the Yankees; is that right?
>
> MR. NAGER: The ability to compete. Yes.
>
> JUSTICE BREYER: Yes. Okay. I don't know a Red Sox fan who would take a Yankees sweatshirt if you gave it away. I mean, I don't know where you are going to get your expert from who's going to say there is competition between these two products. I think they would rather — they would rather wear a baseball, a football, a hockey shirt.
>
> MR. NAGER: ... But you've got to recognize what the competition is for. The competition is

> for fans. And the fact of the matter is, you're right that someone who has lived in New
> York City for a long time is unlikely to be a Red Sox fan and be easily persuaded to be a
> Red Sox fan, but the person who is three years old can easily be persuaded.
>
> JUSTICE BREYER: They have very small allowances at three years old.
>
> (Laughter.)

But the competition between the clubs is to enhance the product so that more revenues will
flow to the club through television, attendance, etc., as the club competed for the loyalty
of fans regardless of geographical location. This point seems to have been missed in the oral
argument. Both the Red Sox and Yankees are competing to attract more interest in their
respective teams and to thus enhance their value and to make them more competitive.
Again, however, the implication of a single-entity holding in *American Needle* could relate
to labor-management relations in the NFL — and a single-entity holding would conceivably
spread this to the *Brown* decision (incorporated by the Curt Flood Act of 1998), which
assumed that each team is an entity, part of a multi-employer bargaining unit.

But a unanimous Supreme Court stopped the owners' single-entity argument in its
tracks. Said Justice Stevens on behalf of a unanimous Court, while noting that there are
many reasons under which independent entities may work collectively and avoid the strictures
of antitrust law: "The NFL teams do not possess either the unitary decisionmaking quality
or the single aggregation of economic power characteristic of independent action. Each of
the teams is a substantial, independently owned, and independently managed business....
[T]he teams compete with one another, not only on the playing field, but to attract fans, for
gate receipts and for contracts with managerial and playing personnel."[37] The *American Needle*
reasoning applies equally to baseball, thus preserving assumptions under which a limited
application of antitrust law was applied to that sport in the Curt Flood Act of 1998.

Thus, again, the remaining issue in a post–*Brown* labor-antitrust arena relates to decertification. When a sports league like either the NFL or the NBA — or indeed MLB itself —
locks out the players, for instance, how might subsequent antitrust litigation proceed? In
the case of the NFL, the 2006–2012 collective bargaining agreement asserts that the parties,
upon commencement of antitrust action, "reserve any arguments that they make regarding
the application of the labor exemption," but at the same time a subsequent provision states
that the NFL "waive[s] any rights they have to assert any antitrust labor exemption defense
based upon any claim that the termination" of collective bargaining status is or "would be
a sham, pretext, ineffective, requires additional steps, or has not in fact occurred."[38] Even
prior to questions relating to whether restrictions on player mobility are valid under a so-
called "rule of reason" and thus not violative of antitrust law, the question is whether the
lockout itself can be violative of antitrust law. *American Shipbuilding* was predicated upon
the assumption that an employer could engage in a kind of preemptive strike or action
when it apprehended that a union would take action against it down the road. But what
happens when there is no union in the wake of decertification? If sports owners cannot
establish that decertification is a pretext or sham, it is difficult to see how *American Shipbuilding* would protect them under labor law and would include antitrust liability. Moreover,
it seems that the basketball guaranteed contract arbitration, which rendered them unenforceable in lockouts as well as strikes, would be inapplicable here with the absence of a
union and federal labor law. A failure to pay would be a material breach of contract as in
Hunter, thus according such players free agent status.

Another issue which will inevitably arise in the wake of decertification relates to the
enforcement of the collective bargaining agreement itself. In this matter the circuit courts

are divided, the Court of Appeals for the Fourth Circuit holding that union majority status is a prerequisite to the enforcement of collective bargaining agreements[39] and the Court of Appeals for the Fifth Circuit holding to the contrary.[40] The matter has yet to come to the United States Supreme Court.[41]

Sports owners will contend that the decertification tactic itself is a failure to bargain in good faith since the union, by depriving itself of majority status, is playing games[42] and has no intent to bargain a new agreement. If the union defends against such a charge before the NLRB by stating that it intends to conclude an agreement, it could meet itself coming around the corner and support the argument that decertification is a sham. (The union will argue that the players have the right to refrain from union activity under federal labor law.)

In any event, even prior to *American Needle*, it seems clear that in minor league baseball, where there is no union and where salaries and conditions of employment are demonstrably inferior to the majors, the Curt Flood Act does not allow the players to sue. The Court in 1953 had ruled in *Toolson v. New York Yankees*,[43] that a minor league player could not sue the Yankees on the grounds that he had been restrained in pursuing his trade when, subjected to the Yankee practice of stockpiling players in their farm system who could advance elsewhere, he was assigned to the Binghamton farm team. In *Toolson* the Court therefore resolved any uncertainty about *Federal Baseball*'s antitrust applicability to the minor leagues as well as the majors. Though it is obvious that the complaint filed in *Toolson* had as its principal objective the ability of the player to progress to the majors more expeditiously rather than to be stockpiled in the rich Yankee system, the Curt Flood Act will not help. It reverses the antitrust exemption only with regard to major league players-owner relationships and leaves intact the progeny spawned by *Federal Baseball* in the minor leagues.[44] Thus, the 1998 act changes only the major league player relations, i.e., Curt Flood's assignment (an issue, as we have seen, that is now addressed by the collective bargaining agreement itself) to the Philadelphia Phillies by virtue of his trade from the Cardinals — and nothing else. (A related issue discussed in Chapter 9 is whether foreign players under agreements such as those negotiated with Japan and Korea are covered by the Curt Flood Act.)

Again, whatever the coverage, the courthouse door under *Brown* and the 1998 statute opens only if the union is out of the picture at the major league level in some sense of the word, either because of its absence or because the subject matter negotiated is something with which the union has had no contact.

Towards the 2002 Collective Bargaining Agreement: Bud Selig's Blue Ribbon Panel

Meanwhile, notwithstanding the collective effort employed in the halls of Congress by players and owners, major league labor difficulties continued in the wake of the 1996 agreement. These problems began to emerge more clearly when Commissioner Bud Selig appointed a Blue Ribbon Panel to examine competitive imbalance in baseball as a prelude to the 2002 negotiations between the parties. (No union or independent representative chosen by anyone other than the Commissioner was part of the panel.)

The Panel made a number of key findings: (1) that large and growing revenue disparities between the clubs were causing problems of "chronic competitive imbalance"; (2) that these problems had become substantially worse during the five complete seasons since the 1994-1995 strike and were likely to continue unless Major League Baseball undertook remedial actions; (3) that the limited revenue sharing and payroll tax had neither produced the intended moderating effects on payroll disparities, nor had it improved competitive balance; and (4) that in a majority of markets, the cost of maintaining a competitive position would result in the escalation of ticket and concession prices. With regard to low-revenue clubs that had benefited from revenue sharing previously instituted, the Panel said: "[S]ome low-revenue clubs, believing the amount of their proceeds from revenue sharing insufficient to enable them to become competitive, used these proceeds to become modestly profitable." Thus, the Panel concluded that the 1996 collective bargaining agreement had not created any "significant 'drag' on player salaries and ha[d] not significantly enhanced competitive balance."

All of this, of course, was prior to the well-chronicled successes of low or bottom payroll teams like Oakland, Minnesota, Montreal, Tony Peña's hard-charging 2003 Kansas City Royals, and most especially the 2003 World Champion Florida Marlins and the 2008 American League (AL) Champion Tampa Bay Rays. Indeed, the Panel, consisting of appointees representing industries or owners themselves (Selig himself remained an owner of the Milwaukee Brewers even subsequent to his time as Acting Commissioner), was not truly independent (some of the same cast of characters, such as the conservative columnist George Will, have re-emerged as part of a new 2009 committee to look at problems of the game in 2010 and beyond). But it failed to take account of the fact that small-market and small-payroll teams (the Panel improperly equated the two definitions with one another) such as Oakland had tied an all-time record, winning twenty in a row in 2002, and in both '01 and '02 won more than one hundred games. The low-payroll Minnesota Twins, who like the Montreal Expos have continuously shed expensive free agents and replaced them with high caliber farm system players, have been in the postseason year after year! More fundamentally, examining the entire history of baseball as have Berri, Schmidt and Brook,[45] one finds that competitive balance seems to have been enhanced, for the most part, since the 1970s and in the early years of the 21st century after the Blue Ribbon Report — the very period in which free agency came into existence!

Finally, in one of its more remarkable conclusions, which attracted the attention of Congress that fall,[46] the Panel stated that "only three MLB clubs have operated profitably over the past five years, despite the industry's revenue growth." The central theme of the report was that the revenue disparity was becoming larger — for example, local revenues were now $12 million for Montreal as opposed to $176 million for the New York Yankees. This was intended as a partial response to the point that there had always been a competitive imbalance and disparity; for instance, in the 1940s teams like the Boston Red Sox and the New York Yankees at the top end were much more successful than the St. Louis Browns, Philadelphia Athletics, and Washington Senators on the bottom. The Panel argued that franchise relocation, so frequently utilized in football, hockey and sometimes basketball, should be an "unavailable tool" to address competitive forces. Why? In fact, the bottom-end clubs in the 1940s had moved to Baltimore, Oakland, and Minnesota respectively. It may be that Oakland, if unsuccessful in pursuing relocation to San Jose or the East Bay, may be the next team to move beyond its immediate market. However, no relocation had taken place in baseball since the Milwaukee Braves (which had moved from Boston in 1953, then went to Atlanta in 1966) and this century's transfer of the Montreal Expos to Washington.

The Panel argued that the differences between the contemporary situation and the one in the 1940s were the extent of the disparity — particularly compared to the other major sports, like football, which has long had a socialistic form of revenue sharing — and the fact that baseball was increasingly in competition with the other major sports for entertainment dollars. Said the Panel:

> There was a time when baseball had the almost undivided attention of sport fans from April to October. Now, however, there are just six weeks between the last National Basketball Association ("NBA") championship game and the first National Football League ("NFL") preseason game. MLB must improve its competitive balance if it is to remain competitive with other sports attractions.

Sports like football and basketball pose a greater challenge to baseball today as each season lengthens and overlaps with the other. (This is a major reason why multi-sport athletes like Stanford's Toby Gerhart — now with the Minnesota Vikings — seem unlikely to follow in the footsteps of such stars as "Bo" Jackson, Deion Sanders, and Charlie Trippi, who played both baseball and football, or Gene Conley, who played baseball and basketball for the Red Sox and the Celtics.) But, assuming that competitive balance does in fact make sports more interesting and attractive, we shall soon see that baseball compares rather favorably in this regard to basketball and football — at least in a number of respects.

The Contraction Issue

Interestingly, the panel rejected the idea of "contraction," deeming it unnecessary to eliminate existing franchises.[47] But at the conclusion of the 2001 World Series, Major League Baseball voted to contract,[48] setting off a firestorm in Congress,[49] as well as prompting litigation and arbitration of the issue.[50] It was thought that this was a shot across the bow of the players union on the eve of the 2002 negotiations, since as many as fifty jobs would be lost, sowing both discord and a depression of salaries in the player ranks.

The owners were stymied in their bid for contraction, principally because of the interpretation given to their lease agreement by the Minnesota state courts.[51] But in arbitration they again faced formidable obstacles, notwithstanding the American labor law presumption that an employer has the right to go out of business — even for antiunion reasons![52]

The owners maintained that the Supreme Court's landmark *Darlington*[53] and *First National Maintenance*[54] decisions, in which it was held that an employer possesses a management prerogative to close or to partially close its operation, were dispositive of the issue. Moreover, under the collective bargaining agreement between the parties, arbitrators had held that the obligation that it thrusts upon the parties to negotiate is compatible and consistent with Supreme Court labor law jurisprudence. The owners relied upon an award of arbitrator Richard Bloch[55] that had held that a major league rule that requires all clubs to conform to a 60/40 ratio of assets to liabilities (contended by the MLBPA to be a "thinly veiled attempt to suppress free agent bargaining")[56] was not bargainable under *First National Maintenance* because there was no showing that the rule had an impact upon jobs or employment conditions. Bloch had concluded that the rule was "clearly designed toward protecting the economic stability of teams ... without a demonstrable impact on players' salaries."[57]

The players contended that *First National Maintenance* and its progeny were distinguishable from the contraction issue. They noted that contraction would necessitate a special procedure to allow the remaining teams to claim the former players of the newly contracted teams and argued that the previous cases did not involve the transfer of employees in the shut-down operations to other viable portions of the enterprise.[58] The MLBPA argued that *First National Maintenance* itself spoke of fashioning the duty-to-bargain obligations in light of the traditions of the industry, the needs of employees, and the like.[59] The union thus emphasized the point that in sports, the players are the product, and that it is difficult or synthetic under such circumstances to delineate (which Bloch did in the 60/40 circumstance) between the entrepreneurial concerns of capital as opposed to labor.[60] The players buttressed their argument with the fact that the 1996 collective bargaining agreement had shaped detailed rules on such matters as revenue sharing between the teams, which would normally be a management prerogative since it involves relationships between the independent clubs and would not thus be part of the bargaining process.[61] The union's point here was that normal considerations of management prerogative, which are beyond the boundaries of the collective bargaining process in labor law, do not apply in an industry like sports or baseball.

Moreover, the MLBPA noted that a series of arbitration rulings involving the amateur draft system, which is not part of the collective bargaining agreement itself, precluded Major League Baseball from making changes that can have an impact upon free agency, notwithstanding the fact that the impact upon employment conditions in the bargaining unit may be less than immediate or direct — the clubs contending that the obligation to bargain was merely over the *effects of the decision* rather than the decision itself, i.e., the circumstances and procedures relating to employment by other existing clubs.[62] The players noted that clubs would not bid for available free agents if they anticipated that better players employed by Montreal and Minnesota might soon become available to them as a result of contraction. Thus the same impact that produced arbitral reversal of changes in the amateur draft system was present here because of its impact upon free agency.[63]

In any event, in the collective bargaining agreement of 2002 the parties resolved the matter through a promise by the owners that they would not contract until at least 2007 and a promise by the players that if the owners did so then, the players would not challenge it.[64] The owners also promised not to institute a contraction of more than two clubs and not to challenge the union's right to bargain over the effects of the decision.[65] Though there continues to be trouble and concern about the two Florida teams, the Marlins and the Tampa Bay Rays, notwithstanding their 2008 championships, as of today, baseball seems to have dropped the contraction matter.

The San Francisco–Oakland–San Jose Fracas

A new relocation dispute of sorts has arisen out of the attempt by the Oakland A's to either obtain a replacement for a more than four-decade-old Oakland Coliseum or to move to another city in the Bay Area — or, if unsuccessful in that effort, outside the Bay Area. Dissatisfied with Oakland's proposals for new stadium sites or the lack thereof, initially the A's expressed an interest in moving to Fremont, California, which is immediately south of Oakland on the same expressway — an arrangement which at one time seemed to be finished but may have now revived.[66] While Oakland made new proposals in 2010,[67] the most serious discussions relate to the A's interest in building a stadium in San Jose — an area which is part of the San Francisco Giants' territorial jurisdiction. The Giants view San Jose as part of their financial base, given the prominence of Silicon Valley and its rich resources in that immediate area. Ironically, the Giants obtained this territorial jurisdiction because the A's gave it to them when the Giants were campaigning for a new stadium in San Jose and considering a move to Florida in the 1980s.

The city attorney for San Francisco has threatened suit in the event of a San Jose relocation on the theory that when the new Giants stadium was built in San Francisco (initially named PacBell — now AT&T), the city provided binding legal agreements to assist in the building of the ballpark which would be violated if its territorial jurisdiction was compromised. States the San Francisco city attorney:

> These agreements include a long-term ground lease and non-relocation agreement with the Giants and its affiliates. The City also has incurred significant financial obligations and expenses, including the development of public areas surrounding the ballpark, and issuance of tax allocation bonds based on property tax increment generated by development of the ballpark.
>
> The City made its commitments in reliance on Major League Baseball's express written acknowledgement that it had no objection to the obligations that the Giants assumed under its legal agreements relating to the development of the ballpark. The City justifiably understood that acknowledgement to mean Major League Baseball would not take any action to undermine the financial viability of the Giants franchise of the Giants' ability to perform its obligations. Yet, tampering with the Giants' established territorial rights would be just the sort of action that the City believed Major League Baseball was in effect promising it would not do.[68]

Both San Francisco and the San Francisco Giants have a great interest in keeping the A's out of San Jose. The Damoclean sword hanging over these negotiations is the A's threat to relocate outside of California altogether (possibly to Charlotte, North Carolina) if they cannot find a site in either San Jose or Fremont or some other municipality in northern California.

In a sense, this is a replay of the successful effort by MLB to relocate the Montreal franchise to Washington, D.C. — a move which was fiercely resisted by the Baltimore Orioles, who possessed territorial rights subsequent to the departure of the Washington Senators. Ultimately, Baltimore acquiesced for a rich television contract, which nonetheless leaves the Orioles relatively moribund as more fans have turned their attention towards the nation's capital to watch the Nationals. It appears that baseball's control of relocation issues is still preserved against club or city attack on the basis of *Federal Baseball* — authority which was relied upon to uphold the move of the Milwaukee Braves to Atlanta.[69] Similarly, notwithstanding whatever implied promise or breach of contract[70] action which would challenge the Commissioner's authority to award San Jose to Oakland in "the best interests of baseball," it would seem that the Giants' litigation would fail on the basis of *stare decisis*. Ironically, the only authority that the Giants could rely upon to circumvent *Federal Baseball* is a district court decision filed by parties challenging the Giants' refusal to relocate to Florida in the early '90s.[71] But, as we see below, most decisions — the issue has not yet gone to the Supreme Court — are to the contrary. On the other hand, the courts may yet reconsider *Federal Baseball* and *Flood*, and, at a minimum, examine more carefully the Seventh Circuit's *Finley* assumption that clubs have waived their right to sue MLB. Perhaps the waiver should be deemed to require a clear and unmistakable waiver in order to bar the Giants from the courthouse door. At a minimum, *Federal Baseball* should be modified so as to provide an arbitrariness or good faith standard so that baseball no longer has a free ride in the world of antitrust.

Contraction and the Antitrust Issue

The contraction cases as well as the San Francisco–Oakland–San Jose dispute have renewed debate about the antitrust exemption for baseball under *Federal Baseball*. The enormous power of organized baseball and its impact upon communities in search of new or existing franchises have been major factors in starting a new round of scrutiny. As noted above, the courts have divided on the question of whether *Federal Baseball* applies outside the context of the reserve clause. The leading opinion at this juncture is *Major League Baseball v. Crist*,[72] a ruling of the Eleventh Circuit growing out of the question of whether the Florida Attorney General could have access to Major League Baseball's records relating to contraction. *Crist* held that decisions about the number of teams participating in league play is related to the "business of baseball" within the meaning of United States Supreme Court authority and therefore immune to antitrust actions.[73] Some, like Professor Zimbalist, have argued that the anticompetitive consequences of antitrust exemption are so egregious that the Court or Congress should or will reverse *Federal Baseball*,[74] though it is generally thought that the impact of such a decision might well have greater consequences for small-town minor league baseball than Professor Zimbalist's analysis admits.[75]

The fact that Major League Baseball's 2002 collective bargaining agreement addresses the contraction issue and the broad sweep of *Brown v. Pro Football* suggest in totality that whether or not contraction or perhaps even relocation issues are within the scope of *Federal Baseball*, the labor exemption might be available to baseball even if the holding is reversed. *Brown* seems to suggest that the answer to such issues arising under the collective bargaining agreement or in the bargaining relationship should come from the NLRB or arbitrators. This could mean that if the reasoning of the baseball antitrust contraction cases can be extended to relocation disputes — like the 1980s litigation over the Oakland Raiders[76] and the San Diego Clippers,[77] in which the NFL's and NBA's respective refusals to authorize relocation were declared to be invalid — the labor exemption that was not asserted in those cases could now operate as a defense and provide for a reversal of those holdings in baseball. This, as stated, is because the issue of location is addressed in the collective bargaining agreement.

The Montreal Expos and the Minnesota Twins were the candidates for contraction or elimination at the beginning of this century. Montreal is now in Washington — and thus far somewhat less successful as a competitive baseball team than it was in its Expo days — and it opened the 2008 season with a state-of-the-art stadium in Anacostia. The Minnesota Twins, also with a new stadium in 2010, have gone on from success to success in reaching the playoffs, though they have not returned to the World Series since 1987 (when they induced all clubs in the majors to get their fans to wave hankies or some kind of paraphernalia) and 1991. It too has been successful in developing a state-of-the-art stadium, which has allowed it to re-sign superstar catcher Joe Mauer (for whom both the Red Sox and Yankees anticipated a vigorous bidding war) and the franchise seems now to have been reinvigorated.

There is one final note here. On the antitrust issue itself none of the Justices who decided *Flood* are on the Court today. And at least on some significant issues,[78] the Court possesses little interest in *stare decisis*. However, I do not anticipate a reversal of either *Federal Baseball* or *Flood*, no matter how badly flawed these decisions are. But time will tell.

Tax System Innovations of the 2002
Baseball Collective Bargaining Agreement

The public and undoubtedly the parties themselves were concerned that yet another strike or lockout would occur when the 1996 collective bargaining agreement expired in

2002. But, *mirable dictu*, for the first time in thirty years the parties were able to peaceably resolve their differences.

The 2002 baseball collective bargaining agreement was obtained on the brink of the union-set strike deadline of August 30. The 20-game winning streak of the small-market Oakland A's that summer had again fostered baseball excitement comparable if not akin to the slugfest between Mark McGwire and Sammy Sosa which had lifted baseball from its doldrums in 1998. The 2001 season had seen Barry Bonds slug 73 homers to break the McGwire record of 70 obtained in '98. Recognition that these feats may have been triggered, in part, by performance-enhancing steroids used by all three players was yet to come. Yet, even prior to this new scandal, which was to renew and exacerbate tensions between the union and owners, the negotiations produced a cliffhanger throughout the summer of '02.

The agreement that emerged — this time without resort to either a strike or lockout — addressed a wide variety of issues. The minimum salary was to be $300,000 in 2003 and 2004, with cost-of-living adjustments thereafter. For the first time, random testing for steroids was introduced. The contract now provided that positive tests resulting in treatment the first time, with suspension after two positive findings, and were to be instituted by Major League Baseball again, an issue which was to consume baseball for the entire period of the 2002 collective bargaining agreement. (This is discussed in Chapter 7.) Moreover, a committee was established to look at the idea of an international draft, given that the sharp increase of Latin American players, as well as those from Japan, Korea, Australia, Cuba, and even Europe, were affecting the competitive balance. (This is discussed in Chapter 9. It should be noted here that no international draft has been instituted as of this writing — though it remains possible that this will be a major collective bargaining issue in 2011.)

The overriding focus of 2002 was the concern expressed in the Blue Ribbon Report to facilitate competitive balance or parity between the clubs and enhance interest in baseball in so doing. Preliminarily, it should be noted that there has always been some doubt about whether competitive balance does translate into a more successful and profitable game. Bill Walsh, the legendary coach of the Super Bowl champion San Francisco 49ers and on two occasions Stanford's coach as well, told me that he thought that game had been more attractive in the dynasty period presided over by his 49ers and teams like the Dallas Cowboys. It was his view that the absence of such excellence contributed to public interest in silly antics like dance routines in the end zone after a touchdown and the various puerile attention-getting gambits of Terrell Owens and more recently Chad Ochocinco of the Cincinnati Bengals. And it seems clear that the rise of the Boston Celtics and the Los Angeles Lakers in the 1980s, emerging into a great rivalry featuring Larry Bird and Magic Johnson, rescued professional basketball from the doldrums of the 1970s and economic decline. Nonetheless, in baseball attendance declined during Yankee hegemony in the 1950s (perhaps because there was no real rivalry with any other team), and thus the baseball assumptions have always been to the contrary.

Thus the major innovations of the 2002 agreement relate to the tax system, which the owners hoped would act as a drag on future salary increases by making big-market clubs less willing to spend. The players favored a split-pool system that, whatever the level of revenue sharing, redistributes more money to the bottom teams and takes less money away from the top teams. They have always wanted the Yankees to drive the market.

The owners, on the contrary, favored a straight-pool system where all of the collected funds would be distributed to all clubs equally. The 1996 agreement provided for a 20 percent tax, the Blue Ribbon Panel called for 40–50 percent, and the owners demanded 50 percent. The union wanted 20 percent to be increased to only 22.5 percent. However, the owners wanted to place more emphasis upon the straight-pool system that would penalize the high-spending clubs more effectively. More clubs would benefit under this system, creating more ownership support.

As Professor Zimbalist has written:

> The players resisted such a substantial increase. Revenue sharing was being called for in the name of competitive balance, but the players were concerned that at such high tax levels it would also function as a strong deterrent to player salary increases. They reasoned something like this. Suppose that George Steinbrenner believes that Jason Giambi will add $20 million a year to the New York Yankees' local revenues. That being the case, Steinbrenner should be willing to offer Giambi a salary of up to $20 million. Now suppose that MLB informs Steinbrenner that it will tax away 50 percent of any local revenue generated by the Yankees. Suddenly, Giambi is no longer worth up to $20 million to Steinbrenner. He is now worth only $10 million, and Steinbrenner's pay offer would be scaled down accordingly.[79]

The 2002 agreement provided for a 34 percent net local revenue tax, an amount that would be supplemented out of the Major League Baseball central fund and that would increase in the later years of the agreement. This central fund amount, which will consist of 25 percent of the redistribution, was to be done on a split-pool basis, whereas 75 percent will take place in a straight-pool system. The system — particularly when viewed in conjunction with the luxury tax discussed below — singled out the high-spending New York Yankees, but its impact on the team appears to be limited. Messrs. Sabathia, Burnett, and Teixeira can all testify to that!

Again, the low-revenue teams have a windfall under both the '02 and '06 agreements because there is no payroll minimum that all clubs must maintain, in contrast to minimum salaries set forth in the collective bargaining agreement. Until 2010, when receipts and distribution of some club revenues were mysteriously released,[80] financial reports filed with the commissioner were not seen by the public or discussed in public, and a number of the lowest-payroll teams, such as Milwaukee, Kansas City, Miami (the Marlins) and Tampa Bay, actually had reduced their payrolls since the revenue sharing concept had come into existence. The revenue-sharing provisions of the agreement, which would shift about $229 million from richer clubs to poorer ones in 2003, did not immediately translate into more spending. For instance, despite receiving $20 million in the 2003 season, Tampa Bay still cut its payroll from $34 million to $20 million. In 2005 Tampa Bay received $33 million in revenue sharing and increased their payroll only by $9 million, from $25.6 million to $35.4 million. In the same year the Florida Marlins received $31 million, but it slashed its payroll from $56.3 million to $15.9 million. The Pittsburgh Pirates, with perhaps the most beautiful ballpark in all of baseball, PNC Park, have not won since 1992. The Pirates received $25 million from revenue sharing in '05 and increased their payroll by $8.6 million. On the other hand, MLB contends that the Pirates spent 3.3 times as much on major league payroll *and* player development than it received in revenue sharing. No figures have been provided to support this.[81] And things are not improving. In 2008, the Buccos received about $75 million from Major League Baseball and had a payroll of $48 million, so the team made a hefty profit before selling even a single ticket![82]

On the other hand, the Toronto Blue Jays received $31 million in revenue sharing in 2005 and used $26 million of it for payroll. Their fortunes and division contending capabilities were enhanced, though they did not win the East in any year from '06 through '09. In 2010 the Florida Marlins, apparently pressured by both MLB and the union, have re-signed established players and "promised to allow the commissioner's office and the players union to monitor their spending for the next three seasons."[83]

Scholarly commentary suggests that revenue-sharing funds are not being reinvested in talent by the "payee team owners and the result is an inferior product on the field," though recognizing the claim that such clubs are investing further in minor league farm systems.[84] In this study the contention is made that "the unintended consequence ... is that the incentive to win (and generate revenue from winning) is in fact reduced for low revenue teams."[85] (The rewards of winning have been clear for some time.[86]) Indeed, economists in a brief to the Supreme Court in an antitrust case in 2009 have submitted that the weight of authority is that revenue sharing is counterproductive and does not enhance competitive balance or parity.[87]

As the recently revealed data established, quite clearly the Florida Marlins were deceptive about their financial revenue-sharing receipts in order to convince government and taxpayers that the club would leave the Miami area in the absence of financial aid.[88] Beyond this kind of problem, there are at least three issues which have taken the bloom off the revenue-sharing rose. The first is that the same incentive for a low-revenue club to spend the dollars that the Red Sox and Yankees spend is not there.[89] A second is that it is difficult for an outsider to estimate club investment in producing a good product simply on the basis of payroll in view of signing bonuses for international free agents, farm team development and the development by most teams in Latin American facilities.[90] All constitute considerable expense. Third, as noted below, there is no indication that revenue sharing has made baseball any more competitive — thus undercutting the argument that it is achieving its objective of competitive balance. Statistically, more progress was made toward achieving this objective prior to the revenue-sharing reforms contained in successive collective bargaining agreements.[91]

Since the weight of evidence is against the proposition that low-revenue clubs will use revenue sharing to produce winning teams rather than to unload established players, is there another way to make revenue sharing work? Professor Michael Lewis properly contends that the incentive to improve and attract fans is diminished by the fact that accomplishing the goal will result in reducing revenue-sharing receipts for the low-revenue teams.[92] Thus his proposal is that a more balanced playing field would be created if "revenue sharing payments [were] increased for teams that attract more fans."[93] His view is that linking revenue sharing to attendance would encourage teams to spend more money on players, win more games and thus obtain higher revenue-sharing receipts by virtue of greater attendance. It is an intriguing and somewhat attractive idea, though it is not clear that this incentive will produce more investment in teams and winning. The collective bargaining agreement states that a "principal objective of the revenue sharing plan is to promote the growth of the Game and the industry on an individual Club and on an aggregate basis.... The Commissioner shall enforce this obligation by requiring ... each Player Club no later than April 1, to report on the performance-related uses to which it put its revenue sharing receipts in the preceding revenue sharing year. Consistent with his authority under the Major League Constitution, the Commissioner may impose penalties on any Club that violates this obligation." No sanctions have been imposed and Major League Baseball has reported that all clubs are expending monies for baseball purposes as contemplated by the agreement, notwithstanding the declining payroll of some of the small-market teams for some of the revenue-sharing periods. Only time will tell whether the Marlins' 2010 pledges will translate into more spending for that club and thus constitute an exception to the above noted trend. Nothing has been heard from the Commissioner about the Pirates and the Royals.

There are two other problems relating to revenue sharing. The first is that differences in revenues do not necessarily mirror differences in markets, a point of confusion set forth in the Blue Ribbon Report itself. For instance, the Seattle Mariners are one of the so-called small-market teams and yet they are consistently in the top half dozen of teams with highest revenues. This has been obtained not only with reasonably good attendance at Safeco Field (though it has declined in recent years before the '09 on-the-field revival), but also because of their lucrative multi-state radio and television contract covering the far West. In the far West, Mariner baseball reigned supreme throughout such states as Oregon, Montana and Idaho, as well as Washington! Conversely, the Philadelphia Phillies are by demographic standards one of the big-market teams and yet, until their recent resurgence, they have been lower in revenue. It would seem that the parity objective should dictate a sharing on the basis of market indicia or, alternatively, on the basis of the effort put forward to spend for baseball purposes consistent with the collective bargaining agreement. Given the fact that baseball, like all sports, relies upon team fans for support, the effort should be made transparent to those fans and the public generally.

Another problem relating to this matter is the financing of stadiums. On Opening Day 2009 the fourth oldest Major League Baseball stadium (after Fenway, Wrigley and Chavez Ravine in Los Angeles) was Anaheim Stadium, which was opened on April 19, 1966.[94] This construction boom[95] has been facilitated by the 2002 collective bargaining agreement which makes deductible from club revenue sharing payments "the Stadium Operations, Expenses' of each Club, as reported on an annual basis of the Club's FIQ [Financial Information Questionnaire]." The contract provision has thus somewhat altered the pattern of stadium financing, with the San Francisco Giants being the only club under the agreement to rely principally upon private financing for the new PacBell prior to its adoption. Now the St. Louis Cardinals have paid two-thirds of the cost for their new stadium, and the wealthy Yankees and Mets are paying the entire bill less property tax, breaks, land costs, etc. The rich are getting richer through revenue sharing deductions provided by the collective bargaining agreement!

The Florida Marlins have offered to put up 42 percent of the costs (and have done so, as we have seen, with false representations) and the Oakland A's have explored a new stadium in Fremont, California, and more recently in San Jose, where the costs, let alone permission to build the park, are as yet undefined. The extent to which the public is actually off the hook in these various new parks is unclear. But what is clear is that stadium growth is a part of the ever expanding baseball prosperity of which the MLBPA is a part and for which the public is expected to pay.[96] Again, the most interesting part of the stadium finance situation is the extent to which the wealthy teams are getting wealthier. The late New York Yankees owner George Steinbrenner who bitterly complained about the 2002 agreement may have obtained "Steinbrenner's revenge" before his death, as the other clubs finance his new 2009 Yankee Stadium through revenue-sharing deductions!

The deductions from revenue sharing are only a part of the picture. What makes new stadiums which are promoted by the collective bargaining agreement so lucrative is the ability of franchises to threaten cities with a move to another location as a vehicle to obtaining governmental assistance.[97] This means that hard-pressed communities must forsake expenditures for schools and transportation if they want to hold on to clubs which threaten to go elsewhere! Oakland and San Jose voters will soon take note!

And then finally there is the problem of the so-called related entities, television stations in which approximately a half a dozen clubs have substantial interest. Some 75–80 percent of club revenues in baseball are derived through local television and other local income. The Boston Red Sox through Nessen, and the New York Yankees by way of YES, have derived considerable revenues from these media outlets. The collective bargaining agreement states that revenue-sharing obligations are applicable to all baseball operations "except those wholly unrelated to the business of Major League Baseball." Apparently an accommodation had been arrived at with the Red Sox but the question of New York Yankee obligations still has not been resolved. Both the Red Sox and the Yankees have prospered mightily under the existing arrangement. The question of applicability of revenue sharing to these new media entities is a factor in the inability to remedy the rich-poor divide.

But it is nevertheless thought that the revenue-sharing process has allowed some of the small-payroll teams, such as Florida and Montreal (which became the Washington Nationals in 2005), to husband their resources and not to send their best players to the contending teams at the time of the trade deadline, as they have done in the recent past. Florida's 2003 success (it won the World Championship that year) may confirm the idea that small-market teams are more competitive under the new agreement (though its sharp decline and trade of front-line players such as Josh Beckett and A.J. Burnett suggests that, as in '97 when they unloaded virtually all of their stars in the wake of that World Championship, they have converted to a small-market pattern when it suited their purpose).

But all of this leaves undisturbed the fact that so many successful low-payroll teams possess excellent baseball acumen and evaluation skills that permit them to compete fairly successfully with their richer cousins. The considerable success of Oakland, Minnesota, Florida and Montreal (prior to its Washington move) was not attributable to the 2002 agreement but rather had its roots in qualities possessed by the personnel of those clubs unrelated to the collective bargaining agreement.[98]

The spectacular emergence of the Colorado Rockies in 2007, their 21 out of 22 victories in what will be forever known as Roctober, was unprecedented and led them to capture the National League Championship. All of this was done with a payroll of $54 million, ranking the team 26th out of 30. Teams on average spend 49 percent of their revenue on payroll, but the Rockies spent only 28.4 percent on the players, ranking them next to last.[99]

In 2003 the low-payroll teams had been more successful than ever. Even the Montreal Expos, forced to be wandering vagabonds who were required to play a substantial number of their home games in Puerto Rico, had a respectable finish. (And in prior seasons, the Expos had been even better!) The Montreal relocation team, the Washington Nationals, owned by Major League Baseball on a limited budget, were contenders for most of 2005, though not in seasons thereafter. Oakland and Minnesota were in the playoffs, even though each was generally eliminated in the Division Series. The same held true in the years to come: as recently as 2006, Oakland and Minnesota faced off against one another in the Division Series, with the former advancing to the Championship level.

These teams made good use of their farm system and operated effectively with a relatively low payroll. Similarly, in 2007 the Cleveland Indians defeated the New York Yankees in the postseason Division Series — when the latter had nearly four times the payroll. They almost accomplished the same mission with the Boston Red Sox, who came back from a 3–1 deficit despite the questionable use of Jon Lester as an extra inning reliever in Game 2; the Red Sox spent twice as much as the Indians. And, in 2009, the Minneapolis

Twins made the playoffs with the seventh lowest payroll in baseball. They were back again in 2010.

Nonetheless, given the fact that the 2002 and '06 agreements do not provide for a minimum payroll, there is ongoing concern that some of the small-market teams will spend their revenue-sharing dollars on "everything from Christmas bonuses for front-office employees to expansion projects for unrelated businesses operated by the teams' owners," rather than on the free-agent market. Again, unsuccessful clubs like Milwaukee and Pittsburgh have maintained that they are spending funds for the purpose of improving their scouting and minor league systems. The 2007 and 2008 successes of Milwaukee — they were in first place in the NL Central Division most of both years — as well as the above-referenced successes of Cleveland and Colorado appear to bear out those claims for that club. So as long as Selig or his successor does not reveal to the public the results of his investigation of team efforts in putting non-payroll monies into baseball and the basis for his conclusions, the burden is on baseball to explain. It has not done so.

Why can't MLB devise an inverse tax on the low-payroll-spending teams? This is an idea that has been bandied about for some time. The teams are collecting from the Central Fund, revenue sharing and local TV and radio and cable approximately $80 million by some estimates. A third of the clubs have a payroll below this and it may be that those teams should be taxed.[100] Surely the Marlins demonstrated considerable acumen by obtaining Hanley Ramirez, once in the Red Sox farm system and now considered to be one of the elite players in the National League. The fans will only turn out if there are those who complement him — and if Ramirez himself is re-signed rather than being allowed to escape through a trade or free agency. Money must combine with judgment to take, in this case, the Marlins to the next step. The public is entitled to know something about the monitoring process.

When first introduced, the new luxury tax presented the most difficulties in the bargaining, although the fact that both sides accepted the concept from the beginning of collective bargaining indicated that the parties might be able to resolve their difference peaceably, as they did. The concept of the luxury tax brings baseball close to a *de facto* salary cap. But it is hardly a hard cap, at least in the sense of either football or basketball (neither of them, for that matter, is entirely rigid); instead, it is designed to *discourage* spending beyond a particular level.

In the 2002 agreement, the negotiated payroll threshold was $117 million in 2003; this rose to $136.5 million in 2006. The tax rate ranges from 17.5 percent for first-time offenders to 30 percent for consecutive offenders, with a rate of 40 percent for teams that are above the threshold in three consecutive years.

The 2006 agreement provides that the tax threshold be $148 million in 2007; $155 in '08; $162 in '09; $170 in '10 and $178 in '11. The luxury or "competitive balance" tax (as it is called by the collective bargaining agreement) is 22.5 percent for first-time offenders, 30 percent for teams whose payroll has exceeded the threshold twice in a row, and 40 percent for those doing so over three or more consecutive seasons. Thus, in 2008, the Yankees were taxed at a 40 percent clip and had to hand over $26.9 million to the Commissioner's Office, while the Detroit Tigers, who had never previously exceeded the threshold payroll, were taxed at the 22.5 percent rate and had to hand over $1.3 million. 2009 marked the first time during the current collective bargaining agreement that the Red Sox did not have to pay any luxury tax.

Whatever the reason — and one can see that many of the patterns have emerged far in advance of the reforms of 1996, 2000, and 2006 — the objective of "hope" focused upon by both Selig and the Blue Ribbon Panel has been realized by certain measures. When one examines won and loss records in MLB — teams winning .600 or more or losing .400 or less — more parity exists in baseball than in basketball and football and by appreciable amounts (Chart 1b).

Patterns have held fairly steady throughout the free-agent period which began in 1975 in baseball and in all the sports from the '70s onward. Hope, when measured by the new teams that have appeared in the postseason, the same is true again (Chart 2).

Again, this compares favorably with both the NBA and the NFL (Charts 3 and 4).

TABLE 5.1. REGULAR-SEASON PARITY
ACROSS PROFESSIONAL SPORTS

Season	MLB	NBA	NFL
1976	18%	28%	79%
1977	39%	32%	75%
1978	14%	41%	54%
1979	18%	41%	64%
1980	14%	50%	71%
1981	18%	52%	57%
1982	11%	43%	61%
1983	11%	57%	43%
1984	4%	39%	57%
1985	29%	48%	68%
1986	7%	61%	79%
1987	7%	52%	68%
1988	14%	61%	71%
1989	11%	56%	57%
1990	4%	63%	75%
1991	7%	70%	75%
1992	11%	59%	79%
1993	18%	48%	57%
1994	7%	70%	54%
1995	14%	59%	50%
1996	7%	52%	57%
1997	7%	66%	30%
1998	20%	62%	70%
1999	20%	59%	58%
2000	0%	59%	71%
2001	17%	66%	68%
2002	30%	48%	53%
2003	20%	48%	81%
2004	20%	48%	66%
2005	10%	48%	84%
2006	7%	38%	53%
2007	0%	48%	59%
2008	17%	66%	59%
2009	13%	55%	—
Average	**14%**	**53%**	**33%**

The above chart lists the percentage of teams in each major professional sport with winning percentages either above 60 percent or below 40 percent (prepared by Mike Scanlon based on the data presented in the *Baseball Reference*, *Basketball Reference* and *Football Reference* websites. See http://www.baseball-reference.com/; http://www.basketball-reference.com/; http://www.football-reference.com/).

TABLE 5.2

MLB	Non-Repeating Playoff Teams	Total Teams in Playoffs	Turnover Percentage	Total Number of Teams in the League	Percentage of League in the Playoffs
1975	2	4	50%	24	17%
1976	3	4	75%	24	17%
1977	1	4	25%	26	15%
1978	0	4	0%	26	15%
1979	4	4	100%	26	15%
1980	4	4	100%	26	15%
1981	4	8	50%	26	31%
1982	3	4	75%	26	15%
1983	4	4	100%	26	15%
1984	4	4	100%	26	15%
1985	3	4	75%	26	15%
1986	4	4	100%	26	15%
1987	4	4	100%	26	15%
1988	4	4	100%	26	15%
1989	3	4	75%	26	15%
1990	3	4	75%	26	15%
1991	3	4	75%	26	15%
1992	1	4	25%	26	15%
1993	2	4	50%	28	14%
1994	—	—	—	—	—
1995	—	8	—	28	29%
1996	4	8	50%	28	29%
1997	4	8	50%	28	29%
1998	4	8	50%	30	27%
1999	2	8	25%	30	27%
2000	5	8	63%	30	27%
2001	3	8	38%	30	27%
2002	3	8	38%	30	27%
2003	3	8	38%	30	27%
2004	4	8	50%	30	27%
2005	3	8	38%	30	27%
2006	5	8	63%	30	27%
2007	7	8	88%	30	27%
2008	5	8	63%	30	27%
2009	4	8	50%	30	27%

This table indicates the turnover in teams appearing in the baseball playoffs. During the 14 years of 4-team playoffs in the years after the advent of free agency, a full 72 percent of the teams appearing in the playoffs did not make it to the postseason in the previous year. Since the playoffs expanded to 8 teams in 1995, this has dipped to the point where half the teams in the postseason had appeared in the previous year's playoffs (prepared by Mike Scanlon based on the data presented in the *Baseball Reference* website. http://www.baseball-reference.com/).

TABLE 5.3

NBA	Non-Repeating Playoff Teams	Total Teams in Playoffs	Turnover Percentage	Total Number of Teams in the League	Percentage of League in the Playoffs
1975	4	10	40%	18	56%
1976	4	10	40%	18	56%
1977	6 (8)	12	50% (67%)	22	55%

NBA	Non-Repeating Playoff Teams	Total Teams in Playoffs	Turnover Percentage	Total Number of Teams in the League	Percentage of League in the Playoffs
1978	5	12	42%	22	55%
1979	3	12	25%	22	55%
1980	2	12	17%	23	52%
1981	3	12	25%	23	52%
1982	5	12	42%	23	52%
1983	2	12	17%	23	52%
1984	5	16	31%	23	70%
1985	3	16	19%	23	70%
1986	2	16	13%	23	70%
1987	3	16	19%	23	70%
1988	3	16	19%	25	64%
1989	3	16	19%	27	59%
1990	3	16	19%	27	59%
1991	3	16	19%	27	59%
1992	4	16	25%	27	59%
1993	3	16	19%	27	59%
1994	4	16	25%	27	59%
1995	3	16	19%	29	55%
1996	3	16	19%	29	55%
1997	4	16	25%	29	55%
1998	4	16	25%	29	55%
1999	5	16	31%	29	55%
2000	3	16	19%	29	55%
2001	2	16	13%	29	55%
2002	4	16	25%	29	55%
2003	2	16	13%	29	55%
2004	5	16	31%	29	55%
2005	5	16	31%	29	55%
2006	3	16	19%	29	55%
2007	5	16	31%	29	55%
2008	4	16	25%	29	55%
2009	3	16	19%	29	55%

The number in parentheses included established ABA franchises that were newly incorporated into the NBA.
    This table indicates the turnover in teams appearing in the basketball playoffs. During the 7 years of 12-team playoffs, only 31 percent — 29 percent if ABA franchises are counted — of the teams appearing in the playoffs did not make it to the postseason in the previous year. This number dips to 22 percent in the 26 years since the playoffs expanded to 16 (prepared by Mike Scanlon based on the data presented in the *Basketball Reference* website. http://www.basketball-reference.com/).

TABLE 5.4

NFL	Non-Repeating Playoff Teams	Total Teams in Playoffs	Turnover Percentage	Total Number of Teams in the League	Percentage of League in the Playoffs
1975	3	8	38%	26	31%
1976	2	8	25%	28	29%
1977	2	8	25%	28	29%
1978	5	10	50%	28 .	36%
1979	3	10	30%	28	36%
1980	6	10	60%	28	36%
1981	6	10	60%	28	36%
1982	10	16	63%	28	57%

NFL	Non-Repeating Playoff Teams	Total Teams in Playoffs	Turnover Percentage	Total Number of Teams in the League	Percentage of League in the Playoffs
1983	5	10	50%	28	36%
1984	3	10	30%	28	36%
1985	5	10	50%	28	36%
1986	3	10	30%	28	36%
1987	5	10	50%	28	36%
1988	4	10	40%	28	36%
1989	3	10	30%	28	36%
1990	7	12	58%	28	43%
1991	5	12	42%	28	43%
1992	6	12	50%	28	43%
1993	5	12	42%	28	43%
1994	5	12	42%	28	43%
1995	4	12	33%	30	40%
1996	5	12	42%	30	40%
1997	5	12	42%	30	40%
1998	5	12	42%	30	40%
1999	7	12	58%	31	39%
2000	6	12	50%	31	39%
2001	6	12	50%	31	39%
2002	5	12	42%	32	38%
2003	8	12	67%	32	38%
2004	5	12	42%	32	38%
2005	7	12	58%	32	38%
2006	7	12	58%	32	38%
2007	6	12	50%	32	38%
2008	7	12	58%	32	38%

This table indicates the turnover in teams appearing in the football playoffs. During the 11 years of 10-team play-offs, 57 percent of the teams appearing in the playoffs did not make it to the postseason in the previous year. This number dipped slightly — to 49 percent — since the playoffs expanded to 12 teams in 1990 (prepared by Mike Scanlon based on the data presented in the *Football Reference* website. http://www.pro-football-reference.com/).

Both the turnover in baseball's postseason and the infrequency of repeat appearances seem to be enhanced by the development of the wild-card system in 1995. All of this seems to fit with the fact that the country is more interested in baseball than ever, as reflected in sharply increasing revenues (discussed in more detail in Chapter 6).

Twenty-one of the thirty clubs were able to get to the championship series during the past decade, fourteen advancing to the World Series and producing eight different winners. As Tyler Kepner has written:

> There was plenty of triumph to go around. At the start of the decade, eight franchises had never been to the World Series. Now there are only three: the Texas Rangers, the Washington Nationals and the Seattle Mariners. The Diamondbacks and the Los Angeles Angels won in their first appearances; Houston, Colorado and Tampa Bay lost.[101]

In 2004, the Red Sox were to win in dramatic fashion after being down 3–0 in the American League Championship Series, the first sports team ever to rally from a 3–0 disadvantage — and in the process quenched a thirst for a world championship that had gone on unabated since 1918. Before Alex Rodriguez's Yankees were able to win even two playoff series, the Townies possessed two world championships ('04 and '07). The Angels won for the first time in their (at that time) forty-two-year history, the Cardinals making it for the first time in twenty-four years, and the Phillies for the first time since 1980, redressing a twenty-eight-year wait. And in 2010 two teams perennially out of the postseason in the past two decades, Cincinnati and Texas, were able to get in! The World Championship went to the San Francisco Giants, who had not prevailed since 1954 when they were in New York City.

At the same time, it must be acknowledged that there are certain teams which are hopeless by virtue of the infrequency with which they appear in the playoffs — and baseball does not do as much to promote parity in this sense of the word (Chart 5), i.e., parity between seasons or the ability to bounce back from a bad one. The bad teams, Kansas City and Pittsburgh, are always the prime illustrations; they continue to languish and do not bounce back. Cincinnati, the first professional team ever in 1869, and once a premier team when it had great dominance in the '30s, '40s and '70s, and again as recently as 1990 when it swept the "Bash Brothers" Oakland A's in a four-game World Series — seemed to be moving down toward membership in this group. But in 2010 the Reds reversed this trend with a Central Division championship.[102]

TABLE 5.5. NUMBER OF SEASONS SINCE LAST PLAYOFF APPEARANCE, BY LEAGUE AND FRANCHISE

MLB		NFL		NHL		NBA	
Nationals	28	Bills	9	Panthers	8	Timberwolves	5
Royals	24	Lions	9	Kings	6	Knicks	5
Pirates	17	Texans	7	Coyotes	6	Bobcats	5
Blue Jays	16	Browns	6	Maple Leafs	4	Thunder	4
Reds	14	49ers	6	Oilers	3	Pacers	3
Orioles	12	Raiders	6	Thrashers	2	Clippers	3
Rangers	10	Rams	4	Sabres	2	Grizzlies	3
Mariners	8	Bengals	3	Islanders	2	Bucks	3
Marlins	6	Broncos	3	Lightning	2	Kings	3
Giants	6	Chiefs	2	Avalanche	1	Warriors	2
Braves	4	Jets	2	Stars	1	Nets	2
Astros	4	Saints	2	Wild	1	Suns	1
Mets	3	Bears	2	Predators	1	Raptors	1
Athletics	3	Redskins	1	Senators	1	Wizards	1
Padres	3	Buccaneers	1	Canadiens	0	Pistons	0
Tigers	3	Seahawks	1	Rangers	0	Heat	0
Diamondbacks	2	Jaguars	1	Devils	0	76ers	0
Indians	2	Cowboys	1	Flyers	0	Bulls	0
Cubs	1	Packers	1	Sharks	0	Jazz	0
White Sox	1	Patriots	1	Blue Jackets	0	Trailblazers	0
Brewers	1	Falcons	0	Blues	0	Spurs	0
Rays	1	Colts	0	Flames	0	Hornets	0
Red Sox	0	Dolphins	0	Bruins	0	Hawks	0
Rockies	0	Vikings	0	Capitals	0	Celtics	0
Twins	0	Titans	0	Ducks	0	Rockets	0
Cardinals	0	Panthers	0	Canucks	0	Mavericks	0
Angels	0	Giants	0	Hurricanes	0	Cavaliers	0
Dodgers	0	Chargers	0	Blackhawks	0	Nuggets	0
Phillies	0	Ravens	0	Red Wings	0	Magic	0
Yankees	0	Eagles	0	Penguins	0	Lakers	0
		Cardinals	0				
		Steelers	0				
AVERAGE =	5.6		2.1		1.3		1.4

Number of seasons since last playoff appearance, by league and franchise (data as of Dec. 1, 2009) (table prepared by Zac Cox).

Moreover, there is a correlation between payroll and performance when one notes that in baseball from 1995 to 2009 a substantial majority of the teams who were at the top were in the top third for payroll spending (Chart 6).

Table 5.6

	Payroll Rank of Team with Best Win %	Payroll Rank of Team with Second-Best Win %	Payroll Rank of Team with Third-Best Win %	Payroll Rank of Team with Fourth-Best Win %	Payroll Rank of Team with Fifth-Best Win %	Payroll Rank of Team with Sixth-Best Win %
2009	1	6	9	4	7	18
2008	6	8	29	4	12	15
2007	2	23	4	1	26	25
2006	5	1	19	14	21	4
2005	6	13	4	1	2	26
2004	9	1	2	8	6	19
2003	3	1	9	23	6	7
2002	1	28	7	15	4	13
2001	11	29	1	17	9	8
2000	17	11	4	26	6	25
1999	3	9	1	11	4	6
1998	2	3	15	14	8	10
1997	5	2	1	7	19	15
1996	4	3	1	18	10	12
1995	9	3	19	6	2	11
1994	27	1	3	8	19	7
1993	7	14	20	1	13	27
1992	11	5	3	12	13	19
1991	14	16	20	2	9	23
1990	10	16	26	20	2	6
1989	12	20	13	9	11	6
1988	14	4	5	11	3	2

Winningest Teams' Payroll Ranks, by year. Example: The team with the third-highest winning percentage in the majors in 2009 had the ninth-highest payroll. (It happened to be the Cardinals.) Teams shaded in dark gray had payrolls in the bottom third of all teams for the particular year; teams shaded in light gray had payrolls in the middle third. Unshaded teams had payrolls among the highest third. From 1995 to 2009, 63 percent of teams who finished in the top six in winning percentage were among the top third in spending on payroll. Only 12 percent of the same group came from the bottom third of spending on payroll (table prepared by Zac Cox).

Third, the fact is that the New York Yankees were winners of the World Championship again in 2009 — their 27th championship in 107 seasons of organized baseball, far exceeding any other team in baseball (the Boston Celtics have a better World Championship record — 17 out of 64!). Even more important, they have been the only team to have been in the postseason every year but one since 1996! (Cartoon)[103] They have won the Eastern Division every year between 1996 and 2006 — something which is far more statistically significant than success in the postseason.[104]

It is not true to say, as Professor Zimbalist has, that the Yankees "didn't buy the World Series."[105] The Red Sox are big spenders too — but the payroll and revenue of no team rivals the Yankees (Charts 5, 6). Of course, a considerable number of factors such as "smarts, good team chemistry, player health, effective drafting and player development, intelligent trades, a manager's in-game decision-making, luck and more" explain much.[106] But Zimbalist himself admits superior resources give a team like the Yankees an extraordinary advantage over virtually all others![107]

Ed Stein United Feature Syndicate

The first World Championship in the Obama Administration — the President's mantra — diminished hope for Yankee competitors (Ed Stein: © *The Rocky Mountain News/*Dist. By United Feature Syndicate, Inc.).

Yet by most measures there is more competitive balance and thus presumably more hope and excitement in baseball as opposed to football and basketball. In baseball only 8 of 30 teams are in the postseason, in contrast to 12 of 32 in football and 16 of 30 in basketball, which means that only the very bad teams in these sports are excluded from the postseason. Granted, the Golden State Warriors produced great excitement in 2007 when they made the playoffs and moved past the seemingly superior Dallas Mavericks. But in basketball and football to a lesser extent, the postseason simply means less as a measure for success, competition during the regular season counts for less, and in baseball the number of new teams reaching the postseason exceeds the others. Ironically, the National Football League, which has had complete revenue sharing through national television (traditionally a key part of its revenue), has complained recently of *lack of parity!*[108]

There now seems to be in substantial measure more parity, viewed in some of the ways described above. Selig has proclaimed that parity has never been better — but attributes this to the reforms contained in the 2002 and 2006 collective bargaining agreements. But, as we have seen, more or comparable competitive balance existed prior to the reforms. Thus, there is indeed more competitive balance, and I would attribute it — as did Harvard's Stephen Jay Gould earlier on — to the fact that the baseball population has grown so considerably, and not only includes black players since the time of Jackie Robinson but now foreign players from all over the globe, particularly Latin America and the Far East. It may also be, as Professor Gould argued, this is the principal reason why no one will hit .400 now and that perhaps even Ted Williams, if he were a player today, could not do so.

What will be the player salary impact of these new mechanisms put in place by both the 2002 and '06 agreements? In the short run, immediately after the agreement, it appeared to be depressing the free-agent market. But that trend has not continued.

Initially, in the run-up to the '02 negotiations, the value of major league free agent contracts declined substantially from the winter of 2000-2001, with nearly 30 percent of free agents receiving salaries under $1 million that winter (up from just 8 percent in 1999-2000). Also, the Boston Red Sox expressed interest in shedding baseball's second-most-generous player contract with slugging outfielder Manny Ramirez through waivers (no one bit!), entered into prior to the new collective bargaining agreement, though their stance may have been attributable to Ramirez's personality as much as anything! And, although MVP shortstop-third baseman Alex Rodriguez was willing to accept a reduction in salary from his record-breaking contract, this was vetoed by the Major League Players Association as inconsistent with the 2002 agreement.[109] Although murmurings of collusion re-emerged in 2007, it seems that this is unlikely.[110] As noted above, a key element in the collusion cases of the 1980s was the refusal of clubs to bid for free agents when their previous team wanted to retain them. The competition between the Boston Red Sox and the Oakland Athletics for closer Keith Foulke in the winter of '03-'04, for instance, as well as the club's futile attempts to dissuade outfielder Johnny Damon and pitcher Martinez from accepting the lures of Gotham, seems to make that precedent inapplicable. The poor state of the economy at the turn of the new century could have been a factor in the downswing at that time. Sabathia, Burnett, and Teixeira, all major Great Recession free-agent acquisitions by the Yankees in the winter of '08-'09, as well as John Lackey and Jason Bay in the winter of '09-'10, all make the current free-agent bidding markedly different from what it was in the 1980s.

Another factor which depressed salaries could be the increased use of minor league contracts for marginal players. But this practice began to take root in the early nineties, well in advance of the last two negotiations — and this salary arbitrator, at least, allowed such salary evidence to be introduced in salary arbitration proceedings at that time.

The same tendency to depress salaries is manifested in the case of the clubs' increased reluctance to offer salary arbitration to incumbent players, allowing them to become free agents and sometimes negotiating with them afterwards on that basis. In 2003 the number of refusals to tender had doubled from what it was three years earlier! In 2008, 43 names were on the non-tender list (Chart 7).

TABLE 5.7

Number of Players Not Tendered Contracts, by Year

2009	42	2004	58	1999	39	1994	35
2008	43	2003	46	1998	32	1993	39
2007	28	2002	34	1997	28	1992	16
2006	50	2001	27	1996	48	1991	13
2005	41	2000	28	1995	45		

(Prepared by Zac Cox based on data provided by Major League Baseball Players Association.)

This refusal-to-tender tactic relegates the players to the market, rather than simply accept the inflated values that are associated with the comparability criteria inherent in the salary arbitration procedures for which the players would be eligible if contracts were tendered. In 2010, for instance, designated hitter Jack Cust of the Oakland A's was non-tendered by that team — and signed by the club once he was on the free-agent market at an amount which was demonstrably inferior to what he would have obtained through salary arbitration.[111]

Of course, these provisions have been in the parties' collective bargaining agreement for nearly 4 decades. Until the past two decades, the owners had an aversion to invoking the right to nontender because of their reluctance to deprive themselves of their investment and risk fan ire produced by the departure of popular players. This is why they were so unreceptive to the Charlie Finley idea that all players should become free agents once their contracts expire. Yet the conduct of the owners, beginning in the '90s and continuing into the early years of this century, seem to support his position. The owners have awakened to the fact that the relatively large number of contenders has depressed the free agent market, one mirror image of this being the willingness of Alex Rodriguez to accept a lower salary with the Boston Red Sox than he received just a few years before with the Texas Rangers. But given the economics noted below, with baseball now awash in ever-expanding revenues, that kind of attitude, expressed just seven years ago by Rodriguez, is a matter of history. Moreover, the willingness of Alex Rodriguez to opt out of a quarter-billion-dollar contract and negotiate a better one suggests that baseball's salaries are moving on a sharply upward trend.

True, because all teams except the New York Yankees (and occasionally the Boston Red Sox) have been attempting to keep their payrolls under the threshold, there is some indication that the 2002 agreement had an impact on salaries. At the same time, trades among the clubs seem to involve money considerations to a greater extent than in the past, and the most important development is the fact that the gap between rich and poor is growing, notwithstanding the collective bargaining agreement. As Professor Zimbalist has noted, "[T]he standard deviation, or the dispersion, of opening-day payrolls actually rose to $27.3 million in 2003 from $24.7 million in 2002, an increase of 10.5 percent." In addition, *Business Week* has referred to

> the still-widening gap between what rich franchises such as Yankees pay their players and the pittance parceled out by their poor relations. Even more worrisome: some clubs that are receiving a windfall in revenue sharing have nevertheless slashed their payrolls.
> In 2002, the payroll spread was $91 million — from the Yankees' League-high $125 million to the Tampa Bay Devils Rays' $34 million. [In 2003], the gap between the same teams [was] a staggering $133 million....[112]

But the players are doing well and the problems that have been anticipated for more than three decades simply have not emerged. A fundamental concern of the Blue Ribbon Committee, it is to be recalled, was that competitive balance would be eroded by the unbridled market. Again, beyond the triumph of the small market clubs both prior and subsequent to the 2002 collective bargaining agreement noted above, the fact of the matter is that from 1977 onward, just as free agency was being felt, there was no year except the strike year of '81 when there were more than three clubs either over .600 or under .400 until the beginning of the New York Yankee domination in 1998. The Blue Ribbon Committee focused upon the period of Yankee dominance when there was in '98 and '99 a slight uptick in very good and very bad teams. As noted above, competitive balance is quite different today.

In 2000 there were no teams over .600 or under .400. In 2006, no teams had a winning percentage greater than 60 percent and only two teams won fewer than 40 percent of their games. In 2007 there was no club above .600 and no club below .400. This was the second year since 1900 when this had happened, the first being 2000. Perhaps the welfare state model earlier championed by the National Football League and adopted in 2002 and '06 has had an effect, though the demonstration of parity seems to be much more deeply rooted given the above noted prevalence of this pattern prior to the recent collective bargaining agreements. And, at the same time, by 2009 this trend seems to have weakened. In 2008, two teams were above .600, and three teams were below .400; in 2009, one team, the Yankees, was above .600, and three teams were below .400.

Again, the luxury tax may have had some slight impact. As noted, the luxury tax is aimed almost exclusively at the Yankees and it may be that the Yankees, having signed left-hander Randy Johnson for the 2005 season with less than unqualified success, deliberately passed on centerfielder Carlos Beltran (he left Houston for the Mets) as too expensive. Perhaps the luxury tax encouraged a more perspicacious Yankee posture.

Yet the Yankees quickly paid $52 million for Johnny Damon, the Red Sox' erstwhile heartthrob, who, like David Ortiz, had performed playoff heroics in '04. Beltran, as noted, went on to sign with the Yankees' market rival, the New York Mets, for an agreement that did not seem to harm his financial progress, though it did not bring the Mets to the promised land. Beltran was caught looking at a third strike for the final out that extinguished the team's '06 pennant hopes — and the Mets somehow managed to collapse in '07 after leading the pack most of the way, thus leaving them with the "left at the altar" feeling.

The Yankees wisely passed on Johan Santana, previously of the Twins, and let him sign with the Mets so as to save their resources for the splurge of '08-'09. Perhaps Yankee acumen was promoted by the luxury tax — but that is hard to prove. Again, if one looks at recent years *in toto*, the case for the impact of the 2002 agreement on salary restraint seems to be a difficult one to make. The sum of $1.1 billion is being spent on free-agent salaries today, with those players making an $8 million average. In '00-'01, 119 free agents received $1.2 billion. Of course, this was the year of both Alex Rodriguez and Manny Ramirez. But in '01-'02 the number had already receded to $784 million prior to the 2002 agreement. As noted above, this figure went down in '02-'03 to $509 million. But in '03-'04 the figure bounced back to $823 million shared among 183 free agents. It understates the matter to say that this trend continued in 2006-2007, when 117 free agents commanded $1.655 billion.

This rebound of salaries is attributable to the financial health of baseball. For the fourth consecutive season at the end of 2007, baseball had set attendance records — and attendance was down by only about 5 million in 2009 despite the worst economic conditions in the general economy in decades! Television contracts outlined below have made the pie even richer. Parity by most standards has never been better! From total revenues of $1.8 billion in 1993, baseball has gone to $3.2 billion in '02, $4.6 billion in '05, $5.2 billion in '06, $6.5 billion in '08, and approximately $7 billion now.

The reasons for this are numerous, though the prognosis which the Blue Ribbon Committee may have had in mind — salary restraints, which would make it easier for small-market clubs to compete — clearly is not the one which has transpired. In substantial part these developments are attributable to a factor which the Blue Ribbon Committee focused upon: the extent to which fans and a substantial number of the 30 franchises believe that their team has a shot at the championship. And this is tied directly to the new division alignment and the "wild card" phenomenon. The root of this is the expansion in baseball which has taken place since 1961, producing many schedule changes as well as the expansion which triggered the wild-card concept in 1993. Again, these developments are not attributable, as Selig and baseball owners would have it, to reforms in the collective bargaining agreements of 2002 and 2006.

Expansion and Divisional Competition

Expansion, after all, diminished the potential for believing that one's team was in the race. In 1961 the American League went from 8 to 10 teams and the following year the National League did the same. In 1966 I went to an entire Red Sox-Yankee series at the end of the year to watch the Red Sox prevail over the Yankees and finish 9th (though New York took 2 out of 3) while the Yankees were dead last in 10th place. Though 1967 was to reward my loyalty with an American League championship and the "Impossible Dream" against 100-1 odds, not many fans would pursue their club's fight for 9th place in a field of 10 with the enthusiasm that I displayed that September.

Divisional play, instituted in 1969, was meant to address this problem. The National League resisted the idea, President Warren Giles stating: "It would be a contradiction of baseball history and tradition to divide the league and then see a team that finished fourth or fifth in percentage playing in the World Series." And the New York Mets led the charge, fearing that they would lose home dates with "big draw" teams like the Dodgers, Giants and Cardinals.

But in '69, when both leagues expanded to twelve teams each, a playoff format was adopted with the best-of-five series before the World Series. The effect, admittedly along with the 1969 divisional reforms, was to make baseball more like football (the National Football League had introduced the wild card concept in 1970), basketball and hockey, which have had extended playoff systems, including a majority of the teams in basketball and hockey, so the failure to make the playoffs means that the club is one of the lower-rung teams. The wild card, created alongside of three divisions in 1994, was designed to put a non-division fourth team with the best percentage in the league into postseason play. This concept contradicts baseball's emphasis upon the victory going to the team that can prevail in a long, hard season that includes the hopes of April, the brilliant sunshine of June, the dog days of August, and the exhausting race to the finish in September! As Sparky Anderson once said: "162 games don't lie."

In much the same vein, the *New York Times* said about the wild-card concept when it was first introduced:

> The new system is phony and demeaning to the game. It may even have eroded some of the competitive motivation within divisions, once teams realized that finishing far behind the leader did not eliminate their chances of making the playoffs. While it is true that the wild card slot provides another kind of incentive for struggling teams, baseball is cheapened when teams with sorry records are playing for playoff spots.[113]

Clearly the wild card has been a part of baseball's success, its critics sidelined as "baseball purists" in a bad sense of the expression. Yet a sense of uneasiness exists about the extent to which the regular season has been denigrated in the process. A major problem is whether all teams will play hard against a team in contention. Bill Rigney, manager of the California Angels in '67, told me of how the Red Sox applauded him after his team's defeat of the Tigers on the last day, which clinched it for the Sox. This problem is compounded in a wild-card situation.

In 2007, for instance, the Arizona Diamondbacks, having clinched the Western Division Championship, removed their regulars from a game against the Colorado Rockies, since the Diamondbacks had to focus upon what was in front of them. The Rockies, however, were still in the race and ultimately tied the San Diego Padres to go on and win against that team in a sudden-death one-game playoff and to sweep all rivals in postseason play, the last of which were the Diamondbacks themselves!

Of course, the league system itself—long before any discussion of divisional play and the wild-card concept—can reward teams with inferior won-and-lost records, as I knew in my first season when the Red Sox won 104 games and yet were defeated in the World Series by the Cardinals, who had an inferior won-and-lost record in the regular season. Divisional play exacerbates this. But, as the *Times* properly said, this problem is perhaps unduly exaggerated with the wild card.

In 2007 the rules were changed so as to attempt to reward those who do well in the 162-game schedule and to give the team with the best winning percentage not only home-field advantage throughout the entire playoffs but its choice of what schedule it wants so that it can more easily go with the three-man pitching rotation on four days' rest. The Yankees took good advantage of this in 2009, going to a three-man rotation because of days off in between its games. The difficulty stressed below is that a large number of games were played following days off—in complete contrast to the day-to-day baseball schedule during the regular season—just to satisfy Fox's desire not to compete with football and basketball and thus push the World Series into the cold month of November! Still, this reward, whether flawed (and I believe that it is) or not, is not the answer to the reward problem because it does not sufficiently address the windfall obtained by the worst team, i.e., the wild card, over the best team.

Commissioner Bud Selig has suggested that the wild-card winner be limited to one home game, in contrast to the two which now precede the championship series.[114] Commentator Bob Costas has proposed that the wild card be ditched, with the division winner with the best record given a bye and the other two division winners play to contest the best team, the drawback here being that the division winner with the best percentage might play in a weak division and thus itself get a windfall. Because of the unbalanced schedule (discussed below) it might be that another avenue through which this could be addressed would be to allow the team with the best record to choose the team that it wants to play. The wild card might be much stronger than divisional winners in a weak division.

The third alternative would be to have two wild cards in each league with a quick two-out-of-three series for them in which the survivor plays the division winner in a four-out-of-seven series, the wild card having two of the seven games at its home.[115] This seems to be the way baseball is going.[116] But part of this proposal assumes that the regular season be shortened, and September less important than October, and that runs up against another development which has taken place over the past decade.

This development is interleague play. Interleague play was first adopted in 1997 and it has created bizarre and unfair scheduling during the regular season. In fairness, the problem of scheduling began even before interleague play, as expansion led to so-called unbalanced schedules. Previously each club had played the other 22 times and divided their games 11 home and 11 away—so that, for instance, the Red Sox could play the Yankees more often than they played other teams in other parts of the country, and the same for the Giants and the Dodgers. In 1962–68 each team played the other 18 times, 9 home and 9 away. Natural rivalries would not be thus undercut by the increase in the number of teams—the objection that the Mets raised to two new divisions in 1969. Though the American League reverted to a balanced schedule in '79 and the National League did so in '93, Major League Baseball adopted an unbalanced schedule again in '01.

As indicated above, the unbalanced schedule, however, distorts the wild card because, for instance, the leaders in the West, like the Angels and the Athletics, will have an opportunity to feast on Texas Ranger pitching,[117] but will only play the Red Sox and the Yankees ten times![118] This problem is made worse by interleague play, in which some teams do not play the same teams in the other league that their rivals play. George Steinbrenner protested when his Yankees had to play the Los Angeles Dodgers, but he was silent when the Red Sox had to do it and were swept in 2002. The Mets complained in 1999 that they had a more difficult schedule with six games against the Yankees than the Giants did with six games against the A's.

Initially, when adopted in '97, interleague play made some sense in that teams played other teams in their same division: the AL Central would play the NL Central, thus promoting natural rivalries, e.g., the Cincinnati Reds against the Cleveland Indians. One problem here is that some teams, like the Seattle Mariners, have no natural rivals. In 2002 the interleague system was modified by rotating divisions, still retaining natural rivalries like those between the Oakland A's and the San Francisco Giants, and between the New York Yankees and the New York Mets. (For some reason baseball seems to believe that the Boston Red Sox and the Atlanta Braves fit this category just because the Braves were in Boston before 1953!) The result of all this is a smorgasbord of different teams playing different teams and with the idea that within and without a team's league, sometimes there will be no even distribution of games between each team's park. This, of course, is fundamentally unfair and at odds with the integrity of the regular season competition, the virtue of which the baseball claims to extol!

And there are other problems as well. For instance, there have been numerous two-game series crammed into the schedule. As Dusty Baker said when at the Giants' helm: "This year we have 26 two-game series. Last year we had six. That means 20 more travel days for somebody."[119] (The Mariners had 28 two-game series that year.) Recently, this scheduling problem has dissipated, but it still exists in some measure nonetheless.[120]

An added difficulty is that this makes more infrequent the romance inherent in three- or four-game series that produce moments one can reflect on for years — for instance, the 16 homers that the Red Sox socked off the Yankees in Fenway in '77, driving "Catfish" Hunter from the mound in the first inning of the first game when he yielded four of them. And then there was Bill Buckner's bases-loaded blast off the façade in Anaheim (as it was before renovation) in '84, when the Red Sox obtained a similar three-game sweep, this time away from home.

The attractiveness of interleague play is, of course, the excitement of having new teams, particularly marquee teams, come in to play in a park. The natural rivalries make sense, but sometimes the Indians and the Reds have not played each other because other teams in other divisions may find the Indians, the Red Sox or the Yankees particularly attractive. The San Francisco Giants have been most pleased to have the Red Sox and the Yankees in their park!

The bottom line is as it always has been: money that is distributed to all the owners and stadiums. As *Baseball Prospectus* noted, "Dollar signs always excite Major League Baseball, so it comes as no surprise when Commissioner Bud Selig says interleague play will continue at least until his term expires after the 2009 season. MLB set an interleague attendance record this season [2007] as 8,795,929 bought tickets for the AL-NL matchups. The average attendance of 34,905 was also a record."[121] On the other hand, it has been argued that once the novelty of interleague play begins to dissipate, the bloom may be off the rose. It is clear that the interleague concept has benefited by virtue of the fact that "[t]he interleague games are heavily skewed towards the optimal calendar slots and, as a result, the other games are skewed the opposite direction."[122] Interleague play usually commences in mid–June, when children are out of school, and what are sometimes long trips can be more easily made to ballparks far away from the suburbs and rural areas.

In a far-reaching and perceptive short essay, Gary Gillette and Pete Palmer[123] reiterated not only the point that most of the games are in June, which is a treat for parents with children who have just been released from school duties and assignments, but that "61 percent of interleague games have been played on the weekend, compared to only 46 percent of intraleague games. Scheduling the bulk of interleague games on weekends provides a hidden favoritism and represents an overlooked factor that dramatically changes any attendance assessment." Moreover, the authors quote Ron Blum of the AP as noting that the Florida Marlins once announced a crowd of 28,599 — but not more than 8,000 were actually in the park, highlighting the difference between attendance figures presumably based upon tickets sold and those actually in attendance. They also make the point that interleague play has undoubtedly diminished the cachet of the All-Star Game and, in my judgment, thereby induced Bud Selig to make one of his most foolish decisions ever: to determine that the home-field advantage in the World Series is based upon the victor of the exhibition All-Star Game — the result of which the players care very little about. Gillette and Palmer argue that, for the same reasons, interleague play may have diminished the attractiveness of the World Series itself, because fans have so frequently seen players from competing leagues playing against one another.

In any event, on the eve of wild-card and interleague play in 1993, as each league had moved to 14 teams, the owners proposed three divisions and extended playoffs for the 1994 season. Donald Fehr, the MLPA leader, responded positively and said: "If this is something the fans want to see, we ought to work toward a method of accommodating it. I assume the owners voted for it, at least in part, because that's the case."[124] Though the union had expressed initial concern about the extension

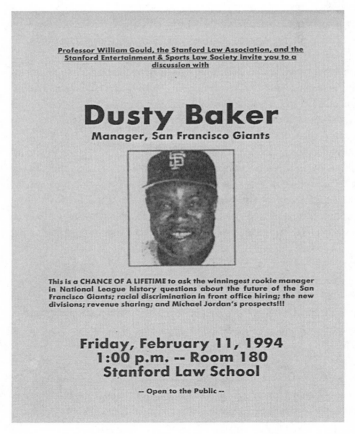

One of the game's most distinguished managers, Dusty Baker, manager of the Cincinnati Reds, Chicago Cubs, and, at the time of this photo, San Francisco Giants. Had his 103 victories been obtained after 1993, the Giants would have qualified for the postseason (courtesy Dusty Baker. Poster prepared by Michael Zubrensky, Stanford Law School '94).

of the regular season schedule from 154 to 162 games in 1961, because of the wear and tear involved in the length of the season, their attitude toward playoffs as well as a wild card was entirely different. The acceptance of each could trigger more compensation, which was not necessarily realized as the season moved from 154 to 162 games.

The '94 strike, of course, made the wild-card issue moot, but in '95 baseball voted to expand by four teams, two in an "expeditious manner."[125] This meant that there would be playoffs between the division leaders and the team with the next-best record, which would become the wild card, the wild card playing the strongest team except when that team was in its own division. Ironically, John Harrington of the Boston Red Sox was the architect of a scheme that did not require the wild card to play the divisional champion with the best record; and in '95, when I traveled to Boston to see Tim Wakefield battered by the Central Division Champion Cleveland Indians in the first wild-card series, the match-up was created by virtue of the fact that Harrington's plan had been rejected. Though there is no substitute for a division championship, the major objective is to get into the playoffs, with wild cards winning the world championship in '97, '02 (both sides in the World Series were wild-card winners that year), '03, '04 and '06. (Indeed, wild-card teams have been successful in football's Super Bowl, with three winning it all!)

One way to both enhance competition and diminish the arbitrariness of interleague play which, as noted, undercuts the integrity of the pennant race itself, is to realign the divisions and perhaps even eliminate the demarcation line between an American League and a National League![126] The separate administration of the leagues as well as their separate umpiring crews have already been eliminated. Lumping together 30 teams into a new set of divisions cutting across the previously established leagues would put the teams, such as Toronto, which has been continuously pushed out of the top spots by Boston, New York and Tampa Bay, into postseason access.[127] Both competition and fairness can be realized if, under any reform, the same teams play the same competition and if more teams with superior won-and-lost records obtained during the regular season have a chance to compete for the World Championship itself.

But in any event, the game is growing exponentially — and much of its success is attributable to increased competition created by the wild card as well as the attractiveness of interleague play. In the final analysis, all sports must share the pie by some mechanism. Neither side can have it all, and although the revenue allocation in any labor-management relationship is necessarily arbitrary, the football and basketball experiences suggest that it can be done (though the latter is so excessively regulated as to be unacceptable to most unions). Unless the baseball players believe that their future salary increases have no limit (that is, until they have 100 percent of the revenues), arriving at an appropriate revenue boundary line is not an insurmountable challenge for the bargaining process, and as of 2011 baseball seemed to be doing well at this. If the parties can continue to meet the challenge, the ensuing stability and certainty in their relationship could make it a less acrimonious one.

The 2006 agreement and the expanded free agency (in the sense that compensation for free agents has been diminished) suggests that all such problems are on a horizon that is considerably distant at present. Baseball has never been so prosperous, a development that seems to move on unabated through the Great Recession of 2007. Beginning with the NLRB's intervention in '95 and the collective bargaining agreement in '96, baseball has indeed drawn back from the precipice and its economic prospects appear to be good. But in the process, for better or for worse, much about the game itself on the field has changed. It is to that matter that we turn in Chapter 6.

Salaries

Off the field, the first and most obvious change is in the area of salaries — a phenomenon which has been at the core of all the debates about competitive balance, luxury taxes, revenue sharing and the like. Salaries have increased more than one hundredfold since Marvin Miller first assumed the position of executive director in the Major League Baseball Players Association, and the figures are even more dramatic when one looks at the past almost sixty-year period.

In 1950 the average player salary was $11,000, which today translates into $98,575. As recently as 1990 that figure was $600,000, worth $991,000 today. On Opening Day 2005 the average salary was $2,632,655. In 2006, 409 players were making at least $1 million. In 2008, 434 players were making at least $1 million, and 85 players reached the $10 million plateau. Median salary held steady for the third consecutive year at the record high of $1 million, and the average salary for the season ending in 2008 was $2,925,679, or an increase of 3.57 percent from the year prior.[128] In 2009 the average baseball salary was just shy of $3 million, with the percentage increase of 2.4 percent since a slight drop in 2004.

As recently as two decades ago Robin Yount of the Milwaukee Brewers led the hit parade of major league salaries with $3.2 million, equaling $4.8 million today. But Manny Ramirez, obtained through the free agency process from the Cleveland Indians, earned $22.5 million per annum until 2009. Alex Rodriguez, whom the Red Sox once sought to obtain from the Texas Rangers (they wanted to deal Ramirez as part of the process), has a quarter-billion-dollar agreement, consisting of $26 million in 2005. Now, as previously mentioned, Rodriguez has gone even higher under an opt-out clause in his contract. Contrast this with the 1940s, when Ted Williams and Joe DiMaggio set new records by negotiating (without any agent, of course) salaries of $100,000 and $125,000 per year, though contemporary player aggressiveness has brought the game back full circle to Babe Ruth. Ruth would have been very much at home in the era of Rodriguez and Ramirez!

To provide some perspective on this matter of salaries, the New York Yankees, who always lead the way financially, went to a payroll of more than $200 million in 2005 and retained that position in 2009 — from $92 million in just the year 2000. The erstwhile Red Sox ace Roger Clemens signed with the Yankees for the second time in 2007 at a $17.4 million salary, which, given the fact that he started playing in June, came out to $5.8 million per month! The Boston Red Sox, attempting to keep apace in second place, went from $77 to $130 million during the same period of time. (In 2006, the payrolls of both the Yankees and the Red Sox declined modestly to $194,464,656 and $120,099,824 respectively, though the former was bumped up over the $200 million mark again through the signing of Clemens.)

In 1990, two decades ago, the teams were at $20,991,318 and $20,983,333 respectively. In today's dollars these team's 1990 payrolls would now amount to $55,017,000 and $54,996,000 respectively. In the wake of free agency in 1977 *the entire payroll* for the Yankees and Red Sox was approximately $3 million for the Yankees and $1,375,000 for the Red Sox!

Revenues

The players have asserted that the owners have not entered into obligations which they cannot afford. Major League Baseball operating income has gone from $765,000, translatable into $5.8 million today, to approximately $130 million in 2005. Again, Major League Baseball revenues for 1993 were $1.8 billion, $3.2 billion in 2002, $4.6 billion in 2005, $5.2 billion in 2006, $5.5 billion in 2007, $5.8 billion in 2008 and more than $7 billion today.

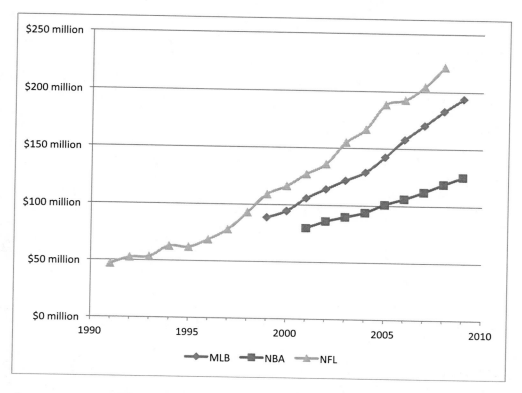

Average team revenue by sport (graph prepared by Zac Cox based on data in *Forbes Magazine*).

As noted above, MLB has unilaterally imposed a 60/40 ratio of assets to liabilities, which the union claims is an attempt to suppress free agent bargaining. But player attempts to thwart such decisions, engaged in without union consent, have thus far failed by virtue of an arbitration award in the 1980s which concluded that the 60/40 ratio rule was not bargainable inasmuch as it was "clearly designed toward protecting the economic stability of teams ... without a demonstrable impact on player salaries."[129] The 2002 collective bargaining agreement suspended the 60/40 rule until 2005–2006 and stated that it may continue "in a manner that does not affect any Club's Major League Player contracting decisions." Judging by the free agent developments in 2006 and '07, club contracting decisions do not seem to have been affected or interfered with to a considerable extent.

In 1950 television and radio revenues amounted to $3.4 million, worth $30.5 million in 2009. In 2000 Major League Baseball signed a $2.5 billion broadcasting contract with Fox Entertainment through 2006, agreed to an $851 million deal with ESPN, agreed to $650 million with XM Satellite Radio, and sold Japanese television rights to its game to the advertising firm Dentsu for $275 million in 2003. In 2006 Fox agreed to pay MLB $257 million per year from 2007 through 2013. Though this constituted a decrease from what Fox was paying, it will be expanding its Saturday coverage from 18 to 26 weeks per season, and they will no longer broadcast any of the division series games and any of the LCS. TBS pays $104 million per year for the right to broadcast all twenty of the division series games and a Sunday afternoon game-of-the-week package. Fox entered into the above-mentioned seven-year contract worth $257 million per year through 2013 and received (1) an exclusive window worth 26 baseball telecasts; (2) the exclusive prime-time rights to the All-Star game and the World Series; and (3) exclusive coverage of the American and National League Championship Series in alternating years.[130]

Gate receipts, through unprecedented attendance records, notwithstanding the decline after the '94-'95 strike (as measured against record-setting 1993), as well as increased ticket prices — $1.60 in 1950 and an average of $25.40 in 2008 — have all helped the revenue stream and financed the rapidly escalating salaries. In 2007, average ticket prices increased 2.5 percent to $22.69, but the 2008 season witnessed a 10.9 percent rise in average ticket price to $25.40. This increase is substantially more than even the 6.3 percent jump in price during the 2005 season. The Red Sox continue to lead the league in average ticket prices, charging fans an average of $48.80 per ticket in 2008. The 1990s parks like Camden Yards in Baltimore, Toronto's Skydome and the new Comiskey Park in Chicago (now called Cellular Field), all were built to hold crowds of more than 50,000; but more recent parks, like those in San Diego and Detroit, have aimed lower, emulating the Red Sox maxim that smaller means higher prices because of demand and supply. Average attendance per game has gone from 16,550 in 1950 to 26,750 fifteen years ago and now to more than 32,000.

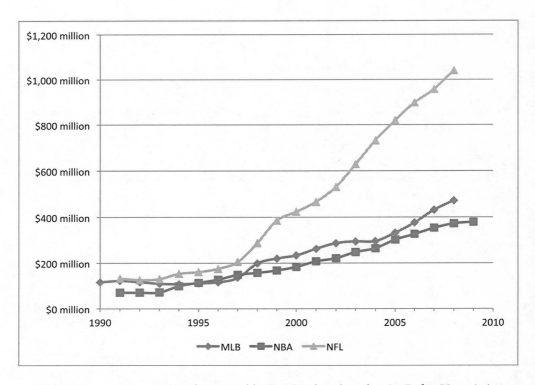

Valuations across sports (graph prepared by Zac Cox based on data in *Forbes Magazine*).

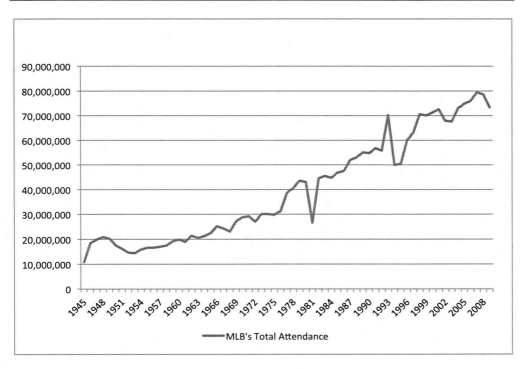

Post–World War II baseball attendance (graph prepared by Michael Scanlon).

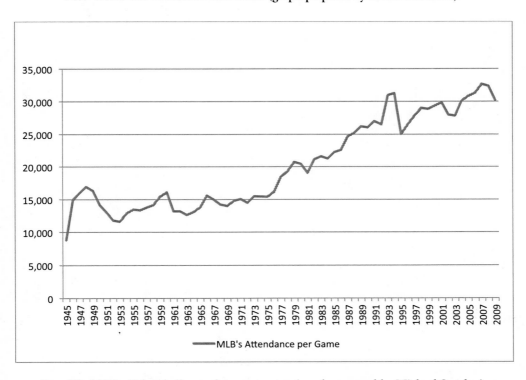

Post–World War II baseball attendance per game (graph prepared by Michael Scanlon).

In 1950 the Philadelphia Athletics franchise value was $2.9 million (worth $26 million today) while the new Washington Nationals, who recently transferred to the nation's capital from the Montreal Expos, fetched a price of $450 million. The average valuation is now nearly $475 million dollars. Revenue is up and so is franchise value. The Boston Red Sox sold to the new ownership for $563 million in 2002, and the Cubs were sold in 2009 for $845 million. The Yankees, purchased by George Steinbrenner in 1973 for $10 million (today's $48.6 million), are now worth an estimated $1.3 billion.

Thus the labor and business changes have all moved in one direction. Many of the new developments are directly attributable to the emergence of the guaranteed contract in the "Catfish" Hunter negotiations and its general acceptance throughout baseball, as well as the investment that clubs have in both pitchers and hitters. All of that in turn is attributable to the free agency procedures negotiated in 1976 and in subsequent collective bargaining agreements.

But the changes in the field are more complicated and frequently related to those that we have seen off the field. And it is to this matter that we turn.

CHAPTER 6

On-the-Field Changes: The Players Speak

Baseball is a game of cycles, as best demonstrated by its long season, in which the prospects for each club can change dramatically over the large number of games that are played (now 162), as well as varying degrees of weather. This is emblematic of the business of things. But the cycles discussed here on and off the field have gone far beyond any given individual season.

Learning the Game

There are a number of changes that have evolved in a continuous pattern during this past half-century plus. The first is that, in contrast to my New Jersey days, children no longer play the game informally on a regular basis, as was the case through the 1960s. In the 1940s we lived, read about, ate, drank, and slept baseball every day throughout the long, hot summer and in the colder March days as well. As Houston Astros pitching coach and former Dodger pitcher Burt Hooton said:

> Older pitchers and players spent a lot of time on their own playing baseball with each other—from young ages on up, there were no adults around, you just got a ballgame together, you went to the schoolyard and played baseball practically all day long. You learned how to play; your instincts became pretty good; you figured out how to win; you were more creative. The evolution of the player today is: most of the time they don't play unless there's an organized workout called or they have select leagues or they have leagues here, leagues there.

Jim Beattie, a pitcher for both the Seattle Mariners and the New York Yankees and subsequently Vice-President of the Baltimore Orioles, says that he played every day informally between the ages of eight and sixteen; this was an important part of building strength and skills relevant to his baseball career. Jon Miller, the broadcaster for the San Francisco Giants and *Sunday Night Baseball*, notes that kids today only play in an "organized" fashion. In contrast to the way that I played as a child, most of the baseball of my sons was played in both Little League and Babe Ruth as well as at the college level (my oldest son played some outfield for Occidental College). This is even more true for my grandson, Joey, who plays in organized and highly competitive baseball tournaments in southern California. Except for our own informal "batting practice" and catches in the driveway or the back yard, as well as running and hitting fly balls on an open Stanford field—probably much more than most youngsters are exposed to — the baseball of my sons was carefully organized.

Then there is the aluminum bat. The aluminum bat has enormous implications for the young players who are learning to play the game — and for many of the changes that have taken place in hitting and pitching. In no other professional sport do the amateur aspirants play with equipment that is fundamentally different in nature from that which will be used professionally. But the fact that players are accustomed to aluminum bats, as opposed to the wooden bats used professionally, has implications which are discussed below.

Talking About the Game

As for the matter of communication about baseball, particularly on the field itself, Yankee catcher Charlie Silvera states:

> When I was a coach with Billy Martin, we had a rule if the catcher two strikes, you go out and remind the pitcher now that he has two strikes, especially in a jam situation. You have to go out and remind them this is what happens in the game. There is not enough talking. There is not enough letting each other know what's going on, calling for a ball. Everybody's quiet, no reminders. This is a game of reminding — do this, don't forget this, remind them, remind them. But nobody does it....
>
> Again, repetition, reminders. But they don't want it. The catchers don't want to go out. A rookie catcher doesn't want to go out and talk to an 8-million-dollar pitcher because he might upset him. True. Our thoughts are "To hell with that." There's no tin gods in our club. I mean, pitchers and Yogi [Berra] would get on him. [Vic] Raschi would say to me — I caught him in Portland — "Get on my fanny when I need it." You don't see that now.... They don't remind them: "Where are you going? You've got your man at second base." You know, people fall asleep. You've got to wake them up sometimes, tell them where they are. Let them know where they are.

Two changes in the game have diminished discussions about the game between players. The first is the switch from railway trains to airplanes as jet travel came in the late '50s and early '60s, and soon thereafter expansion which required plane travel (1958 MVP Red Sox outfielder Jackie Jensen left the game early because he found plane travel to be so stressful). But the players would discuss the game during long train rides when they would be playing cards, eating and drinking together. Airplane travel simply has not allowed for that kind of contact.

The second is that, by virtue of the advent of the Major League Players Association and collective bargaining agreements in the early '70s, players could room by themselves, in contrast to the practice before that. States Red Sox ace Cy Young winner Jim Lonborg:

> You know, I always loved having roommates because it was just an opportunity to really talk about the game of baseball after you had left the clubhouse, and it was just the way life was in those days.... When the union did start to gather some strength, there were more and more calls for individual rooms, if the player wanted it, and the ballclub would have to honor that request. But I don't think I had a private room until I got to ... the Phillies, after a couple of years, probably in 1973, '74 ... they just offered individual rooms to everybody.... I'm not privy to what life is like on the road for the ballplayers now, but I do remember the specialness of having roommates who really loved the game of baseball, and we would spend a lot of time in the clubhouses after ballgames, you know, drinking beers, and guys like Earl Wilson would pick you up, and tell you about all the good things you did in a ballgame, and help you to get your psyche ready for the next ballgame, and to pass — constantly pass on positive

information to make you a better ballplayer, which was the best thing about having a roommate.

Lonborg went on to speculate that the controls on alcohol disrupted some of this camaraderie which, in his view, was a "sad thing ... because there was nothing better than to have a few cold beers ... with your buddies after a victorious game, or especially after a bad game, which can kind of make everything right again."

Cy Young winner Jim Lonborg, ex–Stanford pitcher, the ace of the Red Sox' 1967 "Impossible Dream" (courtesy Boston Red Sox).

The New Players

The advent of black and Latino players, beginning in small numbers in the '40s and '50s from the time of Jackie Robinson of the Brooklyn Dodgers and gradually increasing for the next 20 to 30 years, has been very important. Though the number of black or African American players has declined appreciably, as discussed in Chapter 8, Bobby Doerr's comment in Chapter 1 gives testimony for the proposition that there has been no greater change in the game. More about this later.

Today a disproportionate percentage of the new talent is coming from the Dominican Republic and other Latin American countries like Venezuela, and the Far East (Japan, Korea, and Taiwan in particular) has emerged as well. The advent of such players has coincided with the diminished role of black Americans.

In 1950, when only a small number of black superstars were part of the game, the effect was the most dramatic. Blacks out-hit white players .296–.265, and the All-Star games began to shift in the National League's favor as they possessed the greater number of outstanding black players. The fortunes of teams that excluded blacks, like the Washington Senators, the Detroit Tigers, and the last to integrate, the Boston Red Sox, began to decline in the '50s — though the nearly lily-white Yankees, who brought in Elston Howard in 1955, still flourished. They were the only exception to the rule.

The Players' Size

Another major change is the size of the players. When the Washington Nationals began the 2005 season, the previous dugout occupied by the Senators in the early '70s had to be scrapped because, though the rosters were constant (though the coaching staffs had increased from an average of 3 to somewhere between 7 and 10), the same number of players could not fit in the same space. As Jim Kaat, the former Yankee and Twin pitcher and subsequently a Yankee broadcaster, said: "Someone with Johnny Pesky's physique could not play in the game today."

In 1950 a player who was 5'10" to 6' and 170 to 200 pounds was a big player. The average size of Babe Ruth, Lou Gehrig and the rest of the 1927 Yankees was 5'11", 176 pounds. In 1990 there were half a dozen 200-pound players in the American League Champion Oakland A's lineup. I can recall sitting in lovely box seats in Fenway Park in the spring of 1998 for a Red Sox–Yankee series and noting how big the Yankees were and how unlikely it was that the Red Sox, then of smaller physical stature, would be able to compete effectively with them. ("Mo" Vaughn squeezed a high pop-up to win the first one on Friday night — but the Yankees took 2 out of 3 and the two were by decisive scores!)

The 2009 Boston Red Sox roster averaged 6'1" with a weight of 202 pounds. So-called medium-sized players declined from 75 percent of the total in the late '70s to 45 percent in 2003 — and the larger players enjoyed a greater salary increase from the mid-'80s through this century — 483 percent compared to 300 percent.

Weight training became an important part of baseball conditioning in the '70s. In the 1975 Fenway Park Opening Day between the Red Sox and the Milwaukee Brewers noted above, I witnessed a home run by Fred Lynn which was hit so high that it disappeared beyond the top of the stands and thus appeared as it went off the bat as though it would be a pop-up to the infield. Until the '70s, the conventional wisdom was that lifting weights was not good for baseball players. All of that has changed today. (Lynn's 1975 blast was surely the direct product of the new weight-lifting programs which all players have come to accept — though, as we see in Chapter 7, the problem of steroids and illicit drugs has also been part of the changing size scenario.)

Though this is more difficult to measure, a smaller percentage of the large players today seem to have bulging stomachs. Mickey Lolich, the Detroit Tigers ace of the late '60s and pronounced 1968 World Series fame, had a considerable paunch. Though this matter defies precise measurement, a smaller number seem to fall in that category today.

The Game's Speed

But ultimately, the ambience of the game has been affected by a fairly appreciable change in its length. Again, this may be a matter that moves in cycles. Admittedly, baseball is not the only sport which is criticized for its duration. For instance, of the National Football League it has been said that only 11 minutes of action take place during the entire 3-hour football broadcast.[1]

A little more than sixty years ago the average baseball game was one hour and fifty-eight minutes in length, moving up to 2:38 in 1960. In 2000 this topped out at 2:58 and from 1990 through much of this century the time has hovered between 2:48 and the maximum reached in 2000. In 2006, Oakland A's right-hander Joe Blanton pitched a game the duration of which was 2 hours and 7 minutes in a 7–0 shutout against the Kansas City Royals. In '07 he beat the Twins 1–0 in 1:49. Both efforts were commented upon as remarkable feats!

Now the length of game shows some sign of declining somewhat, down most recently to 2:47. Wrote Richard Sandomir of the *New York Times*: "With rival sports running at faster velocities, baseball cannot afford to let its problematic pace paralyze its recovery [from the '94-'95 strike]."[2] Major League Baseball has taken the view that a number of reforms can quicken the pace of a game that is one of sport's most leisurely: (1) Start innings on time: two minutes and five seconds between innings, with an umpire signaling batting at 1:40. (2) Batters are to stay in the box, something that has been required in both the NCAA and the minors,[3] or else they will be penalized by having a pitch called a strike regardless of its location (but this seems to have happened rarely in fact). (3) Pitchers are to deliver in twelve seconds when the bases are empty—again apparently unenforced (though Detroit manager Jim Leyland told me that he had witnessed instances in which it was enforced). (4) Managers are to have relievers called into the game before they reach the foul line. (Though I thought that the walking entry of relievers as they entered from the bullpen was both stately and dignified—in the '70s they were brought in on little carts, discontinued because of the oil crisis of that era—they now sprint in like joggers in track and field.) As Sandomir writes: "Umpires can prevent incessant or prolonged stoppages by denying a batter permission to leave the batter's box and can order a pitcher to pitch a ball and automatically call it a strike. The rules are in place, but 'there are no parameters for how much clock profligacy is too much,' said Rich Levin, a spokesman for major league baseball."[4]

There are a number of factors at work here. The umpire is told to tell the pitcher between innings that one more warm-up pitch can be thrown at 1:20 out of 2:05 minutes for warm-ups in between innings. At this point the batter is supposed to approach the plate. But some batters do not want to begin to hit until their music is played after the public address announcement is made. Until the 1960s no public address announcements were made in Fenway Park after the lineup had been announced and after the lineup had batted one time around at the beginning of the game. This changed in the '60s—the Giants' slugger Jack Clark was announced to "Staying Alive." At some point in the '90s music was played for specific batters—usually the music that was one of their favorites, just as relief pitchers (and the increased frequency of relief pitchers has increased the length of the game) want their own music (San Francisco Giant closer Robb Nen made an entrance to the particularly dramatic "Smoke on the Water"). Until the '90s at Fenway anyway, there was no music—only the tasteful organist John Kiley, who played between innings and would end each Red Sox victory with three triumphant notes when the game was concluded.

Rather than imposing sanctions such as a strike for a delayed pitch by a pitcher, the umpires will frequently say: "You need to pick up the pace." This problem is compounded by frequent conferences at the mound between catcher and pitcher and infielders and pitcher—the bench being restricted to one or two visits in a particular inning. In the 2009 World Series, Jose Molina, the Yankee backup catcher, made frequent visits to the mound when a runner was on base. Some managers believe that this will undercut the defense's ability to stay alert. Carlton Fisk, when with the White Sox, was regarded as a frequent offender.

The overriding theme here—as with pitchers and batters backing off and in and out of the home plate area and the pitcher's mound—is what Mike Port, the respected Vice-President of Umpiring, calls "too much information." In an age of video replays and observation of the other team's tendencies, let alone its ability to steal signs as the Yankees apparently thought the Phillies were doing in the '09 World Series, the potential for delay grows considerably. There is what Port calls a "preponderance of information" which interferes with the speed of the game. It may be that the new Selig committee will fashion new rules relating to the frequency of any kind of visit to the mound when it reports.

But there is more here — Tom Verducci[5] has pointed out that major league pitching stats in April 2010 averaged 7.1 strikeouts per innings, the highest rate of all time, a statistic that has continuously increased since the 1980s. During the same period the team walk rate of 3.7 per 9 innings was the highest since 2000. This means, he notes, that there are 10.8 non-contact plate appearances per 9 innings, up 37 percent from 1980 and 24 percent from the year of the pitcher, 1968. The Red Sox and the Yankees are the most notorious long-game artists because of their ability to engage in wars of attrition to get the pitch count up.[6] This is because the Red Sox and Yankees are so disproportionately represented among players who have faced the greatest number of pitches per plate appearances for 2009.[7]

Inevitably this problem is tied to two others — the number of pitchers employed and the rising significance of pitch counts for each pitcher. A variable most associated with the length of the game is the number of pitches thrown.

Of course, there are other problems as well. As noted, the strike zone is one of them. Bobby Cox, the manager of the Atlanta Braves, said to me that many pitches that he believes to be strikes are called as balls, and Dusty Baker has affirmed this to me in a number of conversations. This is in part attributable to the reluctance of umpires to call the so-called high strike at the letters.

Moreover, in the wake of September 11, 2001, all of the teams took to playing "God Bless America" in the 7th inning — the Yankees also including references by announcer Bob Sheppard to the Iraq war and how it was a struggle for democracy (which it was not) — even though "The Star-Spangled Banner" had already been played at the beginning of the game. Surely the 7th inning, which includes standing up in the bottom of the inning (when one supports the visiting team one stands up in the top of the inning) and "Take Me Out to the Ball Game" consume enough time already.

In some measure, however, I subscribe to the view expressed by Tigers manager Leyland when he said to me, "If you go to a good movie, the time doesn't matter. On the other hand, if you go to a bad one you want to leave it right away." In an era when baseball is competing with other sports, however, this view does not seem to get a lot of attention. Some of the problems seem to be fairly intractable, such as the lengthening of games through extended commercial breaks and pitching changes — and there are many more pitching changes! As Colorado Rockies coach Marcel Lachemann said:

> They talk about speed of the game relative to years ago, but you've added 2–2.5 minutes for radio and TV between every inning; 2–2.5 minutes with every pitching change. It used to be the guy would come in, throw his pitches and be ready to go; well, now you have to wait for that commercial to be over. It goes back to the fact that we're in the entertainment business and you need to get the dollars. I don't think the game takes that much longer. When Mike Hargrove used to play, we called him the human rain delay — nobody made a big deal out of it. As long as the fans have action, they don't care.

Mike Port notes that it is the *pace* of the game rather than the *length* of the game which ought to be critical. Port states that a game can be quite interesting even if it goes three and one-half hours and the score is 5–4 — and not 1–0. The objective of the umpires is to keep the game moving, and within the context of rules which allow for frequent visits to the mound by players, he believes that the game is being handled well by the umpires. Port says: "Do we want the players to have their own headsets so that information can be transmitted to them that way, such as is done with quarterbacks in football?" He contends that that might offend sensibilities and the ambience of the game considerably more than the pace does.

Finally, advertising is particularly valuable in the postseason games, and it is no coincidence that the length of the spectacular 2003 postseason play — the Red Sox and Yankees were the prime culprits — ballooned to 3:25. In 2007 a Saturday night postseason Red Sox-Indian game of eleven innings went to 1:30 A.M.! For reasons noted below, the multiple pitching changes, during which more advertisements and commercials are run, will not diminish appreciably. Short-run commercial interest and the perceived need for the owners to enhance revenues go against the grain of shorter games. To compound matters, the importance of pitch counts, in which hitters have become more adept at fouling off pitches, is another important factor, particularly in some of the contentious Red Sox-Yankee games which have received so much attention in this past decade. And this, in turn, means more time taken for the entry of relief pitchers.

And to compound matters further, during the postseason period, the effort to get the West Coast audience means that many games cannot start before 5:00 P.M. Pacific Daylight Savings Time-which means that they begin after 8:00 P.M. in the East. This means that these games, which are often contentious and hard fought, will sometimes, as was true in 2004 American League Championship series, run into extra innings that are played until midnight or after on the East Coast. In 2007, because of the concern with keeping the Red Sox — Cleveland ALCS at prime time — 5:00 P.M. Pacific and 8:00 P.M. Eastern — the spectacularly exciting Colorado-Arizona NLCS was being played, and indeed started, long after most Easterners had retired for the night.[8]

Aside from exhausting the old fans, the next generation of baseball's fan base must turn in to bed when the games are just beginning. And to make matters worse, the mandate of advertising means that baseball is unwilling to play one single contest in the World Series games during the daytime, as was done traditionally until 1971. Again, a generation of young fans loses out through decisions of this kind. Though short-term profits do well under such circumstances, this does not seem to be a good way to do business in the long run.

The Minor Leagues

Another important change which affects so many issues arising in baseball today is the decline of the minor leagues. Again, one must be careful to qualify this commentary with the importance of baseball's cycles. In the '40s and '50s there were seven layers to the minor league system, going from Triple A through class D. The televising of major league baseball initially decimated the minor league system, leaving it with four levels, if one counts class A, rookie league, as a separate step. Now, however, the minor league system has achieved a measure of revival as, beginning "in the 1980s, when a new breed of businesslike well-heeled owner began expanding the market, bringing not only new cash but the expectation of making money."[9] In 2007 minor league baseball, like its major league counterpart, broke all attendance records![10]

In 1949 there were 448 minor league baseball clubs and 59 leagues before the decline noted above. At that point annual attendance was 39.8 million, plummeting to 9.7 in 1962. But now it has resurrected to 34.7, producing ten million market values at the Triple A level, as well as a growth of new independent leagues which have become recruitment grounds for MLB!

Still, the number of farm hands in the minors competing for major league jobs is dramatically less than what it was more than six decades ago. In 1950 there were 26.7 minor leaguers per major league job. In 1990 this had declined to 5.9, coming back to 8.3 in 2002. This means that a number of people looking over the shoulders of major leagues has declined by approximately 60 percent in the past half century. This fact, along with extended continental travel schedules, seems to be responsible for the idea that players should have an occasional day off, and perhaps the number of players who are on the disabled list due to injuries like pulled groins. The ball players from the '40s through the '60s maintained that they would have found a way to play through some of these injuries, given the competition waiting in the wings. Charlie Silvera sums it up well:

> Casey [Stengel, manager of the Yankees in 1949 and the '50s] did a good job because he controlled everything. He didn't care if you didn't feel well. If you showed up — just like with Yogi [Berra, Yankee catcher]. For instance, one day I'm sitting there at the clubhouse, I gotta get out there early to make sure my uniform was still there and somebody else hadn't taken it. So anyway, the trainer came in, and Casey used to walk around the clubhouse. The trainer came in and said, "Casey, Yogi just called and says he doesn't feel well. He's not going to show up today." And Casey said, "You tell him to get his fanny out to the ballpark. I might need him." ... Yogi never pulled that again. He always came out to the ballpark. And he was there. He's going to be a better player than I am, even if he isn't feeling well. Potentially I mean with the bat.... [Certain left-handed hitters] get out of line with a left-handed pitcher.... [Todd] Walker [Red Sox 2003 second baseman], he'd take a hike. You think Williams would do that? You think any of those Red Sox or any of those Yankees would do that? They were paid to play. They had a certain amount of pride.

But, as noted, the decline of the minors means that there are fewer players with the capability to look over the shoulder of a major leaguer and threaten him with immediate job loss. At the time of Stengel, Berra, and Silvera, colleges were not important as part of the *de facto* farm system or a recruiting ground. As noted in Chapter 1, college baseball has never enjoyed the popularity and revenue possessed by football and basketball in substantial part because of the fact that the college game came along after the pros had established themselves and the frequency with which the game is played. In football and basketball the opposite was the case, with college football emerging at least a couple of decades before the National Football League, and in the case of basketball substantially in advance of the first major professional league, the Basketball Association of America, in 1946.

As Reds Manager Dusty Baker notes, now the colleges have become a surrogate for the minors, particularly at the B and C level. As Baker said:

> Now, they're using the college level as class B and C, which really saves money at the big league level. Plus, when I came up, they preferred high school players, possibly because some of the kids were more mature coming out of high school; most of them had more sense of responsibility. Whereas, now, they would prefer a college player because he's used to being away from home, it's not as big a risk on investment, you get a return on your investment in a shorter period of time — you give a kid a bunch of money and in 2 years, he's in the big leagues, whereas a high school player, you figure it'll take 4 or 5 years to get to get to the big leagues.

College players who are not drafted out of high school or who do not commit to a team prior to enrollment in college are not eligible for the amateur draft process until the completion of their junior year.

The overall result of this is that players have less of a portfolio prior to their arrival in the major leagues and require more on-the-job training at that stage. For instance, in pitching, in 1950 there were seven 20-game winners in Triple A. In 1990 there were none in all of the minor leagues! The same was true in 2006. In 1950 there were nine players with thirty homers or more in the minors. In 1990 there was one in all of the minor leagues. In 2006 the trend had reversed, with 6 30HR hitters in AAA, 2 in AA, and none in A. Either power is emerging anew or players are being provided more seasoning in AAA and AA.

The phenomenon of declining minor league portfolios is the mirror image of the emergence of first-rate college baseball programs like those at Stanford, the University of Texas, Southern California and Louisiana State. These programs are a factor in the decline of the minors, though attendance and franchise value have had a considerable resurgence over the past two decades. As in football and basketball, the colleges nonetheless remove the expense burden from the major leagues.

However, they operate under playing practices which are dissimilar in a number of respects. As St. Louis Cardinals manager Tony LaRussa says:

> A good college program gives a player certain pluses in his development. It's not the same as if he played April to September in the minor leagues, day-in, day-out. All you're doing is grooming your-self to be a major leaguer — it's not the same. College isn't bad, but if you're talking about a quality minor league development program where all you do from April to September is work on being a good major league player, you can't compare that with going to college and studying and working out.

One classic example of the differences is the fact that so many pitches in college ball are called by the coach from the bench, whereas this is a rarity at the professional level. As managers like Dusty Baker and Jim Leyland note, signals are often flashed for pickoff throws, pitchouts and even conferences at the mound in the majors, but rarely the pitch itself. Says Baker:

> The only thing we call are pitchouts, throwovers, and stepoffs to stop the running game. But I believe in letting the catcher call the game because he's underneath the hitter, he's working with the pitcher, he knows what his best pitch is, what his other pitch is. What hurts us is, by the time we get a lot of kids out of high school and college, especially catchers and pitchers, they've never called a pitch. All the pitches come from the bench, so we get them and we have to school them on how to call a game. It's like being a passenger in a car: you'll never learn your way around town until you learn to drive.

True, in the 1987 National League Championship playoffs between the St. Louis Cardinals and the San Francisco Giants, Giants manager Roger Craig was televised in the dugout flashing signals on every pitch. Though it was generally assumed that most of these signs were meaningless and had nothing to do with most of the pitches thrown by his hurlers, in fact, Craig's policy was to call pitches from the dugout. However, this appears to be the exception to the rule.

With regard to the colleges, Lachemann, when asked if colleges are a surrogate for the minors, replied:

> Not really. I'm sure there's a lot of very good instruction going on in college baseball, but college coaches are there to win so they can keep their jobs, not for development. In the minors, you're still trying to win but you're there mainly to develop players. So you will pitch guys who might not be very good right now but, down the line, they're going to learn how to pitch — those aren't going to pitch in college. A lot of your college pitchers who come out who've done real well — for a lot of them, that's as far as they're going to go. Guys that may have a lot of physical ability but don't know how to pitch quite yet, they get kind of pushed aside because you have to win in college ball, there's an urgency to win right now. You can't develop a guy for 3 or 4 years down the road because he'll be gone.... You're not pitching that much, you're not on a 4-day rotation, the whole series is on the weekend, and if you're not abusing people, they're probably just going to pitch one game if you're a starter, so you're

basically pitching one game a week. You get into a minor league system and now you're pitching on a 5-day rotation and learning how to pitch — it's what it's all about. The other thing — it's not a knock against college coaches — there's a lot of programs where almost all the pitches are called, so the thought process isn't being developed like it is where you have to think for yourself, learn to call your own pitches, and do all the other little things.

It seems clear that the minor leagues remain an important part of baseball training. While the Curt Flood Act of 1998 did not affect the minors directly, it is often said that *Federal Baseball* should not be reversed *in toto* because of its impact upon the minors: the territorial monopoly given to teams like San Jose or Fresno would be eroded if antitrust law were applicable. But still the question is whether this would mean the decimation of the minor leagues or any other serious impact.

The rise of the independent leagues in so many of the minor-league markets suggest that the answer to this question is not as easy as it has been assumed. Congress should take a careful look at this so as to assess the empirical evidence that has emerged with the independents — their salary structure is obviously lower than the minors — and whether this suggests a viability which can be preserved even with a more sweeping reversal of *Federal Baseball*.

The Pitching–Hitting Balance of Power

It was a precipitous decline in hitting and an excellence in pitching — quite the reverse role of the past few years — which set in motion the series of changes in baseball beginning in the 1960s. It all began with the success of some of the hard-throwing brushback pitchers like Bob Gibson of the St. Louis Cardinals and Don Drysdale of the Los Angeles Dodgers. Carl Yastrzemski won the batting title in 1968, hitting only .301, the lowest average to win a title since George (Snuffy) Stirnweiss's batting championship of .309 in 1945. Meanwhile Bob Gibson mowed down National League hitters with an unbelievably low ERA of 1.12 in '68, and Luis "El Maestro" Tiant, whose career revived with the Boston Red Sox in 1972, possessed a 1.91 ERA at that point. Changes were necessary to produce more offense and consequent excitement for the fans.

It was one thing to sit behind home plate as I did in 1980 and watch the fabulous Mike Norris's sweeping curve ball as he reached new heights for the Oakland A's. It was exciting to see the tremendous break in the ball when Tom Gordon emerged with the Kansas City Royals in 1989 and to witness the big breaking curve that came off the fingers of Bert Blyleven as he toiled for the Minnesota Twins. But the average fan was not as interested. More excitement and offensive production were demanded, and those demands were soon met.

In 1969 the pitching mound was lowered from 16 to 11 inches. Though the rule was unevenly enforced (it is said that Koufax and Drysdale did better at Chavez Ravine because the mound was even higher there), this was obviously done in direct response to the Gibson performance.

Equally important, the American League introduced the designated hitter rule in 1973, which allowed a non-position player to hit in the place of the pitcher. The objective here was to create more offense in the lineup — more runs, more hits, more runs produced and more home runs. Many veterans who were about to retire because of the decline in their fielding abilities, like Orlando Cepeda of the San Francisco Giants, saw their careers extended — in Cepada's case as a DH with the Boston Red Sox in '73 when the rule was first instituted. And the rule is undoubtedly a major factor in the superior batting records in the American League and its general superiority — a role reversal from the National League's dominance in the 1950s, the product of the disproportionate number of black hitters in that league.

Decades of strategy had been based upon the role of the pitcher as a hitter and whether a manager should pinch hit for him in a given situation. This was now cast aside in the interest of more offensive production and putting the ball in play. The role of the manager and managerial strategy seems to have been diminished in the American League as a result. The late Bill Rigney, infielder for the New York Giants and manager of the California Angels as well as the San Francisco Giants, said:

> With the DH, [managing] has to be different because you don't have to make a decision about hitting for the pitcher. With the pitcher hitting in the National League, the 6th inning is the toughest inning for the manager; that's the decision inning — "Should I let him hit? He's still pitching pretty good and we're only a run down but the bases are full." I've always felt this way about managing, even with the DH: after 6 innings, if our club hasn't put our guy ahead, then it's my game to win or lose — me, the manager, I'll make the decision. Even though you're pitching a shutout, we're 0–0, I've had enough, you've had enough, that's it. If we have a lead, then I operate differently, but I think the 7th, 8th and 9th are the manager's innings where he has to make the proper decisions.

Still, managers like Jim Leyland and Tony LaRussa, who have also managed in both leagues differ. States LaRussa:

> I think that's one of the misconceptions of the American League. In my opinion it's harder to handle an American League pitching staff than a National League one because every decision you make is based on who you think should pitch to that next hitter. A lot of times it's very tough — a guy is starting to lose it but he's doing OK and you don't know about your reliever. In the NL, if the pitcher is coming to bat, you take him out of there. So I think it's tougher managing an AL pitching staff. That stuff about switches is overplayed.

The decline of the bunt was in part promoted by this change because pitchers (as well as other weak hitters in the lower part of the order), who did not normally possess good hitting skills, were taught to bunt to advance runners on the bases. As bench coach DeMarlo Hale of the Red Sox said to me: "We're not a bunting team ... you have to know your personnel, and you've got to manage your personnel."

Again, the DH rule meant that power-hitting players who were either poor defensively or whose physical condition had deteriorated so as to undercut their ability to move quickly in the field saw their careers extended. Correspondingly, the careers of .217 career hitting shortstops like Del Maxvill, who played for the Cardinals in the '60s and '70s, came to an early end. Said Lonborg:

> I think the quality of the lineup, one through eight, is probably much stronger now than it was then just because the development of the players — the guy that's hitting number eight is probably a .260 hitter, a .270 hitter, where in those days you did have the pitcher who was, you know, not much of an issue, and you did have your eighth hitter who was probably your Del Maxvill, your Ray Oyler–type of ballplayer, and maybe even your seventh hitter was suspect — except for the great teams, like some of the great Cardinals teams and the Pirates teams in those days, and the Cincinnati Reds in the '70s had strong lineups all the way through.... I really think the quality of the hitters in the lineup, in the American League, especially ... provides a lot more strength one through nine in those days just because they don't — they want young guys who can hit .260, .270, maybe a little bit of pop. And that wasn't the case forty years ago.

The early '70s also brought a new-found focus upon physical strength for the hitter to produce more and, as noted, the aluminum bat was introduced in all of amateur baseball so as to reduce the cost associated with wooden bats, which were so frequently broken.

Little League first used the aluminum bat in 1971 and the NCAA permitted its members to use them in '74, a move fueled by economic concerns because of the high cost of replacing broken wooden bats. The primary benefit ultimately was seen as the increased performance potential of aluminum bats, which produced more hits and runs. Today the aluminum bat has become the standard one at virtually all levels of amateur baseball, though it is not required. The safety of such bats, because of the rapid speed at which the ball is propelled and the consequent injuries for pitchers, has been an ongoing controversy.[11] But today there is a fundamental dividing line between amateur and professional baseball: virtually all amateur baseball uses the aluminum bat and all professional baseball uses the wooden bat. The latter adheres to its position because of the view that the aluminum bat is inconsistent with the game's integrity, and that one of the sweetest sounds of the game is the crack of the bat as the ball is hit. But there are problems aplenty by virtue of this difference between amateur and professional — a difference which does not exist in any other major sport!

The introduction of the aluminum bat made it difficult for pitchers to pitch inside. If a pitch was on the inside of the plate a hitter could produce a base hit and in some instances a long ball as well. When a hitter with a wooden bat was jammed in on the fists he would be "sawed off" with a broken bat flying in different directions. As Dusty Baker has said, hitters have been fearful of swinging at inside pitches with wooden bats because they would get "piano nails or electric tape." Particularly if the weather was chilly, from the time of sandlot ball onward, anyone who played the game did not want to get a pitch on the hands of the wooden bat. Jim Lonborg spoke to me about the way in which Red Sox pitching coach Sal "the Barber" Maglie, the former hard-throwing pitcher from the Giants and Dodgers in the 1950s and erstwhile Mexican leaguer, had taught him, Lonborg, to pitch inside effectively with the "brushback" pitch which so infuriated the Yankees one warm June night in New York. Much of this changed with the aluminum bat because of the good results for the hitter when pitched inside — and this had an impact on the behavior of both the hitter and the pitcher.

Pitchers at the amateur level were now afraid to come inside because of the enhanced advantage for hitters with the aluminum bat and the ability of so many hitters to produce base hits on pitches that would produce nothing with wooden bats. As former Dodger pitcher and Houston pitching coach Burt Hooton says:

> Guys don't have control inside yet because they've never been taught to pitch close to a human being. And when you pitch close to a human being, there's a fear factor that you're gonna hit him — you don't want to hurt anybody. But the other side of the coin is you have to play the game and pitching inside, knocking somebody off the plate a little bit, is part of that game. Your intent is not to hit them, your intent is to let 'em know: hey, I'm not gonna give you a free ride to that outside part.

Says Baker:

> Back in my day and even before me, they'd see if you could hit a fastball; then they'd see if you could hit a breaking ball; then they'd see if you could hit a changeup; if you hit all those, they'd try to intimidate you and see if you could hit on your back. Nowadays, that doesn't work because they have the no-knockdown rules. Imagine Willie Mays and Hank Aaron hitting with the league reprimanding Gibson and Drysdale for throwing at them. Now pitchers can be ejected for throwing at you where, before, if a pitcher wanted to throw at you 4 times,

he could throw at you 4 times and nobody said a thing. That's big. That's real big. Imagine guys like Barry Bonds that stand on top of the plate: how many times would Gibson or Drysdale have drilled him? Especially with no arm pad — he'd have been drilled every day.

Contrast this with how Jim Kaat describes Yankee third baseman Alex Rodriguez diving into the pitch with his left shoulder. States Kaat:

Alex Rodriguez ... dives into the ball with a shrugged shoulder, and they're just not accustomed to being pushed off the plate. So a lot of times those pitches are 6–8 inches inside. And because it's such a surprise to the hitter, right away they want to go to the mound. I think that's what provokes more fights. And years ago if you threw the ball up and in to the guy, he was almost proud that you had that much respect for him that you would knock him off the plate. It's kind of a badge of honor.

Former Boston Red Sox first base coach Lynn Jones says:

Hit batsmen and guys charging the mounds — a lot of it is unnecessary, a lot of it is showmanship, a lot of it has nothing to do with the game itself. If you watch the game and understand its development, you understand that guys will charge the mound when they get hit by a curveball, but it's not the situation to be hit, so they misread the situation and don't act accordingly. The problem with a lot of it is that the umpires have an edict making them get involved with how the game is supposed to be developed as far as gamesmanship and sportsmanship. This game has been played for a long time and teams will police themselves: if you need to get hit, you get hit. Ninety-nine percent of the time, that other team knows why, but when somebody throws inside and gets knocked down accidentally and the umpire doesn't understand the overall reason, he throws a warning and then the other team wonders why because there's no clearcut reason. Teams will police themselves in the sportsmanship of the game.... It used to be that when you got hit, there was a purpose for getting hit. If you took a 3–0 hack because you were trying to go deep and you fell down and the next pitch was up and in, then OK — I missed my shot and he had his shot. If he hits me, I go to first base and the next guy comes up. If I had 3 or 4 hits in a game and I owned that pitcher, I expected to get thrown at — that was part of the game. Now, that's not part of the game because the umpires and the commissioner's office have taken that away from the pitchers.

More than twenty years ago, Dr. Bobby Brown, the former third baseman for the New York Yankees and president of the American League, commented on the changes in attitudes vis-à-vis players and hitters:

The only change is that there's more of a tendency for hitters and pitchers to try and confront each other in a physical manner. We had very little of that in my day. A pitcher throwing close to hitters was not unusual. Occasionally a hitter would get hit but if the ball came close, since the hitter expected that it might come close, he didn't immediately charge the pitcher. There were other ways to retaliate besides having that one-on-one confrontation and then team-on-team confrontation. It happened occasionally but not very often. There were other ways that you tended to try and even the score up. You just remembered [what happened] and didn't answer in the next 5–10 minutes.

Of course, the DH rule has exacerbated this problem, given the fact that the pitcher does not bat in the American League and the attempt to retaliate against a perceived culprit, a pitcher who is deliberately throwing at the hitter, is gone. In the National League, where the pitchers hits, there is a potential to retaliate. Says Bill Bavasi, former general manager of the Seattle Mariners:

I think hitters should get hit more and they should get hurt more because they dive; they have no fear. Look at tapes of Yogi Berra hitting or Roy Campanella — we all got yelled at for stepping in the bucket — that's all they did was step in the bucket because their first movement was to avoid getting hit. Their styles of hitting were not like they are now; now they're just diving in.

And there is another factor here as well, which Milwaukee Brewers Coach Dave Nelson stresses, i.e., the involvement of managers and coaches in this process and the extent to which they can have fingers pointed at them for the making the wrong decision:

> There are pitching coaches who believe in pitching away because that's how they want to get their outs because it's hard to find good pitchers who can pitch inside. A guy tries to pitch inside and misses, well, that pitch is out of the yard. More mistakes are hit inside than away — the coach figures that if the pitcher makes a mistake away and the batter hits it out, then I'll tip my cap to him, but if he makes a mistake inside and hits it out, then that's on me. So they'd rather pitch away — they'll pitch in a little bit to keep a guy honest.

And the number of hit batsman has increased appreciably since 1946. The number of instances in which batters are hit has skyrocketed from an American League average of 17.88 in 1946 to 63 in 2003. National League statistics, while not as dramatic, nonetheless have witnessed a threefold increase in the average number of hitters who are hit by pitches. (See chart).

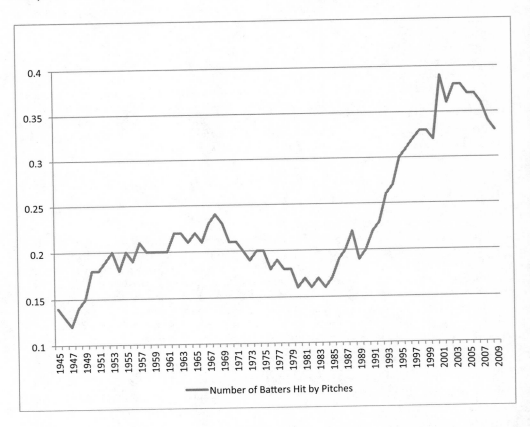

Numbers of batters hit by pitches per game (prepared by Mike Scanlon based on the data presented in the Baseball Reference website. See http://www.baseball-reference.com/) (courtesy David W. Smith of Retrosheet. A copy of the original graphs in the paper can be found at: "From exile to specialist: The evolution of the relief pitcher," Retrosheet.org, June 23, 2000, p. 1.1).

The AL-NL differential statistics established a reasonably clear nexus between hit batsmen and the introduction of the DH rule since the NL does not have the DH. From 1973 through the mid–1990s the rate of hit batsmen in the AL was anywhere between 3 percent and 30 percent higher than the NL. Theories have been traditionally advanced, including: (1) the "moral hazard theory," which is that AL pitchers don't fear retaliation with the presence of the DH and are therefore more apt to hit opposing batters because they don't bear the cost of their actions directly; and (2) the "lineup composition theory" that since the DH and others in the lineup are greater offensive producers, the pitcher is more likely to hit them than a typical weak-hitting full time pitcher.[12] Lee A. Freeman suggested a variation on this theme that says AL pitchers do not have an opportunity to ease up their delivery to opposing pitchers, because they wanted to pitch inside to increase the chances of hitting those batters.[13] Two other factors complicate this story somewhat: (1) the rate of hit batsmen in the AL exceeded the NL prior to the introduction of the DH, going back to 1967; and (2) in the 1990s the gap compressed and was even.

Some believe that the differential in hit batsmen in the leagues is caused by the fact that American League umpires (this is prior to the merger of the AL and NL umpires into one body) used the old-style "balloon" chest protector, and that this forced them to stand more upright and therefore call more high strikes. The difficulty here is that there is no shown correlation between high strikes and hit batsmen. It may be that the compression of the differential between the AL and NL in the '90s is due to the implementation of the so-called "double-warning rule" in 1993, which raised the cost of hitting batters, because the cost was placed upon the pitcher and manager, who could be immediately ejected and sanctioned further. Also, the double-warning rule was instituted just at the time of expansion, when there were more inexperienced pitchers who may not have known how to pitch inside. The idea of Bradbury and Drinen is that this gave NL pitchers less fear because they know that the opposing team dare not hit them or they will suffer, whereas AL pitchers have more fear because of the possibility that they could be ejected even without the double-warning if the umpire believes that the pitcher is deliberately throwing at the hitter in an egregious fashion.

It seems as if the evidence supports the view that the better batter composition rule is the correct one, i.e., that "better batters are positively associated with hit batters."[14] Moreover, the evidence supports the view that teams hit batters as a form of retaliation because the pitchers are more likely to be hit the inning after hitting a batter. Further, since there are more, better batters in the AL, it follows that this may be a factor in the greater number of hit batsmen. In the AL the pitcher cannot be hit because he does not bat.

And then there is the matter of equipment that hitters have taken to wear just over the past two decades.

As big sluggers in recent years such as "Mo" Vaughn, David Ortiz and Barry Bonds have taken to wearing protective elbow pads and gear, the Commissioner of Baseball in the Major League Baseball Players Association agreed in 2000 to standardize elbow protective equipment, providing that a player's elbow protection pad cannot exceed ten inches in length and that a "non-standard" pad cannot be used in the absence of certified injury. The view has been that this agreement changes nothing and that players will continue to lean and dive into the pitch with relatively little fear. In fact, this is because the changes have made hardly any difference because the big hitters were wearing pads that were rarely longer than twelve inches in any event. As Jim Kaat said: "The protective equipment allows hitters to dive in, gives pitchers less control and in the process we have more hand injuries because the hitters are not holding their hands back." Says Billy Wagner, while performing as the New York Mets' closer: "It's getting ridiculous. It's to the point you can't throw a ball inside, the guy just leans in and takes it. Pitchers need to make a living in there, but a lot of times you just can't."

Says former Chicago Cub third baseman Ron Santo: "They pitched inside when we played." This is confirmed by his teammate Billy Williams, who says: "We couldn't step in covering the home plate ... we couldn't do that ... some pitcher like Don Drysdale would say 'You better unloosen your top button.'" Santo speaks about being hit in the face by a ball when he was twenty-six years old. So many of the ex-players speak of being pitched hard inside as a "badge of honor and respect." The pitcher backed you off because you were so dangerous and you expected and understood that. As Dusty Baker said: "You expected to get knocked down"—particularly after you or one of your teammates had enjoyed success at the plate!

Not so today. The pitchers coming inside on hitters will produce a glare, and the hitter may threaten or actually charge the mound. But in an interview with the *Boston Globe*, Umpire Director Mike Port said that there had been an appreciable drop in the number of instances where hitters were changing the mound in the past few years because of the penalties imposed for it.

Of course, there have been fights about inside pitches for more than four decades. As noted, Red Sox ace Jim Lonborg turned his game up a notch when the club's pitching coach Maglie taught him to pitch inside. In June 1967 Lonborg's pitching caused the Red Sox and Yankees to square off in Yankee Stadium with players from both clubs emptying the benches to challenge one another. As Lonborg said: "If I've got a hitter that's thinking a little bit more about the inside part of the plate, now I can get to the outside part of the plate and not have him take as a good a swing as he would have if he knew that I never could get that ball to the outside part of the plate." In any event, the fact that the number of hit batsmen is increasing testifies to the newly acquired confidence of offensive-minded hitters as well as to a lack of training and experience for pitchers in the arts provided by Maglie to Lonborg.

Obviously, this has had considerable implications for pitching itself. Until the 1960s hitters did not even have a helmet and thus were arguably more expert in getting out of the way of a pitch. Pitchers have had to take this into account, and yet they have not seemed to have done so effectively.

Bob Boone, an all-star catcher and manager with a number of big league clubs and (along with Lonborg) a product of the Stanford baseball program, points out that pitchers are penalized for throwing inside because Major League Baseball wants to protect the investments that have emerged as a result of the long-term guaranteed contracts fostered from the time of "Catfish" Hunter. Some maintain that with this change, umpires have become more reticent in calling the inside strike.

According to Boone and others, like Jim Palmer of the Baltimore Orioles, it is the absence of command that makes the game so much different today. Says Boone:

> Command is what allows you to pitch inside. If you throw inside just to knock people down and those pitches are balls, you're facing hitters in a hitters' count. They're all better in hitters' counts. A wasted pitch inside just gives the hitter a better chance.

For Jim Beattie this inability to throw inside—what former Angels and Red Sox second sacker Jerry Remy says is a "lost art for pitcher"—has changed the game in basic respects.

Pitchers do not have, says Beattie, like Boone and Hooton, good control or command and don't have the control of the strike zone with their fast ball.

The result is that they work on more breaking stuff and thus pitch up and down rather than in and out. They pitch this way in order to miss the aluminum bats. Jim Kaat, former Twin and Yankee left-hander and broadcaster for the Yankees, says:

> With the metal bat, pitchers are more geared to thinking they have to miss the bat completely; they have to strike the guy out because with an aluminum bat, if you get any part of the bat on it, you can get a hit.

Thus, as Beattie says, the pitching game became more "up and down" rather than in and out. Beattie notes that this way of pitching affects arm strength, which cannot be built up with curves as well as with fastballs. The late Earl Wilson of the Boston Red Sox and Detroit Tigers, paraphrasing General Douglas MacArthur on victory at the time of the Korean War, told me that there is no "substitute" for the fastball. Lonborg agrees:

> I still think that there's a lot to be said for pitching in and out, as opposed to up and down, because not everybody can pitch up and down, but everybody can pitch in and out. You know, if you have a fastball that moves a lot, and stuff like that, sometimes it's not going to move if it's up, but it's always going to move if it's in, so that's where I think you've got to keep, you know, with the strength of the arm action itself.

But in Beattie's view, diminished arm strength that was normally associated with the development of a fastball at an early stage has directly affected the endurance of pitchers. This, of course, has produced the consequent emphasis upon pitch counts and diminished complete games as well as innings pitched.

The new pitching means pitch counts matter above most other considerations. Indeed, the stadiums built over the past decade generally give the pitch count to the fans on the scoreboard — and the old ones, like Fenway Park, have built in this feature. It is such an important aspect of the game that it is essential to the calculation of the fan as well as everyone else. Contrast this with the remarks of Hall of Famer Billy Williams about his time with the Chicago Cubs and the pitchers of his era: "Those guys were trained to pitch until they got tired." As Charlie Silvera, former New York Yankee catcher and backup for Yogi Berra, says:

> When we played there was no such thing [as pitch counts]. They started following pitch counts in the '70s if a guy had a tender arm. [When I played] the pitcher would let you know — you could tell by the crack of the bat if we weren't doing well. The catcher would ask if you're doing well and you'd tell him. You've been around long enough, you can tell when a pitcher doesn't have it.

Says Red Sox television broadcaster and former second sacker Jerry Remy:

> I'll be honest — I played behind Nolan Ryan [when he played with the Angels] and I never thought about a pitch count, nor did he. He had many games where he threw 150 pitches. That's another change in the game: trying to protect arms.

Indeed, though it is undocumented, Ryan claims he threw 259 pitches in an extra-inning game. Warren Spahn and Juan Marichal hooked up in a complete 16-inning contest which they both finished!

Says Silvera:

> Young kids in the minor leagues are having Tommy John surgery. You can throw with a sore arm; you can't throw with a bad arm. A bad arm is when you can't even lift your arm — your

arm was so sore you couldn't even comb your hair. You can pitch through some pain. Now, some of these people get a twinge and it bothers them and they shut 'em down. Johnny Sain would just go take a hot shower to loosen up.

But Leyland states that pitchers were simply pitching when they were hurt and that this was undesirable. Vivid testimony for this is provided by the erratic and talented fastball wild-man lefty of the Boston Red Sox from the early '50s, Maurice "Mickey" McDermott, who in July of 1951 pitched seventeen innings of a nineteen-inning struggle with the White Sox and threw approximately two hundred and forty pitches in his estimation. Said McDermott: "I was having a great time. I didn't want to come out." Two weeks later he pitched another sixteen innings as the Sox triumphed over the Indians, struck out fifteen Cleveland Indian batters and walked only one. In that one he estimated that he threw two hundred and thirty pitches. After that he spent three days in the hospital recovering.

In 2003, Milwaukee Brewers pitcher Jeff Suppan (at that point with the Pirates) said to me: "These days every pitcher is going to have surgery. It's inevitable." Pitching coach Ray Miller, in a *New York Times* interview, says this:

> "In my first 10 years in the big leagues," he said, "if a pitcher has something bothering him, the trainer said go to the doctor's office tomorrow morning. The guy said it's not that bad and he pitched through it. Now you have an orthopedist in the clubhouse every day. This pitcher is making $3 million a year. If he says he's a little tender, the doctor is going to say I think you should rest him. He's not going to say pitch through it and have the guy go out and get hurt."[15]

The contrast is demonstrated vividly by Dusty Baker's experience when he managed the San Francisco Giants:

> Guys aren't going as deep because they're conditioned by the pitch count. I had one guy [with the Giants] come up from the minors, William Van Landingham, he had a no-hitter in the 7th inning with, like, 96 pitches, and he was tired to death. He gave up a hit in the 8th so I went out to check on him ... he was dead tired because he had never thrown over 100 pitches. A lot of it depends on the person. There were some guys, like Nolan Ryan, who were just getting warmed up at 100 pitches. A strikeout guy is going to throw more pitches than a control pitcher, big time — you figure he's going to at least throw 4–5 pitches for every guy.

Again, this goes back to training. College pitchers throw infrequently, often once a week on the weekend. In the minors, pitchers are kept on an extremely careful and limited pitch count. This is to be contrasted with college ball where, for instance, Jeremy Guthrie, threw 144 pitches for Stanford against Cal State Fullerton in a 13-inning classic game in the NCAA regional opener. But Guthrie was lifted on Mother's Day five years later by the Baltimore Orioles when his pitch count had barely reached the '80s, only to see his potential victory frittered away by a bullpen which allowed the Boston Red Sox to win it in the 9th, 6–5, on a Julio Lugo infield hit!

While it appears that the number of pitches thrown on average by starters between '89 and '05 are virtually the same,[16] long outings are dwindling. In 1994 the number of games in which pitchers threw at least 120 pitches was 461, increasing to 544 in '96. In '01, '02 and '03 the numbers were 242, 224 and 228, a downward trend to less than half what it was in '96.

One reason for this is the hitters themselves. As noted above, the number of hitters who can work the pitcher into deep counts is increasing. The newfound emphasis on on-base percentage (obp) means that many hitters are far more selective. And the increasing size of players means that more can hit for power. The home run explosion is mirrored in the fact that the lineup has fewer soft spots on which the pitcher might coast. The DH in the American League has made this particularly true in the junior circuit. "Batting averages are higher today, meaning more balls are put in play and pitchers must face more batters to get out of an inning."[17] Pitching has simply become more stressful. "Strikeouts and walks have increased as a percentage of played appearances for 80 years, with a sharp uptake since the 1980s. Even plate appearances that result in the ball being put in play take more pitches, as hitters work deep counts."[18]

Professional hitters, even without the aluminum bat (generally associated with an upswing in the number of home runs in the college game),[19] have witnessed the augmentation of their bats. Led by Barry Bonds, many have moved to maple bats from ash bats, and others noted that Bonds used the maple bat to hit his 73 home runs in 2001.[20] Now some hitters have turned to so-called "beech bats."[21]

Bat handles used to be thicker, states Bobby Doerr, who noticed this phenomenon even as a player. Today the object is to generate greater bat speed now and thus the handles are thinner. A wide variety of distributors — in the '40s it was essentially the Louisville Slugger people, as opposed to more than a hundred distributors now — tailor the bat to the particular player. Says Ron Jackson, the former hitting coach of the Red Sox:

> Guys use thinner-handled bats now. That causes the bat to break.... One reason why players went to lighter bats is because of aluminum bats — they're light. You pick up an aluminum bat and it's light. Now they want the same size and weight as the aluminum bat they used in college. They go to the wood and try to get the same weight — the ball hits the bat and it's more likely to splinter.

(A byproduct of this development is the more frequent incidents of wood flying all over the infield, sometimes in five or six pieces! This has become a substantial safety issue for both players and spectators.[22] Some believe that the large number of manufacturers is responsible for the increase in this dangerous phenomenon.) This quicker speed has helped foster the offensive revival. While home run hitters always drove Cadillacs, these bats make it possible for the players and their agents to make a more effective presentation in salary arbitration or free agent negotiations.

Specialization and the Five-Man Rotation

As a result of the offensive revival, new roles were developed for the pitcher, and a new era of specialization was brought into play. Beginning in the late '60s or early '70s clubs began to go to a five-man rotation rather than the four-man or, more precisely, four-day rotation in which one or two aces would take the ball every 4th day, which had existed for all or most of the century. This appears to have begun with the New York Mets during their own "Impossible Dream" of 1969 when that club was able to use a surplus of outstanding young talent down the pennant stretch — Koosman, Seaver, Gentry, McAndrew and a young (and still somewhat wild) Nolan Ryan. Indeed, Ryan has said that Tom Seaver was the first pitcher he encountered who wanted the ball every 5th day rather than on the 4th day — though Bob Gibson pitched every 5th day before Seaver reached the majors. "No team has used a four man rotation for an entire season since Toronto in 1984."[23]

In the four-day rotation it was not uncommon for the best pitchers to get more than forty starts a year — in 1973 twelve pitchers reached that plateau. But from 1979 through the late '80s there was only one per annum to do it. Initially, as *Baseball Prospectus* has noted, the five-man rotation meant that the best pitcher on the staff threw every fifth day and that that would be accomplished even if the fifth starter was bumped from the rotation. Every fifth day, as opposed to every fifth game, produced approximately thirty-six starts a year in a 162-game schedule. But here also the number of pitchers making thirty-six starts declined to thirty-one and thirty-three in '73 and '74 respectively, all the way down to one pitcher in 1998. Now, the five-man rotation has become so sacrosanct that a day off in the schedule would mean that the ace starter or anyone else who was next in the rotation would get five days of rest — a factor encouraged in some situations where starters like Pedro Martinez in his Boston Red Sox days was considered to be fragile and indeed *in need* of five days' rest or more! In 2007 the Sox seemed to follow the same pattern with both Curt Schilling and Daisuke Matsuzaka, the former because of his age (40) and the latter because the season is longer in the United States than in Japan and it was feared that this would take its toll on the arm of the young Japanese ace.

As *Baseball Prospectus* has noted: "From 1999 through [2001] ... the Red Sox tried their damnedest to give him [Martinez] five days of rest when they could. Pedro is not a large man at 5'11", 170 pounds, and the Red Sox were tacitly admitting that Pedro's small stature meant that they had to personalize their care of him to account for his particular situation." The limitation of the five-man rotation concept is that the quality of the fifth starter, particularly in the era of major league expansion and minor league reduction — recall the performances obtained by minor league pitchers prior to major league experience — meant that starting rotations were weakened. Silvera, looking back to the four-man rotation, says:

> We always figured games were won by the starters. The 5th guy is the 5th worst starter and is generally the guy you can't really depend on. We had 5 starters in those days: we played double headers so you had to have a 5th starter. We didn't have any specialists in the bullpen. Sure, we had long men, but we didn't have a closer that HAD to pitch the 9th inning; we didn't have a setup guy who HAD to pitch the 8th. I think baseball, like a lot of things in life, is controlled by a mob mentality — everybody goes along with the thinking of the day.

Jim Kaat echoes this in stating that the five-man rotation was one of the "worst things" ever to happen to pitching:

> The 4-man rotation works out perfectly: you pitch today, then you're a little sore, the next day you toss a bit, the 3rd day you begin to recover, the 4th day you're right back ready to pitch. When you're pitching on a regular 4-man rotation, I think your between-start routine is easier to manage and your control is a little sharper when you go to the round versus the 5-man rotation, particularly today because it's not only a 5-man rotation. But very seldom does the pitcher pitch 9 innings, so you're pitching 6 innings and now you have to wait another 5 days before you go out there again. You spend a lot of time between starts either in the weight room or doing physical training before you get back out to the mound, so now it becomes more of a physical fitness routine than it is being sharp; pitching is touch and feel and control, and that part is secondary to the power and strength part.... With a 4-man rotation, you get your best pitcher out there 6–7 more times a year. If you do that, you could carry 1–2 fewer pitchers and fill out your bench.

In response, Bob Boone, when managing the Kansas City Royals, attempted to institute a 4-man rotation — as did Clint Hurdle subsequently with the Colorado Rockies — and they both had difficulties. The attempt to go back to the four-man system by Boone and Hurdle (who was operating in the high air of Denver) did not succeed, in the view of *Baseball Prospectus*, because Boone's experiment did not adequately monitor pitch count. Stated Boone: "The trial was scrapped after [Kevin] Appier and Chris Haney suffered arm problems." The downfall of the experiment was that Boone did not compensate for his starters' decreased rest by limiting their pitch counts. On the contrary, Appier threw 141 pitches in a start shortly before he went into the tank.

As noted, pitch counts have become so important — most managers are reluctant to use most pitchers far beyond 100, although the sturdy hurlers still approximate 125 to even 150 pitches — that now it has become *de rigueur* to place pitch counts as well as the pitchers' velocity on the scoreboard in most ballparks so that the fans are in a position to make their own judgment about how tired the pitcher is or is supposed to be and when he should depart. In 2007 the ability of Daisuke Matsuzaka to throw into the mid–120s of the pitch count, as he did that season against both Detroit and San Diego, was viewed as particularly remarkable! Matsuzaka developed arm trouble even during his fine 2008 season, as well as in 2009, when he was hurt training for the World Baseball Classic — and he developed more problems in 2010!

Paradoxically, the five-man rotation should leave the starters more rested — but the number of innings pitched by starters has declined appreciably. For instance, in 1946 Bob Feller led the Major Leagues by throwing 371 and $1/3$ innings. In '48 Johnny Sain reached 314 and $2/3$, and his rotation mate Warren Spahn ("Spahn and Sain and two days of rain") came in for 302 and $1/3$ in 1949. Robin Roberts led the majors from '51 through '55 and posted in the three middle years innings pitched of 330, 346, and 336. The horrific exploits of Micky McDermott in the '50s have already been noted!

In 1971 Mickey Lolich turned in 371 innings, and knuckleballer Wilbur Wood did 359 in 1973, with the White Sox. Since 1980 and Steve Carlton's 304 innings pitched, the closest anyone has come to 300 innings is Bert Blyleven's posting of 293 in 1985. Indeed, when Toronto pitcher Roy Halladay threw 266 in 2003, it was generally thought that excessive work was responsible for his lackluster performance in '04.

In the 2007 postseason, apparently Manager "Tito" Francona of the Red Sox felt that ace 20-game winner Josh Beckett could not come back on three days' rest after throwing 80 pitches in the first game against Cleveland. But as recently as 2003 Beckett had thrown 108 pitches in game three for Florida against the Yankees and 107 in game six when the Marlins won it all in the World Series itself. As recently as 1986 Roger Clemens, in the postseason against the Angels, having thrown 140 pitches in game one, came back and shut out the opposition until the 9th inning on three days' rest, throwing 134! The number 2 pitcher, Bruce Hurst, threw 127 pitches in game two and, again on three days' rest, threw 101 in the fateful game five, when the Sox staved off elimination by virtue of Dave Henderson's 9th-inning home run! Reliever Calvin Schiraldi pitched three innings in game four and came back the next day to pitch two and hold the Angels off.

The picture has changed. And of course, it is no surprise that the number of complete games has dropped precipitously during the same period of time. Here the decline is even more dramatic if one views it from a century perspective, beginning in 1908 when the average number of complete games was 105 per team per decade. Now the average number has gone from 56 in 1948 to 24 in 1988 and 10 in 1998. In 2006, the average number of complete games per team was only 4.77. Of course, some of the efforts of workhorses like Curt Schilling, the hero of the Boston Red Sox' postseason efforts in 2004, are well chronicled — but these are the rare exceptions and not the rule. But the contrast between pitchers like Robin Roberts, who between '52 and '54 turned in 30, 33, and 29 complete games, is vivid. Juan Marichal of the San Francisco Giants averaged 24 complete games between 1964 and '69. (See chart.)[24]

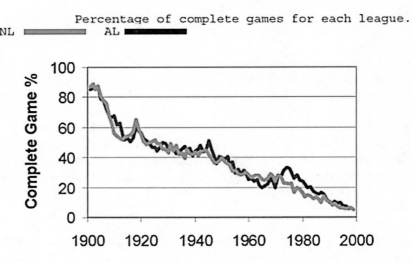

Percentage of complete games for each league.

More rest, fewer innings pitched and fewer complete games — this was the pattern in place at the turn of this century. The guaranteed contract over these past three and one half decades — which incentivizes teams to protect their investment — has been a major factor in producing this change. There has been some pushback against this, most notably in the case of Nolan Ryan, now president of the Texas Rangers, who has maintained that pitchers should be trained to be accustomed to a greater number of innings and freedom from pitch counts. But there is controversy relating to younger pitchers who are allowed to throw a large number of pitches[25] — and, of course, the players cannot simply start to do this when they reach the Major League level. It is all about what players are used to doing.

With fewer innings and complete games pitched, enter the so-called "quality start," which has come to mean unofficially six innings pitched and three earned runs allowed — at that point it is to be turned over to the bullpen with the starter producing what is a relatively undistinguished 4.50 ERA. Says former San Francisco Giants manager Felipe Alou:

> The guys now don't throw as many innings. Juan Marichal threw 240 complete games. Right now, they baby the pitchers and it starts in the minor leagues. With all this babying, guys are still getting hurt left and right. When I was playing, most teams had only 9 pitchers, sometimes 8, because [the starters] could throw complete games. You have Juan Marichal, Jack Sanford, Sam Jones, Billy Pierce, and Johnny Antonelli on your staff, it was usually a 9-inning affair — you didn't need other pitching. Nowadays, guys only pitch to maybe the 7th inning.

But as Jim Beattie notes, "Every pitch that pitchers throw today is much more stressful and tougher than pitches they threw 30 years ago.... Throwing 150 pitches 30 years ago was not as stressful as throwing 150 pitches today in a ballgame." As noted, in part this is attributable in the American League to the presence of the designated hitter and the fact that there is no real weak spot in the lineup. In this century both the Red Sox and Yankees have become masters at this process — a major factor in making both teams big run-producing machines. Some sub–.200 hitters like Del Maxvill of the Cardinals were placed in the lineup because of their glove; rarely does that happen anymore.

Then, as Beattie notes, "working the count" by batters is a "bigger deal" because of the pitch count, and hitters, taught to take and to foul off pitchers, deliberately trying to "get into" the opposition's bullpen. Thus, Beattie is of the view that, notwithstanding the Boone-Hurdle initiatives, it is unlikely that baseball will go back to a four-man rotation.

At least in the foreseeable future the 5-man rotation and relief specialists are here to stay. In any event, the return to a four-man rotation could not be started at the majors but would have to be inculcated at the lowest rungs of the minors — and that is not happening!

This has meant enlargement of pitching staffs and a greater need for so-called specialist relievers, which were unknown in previous years when the save was not even a statistic. In the 1940s through the '70s a number of outstanding relief pitchers emerged and "fireman of the year" awards were given to such worthies as Smokey Joe Page of the New York Yankees, who blinded power-hitting Red Sox players in the 1947, '49 and '50; Johnny Murphy, who preceded Page in '46 and went on to serve with the Red Sox in '47; Hugh Casey (he posed in photos in a fireman's hat), relief specialist for the Brooklyn Dodgers in their classic World Series matchups with the Yankees; Ellis Kinder of the Boston Red Sox, purchased from the St. Louis Browns, and who, after a 23–6 season in 1949, was found to be more suitable for relief stints; Jim Konstanty of the 1950 pennant-winning National Philadelphia Phillies, whose 74-game production appearances in 1950 set a record which was not broken for years to come.

But there were two overriding factors at this point. In the first place, relief pitchers, notwithstanding the performances of outstanding pitchers like those just identified, were generally the pitchers who were not good enough to start. They were demoted to the bullpen and consigned to a lower status.

A second characteristic, which lasted through the early or mid–'80s, was that relief pitchers pitched a considerable portion of the game. It was not unusual for Page, particularly following on the heels of an Allie Reynolds starting stint, to pitch three or four innings. The same was true in the '70s of Rollie Fingers of the Oakland A's, Bill Campbell of the Boston Red Sox (but this, along with reliance upon the arm-straining screwball, may have shortened Campbell's career and also that of Page), and Bruce Sutter, who was to obtain the new "Rolaids" award, which was created in the '70s for relief pitching.

In the late '80s Tony LaRussa, then managing the Oakland Athletes, who won the American League three years in succession between 1988 and '90, developed a new refinement. In the first place, his reliever Dennis Eckersley, an erstwhile twenty-game winner with the Boston Red Sox, was found suitable by LaRussa and his staff for one inning of relief. The conventional wisdom came to be that the closer should only pitch one inning — and subsequently some of them, such as Robb Nen of the San Francisco Giants, did not come into the game with men on base and were unable to hold the runners on when they were on base. There have been a number of relievers besides Nen whose degree of specialization precluded them from entering in the middle of an inning with men on base. On the other hand, it is felt that Red Sox closer (that is what they are called these days) Jonathan Papelbon turned the tide for the Red Sox in the critical game 2 of the 2007 World Series by picking off Matt Holliday at first base!

But now LaRussa produced a new twist. In the eighth inning, prior to Eckersley's appearance in the ninth, the A's had two "set-up" men who would pitch to a lefty or a righty generally (but not always) in accord with the percentages to hitters who hit from the same side of the plate. Thus left-hander Rick Honeycutt was called upon to get the left-handers. (A pitcher is deemed to be more successful against a hitter who swings from the same side that the pitcher pitches; e.g., a lefty who bats from the left is more vulnerable to a left-handed pitcher, because the breaking ball will break away from such a batsman, whereas the lefty's pitch will break into the righty, generally making the righty's swing versus the lefty more likely to produce a hit.) Sometimes, however, Honeycutt would go after righties too and confound the percentages. The Red Sox, with their 1986 American League

Championship team, for the first time in that club's history used a lefty, Joe Sambito, whose sole function was to pitch to one or two left-handed hitters late in the game! Under ideal circumstances, Red Sox manager Terry Francona has used lefty Javier Lopez in that role in '06 and '07 — a slot to which the latter successfully returned with the 2010 World Champion Giants. (Lefty Hideki Okajima confounded all of this in '07 when he was able to pitch to right-handers even more effectively than left-handers for the Sox!) This has meant more pitchers in the bullpen and more areas of specialization.

The LaRussa innovations are in a sense the mirror image of what Casey Stengel did with hitting lineups for the Yankees beginning in 1949. No one before him had made such generous use of platoon hitters like Gene Woodling, Hank Bauer, Cliff Mapes and Johnny Lindell, alternating with one another to good effect. Their Red Sox rivals seemed slow and lumbering with a set lineup which could not sub one hitter for another depending upon the emergence of a righty or lefty.

Following the LaRussa pitching model, in which he used Honeycutt and Gene Nelson so frequently in the seventh and eighth innings prior to Eckersley's entry, other managers began to use so-called set-up men. Some pitchers are paid to be set-up men and are compensated in salary arbitration and in free agency accordingly. Some are so-called long or middlemen, who may come in the third or the fourth or the fifth and act as a bridge to the set-up man and closer. Indeed, recent versions of the Oakland A's as well as the bullpen-rich 2007 Seattle Mariners have witnessed a virtual train of relievers lined up in the bullpen ready to face each new situation. (See chart.)[26]

Says Felipe Alou:

> They're paying the closer millions of dollars to pitch in the 9th inning so I have to bring him in then. At the end of the day, the guy making $10 million to close, I have to bring him in. If I lose the game with that guy, well, management told me he was the closer.

As Marcel Lachemann says, if the manager does not use the pitcher in his assigned role and the game gets away from the club then "they're second guessing" the manager. It's his judgment which is on the line.

This leads to some bizarre results. On June 13, 1992, Red Sox reliever Greg Harris, in the midst of an excellent year with the team, relieved Joe Hesketh with one out in the Toronto Blue Jay seventh. Harris retired the next two batters to end the inning and he retired the side 1-2-3 in the eighth with a 5–2 lead. Jeff Reardon came in to start the ninth and promptly got the first two batters on a pop-up and fly out. But then he began to look very shaky indeed. After Kelly Gruber got an infield single, John Olerud doubled, scoring Gruber. Eventually Candy Maldonado struck out to end the game and the Red Sox won it 5–3. When I queried Red Sox Manager Butch Hobson after the game as to whether he had thought about going with his set-up man into the ninth because he was retiring hitters repeatedly, he said: "I would have to be certified to a mental institution to do such a thing! I have the best closer in all baseball in the bullpen and I'm not going to avoid using him under that circumstance."

But a few years earlier, in the contentious 1986 playoffs between the New York Mets and the Houston Astros, in game three, starter Bob Knepper left the game after seven innings of pitching with a 5–4 lead when the Astros pinch hit for him in the top of the eighth. Charlie Kerfeld came on and pitched the eighth, retiring the Mets in order. That was the end of his assigned role. In came the man with the relevant specialty, Houston closer Dave Smith, who promptly lost the game to the Mets on a Lenny Dykstra home run! Kerfeld was

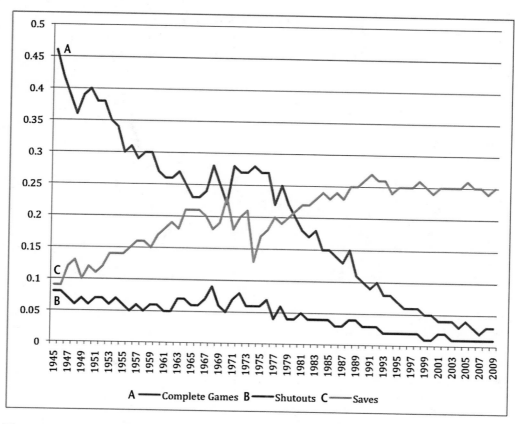

The rise of the reliever in post–World War II baseball (David W. Smith, "From exile to specialist: The evolution of the relief pitcher," Retrosheet.org, June 23, 2000, p. 2).

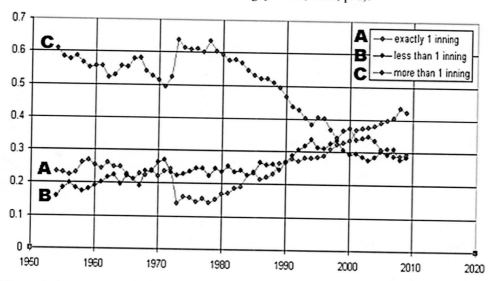

This graph shows the fraction of AL relief appearances lasting less than one inning, more than one inning, or exactly one inning. The data excludes 3-out save appearances. *More on AL relief appearances, available at* http://www.baseball-reference.com/blog/archives/4188 (graph prepared by Michael Scanlon) (courtesy David W. Smith of Retrosheet. A copy of the original graphs in the paper can be found at: "From exile to specialist: The evolution of the relief pitcher," Retrosheet.org, June 23, 2000, p. 1.2).

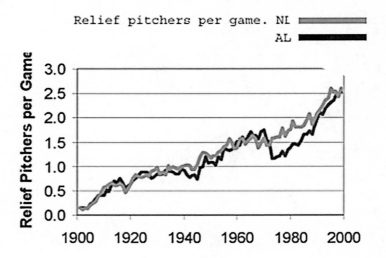

doing well that day. Perhaps Smith got out of bed the wrong way that particular morning. The specialist role assigned to each precluded any flexibility in the manager's decision-making process.

This kind of specialization means that more pitchers must be carried on the roster, some clubs carrying 11, 12 or 13 pitchers on a twenty-five-man roster. In the '60s and '70s managers occasionally began to use the so-called double switch whereby, late in the game when a relief pitcher was utilized, a defensive replacement would take the pitcher's place in the lineup, particularly when the pitcher was due to bat fairly early. Thus the substitute infielder or outfielder or even catcher would serve as a kind of *de facto* pinch hitter. Says Dusty Baker:

> [Tony] Lasorda [the Dodgers manager and subsequently general manager] used to use [the double-switch] with us [when Baker was a player for the Dodgers]. Now we have to use the double-switch more because we have 11 or 12 pitchers; you don't have as many bench guys, therefore you have to double-switch or else you're going to run out of bench players rather quickly. You have 10 pitchers, I can pinch hit all day because I have 8 guys on the bench; you look at these guys now: they have 12 pitchers but 5 bench players so you have to use them wisely. You used to use a bench guy as camouflage: you'd send one guy up there knowing they were going to bring this pitcher in, then you'd call him back and put another guy up there, the guy I might have really wanted up there in the first place. You can't do that. When we came up, they had 10 pitchers, which is another reason the starters went deeper in the game: you only had 4 starters and 6 relievers. And if you didn't stick with your starting pitching, you could go through your whole bullpen in 3 days and then everybody's tired.... The double-switch requires you to have a stronger bench. But at the same time, it's designed, not for your bench, but to conserve pitching — so your pitcher can go another inning and not have to hit; you don't have to pinch hit for him. You're conserving your bench and stretching out your pitching. It's designed to keep that pitcher in the game longer.

More areas of specialization produced not only more pitchers per game but also more pitches, which, as noted above, had the effect of lengthening the games. One paradox here is that although baseball seems to have more careful hitters who are willing to take a pitch and not swing at the first one, players overall have become more free-swinging at the plate as the number of strikeouts has gone up.

The Knuckleball

This is an extremely peculiar pitch which has been discussed in some detail by former Yankee hurler Jim Bouton in his classic *Ball Four*. One of the best pitchers throwing it in my childhood was Emil "Dutch" Leonard, who pitched in the '30s and '40s, and whom I can recall tossing it for the Washington Senators after World War II. Others like Hoyt Wilhelm threw the pitch until he was 49. Wilbur Wood became more expert at it when pitching for the White Sox after a tour of duty with the Red Sox. (He once pitched both ends of a double-header.) Tim Wakefield, who threw it both for the Pittsburgh Pirates and the Boston Red Sox, says:

> Throwing a knuckleball doesn't really put a whole lot of strain on your arm, if you're throwing it correctly and you're used to throwing it, which enables me to be able to be as versatile as I am, to be able to start one day and maybe throw out of the bullpen the next couple of days, if the bullpen needs help. It's like I'm a pitcher and a half. I can start and go six or seven innings and then maybe a couple days later if the bullpen needs help I could throw an inning or two in the bullpen and then make my next start.

The Niekro brothers, Joe and Phil, both threw it successfully. Joe retired at the age of 43, and not because of a sore arm but rather because he needed a hip replacement, which made it difficult for him to cover first on infield grounders. Charlie Hough of the Los Angeles Dodgers and Tom Candiotti of the Cleveland Indians and numerous other teams were expert at it as well.

What is the knuckleball? As Wakefield said to me: "Technically it's called a knuckleball but you don't hold it with your knuckle. I hold it with my fingertips and my fingernails."[27]

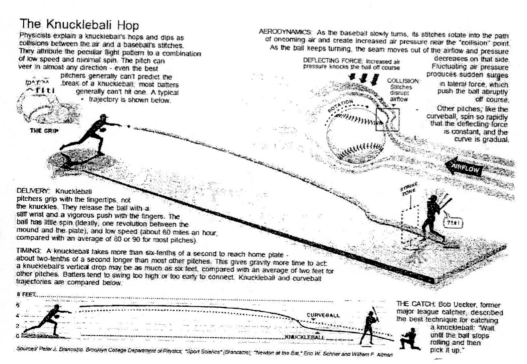

The peculiarities of the knuckleball (courtesy the *New York Times*).

The knuckleball seems to stand still and does not turn, taking a pronounced dip at some time prior to or at the plate. Says Wakefield:

> I try to throw it without any spin, and the way the aerodynamics works around the ball, it forms a small air pocket right behind the ball, which causes it to move all over the place. You know, with the wind going over the ball, because you're throwing it without any spin it's catching the seams and it's bouncing around like a butterfly.

As Wakefield says, it is not held by the knuckles, but rather by the fingertips or fingernails, and "when I release it, I try to release it with my thumb and ring finger at the same time and then guide it out with my index finger and my middle finger. And you try to throw it without any spin almost every time." It appears that warm muggy conditions when the air is heavy helps the knuckler. Bouton said if you do not possess it in the sense that it does not take a big break, the pitcher is throwing batting practice and big league hitters will hit countless long drives and home runs. Even when successful and obtaining a victory, Wakefield, pitching over five innings in a game where the Red Sox outscored the Tigers 11–9, yielded 6 home runs, a record for a game in which a pitcher gave up that number of home runs and nonetheless obtained the victory.[28]

Very few pitchers throw it today and the reasons appear to be threefold: (1) because, as Wakefield states, "It's ... very tough to control and it's more of a feel pitch and a lot of guys don't really have the feel of throwing a knuckleball"; (2) most major league scouts and teams seem to be focused upon obtaining pitchers who can throw at least 90 miles per hour; and (3) a small number of minor league teams diminishes the potential for teaching the pitch and it is generally seen as a pitch that is difficult to teach. Wakefield, who has at times thrown 102 out of 105 pitches as knuckleballs, has pitched into his 40s, as did many knuckleballers before him. He says now, "I think it's a dying breed."

The Way Hitters Have Changed

In the 1940s and '50s the great sluggers like Ted Williams could indeed produce a dramatic bases-loaded swinging strikeout of the kind that I heard over the radio in our home in 1946. But *in toto* Williams and other outstanding hitters were unlikely to strike out. He had great on-base percentage (OBP) — an idea discussed in the much-publicized *Moneyball* as though it was a novel one originating with the turn-of-the-century Oakland A's — and his high batting average was attributable to both his selectivity and to the fact that his plate appearances which did not result in walks always saw the ball in play.

In essence the prototype of the new player of the late '60s and '70s was personified by Reggie Jackson, who swung from his heels with both the Oakland A's and the New York Yankees and could produce dramatic, clutch results — particularly the three World Series home runs that he launched against the Dodgers in 1977. As dangerous and crowd-pleasing a hitter as he was, Mr. October could hit quite often in the .260s. Says ex-Yankee second baseman and San Diego Padre broadcaster Jerry Coleman:

> You go back to DiMaggio, he'd strike out only 13 times in over 600 at bats; Sammy Sosa struck out 170 times. Even though he hit 66 home runs, what happened to those other 170 at bats? Reggie Jackson struck out 2600 times.... Those things, if you're a manager, are disgraceful. But you hit a home run and everyone goes nuts. So the dominance of the home run is the most dramatic thing that has changed.

Says Johnny Pesky:

> The thing is, we didn't strike out as much. Today, we have more free swingers. More guys want to hit the ball for distance.... To me, it was embarrassing to strike out. Embarrassing. If you hit the ball, you had a chance. That's the theory I always went by.

Says Bob Boone about his son, ex-Seattle Mariners second baseman Brett Boone: "He strikes out 110 times!"

In the fateful year of 1946, slugging Pittsburgh Pirate outfielder Ralph Kiner led the way with 109 strikeouts. The next three years between 1947 and '49 saw top figures of 110, 102 and 92. (These were established by Philadelphia A's shortstop Eddie Joost, Cleveland Indians slugging outfielder Pat Seerey, and Duke Snider, the "Duke of Flatbush," of the Brooklyn Dodgers.) The above-mentioned Reggie Jackson, as he moved into the role of one of baseball's leading and most spectacular sluggers, led the way in 1968 with 171! And Bobby Bonds (Barry's father) took the lead away from him in '69 and '70 with 187 and 189. Generally speaking, today the average is in the high 180s. The number of strikeouts in the game from 1950 through the present era has doubled, a factor which has played a role in lengthening the time of games. In 1950 there were slightly fewer strikeouts than walks (5:6) but now the strikeout to walk ratio is nearly 2–1.

When one looks at the premier '40s and '50s stars as judged by batting average and home runs, Williams is 0.092 strikeouts per at bat, Joe DiMaggio 0.054 and Stan Musial 0.063. Contrast this with the upward movement of the '50s and the '60s, with Carl Yastrzemski at 0.116, Frank Robinson at 0.153, Hank Aaron 0.112, and only Mickey Mantle moving into the real modern era at 0.211. Reggie Jackson in the '70s and '80s group is at 0.263; Mike Schmidt at 0.225; Jim Rice at 0.173. Only Barry Bonds, Ken Griffey and Frank Thomas among the contemporaries compare favorably at 0.157, 0.180 and 0.167 respectively. The big sluggers of this period — Mark McGwire at 0.258; Manny Ramirez at 0.220; Alex Rodriguez at 0.204; and Sammy Sosa at 0.261 — are the closest to the Bonds and Griffey pair.

The batting averages of these contemporary big boppers are not as spectacular as those of either Williams or Stan Musial, or even Yankee centerfielder Joe DiMaggio. Williams, after all, was the last man to hit .400, reaching the august .406 average in 1941. No one, not even Williams himself in the late '50s, when he hit .388, has seriously challenged the mark since then. The Boston Red Sox, Williams's team, was the last Major League team to hit .300, reaching the .302 mark in 1950, twenty-three years before the designated hitter rule inflated American League averages.

Could Williams have done it subsequently? Or under today's circumstances? I put this question to Johnny Pesky when he was coaching the Red Sox in 1988 and he said: "Well, he's 70 years old today." But Jerry Coleman, who opposed Williams on the Yankee side of things in the late '40s and '50s said that there are special circumstances not present today:

> It was the gloves and the fields. You ever see Frank Crosetti's glove? It was as big as the palm of my hand. If you didn't catch with 2 hands you couldn't catch it; and to catch a ball with 1 hand was one of life's great miracles. I think it's tougher now because the gloves are so big and the fielders are agile.

Says Charlie Silvera:

> I think a lot of it had to do with a lot of day games, a lot of hard infields. The old St. Louis ballpark was shared by the Browns and the Cardinals — they had no grass! They had to put green dye on the infield! It was like playing in a parking lot — there were a lot of balls that

went through. In those days, the home run wasn't as big and there were a lot of slap hitters like the Waners.

Red Sox outfielder (1972–90) Dwight Evans said that he thought that Williams would have a difficult time given the wide variety of pitches, particularly the splitter and the forkball, which looks like a fast ball but which goes into the dirt at the last moment.

On the other hand, Johnny Pesky is of the view that the pitches today are essentially the same as those that were used by pitchers in his generation. Says Burt Hooton: "The split finger is a new pitch, but it probably came about because a guy couldn't throw a real good curveball or slider so he found something else." And Jerry Coleman says: "The slider is a pitch that came after World War II. It was curveball, fastball, change up. Now you have the slider, splitter, sinker." But says Dusty Baker:

> There's no pitch that's thrown now that wasn't thrown before but with a different name. Guys say there weren't split fingers — well, they called them forkballs; they say guys didn't have a changeup — they called them palmballs; they didn't throw sliders — they called it the out-shoot; they say there were no sinkers — they were in-shoots; the curveball was called a drop. You have to also remember that guys used to load the ball up. Now they're going back to loading the ball up because no one is enforcing it — this is the first year in awhile where they busted a guy for using a foreign substance. Imagine trying to hit with a foreign substance. Back in my day and even before me, they'd see if you could hit a fastball; then they'd see if you could hit a breaking ball; then they'd see if you could hit a changeup; if you hit all those, they'd try to intimidate you and see if you could hit on your back.

Perhaps the late Stephen Jay Gould has provided the best answer by noting that baseball, in the Williams era, had only a token number of black players, who were just coming into the game during Williams's last thirteen years (none were in when he hit .406), and that the great Latin and Asian superstars were not yet on the scene. The fact that more talented players who were not there in 1941 may mean that today's competition from the mound (remember that the Japanese and Koreans are disproportionately pitchers) would make it more difficult for Williams today, notwithstanding the change in the sacrifice fly rule, which, as we have seen, would have made his average .411 instead of .406.

But in any event, home run production — at which Williams, who had 521 of them during a career shortened by World War II and the Korean War, was proficient — has soared and the customers have responded by voting with their wallets. Of course, expansion has doubled the number of teams and consequently the number of players.

But consider this comparison — in 1950 the number of players with 40 or more home runs was one. In 2000 it was sixteen. In 2009 there were none, but fifty-four players hit twenty-five or more homers, the fourth highest number in the decade and the sixth in history. The number of players with one hundred or more RBIs during the same period of time had gone from twenty-two to thirty-three — but the latter was the lowest in a full season since 1993! The number of home runs per game has increased from 1.79 in 1952 to 2.25, reaching a high of 2.34 in 2000, and runs per game has edged up less dramatically.

And as this story has unfolded, Seattle Mariners president Chuck Armstrong notes the fact that it was difficult to get baseball and the public to focus upon Ichiro Suzuki's record-breaking performance for hits produced:

> No one outside of Seattle seems to be excited about Ichiro having a chance to break [George] Sisler's hits record. Sisler's mark has been around longer than Ruth's mark — it was started in 1920, for Pete's sake — and here's the first guy since I don't know when to come close to breaking it. You used to see players choke up and try to find holes — Texas Leaguers were a part of their game — Ichiro is a throwback that way.

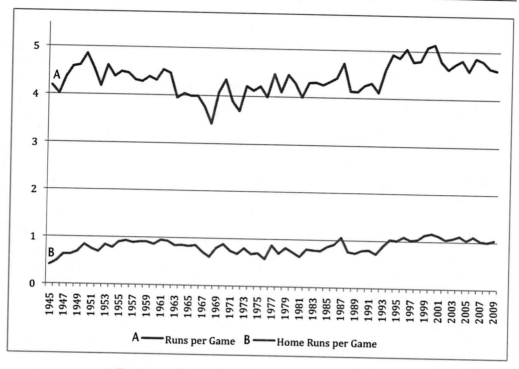

Offensive production (graph prepared by Michael Scanlon).

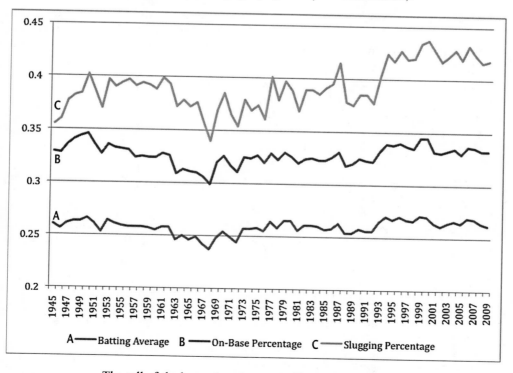

The roll of the batter (graph prepared by Michael Scanlon).

Speed on the Bases

Such is the power game in baseball, it has actually declined to nearly one stolen base every other game. (In 1990 the speed game, exaggerated by the existence of Astroturf, which came and went from the '70s through the '90s, had tripled the number of bases stolen.) The ideas promoted by Earl Weaver, manager of the Baltimore Orioles in the '60s and '70s, have won out. His maxim was to play for the big inning and to allow the power hitters to deliver rather than to take chances with stolen bases. The stolen base, still critical to the game as Dave Roberts's clutch steal against the New York Yankees in game 4 of the 2004 American League championship playoffs can attest to, has declined in number as the size of the players has expanded and grass in the ballparks has been restored in place of Astroturf.

Attempts at stolen bases since the mid–'80s have declined by thirty-six percent. Clubs are doing a simple cost-benefit analysis which concludes that the "reward of the extra base is not worth the risk!"[29] As one commentator has said:

> Having a runner on second base is obviously better than having a runner on first, but the gap is not enormous. A team with a runner on second and no one out will score about a quarter of a run more on average than a team with a runner on first and no one out, according to *Baseball Prospectus*, a web site and scouting guide. So stealing second with no outs is worth about 0.25 runs.
>
> Being thrown out — then having nobody on base with one out — reduces the number of runs a team can expect to score by 0.64. The out is more than two and a half times as bad as the steal is good. So to break even, a team needs to steal almost three bases for every one time it is caught. The caution of today's managers starts to look smart.[30]

As Paul Burdick and Kevin Quinn have made clear in an exhaustive study, the stolen base process has gone through a number of cycles.[31] They point out that stolen bases plummeted in the 1920s when the home run came in with Babe Ruth and did not re-emerge until the 1960s, a few years after Jackie Robinson had come and gone. Not until 1951 was the important statistic of caught stealing (recall its importance in the Luis Polonia arbitration) recognized.

The Negro Leagues had emphasized the stolen base, long after it had fallen out of fashion in the Majors. Individual stolen base threats like Maury Wills became important. Willie Davis and Luis Aparicio had a success rate above 75 percent, with Wills close behind at 73.8 percent. Stolen bases were on an upward trend through the beginning of the '70s. Then, with Lou Brock's 551 steals for the decade, 14 players stole over 200 bases each. The Boston Red Sox slugged their way to more runs in the decade of the '70s than even the Cincinnati Reds — but the Big Red Machine was more successful with speed as well as power. The Oakland A's, the one true dynasty of the '70s, stole more than any other team in the decade. Rickey Henderson's 512 steals "paced the attack."[32] Write Burdick and Quinn:

> While some teams continued their pace of the 1980s, more NL teams joined a growing list of AL teams who were getting far more selective in terms of running. New stolen base stars like Kenny Lofton and Barry Bonds were still emerging, and established stars, including Rickey Henderson, kept up their act. By the second half of the decade, the top teams from either league, the Braves and the Yankees, were nearer the bottom of their leagues in steals than the top.
>
> This does not reflect the demise of the running game similar to what we saw in the 1920s. While attempts are down, teams are actually getting much better at stealing bases.
>
> The Thorn and Palmer data imply that, on average, a team will score about .30 additional

runs with a runner on second with one out than with a runner on first with one out. But a team will score about .60 fewer runs with no runner on first with two outs than with a runner on first and one out. Thus, we get the standard break-even threshold that has served as a baseball rule of thumb for stolen base effectiveness at two for every three attempts or about 67%.... The success rate has been generally increasing since 1951, and has been above the break-even point consistently since the 1980s.[33]

The steroid-fueled '90s saw power again push the stolen base back into the subordinate position that it had been in from the '20s through the '60s. It has reverted in the first decade of the 21st century to the cautious cost-benefit status alluded to above, though the 2010 Tampa Bay Rays run with abandon as well as slug.

Some of the same analysis has diminished the use of the bunt to advance the runners, though here the comparison is between a runner at second with one out and at first with no outs. Bunting, after all, is another manifestation of so-called "small ball." The downward trend seems clear.[34] One reason is statistical probabilities, which have been relied upon particularly by the A's, the Blue Jays and the Red Sox. States a recent *New York Times* article:

> According to *Baseball Prospectus*, which analyzes statistics, teams with a runner on first base and no outs scored an average of 0.896 runs an inning last year. Teams with a runner on second and one out scored an average of 0.682 runs, meaning their chances of scoring decreased if they sacrificed the runner ahead.
>
> The statistics showed that teams with a runner on second and no outs scored an average of 1.142 runs while having a runner on third with one out produced an average of 0.945 runs, another reduction. Finally, teams with runners on first and second and one out scored 1.51 runs on average while a situation with runners on second and third and one out produced 1.35 runs, another example of the bunt's hurting, not helping, a rally.[35]

But bunting is more situational, defying generalized statistical probabilities. The failure of Alex Cora of the Red Sox to bunt against Seattle in June 2007 with a runner on and no outs not only produced an out with no advancement in that given case but also seemed counterproductive given the availability of better hitters waiting on deck and in the dugout. States Jim Beattie:

> I remember playing Gene Mauch, we had the first or second inning, he'd sacrifice bunt in the first or second inning because he felt like getting men in scoring position was the most important thing. I think that the idea of the sacrifice bunt should be used but only when you have to score one run. When you win a ballgame with one run, the sacrifice bunt comes into play, but when you're looking to score a couple runs, or one run is not going to do it, then the sacrifice bunt gives up an out, and when you're trying to score more runs, that's not what you want to try to do. You've only got twenty-seven outs. To move it that way, you lose those outs, you lose opportunities to score more runs. But the sacrifice bunt can come into play later on in the game when you only need to score one run....
>
> ... It kind of depends on who's following after you have the sacrifice bunt. I mean, the number six hitter gets on and you have a sacrifice bunt so all of a sudden by the seventh hitter, now you've got the eighth and the ninth guy, you're probably not going to have a good chance of driving the guy in anyway. So it may depend on what the quality of the hitter is after the sacrifice bunt or what the quality of the hitter is after the guy on first base gets on there with one out or no outs.

It is thought that fewer hitters, particularly in the DH American League, have the ability to execute the bunt. (In the National League the pitchers who hit for themselves are frequently called upon to bunt.) States Charlie Silvera:

> I think the game has developed into scoring, home-run with the lively ball, and there's stronger people, smaller ballparks, they've forgotten how to win a one-run ballgame. There

are times when you're going to face a good pitcher and one run means an awful lot. There are too many times when the bunt situation comes up that the pitchers don't know how to bunt and a lot of times when the bunt situation comes up and the pitcher gives a lollipop for their guy to bunt, more or less, *here*, throws it up there, half speed, ³⁄₄ speed, and bunts it and they get the guy over. Billy Martin, get back to him again, let's say before the DH started I would pitch to the pitchers in batting practice, and those pitchers, if they didn't get a runner over in the game before, Billy would say, "Don't let them hit today. Let them bunt for 20 minutes." Well, you bet that they learned how to bunt. So they took their hitting away. Well, you can't do that now. But we did it, just the little things.... The bunt has its place, and there are times when you definitely have to bunt. There are some lousy hitters, I mean, what are you going to do, are they going to strike out? You might as well try to get them over. The pitchers in the National League, especially.

But nonetheless, Bob Boone states that his father Ray Boone, of both the Indians and the Tigers, maintained that very few people could execute the bunt in the '40s and the '50s and that the "good old days" comparison is based upon faulty memories. Says Boone: "The question about bunting comes up all the time. You hear: 'Oh geez, they don't bunt as well as they used to. It's a lost art.' But my dad said, 'Hell, we couldn't bunt in the '50s either ... it was always that way.'"

In any event, the same statistical probabilities have come into play here — more substantially against the bunt as opposed to the stolen base — because the object is to give up an out, a sacrifice (it is after all a sacrifice bunt) which is not involved in a stolen base. Dave Nelson sums it up succinctly: "Speed goes in cycles ... because of the new ballparks, teams are getting away from speed and going more for power." And, it goes without saying that power is more statistically measurable than the little things like hitting to the right side of the infield to advance the runner as well as bunting successfully — and salary arbitration in particular makes available statistics more central to player evaluation.

"Caught stealing" becomes an official statistic in 1951, so the date for the years before then is based on reconstructions and not very accurate (graph prepared by Michael Scanlon).

The Ball and the Parks

There are a number of factors in making the game more of home run production rather than bunts and steals. Bob Boone, for instance, believes that the ball is livelier and has been for some period. He believes that the sudden rise of thirty-plus home run hitters like Pete Incaviglia, Wally Joyner, and Mark McGwire in 1986, and particularly in '87 when home runs took off, was due in part to the lively ball. Boone said the ball "feels different" and in the '80s he saw "little guys hit them out going the other way [to the opposite field]." Similarly, ex–Florida Marlins Manager Jack McKeon has said: "The ball is livelier; it's smaller."

As noted above, the ballparks are different in terms of their dimensions, and the fact that they have become so hitter-friendly is surely a major factor in the way in which the games have moved. The late '60s and '70s produced "cookie cutter" concrete jungles in cities like Cincinnati, Pittsburgh and Philadelphia, and for awhile dimensions seemed to be pitcher-friendly. But the trend since 1945 and '50 is obvious. Except for the right field line, the pattern in left and center has been to reduce the distance between 10 and 20 feet.

Indeed, in 1940 the most distant part of the park on average was 448 feet, compared to today's 409. Granted, those like Alex Rodriguez felt that they lost ten homers every year in one of the new attractive state-of-the-art stadiums, Safeco Field of the Seattle Mariners. Similar complaints have been made by Juan Gonzalez about the expanse of left field in Comerica Park of the Detroit Tigers (the fences were brought in for Gonzalez). And on Opening Day of 2004, when Petco Stadium was inaugurated in San Diego, one of Barry Bonds's patented blasts seemed to fall just so short of what has come to be regarded as a pitchers' park. But in the main, the new stadiums of the past twenty years have been patterned after one of the most attractive state-of-the-art parks of them all, the Baltimore "Orioles' Park"—generally referred to as Camden Yards. Both Denver and Arizona are at high altitudes—and this makes the ball fly. In the '90s Kansas City moved the fences in, making their park a home run haven. But they were moved out again in 2003 when the home run average turned out to be 200 per season and, as we know, the new Yankee Stadium has played a critical role in that team's home run production—136 homers, compared to 112 in the old Stadium in the Mantle-Maris 1961 onslaught.

Strike Zone

The strike zone—the subject of much controversy as major league baseball has sought to make it uniform—has been felt to be a factor. Before the 1963 season the strike zone was expanded, perhaps in response to Roger Maris's home run record in 1961. In 1969 "the top of the strike zone was moved from the shoulders to the armpits; in 1988, the upper limit became the 'horizontal line at the midpoint between the top of the shoulders and the top of the uniform pants.'"[36]

But the situation now is more complicated. "Strike called at the letters" was something that we heard as children on the radio frequently. Strikes have not been called at the letters, the umpires favoring a lower strike zone in recent years—sometimes below the knee itself—or at least at the small of the knee! Mike Port, MLB Vice President for Umpires, says that today umpires will call a strike slightly above the waist but in most instances not much further because of the cultural acceptance by all teams of the new strike zone. Both clubs will be "barking" at an umpire who calls a strike at the letters, states Port. And no one proves the point more dramatically than the notorious lowball hitter, Red Sox DH David Ortiz, who rails against any strike above the belt.

Today's baseball has 27 more pitches than in 1988, apparently the oldest official pitch counts, "equal to nearly an extra full inning of play — although stronger players, smaller ball fields and tighter baseballs also give pitchers more incentive to work around the strike zone."[37] The high strike was called for power pitchers who would be able to go right after hitters who are now running up deep counts — though a difficulty here is that most pitchers, in substantial part because of the aluminum bat, are taught to pitch low. But if the strike were called at the letters, as we heard it called so frequently on the radio in the 1940s and '50s, it is quite possible that games would move more quickly; however, attempts to return to this standard were made in both 1999 and 2001 and they failed.

The overriding objective of former San Diego Padres President Sandy Alderson, when he was Major League Baseball Vice-President, was to obtain the uniformity through a machine called QuesTec. The difficulty here is that strike zones are going to appear to differ inevitably with umpires, as well as their size, which determines how far they can get down on the pitch. The elimination of separate American and National League offices has led to the rotation of umpires throughout the entire Major League Baseball system. But, though this change has supposedly eliminated league differential practices or policies, a consequent lack of familiarity with the tendencies of each umpire has created new uncertainties.

Dusty Baker often quotes Hank Aaron's comment: "Keep the umpire in the equation." There would be inevitable subjectivity, Aaron noted. Pitchers, of course, stated that umpires, concerned with grade consciousness as the result of QuesTec, err on the side of caution, i.e., balls rather than strikes. As noted above, Bobby Cox concurs with Baker.

But the fact is that most fan observations are derived from television, and television cameras are on an angle.

> The Red Sox telecast on NESN is one of only three in Major League Baseball that places its main camera directly behind the pitcher in straightaway center field. The other 27 clubs ... put the camera off-center, about 10 to 15 degrees toward left field. That offset angle means the vast majority of baseball fans get a skewed sense of the pitcher-hitter confrontation, the matchup at the very heart of baseball.[38]

In any event, it is thought that the new strike zone and what some allege to be a promotion of more strikes is helping the hitters. As Murray Chass has written:

> Umpires were told before the season to stop calling strikes on pitchers off the corners of the plate. In recent years, the strike zone had spreadhorizontally. At the same time, umpires were told to call strikes on pitches two inches above the belt. For years, pitches above the waist had been called balls.[39]

Mike Port states that baseball has been successful in reducing the pitches called strikes east-west off the corner of the plate, where it was thought that some of the Atlanta pitchers, in particular, benefited unduly. It is the above-referenced up and down problem that Port notes that needs more work.

But rule 2.00 of the Official Baseball Rules is quite clear. It states:

> The STRIKE ZONE is that area over home plate the upward limit of which is a horizontal line at the midpoint between the top of the shoulders and the top of the uniform pants, and the lower level is a line at the hollow beneath the kneecap. The Strike Zone shall be determined from the batter's stance as the batter is prepared to swing at a pitched ball.

The last sentence, however, always gave hitters like Ricky Henderson an enormous advantage because he was truly screwed up into a contorted stance which seemed to provide for no strike zone at all. The fact of the matter is that umpires appear to rarely call the strike at the letters as they should under rule 2.00 and, as Port noted, generally speaking are reluctant to go much above the belt.

It seems unlikely that Major League Baseball has a duty to bargain with the umpires about the strike zone because the strike zone under the labor law established by the Supreme Court truly relates to the nature of the game itself. But the question, should it be raised by the players in a duty-to-bargain case in the future, is a closer one given the fact that the way in which strikes are called clearly affects both hitters and pitchers, their conditions of employment as well as their wages obtained in negotiations and salary arbitration proceedings. This is a close question which would seem to suggest that it should not be done unilaterally without player involvement under both the collective bargaining agreement and federal labor law. States Port: "The batters want a strike to be a strike. The pitchers want more room around the plate." Beyond the strike zone itself, there are other changes in the hitter-pitcher balance of power as well. The paradox, given the number of strikeouts taking place, is that there is much more care and attention given to the details of the hitting process.

But clearly the biggest change of all is the video process for all players. Each hitter's and pitcher's strengths and weaknesses and tendencies are examined in detail. It is said that Curt Schilling had taken to studying video with increasing intensity when his ability to throw the fastball in the mid–'90s declined. Says Lynn Jones:

> I think the big thing that has changed since we came up is that it's so visual now. Everybody goes to the video right after their at bat. It's instant replay and you can analyze your swing, where the pitch was at, what the location was — there's more things that you can look at immediately. We couldn't do that back then, we had to memorize it, we had to visualize up here — there's a big difference in the game because they have to see it; they don't remember it as much. The good hitters do, they remember all those; the good pitchers remember those, but most don't because they know they just go to the monitor to find out.

Some say that the difficulties endured by Barry Zito with San Francisco during his first four years there, after a relatively distinguished career in Oakland where he won a Cy Young award, are attributable to the fact that players could see that the angle of his delivery tips the kind of pitch that he will throw. Of course, the scrutiny of pitchers to see whether they are tipping them has always been part of the game. But today the game is indeed more scientific and sophisticated.

Uniforms

Uniforms are extremely important to the game and it might be said that most fans loyal to a club are loyal to the uniform. "Typically fans follow teams, not players. Jerry Seinfeld has observed that people can hate a player who plays on an opposing team, then love the very same player when he plays for their team. For Seinfeld, this means that people are really just 'rooting for clothes.'"[40]

I can recall in the late '70s and early '80s, at the time of the free agent exodus from the Red Sox, as Fred Lynn, Rick Burleson and Carlton Fisk departed (the first two through trades entered into because the Red Sox knew that they would lose those players through free agency), friends asked me how I could still identify with the club. But my view was that, notwithstanding a certain measure of loyalty to the alumni as they went to new teams, I could always identify with the club not only because of the characteristics of the home field of Fenway Park, but also the uniform. The Red Sox' home uniform remains almost identical in 2011 to what it was in 1946: a white uniform with RED SOX in red letters across the front. Another extremely attractive one was the Tigers' home uniform, which was white with a large black old-English D on the front of the uniform. The major change is that occasionally the club will wear red or blue jerseys on Sundays or particular occasions, which used to be worn just in spring training.

The road uniform was always important, the Red Sox having a stately and dignified gray with the black letters BOSTON across the front. Suddenly in 1990, through the initiative of then General Manager Lou Gorman, this changed so that there was a stripe down the side of the pants-but even more horrible, names placed on the back of the uniform. When this happened in 1990, Dwight Evans said to me: "I feel like a California Angel."

At the beginning of baseball's existence, however, there were not even numbers. Spectators were presumed to know the players without identification.

The first attempt to identify individual numbers on uniforms occurred with Cleveland in 1916. The numbers were attached to the sleeve, not the back. The idea then disappeared and was not seen again, except briefly by the Cardinals in 1923, until 1929 when the New York Yankees took the field with large numbers on their backs. This apparently inspired considerable ridicule, similar to that aimed at the change of the Red Sox in 1990 when they put *names* on their uniforms. Initially, the numbering went by the position in the batting order, and this is why Ruth had the number 3 and Lou Gehrig was given 4. By 1932 all the major league teams had numbers, and in 1952 the Brooklyn Dodgers repeated the numbers in front of the home jersey. Many others teams have copied this idea. In the '60s numbers began to appear on the sleeves, and by the '70s some clubs even put numbers on the trousers.

Names on the back of uniforms was inspired by TV coverage, the Chicago White Sox being the pioneer of this idea in 1960. The Yankees, however, who initiated numbers, have never displayed names on either their home or road uniforms, and the Red Sox and the San Francisco Giants have continued to refuse to display names on their home uniforms. I had always thought that the idea was not only gauche but also showed a lack of knowledge of the team — and it is interesting to note that the idea did not spread quickly because of fear of lost revenues through lower scorecard sales. But it must be admitted that some of the same arguments could be made about numbers which even a purist like myself finds acceptable (and my objections about the lack of a cognoscenti applies equally to the fact that players are announced throughout the game, rather than only on their first appearance, as was the case in the 1940s).

One other matter relating to baseball uniform attire has changed considerably over the years since the immediate post–World War II era. Modern players have taken to wearing uniforms in a loose, almost baggy, pajama-like fashion, perhaps imitating the style of dress that one sees young people wearing, particularly in urban areas. In basketball this translates into pants that are worn lower, sometimes going considerably below the knees. Except for outliers like ex–St. Louis Cardinal shortstop Brendan Ryan, for instance, in baseball this means one cannot see even the sock, a result that seems regrettable for a team like the Red Sox. I remember seeing Bobby Doerr in a 1940s *Sport Magazine* adjusting his stirrups before a game.[41] Mike Timlin wore his socks high, as it was done when I was a child. But it appears as though he was the only member of the 2007 World Champion Red Sox to do so.

In my view, both Detroit and Cleveland always had distinguished gray road uniforms with the names of the city in print. Now, for reasons best known to themselves, they have transformed the city name on their uniforms worn away from home into cursive writing. The old road uniforms were far more dignified.

The uniform, of course, is fundamentally distinct from the play engaged in on the field itself. It provides continuity and a link between the past and the present, which baseball more than any other sport preserves. It helped me to survive the doldrum-filled 1950s that afflicted the Red Sox.

CHAPTER 7

Cheating, Drugs and Other Forms of Problem Behavior

Mel Allen, the charming, folksy and articulate announcer for the New York Yankees during my childhood—he was undoubtedly the best baseball announcer I ever heard—commented frequently that baseball players were "just like everyone else." They were no better or worse, said Allen, than people in other walks of life. I shall always remember the strong dissent to this idea registered by my father when we would hear it on the radio. It was his view that baseball players were a "cut below" the average person and that their lifestyle warranted more scrutiny and skepticism.

This view, formed at a time when college-educated players were still a substantial exception to the rule in baseball and when the all white complement of players came disproportionately from the rural South, was undoubtedly rooted in the flamboyance of some players, like Babe Ruth, whose alcohol-fueled carousing and wenching raised many eyebrows. It surely had something to do as well with the scandals—particularly those involving gambling—of the early twentieth century in organized baseball. But there was more.

As Roger Kahn has written about baseball players of the early and mid–twentieth century: "Many pitchers developed a side occupation good in both winter and summer. That was drinking whiskey.... Fine pitchers worked a four-hour week. Leisure and the transient nature of the business were doorways to a boozy life."[1] The recent disputes and difficulties with steroids and other performance-enhancing drugs in baseball and professional sports generally are properly understood against the backdrop of other issues. When it comes to controlling the use of drugs, baseball has found itself placed in unflattering comparisons with other sports like football[2] and basketball, notwithstanding the fact that hockey took a considerable amount of time to address this issue in any fashion.

How are other problems of a similar nature addressed? San Francisco Giants outfielder Barry Bonds, in a well-publicized interview in 2005, rhetorically posed the question: "What is cheating?"

Baseball has indeed confronted this question in a wide variety of contexts. How are prohibitions to be enforced? What kinds of sanctions are levied against those who are found to offend the policy? And, more fundamentally, should drugs which enhance performance be prohibited at all? How does one distinguish this from, for instance, Viagra (which some athletes consume for competitive status on the field of sports!) or Tommy John surgery, which reconstructs pitching arms and is now common even among high school players?[3] What about the steroids which can be obtained with a prescription, like cortisone and prednisone, which have been openly used by players in a variety of sports for at least four decades and which are used openly by Bonds today to deal with arthritis?

Some of my students at Stanford Law School have suggested that since attendance records are booming, there is no need to focus upon these and related issues. Recall that this was the point made by Hall of Famer Joe Morgan on Sunday Night Baseball. Given the popularity of professional wrestling, some have even questioned whether prohibitions against gambling are appropriate.[4] States one writer: "The only real outrage displayed by fans in recent days was not in regards to sport, but to the government charge that [Atlanta quarterback Michael] Vick helped operate a dog-fighting ring that killed under-achieving animals by hanging, drowning and bashing them into the ground."[5]

Should, however, the most basic public reaction be dispositive on the question of acceptable behavior for professional athletes? To what extent are partisan fan reactions relevant at all? Barry Bonds is not booed in San Francisco, and at least until recent slumps, David Ortiz heard nothing but cheers in Fenway. Now that he has proved to be so successful in the postseason in 2009, as we see below, Alex Rodriguez has seen the past forgiven. Mark McGwire's tearful confession induced a cascade of hosannas from St. Louis Cardinals fans. Along with the question of the relationship between drugs and actual performance, these are some of the most fundamental and perplexing aspects of this issue.

The 2005 Baseball and Professional Sports Steroid Hearings, and the impatience expressed by many members of Congress regarding the penalties to be given to drug users, highlight the fact that there are perceived special problems here, arguably akin to gambling, which are not to be treated in the ordinary fashion. Belatedly, baseball moved into the business of drug testing, with particular focus upon performance enhancement, in 2002 and '05 with policies which provide clearly for a fairly detailed series of steps, including penalties. But the Anabolic Steroid Act of 1990 had made possession of such drugs to be unlawful for a decade and a half before baseball gave the matter its attention — even though critics of drug testing and regulatory initiatives by baseball continued to state that there was nothing unlawful about drug use until the '02-'03 period! Indeed, from 1971 onward, Major League Baseball had a drug policy which prohibited the use of prescription medications without a valid prescription, and presumably this prohibition applied to steroids even before the 1990 legislation. And, as we shall see, drugs and their prohibition by Major League Baseball were a constant source of controversy — again the assumption being that inappropriate drug use was impermissible in baseball.

At the March 17, 2005, House of Representatives hearings, Association Executive Director Donald Fehr said that the approach to the drug offense arena was that of progressive discipline. This is the approach undertaken by all of the major professional sports and in labor-management relations generally. The disputes about discipline relate to the question of whether baseball (or some other employer) has disciplined a player without "just cause."[6] But progressive discipline has meant something different to baseball than to the other sports.

The National Football League, which tests for anabolic steroids, growth hormones, and diuretics and other masking agents, as well as ephedrine and other selected stimulants, and dietary "supplements" containing prohibited substances, has a penalty policy for sanctions for testing positive. The player receives a four-game suspension for the first positive test; a six-game suspension for the second one; and a minimum one-year suspension in the third instance. The National Basketball Association prohibits steroids, amphetamines, cocaine, marijuana, and selected other substances. The NBA imposes a five-game suspension in the first positive test; a ten-game suspension for the second one; and a twenty-five game suspension in the third instance. The National Hockey League, which only tested for players already in the league's substance abuse and behavioral health program until 2005, had no publicly established policy at the time of the congressional hearings — though players who are abusers can seek help the first time without being exposed or suspended. But the 2005 hockey agreement tracks the other major sports in these areas.

How do professional sports properly fit into the progressive discipline model and what are the appropriate sanctions and policies? Does progressive discipline have any relevance to drug problems and related matters?

Arbitrators, in interpreting the just cause provisions of collective bargaining agreements, have obliged management not to take disciplinary action against employees in the absence of just cause for so doing and have placed the burden upon the employer to establish just cause through a preponderance of evidence or, in the view of some arbitrators, even more exacting standards. The assumption of progressive discipline is that counseling and suspension will come prior to discharge in that they can correct employee behavior before the most severe sanction of discharge is imposed. But in the collective bargaining process there are always certain offenses which constitute exceptions to the principle that progressive discipline or a graduated series of penalties ought to be employed, such as dishonesty, theft, violence on the job, violent insubordination to supervision or management, and intoxication on the job. Under some circumstances, these are all forms of conduct which may warrant immediate dismissal.

In professional sports the analog to immediate dismissal is suspension for life and the near analog is a substantial suspension of a number of years or even a year, given the short playing career of professional athletes. Are there offenses in professional sports which are comparable to dishonesty, theft, violence and the like which would carve out an exception to progressive discipline? In the pre–2005 period, baseball was satisfied to simply require counseling of anonymous rule breakers for a first offense. This is the kind of progressive discipline that would be applied to most non–theft-dishonesty-violence rule infractions in industry generally, and it was an adherence to this approach which was one of the factors producing anger and outrage on the part of Congress as it addressed these issues in 2005. The baseball's union and industry allies on this issue, such as Murray Chass of the *New York Times*, quickly rushed to its defense when he wrote:

> [Congressman Henry] Waxman can thrust himself front and center on national television and have his own fifteen hours of fame.... I wanted to ask [Congressman Tom] Davis and Waxman about steroids, but I also wanted to ask them why they are so concerned about the potential dangers in steroids when they ignore the 400,000 deaths each year that the United States surgeon general has said are related to smoking.... "Why should baseball have to drudge up its dirty past and the National Football League does not" creates a double standard that must rightfully make Selig crazy.[7]

Yet this point, which was so frequently voiced by baseball insiders until the past few years, is both superficial and wrongheaded. The fact that there are other issues which need examination, inquiry and regulation does not argue against regulation in baseball. Baseball's obdurate and uncooperative backward approach has invited the so-called "double standard." When one considers the kind of sanctions that should be imposed, inevitably the discussion must focus upon comparability of performance-enhancing drugs to other issues like gambling and other forms of heinous behavior by athletes.

The concern with gambling goes back a considerable amount of time, given its obvious impact upon the integrity of the game. The 1877 Louisville Grays, prior to the advent of organized baseball as we know it today, was the first of the gambling scandals in this unprecedentedly commercialized sport. The 1919 "Black Sox" scandal, described below, as well as Cincinnati Reds superstar and manager Pete Rose's involvement in betting on games of his own team while he was its manager, have resulted in suspensions for life. In neither instance was a prior offense considered to be a prerequisite to the ultimate penalty.

Of course, Rose, as manager of the Reds, was not covered by the collective bargaining agreement between the players and the owners. Collective bargaining and collective bargaining agreements in baseball were not in existence at the time of the 1919 World Series "Black Sox" gambling scandal. Indeed, collective bargaining for most of the population, outside of skilled craftsmen and some miners and garment workers, did not exist at all!

Prior to the advent of collective bargaining in basketball, players have been expelled for gambling. In *Molinas v. National Basketball Association* a federal district court held that "a disciplinary rule invoked against gambling seems about as reasonable a rule as could be imagined."[8] The court held that a player wagering on his own team could be suspended from the NBA for life, the league characterizing the plaintiff as a "cancer on the league" which must be "excised." Said the court:

> When he [Molinas] chose to place a bet this would indicate to the bookmakers that a member of the Fort Wayne team believed that his team would exceed its expected performance. Similarly, when he chose not to bet, bookmakers thus would be informed of his opinion that the Pistons would not perform according to expectations. It is certainly reasonable for the League and [the Commissioner] ... to conclude that this conduct could not be tolerated and must, therefore, be eliminated. The reasonableness of the League's action is apparent in view of the fact that at the time, the confidence of the public in basketball had been shattered, due to a series of gambling incidents. Thus, it was absolutely necessary for the sport to exhume gambling from its midst for all times in order to survive. The league ... could reasonably ... restore and maintain the confidence of the public vital to its existence ... and ... apply the most stringent sanctions. One can certainly understand the reluctance to permit an admitted gambler to return to the league, and again to participate in championship games, especially in light of the aura and stigma of gambling which has clouded the sports world in the past few years.[9]

Thus the right to refuse reinstatement of the basketball player in question was upheld.

Today, under the collective bargaining agreement between the parties, which includes the NBA constitution, the Commissioner "shall direct the dismissal and perpetual disqualification from any further association with the Association" if "after a hearing [the player has been found by the Commissioner] to have been guilty of offering, agreeing, conspiring, aiding, or attempting to cause any game of basketball to result otherwise in on its merit." And in the same section the Commissioner is given "final, binding and conclusive and unappealable" authority regarding players who wager on the outcome of any game in the league, though here the punishment, while "within the absolute and sole discretion of the Commissioner ... may include a fine, suspension, expulsion and/or perpetual disqualification...."

The approach in baseball is different. Article XI of the collective bargaining agreement states that a grievance which involved the interpretation or compliance with the agreement "shall not mean a complaint which involves action taken with respect to a Player or Players by the Commissioner involving the preservation of the integrity of, or the maintenance of public confidence in, the game of baseball." While this portion of the contract between the parties does not mention gambling and thus theoretically affects the use of drugs in the game (in 2005 the Commissioner Bud Selig intimated that he might use this contractual provision to exercise power in the drug-testing arena), apparently it has been understood that its purpose relates to gambling. Here also the owner or the Commissioner is given "full, final and complete disposition" of the matter and the decision has the same effect as an arbitration award where disputes are properly within the grievance arbitrator's jurisdiction. Some of the recreational drug arbitral decisions suggest that this contract language has direct relevance to drugs and that this gives the Commissioner the authority to act in the areas under appropriate circumstance.

The issue of gambling as it relates to bargaining unit employees covered by the collective bargaining agreement appears to have faded in significance — principally because the players are paid so well. It is to be recalled that the White Sox were allegedly tempted to accept bribes and "throw" the 1919 World Series, in part, because of the penurious and mean-spirited conduct of owner Charlie Comiskey. Mean-spirited many of today's Lords of Baseball may be — but the dynamics, even for low-payroll teams like the Florida Marlins, Tampa Bay Rays and Kansas City Royals, are such that it is difficult for them to be penurious by the standards of most Americans today.

Yet, everything is relative in life. And with so much money in and outside of sports relating to the games, the problem of temptation for even the well-paid can never be completely dismissed, given the abbreviated career duration of the average athlete. Moreover, as the 2007 basketball referee scandal highlights, temptations for the considerably less well-paid adjudicators is an ongoing problem. And the Washington Wizards' Gilbert Arenas gun dispute of 2010 highlights the problem of off-the-field or court conduct such as gambling and its inevitable relationship to what happens in or near the game itself.

Other problems aside from gambling which affect the ability of baseball to promote the game remain. Principal among them is the problem of violence, particularly when engaged in on the playing field. Violence (discussed below) has been highlighted by recent events in basketball as well as baseball. One of the most prominent disputes arose as Coach Don Nelson's 1990s version of the Golden State Warriors began to disintegrate and various players looked for easy ways to find an exodus from what the players perceived to be a sinking ship. When basketball star Latrell Sprewell choked his coach while playing for the Warriors, the club and commissioner suspended him and the matter was taken to arbitration.

This is a very serious problem. Contrary to the *Sprewell* arbitration opinion, the matter of violence by a player against a coach is not comparable to violence between players. Generally, arbitrators have held that employee violence against supervisors is one of the cardinal sins which can justify dismissal without a prior offense because of its direct challenge to both order and production. The *Chacon* 2010 baseball arbitration, whereby a guaranteed contract was voided when a player attacked the general manager, properly recognizes this point. Yet the arbitrator in *Sprewell* compared this attack with other altercations between players themselves as he modified the substantial penalty imposed upon the player in question.[10]

Nonetheless, these matters do pale next to gambling, which is *sui generis*. Notwithstanding the apparent attractiveness of professional wrestling, gambling affects the integrity of all sports, baseball included. This is because, in contrast to *pure* theater and entertainment of that variety to which it bears a more than distant familial resemblance (recall that 1946 Yankees–White Sox double-header and my father's wry reaction to the Chicago White Sox manager's histrionics), the essence of the game's attractiveness to the watching public is the uncertainty of the result. This is the key element in its dramatic presentation and provides a contrast to other forms of entertainment where the story line and conclusion are frequently well known to the audience. Rare is the game which is so compelling that the baseball audience will watch a tape of it from beginning to end once it knows the end result! The difficulties that ESPN has had obtaining an audience for historic games supports this proposition.

Thus the bedrock of sports is its implacable hostility to gambling, whether it involves the games' result or point spread, at least from the time of the infamous "Black Sox" scandal of 1919, when leading members of the Chicago White Sox allegedly threw the World Series in which the White Sox had been favored against the Cincinnati Reds. The famous "Say it ain't so, Joe" is the comment that a child reputedly made to "Shoeless" Joe Jackson, the White Sox outfielder (supposedly at least complicit in the scandal) who was baseball's hitting machine, unrivaled until the development of Babe Ruth and the advent of Ted Williams in 1939. Exclusion via suspension from the game of baseball for life was reaffirmed anew in the case of Pete Rose in 1989, though his gambling offenses took place when he was a manager and not a player. Accordingly the issue of gambling has never been addressed under the collective bargaining agreement, i.e., whether the Commissioner's authority to impose any sanction in the "best interest of baseball" is under all circumstances compatible with, and more precisely, beyond the just-cause provision of the collective bargaining agreement, which protects bargaining unit baseball players against disciplinary sanctions by both the Commissioner and the clubs that are unjust.

Rule 21 of the Major League Rules prohibits gambling on baseball and other related conduct such as rewarding opponents through such methods as "grooving" a perfect pitch to allow a hitter to have a home run. Even Barry Bonds would admit that since the Black Sox 1919 scandal such conduct is recognized as "cheating" that can affect the integrity of the game. Illegal use of performance-enhancing drugs should be viewed as cheating and, as we see below, this is one of the bases for its prohibition and regulation in baseball.

It is said that the policy as it relates to gambling was in fact applied inconsistently long before collective bargaining. The involvement of yesteryear greats like outfielders Ty Cobb and Tris Speaker and the Red Sox pitching hero of 1912, Smokey Joe Wood, with gamblers, and the first "Dutch" Leonard with gambling on baseball games itself, has been well chronicled.[11] But, notwithstanding what many regarded as the convincing nature of the charges against these superstars of their day, no action was taken by Commissioner Kenesaw Landis, whose office was created so as to combat the 1919 Black Sox scandal.

Again, since then, the problem of gambling has subsided to the background. The issue of drug-taking by baseball players has overtaken all of that, at least during the past three and a half or four decades.

In 2005, at the Baseball Steroid Hearings conducted by the House Government Operations Committee, the question of whether gambling is comparable to the consumption of drugs when engaged in by baseball players was put to Major Baseball League Players Association Executive Director Don Fehr, but he avoided a direct response to the question, noting correctly that the gambling issue had not arisen in connection with bargaining unit employees. When questioned about why a series of penalties were to be imposed upon players beginning with relatively abbreviated suspensions — Republican Congressman Christopher Shays characterized the agreement as providing for "five strikes and you're out" — Fehr cited the practice of progressive discipline as well accepted in labor-management relations. As noted, this practice obliging employers to counsel and suspend employees prior to taking more severe disciplinary action such as discharge — or in the case of baseball, suspension for life or for years — has been used in private industry and the public sector. Neither

Congress nor Fehr directly addressed the question of where drug offenses, in the hierarchy of misconduct, precisely lie.

Is there something peculiar about drugs in a competitive sport — a competition not present in other forms of entertainment like theater and movies — which makes it akin to gambling or more serious than the kind of misconduct which normally comes before arbitrators? As we shall see, the labor arbitration cases in baseball dealing with drugs focus, in part, upon harm that can be done to the industry, which is inevitably rooted in public acceptance. It seems that the universal condemnation by the public heaped upon gambling at the beginning of the previous century and today is not completely present in the drug cases.

True, Barry Bonds, who has been the subject of much discussion involving performance-enhancing drugs, was booed lustily in many ballparks throughout the country. Yet he was not booed in San Francisco while a member of that team — quite the contrary! On Opening Day in '05, '06 and '07, as Bonds's involvement with drugs was chronicled by the grand jury testimony provided in the BALCO case, in which Bonds, along with Jason Giambi and Gary Sheffield of the Yankees, were found to have taken anabolic steroids, Bonds was *cheered* lustily by the crowd in Pac Bell Park (now called AT&T) in San Francisco. Giambi was cold-shouldered by Yankee fans after his grand jury testimony, in which he admitted to steroid consumption, was revealed. But when his physical condition and batting performance recovered, he was welcomed back by the Yankee Stadium throng unqualifiedly. Most dramatically, Alex Rodriguez, who first denied and then implausibly affirmed drug taking in the relatively distant past, received absolution in the wake of the 2009 World Series. Stated Harvey Araton in an article which spoke of "redemption": "2009 may go down as the year in which fans forgave baseball because of Rodriguez's 'astute apology' and his formidable performance in the 2009 World Series!"[12] Araton, nimbly recognizing that he was writing for a New York paper, nonetheless cited a cultural anthropology department chairman at Duke University as the authority for the proposition that Rodriguez had received a "standing ovation from the court of public opinion."[13] Subsequently, he has been linked to a Montreal doctor who allegedly promotes the use of HGH, human growth hormone, for which no baseball testing exists at present.[14] He has been contrasted to his unrepentant teammate Roger Clemens, whose defiance has produced a perjury indictment.

Most Giants and Yankees fans frequently offer one of a number of explanations: (1) "Everybody's doing it"— though those of previous generations, against whom Bonds's records are being compared, clearly did not do it; (2) there is no relationship between drug taking and performance; (3) it has not been proved in an adjudication where witnesses are presented and there is an opportunity to defend himself that Bonds and others similarly situated are using these drugs.

Beginning with the Olympic movement and the scandals of the '60s and '70s particularly those involving East German track athletes and swimmers, there has been a refusal to countenance performance enhancements by the World's Anti-Doping Agency (WADA), particularly when they are dangerous to the health of the athlete or they violate "the spirit of sport."[15] Yet the tradition of doping in athletics is longstanding, going back to the third century B.C., when hallucinogens were taken by the Greeks — and in modern times from 1886, when an English cyclist died of an overdose of what is known as "trimethyl" during a race between Bordeaux and Paris. In the Roman era, stimulants were used by gladiators in the well-known Circus Maximus. Only in 1968 did the International Olympic Commission medical commission ban a list of prohibited drugs for the '68 Winter Olympics.

Since then there have been attempts to regulate and to catch up with developments in technology and science. Professional athletics have been relatively slow to regulate because of both the concern by owners that such problems are, at best, a diversion from the public's enjoyment of the games and thus a potential interference with profits, as well as the existence of unions (baseball has been the strongest and most obdurate in this matter) which have sometimes fought vigorously against any attempt to interfere with so-called rights of privacy.

In any event, the problem of drugs in baseball—where, as we have already seen, the union is strong and vigorous in protection of its members—if not the equivalent of gambling, is something out of the ordinary and different from a wide variety of other types of misconduct.

Again, unlike gambling, which is a more extreme form of straight-out dishonesty, the unions have argued for the relevance of a policy of progressive discipline, which is bound up with just-cause language in collective bargaining agreements, that proceeds upon the assumption that the employees' attitude and behavior can be altered so that he or she can do the job more effectively. In connection with the steroid problems of the '90s, however, the issue was enhancement, i.e., that the player was enhancing his competitive position in the game by virtue of an unfair advantage. Though this conduct, in contrast to recreational drugs, constitutes a direct analog to dishonesty, one cannot say that possible rehabilitation is out of the question.

Enhancements are a more complex issue—first because, as noted, they do not produce universal condemnation among the public. A substantial number of those who care about baseball and sports are bothered only a little or not at all if one of the hometown heroes produces good results. As we can see, this applies to Bonds, Giambi and Rodriguez. And similarly, David Ortiz was welcomed back warmly in '09 (Manny Ramirez had already been forgotten in the distant past) when he was revealed to be on the 2003 list of those who had tested positive. (Of course, Ortiz—unlike the four immediately forementioned, was not a jerk, but rather a likeable Big Papi.)[16] The .240 hitter would get different treatment by the public.

It seems possible that where individual player sports, like cycling, tennis and swimming, for instance, are affected by drugs, the public's reaction may be somewhat different. After all, the team sport encourages rationalization and justification for anything that an individual player is doing, so the question is always asked whether the team effort and record been changed or appreciably changed. Will the same be true in individual sports? At the same time, proponents of drug enhancement legalization say that: "[I]t seems inhuman to ask athletes to pedal their bikes at great speed some 2,200 miles in three weeks [in the Tour de France], often up torturous mountain passes, without chemical assistance."[17]

Second, in contrast to recreational drugs (or at least their use by some athletes), performance-enhancing drugs do not, at least in the short run, impair effectiveness, but rather improve it in a number of respects (though this itself has been a disputed matter). For instance, fitness is a prerequisite (perhaps ignored by such baseball worthies as Babe Ruth, who consumed considerable quantities of alcohol and kept irregular hours during the baseball playing season), and this is generally associated with exercise, calisthenics, running, and in more recent years a regimen of weight lifting, which has made baseball players stronger and presumably more able to hit home runs. Moreover, as my colleague Professor Henry Greely has noted, while athletes have been precluded from increasing the number of their red blood cells through injections of Epogen or Procrit—it is a "serious violation of the antidoping rules"—the sale of high-altitude oxygen tents that control the atmosphere so as to provide lower-than-normal levels of oxygen (the body compensates by producing more erythropoi-etim and thus more red blood cells), as well as low oxygen breathing mass systems, have not been banned. States Professor Greely:

> All of these athletes gain a competitive advantage from having above-normal amounts of red blood cells as a result of having above-normal levels of erythropoietim. In two of the cases this advantage is completely uncontroversial, in one it is slightly controversial, and in another it continues to be debated, and in one, but only one, it is banned. Why? What makes the injection of Epogen or Procrit an improper way to enhance athletic performance?[18]

Professor Greely sees "plausible explanations" in prohibiting performance-enhancing drugs, but no "compelling ones."[19] First among them are the potential safety risks—par-ticularly of anabolic steroids as well as amphetamines. At the same time, non-drug enhance-ments, like conditioning during hot summer days, particularly in football where heavy equipment is worn by players, have been known to produce death. My view is that this is similar to Murray Chass's no-smoking argument requiring that all problems be addressed before any (in this case drugs) can be taken on. Some practice sessions like football players in extreme heat need to be more carefully regulated as well as drugs.

The safety argument with regard to anabolic steroids is the strongest of all. Players like Jason Giambi of the Yankees, who suffered from a tumor on his pituitary gland in 2004, may have imperiled their immediate (or not so immediate) health. Congress began its 2005 Baseball Steroid Hearings with testimony from the parents of young players who had emu-lated major league players by taking steroids and who suffered from increased irritability and mood swings, and in some prominent instances committed suicide. The 2007 landmark Mitchell Report[20] stated emphatically that there are "sufficient data to conclude that there is an association between steroid abuse and significant adverse effects" including psychiatric and cardiovascular problems, liver injury and harm to the reproductive system. Moreover, states the Mitchell Report: "There also appears to be a connection between steroid use and an increased risk of tendon tears in athletes." It is of some interest to note that a number of prominent players who have been mentioned as drug users seem to have suffered sub-stantial and lengthy muscle injuries, McGwire being prominent among them. And Mitchell also said that human growth hormone, the prohibition of which is now also part of baseball's drug policy, can also have adverse consequences, e.g., "acromegaly, the overgrowth of bone and connective tissue that leads to protrusion of the jaw and eyebrow bones, and gigantism, the overgrowth of the entire body in children or adolescents," the latter of which cannot occur in adults because growth zones are sealed. The consequences include "cancer, impo-tence in men, menstrual irregularities in women, cardiomyopathy, hypothyroidism and arthritis."[21]

What do steroids accomplish for the player? There has been little actual discussion, though much debate about the relationship between performance enhancement in baseball and performance, and indeed ongoing skepticism about the gains to be obtained through HGH, abound.[22] McGwire maintained that steroids had not enhanced his hitting ability and were not responsible for his 70 home run record year in 1998.

There seems little doubt that, in football for instance, 350-pound linemen can fre-quently push smaller people out of the way. Baseball is relatively complex. Are steroids or other enhancement drugs responsible for an offensive power surge in baseball? In this con-nection, it is interesting to note that most of the players who have been identified as having tested positive for prohibited drugs in the early days of 2005 drug testing revisions are not power hitters, but rather pitchers and utility players who presumably have used steroids for their recuperative benefits for injured players. In some respects, this use of these drugs can be analogized to cortisone which, as ex–New York Yankee and Twin pitcher Jim Kaat advised me, were used on players in his generation in the '60s and '70s with considerable frequency. (This continues to be the case today.) Pitchers attempt to recuperate from the wear and tear and stress of throwing a ball, in some instance, more than one hundred times on a given day. Just as was the case with cortisone in the '60s and '70s, the new round of drugs are designed to permit players to come back from injuries more quickly.

However, the cortisone and prednisone variety of the steroid family which are prescribed by medical physicians are designed to *maintain* performance, not *enhance* it. But the demarcation line is sometimes somewhat synthetic. Drugs which maintain performance are banned in the Olympic Games because it is believed that users gain a sense of euphoria which can be helpful in a competitive setting. Baseball is not in line with this international consensus, attempting to draw a bright line between maintenance and enhancement.

Steroids are assumed to have been responsible, in substantial part, for the dramatic increase in home run production. Of course, as baseball officials never tired in asserting, the smaller ballparks, beginning with Baltimore's Camden Yards in 1992, and the expansion of clubs to thirty, which has diluted pitching more than hitting, have played a secondary role. It is thought that both the owners and union ignored the steroid problem in 1998 because it brought baseball back from the abyss in which it was lodged after the World Series — canceling '94–'95 strike — and that McGwire and Sosa were steroid users whose careers quickly declined as baseball began to take a firmer regulatory stance in '02, or who were overtaken by injuries generally associated with steroids.

David Leonhart in the *New York Times* has noted that the upswing in home runs was sharper in '96–'97 than in '98 and that the case for increased revenue as a result of the '98 season in attendance and television has not been clearly made. But clearly, in the wake of the strike, the home run ball has achieved an "almost absurd dominance," at least until the years 2004 and '05. The forty- and fifty-home-run-per-year plateau was assaulted with more frequency. Yet ex–San Diego Padre President Sandy Alderson, until recently Vice-President of Major League Baseball, and Will Carroll have nonetheless noted the other factors, i.e., expansion, the size of ballparks, and the fact that some say that the ball itself is "juiced." Carroll, however, notes that except for the 1993 expansion, homers have generally fallen back to previous levels within a year or two of the arrival of the new teams, and that some of the new parks — like Comerica in Detroit, Petco in San Diego and AT&T in San Francisco — are pitchers' parks. The fact is that the power (and in some measure batting averages) continued to soar upwards from 2000 until '06, falling back in '07, '08 and '09. This is no doubt attributable to the tightening of drug testing, and the publicity provided by the landmark book *Game of Shadows* on BALCO, the Mitchell Report, and also the litigation about the confidentiality of the drug testing.

Yet the nexus between drugs and performance is disputed by some altogether. Though the hitting of the baseball is a hand/eye coordination phenomenon, the enhancement drugs may enhance that particular attribute. My friend and colleague, the late Leonard Koppett, argued endlessly with me that Barry Bonds's performance could not be enhanced through drugs because of his superior coordination and eyesight, wrists, strength, etc. But the fact is that most balls are hit only a few rows back into the stands and the strength — whether associated with steroids or weight lifting or other measures — undoubtedly provides that extra distance for a large number of home runs. As author Howard Bryant (author of the book *Juicing the Game*) noted, the "assumption" of talent was a "given." He noted that the fact that steroids could not enhance one's ability to hit the ball was irrelevant; that wasn't at issue at all, but rather the question of whether the ball could be hit better! Said Bryant:

> Steroids were, in many ways, perfect for baseball. Anabolic steroids enhanced quickness, which was crucial to a baseball player's swing or ability to steal a base. They built muscle mass, even without exercising, giving players unprecedented power and increased aggression.... [They] allowed athletes to heal faster from injury. Recovery speed in a sport like baseball with so many games and so few days off was especially advantageous.[23]

The recovery or healing function was particularly important to aging athletes as they moved into their late thirties. This is what prompted the otherwise irascible and frequently irrational Senator Jim Bunning of Kentucky, a former left-handed Hall of Fame pitcher with the Detroit Tigers and the Pittsburgh Pirates, to compare hitters like Bonds, who is now in his forties, with Williams at a similar age. Though Williams continued to hit well (except for his penultimate year of 1959), age took its toll on both batting average and home run production.[24]

As Alan Schwarz has noted in discussing *Baseball Prospectus* projections relating to Bonds:

> Entering 2000 at age 35, Bonds was producing seasons with roughly thirty-seven home runs and a .288 batting average. His skyrocketing performance in the five seasons since, particularly while moving from the good hitter's park (Candlestick) to a horrible one (SBC), is all but unprecedented in baseball history. Had Bonds aged at a typical rate, he would hit .272, not .339, and hit 142 fewer home runs, 116 instead of 258.[25]

In contrast, Bonds's performance has moved sharply upward in unprecedented fashion in the last five years prior to his injuries in 2005. Bonds's enormous change in physique during this period of time attracted a great deal of attention and, coupled with the BALCO testimony and the detailed fact finding of *Game of Shadows*, it seems likely that Bonds would have been more than 100 home runs away from Aaron's record when he broke it in 2007.

Some commentators like Will Carroll have derided the significance of Bonds's performance by highlighting the fact that other sluggers like Hank Aaron, Willie Stargell and Carlton Fisk had increased home run production as they moved into their late thirties and sometimes their early forties. But this misses the point. For Bonds is not only hitting home runs, his entire statistical portfolio has moved upward — particularly batting percentages as well as runs batted in. Though Bonds is an extraordinary player, he would not be a lifetime .300 hitter (in fact, at the time of his record-breaking 756 he was only at .298) without the benefit of the late '90s and early twenty-first century. Again, that, along with his changed physique and some of the injury problems that he had in '05 as well as the information contained in *Game of Shadows*, is what makes him so suspect.

Wherever one places steroids in the hierarchy of cheating, what is unique and peculiar is the increased risk of injuries and the great potential for injury to tendons in particular. It is thought that Mark McGwire's premature retirement was attributable to the fact that his frame could not withstand the muscle mass created by steroids. Similarly, in '05 and to a lesser extent in '06, Bonds's long absences and physical difficulties have been thought to be attributable to steroids as well. As noted, Giambi suffered from a tumor on his pituitary gland in 2004, a phenomenon generally thought to be associated with steroid use. Paul Byrd, who in 2007 admitted to taking Human Growth Hormone, suffered from the same problem as well. Indeed, David Ortiz had mysterious wrist difficulties in '08 and '09.

As the Mitchell Report noted, the long-range consequences of steroids are arguably even more considerable. MVP Ken Caminiti of the San Diego Padres openly confessed to his use of steroids and its role in mental and physical difficulties prior to his premature death. Congress has heard testimony from the parents of young people who have emulated established players who in some instances have suffered from "'Roid Rage," mental depression, increased irritability, mood swings and suicide.

And steroids are only part of the problem. Thanks to the efforts of Senator Orrin Hatch of Utah (whose son has acted as a lobbyist for health supplement facilities), President Clinton signed into law the Dietary Supplements Health and Education Act (DSHEA), which theoretically was designed to provide consumers with more medicinal remedies but, in practice, shifted the burden of proof relating to product safety from the manufacturer to the Food and Drug Administration (FDA). The result was a boom for the supplement industry and, for instance, the use of legal so-called steroid precursors like androstenedione, used by Mark McGwire during his home run record-setting year of 1998. (This was the drug that an inquiring reporter discovered on McGwire's locker shelf, resulting in his ban from the Cardinals' clubhouse.)

Second, there is the matter of human growth hormones, used by a number of major leaguers including ex-pitcher Jason Grimsley and others whom he named in an affidavit submitted to the United States government. As the Mitchell Report suggested, this may well be the continued enhancement drug of choice by a number major leaguers because it is not "detectible in any currently available urine test."[26] As allegedly reported in the Grimsley affidavit, these drugs were used by Yankee pitcher Roger Clemens (whose physique has changed enormously since the '90s as well) and his sidekick with both the Yankees and Astros, lefty Andy Pettite. On the eve of the seventh game of the American League Championship in 2007 between the Red Sox and the Indians, the *San Francisco Chronicle* reported that Paul Byrd, whose old-fashioned windup was of the kind that my father and I had admired in the 1940s, had purchased HGH from '02 through '05 until the eve of its prohibition by MLB.[27]

And lastly there was the problem of amphetamines, or the so-called "greenies" made openly available in clubhouses to players who consumed them in large quantities. Marvin Miller of the Major League Players Association noted that the players and the union had nothing to do with this drug, but that it was made available to them by the owners. This became an important drug of choice with expansion and the increased travel and jet lag associated with change in time zones from coast to coast. They appear to have been used by many players with considerable frequency.

In order to gain some understanding of where we stand now and, more particularly, what type of baseball disciplinary action could have been taken against Barry Bonds and the also indicted ex-pitcher and Cy Young winner Roger Clemens[28] subsequent to indictment or conviction, or either player's revelation as a drug abuser through baseball's own investigative efforts, it is important to look back to the arbitral law which has evolved on drugs since the '80s.

The 1980s situation involving drug policy was completely different from the situation today. Yet ironically it laid the foundation for the drug-testing changes in the collective bargaining agreement instituted in '02 and '05.

This began in 1985, when testimony about the use of cocaine emerged in a Pittsburgh case in which nineteen major leaguers testified or were implicated, and one individual was convicted of selling cocaine to baseball players. Peter Ueberroth, then Commissioner of

Baseball, suspended eleven players for cocaine use and pushed for a strict drug-testing policy which was never implemented. Drug testing was to be pushed to one side, although numerous disputes arose out of suspensions of players in the wake of the '85 scandal. And baseball initially promoted a drug-testing policy applicable to all in MLB except players — then, in a case discussed below, attempted to insert drug-testing clauses into individual player contracts of employment.

The first adjudication arising under the collective bargaining agreement — it arose prior to the 1985 criminal trial in Pittsburgh — involved Hall of Fame pitcher Ferguson Jenkins, who achieved prominence with the Chicago Cubs, the Boston Red Sox and the Texas Rangers. Jenkins was with the Rangers when he was suspended by Commissioner Bowie Kuhn after being arrested by Canadian police at Toronto Stadium during the 1980 season before the start of the game between the Texas Rangers and the Toronto Blue Jays. Jenkins was charged with possession of 1.75 ounces of marijuana, 2.2 grams of hashish and 3.3 grams of cocaine. These substances were reportedly found in Jenkins's luggage by Canadian customs officers as the team's luggage and equipment were being moved through customs after being unloaded from the Rangers' charter flight from Dallas to Toronto. Jenkins was not present with his luggage at the time these substances were claimed to have been found.

The Canadian authorities released Jenkins within an hour or so of his arrest and a trial date was set for December. Commissioner Kuhn, upon learning of the arrest, contacted Jenkins's lawyer and arranged for a so-called "investigatory interview" of Jenkins with his lawyer present — an interview conducted by Major League Baseball's director of security for the Commissioner's office. Fehr, then general counsel for the Players Association, and an attorney from the Commissioner's office were present. Jenkins was advised by his lawyer not to respond to a line of questioning dealing with this incident as well as questions relating to his alleged possible prior illegal drug use.

Arbitrator Raymond Goetz noted that the Players Association did not question the basic authority of the Commissioner to investigate unlawful use or possession of drugs by players, nor his authority to impose penalties against players who refuse to cooperate in such investigations. The arbitrator held — and this is a policy that has been followed for the past quarter century — that disciplinary action arising out of, in this case, the failure to cooperate with a drug investigation or drug use itself was governed by the collective bargaining agreement's "just cause" provisions under which the Commissioner or the club has the burden of proof through a preponderance of evidence to establish that such action has been instituted for just cause. In the *Jenkins* matter the Commissioner's discipline did not deprive him of pay but rather his ability to perform in major league games. The arbitrator quickly concluded that this was discipline within the meaning of the agreement and the parties' practices, notwithstanding the provision of pay and benefits.[29]

Arbitrator Goetz held that the arrest itself could not provide a basis for finding just cause for the action taken since under both Canadian and American law a criminal defendant is presumed innocent until proven guilty. Though he acknowledged in his opinion a few exceptional circumstances such as the unwillingness of fellow employees to work alongside of an individual where violence had been involved, this was not the case here. Said Goetz: "In all likelihood, Jenkins's teammates are most anxious to have their leading pitcher returned for the crucial closing weeks of the season." On the more significant question of whether Jenkins's appearance in a uniform while under arrest would undermine public support for baseball or create a public relations problem for baseball, the arbitrator concluded that this lacked "proper foundation."

Arbitrator Goetz noted the "well founded apprehension of the Commissioner and the public about unlawful use of drugs in professional sports," but concluded that the suspension mandated with regard to this incident, and the assumption about public reaction to it, seemed "unwarranted." Said the arbitrator, while noting that there was no evidence of any critical commentary by the press or others: "Can it really be supposed in the present-day attitudes about matters of this kind that any significant number of baseball fans would withdraw their support if Jenkins were allowed to appear in uniform with the Rangers before he has had his day in court?" Because Jenkins would be tipping his hand at his criminal prosecution if he had responded to questions posed to him by the Commissioner's representative and thus would have jeopardized his defense, and the fact that the arrest was for "simple possession of small quantities of untested substances" and thus did not present allegations relating to more serious unlawful activities, in light of his past record and the severity of the penalty, the grievance was sustained and Jenkins was restored to active status with the Rangers immediately.

But the facts and arbitral commentary began to change as the 1980s unfolded. First, a series of arbitral cases involving the convictions of some baseball players like Willie Wilson, Jerry Martin, Willie Aikens of the Kansas City Royals, and Vida Blue, the outstanding left-hander for both the Oakland A's and the San Francisco Giants, created a new arbitral jurisprudence. The same was true of the Pittsburgh trials which followed these cases, and further proceedings where the Pittsburgh Pirates sued slugging outfielder Dave Parker for contract damages after his departure to the Cincinnati Reds for his involvement in recreational drugs while he played for the Pirates.

But the *Wilson* arbitration, which involved both Wilson and Jerry Martin, set the stage for much of what was to follow. Both Wilson and Martin were sentenced to one year in prison with all but three months of the term suspended and they were fined $5,000 and $2,500 respectively for possession of drugs. Each of them was placed on probation for two years commencing with his release from prison. The Commissioner, based upon the criminal convictions and the acknowledged use of illegal drugs, imposed a one-year unpaid suspension on each player. The players were required by virtue of the Commissioner's edict to remain in probationary status until the end of the court-imposed probationary period. The Commissioner cited major league rule 21(f), binding upon the players by virtue of the Uniform Players Contract (itself incorporated in the collective bargaining agreement), which speaks of conduct which is not "to be in the best interests of Baseball," and article I, section 2, of the collective bargaining agreement, under which the Commissioner may investigate practices suspected of not being in the "best interests of the National Game of Baseball." The Players Association did not contest the Commissioner's authority to issue a disciplinary suspension in connection with drug-related activities, but rather both challenged the additional probationary period as beyond the Commissioner's authority, and argued that the medical examination authority given to the clubs constituted an exclusive means of determining whether the players are acting properly.

In the *Wilson* case the arbitrator rejected the idea that the players' contract relating to medical treatment by the clubs would "somehow preempt" the disciplinary authority of the Commissioner. Again, the just-cause provision was invoked as a limitation upon the Commissioner's authority. Arbitrator Richard Bloch noted that "there can be little question" that rule 21(f) prohibiting conduct "not in the best interest of Baseball" was relevant and that the conduct of the players was thus "a matter of legitimate concern to the Commissioner." Said the arbitrator:

At its worst, to the extent cocaine use becomes habitual or addictive, a player risks both an increased chance of physical deterioration, and a dangerous involvement with the criminals who sell the drug. That involvement may lead to control of the player either because of the addiction or because of the risks of exposure. The consequences of such control over any part of the game are so obviously disastrous as to require no elaboration.... Nor can there be serious doubt that this type of employee misconduct is of serious impact on the employer. Because baseball players are highly skilled, well compensated and constantly visible, they deserve and receive national attention. Neither the players nor the industry escapes the publicity. And, drug involvement, because of its threat to athletes' playing abilities, because it is illegal and because of the related connotation of inroads by organized crime, constitutes a serious and immediate threat to the business that is promoted as our national pastime.[30]

In *Wilson* the players were convicted of criminal possession of drugs and, as the arbitrator emphasized, cooperated with the Commissioner. This was different from *Jenkins*, where an arrest and not a conviction was presented, and where it was possible to dismiss the harm to the game posed by Jenkins's participation in Rangers games while the matter was being resolved. But even in *Wilson* the arbitrator employed reasoning now discussed in connection with steroids when he noted that it was impossible to determine if drugs had harmed the Royals' performance on the field and their ticket sales, it being in his words "impossible to quantify." Thus, the arbitrator rejected the association's position that the Commissioner's authority to fashion a probationary period for the players involved was somehow preempted by the clubs' contractual right to institute medical examinations. But the arbitrator nonetheless concluded that a penalty beyond the one-year suspension was not consistent with the just cause requirement. The arbitrator's reasoning was that not only had the players provided immediate and open cooperation, but that they had been "hit very hard" by the judicial system by virtue of receiving the maximum prison sentence and maximum fine, even though the players' drug involvement was "limited." Said the arbitrator: "There is no evidence, and there is no assertion by the Commissioner that Wilson and Martin ever used cocaine on the job or that their play was in any way affected by it."[31]

But the opinion noted that, notwithstanding the modification of the penalty imposed by the Commissioner, "the problems of drug involvement are of real concern"—and in a subsequent decision involving Atlanta Braves pitcher Pascual Perez, while dismissing the evidence against Perez, the arbitrator noted that the problem of the drugs was "vital."[32] Again, in the *Hoyt*[33] case, in which the penalty imposed upon the San Diego Padres and the erstwhile Chicago White Sox right-hander was set aside, the arbitrator again acknowledged "baseball's legitimate and substantial interest in eliminating drug use among players and non-player personnel."[34]

In *Hoyt* the Padres' pitcher pled guilty to the possession of various controlled substances while crossing the border from Mexico to the United States. He was convicted of a misdemeanor for possession and provided a minimum sentence of 45 days and a fine of $5,000, as well as five years' probation conditioned *inter alia* on random testing, psychiatric counseling and abstinence from narcotics, marijuana, LSD or other dangerous drugs. The Padres terminated his contract almost immediately for violation of club policy relating to drugs and failure to adhere to warnings. Commissioner Ueberroth, once Hoyt had completed his sentence, declared him ineligible for the 1987 season and stated that his reinstatement in 1988 or sooner would be conditioned upon participation in a rehabilitation drug program as well as an appropriate drug-testing procedure supervised by the Commissioner's office. Both sanctions were challenged as without just cause—and again, the arbitrator agreed with union's position.

This time the reasoning was predicated upon the fact that Hoyt had never used cocaine during his major league career — there was not a "sliver of evidence" to this effect, said the arbitrator — nor was there evidence of recreational use of illegal drugs. Valium, used by Hoyt here, was illegal only when used without a prescription, as he did, in contrast to cocaine which is illegal *per se*. The arbitrator concluded that the club had not conducted an appropriate investigation in consideration of the specific nature of the offense and had not fashioned a disciplinary sanction which was responsive to it, and thus did not carefully weigh all the facts as "just cause requires."

The arbitrator also set aside the Commissioner's one-year ban because of its inconsistency with prior action. In this connection, the arbitrator noted that the players penalized by the Commissioner in the Pittsburgh trial dispute — where both the sharing and distribution of drugs to others was involved, as well as the introduction to drug dealers — involved a one-year suspension for the entire 1986 season but, in lieu thereof, 100 hours of community service for the following two years, as well as contribution of 10 percent of the base salary and random testing. The players chose the latter alternative. Also noted was the use of cocaine in *Wilson* and the heavy involvement in cocaine in the *Vida Blue* case. When viewed from the perspective of misconduct of others, the arbitrator held that a year's suspension was not consistent with just cause in *Hoyt*. However, the arbitrator viewed the lesser penalty of sixty days' suspension as appropriate.

On the other hand, Arbitrator George Nicolau upheld the Commissioner's suspension of the Atlanta Braves' centerfielder Otis Nixon for just cause under the Agreement.[35] Here, Nixon had been tested for cocaine use under a random testing program to which he was subject due to his use of illegal drugs in 1987 when he was in the minor leagues. When positive results for cocaine emerged from testing in September '91, the Commissioner imposed a sixty-day suspension. This suspension barred Nixon from playing in the remaining game of the '91 season, the League Championship Series, the National League Championship Series and the World Series if Atlanta participated, as indeed they did. In *Nixon* the arbitrator upheld the position of the Commissioner and distinguished *Wilson* inasmuch as they were first-time offenders and Nixon was a second time offender. Moreover, *Hoyt* was distinguished inasmuch as those offenses occurred off-season and did not involve cocaine, whereas Nixon's problems arose in the context of his team "battling for division title." Sounding a theme in *dicta* which would emerge again, the arbitrator noted "apparent declining [drug] use within the industry," but nonetheless concluded that the Commissioner had acted properly in relying upon deterrence in fashioning the penalty.

The reasoning of both *Nixon* and *Hoyt* seem sound. But some of the *dicta*— that portion of the opinion which contains language unnecessary to the precise conclusion in the case — in both cases missed the mark considerably. Said Arbitrator Nicolau in *Hoyt*:

> It should also be noted, in response to an argument advanced from theCommissioner's behalf, that Hoyt's suspension was not imposed at a time when the problem of drugs in baseball was accelerating. By all available evidence, the early '80s trend discerned by the Commissioner and others had been reversed. Thus, the "growing problem/growing sanctions" argument does not hold.[36]

This language seems ironic considering a number of developments both before and after *Hoyt*. The first problem is to be found in the facts of the *Steve Howe* arbitration.[37] Here an outstanding left-handed relief pitcher, at this point with the New York Yankees, had been hospitalized for drug-related treatment on six occasions and suspended from baseball six times. In 1990, two years before the arbitration in question, the union had grieved the

Howe suspension because of violations of his drug after-care program, and the Commissioner had agreed to permit Howe to return under certain conditions. Howe was provided a stringent after-care program which entailed testing as many as three times per week for the remainder of his career, and the Commissioner directed that he, Howe, be removed from baseball in the event of a positive drug test. When Howe was arrested and provided a guilty plea in an off-season incident for possession of cocaine, Commissioner Fay Vincent banned Howe for life.

Again, Arbitrator Nicolau held that the suspension for life was not consistent with the just-cause provision. He noted that the Commissioner, while conditioning his 1990 return on regular testing and a caution to the effect that Howe be tested every other day, created a policy which was not heeded and implemented by baseball. Since baseball had not implemented regular testing, the arbitrator concluded that Howe had not been provided with a fair shot at success. Again, ironically, the arbitrator said: "All available evidence supports the proposition that drug use in organized baseball is not what it appeared to be some years ago.... There has not been an 'initial offender' in the Major Leagues since 1989 and those who unfortunately repeated an offense are concededly no more than a handful."[38]

But, of course, at the very time of the *Howe* arbitration, another different kind of drug problem was developing, i.e., steroids and HGH. In order to gain understanding of it one needs to backtrack to 1984.

In 1984, in the wake of the *Wilson* and *Perez* arbitrations, baseball and the Players Association negotiated a reasonable cause arrangement for the testing of players. But when MLB could not extend this program to random testing in the teeth of Players Association resistance, it unilaterally discontinued it. Without random testing, the problem then and now with reasonable cause procedures is that the parties who are in a position to invoke such a standard have no interest in doing it. Neither the players, who would be regarded as snitches, nor the owners, who might be depriving themselves of much-needed talent, would see it as necessarily in their interests to take this step. Thus, there was a need for some other policy.

Meanwhile, as noted above, the clubs, following the conclusion of the '85 season, insisted that players include in their uniform players' contract a special covenant providing for drug testing. But in Panel Decision No. 69,[39] these drug-testing clauses introduced by the clubs were held to be in violation of the Agreement because they did not confer a "benefit upon the player" as the Agreement requires in connection with special covenants between players and owners. Arbitrator Thomas Roberts noted that this drug-testing policy was inconsistent with the Agreement's requirement that such terms and conditions of employment be negotiated only with the exclusive bargaining representative, the Players Association, as required by the contract. Thus, by virtue of the 1986 Roberts award, neither the clubs or the Commissioner could obtain drug testing. This also explains why, as Arbitrator Nicolau noted, all was quiet on the drug violation front in the late '80s and early '90s except for the *ad hoc* arbitrations, which raised the question of whether discipline imposed upon players who had been involved with recreational drugs — as in the *Hoyt*, *Nixon* and *Howe* cases — were consistent with just cause. But there were many warnings that a darker cloud was hovering over baseball, including a famous Jose Canseco incident in 1988 in Fenway Park, where the fans shouted "steroids, steroids" and he simply flexed his muscles and laughed.

Then, in the wake of the 1994-95 strike, came the upsurge of home run and power production most prominently illustrated by the 1998 home run race to break Roger Maris's thirty-seven-year-old record of sixty-one homers conducted by Mark McGwire and Sammy

Sosa (both broke the Maris record). Only Cal Ripken's dramatic 1995 leap over the Lou Gehrig consecutive-game record was comparable in overcoming baseball fan disillusionment in the wake of the strike. Then came Barry Bonds's 2001 mind-numbing, record-setting 73 home run achievement. As noted above, Bonds, whose physical appearance and upsurge in performance in his mid– and late thirties attracted considerable curiosity and skepticism, provided for more attention to be given to the question of steroids.

But BALCO was still three years away. And until the 2002 collective bargaining agreement, drug testing was resisted by the Players Association, principally upon privacy grounds, even though the issues were quite different from the recreational drugs in the '80s and '90s involving the arbitration awards noted above. Another argument of those resisting drug regulation was that performance-enhancement drugs, while obviously cheating, was cheating which was akin to scuffing balls, or placing foreign substances on a pitcher's hand or glove — something that Hall of Fame pitcher Gaylord Perry was accused of, and a matter that resulted in a ten-day suspension for Los Angeles pitcher Brian Donnelly in 2005. It was also analogized to corked bats (a 2003 incident involving Sammy Sosa seemed to implicate him in this practice) or sharpening spikes so as to take unfair advantage of an opposing player in a manner which would injure him.

The 2002 collective bargaining agreement provided for drug-testing procedures for the first time (thus prompting a number of the uninformed to state that drugs in baseball have only been illegal since 2002). This proved to be a departure from previous negotiations in a number of respects. In the first place, as noted in Chapter 1, the 2002 agreement, which addressed comprehensively revenue sharing and a luxury tax system aimed at the rich clubs, was the first agreement since the 1960s resolved without resort by one side or the other to economic warfare, i.e., the strike or lockout. Don Fehr, in a statement quoted by the Mitchell Report, said that owners had never brought a drug-testing proposal to the main bargaining table during that fall, winter and spring of '94-'95. Thus, for the first time in 2002, albeit in a far more limited fashion than that which had been employed in football and basketball, drug testing was introduced.

The agreement provided that during the regular season, including spring training, all players would be subject to two tests at "unannounced times" during the 2003 season. Prohibited substances were "any and all anabolic androgenic steroids covered by Schedule III of the Code of Federal Regulations' Schedule of Controlled Substances." Again, such substances have been outlawed at the federal level since 1990. Arbitrators, interpreting the just-cause provisions in collective bargaining agreements in industries other than baseball, have frequently sustained sanctions imposed on employees for violations of federal or state law.

The 2002 agreement provided that 240 players selected on a random basis would be tested in 2003. More players would become subject to unannounced random tests if 2 percent of the players tested positive. On the other hand, if the players passed the test, the clubs would recede from their previously expressed demand that players be tested for a wide variety of drugs.

In 2003 somewhere between 5 and 7 percent of the players taking the steroid tests tested positive for the drug. Thus in 2004 a more extensive testing program was introduced, but one which contained a number of limitations: (1) the failure to include non-steroid drugs like amphetamines; (2) what were perceived to be relatively light sanctions in the form of suspensions and fines for the first four offenses; and (3) no random testing during the off-season. Specifically, confidentiality of player participation and the results were to be preserved, and five steps were devised for players who tested positive. The first step was that the player would be placed on the so-called "clinical track" without any sanction. The next three were fifteen, twenty-five and fifty-day suspensions and, in the disjunctive, fines going from $10,000 to $50,000. The fifth positive result step was a one-year suspension or up to a $100,000 fine.

But in late 2004 public dissatisfaction with these procedures began to emerge. It started with the revelations about steroid use in the so-called BALCO case in San Francisco, in which major league players were called to testify about provision and receipt of drugs. The *San Francisco Chronicle* was able to obtain access to grand jury testimony provided by such superstars as Bonds, Giambi, former Giants catcher Benito Santiago and Gary Sheffield. The testimony showed that Giambi admitted to the use of steroids. Subsequently the *New York Times,* in a series of articles by Murray Chass, showed that Giambi had insisted upon the removal of steroids as prohibited conduct in his individual contract of employment with the New York Yankees and that the Yankees had acceded to his position.[40] Bonds, who subsequently said that he "did not know what cheating was," said that he did not know he was using steroids but thought that he was using "flaxseed oil" when using the steroid known as "the clear." His testimony was viewed by practically every observing member of the public as unbelievable and deceitful — though in 2011 a jury refused to convict him of perjury.[41]

BALCO put pressure upon the Players Association and the owners to go back to the bargaining table and to do what Marvin Miller had never allowed when he was Association director, i.e., a mid-term modification of the collective bargaining agreement, in this case on drug testing. Meanwhile, urine samples of major league baseball players, undertaken with the promise of privacy in the collective bargaining agreement, were seized by federal agents serving a search warrant on a laboratory in Las Vegas. Said my colleague Professor Robert Weisberg in the *New York Times*: "A search warrant is sought ... when you don't trust the person from whom you are getting the evidence not to destroy or hide the evidence."[42] Players whose urine samples were said to be included were Bonds, Giambi and other noteworthies such as the above-mentioned Sheffield, Santiago and outfielder Armando Rios.

Now pressure began to build upon the parties to make changes. The *New York Times* editorialized in a piece entitled "Baseball Shame" that "nothing has changed." Said the *Times*:

> Gene Orza, the union's No. 2, offered the lame comment the other day that steroids were no worse than cigarettes. This is the same Mr. Orza who said last year when the first year's test results were announced, that the problem was under control.[43]

The *Times* did not note that their own columnist, Murray Chass, had offered the same "lame" justification. The *Times,* noting Olympic athlete testing, which provided for sanctions of one year in the first instance and life time banishment the second time, around said:

> This is the kind of program baseball needs. It is obviously too late to restore the credibility of baseball's record but is not too late to level the playing field. And it is never too late to begin educating the next generation of players.

Meanwhile, a well-publicized book, *Juiced,* by former Oakland A's slugger Jose Canseco, was published, in which he alleged, among other things, that he had injected Mark McGwire with steroids when the two of them were together in Oakland as the "Bash Brothers." This book produced yet more attention and the ultimate involvement of two House committees which held hearings in the spring of '05.

BALCO had prompted baseball to negotiate the first modification of its collective bargaining agreement in late '04 and early '05. Now the sanctions became different, consisting of ten, thirty, and sixty days for the first three offenses, one year for the fourth, and the final one to be within the Commissioner's discretion. But the flap over Jose Canseco set the stage for considerably more extensive congressional inquiry than had been the case previously, as well as possible legislative intervention. Senator John McCain (R-AZ) had threatened and cajoled baseball prior to 2005, and now lay in the wings as the House Committee on Government Operations began an inquiry fueled in substantial part by the Canseco book. Thus, on February 24, House Government Reform Committee Chairman Thomas Davis (R-VA) announced that he would hold hearings to which Bonds and Giambi would be called to testify with bipartisan support (neither of them was ultimately called when hearings were held). Baseball did not do itself much good when it indicated a reluctance to testify, or to provide information in the absence of subpoenas about how it had responded to the drug issue through the collective bargaining process. Using a line that was frequently taken by Fehr and the union, Chass of the *New York Times* said: "Congress should know the system is working."[44]

Even more damaging was MLB's apparent threat to discontinue its drug-testing program if Congress or some other government entity intervened. And, equally unfortunately, when it cooperated, baseball produced a document, *Major League Baseball's Joint Drug Prevention and Treatment Program*, which in its Discipline Provision, Section 9, differed from the way in which the program had been advertised to the public and the Congress. Specifically, the Agreement presented was phrased in the disjunctive so as to allow players to be fined rather than be suspended for a specific period.

In the first place, as both Chairman Davis and ranking minority member Henry Waxman noted in a March 8, 2005, letter, with a week to go before hearings scheduled for March 17, Major League Baseball had "failed ... to provide copies of its drug policies." But the worst was yet to come. On March 16, the same Congressmen sent another letter to both Selig and Fehr stating that the policy was too narrow in scope, excluding some anabolic steroids, novel or "designer" steroids, and amphetamines. The March 16 letter, referring to the fines which appeared in the policy, said: "The fourth violation may be punished by either a 'one year suspension or up to a $100,000 fine.' One hundred thousand dollars is less money than some players earn in one game."

At the March 17 hearing, Rob Manfred, baseball's top labor relations executive, provided a curious performance, stating that the language was incorrect in the Agreement which had been provided to the parties. This rather egregious error, reminding many of Major League Baseball's legal errors in past labor arbitrations, such as the conspiracy cases in the 1980s in which baseball had been found to have illegally colluded in bidding for free agents, and the NLRB's finding that the owners had not bargained in good faith in the 1994–95 strike, put Manfred in hot water. Murray Chass of the *New York Times* apologized for Manfred and organized baseball when he wrote: "The committee members, however, chose to ignore Manfred's explanation. They were looking for an issue, they found it and they weren't about to let it go. Probing steroids use wasn't enough. It was as if the committee saw blood from an open wound and attacked."[45] Bruce Jenkins of the *San Francisco Chronicle* had a much more sensible view of what transpired that day. Said Jenkins:

> Rob Manfred, baseball's vice-president in charge of labor issues, was the man responsible. If you weren't sure of that, you got the picture when Selig, at one point of questioning, pointed his thumb in hitchhiking-like gesture toward Manfred. Let's be clear that this is one of the most important documents in the history of the sport. And there's a blatant error in its most crucial passage? Who edited the thing, Smokey the Bear?[46]

Congressman Waxman (D-CA) provided an eloquent opening statement in which he chronicled the longstanding series of investigations by the Congress into drug use in professional sports and noted that in 1973 the House Committee on Interstate and Foreign Commerce had said that "drug use exists ... in all sports and levels of competition." The congressman referred to a 1995 article in the *Los Angeles Times* in which a major league general manager cited widespread use of steroids in baseball: "In response to that story Commissioner Selig said, 'If baseball has a problem, I must say candidly that we were not aware of it. But should we concern ourselves as an industry? I don't know.'" This comment is obviously disingenuous. As noted above, even during the 1988 playoffs between the Red Sox and the A's after Jose Canseco's dramatic home run off Roger Clemens in game one, the Sox fans had taunted Canseco about steroids. Was MLB unaware of this?

And, amazingly, on the eve of the 2005 hearing itself, Selig was heard to opine during an interview at a San Francisco Giants-Kansas City Royals exhibition game in Scottsdale, Arizona:

> "I keep saying is there something I missed?" said Selig, referring to steroid use in the '80s and early '90s. "There are a lot of people saying it now but I didn't read any of that or hear any of that then. The retrospect of history is most interesting, and I guess I'm going to have to determine somewhere along the line the accuracy of it."[47]

Said Selig in the same interview: "If I'm going to do a historic retrospective, we'll do it ... but I'm not sure that's either fair or reasonable."[48]

Many argued that there could be no question of illegal conduct prior to the revision of the drug testing procedure in 2003. This view was rooted in the idea that conduct could not be viewed as impermissible because no drug testing regimen was put into effect prior to that. But again what this kind of thinking overlooked was the fact that Congress had prohibited a list of anabolic steroids since the Anabolic Steroid Act of 1990, and that there could be "just cause" for sanctioning players who violated the law. This kind of argument confused drug testing — put in place by baseball in 2002 — with the prohibition of drugs which had existed since 1990.

True, drug testing had been struck down as invalid under the collective bargaining agreement in connection with recreational drugs in the '80s. But, as we have seen, this did not affect the ability of the Commissioner and clubs to discipline players for using these kinds of drugs under some circumstances. Subsequently 2004 legislation added hundreds of steroid-based drugs and precursors including Mark McGwire's androstenedione (already prohibited by the National Football League) to the list of anabolic steroids and ultimately Major League Baseball included all of these in its own list of banned substances.

Some, like Professor Zimbalist, have contended that Selig, though he could have acted more aggressively and consistently, nonetheless discharged his responsibilities properly and that little was known beyond baseball's experience with recreational drugs in the mid-'90s.[49] Tied to this line of argument is the proposition that the Players Association was the principal obstacle. As we have seen already, the Players Association was an obstacle — but, as events during '05 and '06 bore out, much was known and certainly enough to induce the Commissioner to take action. After all, Mark McGwire had been identified by the Associated Press as in the possession of androstenedione. Manager Tony LaRussa of the St. Louis Cardinals had threatened to bar the reporter from the clubhouse because of this invasion of McGwire's privacy. Subsequent to Jose Canseco's book Tony LaRussa said that Canseco frequently laughed about drugs, making it clear that he was aware of Canseco's reported activities, and yet did not turn him in. Other managers spoke of their unwillingness to act as "snitches" in reporting drug conduct and behavior. The fact is that rather than act out of a vigorous or genuine manner to combat drugs, the problem was viewed as a noisy inconvenience which interfered with the hit parade and renaissance that baseball was enjoying in post-strike '94-'95 era and the years immediately thereafter.

This was then the posture of organized baseball in the spring of 2005 before Congress. The House of Representatives committees on March 17, in hearings that were held in the immediate aftermath, hardly distinguished themselves — after all, the leadership consisted of the same sordid bunch who had been responsible for the Clinton impeachment hearing fiasco and enormous waste of taxpayer money associated with that and various other schemes. On March 17 the House committee charged with drug testing did in fact engage in considerable grandstanding and showboating. Again, however, the response of Selig and baseball diverted attention from this, as did the memorable comments of Bonds when questioned by journalists during 2005 spring training about BALCO. Said Bonds:

> I don't know what cheating is. I don't know if steroids is going to help you in baseball but [referring to the baseball reporters who queried him about steroids, he said] all you guys lied! ... All of y'all and the story have lied. Should you have asterisks behind your name? All of you lied. All of you said something wrong. All of you have dirt. When your closet's clean, then come clean somebody else's, but clean yours first, okay?[50]

Bonds also attempted, with some measure of success, to make this a racial issue. In the same "I don't know what cheating is" interview, Bonds, when asked whether he was receiving greater scrutiny in '05 as he approached Babe Ruth's 714, said: "Because Babe Ruth is one of the greatest baseball players ever and Babe Ruth ain't black, either ... blacks, we go through a little bit more. That's the truth, unfortunately. I said it. I'm not a racist, but I live in the real world."[51]

Overlooked in any of the commentary or apparent questions was the fact that Hank Aaron, whom Bonds had in his sights at that point, was black as well. But, in the same vein as the O.J. Simpson fiasco in the '90s, the public seemed to divide on racial lines when viewing the acceptability of Bonds's statistical record, notwithstanding his apparent use of steroids. And the constant mantra on California Bay Area talk show stations was that, whether Bonds had used steroids or not, probably others had as well and Bonds was the best of them. This comment turned out to be true as the Mitchell Report chronicled the pervasive and widespread abuse in the game. Such superstars as Manny Ramirez and David Ortiz were subsequently identified as having tested positive — and the rivals of the 1998 race to top Roger Maris's 61-homer season in 1961 conducted by McGwire and Sosa, both of them now implicated in steroids. But, of course, that missed the point because Bonds was being compared with others like Aaron, Roger Maris and Babe Ruth, who had not benefited from enhancement drugs. It is Bonds's contemporaries who were engaged in the same kind of conduct — and time was to show that there were a good number of them — who should be judged by the same standards.

Meanwhile, the story would not go away. In the first place, the Government Reform Committee expanded its hearings to cover football, basketball and hockey, depriving critics of one of the so-called "double standard" arguments. Initially the National Football League was highlighted and praised as a foil to Major League Baseball. NFL representatives noted that only 111 players had tested positive since 1989. The Committee, through both Congressmen Davis and Waxman, noted that the NFL had cooperated with the Committee (it recalled that baseball flirted with the idea of non-cooperation right until the eve of the March hearings) and called upon the NFL for advice on how to deal with Major League

Baseball! But more careful scrutiny of the NFL itself was invited when, on the highly respected CBS television program *60 Minutes*, it was revealed that three members of the Carolina Panthers were found to have tested positive just prior to the 2003 Super Bowl. It was noted that there were now 350 linemen who weighed more than 300 pounds! Were NFL players being tested as frequently as they should be? Were new designer drugs escaping detection? Now the NFL began to insist on new standards beyond the previously established ratio between testosterone and epitestosterone contained in a person's body. The NFL, previously satisfied with a ratio of 6–1 as a basis for establishing a positive for the urine sample, now sought a 4–1 ratio.

Hearings were now extended to the Commerce and Trade Subcommittee of the House Energy and Commerce Committee, chaired by Congressman Cliff Starns (R-FL), who began with a more critical look at the NFL. Soon the National Basketball Association, always considered to be light years ahead of the other leagues in any area of reform, saw its own policies derided as "pathetic" and "a joke." A series of questions were asked. Why were NBA veteran players tested only once a year, in the pre-season? Why was cocaine subject to a penalty of a year suspension and steroids only four games? No good answers were provided, and notwithstanding union executive director Billy Hunter's assertion that an infinitesimal number of basketball players had tested positive, Commissioner David Stern, with no real objection from Hunter, seemed to be promising firmer testing policies. In the 2005 collective bargaining agreement negotiated in June of that year, players were now to be subject to four random tests during the season and a new set of penalties — ten games for a first offense and a lifetime ban for a fourth positive test were now instituted. Stern, a month earlier, had said to the House Committee on Energy and Commerce: "Our program will get much stronger ... but if Congress sees fit to legislate, we will meet and exceed any standard you set."[52]

Then in late May a much-anticipated legislative proposal emerged in the form of the Clean Sports Act, introduced by Senator John McCain, who was joined by Congressman Mark Souder (R-IN) and Messrs. Davis and Waxman, along with Congressman Cummings (D-MD).[53] Senator McCain expressed the view that it would be important to establish testing standards akin to those employed by the Olympics — and thus the McCain Sports Act provided for a two-year suspension for a first positive test and a lifetime ban for the second. The threat of this legislation produced a new round of bargaining with yet more changes in the drug policy negotiated between labor and management.

Drug Law Reform in Baseball

But meanwhile a number of legal hurdles to the Act, or McCain-Davis as it was called, emerged. Could Congressional legislation trump a collective bargaining agreement just as the United States government criminal drug prosecution employed, for instance, in the BALCO case could trump the contractual right to privacy in a urine test established by the collective bargaining agreement?[54] In BALCO-type investigations — contrary to the assertion of baseball union lawyer Gene Orza[55] — it is clear that the government's seizure of employer tests is not limited or governed by a requirement that the employer itself have probable or reasonable cause to seize. Thus, the Court of Appeals for the Fourth Circuit has held that a party "acted in a private capacity, then government activity is not implicated and the Fourth Amendment does not apply.... [T]he Fourth Amendment ... does not protect against searches, no matter how unreasonable, 'conducted by private individuals acting in a private capacity.'"[56]

Moreover, it seems clear that properly enacted legislation overrides provisions of a collective bargaining agreement addressing drugs and drug testing. For instance, where racial and sexual discrimination were engaged in prior to the civil rights legislation of the 1960s, collective bargaining agreements which provided for such were superseded by the dictates of fair employment practices law.

Here also the question of the Fourth Amendment to the Constitution, which protects against "unreasonable searches and seizures," is presented. Murray Chass of the *New York Times* said about McCain-Davis: "The senator and the representatives seemingly ignored the Amendment in their haste to punish Major League Baseball and other professional leagues for not imposing egregious penalties on players for testing positive for performance-enhancing drugs."[57] Most of the Fourth Amendment cases involve governmental employees, since only government action is regulated — particularly among those employees who are involved with public safety or security in some sense of the word. Also, the Chass line of argument ignored the testimony that had been presented to Congress about the harm caused to young people who emulated the drug enhancement behavior, let alone an interest in preserving competitive integrity in baseball.

The leading random drug-testing case involving athletes — it is not alluded to by Mr. Chass — is *Dimeo v. Griffin*,[58] involving jockeys in horse racing. In this case the Court of Appeals for the Seventh Circuit, in an opinion authored by Judge Richard Posner for the 7–4 majority, held that the owner of Racing Boy constitutionally promulgated a rule requiring jockeys as well as other participants in horse races in Illinois to submit to random drug testing not based upon individualized suspicion of wrongdoing. The court noted that horse racing in Illinois and elsewhere is highly regulated because (1) it is dangerous to jockeys; (2) it is a magnet for gambling; and (3) it grows out of a "long history of fixing, cheating, doping of horses, illegal gambling, and other corrupt practices."[59] The court said that Illinois had a "dual concern with the use of illegal drugs by participants in horse racing": (1) personal safety of participants who might be killed or injured in accidents; (2) a financial concern.

The court then noted that for most men, though urination is a private activity, they urinate "side by side in public restrooms without embarrassment even though there is usually very little, and often no, attempt to partition the urinals."[60] The court said that athletes are subject to frequent medical examinations and that privacy concerns were not as strong under such circumstances inasmuch as "the more habituated he [the athlete or individual] is to them, the less sensitive he is apt to be." Noting that all individuals provide a urine sample in connection with their annual medical examination, the court noted that here the individual had "voluntarily traded away some sense of privacy by undertaking this job." In the sports cases, said the court, particularly in horse racing, "the incremental invasion of privacy is very slight; the physical danger of drug use — not only (or always) to the user himself, but also to other participants ... is acute; and there is in addition a substantial state financial interest (the pari-mutuel revenues), which is comparable with the interests in maintaining an efficient and productive work force."[61]

The issue has not yet reached the Supreme Court — though in cases involving non-athlete employees the Court has generally approved random testing notwithstanding the Fourth Amendment applicability to such matters. The Supreme Court has declared unconstitutional drug tests for political candidates, but it did so because there was "no evidence of a drug problem among State's elected officials" as well as their involvement in jobs which involved safety.[62] A very different record for legislative history could be compiled in connection with Major League Baseball players — the Mitchell Report would be Exhibit 1 in this connection!

The basis for legislation in both horse racing and baseball is the health and safety of the players (in horse racing, jockeys) as well as the public, the frequency of drug use, and the integrity of the game, which is a business in interstate commerce subject to regulation by the labor laws. The same relatively minimal intrusion on privacy as found in the horse racing context would be applicable in other professional sports. While, as the dissent noted, the idea that the players are more subject to regulation because they voluntarily ceded their privacy is probably the weak reed in the analysis, other elements are present.

Arguably there is one factor contained in *Dimeo* and horse racing not fully present in baseball: the financial involvement of the state in horse racing. But the state's financial interest in the industry received relatively little attention in the majority opinion of Judge Posner — a factor noted by the dissent itself. Moreover, the financial assistance provided to most baseball stadiums may partially diminish this distinction between baseball and horse racing, although horse racing is more directly tied to the state and its interest in obtaining revenues.

The Supreme Court has been closely divided in the drug-testing cases. But, in the absence of a substantial change in the Court's composition, much of Judge Posner's analysis in the *Dimeo* majority position would probably carry the day in baseball and other professional sports. In any event, the threat of legislation and constitutional problems with it diminished once baseball was able to resolve its differences on drug testing with yet a new program providing for additional scope and sanctions in November 2005.

Selig, who had just a few months ago expressed the same sense of satisfaction with the status quo that he had articulated for more than a decade, now saw the congressional handwriting on the wall and, once again, moved to catch up with the events that were pushing him on. Fehr, in responding to Selig's newfound call for action, opined that he could not understand a sense of dissatisfaction with the policy which just two months earlier had been adopted. Fehr stated that he could not understand why there was a necessity for a change when it was impossible at that point in '05 to see whether the recently adopted changes were working or not. Yet after the May hearings, Commissioner Selig said in an open letter to baseball fans that he would support government intervention along the lines of Olympic rules if the matter could not be resolved through collective bargaining with the union. On May 18 Congressman Joe Barton (R-TX) said: "In a perfect world I'd rather this just be done in collective bargaining or voluntary acceptance by the players in respective sports ... but obviously we don't live in a perfect world. And in this case we need federal intervention. I think we've gone too long."

No legislative action was taken, and in the fall of 2005 the parties agreed to their second revision of the drug-testing policy. This provided for a number of reforms including: (1) more frequent testing; (2) the idea of a new independent agency to monitor test results; (3) a broadening of the scope of drugs to be covered by the policy, including amphetamines; and (4) new penalties for offenses which would begin with fifty games, proceed to 100 games the second time around (two-thirds of the season), and culminate in life suspension — three strikes and you're out.

What Does the November 2005 Agreement Mean?

Baseball has now asserted that, since fewer players are failing the drug tests in 2006 and beyond under the new policy, then the policy is a success. As of August 11, 2006, thirty-four players in the majors and thirty-two in the minors had tested positive — in 2005 the figure was eighty-six at that time, ultimately reaching ninety-three, with eighty-one in the minor leagues and twelve in the majors. Said the same Rob Manfred who had testified in 2005 in defense of changes made earlier in the year: "We believe that the programs are working.... When you make penalties much more severe, as we have, fewer people will be willing to take the risks."[63] Clearly the drug policy, by its inclusion of amphetamines, which constituted the major abuse in baseball from the '70s onward, is an improvement in many respects. Note, however, a player who tests positive for amphetamines receives mandatory testing after the first offense is not identified and would not be included among the current list of violators.

But the greatest concern relates to the possibility that players may be beating the tests and that there are abuses which are not reached by the tests. Players are tested for steroids in the off-season, but the tests do not involve many of them. Baseball can conduct a maximum of sixty random out-of-competition tests, a small number of the total pool of eligible players, which constitutes 1200. The odds are that the average player cannot be reached in the off-season and can prepare effectively for the testing, which takes place during the first days of reporting. Moreover, in 2010 only 3 percent of the tests were conducted during the off-season.[64] Well in advance of his testimony to Congress which led to a perjury indictment, 350-game-winner Roger Clemens, whose physique, like that of Bonds, has changed enormously since the '80s and '90s, took to remaining as a free agent until the beginning of the season in May or June. This has happened during his most recent years with the Houston Astros and the New York Yankees, and he has been viewed as a free agent not under contract to any team and thus not subject to any testing during the off-season, as well as a portion of the season itself! (An NFL player protesting drug testing has asserted that he is not an employee subject to the NFL's procedures because he is a free agent.[65]) The players who are under contract are advised that the test will take place at the time of the spring training physicals.

There are problems even with regard to the tests during the season itself. Antidoping experts are concerned that baseball must rely upon club officials to watch over players at the time that they take the tests, stating that this is illustrative of "a flawed system."[66] Said the *New York Times*: "They [the antidoping experts] question why players are not more closely chaperoned when they are to be tested and why, in some cases, they are given so much time to provide a sample. And they say that far more random tests should be conducted."[67]

A general manager told the *Times* that collectors routinely showed up 4 hours before a night game, at about 2:30 P.M. in most cities. If a player spotted the collector he could then alert teammates not to take amphetamines that day. The same general manager said that by varying the times that the collector would appear, baseball could provide a greater deterrent. Indeed, it has been revealed that drug testers contracted by the League "routinely alert team officials a day or more before their arrival at ballparks for what is supposed to be random, unannounced testing of players. By eliminating the surprise factor, the practice undermines the integrity of the testing program, an antidoping expert said."[68] MLB defended this by stating that "team officials are not supposed to tell players that tests will be conducted."[69]

Players tested in the off-season have been called and told what time the next day the collector would arrive. This contrasts with the Olympics, whose athletes must provide information as to where they will be and where testers can show up at any time unannounced. "If the athlete who is to be tested is not at those locations, the representative calls to notify him or her about the test. The athlete then has a two-hour window to report and provide a sample."[70]

Not only does baseball differ from Olympic procedures, but the number of drugs prohibited by the Olympics is substantially wider in scope. Baseball defends its policy by stating that many over-the-counter drugs that are available are prohibited by the Olympics, a defense which most experts find unsatisfactory.

Tests attempting to examine the proportion between testosterone and epitestosterone, in baseball as well the NFL, have followed the Olympics in providing a 4–1 ratio, although there are many who believe that a 3–1 ratio contains significant performance enhancement. Moreover, it is said that Olympic athletes are able to reduce their epitstest by flicking powdered epitstest in their pockets and thus instantly lowering their ratio.

Additionally, there may be loopholes in the drug tests themselves. For instance, the endurance booster EPO increases the blood's capacity to deliver oxygen. A policy has not been worked out on this. Similarly, as noted above, human growth hormones may be the biggest problem of all. In the Mitchell Report, it was stated that, while baseball players had turned away from steroids, they probably were using human growth hormone in their place. Stated Mitchell: "The information obtained in this investigation suggests that the use of detectible steroids by players in Major League Baseball has declined but the use of human growth hormone has increased."[71]

The Jason Grimsley bust indicates the problem is widespread. Baseball does not have in place tests for human growth hormone although some believe that it can be tested through blood samples.[72] But no one in baseball on either the owner or player side has proposed blood testing.[73] And, it must be admitted, it is not clear whether blood testing can accurately provide information about human growth hormones (HGH), though the Olympics have tested for HGH with blood samples for some time. Accordingly all of this indicates that the statistical data about positive tests, however comforting, may not reveal the full extent of drug abuse in baseball. As the October 2007 Paul Byrd revelations suggest, the "steroids" era may have lasted with us well into the twenty-first century.

In the wake of the publication of *Game of Shadows* by *San Francisco Chronicle* reporters Fainaru-Wada and Williams,[74] Selig appointed Senator George Mitchell, part owner of the Boston Red Sox and former Democratic Senate Majority Leader, to investigate drug abuse in baseball. The retrospective which Selig had previously appeared to oppose was now in order. In contrast to the United States government, of course, Mitchell had no subpoena power, but could have turned to the Commissioner to impose sanctions for those who did not cooperate.

The 2007 Mitchell Report stated that "[for] more than a decade there has been widespread illegal use of anabolic steroids and other performance-enhancing substances by players in Major League Baseball, in violation of federal law and baseball policy."[75] The report referred to a "minority" who had offended. The report implicated management as well as players, for instance, and pointed out that Peter Magowan, President of the Giants, and GM Brian Sabean had been alerted to Barry Bonds's behavior and involvement with the trainer Greg Anderson, who was thought to be supplying Bonds — but no action was taken by either of these individuals. The Red Sox had speculated aloud through e-mail communications about Greg Gagne's reputed drug taking when considering his acquisition in 2007. The owners thus bore considerable blame — but no action was taken against them by the Commissioner, nor was it recommended by his appointee Senator Mitchell.

Mitchell stated that the Players Association had been "largely uncooperative" and that the players, having received a memorandum from the Players Association discouraging them from cooperating with the investigation, "almost without exception ... declined to meet or talk with me."[76] Of active players, the only one to do so was Frank Thomas, then of the Toronto Blue Jays. Of five hundred former players, only sixty-eight were willing to cooperate, and of them three did so with law enforcement. Mitchell maintained that baseball's drug testing regimen and program was the strongest of any in the professional leagues. Yet this is belied by the observation of independent observers in the *Wall Street Journal* who place baseball down towards the bottom[77] and the fact that the program has appeared to be so poorly enforced, at least at the time of Mitchell. Said Mitchell: "Almost without exception, before this investigation began active major league players were not interviewed in investigations into their alleged use of performance enhancing substances."[78]

Even after Mitchell, so far as the public is aware, little has been done to inquire about Alex Rodriguez or Ortiz or Ramirez or McGwire, for that matter. Ramirez's fifty-day suspension in 2009 was a relatively small price to pay given his $22 million per annum salary! Not only were no steps taken vis-à-vis Sabean and Magowan on Bonds, but also the report chronicled the fact that players seem to have been tipped as to when tests were to be taken, and union officials could not be interviewed in this connection.[79] This is remarkably similar to the earlier pre–2002 situation. Testing could be triggered by reasonable cause but where "tests were administered long after the allegations were received, and no suspected player ever tested positive for steroids in these tests."[80] Accordingly, Mitchell made a series of proposals for baseball, most of them prospective in nature because of his concern that the investigation of the past would be counterproductive in opening up old wounds and the like.

First, he proposed that the testing program be administered by a truly independent authority with "exclusive authority over its [the testing program's] structure and administration."[81] Equally important, the report recommended a new investigations unit which would look into drug policy violations outside of the testing system itself. Said Mitchell when speaking of the past:

> To prolong this debate will not resolve it; each side will dig in its heels even further. But it could seriously and perhaps fatally detract from what I believe to be a critical necessity: the need for everyone in baseball to work together to devise and implement the strongest possible strategy to combat the illegal use of performance enhancing substances, including the recommendations set forth in this report.[82]

Nonetheless, the report chronicled examples of past violations by numerous players, some of them quite well known, such as fireballing ace Roger Clemens. And equally important the report noted that minor league testing, introduced prior to 2002 unilaterally (there is no union in the minors), had produced a sharp reduction in the number of positive tests.[83]

Accordingly, Mitchell urged the Commissioner to "forego imposing discipline on players for past violations" unless "the conduct is so serious that discipline is necessary to maintain the integrity of the game."[84] The hope was, as the report said, to bring this troubling period to a close, and the assumption was that the violations were "distant in time." This, of course, was before the ongoing dispute and litigation about the 2002 list and new revelations in 2009 about violations there. These developments make it unlikely that the steroid era and its revelations are behind us.

A key element of the Mitchell recommendations was the creation of an independent investigation unit to examine drug violations. Perhaps this unit has looked at Rodriguez, Ramirez, Ortiz, Clemens, Giambi and others — but little is known about what, if anything, these investigations have accomplished. Moreover, there is no indication that any investigation of Mark McGwire was conducted in 2010. McGwire arranged for interviews on the MLB television network and was promptly praised by Selig. Selig immediately proclaimed that the steroid era was over. Said Selig: "The use of steroids and amphetamines among today's players has greatly subsided and is virtually nonexistent as our testing results have shown.... [T]he so-called steroid era — a reference that is resented by the many players who played in that era and never touched the substances — is clearly a thing of the past, and Mark's admission today is another step in the right direction."[85] But the fact is that little is known about this point, and Selig's quick reaction suggested that he was more interested in covering up the past as opposed to a genuine investigation. From whom did McGwire and others get the drugs? Who told them that the drugs were helpful to them and how were they to be helpful to them? A host of questions need answering that baseball does not seem interested in asking in a kind of truth and reconciliation proceeding.[86]

There is still no testing for HGH and baseball has performed poorly in its previous steroid drug testing initiatives. Moreover, as Professor Fidler of Indiana Law School has noted along with the important movie, *Sugar*, steroid use is widespread in Latin America, particularly in the Dominican Republic, where players are desperate to escape a life of extreme poverty. And in the second decade of this century, baseball's testing program is considered to be inferior to that of all other professional sports.

What has been the impact of Mitchell? In the immediate aftermath of the Mitchell Report, baseball, through Selig, said that it would adopt all of Mitchell's recommendations except those that required collective bargaining. Previously, Murray Chass churlishly contended that the Report "uncovered little" because the numerous names of players were not uncovered by himself but rather through tipsters.[87] Mitchell was even attacked for not providing the union with a copy of the report prior to its release, as was done with the Commissioner. Said Chass: "Mitchell apparently wouldn't give it to the union because the union refused to cooperate with the investigation. Such juvenile behavior is beneath a man of Mitchell's stature."

There is no doubt that the overriding thrust of the report, notwithstanding the fact that Mitchell was appointed by Selig, was to give the lie to Selig's numerous protestations over the years that he knew little, if anything, about the true state of drug affairs. The Mitchell Report highlighted the corruption that permeated baseball from top to bottom.[88]

Now, as noted, the focus has spread beyond performance-enhancing drugs to stimulants like amphetamines which baseball belatedly prohibited.[89] This process is not transparent as is that relating to performance-enhancing drugs in the sense that players counseled or penalized are not identified. But in the steroid arena, the focus has now come to have centered on the number of medical exemptions for both performance-enhancing drugs and amphetamines — they have been substantial.[90]

In April 2008, MLB having stated that they would not discipline players named in the Report but rather request community service, negotiated a new drug policy with the union.[91] The April changes increase the number of random tests and powers of the administrator who oversees testing. Contrary to Mitchell's recommendations, the administrator "does not have input into how the testing program is designed."[92] Mitchell's view was that the report had held up "well."

But while power production had declined — many of the players' names in the Mitchell Report had seen their numbers enhanced during the years in question[93] — most players remained in the game and most did not confess. Clemens, who like Rodriguez (he had denied before confessing) and Bonds (he continues to deny), became baseball's most celebrated figure implicated in the scandal.[94] Clemens's denial produced a comprehensive indictment for perjury.

McGwire's contention that steroids did not help him with his hitting does not pass the laugh test, as catcher Carlton Fisk noted in characterizing it as a "crock." Fisk has said regarding McGwire: "There's a reason they call it performance-enhancing drugs.... That's what it does — performance enhancement. You can be good, but it's going to make you better. You can be average, but it is going to make you good. If you are below average, it is going to make you average."[95] Similarly, Fisk Hall of Fame colleague Ferguson Jenkins has stated that McGwire owes an apology to the pitchers who gave up his home runs.[96] But otherwise, quiet reigns until the next revelation.

Now, aside from the drug policy itself, discipline in the future will be handled by the arbitration process and some of the case law noted above. Recall that in the *Jenkins* matter the arbitrator held that the "simple possession of small quantities of untested substances, did not in itself provide the basis even for suspicion as to involvement in any more serious unlawful activities by a Player such as Jenkins." The arbitrator looked to the question of whether there was independent evidence in the form of clubhouse or player testimony to provide a basis for concluding that Jenkins was involved in unlawful activity. Moreover, the arbitrator concluded that it was "highly improbable that the refusal to answer these questions under these circumstances would convert Jenkins overnight from a popular professional athlete to a pariah in the eyes of the public." The arbitrator also relied upon Jenkins's long service and the "public esteem" in which he was held.

It seems doubtful that many of these findings could be made in connection with Barry Bonds and others who have been implicated. The performance-enhancing drugs are a far more serious matter than those presented in *Jenkins*. Bonds hardly seems to be held in comparable public esteem. On the other hand, certainly all the evidence is that the San Francisco Giants would have had no difficulty drawing crowds to see Bonds, whether he had been indicted or not — and the same may be true of any other team that had signed him. Witness the "redemption" that has been accorded the partially confessed wrongdoer, Alex Rodriguez. Both he and Mark McGwire now want to move on. Perhaps visits to other stadiums would get him the opposite reception to the one he received in San Francisco — though most of the evidence is that crowds are swelled by the controversial nature of Bonds's behavior as well as his great performance, and that, at least in the short run, it will be difficult to show that the divided reaction to him will harm baseball, the Giants, or any other team which employs him within the meaning of *Jenkins*.

Another arbitration case which has a direct bearing on this is that involving John Rocker, the former relief pitcher for the Atlanta Braves and other clubs. In *Rocker*, it is to be recalled, the pitcher gave statements to *Sports Illustrated* in their December 27, 1999, issue which Commissioner Selig viewed as "profoundly insensitive and arguably racist ... [which] harmed your reputation, have damaged the image and goodwill of Major League Baseball and the Atlanta Braves, and have caused various other harms to the Club and the game." The question in *Rocker* was whether the discipline imposed for conduct which was not "in the best interest of baseball" constituted just cause within the meaning of the collective bargaining agreement. A suspension from spring training in 2000 and with pay until May 1, 2000, along with a required contribution to the NAACP or a similar organization dedicated to the goals of diversity, as well as participation in diversity training, was held to be without just cause. The arbitrator held that a suspension with pay until Opening Day, April 17, was sustained, and that $500 rather than the $20,000 imposed for charitable organizations was sustained, as well as a requirement to participate in an in-season program of diversity training established by the Major League Baseball Employee Assistance Program.

As relevant to the drug testing issue, however, the arbitrator held that even if Rocker had a First Amendment free speech right to "speak his ... mind regardless of the offensive or hateful nature of the speech [this] does not, under a just cause standard, necessarily preclude an employer from taking appropriate disciplinary action where such speech, even if off-duty, has a negative on the employer's business." But the arbitrator concluded that the impact on baseball as a business was not what the Commissioner maintained it was. Said the arbitrator in *Rocker*:

> There seems little doubt that because of the breadth of his verbal offensive and the harshness of its tone, his remarks caused as strong reaction, as has been reflected in media coverage. The evidence, however, does not fully support the Commissioner's claims as to the resulting harm. Although there clearly will be some increased security costs, at least temporarily, there is no hard evidence that either the Braves or Baseball, generally, actually has suffered or likely will suffer from reduced attendance or other loss of income because of Rocker's comments.[97]

This sounds remarkably reminiscent of the comments of students at Stanford Law School in my Sports Law seminar who believed that the NFL's crackdown on violent players was wrong suited because attendance was not declining and the players not falling out of favor with the public. Again, *Rocker*, like *Jenkins*, suggests that the Commissioner, if limited in its discretion by the just-cause provision of the collective bargaining agreement rather than possessing authority to move against those involved in drugs simply on the basis of his best interests of baseball authority as it relates to gambling, will have to show actual and possible immediate harm. Again, this would be difficult to do in the case of Bonds in San Francisco and arguably problematic in other ballparks. Even on the road, where Bonds was the object of near-unanimous derision because of apparent steroid use as well as his difficult personality, the stadiums have been full — particularly as he moved close to the all-time Hank Aaron record.

Nonetheless, I am of the view that the economic standard, whatever evidence is produced should there be indictments in the future, is not entirely dispositive. This is because *Rocker* viewed as relevant the "significant degree" of "detrimental" harm to the reputation of the Braves and of baseball and concluded that the Commissioner had a "legitimate basis" for imposing some penalty upon the pitcher. Moreover, *Jenkins*, like *Howe* and *Rocker* itself, reiterates the view that each case must be based upon its peculiar circumstances. If penalties cannot be imposed upon Bonds because of the divided view of the public about his behavior and the unwillingness to equate it with gambling, what becomes of the cases involving less important and controversial players? Because they do not possess or threaten existing records, the home team may care less and so will the opposing. Should there be different standards depending upon the visibility and controversial nature of the player in question? It would seem that the arbitral jurisprudence allows the Commissioner, with evidence about harm to the reputation as well as perhaps income of baseball, to impose some kind of sanction upon Bonds and others indicted or penalized by the result of the Mitchell investigation, or some other body in connection with performance-enhancement drugs. But the Commissioner thus far seems unwilling to do so.

Another problem which may limit effective drug policy enforcement in baseball is the Court of Appeals for the Eighth Circuit decision in *Williams v. National Football League*,[98] in which the court held that state law, like federal, governs the enforcement of the collective bargaining agreement prohibition of drugs. This means in many jurisdictions that part of the policy, like testing away from the workplace, may have to fall away — and it is this prospect which has led the National Football League to urge Congress to reverse or partially reverse it.[99] The MLB drug policy will be adversely affected as well.

Finally, involvement of the medical profession and MLB cannot go unmentioned. The fact is that many clubs today — I am aware of the San Francisco Giants' practice in particular — require physicians who are team doctors to pay the team for the privilege of performing for them. Many in the medical profession see this as unethical and a practice which compromises the Hippocratic Oath. To whom does the doctor owe his loyalty in examining the player-patient? The club needs to have the player perform in order to attract crowds and revenues. True, pitcher Jim Lonborg, as he told me, rushed himself back into action in 1968 — and Curt Schilling, when he had a torn tendon which bled into his sock during the 2004 postseason games, wanted to perform regardless of what doctors and owners told him. Schilling was never the pitcher again that he was in 2004. The same was true of Lonborg in 1968 after his '67 Cy Young season (though he did have a comeback with the Philadelphia Phillies in the '70s). Baseball or Congress or the medical profession must crack down on this practice of requiring physicians to pay for the privilege of performing. It is they who must be paid for their services if they are to meet their ethical obligations.[100]

Drug Sanctions—The Record Books

The purchaser of the ball that was the 756th home run by Bonds has made an agreement with the Hall of Fame that the ball will possess an asterisk. What should be done with Bonds's record — and the records of those who are similarly situated? The sprinter Marion Jones, upon admitting that she took the "clear," was obliged to return her Olympic medals — and even those who participated with her in relay races were similarly sanctioned. Should Bonds have his record stricken from the record books, as legislation proposed by Senator James Bunning provides? Is an asterisk sufficient? Does the fact that a wide range of players are now implicated change matters? The San Francisco Giants baseball announcers, for instance, have interviewed Bonds respectfully and reminisced about his matchups with Greg Gagne (in Gagne's Dodgers days) when considerable heat seems to have been generated by drugs on both sides of the equation!

The difficulties here are numerous. The first is that we do not know what Bonds may have been able to do without the "clear" or other drugs of a similar nature. But we do not know what Jones would have been able to do in her track meet. The baseball scenario is arguably more complicated because of the fact that it is not simply a race between a number of people but rather a competition which involves human beings on the other side and particular kinds of pitches, the differences in ballpark size, the weather, defense and the like. The fact is that Jones might have won her track races even without performance-enhancing drugs. There is always speculation and uncertainty involved in any remedy of this kind. At the minimum a sanction at least in the form of an asterisk — an officially placed cloud which exists in any event — should be placed over the record of those implicated in Mitchell, and those named and mentioned by the BALCO revelations if they are revealed or investigated by the Commissioner in the future — admittedly a remote possibility. As a retired outfielder said to Rodriguez during a private dinner between the two: "What kind of discount should there be for any records obtained when you are considered for the Hall of Fame?" Whether it is characterized as a discount or asterisk, the policy is most generous and lenient compared to that of the Greeks in the first Olympics, where cheating resulted in a ban for life and the names of cheaters were placed on statues and monuments built thereafter.

It does not do, as Ken Burns argued recently, to say that the failure of baseball to place an asterisk on the Cincinnati Reds' triumph in the 1919 World Series, when they benefited from the dive of the Black Sox, is relevant. Cheating of some or all on one side does not deprive the resulting victory for the winner. The Reds should not be penalized for the misconduct of the White Sox in 1919! But Bonds, McGwire, A-Rod, Clemens and other record holders should be the recipients of ostracism.

Penultimately, there is the question of race. Ruth, not Aaron, produced his records in a segregated era. Presumably he did not face the same vigorous competition that Bonds did, and to some extent, though the number of qualified blacks was still unrepresented at that time, Aaron did as well. In the first place, as far as we know, Ruth himself did not screen out black pitchers, though it must be said that all players of that era are in some measure complicit with segregation. (Ironically, Ruth was deeply hurt and upset by racial taunts of which he was the object, based upon the rather widespread view that he was black![101]) Bonds is a direct actor in his competitive advantage. There is no doubt that both factors skewed the statistics which each player was able to compile. But Bonds seems to differ in the sense that he is directly responsible for the fact that his playing field is not level.

Moreover, even if one looks at the period in which Hank Aaron broke Ruth's record, baseball cannot be said to be desegregated. In papers submitted by former black players to the Court of Appeals for the Ninth Circuit, which the court adopted (discussed in Chapter 8), it was stipulated that the MLB had a quota of two black players per club. Aaron as well as Ruth did not face the very best pitchers in a nondiscriminatory environment.

Closely tied to this is the argument that Bonds, like O.J. Simpson, is being picked upon because he is black. As we have seen, Bonds himself promotes this idea — and so also does William Rhoden of the *New York Times.* He attempted to compare Bonds's situation with that of the first black heavyweight champion Jack Johnson, who *was* persecuted as well as prosecuted by the United States government because he consorted with white women and the white public resented a black heavyweight champion — in contrast to Bonds's situation, in which he is being attacked because it is said that he engaged in illegal conduct which is injurious to one's health as well as unparalleled arrogance. Rhoden's theme is that Bonds, along with other elite black athletes like Marion Jones and Michael Vick, are the only ones who are being pursued as the focus of federal investigations. Writes Rhoden:

> My issue has to do with an apparent double standard that has focused, thus far, on black athletes. I'm waiting for the dragnet to pull in a more diverse bounty of high-profile athletes....
>
> No one is defending Vick, Bonds or Jones; I am just shining the light on what appears to be a troubling imbalance in the pursuit of justice. I'd like to see an entire boatload of athletes being delivered as part of a far-flung, far-reaching investigation into the so-called steroid era, but an era is not made up of two athletes.
>
> Perhaps in coming months there will be a larger pool of mega-athletes named being the subject of suffocating investigations — a bit of diversity in the pursuit of justice. Let's examine the breadth and depth of performance-enhancing drug use in the so-called steroid era.[102]

This point of view seems to me to be patently silly. As Rhoden himself concedes, in fact a number of white athletes have been pursued — they simply do not possess the "stature" of Bonds or Jones. Therefore, Rhoden reasons that the government has no "appetite for bringing down white mega-heroes." Moreover, so far as I am aware, Rhoden has not commented upon the relevance of Clemens's indictment in 2010 to his thesis. The indictment of Clemens, a white player comparable to Bonds, seems to interfere with this theory. Regrettably, as in the O.J. Simpson fiasco, a substantial portion of the black public actually believes the Rhoden argument about Bonds! One hopes that all of those in the steroid era will be identified, ostracized, and where possible, penalized.

Bonds and Clemens, like Williams, DiMaggio, Musial, Mays and Aaron before them, get the attention because, black or white, they are part of the elite group. The same is true of McGwire now—though he is not a hitter who belongs in the category of any of the players noted above. Such individuals always invite scrutiny whatever their race. Justice needs to be pursued regardless of color.

Beyond the issue of race itself, Bonds has placed himself in a special situation. Other elite baseball players, both black and white, appeared before the BALCO Grand Jury. But only Bonds refused to admit that he consumed steroids—and only Bonds appears to have lied. True, Bonds has an extremely unpleasant personality, which brings considerable attention to himself (so does Clemens). But his evasiveness and alleged perjury before the grand jury is the key element in the fact that he is being singled out.

Accordingly, it seems to me that at a minimum the asterisk is an appropriate sanction, for Bonds and those like Clemens, Mark McGuire, and the subsequently identified Sammy Sosa, Manny Ramirez and Alex Rodriguez—reflecting some cloud or doubt about what transpired in the '90s and the early part of this century. If judicial findings are made about drug use on the basis of testing and independent testimony, it may be that Bonds's record should be stricken altogether! This is the approach taken by the Olympics with Marion Jones. This was the approach taken by the ancient Greeks! Why should baseball be different?

The Hall of Fame

Both Shoeless Joe Jackson and Pete Rose have been barred from the Hall of Fame for their gambling activities. Mark McGwire has thus far been denied admission by the vote of writers who, apparently, are influenced by his conduct in 2005 when he refused to say anything about drug consumption in "the past." The same fate may await others.

In some respects, the treatment of Jackson and Rose has always seemed to involve a double standard given the fact that others like Cobb and Speaker, who were close to gamblers, are in the Hall. Indeed, it is thought that Speaker and Cobb, accused of fixing a 1919 game, executed a sworn affidavit that listed every cheating affair that they had heard of and that Commissioner Landis backed down, unwilling to confront them![103] And the Jackson and Rose cases have not shown actual interference with on-the-field competition, though anti-gambling policy is properly rooted in the view that those involved in baseball must be like Caesar's wife, i.e., above suspicion of malfeasance. If, in fact, Bonds and others are shown by drug testing and independent testimony to have consumed drugs independent of the outcome of perjury proceedings, it seems to me that denial of admission to the Hall of Fame is appropriate because of the fact that the integrity of the game itself was interfered with and that competition was not fair. Criminal conviction arising out of this would make the case for exclusion stronger. This has nothing to do with moral character or the idea that the Hall of Fame should maintain the standards of churches.

An Addendum on Other Forms of Cheating

Steroids, whether used by hitters for greater offensive capabilities or pitchers to allow them to gain both strength and recuperative improvement, are a form of cheating—just as is gambling. But as noted, some of those who believe that the problem has been exaggerated think of it as akin to other kinds of cheating which have been regarded as less serious than gambling. For instance, the corked bat, which is hollowed out so as to give the batter greater bat speed, thus presumably power, has been found to have been used about half a dozen times in the last fifteen years. The most prominent of these examples was Sammy Sosa, still a Chicago Cub in 2003 in the wake of some of his great home run years. He was suspended for seven games. This seems to be the general framework for penalties, the greatest number of games imposed upon Billy Hatcher (eight games) as well as Wilton Guerrero (also eight games).

But the most fascinating and more frequently used techniques arise out of the prohibition of the spitball, which was made illegal in December 1919 for the 1920 season, so as to facilitate the offensive production that was to come. Though never as important as the fastball or curve, a number of pitchers relied upon the spitter, one of the most prominent being Jack Chesbro, who won forty-one games in 1904 for the New York Highlanders (the Yankee predecessors). Big Ed Walsh used the spitball to get forty victories for the 1908 Chicago White Sox. The spitball would add a slippery substance to the ball which changed its behavior; so also did nicking the ball's surface so as to change the grip and release by the pitcher. But in 1920 all of this was to come to an end just as Babe Ruth was beginning to hit some of the many homers which would fly out of Yankee Stadium, the "house that Ruth built," three years later. The spitball was then banned. Pitching was disadvantaged and hitting, particularly the home run, were enhanced.

The spitballers were "grandfathered" in — that is to say, those who were identified as individuals who had thrown the pitch in the major leagues were allowed to continue to throw it until their careers ended. The last of them was in 1934.

Since the spitball was banned in 1920, a number of players have been penalized for throwing it. Two prominent examples are Nelson Potter, the Saint Louis Brownies ace pitcher during and immediately after World War II, and Gaylord Perry, who was often suspected of loading the ball with saliva. Each pitcher received a ten-day suspension. The rules apply not only to the spitball by prohibiting a pitcher from "bring[ing] his pitching hand in contact with his mouth or lips while in the eighteen-foot circle surrounded the pitching rubber" but also to apply to various foreign substances. Rule 8–12 prohibits a pitcher from applying a "foreign substance of any kind to the ball," and forbids him to "expectorate on the ball, either hand or his glove."

The pitcher is prohibited from rubbing the ball on his "glove, person or clothing" and from defacing the ball. The penalty is to call the pitch a ball, warn the pitcher and announce it over the public address system, and in the case of a second offense, to disqualify the pitcher from the game. Though the opposing team may take the play — the ball with a foreign substance or spit may be hit for a home run — the warning and, for the second offense, the disqualification are nonetheless instituted. If, on the other hand, any player has "on his person, or in his possession, any foreign substance" for purposes of doctoring the ball, the penalty is immediate ejection.

A number of pitchers have been ejected during the past thirty years or so. One of the most recent is Brian Donnelly of the Los Angeles Angels, who had pine tar in his glove and was immediately ejected and then suspended for ten games. Most of the penalties imposed seem to be ten days, though relief pitcher Jay Howell received only a two-day suspension for the same infraction. On the other hand, Brian Moehler, caught in 1999 with a small piece of sandpaper to scuff the ball, received ten days, as did Kevin Gross for the same offense in 1987. Joe Niekro of knuckleball fame used an emery board to deface baseballs just before the Gross incident and received the same penalty. In 1980 Rick Honeycutt was caught with a thumbtack, which caused him to bleed. He received the 10-day penalty.

Pitchers point out that their infractions draw a slightly higher average suspension than those imposed for corked bats, notwithstanding the Jay Howell penalty. But regardless of any discrepancy between penalties imposed upon hitters and pitchers, the overriding point is that there is enormous difference in the discussions about sanctions for these offenses as opposed to drugs — particularly under the latest revisions of the baseball collective bargaining agreement in 2005 and '08. But the public health concerns with drugs would seem to argue for different sanctions in connection with this kind of cheating.

A Further Addendum on Violence and Conflict Between Players and Fans

A series of incidents involving both fans and players over the past few years have dramatized a number of unhealthy trends in baseball, not the least of which is (1) an inordinate consumption of alcohol by fans; (2) changing standards with regard to obscene language; and (3) the geographical placement and proximity of fans and players to one another. The NBA Pacers-Pistons fracas[104] in November 2004 was, as Arbitrator Roger Kaplan cited in his opinion, "one of the worst if not the worst, in the history of sports since the advent of collective bargaining."[105] In this case Arbitrator Kaplan upheld a season-long suspension of Indiana Pacers star Ron Artest for charging into the stands, trampling on spectators and attacking an individual who was in fact the "wrong person," not the one who had attacked him by throwing a paper cup at him. In denying the union's grievance protesting Artest's season-long suspension and rejecting the NBA Players Association's reliance upon baseball's suspension of Texas Ranger pitcher Frank Francisco for only sixteen games when he threw a chair at an Oakland fan, Arbitrator Kaplan said: "The NBA should not have to justify its decision based upon what commissioner in other sports have done in penalizing their athletes. It is fundamental that previous incidents within your own sport are paramount to determining appropriate penalties."[106]

The arbitrator, however, was required to distinguish the lesser penalty of sixty-eight games provided by another arbitrator to Latrell Sprewell, who attacked and choked his coach during a practice session a few years earlier.[107] As I have said, in my judgment, the *Sprewell* award was deeply flawed[108] because it relied upon the absence of comparable penalties for violence to set aside this one — ignoring the fact that in no instance of previous violence in the NBA or other professional sports had a player choked his coach! But in the Pacers-Pistons matter the arbitrator distinguished *Sprewell*, concluding that the player's past record was distinguishable from that of Artest.

The arbitrator, however, concluded that one of the other offenders, Jermaine O'Neal, was the victim of an excessive penalty, and in order to set this penalty aside, the arbitrator was required to address an issue which is involved in baseball altercations as well. The basketball collective bargaining agreement at that time gave the Commissioner "sole and exclusive authority" to hear appeals involving "on the court" behavior.[109] Here, since the violence occurred in the stands, the question for the arbitrator was what constituted "on the playing court" behavior. Said Arbitrator Kaplan:

> The confrontation between players and fans, spectators and even arena personnel is distinctly different from the type of "on court" or "in the game" conduct such as flagrant fouls, fights

between players, hard picks, elbows and confronting referees. It is clear that the genesis of the altercation occurred when a spectator threw a cup of liquid on Artest while he was off the court and lying on a table.... The Union's argument that [contractual provisions referring to the playing court or court] should be construed narrowly is persuasive. On this basis the Arbitrator was thus able to review the suspensions to determine whether or not they were provided with just cause for the conduct in question.[110]

This is to be contrasted to the collective bargaining agreement in baseball: under Article XI(C) the Commissioner has "full, final and complete disposition of the complaint" when it arises out of "conduct on the playing field *or* in the ballpark."[111] Thus in baseball the Commissioner, albeit with a special appeal system in his office, has full authority to resolve matters that arise, for instance, when players become involved in disputes with fans and player altercations on the field.

These contract provisions, of course, involve disciplinary actions taken against players and, in my judgment, Commissioner David Stern was well justified in taking very severe action in response to the unacceptable behavior of the players involved. In some respects the Pacers-Pistons matter is reminiscent of 1912, when Ty Cobb, prior to the advent of a union or collective bargaining, attacked a heckler (who had lost parts of both hands in a work accident), punching, kicking and spiking him in the stands. Cobb was thrown out of the game and American League President Ban Johnson suspended him indefinitely. When eighteen members of the Tigers protested by striking for two days, they were fined $50 for each day they missed. While there was talk of a league-wide strike, it did not materialize. Cobb was suspended for ten days and fined $50. Johnson determined that "direct responsibility for the unfortunate occurrence rests upon the player."

In 1995 Tony Phillips and Chili Davis were each fined $5000 by the American League for separate incidences of assaults upon fans (Phillips got into a shoving match with a fan behind the left field stands and punched him in the face; Davis, in response to taunting by a Milwaukee fan, approached the supposed offender and poked him in the face, though fans maintain that Davis swung at the wrong heckler). The incidents of 1912, 1995 and 2004 in baseball and basketball, respectively, highlight again the skepticism that many have about whether, as Mel Allen asserted on the radio in the 1940s, professional athletes are similar to the general population.

In 2004 Texas Rangers relief pitcher Frank Francisco was suspended for sixteen games for throwing a folding chair into the stands from the bullpen and hitting the wife of an individual who had repeatedly heckled the pitchers in the Rangers' bullpen. It is the Francisco incident itself that especially emphasizes the fact that fans are a very important part of what appears to be a growing problem — and all too frequently the clubs are complicit in this.

For instance, the same year as the Francisco incident, my oldest son and I were in Anaheim Stadium when we were subjected to profane, abusive and drunken behavior by a young man who claimed he was a season ticket holder. Initially, this conduct had been aimed at others, but when the individual said to me that he had perhaps gone too far with one of his more recent outbursts, I agreed with him and told him that he had gone too far in that the volume of his voice and the content of his language were not only unsuitable to me and my son but also to families in the immediate area. He responded by saying that there was "too much noise" and "I can't hear you" and "I paid the same for the same ticket you paid for." When we could not get the ushers to do anything about this conduct we complained to the Angels, who claimed that they took unspecified disciplinary action against the usher in question. But no action was taken against the fan and no response was provided to our insistence that this be done by either the Angels or Major League Baseball itself.

In a series of articles in the *New York Times*, Clyde Haberman stated that what the New York Yankees really needed was "new fans" rather than new players or a new manager. Said Haberman about Yankee Stadium: "If you sat, as I did, in the upper deck along the third-base line, you were in the company of scores of young men wearing the glazed, dull look of the hopelessly inebriated. Some had arrived in that condition."[112] Haberman railed against the "oafs" and "louts," continuing:

> If it wished, the team could do more to discourage the louts. Rules posted on its Website make clear that fans "using foul language, making obscene gestures, smoking or appearing to be in an inebriated condition will be ejected from the ballpark." Ha! The stadium would be half empty if the ball club ever made good on that warning.[113]

Though the problem of the obscenities is hardly new to baseball — I recall being at Fenway Park with my parents in 1977 and becoming upset and embarrassed at the profanities being used in their presence — it appears that the problem exists in a number of parks. Haberman wrote: "Unruly fan behavior, some of it going beyond merely crude to plainly criminal, is a constant worry at sporting events everywhere."[114] Alcohol is a basic element in the problem and, of course, beer has been part of baseball from its inception. Said Haberman: "The October column [cited above] raised the possibility of cutting off beer sales earlier than is done now, after the seventh inning. But many e-mail writers said we would see world peace before that happens."

However, baseball seems to draw the line when fans directly interact with players. In Wrigley Field in '95, when a Cubs fan ran onto the field to yell at Cubs relief pitcher Randy Myers, he was banned from Wrigley Field for the entire '96 season. When Gary Sheffield fielded a ground ball in the Fenway Park right field corner in April 2005, a fan appeared to take a swing at him and Sheffield was doused with beer. The fan in question had his season ticket revoked for the entire 2005 season, and the individual who doused Sheffield with beer was prohibited from buying tickets for the rest of the year. The Boston police applied for criminal complaints against the offending fans. Said *The New York Times*:

> Fans heckling players is as old as sports. For many of us, athletes are the guys who sit in cages at an amusement park, waiting to fall in a tub of water if we hit the right button.
> We can boo. We can shout vulgarities, talk about their mothers, comment on the most embarrassing details of their personal lives. That is the covenant, and most players accept it....
> In too many instances, fans have crossed the line and baseball had better push them back. There is a tragedy waiting to happen.[115]

But frequently little or no action has been taken. In 2002 two fans jumped out of the stands in Chicago's Comiskey Park and attacked Kansas City Coach Tom Gamboa, who lost his hearing in one ear as a result of the attack. One of the individuals brought a knife onto the field — but he was given thirty months' probation and ordered to perform eighty hours of community service, though he was subsequently jailed for violating his probation. The following year, when fans ran on the field and attacked an umpire at the same park (now called US Cellular Field), three of them paid a $100 fine and spent one night in jail. In the very same month, when an Oakland fan hit Chicago outfielder Carl Everett on the head with a cell phone, he was not tried or penalized. The same is true of the fan who poured beer on Jason Giambi in Oakland in 2005.

Of course, a fundamental part of the fan behavior problem is alcohol. This is what fueled the incident to which my oldest son and I were exposed in the Anaheim Stadium, and in part, this was the focus of a league-wide code of conduct that David Stern implemented in basketball subsequent to the November 2004 incident. This is what made Clyde Haberman ruefully comment that "world peace" would break out prior to restrictions upon alcohol. The fact is that the volume of alcohol sold is important to the bottom line in sports. While the Red Sox took firm and prompt action vis-à-vis their fans in the Gary Sheffield incident, a study showed that alcohol sales had jumped twenty percent from 2003 to 2004 and the complaints about rowdy behavior around the ballpark were on the increase. (At the same time, Fenway Park is one of the most aggressive in fighting back, announcing a telephone line to call in the event of untoward incidents. Now many other stadiums have followed suit.)

The language employed by fans, both orally and by way of written signs, is offensive by any standards in an increasing number of instances. While a number of stadiums and arenas have stopped beer and alcohol by a certain time in the game — this is part of the NBA reform — the fact is that the problem needs greater attention. In addition to the reforms instituted, it may be necessary to introduce stamping of an individual's hand similar to the practice at nightclubs, for instance, to determine how much alcohol has been consumed by a given individual. Again, there is no way that alcohol and its consumption can be separated from these problems. It must be addressed by organized baseball in the coming years.

The Bullpen in Major League Stadiums as a Factor

The location of the bullpen in major league stadiums is part of the picture — probably a major part of the picture — in interaction between fans and players which can lead to violence. As noted, taunting of players by fans is part of the game, as is banter back and forth between the fans themselves. But in a number of instances the location of the bullpen seems to have been a factor in altercations and violence between players and fans. This problem has been exacerbated by the new ballparks, which have enhanced more proximity between the players and the fans, an objective which has served baseball well in attracting new fans. But this proximity, particularly within the context of bullpens, is a problem.

In the Oakland incident, in which a near melee broke out between the Texas bullpen and Oakland fans, the Oakland fan whose wife was struck by a folding chair indicated that he had purchased those seats next to the Oakland bullpen specifically so as to taunt and heckle the visiting team's pitchers. This is made possible by virtue of the fact that in Oakland the bullpens are located on the field along the baselines near the stadium seats.

Of the thirty Major League ballparks or stadiums, only seven have their bullpens located on the field along the baselines, 6 of which are in the field of play itself. The remaining twenty-three stadiums have placed their bullpens beyond the outfield fence, more generally, so as to comport with the traditional way ballparks were laid out. This shows that the fans can be separated from the players.

True, some of the old parks had their bullpens on the field, as was the case in Oakland. Tiger Stadium in Detroit was one of them prior to its demise in 1999. The old and charming Ebbets Field in Brooklyn, where the Brooklyn Dodgers played prior to their move to Los Angeles, also had the bullpens on the field. The new stadium of the New York Mets, opened in 2009, has the same organization of Ebbets Field because the Mets' CEO Jeff Wilpon has said that he wants to keep most of the "motif" of Ebbets Field at the Mets' new park. But the new ballparks in Minnesota (2010), the Bronx, where the New York Yankees play (2009), and Saint Louis (2006) have bullpens beyond the field of play.

Today the ballparks of the Chicago Cubs, Florida Marlins, Minnesota Twins, Oakland A's, San Diego Padres, San Francisco Giants and Tampa Bay Rays all have their bullpens along the lines. In Joe Robbie Stadium, the present home park of the Marlins, though the bullpens are located down the baselines, a wall separates them from the field of play. The new home of the San Diego Padres at Petco Park is also a bit of an aberration inasmuch as the visitors' bullpen is in the right field corner but that of the Padres is located beyond the outfield wall in left center. This came about because of the location of the Western Metal Supply building in the left field corner — reminiscent of how the warehouses across Euclaw Street from the Orioles park in Camden Yards in Baltimore precluded the placement of a wall down there. The design by well-known HOK, which kicked off the current boom in stadiums with the construction of Baltimore's in 1992, exposes the pitchers seated in the right field bullpen to the afternoon sun, which is in their faces. The Padres, initially intending to use this bullpen as their own, moved theirs beyond the outfield fence, where the pitchers would be shielded from the sun's direct heat. In Denver's Coors Field, the visiting team's bullpen seems to be lost among the trees beyond the fence, making it difficult to determine who is actually warming up!

Some of the traditional bullpens in the outfield were cavernous, and the echo of the ball cracking in the catcher's mitt could resound well beyond the confines of a concrete wall. But others, such as in Baltimore's Camden Yards, are more accessible to the fans, adjacent in that case to an elevated picnic area open to the fans, where they can yell in and conceivably throw objects at the pitchers. Thus even the location of the bullpen beyond playing field parameters is not a fail-safe method.

One of the ugliest incidents between players and non-playing personnel occurred in Fenway Park's bullpen — again, beyond the confines of the playing field itself — when Yankee relief pitchers Jeff Nelson and Jim Garcia attacked a Red Sox employee because he was cheering for the home team. (The players were criminally charged with assault but avoided going to trial by agreeing to perform fifty hours of community service and undergoing anger management counseling; the employee filed a civil action for $33,785.) But the bullpen distance in Boston is likely to make Oakland-type confrontations less frequent.

Quite obviously there is an incentive to put the bullpens on the field because that proximity may sell more seats and produce revenue. But not only does this create the greater potential for confrontation between players and fans but also bullpens on the field are unsafe for the players. Both outfielders and infielders frequently have to run up to the hill of the pitching mound and dive onto the hard substance of a mound as well as the rubber. This is what happened to San Francisco Giant outfielder Dustin Mohr in 2004 when he injured his ankle badly. The proper location of bullpens embedded in the outfield will diminish the potential for conflict as well as the safety hazards associated with chasing fly balls, foul fly balls or popups down the line.

Performance-enhancing drugs are hardly the first instance of cheating. There are a variety of ways in which players and teams attempt to obtain an advantage and some of those have been outlined above. Others involve sign stealing; the Giants were apparently able to read and relay signs that would tell them what pitch was coming during the 1951 pennant drive that they won with Bobby Thomson's home run! Indeed, the Philadelphia Phillies have been accused of stealing signs illegally with the use of binoculars.[116] Though no precise ethical standards have ever been established here, baseball appears to prohibit the use of binoculars though "[p]layers, managers and coaches are allowed to steal signals ... [but not through] cameras, binoculars or any method beyond their eyes to do so."[117] Similarly, the National Football League prohibits the taping of other team's signs, as the New England Patriots discovered when they were found guilty of engaging in this conduct against the New York Jets.

The "hidden ball trick"—I saw Marty Barrett do it for the Red Sox in Anaheim in 1985 as he snuck in behind an unsuspecting runner to tag him out—is as old as the game, and yet some players believe that this is not acceptable. A contemporary of Barrett who was replaced by him in the Sox lineup at that time, Jerry Remy, now a Red Sox broadcaster, said that someone who uses the hidden ball trick should be ready for a "punch in the nose." Yet it is something that we would do frequently on the Station Field in Long Branch, New Jersey.

A controversy which is somewhat akin to this emerged out of Alex Rodriguez's alleged trick played on Toronto Blue Jays infielders when he was rounding the bases and shouted "I got it," causing the players to let the ball drop. Whatever the truth of the matter— Rodriguez denied this, though New York Yankee manager Joe Torre reprimanded him for it—it seems difficult to distinguish from runners who routinely attempt to shield defensive players from ground balls until the last second so that they, the fielders, will not have a good chance to field the ball successfully. In both instances the runners are attempting to distract the infielders and not give them a fair chance to play the ball. (This contrasts with Rodriguez's 2004 American League playoff incident: he slapped the ball out of Bronson Arroyo's glove when he was covering first base, a violation of the rules.)

The game has also changed through formal aids that the players have, such as body armor for the hitters, and even before that, batting gloves that came to be worn by virtually all of the players, as well as helmets in the '60s.

Any advantage will do, and yet what seems to be fairly peculiar and *sui generis* about drug taking is that it involves not simply dishonesty but also a public health threat. Though much of society takes many drugs indiscriminately, the fact is that steroids and amphetamines are not only harmful to those who play the game and the public generally, but also, when one examines the most notorious situation—i.e., that of Bonds in 2007—one finds that drug use dramatically enhances performance on the field, not simply maintaining it.

Baseball, on both the union and owner side, was slow to address this matter. The institutions, to an even greater extent than players like Bonds, Clemens, Giambi, McGwire and Sosa, stand responsible in the dock of public opinion. It trivializes this major break with the past to analogize drug use to the scuffing of balls, the throwing of spitballs, etc. It is of a different order, notwithstanding the fact that other factors as well may be responsible for the artificial home run barrage of the '90s and this century. Baseball has not met its responsibility in this arena and it must do so in the years to come if it is to remain faithful to its public trust.

CHAPTER 8

The Growing Problem of Race in Baseball

I hope someday Satchel Paige and Josh Gibson will be voted into the Hall of Fame as symbols of the great Negro players who are not here only because they weren't given the chance. — Ted Williams, upon his induction into the Hall of Fame in 1966.

In a sense it has come full circle. Blacks were excluded, ostracized and discriminated against at baseball's beginnings. In dramatic and historic fashion Jackie Robinson broke the color bar when he joined the Brooklyn Dodgers in 1947 after serving a year of apprenticeship with the championship Montreal Royals in '46. But in the early twenty-first century the role of blacks in America's national pastime is substantially diminished from what it was in the first few decades subsequent to Robinson's advent.

In the 1860s, when baseball was first played by amateurs, the game was integrated for a limited period of time as both blacks and whites played on integrated teams in the New York area. But it could not last. In 1867 the first professional league, the National Association denied access of membership to the Pythians, an all-black team from Philadelphia. Amateurism began to become professionalism as the Cincinnati Red Stockings played from 1869 onward. Here a small number of blacks began to be involved with the game, and between the late '60s and the late '80s there were a number of professional black players.

Some outstanding black players were part of the scene in this period, John "Bud" Fowler and Moses Fleetwood Walker being in the forefront. Walker, an Oberlin College student and catcher at that institution, became the first black player in the majors when his team, the Toledo Blue Stockings, joined the American Association, at that time recognized as being one of two major leagues. But Walker had considerable difficulty and was treated poorly by his own teammates and pitchers who threw to him-as well as by opposing teams, crowds and hotels that excluded blacks. Fowler, the first professional black player, at the nineteenth century's conclusion became the last black ball player to play regularly in the white minor leagues. Between 1878 and 1899 thirty-three black players were part of "white baseball."

Some of the white players, in a manner eerily similar to what was threatened by at least one opposing team in the twentieth century when the color bar was broken in the late 1940s, refused to take the field with blacks at all. One of the standout players, Hall of Famer Adrian "Cap" Anson, was a leader in this effort. In 1883 when his team, the Chicago Nationals, were scheduled to play against Toledo, Anson would not take the field because Walker was playing for Toledo. In this inhospitable environment the number of blacks began to

decline as Jim Crow and "separate but equal" came to dominate the country in the '80s and
'90s.

States Jules Tygiel in his classic book, *Jackie Robinson and His Legacy*:

> By the close of the decade [the 1880's] only a sprinkling of blacks remained in the minor
> leagues. In 1889 the Middle States League invited two black clubs, the Gorhams of New York
> and the Cuban Giants, to enter competition. The following season, the league, renamed the
> Eastern Interstate League, again included the Giants, as well as a Harrisburg team which
> fielded at least two black players. When Harrisburg deserted the circuit to join the Atlantic
> Association, the league disbanded. Harrisburg retained its two black players and the following
> year added several others, causing sportswriters to nickname them the "Polka Dots." The
> Cuban Giants meanwhile enlisted in the Connecticut State League, which also proved short-
> lived when the league collapsed in the middle of the 1891 season, the Giants returned to barn-
> storming, their career in organized baseball at an end. "By 1892 the color line was firmly in
> place. Despite brief appearances [by a number of black players] in 1895, teams in organized
> baseball fielded no blacks. Nor did they invite black clubs to join any major or minor
> leagues. The Acme Color Giants, who played half a season in Pennsylvania's Iron and Oil
> League in 1898, represent the sole exception. After winning only eight of forty-nine games,
> the team mercifully disbanded. At the dawn of the Twentieth Century, the national pastime
> was a Jim Crow enterprise.[1]

As the door shut in the white leagues, blacks began to rely increasingly on their own teams,
just as separate black universities, social clubs, and musical groups began to emerge in the
era of segregation. The above-referenced Cuban Giants were prominent among them and
at the turn of the century there were five such major teams, soon to grow to nine operating
generally within the vicinity of Philadelphia. These teams were barnstorming teams that
sought competition where they could find it.

In the 1920s Negro leagues began to form, but the barnstorming tradition persisted
for black baseball so that even members of leagues would barnstorm and play elsewhere.
Tygiel, again, estimates that only a third of a season's 200 games counted in the league's
standings. Sometimes the black teams played white major league teams, though Commissioner Landis ultimately prohibited this kind of competition.

The black teams could play year-round because of winter opportunities available in
Cuba, Venezuela or Mexico, where they received fan attention unknown to them in the
United States in either the black or white world.[2] Serious competition existed alongside of
showboating in much the same manner as the Harlem Globetrotters displayed in basketball.[3]
In the mid–'30s and '40s Satchel Paige, referred to by Williams at his Hall of Fame induction, became the quintessential illustration of both extraordinary skill and showmanship.
The classic example is when Paige would call in all his outfielders so as to demonstrate how
he could strike out the side. Tygiel notes, however, "Paige never attempted these feats against
tougher competitors."[4]

The rules that developed in white baseball did not apply. For instance, the ball could
be doctored in any way. Cool Papa Bell, one of the Negro League's outstanding players,
reflecting on the "Vaseline Ball," stated, "It had so much Vaseline on it, it made you blink
your eyes on a sunny day."

The teams frequently played in the white stadiums such as Yankee Stadium in New
York — but they were not allowed to use the lockers, showers and other facilities. The games
could be canceled quickly if the white teams who owned or leased the facilities wanted to
use them for other purposes such as a concert or boxing match. Poor training, difficult traveling, generally on buses, and segregated hotels made the living conditions difficult. Where

there were no hotels the players simply slept on the bus or outside the park itself. Nonetheless the legends associated with both players and teams flourished. Among the most prominent beyond Paige himself was Josh Gibson, the powerful home-run-hitting catcher who thought that he might be the first to break Major League Baseball's twentieth century color bar. He is reputed to have died with a broken heart in 1946 when the opportunity was not provided.

The great teams of this period were the Chicago American Giants and the Pittsburgh Crawfords, both of which provided the basis for the Negro National League. Gus Greenlee owned the Crawfords Bar and Grill "On the Hill," and a good deal of gambling and numbers operations as well. The criminal basis for the operations of some black entrepreneurs, as well as the power of so-called booking agents who arranged schedules, diminished the ethical and legal standards that existed in the Negro Leagues.

The Negro National League of its time reached its apogee at the time of the Negro League East-West game in Chicago, which showcased black talent to the white world in World War II days. The performance of Jackie Robinson with the Kansas City Monarchs in 1945 made his talent more widely known, and thus helped to provide the basis for the attack on the color line in organized baseball.

Of course, there were a number of players who may well have been black who played in organized baseball during this period. They could be identified as Indians, Cubans or Mexicans, and it was thought that many such players passed as white. As noted above, Ruth was sometimes thought to be of black parentage, though most modern writers are skeptical of this. In any event, as Leigh Montville in his classic biography of Babe Ruth has noted, Ruth was taunted with racial epithets when he played with the Yankees and this hurt him deeply.[5]

Commissioner Landis and others denied the existence of the color bar, stating, "Negroes are not barred from organized baseball ... and never have been in the 21 years I have served." But baseball, disproportionately populated by Southerners (whose skills could develop because of the better weather year-round, and for whom a rural undeveloped economy allowed for fewer opportunities in other businesses) remained resistant. It was thought that some players in the 1920s and before, like Rogers Hornsby and Tris Speaker, were members of the Ku Klux Klan! The New York Yankee outfielder, Jake Powell, said in a radio interview that he was an off-season "cop" who obtained "pleasure beating up niggers and then throwing them in jail."

Eddie Collins, general manager of the Boston Red Sox, maintained that no black players had applied, and it was often said that there were no blacks who were of major league caliber. But Dizzy Dean, who often barnstormed with Satchel Paige, recognized that there were black players of considerable talent.

World War II hastened the winds of change. Though American troops were segregated in all branches of the Armed Forces — General Eisenhower, later elected president in 1952, testified in support of segregation — hypocrisy and the double standard of segregation and inferior conditions kept blacks out. But, as Tygiel has noted,[6] the Chicago White Sox, Pittsburgh Pirates, and even the notoriously racially exclusionary Washington Senators, began to make noises about providing a chance to black players in the majors.

The population shift of so many blacks from South to North made the black market a potential audience, given the fact that all of the teams were in the North. It is said that Bill Veeck, later president of the Cleveland Indians, attempted to purchase the Philadelphia Phillies, announcing that he would hire black players. Landis shortly thereafter allowed the sale of the team to be made to an owner for half the price — an owner who was subsequently banished for betting on his own team.

Nineteen forty-five, the end of the war at hand, was the eve of the watershed. Landis was to die of a heart attack in 1944, and this "eliminated one of the most implacable and influential opponents of integration."[7] The owners were to hire former Democratic Senator from Kentucky, A.B. "Happy" Chandler, who seemed to be opposed to further exclusion.

Meanwhile, a drama was to unfold in Boston when Isadore Muchnick, a white politician representing a predominantly black district in the Hub, threatened to deny Sunday permits to the Red Sox and the Braves on the grounds that they had not given an opportunity to blacks. Muchnick contacted columnist Wendell Smith, who promised to provide prospects for a tryout and produced Jackie Robinson, then still with the Monarchs; Sam Jethroe, who was later to play in the farm system of the Brooklyn Dodgers, and ultimately center field for the Boston Braves; and Philadelphia Stars second baseman Marvin Williams. The players went through a tryout on April 16, 1945, and it is said that Robinson tattooed the "Green Monster," the thirty-foot-high wall in left field. But none of the players heard from clubs thereafter and it was said that someone had shouted out, "Get the niggers off the field."

The next portion of the chapter to unfold involved the entrance of Branch Rickey, general manager of the Brooklyn Dodgers, who, in considerable and dramatic secrecy, approached Robinson and signed him to a contract with the Montreal Royals in the Triple A International League, for the 1946 season. This is a story which has been recounted in detail by many,[8] and Robinson's ability to overcome the extraordinary amount of hostility in 1947 when he played for the Dodgers — racial taunting by Philadelphia Phillies Manager Ben Chapman and his players, and an alleged refusal to play by the modern "Gashouse Gang," the St. Louis Cardinals — is well chronicled. Enos Slaughter and Joe Garagiola were two of the worst offenders.

Within weeks of Robinson's arrival in Brooklyn in 1947, Larry Doby, a .400-plus hitter with the Cleveland Eagles of the Negro National League, was hired by Bill Veeck's Indians on July 5, 1947. Though the *New York Times* stated on July 6 that he, when introduced to the Indian players, was "greeted ... cordially," in fact, as he told me, most ignored him and would not shake his hand. Robinson, of course, endured such ostracism in baseball that Pee Wee Reese was thought to be courageous by putting his arm around him on the field. Later, when the Cleveland Indians became World Champions in Doby's second season of 1948, he and Steve Gromek, one of the Tribe's leading hurlers, were photographed hugging one another in the club house after their victory over the Boston Braves — a photo that was featured throughout the world!

The achievement of Robinson can never be gainsaid. He, along with Doby and later pitcher Dan Bankhead of the Dodgers, produced the integration of baseball in the twentieth century. But, more important, the summer of 1947 had a lasting impact upon American society. All of this came about a year before President Harry Truman desegregated the Armed Forces in 1948, a reform which took place notwithstanding General Eisenhower's testimony supporting segregation among the troops.

The advent of Jackie Robinson, and then Doby and Bankhead, took place a number of years before the major Supreme Court decisions began to establish the handwriting on the wall for separate but equal,[9] and seven years in advance of the landmark ruling of *Brown v. Board of Education*[10] holding that separate but equal in public education was unconstitutional. It was well in advance of the Montgomery Bus Boycott, which began Dr. Martin Luther King's campaign for civil rights, and the demonstrations which led to comprehensive antidiscrimination legislation beginning in the late '50s and '60s. Robinson's audacious and lonely courage in his struggle against segregation in baseball was repeatedly cited as both precedent and inspiration in the drama that was unfolding in the United States. As Leonard Koppett wrote:

> What is so hard to remember now (and completely unknown to younger people) is the devastating fact that until Jackie Robinson, there was no pressure whatever from the "decent" people to break the color line that all accepted.... So when all is said and done, as much as Robinson meant directly to his own people — as an example and inspiration and pioneer — he meant even more to the white society. He did more than any other single human being could do to focus their attention on the inequities of a system in which lily-white baseball was only one small symptom. The consequences of the waves his appearance made spread far beyond baseball, far beyond sports, far beyond politics, even to the very substance of a culture.[11]

Meanwhile, the push forward continued, ever so slowly and hesitantly, on the baseball field itself. In small numbers, the Negro Leaguers were to follow in the wake of both Robinson and Doby. But those early stars — the most prominent names are Dodger catcher Roy Campanella, pitcher Don Newcombe, New York Giant Monte Irvin, Cleveland slugger Luke Easter and Satchel Paige himself in 1948 — were only tokens. Nonetheless, their disproportionate acceptance in the National League accounted for the dominance of the NL in the '50s and the decline of all-white clubs like the Detroit Tigers and the Boston Red Sox (the last to integrate, with Pumpsie Green in 1959). The New York Yankees eventually escaped from complete racial exclusion, not hiring catcher-outfielder Ellie Howard (the first black player to play for the team) until 1955!

In the case of Howard, substantially before his signing, the Yankees were aware of the considerable talent of Willie Mays. "The tactics of [George] Weiss's scouts and the relationships maintained in the front office demonstrated the team's institutionalized discrimination."[12] But when Mays was signed by the Giants he hit .353 for Trenton in 1950 — the very year the Yankees purchased Howard from the Monarchs. Five years later, when "Mays had become the symbol of the Giants" and had been named as MVP in the National League (that was the year that he made his spectacular over-the-head catch against the Cleveland Indians in the World Series), Howard advanced to the majors.[13]

Pumpsie Green, the first black Red Sox player in 1959 — when the Red Sox were the last team to integrate (courtesy Boston Red Sox).

As Steve Treder has so brilliantly written, all ball clubs, even the relatively enlightened Brooklyn Dodgers and Cleveland Indians, made it difficult for black players to advance during this period.[14] Time and time again ownership found inferior white players to promote ahead of them, a policy not entirely dissimilar from some that have followed in this new century.

The Boston Red Sox appeared to have been even worse. After passing on Jackie Robinson, they passed on Mays as well, overlooking scout recommendations in the process. Instead the Sox first reached out to Lorenzo "Piper" Davis from the Negro Leagues after his best years were behind him. Finally, after he tattooed the ball in spring training when Pinky Higgins was still at the helm, Pumpsie Green emerged on the scene on July 21, 1959.[15] The power-hitting ex-catcher and hard-throwing hurler Earl Wilson was to follow soon thereafter as the Red Sox' second black player. But as Wilson told me more than two decades ago, the Red Sox "should have made clear" that he and Pumpsie "were to be treated equally" with white players.

It was not to happen. The following spring training of 1960 — a year when Green stuck with the team but Wilson was sent to the minors — was, in Wilson's words, an "extremely tough environment." The two of them, Green and Wilson, could not go into restaurants in the South, and either one of them had to go to the back of the restaurant or stay hungry. Wilson told me that he always said that he was not hungry and just stayed on the bus.

For Green, having been raised in northern California, this was something of a culture shock. But Wilson — who hailed from the Deep South of Louisiana — had already been exposed to this while playing for Red Sox farm teams like Montgomery, Augusta, and Columbia, South Carolina. And, of course, the club's two main farm teams were in Louisville and Birmingham. Wilson noted that his eventual transfer from Montgomery to Albany constituted something of an improvement. He told me that the team in Montgomery had Rebel flags sewn onto the uniforms and he had torn his off. Some players, he said, were "blatant racists." Yet as he made his way to the majors and traveled to other southern towns like Jacksonville, for instance, where there were four or five blacks on the team at that time, there was "a little group of us who tried to make each other comfortable when we went into each other's towns."

Wilson told me that though blacks at that time "caught hell," and couldn't live in the hotels, he nonetheless dismissed it as something that allowed him to live in private homes with good home-cooked meals and without a curfew. And he credited a number of players and officials in the Red Sox organization as friendly and encouraging — particularly Johnny Pesky, Dick Radatz, Chet Nichols and Don Schwall. Even subsequent to his departure to the Tigers in 1966 he maintained friendships with Red Sox players like Cy Young winner Jim Lonborg and power-hitting catcher Bob Tillman. He looked back with fondness at 1961 and his work under Pesky at the Red Sox farm team in Seattle. But none of this diminished Wilson's bitterness over his 1960 demotion, when *Boston Globe* writer Larry Claflin had told him that some in the Sox organization were saying that newspapers were "wasting their film" on Wilson because of his well-chronicled wildness. Noted Wilson, other hard throwers were wild during the same period of time in their respective careers — like Sandy Koufax and Nolan Ryan. Their teams, Wilson noted, were patient with them.

That summer of 1960, my labor law professor at Cornell Law School got me a summer clerkship with the United Auto Workers in Detroit. As soon as I arrived in town, I immediately went to Tiger Stadium on a brilliantly sunshine-filled Sunday afternoon when the Sox pulled in. I noticed that there was a new black player in the Boston dignified gray uniform, who was now shagging flies in the outfield before the game. This was centerfielder Willie Tasby, the first black player ever obtained by the Red Sox in a trade—in this case for light-hitting Gene Stephens, he of late-inning replacement fame for Ted Williams when he would leave the game in the seventh or eighth inning in the late 1950s. In 1962 I was back again in Detroit with the UAW. Tasby was now gone, and Pumpsie Green had his lowest-hitting year at .231 and was soon bound for the losing New York Mets in '63. But now it was Wilson's turn on the big stage and he did not disappoint, throwing a no-hitter on the West Coast and a two-run outing against the Detroit Tigers which I witnessed—a performance in which he seldom faltered, the two runs yielded being two towering homers by Rocky Colavito. Wilson and Bill Monbouquette were the steadying influences in the Sox rotation in those years.

But then came the spring training of 1966 and an incident where Wilson was refused service in a Florida club. When I asked him whether the Red Sox had come to his defense he said: "The Red Sox were the cause of the problem.... I was told that this was fine," and asked not to comment upon it. But, said Wilson, "I couldn't do any good with my life that way—it was more important than playing with the Red Sox."

Paradoxically, that was the year when the Red Sox brought in a number of black players. This was the first year for hard-hitting infielders Joe Foy and George Scott, Lenny Green having come to the club the previous year—and second baseman-centerfielder Reggie Smith was to be called up at the tail end of the season. When hard-throwing reliever John Wyatt and the weak-armed Jose Tartabull were obtained, Wilson said that he and his roomie Green laughed and said: "Somebody has got to go." The very next day the telephone rang in their room and Green picked it up. But the call was for Wilson with Sox Manager Billy Herman on the line. Herman told him that he, Wilson, had been traded to the Tigers for Don Demeter, who had not exactly burned down the fences with his play in the Motor City. Wilson said he was not sure that the trade was racially motivated but it came soon after both the increased number of blacks and the Florida incident. Said Wilson: "I can't say that I was the best pitcher around—but I was the best that the Red Sox had!"

And he was to go on and play a key role in the Tigers' 1968 World Championship season. There his pitching improved remarkably, tutored by Coach Johnny Sain of "Spahn-and-Sain-and-two-days-of-rain" fame with the Boston Braves. (Wilson said, laughingly, he and Montbouquette were not of the same caliber.) Their teammates, such as infielder Dick McAuliffe, were supportive. After Wilson had been battered by the Washington Senators in a rough outing, McAuliffe said to him: "Don't worry about that—you're going to win a lot of games for us." And he did, going 13–6 in the remainder of the '66 season, 22–11 in '68, with 29 more to come in the next three seasons.

Yet, in spite of the Earl Wilson trade, it seemed as though things were beginning to change with the Red Sox. The '67 Impossible Dream saw not only Smith, but also Wyatt, Scott, Foy and Tartabull all play key roles. In August they were joined by ex–Yankee Elston Howard, whose intelligence and defensive ability steadied the rotation, though his hitting skills were in decline.

But all of this soon evaporated. My sons and I witnessed rookie Lynn McGlothen flirting with a no-hitter one lovely Fenway summer night in 1972, his work subsequently ruined when Bill Lee squandered the game with a bases-loaded round-tripper to Bill Freehan over the Green Monster. McGlothen's tenure was brief before his departure to St. Louis and then on to San Francisco. Thereafter, in 1976, Canadian Hall of Famer Fergie Jenkins could not demonstrate the dominance that he displayed with every other club for which he pitched!

Thus the '70s retrogressed from the '60s. The late Larry Whiteside, the first African American baseball writer ever on the Red Sox beat (or, for that matter on any baseball beat) arrived in town in 1973 urging the Sox not to trade Reggie Smith in his columns for the *Boston Globe*. He gently chided the Red Sox about Smith in one of his first columns that year. Wrote Hall of Famer Whiteside: "How can I convince the Red Sox that now is not the time to trade Reggie Smith? I've been looking for a fourth for a hand of bid whist for years, and with Reggie, Tommy Harper, and maybe Cecil Cooper, we can finally get one going."[16] But trade him they did — and Whiteside was right there in the fray to capture Smith's anger over the unwillingness of Sox management to tolerate outspoken blacks. Indeed, Whiteside went on to criticize the team again in 1979 for a presence of black and Latin players which was "more imagined than real. Outfielder Jim Rice and first baseman designated hitter Bob Watson are the only two black players on the club."

For a period of time power-hitting Hall of Famer Jim Rice was the only African American on the team. It was in a run-up to this period in the late '70s in which I heard a white spectator shout from the Fenway stands: "George Scott, you are a slave." No official or fan did anything to address this racist insult!

And then came the nadir, a major dispute with erstwhile fleet-footed, base-stealing centerfielder Tommy Harper, who had come across to the team in that above-referenced Milwaukee trade which sent Scott away. Harper blew the whistle on the club in the mid–'80s, revealing a team arrangement for white players to attend segregated functions in spring training and noting that black players were just as unwelcome as they had been in the days of Pumpsie Green and Earl Wilson in the '50s and '60s!

A complaint was filed with the Massachusetts Commission Against Discrimination, ultimately leading to a settlement in which the Red Sox pledged to do better at recruiting blacks at all levels. I wrote in the *Boston Globe* that the Red Sox "short changed" blacks, examining the history that goes back to the immediate post–World War II era. Shortly thereafter came two remarkable developments: a scathing article by Will McDonough of the *Boston Globe* excoriating "biggies" like the *New York Times*, CBS and ESPN, and my *Globe* article in "even our own humble little publication right here." McDonough claimed that Harper was simply dismissed because he was on the wrong side of an internal ownership dispute. Said McDonough about Red Sox owner Tom Yawkey, who had presided over the team from 1933 until his death in the '70s when he was succeeded by his wife:

> I knew Tom Yawkey, the man to whom they trace all of his alleged racist history. I never thought he was racist. But I wasn't as close to him as Joe Cronin and Dick O'Connell were. These two former Sox general managers knew him as well as anyone in Boston. Over the years, I asked both if Yawkey ever suggested they do anything racist. The answer was no.

This read like a bumbling defense to a fair employment practice complaint in the old days when they were first filed in the '60s and '70s. McDonough, like other defenders of racially exclusionary practices, seemed to say: "Others who are in my country club say that I am not racist and therefore I must not be."

On responding to my point in the *Globe* that the trading of Cooper for Scott manifested stupidity as well as racism, McDonough said the following:

> A few days ago, William B. Gould IV, identified as a professor in labor relations at Stanford, wrote a piece on Red Soc racism for the *Globe*'s oped page. He was eminently qualified because he grew up in New Jersey and now resides in Palo Alto, Calif. To prove some points, he wrote that the Sox traded pitcher Earl Wilson to Detroit for a mediocre center fielder (Don Demeter) who was white. He never mentioned Lenny Green, John Wyatt, George

Hall of Famer Larry Whiteside of the Boston Globe, the first black baseball writer for any major American newspaper — he integrated the press box. Here, he is shown with his colleague, Joe Giuliotti of the *Boston Herald*, in the background (courtesy Elaine Whiteside and Joseph Giuliotti).

Smith, Al Smith, Roman Mejias, Jose Tartabull ... all black. All acquired in the same time period.... That's how dumb I am. I never knew that trading one black player for another was a form of racism. That's why I am grateful to Gould, CBS, The *Times* and the rest for straightening me out.

The McDonough piece demonstrated quite clearly that the mid–'60s and early '70s had been almost a blip on the screen. His article made it clear that the legacy of ex–Sox manager and hanger-on, Pinky Higgins, who told Al Hirschberg in the '50s that "no niggers will play on my team," was alive and well. Earl Wilson said to me three years after that exchange: "Are all the Tommy Harpers wrong?"

But then in 1986 there were more developments. First, in a trade with the Yankees for the "Hit Man," Mike Easler, who had joined Rice in the early '80s as one of the team's few black players, the Red Sox brought over Don Baylor from the Yankees. Baylor, the first real black leadership presence in the clubhouse, voiced annoyance with the game's impediments to blacks who would be managers and executives. He said to me, while glancing around the clubhouse in a series between the Angels and the Red Sox in Anaheim that May: "Walk through this place. The only blacks that you will find are custodians and cooks." But Baylor also said that he had been treated well by the Red Sox.

And soon to join him that summer was the talented centerfielder-right fielder, Dave Henderson, acquired from the Seattle Mariners. He was to deliver the greatest home run in Red Sox history and one of the greatest ever in baseball, witnessed by my oldest son and myself in the October Anaheim sunshine, when he rescued the Red Sox from the oblivion of playoff defeat and delivered a 2–2 count home run to left field over the head of Brian Downing, who slumped against the left field wall as the ball disappeared into the seats. Now (at least until the World Series' 6th game, in which Henderson again performed heroics) the magic was back. The Red Sox had won another Eastern Division and American League championship assisted mightily by Baylor (his center-field shot which, eluded the leaping Gary Pettis, had brought the Sox within striking distance), Henderson, and the irascible and volatile Dennis "Oil Can" Boyd, who was the third hurler in a strong rotation led by fire-balling Roger Clemens and lefty Bruce Hurst. But Henderson was soon dealt away the following year, and Boyd developed a sore arm after an exquisite spring training performance in Vero Beach, Florida.

Soon there were to be other black stars on the team — but never a substantial number. Ellis Burks patrolled center field and then, when hobbled with injuries, right field. He could hit for average and power subsequent to his arrival in 1987, but in a controversy with Red Sox management about the need for surgery on his ailing back, he departed as a free agent. Tom "Flash" Gordon was to appear in 1996 after his best years in Kansas City, when he, along with Bert Blyleven, was reputed to have the sharpest breaking curve balls in the majors — or so it seemed to me when I saw both of them. Subsequent to his appearance in the 13th inning of a 1997 Oakland A's game, he became an ace reliever for the Sox. But he too left in a dispute about injuries.

Then there was the most spectacular star of them all in this period — Maurice "Mo" Vaughn, who hit long and towering homers, tagging them authoritatively from the early '90s until his departure to the California Angels at the conclusion of the '98 season. He unloaded a particularly memorable bases-loaded, come-from-behind grand slam homer in the ninth in the team's home opener on Good Friday '98 to win that game against the Seattle Mariners. But, like other African American stars before him, he took the free-agent route out of the Hub.

The new ownership's policies in this century have been far beyond anything that one could imagine in the country club days in previous decades, when utility infielder Frank Duffy spoke of the team's individualism as reflected through "25 guys in 25 cabs." The team has been more visibly committed to racial equality policies in the Boston community, as evidenced by the establishment of scholarships for minority youth through the leadership of former Vice President Charles Steinberg. The club cracked down quickly on the alcohol-fueled abuse of the Yankee black star Gary Sheffield in 2005.

The April 15 date of Jackie Robinson's arrival is commemorated annually by the team. The Red Sox have a black coach, DeMarlo Hale, who has been singularly successful in the third-base box — the thinking coach's position and the controversial hot seat in Boston — and has now been promoted to the number-two position of bench coach. On the field, the black Latin players have been the major attractions, especially "Big Papi" David Ortiz, Pedro Martinez (since departed from the New York Mets and Philadelphia Phillies), and, of course, the controversial Manny Ramirez, whose troublesome behavior in the summer of '08 induced management to deal him to the Los Angeles Dodgers. In recent years, however, the only black American on the team has been centerfielder Coco Crisp, who was traded to the Kansas City Royals at the conclusion of the '08 season — and in '10, outfielders Mike Cameron, Darnell McDonald and Bill Hall signed on, with Carl Crawford to join the fold in '11.

For the Red Sox, like baseball generally, 2011 is considerably different from 1946. In 1946, when I threw in my lot with the Carmine Hose, there were no black players at all in the major leagues. As the Red Sox turned out to be the last to integrate, I have justified my loyalty to the club in the same way that I have expressed my loyalty to the United States. While each institution is badly flawed, my view was that I had a commitment to change and reform, not to depart. This remained so even when I became the object of the racist vitriol of Will McDonough. In any event, the policies of ex–Red Sox Vice President Charles Steinberg and the new ownership in particular have translated into improvements — just as has been the case with the United States itself.

In baseball generally there remain two ongoing issues perhaps more than arguably related to one another: compensation for past discrimination, and steps to remedy the decline of black players in the majors, as well as the small number of managers and front office people in the majors. On the question of recompense, both to the players who came in relatively late in their careers (after all, Robinson was a 28-year-old rookie), and to those who never made it at all (Negro League standouts like Ray Dandridge only made it to Triple A with the Minneapolis Millers), it has taken two forms.

The first is the Hall of Fame issue which Ted Williams addressed in 1966. Four years after Williams's comments, Commissioner Bowie Kuhn created a committee for the annual induction of players who had at least ten years of seniority in the Negro Leagues and who were ineligible for regular Hall election. Initially, when Satchel Paige was inducted in the first round in 1971, the separate Hall was in place — but this was soon changed. The Hall enshrined seven of the best players before the committee's dissolution in 1977, and after '77 the regular Veterans Committee inducted nine former Negro Leaguers as well. But, quite naturally, the veterans favored players whom they knew — and they did not know most of the players from the Negro Leagues, which had become moribund by the 1960s. Many talented black players were overlooked.

Thus baseball sought to remedy this with a new round of inductions in July 2006. This was appropriate action for MLB to take, though the process was considerably short of the ideal. In the first place, it appeared that the Hall of Fame initially intended to make this 2006 process a one-shot deal that could not be revisited, even though future research on the Negro Leagues (records are difficult to come by and the number of former players still living is declining) could reveal more talent. Thus the Hall's Dale Petroskey said: "As more information comes to light down the road, the door is always open to the possibility of perhaps further consideration."

But a second problem relates to the evaluators, both at the five-member screening committee level and the full 12-member voting group, which, according to Cooperstown, possessed "expertise in African-American baseball history."

None of the living former Negro Leaguers participated. This seems particularly puzzling when one considers the fact that some, like Monte Irvin, have both been voted into the Hall of Fame and called upon by MLB itself as troubleshooters in the past. They and others may not have seen the relevant players, but many have learned about them anecdotally and read about them as youngsters.

Third, some of the selections are puzzling. In the first place, five of the 17 selected are baseball executives. The Negro League players are being recognized because they would have been in organized baseball absent discrimination. Can the same be said of the Negro League owners and executives? Though discrimination by many outside of baseball may have been responsible, they did not possess the necessary capital or connections to be part of the big show.

And if owners and executives are part of the pool, shouldn't one of the very first electees be Gus Greenlee, the owner of the dominant all-star-like team, the Pittsburgh Crawfords?

Greenlee not only presided over the Negro League New York Yankees of their time, but he was also an organizer and president of the Negro National League. And most importantly, Greenlee was the major organizer of the Negro League East-West game in Chicago, which showcased black talent in the white world in World War II days.

Another even more troubling omission is that of Buck O'Neil, who gained fame as part of Ken Burns's documentary, *Baseball*. Curiously, the category assigned to him in the electoral process was that of manager. O'Neil was a good manager, but he had relatively little service. He was also a good player, but not at the level that is normally required for the Hall of Fame. But as an ambassador for baseball as well as the Negro Leagues, O'Neil had no rival. Why he could not have been considered as a "pioneer," a separate and unequivocally legitimate category for election, defies explanation.

These examples spotlight another problem, which is particularly perplexing: the lack of transparency in the process. Of course, as with the writers and veterans, the ballots are secret. But those who choose to reveal their vote and reasoning, both in terms of selection or omission, are free to do so and do so frequently. Yet former Commissioner Fay Vincent, the non-voting chairman of the committee, said: "I don't think the individuals are going to be willing to discuss their individual votes. We agreed we would not do that."

Given the lack of any such agreement among writers and veterans, it is difficult to see why this would be the case. Says Negro League expert and author Joe Riley: "I think that they don't want to speak because they would be exposed as not expert on what they are supposed to be expert about."

As in 1971, when the great Satchel Paige was inducted, the past can never be remedied. Baseball is to be commended for attempting to do so. But the process and substantive results could have been much better. One hopes that it will be in the future.

This remedying of the past for excluded black players has taken another form as well. As noted above, the Negro Leagues became moribund as the gates opened in organized baseball and many black players had no opportunities in either arena. Thus their market disappeared and the Negro Leagues did not provide pension or medical benefits to their former players.[17] Accordingly, MLB in the 1990s agreed to provide certain benefits to former Negro League players: in '93 it created medical coverage for them, and in '97 it adopted a supplemental income plan that provided an annual payment of $10,000. Individuals who played in the Negro Leagues prior to '47, when the color bar came down, were eligible. Some of these players had not played in organized baseball at all but only in the Negro Leagues. Some of these players had played in MLB for a period of time that was too short to make them eligible for regular medical and pension plans.

In 2003, however, a retired Major League Baseball player, Mike Colbern, brought a class action on behalf of himself and other retired baseball players which claimed that Major League Baseball had violated Title VII of the Civil Rights Act of 1964 (the comprehensive antidiscrimination law became effective in 1965) by excluding them from the above-noted medical and supplemental income plans because such plans were limited to Negro League players and thus, it was alleged, discriminated on the basis of race. Other claims were filed as well.[18] They consisted of an alleged "battery" for undergoing cortisone shots and other drugs without informed consent. A district trial court denied this claim and the matter was appealed to the Court of Appeals for the Ninth Circuit.

In *Moran v. Selig*[19] the court, speaking through Judge Stephen Reinhardt for a unanimous panel, concluded that these ex-players had failed to make a prima facie case of discrimination under Title VII, that MLB had a legitimate nondiscriminatory reason for the actions they took, and that these reasons were not a pretext for discrimination. The court first rejected the charge of adverse employment action because, in its view, these kinds of medical or pension programs did not qualify as benefits covered by Title VII inasmuch as they were not part of the employment relationship. Said Judge Reinhardt:

> Although some beneficiaries of the two Negro League Plans may have played MLB baseball for a relatively short period of time, eligibility for benefits is not based on such former employment with MLB or on any employment relationship between MLB and the recipients, Rather, to qualify for the Negro League Plans, a recipient need not be a former MLB player, only a former Negro League player. A former Negro League player who never played for an MLB team is eligible for the benefits even though he was never employed in any way by MLB or one of its clubs. Thus, although they resemble benefits typically conferred on the basis of an employment relationship, the Negro League Plans' benefits are not "part and parcel of the employment relationship" between recipients and MLB nor are they "incidents of employment" of the recipient of MLB. Because the supplemental income payments and medical benefits MLB provides to former Negro League players are not awarded on the basis of an employment relationship with MLB, but rather on the basis of participation in another entity to which MLB had no legal relationship, the receipt of these benefits cannot give rise to a valid Title VII claim. In other words, the fact that the appellants do not receive the same or substantially similar benefits as those provided under the Negro League Plans cannot be considered an "adverse employment action" because the provision of these benefits by the MLB is not an "employment action" at all. Appellants therefore cannot satisfy the critical third prong for making a prima facie case under Title VII.[20]

The court also quoted approvingly from the former players' own brief, which said "the racist culture that permeated baseball from the 1940s through the early 1970s led to an 'unwritten quota of two black players per [MLB] team' after the color barrier was broken, and those two players were usually ... of outstanding talent." The court noted that the players benefiting got to play in the Negro League and the players who challenged this policy did not. The court noted that admittedly all the players who qualified under this plan were black or African-American. Said the court:

> Although the players who qualify under the Negro League Plans are all African-American, it was African-Americans and not Caucasians who were discriminated against on the basis of their race. It is true that only players who played in the Negro Leagues are eligible to receive benefits under the Plans. It is also true, however, that the Negro Leagues were formed to provide the opportunity to play professional baseball to those who were otherwise excluded because of their race. There is no evidence, and it would strain credulity and one's sense of history, to suggest that appellants or any other Caucasians sought entry to the Negro Leagues or would have been willing to play baseball in that forum. In short, the Plans were adopted for the specific purpose of providing benefits to those who had been discriminated against by being denied the opportunity to play MLB and to qualify for MLB benefits.[21]

The court noted that MLB was seeking to remedy its past discriminatory conduct and it acted "honorably and decently."[22] Accordingly the past is being addressed by MLB both through the benefit program upheld by the Court of Appeals and by the less-than-perfect Hall of Fame initiative described above. But there is still the question outstanding of the present situation in baseball in the early part of the twenty-first century.

The world, the United States and baseball have changed dramatically since the advent of Robinson and Doby in 1947. Still, Robinson, who promised Branch Rickey that he would "turn the other cheek" to offensive behavior from white players, managers, umpires and fans, was criticized as he became more aggressive after his successful Rookie of the Year season in 1947. As the Court of Appeals for the Ninth Circuit noted, there was a kind of informal quota which limited the number of black players to two through the '70s in many clubs — particularly players of extraordinary qualities.

Cincinnati Manager Dusty Baker attested to this, as did Don Baylor while still active as a player in the 1980s. The marginal player, or light-hitting utility infielder who had an opportunity to observe the game and thus progress to the managerial and coaching positions, was not very likely to be a black. Thus the quota was in effect — and the Treder article attests to this unequivocally.

The number of black players has been continuously declining for a number of years now — and, like the absence of black quarterbacks[23] in football until Doug Williams with the Washington Redskins, blacks have been underrepresented as pitchers, catchers and infielders, where the action is and where the thinking about the game takes place![24] In the 2005 Major League Baseball season 59.9 percent of the players were white, 8.5 percent were African American, 28 percent were Latino and 2.5 percent were of Asian descent. As the 2005 racial and gender report card, Major League Baseball noted, "This was a three-percentage point decrease for white players and three-percentage increase for Latinos. The percentage of African American players," said the report, "is the lowest it has been in twenty-six years." The report went on to note that there were thirty Asian baseball players in MLB which was four more than the previous season. The number of international players had now increased more than 30 percent! And it seems clear that the rise of Latin American players has coincided with the decline in their African American counterparts.

As of 2008 the numbers had improved somewhat. Black players accounted for 10.2 percent of major leaguers, the most since the 1995 season — in contrast to an all-time low of 8.2 percent, which occurred in 2007. Said Robinson's widow: "I feel encouraged. It's not a huge leap, but it's a step forward."[25] But the 2009 season saw the percentage fall back by 1.2 percentage points to 9.0 percent. In 2010 the number of African American players edged ever so slightly upward to 9.1 percent.[26] But in 2011 the figure fell back to 8.5 — near to the 2007 low.

Thus, the problem remains considerable, and the words of John Shea of the *San Francisco Chronicle* have applicability today: "The void isn't just in rotation. It's in bullpens. In lineups. On benches. Everywhere throughout the majors. The numbers are worth repeating — African Americans constituted 27 percent of big-league rosters in 1975, but 19 percent in 1995, 13 percent in 1999 and less than 10 percent this year."[27]

Tom Verducci had noted the stark contrast a few years earlier when he said the following, decrying the fact that just a generation ago one out of every four big league roster spots was filled by black players. Said Verducci:

> The evidence is on view at every Major League ballpark. On the week-end of June 13–14 [2003], for instance, the New York Yankees and the St. Louis Cardinals met for the first time since the 1964 World Series and drew 165,000 fans to the three-game interleague series at Yankee Stadium. Between them the Yankees and the Cardinals suited up only three blacks: New York shortstop Derek Jeter and outfielder Charles Gipson and St. Louis outfielder Kerry Robinson. When they last played in '64 during the heyday of the Civil Rights Movement, the Yankees and the Cardinals featured six African-Americans combined.[28]

The Hall of Famer Joe Morgan, one of the prominent black players with both the Cincinnati Reds and the Houston Astros in the 1970s, referred to the fact that the 2005 Houston Astros were the first World Series team in more than a half century not to have a single black player on the roster. Said Morgan: "Of course, I noticed it. How could you not? ... But they're not the only ones. There are two or three teams that didn't have any African American players this year."[29] Morgan noted that when he was with the Cincinnati

"Big Red Machine" in 1976 he played alongside three other prominent black players: Ken Griffey Sr., George Foster and Dan Driessen. Cincinnati swept a Yankee team which had ten black players on its roster. Only as recently as in 1995, after the strike had ended, the Atlanta Braves and the Cleveland Indians, confronting one another in that year's World Series, had five black players each at that time. The Pittsburgh Pirates won the 1979 World Series with ten blacks on their 25-man roster. In 1994 all six starting outfielders at the All-Star game were African American: Barry Bonds, Joe Carter, Ken Griffey, Jr., Tony Gwynn, David Justice and Kirby Puckett. All of this has changed considerably.[30] Why has this happened?

Bob DuPuy of organized baseball states: "One reason in the decline of black children playing baseball [is] the 'inability to get instant gratification in baseball; these kids think they can come out of high school and go right to the pros in basketball and football.'"[31] But the idea of instant gratification, so often used as a reason for small numbers of blacks in connection with other employment opportunities, is dismissed by most observers who reject such stereotypes.

True, globalization in baseball has meant that there are fewer jobs for white players as well as black Americans.[32] It must be noted that many of the Latino players, such as David Ortiz of the Red Sox, are black, and indeed, most of the Latino players, if they hailed from the United States, would be regarded as black. The Latin American phenomenon is a difficult one to sort out on the racial issue. When I spoke to Larry Doby about affirmative action in the 1980s, he was particularly bitter about the idea that blacks and Latinos were spoken of interchangeably as "minorities" because in his time he thought that Latinos spoke Spanish loudly in order to avoid identification with black Americans. On the other hand, some of these attitudes have altered in this century, and it appears that obviously black Latinos like Ortiz, Pedro Martinez and "El Tiante" identify with black Americans.[33] Still, the decline of black Americans is troubling.

The number of black players, says Don Baylor, who has managed both the Colorado Rockies and the Chicago Cubs and more recently coached the Seattle Mariners, has declined "[b]ecause the League is looking outside the United States for players they can sign at sixteen and put in their baseball academies until they are ready to come the United States." Clearly the numbers show that Latino players, many of whom would have been barred by the color bar if they had not been sufficiently light-skinned, have come into the game in substantial numbers. This is because the academies referred to by Baylor make them cheaper and the poverty of their nations, particularly the Dominican Republic, make them hungrier — and the game is played with such intensity there.

And there is another related issue. Designated hitter Gary Sheffield stated that teams are more likely to recruit Latino players because they "control them" and they cannot do this with black Americans.[34] This may be related to Sheffield's anger at the Yankees for trading him to the Detroit Tigers at the end of the 2006 season: the Yanks, deeming Sheffield to be expendable, traded him for a Latin player, Bobby Abreu, from Venezuela.[35] The point is certainly a logical one given the desperate economic circumstances of many of the players who are coming from Latin America. Yet it is hard to imagine that superstars like Pedro Martinez are in any way controlled. His idiosyncratic behavior caused the Red Sox much worry during his stay in Boston.

Torii Hunter, the Angels' outfielder, has referred to Latin American ball players as "imposters"— meaning that whatever the skin color, their experience with and degree of racial discrimination is different from that experienced by black American players. Orlando

Hudson has maintained that black veteran agents in 2010 like Jermaine Dye found it more difficult to sign free agent contracts.[36] Perhaps the day will arrive soon, particularly in multiracial California, when "people of color" can be spoken of interchangeably, but these comments by Hunter, Sheffield and Doby before him indicate that the historically favored treatment given to those who speak Spanish is not forgotten.

Commentators frequently note that there is a kind of cultural disconnect in the black community to baseball, young players favoring football and basketball. Of course, there is an economic gap between baseball and basketball, the former requiring the expense of bats, balls, gloves and a large field that these days has to be maintained, while basketball requires only a ball and a court. It is said that the so-called "hip-hop" generation favors football and basketball, particularly the latter—and one can see the advertising that is aimed at the young black audience in basketball in particular. But this is a circular process; in part this is so because of the black involvement and indeed dominance in the game, with approximately 80 percent of NBA players being African-American in recent years.

Why is there such a disparity between baseball and the other sports? Says Baylor, blacks are "no longer interested in baseball—they're interested in basketball or football where they can get to the professional level a lot quicker than toiling in the minor leagues." States Dave Henderson, former Red Sox, Mariner and Oakland outfielder, recently a broadcaster for the Seattle Mariners:

> I think it's basketball. Basketball is more hip-hop. The hip-hop society runs with the NBA and every inner-city kid wants to be a hip-hop guy. You don't have your good athletes playing baseball anymore. I noticed in the Seattle area that [high schools are] dropping baseball teams because they can't field a team. You have to be a good athlete to play professional baseball. None of the black kids are playing baseball in the younger ages, they're playing basketball because they want to be cool and hip-hop.

Regarding the factors which are responsible for the small number of blacks in baseball, it is possible that some of them relate to the way young children are trained to play baseball. In the United States the young child develops through Little League and Babe Ruth, in contrast to the way I played with my friends as a child. Parents go to the games and become involved. But 80 percent of black families are single-parent families in which the father may not play a nurturing role which seems to be so important—particularly if he is not in attendance at the child's game. How major a factor this is remains somewhat speculative. (Neither my mother or father watched any of our Station Field games—nor did any parents, for that matter!)

There is yet another factor in all of this, and it is related to the decline in the minor leagues and the fact that the colleges, particularly for teams like the Red Sox and the Oakland A's, have become a new farm system. The colleges have played an important role in attracting blacks to football and basketball: the poor kid from the inner city, or even others of relatively modest means, are tempted by the full scholarships available in those sports. Full scholarships are not available to the black player who wants to choose baseball because baseball is not a high-revenue college sport and aid of any kind is not available to a student athlete.

According to an NCAA survey taken during 2003-04 only six percent of Division I players (the top college bracket) were black. On the other hand, half the men's basketball players were black as well as 44 percent of football players.

In the 2003 College World Series there were eleven blacks on the eight teams that were playing. In 2005 there were 43 black players in the NCAA Division I-A Men's Final Four basketball and four on the 4 teams in the finals of the College World Series. At times Stanford, one of the premier and most highly regarded baseball program universities, has had no blacks and rarely more than two. And the number of African-American players continues to drop at the college level.

Some believe that the draft system adopted in the '60s tempts high school players away from college. But the prevailing view is that scholarships play a major role. The NCAA limits each college to the equivalent of 11.7 full scholarships in baseball, applicable to as many as 35 players. This means partial scholarships, which discourage players from more economically disadvantaged circumstances from participating. Ross Jones, the University of Florida assistant coach in charge of recruiting, said he "could triple the number of African-American players on his roster within ten years if he had more scholarships."[37] The *New York Times* quoted him as follows:

> "If there's an inequity in any sport, it's in baseball," he said. "It absolutely cripples us. At a place like the University of Florida, if we can give a kid $3000 or $3500 in scholarship money, he's still got to come up with $7000 out of his pocket, and that's for in-state kids. If the kid has to pay, they're not going to do it. They'll play the sport where they don't have to pay a dime."[38]

Stanford coach Mark Marquess, when speaking of the decline of black players, said:

> I think there's a reason for that: the minor leagues. The black baseball player that's talented can sign out of high school and if he doesn't have a lot of money or education isn't that important to him, he can sign for a lot of money which means a lot to his family. That great black player is probably going to sign out of high school because it makes sense financially. The flip-side to that with professional baseball is that the same black athlete who is a football player or basketball player and is potentially a great baseball player, can go to a major university on a full-ride for football or basketball while there are very few full-rides for baseball; there's more publicity for those sports — more recruiting and notoriety. I think baseball is losing a lot of great black athletes to football and basketball because of the lack of baseball scholarships. College baseball has no chance to get that gifted black athlete unless he comes from a family where education is emphasized — that's why Stanford has a good chance to get some of those players.

What can alter this decline both in the colleges and the pros? In the first place, with regard to the pros it seems clear that the NCAA must change its scholarship rules so that baseball is more comparable to football and basketball. But college baseball is under pressure, the University of California nearly eliminating its program altogether for 2012. Meanwhile, football and basketball, of course, will resist any cut in their scholarships and the resistance will be considerable, given that football, in particular, is king! Football has complained bitterly about the fact that the number of scholarships available to them have been cut from the 120s to the mid–80s.

Second, Major League Baseball has initiated a number of programs aimed at inner city youth. MLB itself can do a good deal. It has started to promote so-called urban academies in the inner city via the program RBI, Reviving Baseball in Inner Cities, was founded in 1991. The RBI program is in at least 185 cities globally with 250,000 participants and some major leaguers like Coco Crisp, the ex–Red Sox centerfielder, are graduates.

In 2007 baseball started a new Urban Youth Academy in Compton, California, which began in late February with a $10 million facility which will allow thousands of youngsters to learn to play baseball. Darrell Miller, former Angel catcher and farm director, is the director of this complex. It will be interesting to see what progress develops as the result of this and similar initiatives.

A fundamental problem confronting baseball is that the fields and batting cages in the inner cities are few. During my sojourn in Washington in the '90s I sought out a batting cage to take some cuts. I found that there were none in the nation's capitol, which has a substantial black majority. The only place I could find them was in the surrounding suburbs.

Non-Playing Ranks

Beyond the player crisis, there is the matter of on and off the field non-playing appointments. This widely discussed subject has focused in particular upon the job of field manager, which Frank Robinson was the first to fill in 1975 while a player-manager. This was triggered by the flap over Al Campanis's remark that blacks did not have the "necessities" to be field managers.[39] As of Opening Day 2009, of thirty positions, five were held by blacks, with four Latinos and one Asian-American — though one of them, Cecil Cooper of the Houston Astros, would be fired during the season. Dusty Baker, who managed the Giants for a decade and brought them to within one game of a world championship in 2002, and brought the Chicago Cubs almost as far in 2003, has been managing the Cincinnati Reds since '07 — his third position after a broadcaster stint with ESPN.[40] But former Yankee star Chris Chambliss, an ex-coach for the Cincinnati Reds, has long been mentioned as a possible manager but never chosen — and apparently never seriously considered! DeMarlo Hale of the Red Sox has been interviewed by Seattle and in '10 by the Mets. He may well be the next new face in managerial ranks.

In 1999 Commissioner Bud Selig devised a plan which required teams to interview minority candidates not only for manager — but also for general manager, assistant general manager, director of player development and director of scouting. However, in contrast to the subsequently devised so-called Rooney Rule of the National Football League, no sanctions are attached to the failure to do so, though the Commissioner has stated that he would take action against clubs which did not comply. In the first place, sometimes, as in the case of the Dodgers' hiring of Joe Torre in 2007, the rule was simply waived.[41] Moreover, one of the complaints is that the interviews are *pro forma* in all sports. Though in football, the Detroit Lions were fined for failing to interview a minority candidate when Steve Mariucci was hired a few years back, the penalty is thought to be fairly inconsequential. But in baseball the sanctions are non-existent. It may be that the Commissioner's office should be involved directly in the interview process itself so as to avoid the *pro forma* possibility as well as to stress the seriousness of the Commissioner's interests and involvement. Telephone interviews hardly seem to be those which are undertaken with a good-faith intent to employ minority managers.[42]

Says Don Baylor:

> It's got to be in [Bud Selig's] heart that there be an equal playing field. The minorities know it's not an equal playing field at all. Solutions? People in the league can't be "told" to do something because people tend to run away from orders like that. It has to come from within. From Jackie Robinson's situation 50 years ago, a lot has changed: I've become a manager, some other minorities have become managers, Bob Watson has been a General Manager and now he's handing out fines for the league, Cito Gaston won back-to-back world championships and can't get a job as a manager. [Subsequently Gaston had a second tour of Toronto duty.] We don't have the same people pushing for us to get us out there because we're qualified and can do a great job than some other guys that are managing or in the front office today.

Twenty years ago this issue became front and center when Al Campanis of the Los Angeles Dodgers stated that the blacks could not possess the so-called "necessities" to assume a manager's position. Should the Commissioner's policy be more explicit, containing goals or timetables for recruitment? States Baylor:

> [Teams] know how to get around those things by closing the interview process; by hiring someone as an interim manager for a couple of months and then giving him a long-term deal. It's disappointing how it's done. Even during Ueberroth's tenure when the issue was on the front burner because of Al Campanis, people talked about it but it went away. The Commissioner has other things to do and it isn't a priority in the game anymore.

Another problem here relates to the fact that certain coaching positions, such as third base or the bench coach, are often the line of progression to managerial spots. These are the thinking man's jobs—the kind of job that DeMarlo Hale has had with the Red Sox. Moreover, as the *New York Times* has noted: "Diversity among the third base coaching ranks has been in decline for the past 5 years, from a peak of 12 in 2005 to 7 this season [2010], and the racial disparity between first- and third-base coaches has increased."[43] In 2010 there were 3 blacks at the third base post and at first base 12 blacks and 8 Hispanics. Though the position of pitching coach is not traditionally the line of progression to manager—only Bud Black of San Diego fits in that category at this time—all 30 current pitching coaches are white.

A similar pattern to that of coaches and managers exists at the general manager level, albeit a more pronounced one. At the general manager level only Kenny Williams of the Chicago White Sox and the recently departed Omar Minaya of the New York Mets have been the pioneers. Of the total GMs in 2009, five were minorities—three African Americans and two Latinos. Said the same Bob DuPuy quoted earlier: "Under commissioner Selig's direction, Major League Baseball launched several programs designed to increase African-American representation among our players and minority representation among our managers and front offices."[44] But the jury is out.

Selig, in response to his refusal to move the site of the 2011 All-Star Game away from Phoenix despite controversy surrounding Arizona's illegal immigrant legislation,[45] has deflected such inquiries, stating that he has a first-rate record on minority hiring. The fact is that beyond Kenny Williams and Minaya, little progress has been made. Most of the minority hiring is in the lower echelons of MLB, important as they may be. Baseball needs to take steps forward, particularly in concert with the NCAA, to attract young black athletes to baseball scholarships fully funded so that they can compete with football and basketball and produce more black MLB applicants.

Absent a smoking-gun admission that an owner will not hire blacks or other minorities, there is no way that the law can address this matter. This is because the number of jobs are so few that it would be difficult for a plaintiff to make out a *prima facie* because of a violation of the Civil Rights Act of 1964 which prohibits racial and national origin discrimination. The statistical sample is so small, given the small number of vacancies that occur, that it is impossible to make out a violation of the antidiscrimination statute on the basis of statistics.[46] Evidence which augments statistics is necessary.

Pressure to adopt more race-conscious policies may be the only answer. For instance, Commissioner Selig let it be known that he thought highly of ex–Red Sox and Brewer first baseman Cecil Cooper when he was hired on an interim basis and considered by the Astros. Cooper was hired, though he was subsequently fired. More leadership from the top of this kind is required.

CHAPTER 9

Globalization and Baseball

Introduction

The twenty-first century will witness an acceleration in the globalization of America's pastime and an extended reach of baseball beyond North American shores to foreign fans and players. Not only has the game long been played and appreciated in the Caribbean, particularly in Cuba[1] (which defeated the United States in the 1996 Olympics, split a two-game set with the Baltimore Orioles in 1999, and lost to the United States in 2000),[2] but it has also been played in Venezuela, Mexico, and Japan. Now baseball has taken root in Korea and Australia, and even in such unlikely places as Italy.[3] A true World Series — involving the entire world, not just the teams in the United States and Canada — took place in the form of the World Baseball Classic, hosted by Major League Baseball in the United States, Puerto Rico, and Japan in March 2006, and again in March 2009. These were true international tournaments, regarded as successful in the main, and it seems clear that they will be held again in the future.

Japan and Cuba again in 2009, having been the finalists in the World Baseball Classic of 2006 (the United States having been eliminated earlier in both years), have truly walked onto the world stage. At the penultimate stage of the WBC in 2006, Cuba, through its defeat of the highly vaunted and powerful Dominican Republic lineup, filled as it was with Major League sluggers, received enormous accolades. Korea, which had defeated Japan in three instances prior to the semi-final stage, was praised for its impeccable defensive fielding skills. And Japan, which won it all — in spectacular fashion in extra innings in 2009 — showed that the level of play in baseball in that country and in the Far East in general (the game is still in its embryonic form in China) must be taken seriously.

Said *Sports Illustrated* writer Tom Verducci, echoing earlier quoted comments by Lynn Jones:

> Teams such as Cuba, Japan and Korea, meanwhile, played with the versatility and fastidiousness that were hallmarks of the major leagues more than a generation ago, Korea's nimble fielders flawlessly handled all 173 balls put in play against them. Japan's pitchers struck out more than three times as many batters (60) as they walked (17 in eight games). Except for two doubles and two home runs, the Cuban team beat Venezuela, Puerto Rico and the Dominican Republic with 25 singles.
>
> It was oddly old-fashioned, too, to see in a major league park the game of pepper (in which a batter raps softly tossed balls back at one or more fielders) and infield (pregame fielding practice in which infielders and outfielders throw to bases), as Cuba and Japan did, last Saturday at Petco Park in San Diego. Both drills virtually vanished from the major leagues many years ago.[4]

The globalization of baseball is now evident on the playing fields in the United States.

Players continue to hail from the traditional areas of recruitment, such as the Dominican Republic, Puerto Rico, Venezuela, and Cuba; but many players from Mexico, Australia, Japan, and Korea also play Major League Baseball (MLB), and these countries have thus skyrocketed in importance:

> In the past decade, Venezuela has doubled its number of players on major league clubs — to 65 from 30 — and past Puerto Rico as a supplier of talent to the majors, according to 2005 figures from the Elias Sports Bureau (only the Dominican Republic and the United States supply more). There are 134 major leaguers from the Dominican Republic.... Latinos make up 37 percent of players under contract to major league clubs, according to the Major League Baseball.[5]

Even such countries as Spain, Belgium, the Philippines, Singapore, Vietnam, Great Britain, Brazil, Nicaragua, and the Virgin Islands have placed players in the MLB. And, as noted, the Far East has been important. The Boston Red Sox had been recruiting enough Korean pitchers to prompt a journalist to speak of a Korean Pipeline[6] — and as many as three Japanese pitchers have been on the club's MLB roster at the same time. A perceived dearth of qualified players in North America,[7] an attempt to diminish escalating draft and free agency salary expenses through Latin American player recruitment, Japanese free-agency,[8] the demise of the Cold War with its impact upon both Cuba's defectors[9] and the relaxation of conscription in Korea,[10] and the scramble abroad for new consumer markets[11] and recruits have accelerated the globalization of baseball.

In 2000, the number of foreign-born players on MLB rosters was 312 (forty-four of whom, though counted by MLB as foreign-born, were born in Puerto Rico), constituting 26 percent of all players.[12] That number has moved upward to nearly 30 percent![13] However, this represents a remarkable development which cannot be ascribed to changes in foreign countries alone. After all, baseball is the "national pastime" in the United States of America. As such, baseball has been slow to develop outside the national boundaries — particularly in comparison with the British-born sport of soccer or football, as it is called in every country except the United States (football in the United States is characterized abroad as "gridiron"), and even the slow-moving British game of cricket.

As noted, baseball, in contrast to soccer, which had no clear delineation between professional and amateur play in the early years, was fundamentally commercial and businesslike from the beginning and "more inward looking" during its development.[14] Britain was economically developed at an earlier stage than the United States, and had a more populous expatriate community in the nineteenth century, thus making it easier for the game to reach Europe and South America. The frequency of British tours were much greater than the occasional American venture, the so-called Spaulding trip around the world being the most prominent.

> The frequency of these English soccer tours contrast sharply with the history of U.S. baseball tours. While the English FA [Football Association] helped to promote participation in the game of soccer by accepting all comers as affiliates, and the amateur elites took the game with them to the British colonies at investment outposts around the globe, the promoters of American baseball were occupied with fashioning a successful closed monopoly sports league and incurring the attendant rent-seeking costs. If the United States had had colonies or any significant sum of foreign investment in the late nineteenth century, U.S. elites might have been more active in spreading the game to foreign lands.... Baseball has always been a business, whereas the owners of soccer clubs have often been motivated more by social and political goals.[15]

The tardy development of an American empire, which begins in the Spanish-American War of 1898, also impeded baseball's contact with the world. But as the result of economic and cultural connections, countries like Cuba began to play baseball in the 1860s. Resentment of Spain by the Cuban elites made that country receptive to the development of baseball. The first league sprung up in the 1870s, subsequent to the country's first war of independence against Spain, and many Cubans fled to Hispaniola (the island shared by Haiti and the Dominican Republic), bringing with them their love of baseball.

Similarly Japan developed an early involvement with baseball in the 1870s, twenty years after Commodore Matthew Perry arrived in Tokyo Bay. In the 1880s the large number of American expatriates in Japan promoted greater Japanese interest and a rivalry between American and Japanese teams.[16] Ultimately, Japanese colonialism, involving the occupation of Korea and Taiwan as well as other Far Eastern countries, played a role in spreading baseball. Nonetheless, the principal countries involved in baseball were only those in Latin America and Japan.

The percentage of foreign-born players involved in baseball in the United States in the early part of the twentieth century reflected this pattern of insularity, the exceptions to which were only found in Cuba, Latin America and Japan. In the post–World War II era, almost simultaneous with baseball's integration, the number of foreign-born players began to increase. The bonus baby rule, requiring teams to employ players who received bonuses immediately in the major leagues, adopted by Organized Baseball in 1947, made it difficult for those without resources to hire amateur players signed as free agents. Lower-revenue teams were squeezed and could not give bonuses to outstanding players like Yale pitcher Frank Quinn, who was signed by the Red Sox in late 1948 and received $50,000; Billy Consolo, signing with the Sox for $60,000 in 1952; and Johnny Antonelli, inked by the Boston Braves. The rule required that they be brought immediately to the majors and thus take up one of the spots on a 25-man roster, thus discouraging bonuses for young and promising players.

Quinn, immortalized by David Halberstam's commentary about how the Yankees believed that the Red Sox were going to pitch him on the last day of the '49 season if the pennant was clinched on the penultimate day,[17] pitched two years in which he compiled a 0–0 record in both '49 and '50, going a total of nine games and twenty-four innings! Antonelli never really developed fully with the Boston Braves, though winning all of seven games in the three years of '48-'50, and twelve once the club moved to Milwaukee in 1952. But the New York Giants were to see his full talents realized when he threw two twenty-game-winning seasons with them, as well as going 19–10 in 1959. The point is that the talents of certainly Antonelli and perhaps Quinn were stultified by their immediate promotion under a rule which required it since the bonus paid was more than $6,000. The low-revenue teams could not afford this luxury.

Because of the untoward consequences of this 1947 rule, it was rescinded in 1950. But a new rule which had the same monetary cutoff of $4,000, and which required a player to stay signed on the club roster for two years, was enacted in the 1952 winter meetings. The difficulty with this rule was not only premature promotion but also poor team morale since veteran players were playing alongside relatively highly paid but inexperienced bonus babies.

In 1958 the cutoff was revised upward to $15,000, and any player signed by December 5, 1958, could be drafted by another team after his first season of professional baseball if he was not placed on the Major League club's forty-man roster. It was this rule which required Jim Lonborg's rapid promotion to the AAA Seattle Rainiers, the Red Sox' top farm club, before his call-up in 1965. Sandy Koufax of the Dodgers, later to become one of the greatest pitchers in baseball history, languished with the Brooklyn Dodgers for a number of years and was late in overcoming the wildness which affected his pitching in his early years because minor league status would have exposed him to the draft by another club. Again, the first bonus baby rule had been instituted in 1947, simultaneous with the integration of baseball, which made black talent available to the majors. The more talent that there was, the more concern grew with how to control them — a problem which exists to this very day.

All of the bonus baby approaches and the limitations imposed upon players like Lonborg were awkward and self-defeating in their requirement that players advance quickly to the majors — the requirement to advance constituting a kind of wage control through which teams were discouraged from paying large amounts of money to college and high school players. Soon baseball's first amateur draft system was bought into existence in 1965. This approached the same cost control problem through a new method, i.e., the drafting of a player by one team. Prior to this rule the Yankees had found Mickey Mantle and others and simply signed the best players because they were able to outbid the other teams. Now a player could only be drafted by one team.

In the 1970s the composition of draftees and the signing of players began to change, when more college players began to be chosen than those coming from high school. They had more experience and although many believed that that experience was in no way a substitute for the minor leagues, they had the maturity and independence to be able to live on their own on the road, which high schoolers frequently did not possess. In the 1980s this meant ever-increasing bonuses paid to players who came from the amateur ranks. Though, initially, during the past two or three decades teams had selected more college players, there was a reverse trend towards "prep" school or other high school players, which now again seems to have turned back to college players.[18] Meanwhile, MLB salary escalation, triggered by both free agency and salary arbitration in the last quarter of the twentieth century, and a subsequent desire to find new markets for MLB products and new revenue streams including television broadcasting rights abroad, have made baseball look to the Latin American countries for new talent.

Initially, in the earlier and mid–20th century Latin American talent was recruited from Cuba and Puerto Rico — Roberto Clemente being the most prominent Puerto Rican player in this period. But the Cuban Revolution and the subsequent American embargo stopped most of the flow of players from that country. And, as noted below, it appears that the extension of the draft system to Puerto Rico has diminished the supply of players from that area also.

Free agency, as noted, increased MLB costs and this, in turn, pushed MLB to recruit more players from Latin American countries in an industry which uses free agency for talent recruitment far more frequently than the draft, which is relied upon by football and basketball.[19] The overlay in Latin America, particularly in the Dominican Republic, consists of a growing number of instances of abuses and exploitation emerging in the academies in that country, the recruitment of underage youngsters to play there, and kickbacks to officials employed by American clubs. David Fidler of the Indiana Law School, along with Arturo Marcano, have been leaders in bringing these abuses to the public's attention as well as MLB, and thus far the attempt by baseball has been to simply blame it on the *buscones* who recruit young players for the clubs in their academies.[20] Specifically, "the targets of MLB recruiting in the Dominican Republic and Venezuela are children — defined by human rights law as persons under 18 years of age — from impoverished backgrounds, who are less educated, less experienced, and more vulnerable than their counterparts in North America and East Asia."[21] This is a free agency system which now involves the falsification of age (the age limit for recruitment is 17 years old) as well as the use of steroids[22] given to youngsters and the "hiding" of players below the eligibility age who have access to the academies.

Though in 2002 both sides seemed to be interested in an international draft — particularly the owners because of their concern with high-salary bonuses given to players from Cuba who defect — they appeared to be in doubt about the question of where they could save costs most easily. The international draft had been proposed by the Blue Ribbon Panel,[23] an idea triggered not only by the high-salary bonuses but also because of the growing bonus demands made by amateurs in this country and the inability of small-market teams to compete for such talent.[24]

The Blue Ribbon Commission, consisting of both baseball owners and so-called independent members who tend to be industry proponents, advocated an international draft in the interest of enhancing competitive balance. But, in fact, it appears that the existing system, admittedly strewn with abuses, is economically inviting to the baseball owners, even small market teams, because thirty to forty foreign players can be signed on a budget of $1.5 million compared to $6.2 million (what *one* player might get in the United States) for a similar number of players.[25] Thus, even counting foreign infrastructure and maintenance costs, teams are spending more than seventy percent of their total amateur budgets on the draft, thus reflecting an incentive to hire Latin American players. True, the draft gives exclusive rights to a team to sign their own suggestions while they bid for Latin players to join their academies. As Shawn Hoffman has written:

> But in countries like the Dominican Republic, it's simply a case of oversupply; there are thousands of players competing for a relatively fixed amount of dollars, driving down prices across the board. Meanwhile, if a player is drafted in the States, he is that team's only option if they want to add a top-tier amateur to their system that year. If anything, draft bonuses are probably held down by the low-cost nature of foreign signings, since it gives teams a legitimate alternative.[26]

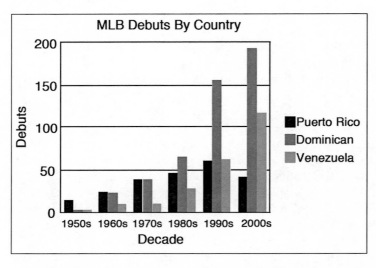

The draft and country origin (courtesy Baseball Prospectus).

The test demonstration of this proposition is Puerto Rico, where the number of players signed has gone down appreciably subsequent to 1990, when the island became subject to the draft. The dilemma for MLB in the Dominican Republican in particular is that the draft will increase labor costs and thus, from its perspective, more effective monitoring may be the best answer. (See chart.[27])

Japan

Problems relating to the recruitment of players from Latin America are appreciably different from those arising out of established leagues in Japan, Korea and even Australia. Perhaps the most dramatic of the new wave of foreign players as it relates to promoting baseball interest abroad has been Ichiro Suzuki (known as Ichiro rather than by his full name). Japanese baseball fans have ordered their daily existence around an early morning telecast which shows his team the Seattle Mariners. Beyond the sale of products in foreign lands, the revenue potential in the United States is considerable. The *Boston Globe* noted that advertiser buying behind home plate in Rangers Ballpark in Arlington, Texas, cost between $120,000 and $160,000 per half inning, if the advertiser buys an entire season's worth of ads.[28] Buying for just a few games cost more per half inning, and the same is true in Kansas City and Seattle. With the advent of Japanese players of superstar quality, many Japanese companies began to express interest in this advertising, aimed as it was at Japanese audiences watching Major League Baseball.

This has created worries for Japanese professional baseball as public interest in the game has declined with the movement of a number of prominent players like 2009 World Series MVP Matsui of the New York Yankees and Iguchi of the 2005 world champion Chicago White Sox. These players bring in their wake a Japanese baseball press corps devoted to the details of their performance on the field and sometimes their lives off the field as well. The return of some Japanese players like Irabu and their effective performance in Japan has built upon the interest in these telecasts. As the *New York Times* has noted:

> Unlike most of the foreigners who play here [the Japanese teams have had a limit upon two "geigjin," or foreigners], the returning Japanese players are more bicultural and bilingual. This has allowed them to win the trust of their teammates, many of whom envy their travels, and bridge the gap between Japanese and American brands of baseball.
>
> In the process, a new breed of Japanese ballplayer has been created: someone with outside experience who, rather than being shunned for the "bad habits" he may have picked up overseas, can now provide leadership on the field and in the dugout. In proving that you can go to the United States and return intact, these players may convince others to try their luck in the major leagues.
>
> On the margins, the returnees have even spiced up the Japanese game, which has fallen on hard times in recent years with the departures of stars like Ichiro Suzuki to Seattle and Hideki Matsui to the Yankees.[29]

Japanese baseball itself saw its own television ratings go down 15 percent as of 2001. As Professor Masaru Ikei has written:

> Ichiro Suzuki's success has brought enthusiasm for American baseball to a new level, lifting spirits here at a time filled with news of economic recession and crime. But it has also created some new worries for fans of the Japanese game. Suzuki's experience may encourage more star players here to leave to join teams abroad. The major leagues, for their part, may expand their efforts to recruit Japanese players. This could deprive Japanese baseball of its best players, leaving it as moribund as the once-mighty Russian ice hockey leagues. Already, TV ratings for the once-popular Tokyo Giants have decreased by one-third. And the Orix Blue Wave, after losing Suzuki, has seen its attendance drop by a whopping 40 percent. Ichiro Suzuki's achievement has added excitement to America's pastime, but it may also mark a turning point for our own.[30]

It is not in the interests of American baseball to destroy Japanese baseball, aside from the unseemliness and potentially untoward consequences of cultural imperialism — nor is it in the interest of baseball to put any league which could possibly provide recruitment streams for MLB out of business. There is an object lesson here. After Jackie Robinson's advent to the Brooklyn Dodgers, baseball skimmed the best players from the Negro Leagues[31] without compensation and thus drove those teams out of business. Says *Baseball Prospectus*:

> The Negro Leagues were simply driven out of business, as the big leagues simply plucked players away with no compensation. Major League Baseball could have paid Negro Leagues for the players they signed. They could have entered into working agreements with Negro League clubs to make them part of the farm system. But as usual, Major League Baseball was only interested in acquiring inexpensive talent.[32]

As I argued a decade ago,[33] there is no reason why agreements entered into between Japan and the United States cannot provide for the trading of players. But a new protocol negotiated between American and Japanese baseball (discussed below) currently prohibits such transactions. It is in the interests of baseball, as it attempts to fashion a true World Series, to have something more akin to a major league in Japan — and perhaps China and Korea down the road. The reinvigoration of baseball in Japan will be more likely in the event that the Far East can compete for American players on the free agent market comparable to the current American pursuit of talent in the Far East. Indeed the commissioners of Japanese and American baseball discussed anew in 2010 the possibility of a future true World Series between the champions of the American World Series and the Japanese Series.

Outside of the playing field itself, another consequence of globalization has been the first marketing arrangement between an American and a foreign team — in this case the New York Yankees and Manchester United — the latter being a team which has long held Yankee-type status in Great Britain and much of the world in soccer (or what the rest of the world calls football). This arrangement allows each team to market in the other's sports terrain without an exchange of money. The Yankees can sell their goods abroad and Manchester United gains access to the American market. Signage is promoted in each team's stadium and a tour of Manchester United in the United States. The idea is to promote baseball interest in Britain and soccer interest in the United States.

But, as the *New York Times* noted, the deal will presumably accrue more to the benefit of Manchester United because of the fact that soccer is much better-known and accepted in the United States than is baseball in Britain, its Commonwealth countries or in Europe generally. One area where the Yankees might benefit would be Asia, given the fact that the British club's games are regularly televised there. Said the *New York Times*:

> Man U bypassed America's fledgling professional soccer league to make a deal with the Yankees because it hopes that the association will make it a recognizable brand in what remains the world's foremost consumer market.
> Still, Man U fans reacted to the news with a who-needs-them disdain. Yankee faithful are equally offended by the idea that a soccer team is needed to help spread the gospel of Babe Ruth, Joe DiMaggio and Derek Jeter. They better get over it. Given today's global marketplace, an all-out merger between such franchises is a distinct possibility.[34]

More recently the Boston Red Sox have obtained Liverpool football clubs in Britain.[35] The first of its kind, it is difficult to determine whether this purchase will be helpful or harmful to Boston and Liverpool respectively.

The only other arrangement like these appears to be the National Football League's deal with the Spanish soccer club Barcelona in its attempt to promote that game in Europe.[36] The NFL has had a European league which operates as both (1) a vehicle to promote football in Europe, and (2) a minor league. Now football, like baseball, basketball and hockey, is attempting to reach the European market through the playing of games abroad — the NFL with recently well-publicized efforts in Wembley Stadium. For both football and basketball the minor league concept in Europe seems to be something of the past or on hold.

As noted above, player interaction across national boundaries has increased as well. In 1999, the Baltimore Orioles split a two-game set with the Cuban national team, with the Baltimore victory in Havana coming in a close game that could have gone either way.[37] Subsequently, Peter Angelos, the Baltimore Orioles owner who spearheaded the contract between Cuba and the Orioles, announced his intention to bring baseball to Greece. The Cuban-American rivalry extended beyond the 1999 Orioles-Cuba exhibitions as the United States triumphed over perennially talented Cuba in the Sydney Olympics.[38] But Cuba was to outshine the United States considerably in the World Baseball Classic in 2006.[39] An opening day game in 1999 was played in Monterrey, Mexico, where baseball has long flourished.[40] The globalization of baseball continued in 2000, when the Chicago Cubs and the New York Mets opened the MLB season in Tokyo,[41] as did the defending champion Boston Red Sox in the same city against the Oakland A's in March of 2008. Both teams played memorable exhibition games in the days prior to the season's opening against the Tokyo Giants and the Hanshin Tigers, when the Americans were dazzled by the Japanese pre-game infield practice, the Japanese skills on the field, and the inspirational songs that the Japanese fans sang for their teams!

Meanwhile, baseball has made some modest inroads in countries that are well established in baseball outside the Americas — Japan, Korea and Taiwan. (Interestingly, as noted, baseball seems to have come to Korea and Taiwan by virtue of the hated Japanese military occupation in the twentieth century.) Japan, which has had organized leagues for much of the previous century and played American All-Stars led by Lefty O'Doul before World War II, has virtually the same rules, though sharply different strategies from the United States. The one major rule difference between the United States and Japan is that Japanese games can be played to a tie because of the dictates of public transportation: after a limited number of extra innings, the game must end with a tie in order to allow the fans to return home on the train before it stops running.

Europe remains a "backwater."[42] As a commentator wrote:

> A couple of aberrations to the contrary — the former Mets manager Davey Johnson taking over the Dutch national team for the current European championships and the Olympic qualifiers, and a handful of big league prospects from the Netherlands signing for serious money in the United States — the sport's European development runs light years behind basketball's.
>
> There were no budding baseball equivalents to Tony Parker or Toni Kukoc, French and Croatian players in the National Basketball Association, when France beat Croatia in the opening round here.
>
> The reality is that the special part of the championships is their ambling pace, their lack of obsession with success in an atmosphere that comes close to charm in its minor-sport modesty.
>
> For all its backers' hoped-for rise in visibility, the expansion of baseball in Europe these days is a breeze, not a whirlwind.[43]

But there are other countries where the game seems to be flourishing notwithstanding the popularity of other sports. For instance, in South Africa, despite the inability thus far to reach the black African majority, the game is growing.[44] The game began in 1898 when American gold miners started a team near Johannesburg. It is particularly strong in the Cape Town area, where players staff most of the lineups in the nearly one hundred amateur clubs. So-called colored or mixed-race players are present in fair numbers in the western

Cape Province. But "blacks remain almost invisible at the top levels of amateur baseball in South Africa, with none on the roster of the national team."[45]

In 2006, WBC South Africa nearly beat a Canadian team which had defeated the United States — and it put up a good battle against Mexico. It was handily routed by the United States 17–0. But it acquitted itself well through its showing in the tournament, returned again in 2009 and will surely be heard from in the future.

Australia has had a nationwide league for a number of years. Israel has established a league recently. And Iran has done so as well.[46] Even Iraq is in the mix, though it may be that all things American are ultimately hated in that country because of the unwise and unlawful invasion of it by the United States.[47] Regrettably, this would be but simply one of a number of byproducts of the 2003 attack which could imperil baseball internationally.

Recruitment of Foreign Players and the Labor Law

Some of the labor and antitrust law derived from the free agency litigation beginning with *Federal Baseball* and proceeding to *Gardella, Toolson,* and *Curt Flood,* as well as the Curt Flood Act of 1998, arguably applies to the recruitment of foreign players to come to the United States. Specifically, the starting point is both antitrust and its labor law exemptions.

Although most of the current MLB conflicts are over the movement of foreign players into the United States, earlier disputes arose when American baseball and basketball players competed abroad. In baseball, for example, the first disputes occurred when prominent American players accepted offers to play in the newly formed Mexican League after World War II.[48] The issues related to contractual obligations and sometimes antitrust law — as did some of the earlier cases discussed in Chapter 3 involving players who were "jumping" from one team or league to another.

Basketball faced a dispute similar to the Mexican League–type issue when Brian Shaw signed a contract with the Boston Celtics in which he promised to cancel his commitment to play for an Italian basketball club the following year. An arbitrator agreed with the Celtics that Shaw's promise was enforceable.[49] The Celtics also had a problem with Yugoslav player Dino Radja, but unlike in the case of Shaw, could not persuade a federal district court that Radja was free of his European obligations.[50] The refusal of USA Basketball to issue unconditional letters of clearance to American players seeking to play in Europe during the 1998–1999 NBA lockout as European teams, required under Federation Internationale de Basketball (FIBA) regulations, raised similar problems.[51]

The effect of *Shaw* and *Radja,* and the European cases arising out of the lockout litigation and the dynamics driving baseball towards the recruitment of foreign players, caused some clubs to institutionalize relationships with teams in foreign countries through "working agreements." The first of these to receive attention in the United States involved a relationship between the San Diego Padres and the Chiba Lotte Mariners in Japan. Murray Chass described the arrangement:

> The San Diego Padres have a new working agreement with a Japanese team that they believe is a significant step in the globalization of baseball. Others, George Steinbrenner [owner of the New York Yankees] for one, are not so sure about the part of the deal that gives the Padres exclusive negotiating rights to one of Japan's best pitchers.[52]

The MLBPA threatened legal and arbitral action if the Padres did not trade Hideki Irabu's negotiating rights to the team of his choice. The MLB Players Relation Committee questioned the authority of the MLBPA to file a grievance on Irabu's behalf. The Committee maintained that the MLBPA could not properly represent a Japanese player who was not already part of the bargaining unit composed of major league players.[53] But several earlier rulings by the courts and arbitrators arguably supported the ideas that the MLBPA could act on behalf of applicant players as well as incumbent players. The significance of these cases is that foreign players who seek access to American professional baseball are applicants — newcomers, arguably in the position of draftees who have triggered litigation in the antitrust and labor law arenas in the United States.

The issue had previously arisen in an American antitrust case, *Wood v. National Basketball Association*.[54] Before the Second Circuit Court of Appeals, Leon Wood, "an accomplished point guard"[55] from California State University at Fullerton, sued under the Sherman Act, arguing that the salary cap and college draft negotiated between the NBA and the NBA Players Association violated federal antitrust law. Noting that the teams were properly regarded as individual employers, whereas the league was not, Judge Winter stated that the draft and salary cap were not "the product solely of an agreement among horizontal competitors but [rather was] embodied in a collective agreement between an employer or employers and a labor organization reached through procedures mandated by federal labor legislation."[56] Accordingly, the court reasoned that federal labor policy precluded a player from obtaining his true market value simply because he was dissatisfied with his salary. Analogizing to collective negotiations between labor and management in construction, maritime, and other industries,[57] the court stated:

> The choice of employer is governed by the rules of the hiring hall, not the preference of the individual worker. There is nothing that prevents such agreements from providing that the employee either work for the designated employer at the stipulated wage or not be referred at that time. Otherwise, a union might find it difficult to provide the requisite number of workers to employers. Such an agreement is functionally indistinguishable from the college draft.[58]

The court noted that "newcomers" like Wood, who sought to bargain as a rookie free of both cap and draft status which limited him to one team, are frequently disadvantaged in collective bargaining relationships primarily because they lack seniority. The Winter opinion rejected the argument that individuals who were not current members of the bargaining unit could not be regulated by collective bargaining agreements and noted that the NLRA "explicitly defines 'employee' in a way that includes workers outside the bargaining unit."[59] Accordingly, the court brought "potential employees" and current employees within the purview of the labor exemption immunity to antitrust liability established by *Wood*.

The Supreme Court had previously accorded protection to applicants under the NLRA, notwithstanding the fact that the statute covers only employees explicitly.[60] On the other hand, the NLRB itself in *Star Tribune*[61] held that, with respect to the employer's bargaining obligations, the employer was under no obligation to bargain with the union over the administration of drug tests to applicants.[62] However, even though applicants were not employees, the NLRB left the door ajar as to whether, under different circumstances, their conditions of employment might be bargainable as an incident of the terms and conditions of the extant bargaining unit of incumbent employees already on the job. Although in *Star Tribune* the drug testing of applicants was too far removed from the interests of incumbent employees for whom drug testing is a mandatory subject of bargaining,[63] the NLRB nonetheless conceded that certain conditions imposed exclusively upon applicants might be deemed mandatory subjects of bargaining if existing employees were "vitally affected" by the applicant conditions.

But the NLRB, during my chairmanship in the '90s, held that an employer is obliged to provide the union with information about applicants so that it may discharge its duty as collective bargaining representative under some circumstances. Said the Board:

> Concerns by a union about possible discrimination in the workplace, including in the hiring process, are relevant to the union's representative function. In fact, as evidenced by the parties' inclusion of a nondiscrimination clause in the collective bargaining agreement, the parties considered possible discriminatory hiring practices as an appropriate subject for bargaining.[64]

In sports, the parties are frequently concerned with the status of newcomers or applicants who are in the college ranks or below. This is certainly the case in football, basketball and hockey. In baseball the Major League Baseball Players Association and MLB do not bargain the draft system itself, and the union does not represent anyone outside of the major leagues themselves — but nonetheless have tied the draft system, in substantial part, to free agents' compensation. This has meant that virtually all rules relating to draftees must be bargained with the union before MLB can change them.

Below, I discuss some of the cases involving the implications of this. But the point is that, just as the Board concluded with regard to no-discrimination clauses in the '90s, there are circumstances in which the parties customarily address the issue one way or another through the collective bargaining process. In these cases it would appear to be appropriate to characterize the subject of applicant conditions as a "mandatory" subject of bargaining within the meaning of the Act — that is, that the parties must bargain about the subject until they are deadlocked or at impasse.

The consequences are threefold: (1) to limit the ability of players to sue leagues on antitrust theories where the subject matter involves applicant conditions because the subject is part of the nonstatutory labor exemption to the antitrust law — this is what the *Wood* case is about; (2) to oblige employers to bargain to the point of impasse with unions about such mandatory conditions of employment involving applicants, i.e., draftees like Wood, even in baseball, where the draft system is not negotiated with the union; and (3) to permit unions to rely upon the evolving case law in grievance arbitration cases discussed below.

Thus, the question of whether applicant conditions are bargainable turns on a case's respective facts and the baseball industry's customs and practices. Reiterating *Wood* eight years later in the 1994-1995 baseball strike in *Silverman v. MLB Player Relations Committee*,[65] the Second Circuit, while holding that conditions of employment such as free agency and reserve clauses are mandatory subjects of bargaining, suggested that the sports draft in baseball might also be considered a mandatory subject of bargaining inasmuch as the conditions of employment imposed on new hires are intimately related to the entire league's salary structure. Writing for the court, Judge Winter reasoned:

> A mix of free agency and reserve clauses combined with other provisions is the universal method by which leagues and player unions set individual salaries in professional sports. Free agency for veteran players may thus be combined with a reserve system, as in baseball, or a rookie draft, as in basketball ... for newer players.... To hold that any of these items, or others make up the mix in a particular sport, is merely a permissive subject of bargaining would ignore the reality of collective bargaining in sports.[66]

True, the court referred to the draft in the context of basketball, whereby players proceed directly to the National Basketball Association from high school or college ranks — in contrast to MLB, where players are almost invariably assigned to the minor leagues which are beyond the jurisdiction of the MLBPA or any union because of the inability or failure to organize players at that level. Nonetheless, the court characterized the word "employee" in the NLRA broadly so as to include individuals outside the bargaining unit. And, most important, the court's language was not limited to basketball or situations where the party's entry into the unit was not necessarily immediate.

Moreover, baseball itself made the draft part of the collective bargaining procedure by establishing draft choices as compensation for free agent losses. Thus, all leagues and unions, in determining player salaries, must necessarily strike a delicate balance between free competition for players and the need for stability and parity of talent. The draft is a necessary component of this give-and-take inherent in the sports bargaining process. Both *Wood* and *Silverman* suggest that the entry of new players from abroad, as well as any future international draft, is subject matter that would affect major league players to which the Curt Flood Act of 1998 would make antitrust law otherwise applicable, notwithstanding the apparent preservation of the principles contained in *Toolson* which preclude antitrust litigation by minor league players.

The most recent judicial pronouncement related to this matter is contained in *Clarett v. National Football League*.[67] This decision suggests that the labor exemption will apply to any challenge maintained by a future Hideki Irabu under the standards of the Court of Appeals for the Second Circuit, and at least as seen by that court, the criteria established under the Supreme Court's ruling in *Brown v. Pro Football*. It is to be recalled that the Curt Flood Act of 1998 changes the law for baseball and provides for the commencement of antitrust litigation under the standards adumbrated in *Brown*. If the Second Circuit is correct in applying the broad sweep of the labor exemption cases involving player access, the claims of foreign players would appear to be stymied under antitrust law. The key question, of course, is whether the Court of Appeals, in interpreting *Brown*, which merely focused upon *when* in the collective bargaining process antitrust law supersedes labor law, was correct in applying this approach to eligibility or player access cases.

In the *Clarett* case, Maurice Clarett, an Ohio State running back, challenged the NFL eligibility rules requiring him to wait at least three full football seasons after his high school graduation before entering the draft. Clarett, who since has encountered difficulties with criminal law, led his team, Ohio State, to an undefeated season and the Fiesta Bowl so as to claim the national championship. Suspended from college competition by Ohio State, and thus forced to sit out his sophomore season, Clarett sought to enter the NFL draft and, when precluded from doing so, challenged the draft eligibility rules. A principal focus of this litigation, as was the case with *Wood*, was the collective bargaining agreement negotiated in this instance between the NFL Players Association and the NFL — and the agreement contained a provision through which the union and the Management Council of the NFL waived their right to bargain any matter not included in the agreement, including the provisions of the NFL constitution and bylaws. The eligibility rules were contained in the constitution and bylaws and were at the heart of this dispute.

The district court had ruled against the NFL on the ground that the eligibility rules which prohibited Clarett from entering the NFL were "blatantly anti-competitive." The court also held that the eligibility rules were a non-mandatory subject of bargaining and that they had not been discussed or negotiated in the sense that the union had received a *quid pro quo* for any waiver obtained and thus the labor exemption was not available. The Court of Appeals, speaking through Judge Sotomayor, the author of the 1995 *Silverman* baseball decision through which the NLRB was able to revive the season, reversed the district court.

The Second Circuit noted that in *Wood* and its progeny,[68] attacks upon a unionized labor market in a collective bargaining relationship with a multi-employer bargaining unit had always been rejected. In *Clarett* the court reiterated its view that the player's antitrust claims were inconsistent with federal labor law because they "imperiled legitimacy of multi-employer bargaining" and that "in the context of sports leagues, uniformity of rules was important for the proper functioning of the sport." Finally, the court noted that its approach was rooted in its view that labor law properly trumped antitrust law because of the expertise of the National Labor Relations Board.

Accordingly, the court held that the labor exemption both before and subsequent to *Brown* has a broad sweep and that, contrary to the district court, the eligibility rules constituted a mandatory subject of bargaining because, like the hiring hall in the construction and maritime industries, they affected employment conditions in the bargaining unit. In the more tenuous part of its reasoning, the court held that the subject matter had been addressed through the collective bargaining process, notwithstanding the fact that they were merely contained in the constitution and bylaws because, these rules were "well known to the union and a copy of the Constitution and Bylaws was presented to the union during negotiations." The union, the court found, had waived its right to challenge eligibility during the term of the collective bargaining agreement and this therefore was part of the bundle of compromises which are part of the collective bargaining process.

Thus, the reasoning of *Clarett*, if applied to baseball, suggests that notwithstanding the Curt Flood Act of 1998, making antitrust law applicable to baseball's major league players, arrangements affecting newcomers including foreign players would be part of the collective bargaining process even though not directly addressed through it or in the agreement. For instance, Major League Baseball and the union have addressed the newcomer issue by establishing a study committee to determine whether an international draft system would apply to applicants abroad. Nothing has come of this to date because of Major League Baseball's current view that economically it still makes sense to use their baseball academies in Latin America, the principal source of foreign players to date, a matter which would minimize salaries and costs in comparison to a draft system. It is possible that a court like the Second Circuit would seize upon such collective bargaining agreement language to use the labor exemption to defeat an antitrust claim by foreign players regardless of whether they are viewed as applicants whose conditions of employment are bound up with those of incumbent players.

The Baseball Draft Arbitration Cases

Even more relevant to this matter were a series of rulings that arose from conflicts relating to the status of baseball free agents, which is part of the collective bargaining agreement, and the amateur draft, which is not part of the agreement. In the first of these cases, the MLBPA filed a grievance alleging that the unilateral adoption by the clubs of amendments to MLB amateur draft rules violated the collective bargaining agreement provisions that protected free agency and prohibited the unilateral change of subject matter if such a change would alter a player's "benefit" under the agreement.[69] Noting that bargaining historically sometimes involved amateur matters and sometimes did not, the arbitrator was of the view that the parties had routinely negotiated the promotion of players to the majors and the demotion of players to the minors. Moreover, the arbitrator concluded that the right to challenge changes in the amateur draft had not been waived by the MLBPA in collective bargaining. Further, the arbitrator believed that the changes in the case before him were significant because they assigned a college-bound player to a club for five years and eliminated the pressure to sign a player upon pain of losing him during the following year. As a practical matter, the opportunity to improve his position in succeeding drafts was foreclosed.

The question before the arbitrator was whether the attempt by the club to promote the signability of such players and to de-escalate costs was consistent with the agreement. Since draft choices are provided as compensation for the signing of free agents, the arbitrator noted that such free agents would carry a "greater burden" in negotiations by virtue of the change. The arbitrator said:

> [T]his is not a case that only affects non-employees not yet in the bargaining unit. It also affects bargaining unit employees because free agency and draft choices are, as of now, inseparable.... [T]he connection is obvious; draft choices and free agency co-exist in the same contractual provision.[70]

Accordingly, a unilateral change in the draft rules was inconsistent with the benefits provided by virtue of free agency. In a second case,[71] the rule that a drafted player was no longer eligible to be signed by the drafting club after he had attended his first class at a university was unilaterally changed to provide an immutable cutoff date of August 15 regardless of whether the player attended class. While the arbitrator did not view this change as profound and fundamental as those addressed in the 1992 decision in which the clubs had attempted to extend the duration of draft control over players throughout and beyond their college careers, the arbitrator noted that the postponement of serious negotiations reflected a measure of bargaining power which would be eroded by the rule change. Here also, in the arbitrator's view, the economic bargain was being altered. And the change was thus prohibited under the same provisions of the collective bargaining agreement. (Subsequently, as noted above, in 2006 the players acceded to the position of the owners and negotiated an August 15 cutoff date prior to attending class, the theory being that clubs would have more leverage if the cutoff time was clear-cut — notwithstanding the fact that there is not a substantial difference between August 15 and the commencement of classes at some universities.)

Finally, in the well-known *J.D. Drew* case,[72] involving the prominent St. Louis Cardinal outfielder who now patrols right field for the Boston Red Sox, prior to the negotiation of his first major league professional contract, the arbitrator considered the draft rules as they related to players who signed with new independent leagues unaffiliated with MLB. The question was whether such a player under contract to one of the new unaffiliated leagues, such as the Northern League and the Western League which emerged in the 1990s, would be subject to a new draft or could be a free agent. Again, the unilateral change in the rules by organized baseball to bring unaffiliated clubs within the requirement that an unsigned player be in a succeeding draft was deemed as inconsistent with the agreement. Said the Arbitrator:

> In the fierce competition which typifies high-stakes negotiations surrounding premium players, whether in the draft or in free agency, a disruption of the [contractual] linkage of draft and free agency which the parties last reconfirmed in their Basic Agreement effective January 1, 1997....[73]

Thus, all of the arbitral decisions provided protections against unilateral changes in the collective bargaining agreement for applicants who were potential MLB employees, but who were outside the MLBPA bargaining unit. It is these very same concerns about potential arbitral holdings relating to the foreign players that — along with potential antitrust liability — induced MLB to support the proposition that a trade could and should send Hideki Irabu to the team of his choosing, the New York Yankees.

The New Protocols Between National Baseball Systems

In the wake of the *Irabu* matter, baseball has negotiated agreements with commissioner's offices of baseball in Japan and Korea. These agreements do not include the MLBPA or the Japanese players' union as a party to them, and thus make the applicability of the nonstatutory labor exemption arguably problematic in the United States, but they appear to have the tacit approval of the union because they eliminate the authority of clubs to make working agreements with baseball teams abroad which provide exclusive or preferential rights to foreign players. Moreover, the union is of the view that Japanese arrangements cannot stand if Japanese free agency — it now consists of a nine-year period — is changed so as to make Japanese player mobility more arduous. Rather than the free-agency framework through which the Cuban and some other Latin American players have bargained with individual teams and the baseball academies sponsored by individual clubs, the arrangements with Japan and Korea have provided for the direct involvement of the national commissioners' offices in the United States, Japan and Korea. These arrangements place substantial limitations upon a Japanese player's negotiating leverage in the case of the Japanese protocol.

The United States–Japanese player contract agreement applies to the recruitment of MLB and Japanese players by MLB and Japanese baseball. (For a number of years Japanese clubs have contracted with two foreigners to play on each individual club in their country.) The agreement states that if any Japanese baseball club wishes to contact and engage a baseball player, "professional or amateur, who is playing or has played baseball in the United States or Canada and/or is under contract with a club that is a member of the National or American League," the Japanese team shall request the Japanese Commissioner of Baseball to determine the status and availability of the MLB player by communicating with the MLB Commissioner's Office. If an MLB player is sought by a Japanese club, they are not to contact or negotiate with the player unless approval is given through the MLB Commissioner. The Japanese club cannot contact the MLB player unless approval to do so is given by the MLB club through the MLB Commissioner. Approval is needed only when the MLB player is on the list of "Reserved, Military, Voluntarily Retired, Restricted, Disqualified, Suspended, or Ineligible." If approval is not needed, then the Japanese club may immediately contact and negotiate with the MLB player. If approval is required, the MLB Commissioner is to transmit to the Japanese commissioner the approval or disapproval of the club.

If an MLB club wishes to engage a Japanese player who has "played baseball in Japan and/or is under contract with a Japanese club," the club must request that the MLB Commissioner determine the status and availability of the Japanese player in the same manner that the status and availability of the MLB player is determined. If no approval is needed, the club immediately contacts the Japanese player. If approval is needed, that contact can be initiated only when the club has provided approval. Similar provisions are provided in the Korean agreement, which was entered into in 1996.

All of these procedures were brought into play by the Irabu matter and the fear on the part of American baseball that litigation would ensue in the absence of new mechanisms. The attempt is to address those Japanese players who have reached an advanced stage in moving toward free agency and thus provide early exit for them with compensation for the Japanese team.

With regard to those players for whom approval is required, the MLB Commissioner posts the Japanese player's availability by notifying "all U.S. Major League Clubs of the Japanese clubs to make the player available." Requests for Japanese club postings are made from November 1 to March 1. Within four business days of the posting all interested MLB clubs are required to submit a bid to the MLB Commissioner "composed of monetary consideration only, to be paid to the Japanese Club as consideration for the Japanese Club relinquishing its rights to the player in the event that the U.S. Club reaches an agreement with the Japanese player." The MLB Commissioner determines the "highest bidder" and that determination is "conclusive and binding on all parties." The Japanese commissioner must then determine whether the bid is acceptable to the Japanese club. If it is not acceptable, then no contact may be had with the player until the next window period. If the highest bid is acceptable, the MLB Commissioner is to award the "sole, exclusive and non-assignable right to negotiate with and sign the Japanese player." If the MLB team cannot come to terms with the player within thirty days from the date that the MLB Commissioner indicates that the bid is acceptable to the Japanese club, the obligation to compensate lapses, as do the negotiation rights of the club, and no contact may be had with the player until the following window period.

No bidding procedures were provided in the Korean agreement, and in both the Japanese and Korean agreements, working agreements of the kind that the San Diego Padres had with Irabu's Japanese club are now prohibited insofar as they give in to the MLB club the "exclusive or preferential rights to contract with players." Similar rules have been established for MLB dealing with baseball clubs located in Italy.[74]

Why did Commissioner Selig enter into these agreements? In the first place, the idea was to avoid future litigation of the kind described above. In the second place, as more Japanese players are recruited, there will always be eighteen MLB clubs which are displeased by virtue of any exclusive or preferential working agreements. This is because there are thirty MLB teams and only twelve Japanese teams. Thus, access for all MLB clubs to Japanese players became an important principle.

Third, the approval mechanisms were included so that Japanese sensibilities about MLB baseball imperialism would not be ignored. The Japanese do not want to see their own professional league become a farm system for MLB and to see their best teams raided for top talent.[75] As noted above, this problem has become more considerable as attendance and TV ratings in Japan have dropped. The problem of American baseball imperialism remains an important one.

And the same holds true for other nations that may fear talent depletion because of an MLB international draft. Thus, the Japanese and other countries also have an interest in restraining and regulating future Irabu disputes.

But there are problems with the Japanese agreement in the United States and perhaps Japan as well. The nonassignability of the rights obtained by the highest bidder is presumably designed to avoid another Irabu situation in which the Yankees were waiting in the wings to receive Irabu's assigned negotiating rights. But teams like the Yankees and Red Sox and other high rollers (it was the Red Sox, after all, which provided the record-breaking $51 million purchase price for Seibu's Daisuke Matsuzaka) will still benefit from the new mechanism because they are most likely to be the highest bidder. This is particularly true given the fact that only monetary compensation may be provided. But transaction arrangements other than those providing for monetary compensation exclusively should be part of the system. It is unclear why a trade between the two countries cannot be arranged unless the Commissioners thought that an agreement could not be negotiated with the player. Yet promotion of trades across national boundaries will lend more credibility to foreign leagues such as those in Japan and promote and enhance foreign baseball, which will lead to a genuine World Series between clubs as well as national teams at some point in the future.

Though under the current arrangement insider preferences are discouraged or prohibited by virtue of the new limitations upon team-to-team working agreements, the fact of the matter is the clubs are more likely to get their players through Japanese teams with whom they have working agreements. The acquisition of 2000 Rookie of the Year relief pitcher Kazuhiro Sasaki by the Seattle Mariners (owned by the Japanese chairman of Nintendo), which has a working arrangement with the Orix Blue Wave of Kobe, is a good illustration.

After the highest bidder wins, the negotiating rights lapse if no agreement is reached with the player within thirty days. Some teams may want to keep the player off the market and to provide the highest bid, knowing that their bargaining stance makes a contract with the player impossible since no dispute resolution mechanism such as arbitration is contained in the agreement. It is unclear how this and other potential abuses by teams can be adjudicated.

Finally, most players who have come from Japan thus far have not come under the bidding mechanism.[76] Most of them have been veteran free agents like Seattle's Ichiro (as noted, the Japanese have a more lengthy 9-year requirement for free agency under their rules) or amateurs. The latter group creates some of the same problems that have afflicted the relationship of MLB with Latin America, such as the signing of underage and relatively immature players. For instance, the San Diego Padres recently signed an eighteen-year-old pitcher from Japan prior to his graduation from high school. While this is not comparable to some of the abuses found in Latin America,[77] it does give cause for concern.[78]

Now, a number of signs point toward disruption of the *status quo*. The signing of Junichi Tazawa[79] by the Boston Red Sox out of one Japan's so-called industrial amateur leagues, whose top players go into the Japanese professional draft, has produced protests on that side of the Pacific. Even more alarming from the Japanese perspective was the flirtation of the outstanding teenage left-hander Yusei Kikuchi with MLB clubs before finally consenting to go to the Japanese draft. The Japanese have responded to the Tazawa incident negatively by stating that this violates a gentleman's agreement and through the institution of a three-year ban against any Japanese player who signs with an American team when he is eligible for and skips the Japanese draft.[80] This is reminiscent of the action taken by the United States against players who defected to the Mexican League immediately after World War II.

Meanwhile, consideration has been given to the possibility of attacking the posting system under the Japanese anti-monopoly law. Though Japanese baseball has shortened the free-agency period from nine to seven years for those who came in during the off-season of 2008-09 (the first change since the present system was shortened from ten to nine in 1997), lack of leverage for Japanese players when they seek to play in the United States, coupled with the bar of those who skipped the draft, will surely invite the pursuit of legal avenues even in non-litigious Japan. It may be that antitrust theories will be propounded in American courts by Japanese players frustrated by the combination of the posting system and the three-year ban.

The next step in the process on this side of the Pacific may be the negotiation of provisions in the MLB collective bargaining agreement which will make it possible for a new MLB–Japan agreement to provide for trades as well as compensation. But beyond such modest reforms, the question of an international draft in the United States—and indeed in Japan as well—may be the next step. Japan has also considered its own international draft and the recruitment of players from outside of its country—a process which could put it on a collision course with the United States.

The existing system will involve baseball deeply in countries abroad, some of which have been late to accept and develop baseball. Moreover, from a competitive-balance perspective, it appears that some of the so-called small-market teams like the Oakland A's, Cincinnati Reds, Colorado Rockies, Arizona D-Backs, San Francisco Giants and San Diego Padres have thrived disproportionate to the Mets, Cubs and Red Sox (though the Sox are now deeply involved in Japan). In any event, MLB continues to believe that its Latin American academies, where large numbers of players are signed at reduced costs, are cheaper than a draft system under which players in this country, such as Stanford University power-hitting outfielder Joe Borchard, obtained more than $5 million from the Chicago White Sox![81]

Yet there are a number of imponderables. First, as Professor Fidler has noted, the scandals and kickbacks involved with vulnerable Latin players seem to continue. Second, it is unclear that a new Dominican and Venezuelan market could emerge in the foreseeable future, notwithstanding the emerging markets, if baseball instituted an international draft—though it can be argued that the "current system will allow baseball to grow organically in countries like China, India and Brazil."[82] Third, there is the problem of Cuba, where escaping players will establish themselves as free agents available to the highest big-market bidder. But their full-fledged involvement with the draft or academies will have to await the departure of Fidel Castro, and perhaps the Castro brothers and those who immediately surround them.

Any effort to establish an international amateur draft system will trigger antitrust litigation pursuant to the Curt Flood Act—and the question affecting Latin American as well as Far Eastern recruits will be whether they can be viewed as rookie applicants who are covered by the antitrust rulings noted above, beginning with *Wood*.[83] But if the negotiated system is addressed by the collective bargaining agreement and thus arguably part of the nonstatutory labor exemption, both *Brown* and *Clarett* may immunize conduct that would otherwise create antitrust liability.

There is another practical issue. With regard to the agreements that MLB has entered into with Japan and Korea, it is possible that *Brown* could provide a shield against antitrust action given the fact that the subject matter involves the bargaining process itself, and the MLBPA was presumably advised, notified, and given an opportunity to participate.[84] The fact that the players' union believes that the arrangement will dissipate if the Japanese free-agency system is altered suggests that there is some measure of union involvement or at least awareness and consequent non-statutory labor exemption.[85] On the other hand, the fact that this approach was formulated without any bargaining with the union could take it beyond the labor exemption.

The thousand-pound gorilla lurking in the room is the extraterritoriality of American labor and antitrust law. Does the case law established in either the labor or antitrust arena apply to conduct engaged in, in substantial part, in other countries such as Japan, Korea, Mexico, Venezuela and the Dominican Republic? These are important issues never considered by the Supreme Court in *Brown* or in the lower court cases involving either *Wood* or *Clarett*.

The Future of International Baseball and Law

Beyond the problems relating to player mobility, there are two major issues relating to international matters in baseball and sports generally which raise extraterritoriality directly. The first relates to professional leagues which are transnational, at this point covering North America and involving the United States and Canada. It is hardly fanciful to imagine that Mexico could soon be part of the equation in baseball and that an international league could, albeit with more defined geographical divisions, extend to other portions of the world like the Far East. Where, for instance, do the Oakland A's go if they cannot locate in Oakland, Fremont, or San Jose? Mexico? Some other city in Latin America?

True, baseball's scheduled games in Japan, Mexico, and the talk of one in Europe are fundamentally sales and marketing initiatives. But if the development of players and leagues continue along the lines described above, it is possible that the leagues can become truly international and that ultimately baseball will produce a real World Series. Of course, there are constraints upon games between Tokyo and New York, for instance, because of the state of transportation and the difficulties in travel, including the jet lag involved. Some players such as Mark McGwire have grumbled about playing abroad, in part, for that reason, and many players on the Red Sox objected to the idea of a baseball opener in Japan in 2008, notwithstanding the fact that the Red Sox have had three (2 in 2008) well-known Japanese pitchers on their roster! Indeed the Red Sox engaged in a short strike in violation of the no-strike clause in the collective bargaining agreement because of a dispute about compensation for their opener in Japan in 2008 — a dispute which seemed to be fueled in substantial part by the reluctance of players to make the long trip as part of the regular season. If foreign leagues are strengthened it is possible that relationships may emerge which result in some kind of cooperation and perhaps postseason competition which is not so filled with jet lag as would be the case with regular season play. And, notwithstanding the failure of the *Concorde*, might there not yet be future breakthroughs in transportation short of a space capsule?

The main problem for major leagues involved in international arrangements is the question of the scope of the law that is to apply to the league in question. This issue first arose in the United States in the 1970s in North American soccer. There the National Labor Relations Board declined to assert jurisdiction over two Canadian soccer teams found to be joint employers with the league.[86] The Court of Appeals for the Second Circuit enforced the Board's order on the joint employer issue, i.e., that the league and clubs were together joint employers of the players — but did not address the question of jurisdiction over the Canadian teams. The Board, itself, had relied upon a number of factors in declining to assert jurisdiction: (1) the teams were owned and operated solely by Canadian residents; (2) their business dealings, such as the location of offices and payment of license fees and taxes, were conducted exclusively in Canada; and (3) the teams were associated with a Canadian soccer association rather than its American counterpart, the United States Soccer Federation.

But the Board ignored the soccer precedent in asserting jurisdiction over Canadian teams during the 1981 and 1994-5 baseball strikes.[87] No one in United States or Canada challenged the Board's jurisdiction.

In a basketball decertification election the Board asserted jurisdiction over Canadian teams and thus applied American labor law to them, refusing to follow the soccer precedent. The regional director held that in soccer what was involved was an initial organizational effort in which bargaining practices and procedures had not been established, whereas in basketball there was a "substantial bargaining history in the multi-employer unit, to which the new franchises had been charted." Said the regional director:

> To the extent that the Board has discretion in this area, this history of league-wide negotia-tions is one of the considerations militating in favor of asserting of jurisdiction over the Canadian teams. Additionally, I recognize that should the Board decline jurisdiction over the Raptors and the Grizzlies, the inherent possibilities for a splintering of results and representa-tion between the American and Canadian teams would not tend to promote stability and industrial relations, clearly a significant consideration.[88]

The regional director also noted that the close affiliation of the Canadian teams with Canadian interests was not present in basketball. It stated that in basketball the teams were fully integrated in the existing unit, in contrast to soccer, in which an organizational effort was undertaken. In essence, the Board's conclusion was that soccer was in an embryonic state at the time of the '70s litigation, in contrast to basketball. In basketball it was noted that there was a functional integration between the teams, particularly on matters such as employee relations, league and rules and regulations relating to terms and conditions of employment for all players on all the teams within the League. Moreover, both sides had taken the position that the American NLRB should assert jurisdiction.

Meanwhile, while the sports cases in the United States seemed to be asserting American labor law extraterritorially over transnational leagues, there are a number of complications on the horizon. The first is that the Ontario Labor Relations Board, in a dispute involving umpires in baseball[89] and referees in basketball,[90] has asserted jurisdiction in labor disputes where some of the umpires and referees were working in Canadian cities. This is in conflict with the American decisions and in some respects it reaches further than those cases because the referees and umpires are employed directly by central offices in New York City, as opposed to the teams, which employ players on both sides of the border. The only contact with Canada is a limited number of games in which the umpires and referees travel there for the purpose of handling those contests.

In a case involving the National Hockey League Players Association and the NHL aris-ing out of the 2004-05 lockout, the British Columbia Labor Relations Board declined to assert jurisdiction over a petition for certification by the players of the Vancouver Canucks[91]—a decision in direct contrast to the position of the Ontario Board. The NHLPA initiated the petition because it wanted to avail itself of the more pro-union Cana-dian provincial labor law, which would have made it impossible for the NHL to lock out the players and then replace them — something which is allowed under American labor law.

When would Canadian law apply and when would American? Would Canadian law apply to both teams when they were playing in Canada? Would the rules change once they moved south of the border to the United States? And, as we have already seen, a major issue in American sports involves drugs and drug testing, the American and Canadian systems having different positions on this. The matter is now substantially complicated by *Williams v. NFL*,[92] which has held that American state law as well as federal law can apply to drug programs and drug testing. Which law would apply? The fragmentation and confusion which would arise undoubtedly induced the British Columbia Board to refuse to assert jurisdiction. In reaching this conclusion, the Board also protected a well-established forty-year-old multi-employer bargaining relationship.

Ultimately, these questions in professional baseball and other sports would be most effectively addressed by some kind of agreed-upon international standard or statute governing this kind of collective bargaining. In the interim it may be that some steps towards this objective will be taken as the result of a genuine world tournament or world cup, in this case the World Baseball Classic.

The 2006 and 2009, World Baseball Classics were on balance great successes and legitimate precursors to a true World Series. The exquisite play of Japan, Korea and Cuba and their attention to fundamentals was refreshing. The up-and-coming teams like South Africa and China will surely be part of the future scene.

Bracketing should be more balanced — i.e., the United States should have been placed with some of the tough Latin American teams in '06 — and '09 was better. The first time around America was given an extraordinary advantage which it could not use well by being placed with Canada, Mexico and South Africa.

Umpires must be selected from all of the countries. A greater balance to the executive committee — important countries like Japan have some representation but Korea has none — should be provided. An erroneous and unusual call by an American umpire in the 2006 U.S.–Japan game could have caused an international incident if Manager Oh had not exercised such restraint.[93]

Players from all teams should be encouraged to play. The best American players from the Yankees, for instance, were discouraged from playing in 2006 by their owner George Steinbrenner. The need exists to provide a unified stand and encourage all players on all teams to be participants, and the Yankees, in allowing Derek Jeter to play in 2009, partially relented.

Finally there is the question of when the games should be held. March was awkward because spring training was just beginning in the United States. "Dice-K" Matsuzaka had his worst of four seasons with the Red Sox because he had shoulder problems attributable to his substantial involvement in the '09 WBC, and particularly the training undertaken prior to the contest itself. "The elephant in the room continues to be the high risk to players who are worth millions to their respective major league teams."[94] Superstars like Ryan Howard, Tim Lincecum and Roy Halladay did not play.

Many of the other teams are in the middle of their schedules which, contrary to the Americans and their position towards the Olympics, they are pleased to interrupt for the purpose of international competition. Though November might make more sense, apparently there is more resistance to this by players who would rather take a vacation from spring training, and who in any event do not want to prolong the long season. Moreover, in order to allow the teams who are participating in the playoffs to have their players involved, the players of the other clubs would have to sit around for two or three weeks before this could begin. But March increases the risk of injury, particularly if the players have not been training in January and February. There is something of a conundrum here but the status quo does not seem to be acceptable. The best of all alternatives would be to disrupt the season for about 10 to 14 days in its midst, as hockey does — but this seems to be unrealistic given the rhythm and the dynamics involved in a regular season pennant chase and the amount of money associated with it.

The WBC was a great effort in both '06 and '09 and needs to be promoted and continued in 2013. It attracted American scout attention to the play of the Asians.[95] The attendance increased by about 55,000 to 801,408. "The semifinals and championship averaged 1.4 percent of U.S. cables/satellite TV households. The average rating for the event's final three games in 2006 was 1.3 percent."[96] The dramatic extra-inning game between Japan and Korea made the WBC even more of a memorable and lasting event in '09 than it had been in '06.[97] The competition needs to be tweaked in some respects, not the least of which is encouraging the United States to make its best players available and to deal with the timing and injury problems. But make no mistake, this is one of the first necessary steps towards effective international competition in baseball — an International World Series.

Conclusion

The changes in the game of baseball since the end of World War II when I first became involved as a nine-year-old on the Station Field in Long Branch, New Jersey, are considerable. Though, with the exception of the designated hitter rule adopted in 1973, the rules on the field itself have essentially remained the same since organized baseball came into existence at the turn of the previous century, the development of the home run by Babe Ruth, the advent of radio broadcasting which was in its infancy in 1921, and night baseball were the big changes in those four decades which preceded our games in the 1940s. Racial integration and free agency — the greatest changes of all in baseball and sports — were yet to come.

Now, nearly seven decades later, as one can see particularly from the testimony of the players themselves provided in this book, there are changes aplenty on and off the field. Not the least of them is the rapid advance of technology, which promises to provide expansion for instant replay, directly or indirectly undermining one of baseball's traditions which has made it so different from other sports like football. Regrettably, there appears to be no alternative to more incursions.

The date when I first fell in love with baseball — 1946 — is the halfway mark between baseball's beginnings on a league basis in the 1870s-1880s and this second decade of a new century which is upon us. My personal observations began in the immediate post–World War II era — an era much closer to the forming of organized baseball in 1901 than we are today to 1946. It is a period that spans President Truman to President Obama. In the 19th century a comparable period would be from the presidency of James Polk and our "Manifest Destiny" and William Howard Taft[1] in 1910, the first president to throw out the Opening Day ceremonial first pitch.

Many of the changes have been on the field. In my view, the DH rule offends the spirit of the game, though not so egregiously as Astroturf (fortunately now in decline) and the use of the aluminum bat in amateur baseball do. As noted, Carl Yastrzemski's batting championship of .301 in 1968 directly led to the lowering of the mound from 16 to 11 inches, thus providing an advantage for the hitter. The strike zone soon narrowed from the letters to something around the belt, even though the rules speak of the armpits.

What is often forgotten, however, is that in the year preceding 1968, when the Sox fell considerably off the pace in their chase of the Detroit Tigers, Yastrzemski was the last Triple Crown winner ever. Only the year before, Baltimore Orioles outfielder Frank Robinson had achieved the same feat. Subsequently, for a variety of reasons outlined in this book, batting and home run production increased enormously, though overall hitting skills did not. And even Yastrzemski and Robinson themselves had possessed lifetime batting averages of only

277

.285 and .294 respectively, hardly in the realm of the hitters like Williams, Joe DiMaggio and Stan Musial in my childhood. Barring new developments in the twenty-first century it seems hardly likely that anyone will ever obtain Williams's .406 batting average of 1941 or, for that matter, the Red Sox team average of .302 in 1950, when Billy Goodman came off the bench due to Williams's broken elbow and captured the batting championship of the American League with an average of .354. These achievements, like Joe DiMaggio's record of 56 consecutive games with a base hit, do not seem to be vulnerable to challenge in the foreseeable future.

This is so, notwithstanding the above-referenced designated hitter as well as the detailed study of opposing pitchers through video, which only the elite hitters like Williams engaged in in the '40s and '50s. (Williams, of course, did it without any kind of video!) The detailed matchups between hitters and pitchers and their past performances are studied by managers in a way never imaginable more than twenty years ago. And the same is true of pitchers, like Curt Schilling and so many others, who use video to study the hitters.

Gradually, beginning in the 1980s, baseball has moved to an era of specialization. Specialized bullpens and increased numbers of pitchers are part of the scene. Indeed, the much-discussed Charlie Finley had even tried to introduce a so-called designated runner in the early '70s, Herb Washington. Like some of the track standouts who tried their hand at professional football, he only had a quick glimpse of the major league scene.

Expansion has produced great changes in the game. Baseball has doubled from the 16 teams whose averages and ERAs I knew in detail in the late '40s. A host of new defensive statistics such as WHIP (walks and hits per inning) have become part of baseball's daily parlance.[2] Now the 30 teams and the layers of championship series which are a prerequisite to advancing to the World Series constitute an enormous hurdle superimposed upon the grinding nature of a 162-game schedule. The World Championship is a much greater achievement than it was in the post–World War II era.

True, as Sparky Anderson said, "162 games don't lie," and the divisional championship winners (even though the divisions are unequal in talent) represent baseball's greatest achievement in recapturing fan interest, attendance, and all of the rich commercial agreements that go with this. But in the age of a wild card, which has existed since the mid-'90s, the view that 162 should be paramount is considered to be

Carl "Yaz" Yastrzemski, baseball's last triple crown winner in the "Impossible Dream" of 1967 (courtesy Boston Red Sox).

that possessed by "baseball purists." With expansion and more teams have come more jet travel and arguably less attention to some of the fundamentals that can only be attained through practice, practice, practice; the demise of infield practice, for instance, has been lamented by Lynn Jones. Games played in Japan by both the Red Sox and the A's against the Japanese Tigers and Giants in early '08 highlight the difference between the United States and Japan dramatically. The same held true for the Japanese and Korean teams in the WBC in both '06 and '09.

However, one problem with the expansion of teams is the dilution of pitching talent. This is so notwithstanding the fact that the labor market has expanded now with the age of globalization and with both Latin America and the Far East filling the new vacancies created.

In the 1940s teams played each other 22 times, 11 in each park. Because home field advantage is important in baseball given the great variance in dimensions, the home team builds itself around those idiosyncratic contours so as to provide an advantage for itself. This is why an equal number of games home and away is vital in order to provide balance and fairness. But interleague play, exciting as it is when rivals such as the Oakland A's square off against the San Francisco Giants, distorts the level playing field and creates situations where there is no home and away match in many circumstances and the same teams do not play the same teams. True, some teams like the San Francisco Giants positively salivate at the idea of playing the Red Sox and the Yankees because of the gate. But it simply is not fair for teams to play different teams and have those games counted towards the championship. This compromises the game's integrity — a vital consideration never as important in other sports like football; long before the National Football League's expansion, a team's given schedule in any particular year influenced its fortunes remarkably.

Putting aside the documented public health dangers involved with steroids, it is somewhat comparable to the drug scandal which will be the epitaph of not only McGwire, Bonds and Clemens, but Selig himself because of owner connivance. Thus the inequities furthered by arbitrary scheduling and competition are simply another subordination of integrity — though admittedly one which poses no harm to anything other than honest competition.

Another by-product of scheduling is the increasing control of it by the networks. Since Fox, for instance, looms so large in the postseason play, it can dictate to Major League Baseball when the Championship Series and the World Series are to begin, making it likely that their revenue-producing advertisements relating to sexual dysfunction and the like can run at 11:00 or 12:00 at night (though they actually run much earlier in the evening), but also depriving the young of an opportunity to see the game on television on a school night or even the weekend itself.

There was a special romance in the colorful foliage at the time of the fall classic and the brilliant sunshine that the games were played in. That is no more, and the problems associated with late-night games grow with each passing year.

Commissioner Selig's determination that the winner of the exhibition All-Star game get home field advantage in the World Series is a positive abomination. Of a number of silly initiatives, this is the silliest of all in an attempt to prop up a game which the players have always regarded as an exhibition and where those who will benefit or lose in the fall classic cannot influence the outcome! Baseball fans noted the good-natured smiles exchanged between Jose Valverde and Marlon Byrd as they struggled against one another in the 2010 game. One would never see that in a game that counts.

Although Commissioner Selig has played a positive role in promoting annual "civil rights" games which are played in one park every year and honoring Jackie Robinson's date of entry in 1947, as well as promoting the candidacy of Cecil Cooper to manage the Houston Astros, the fact is that there are still too few minority managers and individuals in front-office positions. Centerfielder Coco Crisp was the only black American on the entire Boston Red Sox 2007 World Championship team. Baseball, which made enormous strides in reshaping the nation through Jackie Robinson's breakthrough in 1947, has fallen behind the curve and has a considerable way to go here, notwithstanding a slight upward bounce in 2009.

Labor law proved to be a driving force in the changes that took place on the field. It was labor law and, through union leader Marvin Miller, its enhancement of the labor arbitration system which proved to be a key element in player gains. Again, it was the labor arbitration system that produced the major gains by the players, most notably the "Catfish" Hunter case, which resulted in the guaranteed contract. This has a great deal to do with so many of the changes on the field, such as the care with which teams watch over pitchers, with pitch counts, innings pitched, etc.

Free agency was the other major achievement in the 1970s and it led to a series of confrontations in a kind of 30 years' war in which the owners unsuccessfully attempted to recapture the player gains of 1975 and 1976. The mother of all labor disputes, in this case a group of millionaires and billionaires in '94-'95 and the precipice that baseball was on in subsequent negotiations, was triggered by the competitive balance issue — even though the major culprit, the New York Yankees, had gone without a world championship from 1981 through 1996. Indeed, competitive balance was changing as the parties engaged in labor disputes supposedly aimed at the competitive balance issue itself!

Of course, from '96 to '07 the Yankees went to the playoffs 12 consecutive times but did not obtain a world championship in the 21st century until 2009. The rich are able to be much more competitive than others and it must be admitted that the Red Sox, who have made it to the World Series twice in the past six years — one still thrills to hear Red Sox announcer Joe Castiglione's proclamation in '04: "Can you believe it!?" — have a payroll which is second best, only $80 million below the Yankees!

But the small-market teams that possess acumen and developed players can make it, as was made evident by the Cleveland Indians in '07 and the '90s, and their fast start out of the gate in '11, as well as teams like the A's, the Twins, and even the Expos before they moved to Washington. All of this occurred both prior and subsequent to the 2002 and '06 collective bargaining agreements, arguing that the reforms contained in them possess little correlation to success on the field.

And then there are the cardinal sins. Gambling ... all of this had been assumed to be a matter of history, in substantial part because of the fine salaries being paid in all the major sports. But someone forgot about the adjudicators, the referees and umpires, who, while represented by unions, have trailed far behind the players who are the product and make the handsome salaries. National Basketball Association Commissioner David Stern, involved in a recent war of studies about whether referees make decisions based upon race, was soon enmeshed in an FBI investigation of referee Tim Donaghy who, during his last two seasons, was coerced by organized crime members into shaving points and supplying inside information to gamblers. Gambling is the cardinal sin in a business which is predicated not only upon excitement but also genuine uncertainty. The Donaghy matter is a wake-up call to all of the commissioners to engage in more extensive background checks and to recognize that the games, which are awash in money, mean money for those outside the institutions themselves.

Baseball has begun its own check with the umpires, though this has already met with umpire union protest. Minor league baseball's attempt to unilaterally institute background check policies without collective bargaining with the union has produced litigation before the NLRB.[3] Baseball has not experienced anything like this since the Pete Rose gambling fiasco in 1989 and, on the players' side, the 1919 "Black Sox" World Series scandal! But as the Gilbert Arenas fiasco demonstrates, we can never be certain about off-the-field conduct with gamblers, which needs to be visibly scrutinized.

Voice of the Red Sox for the past 30 years, Joe Castiglione. In announcing the last out when the Sox obtained their first World Championship in 86 years, he exclaimed: "Can you believe it!" (courtesy Tayler Aubin).

There are other problems that directly affect the game's integrity. Cleveland Indians pitcher Paul Byrd was revealed to be taking HGH (human growth hormone) just before the seventh game of the 2007 American League Championship Series between the Indians and the Red Sox. Selena Roberts of the *New York Times* and others darkly hinted that the timing might have something to do with the fact that George Mitchell was a director of the Red Sox and was seeking an advantage for his team. Roberts also suggested that the Red Sox were getting a free ride on the steroid issue, notwithstanding the fact that some of its players, like Paxton Crawford, Jeremy Giambi and Jose Canseco (who played for the team in the mid–'90s), were already identified as steroid users. Senator Mitchell felt compelled to issue a statement denying this.[4] In any event, the revelation that both Manny Ramirez and David Ortiz had tested positive in the first group tested in 2003 soon implicated the Red Sox, though they were never as honeycombed with drug users as their rival Yankees.

But the point is that baseball invited conspiracy rumors by putting a part-owner in a conflict-of-interest situation. This policy was followed in the appointment of the Blue Ribbon Panel, which consisted basically of industry insiders and management — the same holds true for Selig's new committee looking at changes in rules.

It is quite clear that the Commissioner is the employee of the owners and yet one would hope, on a matter so delicate as the drug investigation, that he would require independence, notwithstanding Senator Mitchell's extraordinary credentials and his longstanding commitment to the public interest.

Performance-enhancing drugs, be they steroids, human growth hormone or amphetamines, continue to plague the game. The Mitchell Report is just a first draft — and Selig's comments upon McGwire's admissions and Selig's lack of investigative stance toward him and others reveal that the scandal lives on. The bad news is that the steroids era is not over and will not be over until players believe that they cannot obtain an advantage from it without being detected. This is not the situation today, and dark clouds which rival "Shoeless" Joe Jackson's "Say it ain't so, Joe" remain with us.

The problem of performance-enhancing drugs and controversies about discipline may yet emerge anew in the 2011 collective bargaining process. But there will be much more than this, notwithstanding the challenge of HGH, for which Major League Baseball is presently not testing.

The absence of blacks from the field, and the underrepresentation of blacks and minorities in both managerial and key coaching positions as well as the higher echelons of the front office, remain an ongoing and pressing challenge. Though practically none of these matters will be addressed in the collective bargaining process, some form of affirmative action with sanctions at least as significant as those of the National Football League remain vital for the future.

In addition to drugs, at the top of the items to be considered in collective bargaining there will be the international draft, the question of how to induce some teams to spend for payroll and baseball development, new postseason competition rules involving the playoffs, and a renewed attempt by MLB to place limits or a slotting system on draftee salaries. Though the union does not represent the draftees, the matter must be bargained with them. Baseball may push for an international draft with the union in light of the large bonus signings for players from Cuba — more of whom are likely to follow after the demise of Fidel Castro's wake. Like football and basketball it will attempt to regulate salaries among rookies who come within the borders of the United States as well. Most sports have not only done this through the regulation of salaries themselves — it seems unlikely that baseball will develop any kind of salary cap for any players in the future — but also have agreed, in the case of football, to a "slotting" system for high draft rookie salaries. Baseball has attempted to do the same but has been unsuccessful in getting the large-market teams, in particular, to adhere to the system. The union does not want to see big-market spending inhibited. Washington, Kansas City and Pittsburgh might spend more or become more competitive if they could trade high draft choices for established players. It remains to be seen whether these matters can be addressed through collective bargaining in 2011.

Finally, the revenue-sharing revelations of August 2010 will make this matter front and center in 2011 collective bargaining discussions. There will be a resistance to paying clubs that do not use a substantial portion of the monies for payroll, though it seems unlikely that a floor for salary expenditures will be set forth. The union in particular is always reluctant to have any kind of direct regulation of salaries beyond the minimum per player because of a fear of pressure for salary caps — a system which, while it is in existence in football, basketball and hockey, may be particularly inappropriate in baseball, in which so much of the revenues and expenditures necessarily go toward minor league clubs and player development.

The year 2011 marks a new era of peace ushered in by the NLRB's 1995 injunction. After thirty years of warfare, 2002 and 2006 give the parties and the public greater confidence in their ability to resolve these and other issues peaceably this time around.

The game is both game and business. Unlike the theater, both the participants and observers feel some of the same dynamics. Said *Sports Illustrated* a few years ago:

> They [the fans and taxpayers] watch their favorite players come and go through free agency and trades, and see their managers and coaches get shuffled like playing cards. They cringe as the news crawl on their screen reports heinous transgressions committed by their son's hero, whose replica jersey just lightened their wallet considerably. But they come back, because the games matter to them, and because sports fosters a sense of hope.[5]

During the '07 Red Sox-Angels Division series, left fielder Manny Ramirez, who patrolled the same expanse before Fenway's "Green Monster" that those like Williams, Yastrzemski and Rice did before him, commented about a mammoth homer that he hit off the Angel closer Francisco Rodriguez in the second game: "Sometimes he gets me and sometimes I get him."

This was the case with Williams too — only the results were different — and those critical depressing moments in '46, '48 and '49 are simply instances when other very good players got the best of him, as Ramirez did of Rodriguez in '07. Williams tried to succeed at those moments, as did the rest of the Red Sox club, with only Bobby Doerr hitting well in '49 and Rudy York in '46. Quite simply, success was not available at that particular moment. There is no other explanation!

And Ramirez, even when the Sox were down 3 games to 1 against the Cleveland Indians in the Championship series, seemingly in desperate straits, said: "Who cares? There's always next season."[6] This was a shockingly honest comment by one of the gods in whom we had invested our emotions prior to his suspensions for drug use in 2009 and 2011. The players are entertainers, and those like Ramirez meet that standard more than adequately on numerous levels. For the fans, there is always next year.

If Ramirez, Ortiz and others are hitting the ball hard, I and countless others feel good — just as I did when Williams and Stephens were there. I am "down" when the opposite is true. Simply speaking, there is no avoiding that.

The process is fundamentally imaginary ... this is what takes us up there. One fall day in 1969 I could think back to the Brooklyn Dodger fan maxim: "Wait until next year," which Ramirez was echoing, as I watched the Red Sox, already eliminated from the race, experiment with pitcher Sonny Siebert as a reliever as the club came through Detroit for their last visit that year — and, as in many years before and after, I reflected on what 1970 would look like.

We come back because it fosters hope and because, as the *New York Times* said when commiserating with New York Mets fans about the collapse of their team in '07, the game is truly "immortal." It endures, albeit with different nuances, shapes and forms over the years. This is the way it has been since those Station Field years in the mid– and late 1940s.

The game is more exciting than ever, to paraphrase the straightforward and plain-speaking Jim Leyland. Testimony for that proposition is easily supplied by Matt Holliday's headfirst slide to the plate to give the Colorado Rockies the '07 NL pennant in the 13th inning in the month which has come to be called Roctober '07, and whether he touched the plate or not, was out or safe, only made it all the more thrilling!

Most of us who love this game will continue to do so, at least through our heirs — sixty years plus and more ... many more, if Dame Fortune shines upon us all!

Like the tasteful and elegant piano of John Lewis and the ever-so-lovely sounds of his entire Modern Jazz Quartet ... Horace Silver's "Song for My Father" and its stirring eloquence ... and the preacher-like shouts emanating from a tenor saxophone of Stanley Turrentine ... like the Solemn High Mass in Long Branch, New Jersey's, St. James's Episcopal Church, in which the incense rises majestically from the thurible toward the heavens ... as with the Democratic Party and its commitment to equality for all people, promoted more clearly during the time of President Harry Truman when we were playing baseball on the Station Field, and he, in turn, was carrying forward FDR's economic commitment to the little guy ... truly, like all of them, baseball is one of life's eternal verities. May it always be so — notwithstanding the foolish foibles which compromise integrity in the name of commerce by those who run the game — for the generations of my sons and my grandchildren and the generations yet to come.

Chapter Notes

Preface

1. Though I was not aware of it at the time, one of my forebears on my mother's side of the family had played earlier in the Negro Leagues. Harold Gould, *He Came From Gouldtown, to Become a Philadelphia Star of the Negro Baseball Leagues* (2009).
2. Robert C. Berry and William B. Gould IV, "A Long Deep Drive to Collective Bargaining: Of Players, Owners, Brawls, and Strikes," 31 *Case Western Law Review* 685–813 (1981).
3. The decision which relied upon the article is Powell v. NFL, 930 F.2d 1293 (8th Cir. 1989).
4. William B. Gould IV and Robert C. Berry, "Views of Sport; Labor Trouble is Brewing," *New York Times*, Aug. 10, 1986, Section 5, p. 2, Col. 1, Sports Desk.

Chapter 1

1. See generally Brad Snyder, *A Well-Paid Slave: Curt Flood's Fight for Free Agency in Professional Sports* (2006).
2. Michael S. Schmidt, "Mets' Steps Could Allow a Break with Rodriguez," *New York Times*, Aug. 18, 2010.
3. It would seem that this characteristic is shared by many New York City criminals. See Manny Fernandez, "Crime Blotter Has a Regular: Yankees Caps," *New York Times*, Sept. 16, 2010, p. A1.
4. Ben McGrath, "The Extortionist," *The New Yorker*, October 29, 2007, p. 56.
5. The substantial increases obtained by many groups in recent years are discussed in Malcolm Gladwell, "Talent Grab: Why do we pay our stars so much money?," *The New Yorker*, Oct. 11, 2010, p. 85.
6. The most graphic evidence for this proposition is set forth in an illuminating article, Steve Treder, "The Persistent Color Line: Specific Instances of Racial Preference in Major League Player Evaluation Decisions after 1947," *Nine* 10, no. 1 (2007).
7. Report to the Commissioner of Baseball of An Independent Investigation into the Illegal Use of Steroids And Other Performance Enhancing Substances by Players In Major League Baseball by George J. Mitchell, DLA Piper US LLP, December 13, 2007.
8. Basic Agreement Summary, Jan. 22, 2007 (on file with author).
9. This is in reference to a famous late-'90s Nike commercial featuring Atlanta Braves pitchers Tom Glavine and Gred Maddux. "It epitomized an era that had seen a huge drop-off in attendance after the 1994 strike and then a bounce-back driven in large part by ever-increasing home run totals and challenges to Roger Maris' single-season record. As the home runs went up, so did atten-

dance." David Gassko, "Do Chicks Dig the Long Ball?," *The Hardball Times*, Jan. 31, 2008, available at http://www.hardballtimes.com/main/article/do-chicks-dig-the-longball/.
10. Jack McCallum, "Inside the NBA: Game-Fixing and Dogfighting Rock Pro-Sports," *Sports Illustrated*, July 24, 2007, available at http://sportsillustrated.cnn.com/2007/writers/jack_mccallum/07/24/sports.crises0730/index.html.
11. Frederick G. Lieb, *The Boston Red Sox* (1947), p. 60.
12. Harold Seymour, *Baseball: The People's Game* (1990), p. 14.
13. Charles P. Korr, *The End of Baseball As We Knew It: The Players Union, 1960–1981* (2002), p. 1.
14. Bill Keller, "In Baseball, the Russians Steal All the Bases," *New York Times*, July 20, 1987, p. 1.
15. Of course some of the early examples covered by the "bonus baby" rules were required immediate promotion to the Major League level so as to discourage lavish spending. Frank Quinn's move from Yale to the Red Sox and Johnny Antonelli of the Boston Braves were two early examples.
16. Sean Deveney, *The Original Curse: Did the Cubs Throw the 1918 World Series to Babe Ruth's Red Sox and Incite the Black Sox Scandal?* (2009).
17. See Rose/Giamatti Agreement, available at http://baseball1.com/bb-data/rose/agreement.html.
18. Stephen Szymanski and Andrew Zimbalist, *National Pastime: How Americans Play Baseball and the Rest of the World Plays Soccer* (2005), p. 32.
19. See, e.g., Roger I. Abrams, *The First World Series and the Baseball Fanatics of 1903* (2003).
20. In fact the season was delayed, beginning on April 26 so as to give the players time to have a belated spring training and the owners the opportunity to recruit players who had not been previously under contract to them.
21. Tom Verducci, "Good, Old Yankees," *Sports Illustrated*, Nov. 16, 2009, p. 50.
22. Robert Siegel, "All Things Considered: Major League Baseball Doesn't Feel Economic Pinch," Dec. 17, 2010.
23. Buster Olney, "30 is the New 40," *ESPN Insider*, Jul. 27, 2009, p. 40.
24. Tom Verducci, "Big Spenders: After a brief period of financial restraint, clubs are giving huge — and long — contracts," *Sports Illustrated*, Dec. 20, 2010, p. 52.
25. Andrew Baggarly, "Giants notebook: Edgar Renteria says pride caused him to reject San Francisco's $1 million offer," *San Jose Mercury News*, Feb. 21, 2011, available at http://www.mercurynews.com/giants/ci_17439845?nclick_check=1.

26. Tony Massarotti, "Money is No Object," *Boston Herald*, December 7, 2006, p. 84.

27. Mike Vaccaro quotes McGraw as follows: "I know the American League and its methods," he declared in the late summer of 1904, arguing against participating in the Series. "I will not consent to a haphazard box-office game with [AL President] Ban Johnson and company. No one, not even my bitterest enemy, ever accused me of being a fool. I have taken the New York club from last to first in three short years. Now that New York has won this honor, I, for one, will not stand to see it tossed away like a rag." Brush, who was drawn to McGraw's bombast as it mirrored his own, was even firmer in his refusal. Mike Vaccaro, *The First Fall Classic* (2009), p. 36. However, Harold Seymour states that there is "some evidence" to believe that McGraw opposed Brush's position.

28. Telephone interview with Bobby Doerr, Oct. 14, 2009.

29. Larry Tye, *Satchel: The Life and Times of an American Legend* (2009).

30. Timothy M. Gay, *Satch, Dizzy & Rapid Robert: The Wild Saga of Interracial Baseball before Jackie Robinson* (2010), pp. 41–42. The author also dismisses the claim that Ruth hit a towering homer off Paige.

31. *Brown v.* Board of Education, 347 U.S. 483 (1954).

32. Michael J. Haupert, *The Economic History of Major League Baseball*, p. 5:

> During the winter of 1878-79, team owners gathered to discuss the problem of player roster jumping. They made a secret agreement among themselves not to raid one another's rosters during the season. Furthermore, they agreed to restrain themselves during the off-season as well. Each owner would circulate to the other owners a list of five players he intended to keep on the roster the following season. By agreement, none of the owners would offer a contract to any of these "reserved" players. Hence, the reserve clause was born. It would take nearly a century before this was struck down. In the meantime, it went from five players (about half the team) to the entire team (1883) and to a foreman contract clause (1887) agreed to by the players. Owners would ultimately make such a convincing case for the necessity of the reserve clause, that players themselves testified to its necessity in the Celler Anti-monopoly Hearings in 1951.
> In 1892 the minor league teams agreed to a system that allowed the National League teams to draft players from their teams. This agreement was in response to their failure to get the NL to honor their reserve clause. In other words, what was good for the goose, was not good for the gander. While NL owners agreed to honor their reserve lists among one another, they paid no such honor to the reserve lists of teams in other organized, professional leagues. They believed they were at the top of the pyramid, where all the best players should be, and therefore they would get those players when they wanted them. As part of the draft agreement, the minor league teams allowed the NL teams to select players from their roster for fixed payments. The NL sacrificed some money, but restored a bit of order to the process, not to mention eliminated expensive bidding wars among teams for the services of players from the minor league teams.

33. See, e.g., *Philadelphia Ball Club, Ltd. v. Lajoie*, 51 A. 973, (Pa. 1902).

34. Robert Elias, *The Empire Strikes Out: How Baseball Sold U.S. Foreign Policy and Promoted the American Way Abroad* (2010), p. 162.

35. Cf. Brad Lefton, "Welcome Home for a Trailblazer: Nomo is embraced in Japan, years after a contentious split," *New York Times*, May 2, 2010, Sports, p. 3.

36. See Roberto Gonzalez Echevarria, *The Pride of Havana: A History of Cuban Baseball* (1999).

37. Indeed, "[baseball] Commissioner Bud Selig has told his Japanese counterpart he is open to games between the World Series and Japan Series champions, but no steps have been taken for such a matchup." "A True World Series?," *San Francisco Chronicle*, Jan. 8, 2010, p. B3.

38. Interview with Burt Blyleven, May 8, 2004.

39. Mark Fainaru-Wada and Lance Williams, *Game of Shadows* (2006).

40. Mark Fainaru-Wada and Lance Williams, "Bay Area's Role in Vast Steroid Bust: 124 Arrested in Ten Countries — 56 Labs Are Seized by DEA," *San Francisco Chronicle*, September 25, 2007, p. 1; Duff Wilson and Michael S. Schmidt, "D.E.A. Exposes a Steroid Web With China Tie," *New York Times*, September 25, 2007, p. 1.

41. Mark Fainaru-Wada and Lance Williams, "Baseball's Drug Scandal Widens," *San Francisco Chronicle*, November 6, 2007, p. l.

42. *Ibid.*

43. Mark Fainaru-Wada and Lance Williams, "MLB Plans to Talk to Guillen," *San Francisco Chronicle*, November 7, 2007.

44. In this case the Commissioner did not follow established precedent set forth in the drug cases described in Chapter 7. See Michael S. Schmidt, "In Wake of Inquiry, Selig Resets Precedent," *New York Times*, Oct. 29, 2010.

45. Ann Killion, "'Bonds Stands Alone': After His Triumph Bonds Asserts 'This Record Is Not Tainted At All,'" *San Jose Mercury News*, August 8, 2007, p. 1.

46. Michael S. Schmidt, "Clemens Lied About Doping, Indictment Charges," *New York Times*, Aug. 20, 2010, p. 1.

47. Tom Boswell, *Washington Post*, September 1, 2007, pp. E1 and E8.

48. Tom Gatto, "The Great Power Outage of '07," *The Sporting News*, September 17, 2007, p. 56.

49. Global Broadcast Data Base, September 9, 2007, p. 12.

50. "The Fans Speak Out," *San Jose Mercury News*, August 12, 2007, Sports, p. 2C.

51. *The Sporting News*, September 24, 2007.

52. Michael S. Schmidt, "Binoculars in the Bullpen? The Phillies Are Accused of Stealing Signs Illegally," *New York Times*, May 13, 2010, p. B15.

Chapter 2

1. When I resided in Japan in the 1970s, fans were required to return all balls hit outside of the park's playing field.

2. The best description of this is contained in Frederick Turner, *When the Boys Came Back: Baseball and 1946* (1996).

3. "Hey Ba Ba Re Bop" (1945) Written by Lionel Hampton and Curley Hamner.

4. James S. Hirsch, *Willie Mays: The Life, the Legend* (2010), p. 99.

5. Turner, supra note 3 at p. 108.

6. *Ibid.*, pp. 111 and 108.

7. Will McDonough, "Globe Staff, Sox 'Racist': Says Who? Harper Case No Proof," *Boston Globe*, Apr. 17, 1986, p. 51 (response to Gould's op-ed in *Boston Globe*, Opening Day, 1986).

8. *Baseball Digest*, Sept. 1, 2007.

9. Turner, supra note 3 at p. 201.

10. About him, Red Sox fans sang the following song:

"Who hits the ball and makes it go?
Who runs the bases fast, not slow?
Who's better than his brother Joe?
Dominic DiMaggio."

11. James P. Dawson, "Chandler Is Star," *New York Times*, May 25, 1947, p. S1.

12. Elias, p. 16.

13. The debate about set lineups continues to this day. Darren Everson, "The Count: The MLB Leaders in Lineup-Card Tinkering," *Wall Street Journal*, Aug. 11, 2010, p. D8.

14. Gerald V. Hern, "Spahn and Sain," *Boston Post*, September 14, 1948.

"First we'll use Spahn, then we'll use Sain, Then an off day followed by rain, Back will come Spahn, followed by Sain, And followed, we hope, by two days of rain."

15. Tom Wright played intermittently with the Red Sox from 1948 to 1951. He only appeared in 54 games during the 1950 season and 28 games in the 1951 season. In 1952, he had a cup of coffee with the St. Louis Browns, followed by limited pinch-hitting work with the White Sox for 1.5 seasons and the Washington Senators for 3 seasons.

16. See W.P. Kinsella, *The Iowa Baseball Confederacy*.

17. Jonah Keri, "Does Baseball Need Umpires?," *Wall Street Journal*, Oct. 13, 2009, p. 20. "Oddly, in the post-season, when there are even more cameras trained on the field, the number of umpires also expands — to six. This number, too, is a bit of a relic. It came about in 1947 when then-commissioner Happy Chandler decided that the two substitute umpires who usually came to World Series games might as well take the field, too. (What could it hurt?) They were inserted in the outfield. The idea, of course, is that more umpires means better play-calling. But this isn't necessarily true. After Friday's game, Tim Tschida, the umpire crew chief on duty that night, told reporters that while there was no excuse for Mr. Cuzzi's blown call, there was one contributing factor. Umpires spend so little time working in the outfield during the season that it can be a challenge in the postseason. 'Getting into a position is a little bit foreign,' Mr. Tschida said. 'It's a little bit uncomfortable.' In an interview with the *Newark Star-Ledger*, Mr. Cuzzi also said the positioning was a challenge. 'We're not used to playing that far down the line,' he said. 'The instant the ball is hit, we usually start running. I think I may have been looking too closely at it.'"

18. Bruce Weber, *As They See 'Em: A Fan's Travels in the Land of Umpires* (2009). p. 247. This book is the best book-length discussion of the role of umpires in baseball.

19. Murray Chass, "M.L.B. Takes First Step to Add Instant Replay," *New York Times*, November 7, 2007, p. C22.

20. "Selig Names Committee to Examine Facets of Game," *New York Times*, Dec. 16, 2009, p. B14.

21. Paul White, "Do Umpires Need Help?," *USA Today*, Oct. 23–25, 2009, pp. 1A, 2A. See also Jack Curry, "Umpires Are Caught Off Base by Bad Calls," New York Times, Oct. 22, 2009, p. B17; George Vecsey, "A Time to Give Umpires Sympathy," *New York Times*, Oct. 22, 2009, pp. B14, B17; Fay Vincent, "Building A Better Umpire," New York Times, Oct. 18, 2009, p. 10.

22. Pat Borzi, "Playoffs Start, and So Do Calls for a Replay System," *New York Times*, Oct. 8, 2010, p. B11.

23. Bruce Weber, "Umpires v. Judges," *New York Times*, Jul. 12, 2009, pp. 1, 5.

24. They are discussed extensively in Dan Wade, "Expanding Replay: Cons Outweigh Pros in Video Reviews," *Baseball Prospectus*, April 30, 2010.

25. George Vecsey, "Worst Call Ever? Sure. Kill the Umpires? Never," *New York Times*, June 4, 2010, p. 1. See also Jonah Keri and Brian Costa, "Wanted: A Fix at First," Wall Street Journal, June 4, 2010, p. W4.

26. Bruce Weber, "Replay Isn't the Kind of Review That Will Make Umpires Better," *New York Times*, Nov. 7, 2010, p. 11.

27. *NLRB v. Major League Baseball*, 880 F. Supp. 246 (S.D.N.Y. 1995), aff'd *67 F.3d 1054 (2d Cir. 1995)*.

28. Joe Posnanski, "Fisk missed the point: There's more to this story than just steroids," SI.com, Jan. 20, 2010, p. 1.

29. John Shea, "Team isn't getting an A in attendance," *San Francisco Chronicle*, May 5, 2010, p. 1.

30. Hank Greenwald, *This Copyrighted Broadcast* (1999), p. 61.

Chapter 3

1. Robert C. Berry, William B. Gould IV, et al., *Labor Relations in Professional Sports* (1986), p. 60.

2. *Charles O. Finley v. Kuhn*, 569 F.2d 527 (7th Cir. 1978).

3. *Ibid.*, p. 537.

4. *Ibid.*, p. 539.

5. This idea was called into question in the 2009 Yankees–Angels ALC series when the runner was called safe as Angel infielder Erick Aybar was in the vicinity of the bag on an attempt at double play: "[H]is feet were in the so-called neighborhood of the bag in the 10th inning of Game 2 of the American League Championship Series on Saturday. But contrary to enduring baseball mythology, close is not enough. 'There is no such thing as the neighborhood play,' said Rich Garcia, a Major League Baseball umpire supervisor for seven years after spending 25 years in blue. 'You either touch the base or you don't.' ... 'The right call, and in my opinion, a tremendous call,' said Mike Port, baseball's vice president in charge of umpiring." David Waldstein, "The Biggest Secret of Baseball's Unwritten Rules: They Don't Exist," *New York Times*, Oct. 19, 2009, p. D3.

6. Daniel M. Daniels, "Bevens, Big, Modest, Reticent, Hombres Head for Hurling Heights with Yanks," *Baseball Magazine*, June 1947, p. 227.

7. Apparently even Commissioner Bud Selig believes the myth. See Tim Arango, "Myth of Baseball's Creation Endures, With a Prominent Fan," *New York Times*, Nov. 13, 2010, pp. B9, B12.

8. Harold Seymour and Dorothy Seymour Mills, *Baseball: The Early Years* (1960), pp. 4–5.

9. *Ibid.*, p. 7.

10. Robert F. Burk, Never Just a Game: Players, Owners and American Baseball to 1920 (1994) at 14.

11. *Ibid.*, p. 14.

12. *Ibid.*, p. 16.

13. *Ibid.*, p. 29.

14. *Ibid.*, p. 31.

15. *Ibid.*, p. 42.

16. *Ibid.*, p. 51.

17. *Ibid.*, p. 81.

18. Much of the commentary on these cases appears in similar form in Berry, supra note 1 at 48.

19. *Ibid.*, pp. 48–49.

20. Elias, p. 19.

21. *Lumley v. Wagner*, 42 Eng. Rep. 687 (1852).

22. *Metropolitan Exhibition Co. v. Ewing*, 42 F. 198 (C.C.S.D.N.Y. 1890).

23. *Metropolitan Exhibition Co. v. Ward*, 9 N.Y.S. 779 (Sup. Ct. 1890).

24. *Philadelphia Base-Ball Club v. Lajoie*, 10 Pa. Dist. Rpts. 309 (1901), rev'd, 202 Pa. 210, 51 A. 973 (1902).

25. *American Baseball Club of Chicago v. Chase*, 86 Misc. 441, 461, 149 N.Y.S. 6 (Sup. Ct. 1914).

26. This has been brilliantly chronicled in Mike Vaccaro, *The First Fall Classic* (2009). As this book makes clear, like much of this decade — especially 1918 and 1919 — there was considerable proximity between the on-the-field game itself and the gamblers.

27. Leonard Koppett, *Koppett's Concise History of Major League Baseball* (1998), p. 117.

28. *Fed. Baseball Club of Balt. v. Nat'l League of Prof'l Baseball Clubs*, 259 U.S. 200 (1922). See Samuel A. Alito Jr., "The Origin of the Baseball Antitrust Exemption," *The Baseball Research Journal* 38, No. 2 (Fall 2009): p. 86, for a more sympathetic treatment of Justice Holmes' opinion reconciling it to much of the Constitutional dogma existing at the time.

29. *Ibid.*, pp. 208–209.

30. "We freely acknowledge our belief that *Federal Baseball* was not one of Mr. Justice Holmes' happiest days": Salerno v. American League of Prof. Baseball Clubs, 429 F.2d 1003, 1005 (2nd Cir. 1970) (Friendly, J.).

31. G. Edward White, *Creating the National Pastime: Baseball Transforms Itself 1903–1953* (1996), 83.

32. Michael Shapiro, *Bottom of the Ninth* (2009).

33. See *Robertson v. NBA*, 389 F. Supp. 867 (S.D.N.Y. 1975).

34. See *Radovich v. NFL*, 352 U.S. 445 (1957).

35. See, e.g., *Nassau Sports v. Peters*, 352 F. Supp. 870 (E.D.N.Y. 1972); *Phila. World Hockey Club, Inc. v. Phila. Hockey Club, Inc.*, 351 F. Supp. 462 (E.D. Pa. 1972); *Nassau Sports v. Hampson*, 355 F. Supp. 733 (D. Minn. 1972); *Boston Prof'l Hockey Ass'n, Inc. v. Cheevers*, 348 F. Supp. 261 (D. Mass. 1972), rev'd, 472 F.2d 127 (1st Cir. 1972).

36. See *United States v. Int'l Boxing Club of N.Y., Inc.*, 348 U.S. 236 (1955).

37. On the historic role of the Commissioner, see *Finley v. Kuhn*, 569 F.2d 527, 532–35 (7th Cir. 1978). See generally Elliot Asinof, *Eight Men Out: The Black Sox and the 1919 World Series* (1963). For a thorough discussion of the Commissioner's authority see Craig F. Arcella, Note, "Major League Baseball's Disempowered Commissioner: Judicial Ramifications of the 1994 Restructuring," 97 *Columbia Law Review* 2420 (1997).

38. *Milwaukee Am. Ass'n v. Landis*, 49 F.2d 298 (N.D. Ill. 1931).

39. Koppett, *Koppett's Concise History*, p. 193.

40. Compare *Atlanta National League Baseball Club, Inc. v. Kuhn*, 432 F. Supp. 1213 (N.D.Ga 1977) regarding the Commissioner's authority to enforce anti-tampering rule applicable between clubs) with the Chicago National League Ball Club, Inc. v. Major League Baseball F. Supp. (N.D. Ill. 1992), regarding the Commissioner's order to realign clubs held to be beyond his authority under the "best interest of baseball" clause. Cf. Richard Sandomir, "The Slow Creep of the 'Best Interests' Clause," *New York Times*, May 15, 2010, p. B10.

41. See Leigh Montville, *The Big Bam: The Life and Times of Babe Ruth* (2006).

42. John Drebinger, "Gehrig signed by Yanks at Estimated Salary of $35000: Veteran Accepts $4000 pay slash," *New York Times*, Jan. 26, 1939, p. 29.

43. James R. Devine, "The Legacy of Albert Spalding, the Holdouts of Ty Cobb, Joe DiMaggio, and Sandy Koufax/Don Drysdale, and the 1994-95 Strike: Baseball's Labor Disputes are as Linear as the Game," 31 *Akron Law Review* 1 (1997).

44. Donald Honig, *Baseball When the Grass Was Real: Baseball From the Twenties to the Forties Told by the Men Who Played It* (1993), 219.

45. *Gardella v Chandler*, 172 F.2d 402, 408 (2nd Cir. 1949) (Hand, J. concurring).

46. *Ibid.*

47. *Ibid.*

48. *Ibid.*, p. 409.

49. *Ibid.*

50. *Ibid.*

51. *Ibid.*, p. 412.

52. Daniel M. Daniel, "Major Leaguers in 1947 Enjoy Vast Numbers of New Benefices," *Baseball Magazine*, March 1947, p. 334.

53. John Drebinger, "The Reserve Clause," *Baseball Magazine*, July 1951, p. 255.

54. William Marshall, Baseball's Pivotal Era: 1945–1951, 243 (1999).

55. Gardella, supra note 45, p. 415.

56. John Drebinger, "Spring Training — Hypermodern Style," *Baseball Magazine*, March 1951, p. 328.

57. Some of this is set forth in Drebinger, "Spring Training — Hypermodern Style," supra, pp. 327–328.

58. Daniel, "Major Leaguers of 1947," p. 333.

59. *Ibid.*

60. *Ibid.*

61. *Ibid.*

62. See generally *Snyder*, A Well-Paid Slave.

63. Korr, p. 14.

64. See generally William B. Gould IV, *A Primer on American Labor Law*, Chapter 3.

65. See, e.g., *J.I. Case Co. v.* NLRB, 321 U.S. 332 (1944); *Medo Photo Supply Corp. v. NLRB*, 321 U.S. 678 (1944).

66. *Am. League of Prof'l Baseball Clubs*, 180 N.L.R.B. 190 (1969).

67. *J.I. Case Co. v.* NLRB, 321 U.S. 332 (1944).

68. *Ibid.*, pp. 337–39.

69. *NLRB v. Wooster Division of Borg-Warner Corp.*, 356 U.S. 342 (1958).

70. McClatchy Newspapers Inc. 321 NLRB 1386 (1996) enf'd 131 F.3d 1026 (DC. Cir. 1997).

71. *Fiberboard Corp. v. NLRB*, 379 U.S. 203 (1964).

72. Justice Stewart's concurring opinion in *Fiberboard*; *First Nat'l Maintenance v. NLRB*, 452 U.S. 666 (1981).

73. Advice Memorandum from the NLRB Office of the General Counsel on Case 2-CA-34908, Office of the Commissioner of Major League Baseball (May 5, 2003), available at http://www.nlrb.gov/shared_files/Advice%20Memos/2003/dd050503_mlb.html.

74. Case No. 2-CA-38008 charge filed December 1, 2006.

75. *NLRB v.* Mackay Radio & Telegraph, 304 U.S. 333 (1938).

76. Cf. *Major League Umpires Ass'n v. American League of Professional Baseball Clubs*, 357 F.3d 272 (3d Cir. 2004) (upholding arbitral award); Association of Major League Umpires v. the American League and the National League of Professional Baseball Clubs and the Toronto Blue Jays Baseball Club, [1995] O.L.R.B. Rep. Apr. 540 (Apr. 28, 1995) (asserting jurisdiction over dispute arising United States–based baseball umpires when the National Football League hired replacements); National Basketball Association, [1995] O.L.R.B. Rep. Nov. 1389 (Nov. 10, 1995) (asserting jurisdiction over dispute arising United States–based basketball referees when the National Basketball League hired replacements).

77. *American Ship Building Co.* v. NLRB, 380 U.S. 300 (1965).

78. *NLRB v.* Truck Drivers Local Union No. 449, 353 U.S. 87 (1957).

79. Shapiro, *Bottom of the Ninth,* p. 98.

80. Hearing Before the Subcomm. on Study of Monopoly Power of the H. Committee on the Judiciary, 82nd Cong (1951).

81. Gipe, "Yesterday: Ty Cobb's Anger Led to Baseball's First Strike, A Comedy of Errors," *Sports Illustrated,* August 29, 1977, pp. W5–6; Walter, "Baseball's First Strike Was as Rough as a Cobb," *San Francisco Sunday Examiner& Chronicle,* May 31, 1981, p. C2.

82. Marvin Miller, *A Whole Different Ballgame: The Sport and Business of Baseball* (1991), p. 221.

83. See generally Berry, supra note 1, Chapter 3.

84. Ed Edmonds, "A Most Interesting Part of Baseball's Monetary Structure — Salary Arbitration In Its Thirty-Fifth Year," 40 *Marquette Sports L. Rev.,* pp. 1, 6 (2009).

In 1995, ownership proposed a switch from a sole arbitrator to a panel of three for a limited number of hearings. Two hearings were decided by panels and both cases produced victories by management. Believing that the panels produced better results, MLB pushed for a permanent change. One-half of the decisions in 1998 were made by three-arbitrator panels, and in 1999, eight of the eleven decisions were made by panels instead of a single arbitrator. With the transition to all three-arbitrator panels beginning in 2000, the structure of baseball salary arbitration has remained the same for much of this first decade of the twenty-first century.

85. *Kapp v. NFL,* 390 F. Supp. 73 (ND Cal. 1974).

86. In the Matter of the Arbitration between: Major League Baseball Player Relations Committee, Inc. and Major League Baseball Players Association (Panel Decision No. 50 A and B, Salary Guarantee Grievances, Nov. 2, 1983), p. 5 (Goetz, Arb.).

87. *Ibid.,* pp. 3–4, note.

88. *Ibid.,* pp. 5, 6.

89. See Chris Deubert and Glenn M. Wong, "Understanding the Evolution of Signing Bonuses and Guaranteed Money in the National Football League: Preparing for the 2011 Collective Bargaining Negotiations," 16 *UCLA Ent. L. Rev.* 179 (2009).

90. In the Matter of the Arbitration Between Terrell Owens and National Football League Players Association and Philadelphia Eagles and NFL Management Council (Bloch, Arbitrator Nov. 18, 2005), available at ESPN.com.

91. Professional Baseball Clubs, 66 Lab. Arb. & Disp. Settl. 101, 116 (1975) (Seitz, Arb.).

92. Berry, supra note 1, pp. 56–58.

93. *United Steelworkers Trilogy v. Warrior & Gulf Navigation Co.* 363 U.S. 574 (1960); *United Steelworkers v. Am. Mfg. Co.* 363 U.S. 564 (1960); *United Steelworkers v. Enterprise Wheel & Car Corp.* 363 U.S. 593 (1960).

94. *AT&T Technologies, Inc. v. Communications Workers of America,* 475 U.S. 643 (1986).

95. *Kan. City Royals Baseball Corp. v. Major League Baseball Players Ass'n.* 532 F.2d 615 (8th Cir. 1976).

96. In the Matter of the Arbitration between: Major Leagues of Professional Baseball Clubs and Major League Baseball Players Association (Decision No. 32, Alvin Moore–Atlanta Braves, Sept. 7, 1977), p. 13 (Porter, Arb.).

97. In the Matter of Arbitration between Major Leagues of Professional Baseball Clubs and Major League Baseball Players Association, (Decision No. 32, Grievance NO. 77-18, Alvin Moore–Atlanta Braves, Sept. 7, 1977), p. 14.

98. In the Matter of Arbitration between Major Leagues of Professional Baseball Club and Major League Baseball Players Association (Decision No. 37, Grievance

No. 78-15, Re: Michael Grant Marshall vs. Minnesota Twins, Oct. 25, 1978), at 13.

99. In the Matter of the Arbitration between: Major League Baseball Players Association (Richard Tidrow) and Major League Baseball Player Relations Committee, Inc. (Chicago Cubs), (Panel Decision No. 44, Grievance No. 80-19, Nov. 4, 1980 [rev. Jan. 17, 1981], at 20).

100. *Ibid.,* p. 22.

101. In the Matter of the Arbitration between Major League Baseball Players Association and the Chicago White Sox (Panel Decision No. 88, Grievance No. 90-6, Opinion and Award of the Chairman, April 23, 1992).

102. In the Matter of Arbitration Between Major League Baseball Players Association (On Behalf of Ron Gant, Xavier Hernandez and Terry Pendleton) and Major League Baseball Player Relations Committee (On Behalf of Cincinnati Reds and Florida Marlins), (Decision No. 101, Grievance Nos.: 96-4, 96-5, 96-6, Aug. 11, 1997), at 33.

103. Murray Chass, "Deferred Money Puts Snag in Negotiations for Vaughn," *New York Times,* Dec. 27, 2001, pp. C13–14.

104. Murray Chass, "Mets Make Last Tweak and Land Mo Vaughn," *New York Times,* Dec. 29, 2001, pp. C15–16.

105. Jack Curry, "Union Rejects Boston's Rodriguez Bid," *New York Times,* Dec. 18, 2003, p. D1.

106. In the Matter of the Arbitration between American and National Leagues of Professional Baseball Clubs and Major League Baseball Players Association (Panel Decision No. 6, Grievance No. 71-16, Alex Johnson — California Angels) (1971).

107. *Ibid.,* p. 2.

108. *Ibid.,* p. 6.

109. This Matter is discussed in more detail in Jeff Euston, "Contractual Matters: The Restricted List," *Baseball Prospectus,* May 13, 2010.

110. *Mackey v. NFL* 543 F.2d 606 (8th Cir. 1976).

111. *NLRB v.* Truitt, a holding that where the employer invokes an inability to pay in the collective bargaining process it is obliged to open its financial records to the union upon request.

112. *Silverman v.* Major League Baseball Player Relations Comm., Inc., 516 F. Supp. 588, 598 (S.D.N.Y. 1981). See also Murray Chass, "Baseball Poised for Strikes as Judge Denies Injunction," *New York Times,* June 11, 1981, p. D21.

113. Andrew Zimbalist, *May the Best Team Win: Baseball Economics and Public Policy* (1984), p. 81.

114. In the Matter of the Arbitration between: Major League Baseball Player Relations Committee, Inc. and Major League Baseball Players Association, (Panel Decision No. 50A and B, Salary Guarantee Grievances, Nov. 2, 1983; In the Matter of the Arbitration between: Major League Baseball Player Relations Committee, Inc. and Major League Baseball Players Association, (Panel Decision No. 50C and D, Salary Guarantee Grievances); In the Matter of the Arbitration between: Major League Baseball Player Relations Committee, Inc. and Major League Baseball Players Association, (Panel Decision No. 50 F, Salary Guarantee Grievances), Feb. 27, 1984; In the Matter of the Arbitration between: Major League Baseball Player Relations Committee, Inc. and Major League Baseball Players Association, (Panel Decision No. 50 G, Salary Guarantee Grievances), March 26, 1981.

115. In the Matter of the Arbitration between: Major League Baseball Player Relations Committee, Inc. and Major League Baseball Players Association, (Panel Decision No. 50A and B, Salary Guarantee Grievances), Nov. 2, 1983, pp. 28–29.

116. In the Matter of National Basketball Players Association on behalf of Various Players and National Basketball Association on behalf of all Its Teams, Arbitrator John Feerick, Oct. 19, 1998.

117. *Ibid.*, p. 142.

118. *NLRB v. Insurance Agent's Int'l. Union* 361 U.S. 477, 489 (1960).

119. *Ibid.*, p. 55.

120. Zimbalist, *May the Best Team Win.*

121. In the Matter of the Arbitration between: Major League Baseball Players Association (Carlton E. Fisk) and Major League Baseball Player Relations Committee, Inc. (Boston Red Sox), (Grievance No. 80-35, Panel Decision No. 45)(Raymond Goetz, Arb.)(declaring Carlton Fisk a free agent on the grounds that the Red Sox mailed his 1981 contract on December 22nd — two days after the December 20th deadline); Joseph Durso, "Fisk declared Free Agent; Cerone Wins Salary Case," *New York Times*, Feb. 13, 1981, p. A19.

122. In the Matter of the Arbitration between Major League Baseball Players and the 26 Major League Clubs (Grievance No. 87-3) (Aug. 31, 1988) (Nicolau, arb.), p. 7.

123. Murray Chass, "Talking the Talk of Collusion Redux," *New York Times*, February 2, 2003, p. 6.

124. In the Matter of the Arbitration between Major League Baseball Players Ass'n and the 26 Major League Baseball Clubs, Grievance No. 87-3, Panel Dec. No. 79 (1988) (Nicolau, Arb.).

125. In the Matter of the Arbitration Between Major League Baseball Players Association v. Twenty-Six Major League Baseball Clubs, Grievance No. 86-7, Panel Dec. No. 73 (1987) (Nicolou, Arb.); In the Matter of the Arbitration Between Major League Baseball Players Ass'n and the 26 Major League Baseball Clubs, Grievance No. 86-7, Panel Dec. No. 73 (1987) (Nicolau, Arb.).

126. *Ibid.*

127. 2007-2001 Basic Agreement, Art. IV, §12 (criteria for salary arbitration):

(a) The criteria will be the quality of the Player's contribution to his Club during the past season (including but not limited to his overall performance, special qualities of leadership and public appeal), the length and consistency of his career contribution, the record of the Player's past compensation, comparative baseball salaries (see paragraph (13) below for confidential salary data), the existence of any physical or mental defects on the part of the Player, and the recent performance record of the Club including but not limited to its League standing and attendance as an indication of public acceptance (subject to the exclusion stated in subparagraph (b)(i) below). Any evidence may be submitted which is relevant to the above criteria, and the arbitration panel shall assign such weight to the evidence as shall appear appropriate under the circumstances. The arbitration panel shall, except for a Player with five or more years of Major League service, give particular attention, for comparative salary purposes, to the contracts of Players with Major League service not exceeding one annual service group above the Player's annual service group. This shall not limit the ability of a Player or his representative, because of special accomplishment, to argue the equal relevance of salaries of Players without regard to service, and the arbitration panel shall give whatever weight to such argument as is deemed appropriate.

(b) Evidence of the following shall not be admissible:
(i) The financial position of the Player and the Club;
(ii) Press comments, testimonials or similar material bearing on the performance of either the Player or the Club, except that recognized annual Player awards for playing excellence shall not be excluded;

(iii) Offers made by either Player or Club prior to arbitration;
(iv) The cost to the parties of their representatives, attorneys, etc.;
(v) Salaries in other sports or occupations.

128. Tyler Kepner, "With Only 13 Wins, Hernandez Earns Cy Young," *New York Times*, Nov. 19, 2010, p. B11.

129. See James Click, "Baseball Prospectus Basics: Evaluating Defense," *Baseball Prospectus*, March 1, 2004; Ben Lindbergh, "Getting Defensive: Adventures in Team Fielding," February 24, 2009.

130. See, e.g., Greg Bishop, "For Mariners, Prevention Hasn't Been a Cure," *New York Times*, May 16, 2010, p. 2 of Sports Sunday.

131. Richard Sandomir, "Pirates Win For Losing, Financial Papers Show," *New York Times*, Aug. 24, 2010, p. B10.

Chapter 4

1. William B. Gould IV, *Labor Issues in Professional Sports: Reflections on Baseball, Labor, and Anti-Trust Law*, 15 Stan. L. & Pol'y Rev. 61 (2004).

2. *Silverman v. Major League Baseball*, 516 F. Supp. 588 (S.D.N.Y. 1981).

3. Letter from Senator Edward Kennedy, United States Senate, March 3, 2004 (on file with author).

4. See generally William B. Gould IV, *Labored Relations: Law, Politics in the NLRB* (2000).

5. My ideas on this subject are contained in William B. Gould IV, *Agenda for Reform, the Future of the Employment Relationship and the Law* (MIT Press, 1993).

6. William B. Gould IV, "Should the National Labor Relations Act Be Retired? The NLRB at Age 70: Some Reflections on the Clinton Board and the Bush II Aftermath," 26. *Berkeley J. Emp. & Lab. L.* 309 (2005); William B. Gould IV, "The Employee Free Choice Act of 2009, Labor Law Reform, and What Can Be Done About the Broken System of Labor-Management Relations Law in the United States," 43 U.S.F. L. Rev. 291 (Fall 2008), pp. 334–38.

7. Gould, *Labored Relations*, pp. 19–21.

8. Professor Mackenzie is quoted in Gould, supra note 4, p. 18.

9. Murray Chass, "Owners Pull So Hard on Cap, They Can't See Strike in Their Path," *New York Times*, June 7, 1994, p. B11.

10. See generally *NLRB v. Mackay*, 304 U.S. 333 (1938).

11. See generally *NLRB v. Int'l Van Lines*, 409 U.S. 408 (1972).

12. 380 U.S. 300 (1965).

13. See, e.g., John Wawrow, "NHL asks union to disavow threats to punish agents," *USA Today*, Mar. 29, 2005.

14. *The Wages of Wins*, p. 13; e-mail from Roger Noll to the author Jan. 5, 2010.

15. "Just as an employer must bargain with the representative of his employees on grievances so must he about a method of resolving them." *United States Gypsum Co.*, 94 NLRB 112, 131 (1951).

16. *NLRB v. Columbus Printing Pressman Local 252*, 543 F.2d 1161, 1166 (5th Cir. 1976): "We ... hold that such a[n] [arbitration] clause is not a mandatory subject of bargaining, since its effect on terms and conditions of employment during the contract period is at best remote." See also Plumbers Local No. 387, 266 NLRB 30: "The

Board ... has consistently held that interest arbitration, despite its arguable benefits, is not a mandatory subject of bargaining and that neither party can compel the other to negotiate about a contract clause that would, in the event of new contract negotiation disagreement, in effect substitute a third party as final decisionmaker of disputed contractual terms."

17. 518 U.S. 231 (1996).

18. 321 U.S. 332 (1944).

19. *Retail Associates, Inc.*, 120 NLRB 388 (1958); Evening News Assn., 154 NLRB 1494 (1965) enf'd. 372 F.2d 569 (6th Cir. 1967). These rulings have been approved by the Supreme Court in *Charles D. Bonanno Linen Service, Inc. v. NLRB*, 454 U.S. 402) (1982). Cf. El Cerrito Mill & Lumber Co., 316 NLRB 1005, 1006-07 (1995).

20. See generally *American Shipbuilding Co. v. NLRB*, 380 U.S. 300 (1965).

21. See generally *NLRB v. Mackay*, 304 U.S. 333 (1938).

22. See generally *Harter Equip., Inc.*, 280 NLRB 597 (1986); NLRB v. Brown Food Stores, 380 U.S. 278 (1965) (regarding lockouts in multi-employer bargaining contexts); *Int'l Paper Co.*, 319 NLRB 1253 (1995), enforcement denied, 114 F.3d 105 (D.C. Cir. 1997).

23. *NLRB v. Katz*, 369 U.S. 736 (1962); NLRB v. Crompton-Highland Mills, 337 U.S. 217 (1949); *NLRB v. Wooster Div. of Borg-Warner Corp.*, 356 U.S. 342 (1958).

24. 259 U.S. 200 (1922) (holding that the Sherman Antitrust Act was not applicable to baseball). See generally Gould, supra note 4.

25. 29 U.S.C. § 160(j) (2000).

26. For more on the climate during this period at the NLRB, see Gould, supra note 4, at Chapter 7.

27. Memorandum from Arthur F. Rosenfeld, General Counsel, NLRB to all Regional Directors, Officers-in-Charge, and Resident Officers, *Utilization of Section 10(j) Proceedings* (Aug. 9, 2002), available at http://www.lawmemo.com/nlrb/gc02-07.

28. This happened in 1997 and was the first time in the history of the NLRB that any of its employees had ever received this prestigious award, the President's Award for Distinguished Federal Civilian Service. No one from the NLRB has received it since!

29. Much of the above commentary is contained in my memoir of my NLRB service, Gould, *Labored Relations*.

30. Murray Chass, "Baseball Outlook Appears Gloomy," *New York Times*, Feb. 9, 1995, p. B11; Murray Chass, "Baseball's Unreal World," New York Times, Feb. 9, 1995, p. A22.

31. Kevin Fagan, *Drabble* (comic strip), Prince George's Journal, Apr. 26, 1994, p. B4.

32. *Silverman v. Major League Baseball*, 67 F.3d 1054 (1995).

33. Gould, supra note 4, p. 120.

34. Nick Cafardo, "Sox Drop Orioles; Clemens on Target; Vaughn Hits No. 18," *Boston Globe*, June 23, 1995, p. 37.

35. Thomas Boswell, "Reinsdorf Throws Owners the Curve," *Washington Post*, Nov. 22, 1996, pp. B1, B3; Murray Chass, "Owners to Meet Today On Labor Agreement," New York Times, Nov. 26, 1996, p. B9; George Vecsey, "In His Way, Reinsdorf Made Peace," *New York Times*, Nov. 27, 1996, p. B9.

Chapter 5

1. White, *Creating the National Pastime*, p. 23.

2. Harold Seymour and Dorothy Seymour Mills, *Baseball: The Golden Age* (1971), p. 19.

3. *Ibid.*, p. 76.

4. *Ibid.*, p. 66.

5. Murray Chass, "Blockbuster Trade to Become Case of Paying As They Go," *New York Time*, February 17, 2004, pp. C12, C13.

6. See generally Korr, *The End of Baseball as We Knew It*.

7. See, e.g., Michael S. Schmidt, "Agent's Loans to Poor Players Pose Concerns," *New York Times*, Nov. 23, 2010, p. A1. In the major sports, particularly basketball, many of the agents have become powerful forces in the union itself.

8. Sports Broadcasting Act of 1961.

9. Charles C. Alexander, *Breaking the Slump* (2002); Ken Belson, "Apples for a Nickel, And Plenty of Empty Seats: The 1930s Offers lessons on Economic Hardball," New York Times, Jan. 7, 2009, pp. B11, B13.

10. Dave Zirin, "Will pro sports take a body blow?," *San Francisco Chronicle*, Feb. 1, 2009, p. 2; Mark Emmons, "In This Downturn ... Will They Show Up?," San Jose Mercury News, Jan. 20, 2009, pp. 1D, 3D; Josh Levin, "Shake Me Down at the Ball Game," *Sports Illustrated*, June 23, 2008, pp. 14, 15.

11. Howard Beck, "In Some N.B.A. Arenas, the Crowds Are Thin," *New York Times*, Dec. 19, 2008, pp. B1, B14.

12. Stefan Fatsis, "What Recession? We're Ballplayers," *New York Times*, Sunday, Dec. 7, 2008, p. 5.

13. *Ibid.*

14. Richard Sandomir and Ken Belson, "In a Downturn, Corporate Ties Have Put a Bind on Sports," *New York Times*, Mar. 27, 2009, pp. 1, 6; Katie Thomas, "As the Economy Worsens, Is There Money for Play?," New York Times, Nov. 16, 2008, pp. 1, 12.

15. Richard Sandomir, "Red Sox Concede to Hard Times and Will Not Raise Prices," *New York Times*, Nov. 13, 2008, pp. B12, B14.

16. Harvey Araton, "No Recession in the Bronx: Yankees Land Sabathia with Record Deal," *New York Times*, Dec. 11, 2008, pp. B13, B16; Richard Sandomir, "Tax Shelter Helps Yankees Afford Those Big Salaries," New York Times, Dec. 11, 2008, p. B17; William C. Rhoden, "Recession Is a Relative Term in Baseball," *New York Times*, Nov. 17, 2008, pp. D1, D9.

17. U.S. 231 (1996).

18. *Kapp v. NFL*, 390 F. Supp. 73 (N.D. Cal. 1974),vacated in part, 1975 WL 959 (N.D. Cal. 1975) aff'd, 586 F.2d 644 (9th Cir. 1978).

19. See *Kapp*, 586 F.2d at 648.

20. *Mackey v. NFL*, 543 F.2d 606 (8th Cir. 1976).

21. *Reynolds v. NFL*, 584 F .d 280, 289 (8th Cir. 1978).

22. *NLRB v. Mackay Radio & Telegraph Co.*, 304 U.S. at 333. (1938).

23. *Powell v. NFL*, 930 F.2d 1293 (8th Cir. 1989); see also Powell v. NFL, 1960 F. Supp. 812 (D. Minn. 1988).

24. Robert C. Berry and William B. Gould IV, "A Long Deep Drive to Collective Bargaining; Of Players, Owners, Brawls, and Strikes," 31 *Case W. Res. L. Rev.* 685 (1981).

25. William B. Gould IV, "Players and Owners Mix it Up," *Cal. Law*, Aug. 1988, p. 56.

26. F. Supp. 871 (D. Minn. 1992).

27. See *White v. NFL*, 822 F. Supp. 1389 (D. Minn. 1993).

28. U.S. 231 (1996). Justice Stevens wrote a persuasive and perceptive dissent.

29. *Ibid.*, p. 250.

30. E.g., *Textile Workers v. Darlington Mills*, 380 US 263 (1965).

31. U.S.C.A. § 26B (West 2003).

32. 822 F. Supp. 1389.

33. *Clarett v. National Football League*, 369 F.3d 124 (2d Cir. 2004); *Caldwell v. Am. Basketball Ass'n*, 66 F.3d 523 (2d Cir.1995); *Nat'l Basketball Ass'n v. Williams*, 45 F.3d 684 (2d Cir.1995); *Wood v. Nat'l Basketball Ass'n*, 809 F.2d 954 (2d Cir.1987).

34. 352 U.S. 445 (1956).

35. Brief for the NFL respondents, *American Needle v. National Football League*, p. 41 (Nov. 17, 2009).

36. *American Needle, Inc., v. National Football League*, et al. "United States Supreme Court Official Transcript," Jan. 13, 2010, pp. 6–7.

37. *American Needle, Inc., v. National Football League*, 130 S. Ct. 2201, 2208–09 (2010).

38. NFL Collective Bargaining Agreement 2006–2012, pp. 238–239.

39. *Glendale Manufacturing Co. v. Local No. 520, Int'l Ladies' Garment Workers' Union, AFL-CIO*, 283 F.2d 936 (4th Cir. 1960).

40. *United States Gypsum Co. v. United Steelworkers of America*, AFL-CIO, 384 F.2d 38 (5th Cir. 1967).

41. Cf. *Federation of Union Representatives v. Unite Here*, 210 WL 3517388 (S.D.N.Y. 2010).

42. Statement by William B. Gould IV, Chairman, National Labor Relations Board, on *Brown, et al. v. Pro Football, Inc. d/b/a Washington Redskins, et al.* Sup. Ct. No. 95-388, June 20, 1996:

> I am fearful that the Court's decision will invite game playing by the unions in professional sports as they pretend to commit suicide through decertification or defunctness so as to be "sufficiently distant" from the collective bargaining process. This regrettable result — one already employed in football and basketball — may make a mockery of our laws and divert the resources of both tribunals and private parties away from the constructive process of collective bargaining.

43. U.S. 356 (1953). See also *Triple-A Baseball Club Assocs. v. Northeastern Baseball, Inc.*, 832 F.2d 214, 216 n.1 (1st Cir. 1987).

44. The courts are divided on the question of whether *Federal Baseball* applies to issues like relocation and contraction of teams and the United States Supreme Court is yet to address the issue explicitly. In any event, the Curt Flood Act does not seem to directly affect this issue.

45. *The Wages of Wins* (2007), pp. 51–52.

46. "Baseball's Revenue Gap: Pennant for Sale?" Hearing before the subcommittee on antitrust, business rights and competition of the Committee of the Judiciary United States Senate (Nov. 21, 2000).

47. *Ibid.*, p. 44.

48. See, e.g., Murray Chass, "Back to Business: Baseball Votes to Drop 2 Teams," *New York Times*, November 7, 2001, p. A1. Ironically, the 2002 world championship Anaheim Angels were considered for contraction in 2001. See Richard Sandomir, "Angels Were Mentioned in Contraction Talks Before Winning World Series," New York Times, March 12, 2003, p. D3.

49. See "Fairness in Antitrust in National Sports (FANS) Act of 2001: Hearings on H.R. 3288 Before the House Comm. on the Judiciary," 107th Cong. 4–16 (2001).

50. *Metro. Sports Facilities Comm'n v. Minnesota Twins P'ship*, No CT 01-16998, 2001 WL 1511601 (Minn. Dist. Ct. Nov. 16, 2001), aff'd, 638 N.W.2d 214 (Minn. Ct. App. 2002 (preventing the contraction of the Minnesota Twins before the 2002 season because of the team's lease obligations).

51. *Ibid.*

52. See *Textile Workers Union v. Darlington Mfg. Co.*, 380 U.S. 263, 274 (1965).

53. *Ibid.*

54. *First Nat'l Maint. Corp. v. NLRB*, 452 U.S. 666 (1981); see also Dubuque Packing Co., 303 N.L.R.B. 386 (1991), enforced in relevant part, 1 F.3d 24 (D.C. Cir. 1993) (developing a test to determine when an employer's decision to relocate is a mandatory subject of bargaining; the test initially analyzes whether the relocation accompanied a basic change in the nature of the employer's operations); cf. Q-1 Motor Express, Inc., 323 N.L.R.B. 767, 769 (1997) (Chairman Gould concurring) (arguing that the *Dubuque* standard is unsatisfactory for a number of reasons, including the fact that it produces significant litigation).

55. *Major League Baseball Player Relations Comm., Inc. v. Major League Baseball Players Ass'n*, Grievance No. 83-1, Panel Dec. No. 66 (1985) (Bloch, Arb.).

56. Id. at 9; see also Andrew Zimbalist, May the Best Team Win: Baseball Economics and Public Policy (2003), at 98 (stating that "it is clear that the 60/40 rule would function as a back-door salary cap in 2002").

57. *Major League Baseball Player Relations Comm., Inc. v. Major League Baseball Players Ass'n*, Grievance No. 83-1, Panel Dec. No. 66 (1985) (Bloch, Arb.), p. 31. Zimbalist later criticized the 60/40 rule (and the arbitral ruling supporting it) as a de facto salary cap and stated the following about its applicability in contemporary circumstances:

> As of June 2002, when the Selig [60/40] rule was to kick in, the Red Sox had a remaining obligation to outfielder Manny Ramirez of around $120 million. For the rest of the squad, the Sox had approximately another $70 million in long-term obligations. So the team's total in long-term contract obligations alone was roughly $190 million; that is, it was already $60 million plus over the debt limit, without counting the $40 million of pre-existing debt the new owners inherited or the $200 million the new owners borrowed from Fleet Bank to buy the team. The Sox would have to do some massive payroll cutting not to be in violation of Selig's 60/40 rule.

Zimbalist, supra note 55, p. 96–97. However, the 2002 collective bargaining agreement, which allows for a debt service rule, suspends the 60/40 rule until 2005-2006, and it may continue "in a manner that does not affect any Club's Major League Player contracting decisions." 2007–2011 Basic Agreement, available at http://mlbplayers.mlb.com/pa/pdf/cba_english.pdf (hereinafter "Basic Agreement"), p. 190. Meanwhile, no corrective or remedial measures by the Commissioner are to "attempt to influence or interfere with any Club decision regarding a Major League Player's contract, reserve status or roster status. Moreover, the Commissioner shall take no action directed at preventing a Club from establishing its Major League Player payroll budget at a level that the Club deems appropriate." Id at 198 (Attachment 22, § 7).

58. Brief of the Major League Baseball Players Ass'n at 53, *Major League Baseball Players Ass'n v. Thirty Major League Clubs*, Grievance No. 2001-22 (Das, Arb.).

59. *Ibid.*, p. 60–62.

60. *Ibid.*, p. 54.

61. *Ibid.*, p. 62–63.

62. *Ibid.*, p. 85–86 (referring to Major League Baseball Players Ass'n v. Thirty Major League Clubs, Panel Dec. No. 103 (1998) (Eischen, Arb.); *Major League Baseball Players Ass'n v. Twenty-Eight Major League Clubs*, Panel Dec. No 96 (1993) (Nicolou, Arb.); Major League Baseball Players Ass'n v. Twenty-Eight Major League Clubs, Panel Dec. No. 90 (1992) (Nicolou, Arb.).

63. See William B. Gould IV, "Talking About Baseball:

Slugging It Out," *San Francisco Chronicle*, Dec. 2, 2001, p. D5.

64. Basic Agreement, supra note 56, p. 50–51 (art. XV[H] [1]).

65. Id. at 50 (art. XV(H)).

66. Matthew Artz, "Fremont Makes New Pitch for A's," *San Jose Mercury News*, Jan. 9, 2010, p. B1; Carolyn Jones, "Fremont Makes Another Pitch — A's Stadium at Nummi Site," San Francisco Chronicle, Jan. 9, 2010, p. C1.

67. Carolyn Jones, "Oakland Offers 3 Sites on Waterfront for A's," *San Francisco Chronicle*, Dec. 11, 2009, p.1. Jesse McKinley, "The Gloves Come Off in a Bay Area Baseball Dispute," New York Times, Dec. 31, 2009, p. A13; Jon Coté, "SF Threatens Suit if A's Get San Jose OK," *San Francisco Chronicle*," Dec. 18, 2009, p. C1.

68. Letter to Commissioner Bud Selig from Dennis Herrera, "Re: Concerns over Potential Tampering with San Francisco Giants' Territorial Rights," Dec. 17, 2009, p.1. There is some authority that non-baseball entities are outside the exemption. *Henderson Broad. Corp. v. Houston Sports* 541 F.Supp. 263 (S.D. Tex. 1982). But see *McCoy v. MLB* 911 F.Supp. 454 (W.D. Wash. 1995). Cf. *New Orleans Pelicans v. Natl. Assn. of Prof Baseball* 1994 WL 631144 (E.D. La. 1994).

69. *State of Wisconsin v. Milwaukee Braves, Inc.*, 31 Wis.2d 699, 144 N.W.2d 1 (1966).

70. The mere fact that the action sounds in contract is not dispositive of whether the case will be governed by *Federal Baseball* and antitrust principles. *Salerno v. American League of Prof. Baseball Clubs*, 429 F.2d 1003, 1005 (2nd Cir. 1970) (Friendly, J.); *Molinas v. National Basketball Association*, 190 F. Supp. 241, 244 (S.D.N.Y. 1961).

71. *Piazza v. Major League Baseball*, 831 F. Supp. 420 (E.D. Pa. 1993) (holding, contrary to most courts, that baseball's antitrust exemption is limited to issues relating to the reserve system).

72. *Major League Baseball v. Crist*, 331 F.3d 1177 (11th Cir. 2003). See also *Major League Baseball v. Butterworth*, 181 F. Supp. 2d 1316 (N.D. Fla. 2001), *aff'd sub nom*, *Major League Baseball v. Crist*, 331 F.3d 1177 (11th Cir. 2003) (recognizing that Major League Baseball retains a broad antitrust exemption that extends beyond the reserve system); *Minnesota Twin P'shp v. State*, 592 N.W.2d 847 (Minn. 1999) (noting that while baseball's antitrust exemption may be an aberration, it is still a broad exemption that can only be reversed by Congress or the Supreme Court). But see *Piazza v. Major League Baseball*, 831 F. Supp 420 (E.D. Pa. 1993) (holding, contrary to most courts, that baseball's antitrust exemption is limited to issues relating to the reserve clause); *Butterworth v. Nat'l League of Prof'l Baseball Clubs*, 644 So. 2d 1021, 1025 (Fla. 1994) (following Piazza, even though it is "against the great weight of federal cases regarding the scope of the exemption").

73. See generally *Toolson v. N.Y. Yankees, Inc.*, 346 U.S. 356, 357 (1953) (holding that the antitrust exemption extends to the "business of baseball").

74. Zimbalist, supra note 55, pp. 153–56.

75. Daniel C. Glazer, "The Baseball Exemption," *Wall Street Journal*, June 13, 2003, at A6. See generally Lloyd Johnson and Miles Wolff, The Encyclopedia of Minor League Baseball (1997) (providing background on minor league baseball):

Smaller cities like Columbus, Ohio, and Portland, Maine, might be able to support minor-league franchises without financial sustenance from major-league teams, but the Oneonta (New York) Tigers and Lake Eisinore (California) Storms of the world would almost certainly fade into oblivion if left to the vagaries of the free market. As a

minor league baseball official observed following the Crist ruling, "39 million Minor league fans would be upset" if baseball's antitrust exemption was eliminated.

Daniel C. Glazer, "The Baseball Exemption," *Wall Street Journal*, June 13, 2003, p. A6. See generally Johnson and Wolff, Encyclopedia of Minor League Baseball.

76. *L.A. Mem'l Coliseum Comm'n v. NFL*, 726 F.2d 1381 (9th Cir. 1984) (holding that an NFL rule restricting team relocation violated antitrust laws); cf. *Sullivan v. NFL*, 34 F.3d 1091 (1st Cir. 1994) (reversing a jury verdict that awarded substantial damages because of an NFL rule that prevented an owner from selling a portion of a team to the public, reasoning that the jury improperly considered the rule's fairness, as opposed to whether it was a restraint on trade). See generally Katherine C. Leone, "No Team, No Peace: Franchise Free Agency in the National Football League," 97 *Colum. L. Rev.* 473 (1997) (chronicling the litigation surrounding the NFL's antitrust liability and arguing for a partial exemption so that the league can control franchise relocation).

77. *NBA v. SDC Basketball Club, Inc.*, 815 F.2d 562 (9th Cir. 1987) (remanding to trial court for jury determination the issue of whether a rule restricting franchise movement violated antitrust laws).

78. *Citizens United v. Federal Election Comm'n*, 130 S. Ct 876 (2010).

79. Zimbalist, supra note 55, p. 100.

80. Richard Sandomir, "Pirates Win For Losing, Financial Papers Show," New York Times, Aug. 24, 2010, pp. B10 and B13.

81. This is discussed in more detail in Joe Rutter, *Tribune-Review*, June 18, 2006.

82. Bill Madden, "Crying poverty, some MLB owners are laughing all the way to the bank," *New York Daily News*, Aug. 15, 2009, p. 70.

83. Tyler Kepner, "Mariners Join Trend by Signing Hernandez to Long Deal," *New York Times*, Jan. 20, 2010, p. B15; "Marlins say they'll spend more on players," San Francisco Chronicle, Jan. 13, 2010, p. B5.

84. Joel G. Maxcy, "Revenue Sharing in MLB: The Effect on Player Transfers," Working Paper Series, Paper No. 06-15, International Association of Sports Economists (September 2006).

85. *Ibid.*, p. 3.

86. David Pinto, "The Big Picture: If You Win, They Will Come," *Baseball Prospectus*, April 25, 2007.

87. *American Needle, Inc. v. National Football League*, 130 S. Ct. 2201 (2010) (See, Amicus Curiae Brief of Economists In Support of Petitioner.)

88. Jeff Passan, "Marlins' profits came at taxpayer expense," Yahoo! Sports, Aug. 24, 2010.

89. Matt Swartz, "Prospectus Perspective: Acting Like Thieves or Rational Agents?," *Baseball Prospectus*, Aug. 26, 2010; Phil Birnbaum, "The Pittsburgh Paradox: Should the Pirates spend money to win ballgames?," Slate, Aug. 25, 2010.

90. Shawn Hoffman, "Squawking Baseball: Despite the Screams, Revenue Sharing Isn't Broken," *Baseball Prospectus*, Aug. 26, 2010; John Perrotto, "On the Beat: No Problem with the Pirates," Baseball Prospectus, Aug. 30, 2010, pp. 1–2:

The Pirates are quick to point out that they have spent $30.7 million on draft signing bonuses from 2008–10, more than any other major-league club. They gave this year's first-round draft pick, high school right-hander Jameson Taillon, a club-record $6.5 million bonus. Selig say that is a show of good faith on the Pirates' part to their fans that they are trying to build a winning organization.

91. J.C. Bradbury, "Encouraging the Poor to Stay Poor," *New York Times Sports Sunday*, Aug. 29, 2010, at p. 2:

> The failure of revenue sharing to promote competitive balance can also be seen in baseball's historical record. Since its introduction in the mid 1990s, revenue sharing has not made baseball any more competitive than it used to be. Sports economists often measure competitive balance by comparing the standard deviation of winning percentages across teams to an ideally balanced league where all teams are of equal strength, a measure known as the Noll-Scully ratio, which was named after the sports economists Roger Noll and Gerald Scully. As the metric declines toward one, competitive balance improves. The Noll-Scully ratio saw a drastic reduction in the average imbalance in baseball from 2.4 in the 1930s to 1.8 in the early 1990s. Since then, the ratio has not declined any further. Thus, the addition of revenue sharing appears to have had little effect on competitive balance.

92. Michael Lewis, "Baseball's Losing Formula," *New York Times*, November 3, 2007, p. A31.

93. *Ibid.*, p.

94. Neil deMause, "Of Elephants and Fish: The A's and Marlins Seek to Complete MLB's Stadium Sweep," *Baseball Prospectus*, March 18, 2007.

95. See generally, Ken Belson, "As Teams Abandon Stadiums, the Public is Left with the Bill," *New York Times*, Sept. 8, 2010, p. 1.

96. Neil deMause, "How Much Is That Stadium in the Window?: Determining the True Public Costs of Big-League Ballparks," *Baseball Prospectus*, November 8, 2005; deMause, "Stadium Watch 2007: The Updates," Baseball Prospectus, March 4, 2007; Doug Pappas, "The Numbers (Part Two)," *Baseball Prospectus*, December 12, 2001; deMause, "The Next White Elephant?: Another Try in Oakland," Baseball Prospectus, August 15, 2005; deMause, "Amazin' Savings: How the Mets Plan to Pass the Buck on Their New Park," *Baseball Prospectus*, January 23, 2006; deMause, "The Evil Empire Strikes Back: Steinbrenner's Plan to Have Other Teams Buy Him a Stadium," Baseball Prospectus, August 1, 2004; Andrew Zimbalist, "Financing A New Yankee Stadium: The Devil Is in the Details," *Baseball Prospectus*, January 30, 2006; deMause, "Bronx Bummer: The Yankees' Stadium Deal, Revisited," Baseball Prospectus, February 16, 2006.

97. San Francisco, with little direct assistance though considerable aid through infrastructure, is the exception rather than the rule. Most of the franchises which have seen new stadiums have obtained money from public coffers which could otherwise go towards providing for schools, transportation and the like. This has been well chronicled in Neil deMause and Joanna Cagan, *Field of Schemes: How the Great Stadium Swindle Turns Public Money into Private Profit* (2008).

98. Bob Nightengale, "Small-payroll teams turning the tables," *USA Today*, Aug. 12, 2010, p. 1C.

99. Vince Gennaro, Yahoo! Sports, October 31, 2007.

100. Jason Stark, "Pushing for a Minimum Payroll Threshold," ESPN.com: Baseball, Nov. 19, 2009.

101. Tyler Kepner, "The Yankees, and Everything in Between," *New York Times*, Dec. 27, 2009, p. 7.

102. See John Shea, "Baker Revels in Revival of Young Reds," *San Francisco Chronicle*, June 6, 2010, p. B6.

103. Ed Stein, "United Feature Syndicate," *New York Times Weekend Review*, Nov. 8, 2009, at p. 2.

104. Curiously, economists who attack the idea that there is a correlation between payroll and performance put forward performances by low-payroll clubs in obtaining world championships — even though a number of those clubs performed more poorly through the statistically significant 162-game championship season. "Thirty teams participate in Major League Baseball today. In 2001, Arizona was ranked eighth in payroll yet won the World Series. In 2002, the Anaheim Angels were ranked fifteenth and won the fall classic. In 2003 the Florida Marlins won the World Series with a payroll that ranked twenty-fifth out of thirty teams ... in 2005 the White Sox took the title with a payroll that only ranked thirteenth in baseball. And in 2006, the Cardinals took the title with a payroll ranked eleventh. So the seven years following the Blue Ribbon Panel years hardly suggests that payroll dictates ultimate success" (Berri et al. *The Wages of Wins*, pp. 37–38). But this does not go to the more statistically significant 162-game series; in addition, the Angels, Marlins, and Cardinals were wild card teams.

105. Andrew Zimbalist, "The Yankees Didn't Buy the World Series," *The Wall Street Journal*, Nov. 16, 2009, p. A23.

106. *Ibid.*

107. *Ibid.*

108. Greg Bishop, "In N.F.L., Parity is Taking a Turn for the Worse," *New York Times*, Oct. 15, 2009, pp. B1, B17.

109. Bob Hohler, "Union Proves Mighty Foe," *Boston Globe*, December 19, 2003; Jack Curry, "Not Dead Yet: Rodriguez Trade Shows Signs of Life," New York Times, December 20, 2003, pp. B15, B18.

110. Murray Chass, "Is It Collusion or Friendly Chats?," *New York Times*, November 9, 2007, p. C13.

111. Susan Slusser, "Free-Agent Cust signs 1-year deal with Oakland," *San Francisco Chronicle*, Jan. 8, 2010, p. B3.

112. Mark Hyman, "Baseball's Playing Field Gets Even Less Level," *Business Week*, Sept. 29, 2003, at 66.

113. "Virtual Baseball," *New York Times*, September 4, 1995, editorial column 2, p. 14.

114. Jack Curry, "Selig Ponders Alteration to Wild Card," *New York Times*, October 14, 2006, p. B13.

115. Bob Costas, "Playoffs Even a Purist Could Love," *New York Times*, September 21, 2003, p. 10. A variation on this theme would provide for expanded playoffs with ten teams rather than eight. "Jeff Fletcher, Bud Selig: MLB Playoff Expansion Possible," Aol.com, Nov. 18, 2010: "The obstacles seem to be whether the two wild card teams would meet for one game or a best-of-three series, and if it's the latter, how to minimize the impact of the extra off days on the division winners." See also Bruce Jenkins, Plan For More Wild Cards Could Work, With Tweak," San Francisco Chronicle, Sept. 11, 2010, p. B2; Christina Kahrl, "Prospectus Perspective: Four and No More," *Baseball Prospectus*, Nov. 4, 2010.

116. Joe Sheehan, "More Is Less," *Sports Illustrated*, May 2, 2011, pg. 28.

117. This illustration had more validity before 2010 when the Rangers developed considerable pitching strength for the first time in their history.

118. Alan Schwartz, "In Baseball, Searching for Balance and the Scheduling Vortex," *New York Times*, March 25, 2007, p. 10.

119. David Bush, "Whole New Ballgame: Interleague Play Begins Tomorrow," *San Francisco Chronicle*, June 11, 1997, p. D1.

120. http://losangeles.dodgers.mlb.com/content/printer_friendly/cin/y2008/m04/d21/c2565018.jsp

121. John Perrotto, "Year Ten: Interleague Action," *Baseball Prospectus*, June 27, 2007.

122. Jeff Hildebrand, "Interleague Play: An Attendance Study," *Baseball Prospectus*, December 28, 2004.

123. "Interleague Attendance Boost Mostly a Mirage," *Baseball Research Journal*, Jan. 1, 2006.

124. Murray Chass, "Owners Favor Realignment, More Playoffs," *New York Times*, Mar. 5, 1993.

125. Murray Chass, "In Baseball, No Games But the Game is Expanding," *New York Times*, Jan. 21, 1995.

126. See Matthew Futterman, "The Movement to Make Baseball Whole Again," *Wall Street Journal*, May 7, 2010, p. W1 and W5.

127. *Ibid,*. See also Jayson Stark, "Realignment Idea Isn't So Rad, Baseball America," May 3–16, 2010, p. 43.

128. http://mlb.mlb.com/news/article.jsp?ymd=20080 401&content_id=2479371&vkey=news_mlb&fext=.jsp& c_id=mlb

129. *Major League Baseball Player Relations Comm., Inc. v. Major League Baseball Players Ass'n*, Grievance No. 83-1, Panel Dec. No. 66 (1985) (Bloch, Arb.) at 31.

130. Fox landed the contract to air the ALCS games in 2007, 2009, 2011 and 2013, and the NLCS games in 2008, 2010 and 2012. Under the deal, the first World Series game will be played on the first Tuesday night after the completion of the LCS instead of Saturday night as in the previous contract. FOX also retains the rights to broadcast *This Week in Baseball*, MLB's award-winning, youth-oriented magazine show which precedes the FOX *Saturday Baseball Game of the Week*.

Chapter 6

1. David Biderman, "11 minutes of action," *Wall Street Journal*, Jan. 15, 2010, p. W1, 5:

So what do the networks do with the other 174 minutes in a typical broadcast? Not surprisingly, commercials take up about an hour. As many as 75 minutes, or about 60% of the total air time, excluding commercials, is spent on shots of players huddling, standing at the line of scrimmage or just generally milling about between snaps. In the four broadcasts *The Journal* studied, injured players got six more seconds of camera time than celebrating players. While the network announcers showed up on screen for just 30 seconds, shots of the head coaches and referees took up about 7% of the average show.

2. Richard Sandomir, "Batter Up: Let's Dawdle, Kick Dirt and Play Ball!," *New York Times*, May 30, 1995, p. B10.

3. "Batter's Box Rule Aims to Speed Pace in Minors," *Baseball America*, March 14–27, 2005, p.3.

4. Sandomir, *ibid*. See also the enforcement of strict time limits in a Southeastern Conference baseball tournament forced against pitchers and batters and requiring teams to take their allotted positions in 108 seconds after the completion of the previous inning. Mike Tierney, "Boys of Summer, Leisurely No More, Are Put on Clock at SEC Tournament," *New York Times*, June 1, 2010, p. B11. See also Steven Goldman, "Prospectus Perspective: Four Hours of TV, 10 Minutes of Action," *Baseball Prospectus*, Oct. 22, 2010.

5. Tom Verducci, "Why an essential part of the game's romance is in decline," SI.com, May 4, 2010.

6. Richard Sandomir, "Got All Night?," *New York Times*, May 6, 2010, pp. B11, B14; Mike Lopresti, "Yankees–Sox marathons can be a drag," USA Today, April 15, 2010, p. 3C; Tyler Kepner, "Umpire Blasts Yanks' and Red Sox' Pace," *New York Times*, April 19, 2010, p. B14.

7. Russell A. Carleton, "Baseball Therapy: Why Are Games So Long?," *Baseball Prospectus*, May 3, 2010.

8. Richard Sandomir, "Viewer Up! Not When it Comes to the N.L.C.S.," *New York Times*, October 17,

2007, p. C16: "But it is evident that those 10 o'clock starts disenfranchised many Eastern fans sleeping well before the seventh-inning stretch, even while they accommodated those in the Western and Mountain zones. It is also obvious that Phoenix, the No. 12 television market, and Denver, which is No. 18, do not yield the type of viewership boost provided by teams from Los Angeles or New York, or even Boston, which has 900,000 more TV homes, and more stars for Fox to promote, than Cleveland"; Joe Lapointe, "A Day at the Ballpark? More Like a Late Night," *New York Times*, October 15, 2007, p. D2.

9. Richard John Pietschmann, "Monied Interests Departures" (March/April 1998), p. 77.

10. http://mlb.mlb.com/news/press_releases/press_rel ease.jsp?ymd=20071002&content_id=2245590&vkey=pr _mlb&fext=.jsp&c_id=mlb.

11. In the interest of safety, new bats have been introduced in college which have apparently diminished power. "New Bats Could Drastically Alter College Game," *Baseball America*, Oct. 18–31, 2010, p. 44.

12. This is set forth in Dan Fox, "Schrodinger's Bat: The Moral Hazards of the Hit Batsman," *Baseball Prospectus*, May 18, 2006.

13. Lee A. Freeman, "The Effect of the Designated Hitter on Hit Batsmen," 33 the *Baseball Research Journal*.

14. Bradbury and Drinen, "The Designated Hitter, Moral Hazard and Hit Batters: New Evidence From Game-Level Data," *Journal of Sports Economics*, 2006. See also Buehler and Calandrillo, "Baseball's Moral Hazard: Law, Economics, and the Designated Hitter Rule," 90 *Boston University L. Rev.* 2083 (2010).

15. Murray Chass, "Throwback Pitch May Be What Baseball Needs: More Rest, Fewer Innings Is Now the Norm of Pampered Staffs," *New York Times*, June 29, 1997, p. 8.

16. Benjamin Hoffman, "Complete Games Are Dwindling, But For a Reason," *New York Times*, April 9, 2006, p. 4.

17. *Ibid.*

18. Joe Sheehan, "Why 100 Pitches Don't Go As Far As They Used to," *New York Times*, April 15, 2007, p. 10.

19. Ed Guzman and Kirk Johnson, "More Hits, More Runs, And More Concerns: High-Tech Bats Overpower the Game," *New York Times*, August 23, 1998, pp. 1, 4.

20. Rafael Hermoso, "Sluggers Can Be Particular About Their Bats," *New York Times*, May 7, 2002, p. C21; Stan McNeal, "More equal than others," *The Sporting News*, June 2, 2003, pp. 24–27.

21. Stuart Miller, "Muscle beech," *The Sporting News*, May 13, 2005, p. 30.

22. Thus far the ban on these bats has been resisted by MLB. See Nightengale, "Maple Bat Ban Unlikely in MLB," *USA Today*, Sept. 21, 2010, p. 16.

23. David Kiefer, "Rockies Manager Says 4-Man Rotation Could Work," *San Jose Mercury News*, May 30, 2004, p. 7C.

24. David W. Smith, "From exile to specialist: The evolution of the relief pitcher," Retrosheet.org, June 23, 2000, p. 1.

25. Harvey Araton and Andrew Keh, "Pitch Counting," *New York Times*, May 13, 2010, p. B14.

26. Smith, "From exile to specialist," p. 2.

27. See Jack Curry, "Pitch Floats Like a Butterfly, Stings Like a Bee," *New York Times*, August 31, 1992, p. B9.

28. "Wakefield Can't Keep Ball in Park, but Still Earns Victory," *New York Times*, August 9, 2004, p. D3.

29. David Leonhardt, "The Threat of a Stolen Base Can Add Value to an At Bat," *New York Times*, May 8,

2005, p. 9.

30. *Ibid.*, p. 126.

31. Paul Burdick and Kevin Quinn, "Whither or Whether the Stolen Base?," *Nine* 17, no. 2, p. 122.

32. *Ibid.*, p. 127.

33. *Ibid.*, p. 128.

34. Jack Curry, "No More Easy Outs: Statistics-Minded Executives Put Low Value on Bunting," *New York Times*, Aug. 17, 2003, section 8, pp. 1, 3: "Since 1983, the most sacrifice bunts in the majors was 1,811, in 1993. Last year, there were 1,633, a decrease of 9.8 percent. In the same time frame, the most bunt hits were 693, in 1992. Last year, there were 643, a reduction of 7.2 percent. The decline has not been steady, but the trend is clear."

35. *Ibid.*

36. Stuart Miller, "Keeping Score: A Slow Burn Over a Reluctance to Call High Strikes," *New York Times*, Aug. 9, 2010, p. D6.

37. *Ibid.*

38. Greg Hanlon, "You Call That a Strike?!: Why Does Major League Baseball use an outdated, misleading camera angle to show the batter and pitcher?," *Slate*, June 25, 2009.

39. Murray Chass, "Home Run Barrage Contributes to the Rise in Scoring," *New York Times*, May 23, 1999, p. 32.

40. Berri, Schmidt, and Brook, *The Wages of Wins*, p. 1.

41. "For the Love of the Stirrup," posting of Phil Hecken to uniwatch.com (Mar. 28, 2010), available at http://www.uniwatchblog.com/2010/03/28/for-the-love-of-the-stirrup/.

Chapter 7

1. Roger Kahn, *The Head Game: Baseball Seen from the Pitcher's Mound* (2000), p. 287.

2. Football seems to have received less attention, though the drug problem may be as substantial or more so as compared to baseball. See, e.g., Michael S. Schmidt, "Drug Use May Cost Cushing N.F.L. Rookie Award," *New York Times*, May 11, 2010, p. B11.

3. Mike Dodd, "Saves Leader: Tommy John," *USA Today*, Jul. 19, 2003, p. C1.

4. Jaré Longman, "The Deafening Roar of the Shrug," *New York Times*, July 29, 2007, sect. 4, pp. 1, 4.

5. *Ibid.*, p. 4.

6. This is the language of the collective bargaining agreement between the Players Association and the owners.

7. Murray Chass, "Baseball: Cooperate or the Bogey Man Will Get You," *New York Times*, January 30, 2007, p. C15.

8. 190 F. Supp. 241, 244 (S.D.N.Y. 1961).

9. *Ibid.*

10. In the Matter of National basketball Players Association (Latrell Sprewell) and Warriors basketball Club and National Basketball Association, Opinion & Award (1998) (Freerick, Arb.), p. 100, n. 10.

11. See generally Koppett, *Koppett's Concise History of Major League Baseball.*

12. Harvey Araton, "In Yankees Slugger, A Lesson for Redemption in the Steroid Era," *New York Times*, Nov. 3, 2009, pp. B1, B14.

13. *Ibid.*, p. B14.

14. Michael S. Schmidt, "Rodriguez Denies Doctor Gave Him Performance Drugs," *New York Times*, April 3, 2010, p. B8; Michael S. Schmidt, "Investigators Want

to Talk to Rodriguez Assistants," *New York Times*, April 8, 2010, p. B16; William C. Rhoden, "A Sudden Chill in a Carefree Spring," *New York Times*, March 9, 2010, B14; Katie Thomas and Michael S. Schmidt, "Surgeon Isn't Happy After Galea Admits Treating Rodriguez," *New York Times*, March 9, 2010, p. B12.

15. See World Anti-Doping Code, available at http://www.wada-ama.org/rtecontent/document/code_v3.pdf.

16. *Cf.* Michael S. Schmidt, "Stars of Red Sox Title Years are Linked to Doping," *New York Times*, Jul. 31, 2009, pp. A1, B12; Joe Posnanski, "Baseball's Loveable User — He is a First in the Steroid Era: A Cuddly Star Turned Culprit," *Sports Illustrated*, Aug. 10, 2009, pp. 14, 15. However, Ortiz maintained that he did not knowingly take steroids and this appeared to be acceptable to the Red Sox, the Union and MLB. Michael S. Schmidt, and Katie Thomas, "Apologetic Ortiz Says He Didn't Use Steroids," *New York Times*, Aug. 9, 2009, p. 3; "MLB Exec Dupui Takes Boston's Ortiz at his Word," *San Francisco Chronicle*, Aug. 10, 2009, p. 33. With so many other players, the League information which triggered focus upon Ortiz, as with other players, came from records which were presumed to be confidential under the collective bargaining agreement. Clark Hoyt, "Baseball's Top-Secret Roster," *New York Times*, Aug. 9, 2009, p. 8.

17. Jaré Longman, "The Deafening Roar of the Shrug," *New York Times*, July 29, 2007, sect. 4, p. 4.

18. Henry T. Greely, "Disabilities, Enhancements and the Meaning of Sports," 15 *Stan. L. & Pol'y Rev.* 99, 114 (2004).

19. *Ibid.*, p. 129.

20. Report to the Commissioner of Baseball of an Independent Investigation into the Illegal Use of Steroids and Other Performance Enhancing Substances by Players in Major League Baseball (George J. Mitchell, DLA Piper USLP, Dec. 13, 2007), pp. 5–8.

21. *Ibid.*, p. 10.

22. Ian Austen, "H.G.H.'s Conundrum: Does Costly Treatment Enhance Performance?," *New York Times*, Dec. 20, 2009, p. 2.

23. Howard Bryant, *Juicing the Game*: Drugs, Power, and the Fight for the Soul of Major League Baseball (2005), pp. 182–183.

24. See generally http://www.baseball-reference.com/w/willite01.shtml.

25. Alan Schwarz, "Finding a Power Stroke When Most Hitters Start to Fade," *New York Times*, December 12, 2004, p. 4.

26. Report to the Commissioner of Baseball supra note 20 at SR–35. See Michael S. Schmidt, "Baseball Using Minor Leagues For a Drug Test," *New York Times*, Jul. 23, 2010, pp. A1, B12 (describing the use of blood testing for minor leaguers who are not protected by a collective bargaining agreement).

27. Lance Williams and Mark Fainaru-Wada, "Drug Scandal Hits the Playoffs," *San Francisco Chronicle*, October 21, 2007, pp. 1, 12.

28. Michael S. Schmidt, "Clemens Lied About Doping, Indictment Charges," *New York Times*, Aug. 20, 2010, pp. A1, B13; Katie Thomas, "Clemens, Once Under Oath, Is Now Under Indictment," *New York Times*, Aug. 20, 2010, pp. B10, B13; Devlin Barrett, "Clemens Is Indicted on Perjury Charges," *Wall Street Journal*, Aug. 20, 2010, p. A3. Some have said that the indictment is constitutionally flawed because Congress had no legislative purpose in the hearings, but for reasons which are explored in this chapter about Congress's long-held interest in this subject, that is clearly in error. Michael S. Schmidt, "Pos-

sible Flaw Could Turn Clemens Case, Expert Says," *New York Times*, Aug. 21, 2010, pp. B8, B11. A rather silly and often-heard defense of Clemens and others similarly situated is set forth in Ross Douthat, "What Roger Clemens Wants," *New York Times*, Aug. 23, 2010, p. A19.

29. In the Matter of the Arbitration between Major League Baseball Players Association and Major League Baseball Player Relations Committee, Inc., Grievance No. 80-25, Panel Decision No. 41 (1980) (Goetz, Arb.), pp. 11–12.

30. In the Matter of the Arbitration between Bowie K. Khun and Major League Baseball Players Association, Gr. Nos. 84-1 & 84-2, Panel Decision No. 54 (1984), pp. 6–8.

31. *Ibid.*, p. 11.

32. Major League Baseball Players Association (Pascual Perez) gr. no. 84-9 (Richard I. Bloch, April 27, 1984).

33. Major League Baseball Players Association (LaMarr Hoyt) and the San Diego Padres Baseball Club and Peter V. Ueberroth, Commissioner of Baseball (George Nicolau, panel decision no. 74; grievance nos. 87-267, July 2, 1987).

34. *Ibid.*

35. In the Matter of Arbitration between Major League Baseball Players Association and the Commissioner of Major League Baseball (Grievance 91-16; Suspension of Otis Nixon, March 2, 1992).

36. *Ibid.*, p. 44.

37. In the Matter of the Arbitration between Major League Baseball Players Association and the Commissioner of Major League Baseball (Suspension of Steven Howe), Grievance 92-7, Panel Decision No. 94 (1992).

38. *Ibid.*, p. 50.

39. Panel Decision No. 69

40. See, e.g., Murray Chass, "The Yankees Have Met the Enemy and it is Tellem," *New York Times*, Nov. 10, 2005, p. D1.

41. George Vecsey, "Shadows of Doubt," *The New York Times*, Apr. 14, 2011, pp. B13, B14; Juliet Macur, "Bonds Guilty of Obstruction, But Not of Perjury," *The New York Times*, Apr. 14, 2011, pp. A1, B14; Lance Williams, "Bonds Is Guilty of Obstruction," *The San Francisco Chronicle*, Apr. 14, 2011, pp. A1, A8, A9.

42. Carol Pogish and Jere Longman, "Urine Samples Are Seized in BALCO Case," *New York Times*, April 10, 2004, pp. B7, B8.

43. "Baseball Shame," *New York Times*, March 6, 2004, p. A26.

44. Murray Chass, *New York Times*, March 7, 2005.

45. Murray Chass, "Congress Holds a Hearing and Invites Confusion," *New York Times*, March 18, 2005, p. A20.

46. Bruce Jenkins, "McGwire Helped Selig Dodge a Bullet," *San Francisco Chronicle*, March 19, 2005.

47. John Shea, "Selig Wonders: 'Is There Something I Missed?,'" *San Francisco Chronicle*, March 13, 2005, p. D3.

48. *San Jose Mercury News*, March 14, 2005.

49. Andrew Zimbalist, *In the Best Interest of Baseball? The Revolutionary Reign of Bud Selig* (2006), pp. 195, 198.

50. Chris Haft, "Bonds Swings for the Fences," *San Jose Mercury News*, Feb. 23, 2005, pp. 1D, 7D.

51. *Ibid.*

52. Richard Sandomir, "Congress Challenges Leagues on Their Drug Policies," *New York Times*, May 19, 2005, p. A28.

53. Lynn Zinser, *New York Times*, May 25, 2005, p. C20.

54. *United States v. Comprehensive Drug Testing, Inc.*, 513 F.3d 1085 (9th Cir. 2008); U.S. v. Comprehensive Drug Testing, Inc., 621 F.3d 1162 (9th Cir. En Banc 2010); and *U.S. v. Richardson*, 607 F.3d 357, 364–365 (4th Cir. June 11, 2010).

55. Email from Gene Orza to the author, June 12, 2010.

56. *United States of America v. Richardson*, 607 F.3d 357, 364–365 (4th Cir. June 11, 2010).

57. Murray Chass, "Testing For Steroids Ignores the 4th Amendment," *New York Times*, June 2, 2005, p. C23.

58. 943 F.2d 679 (7th Cir. 1991).

59. *Ibid.*, p. 681.

60. *Ibid.*, p. 682.

61. *Ibid.*, p. 685.

62. *Chandler v. Miller*, 520 U.S. 305 (1997).

63. Jack Curry, "Baseball Asserts That Fewer Players Failed Drug Tests," *New York Times*, August 11, 2006, p. C12.

64. Michael S. Schmidt, "M.L.B. Report Casts Doubt on Rigor of Drug Testing," *The New York Times*, May 6, 2011, p. B11.

65. "Bryant Says Drug Testing Does Not Apply to Him in Lawsuit," Associated Press, Oct. 17, 2007, available at http://sports.espn.go.com/nfl/news/story?id=3068435.

66. Jack Curry, "To Tighten Drug Tests, Teams Are Secretly Monitoring Players," *New York Times*, April 1, 2007, pp. 1, 7.

67. *Ibid.*, p. 1.

68. Michael S. Schmidt, "Baseball's Drug-Testing Policy, Pushed As Random, Alerts Teams," *New York Times*, October 31, 2007, pp. A1, A18.

69. *Ibid.*, p. 1.

70. Curry, supra note 63, p. 7.

71. SR-23.

72. Michael S. Schmidt, "New Tool Could Help in Testing for H.G.H.," *New York Times*, March 29, 2010, p. D1.

73. John Manuel and Josh Leventhal, "MLB Delays HGH Testing," *Baseball America*, March 22–April 4, 2010, p. 3.

74. Mark Fainaru-Wada and Lance Williams, Game of Shadows: *Barry Bonds and the Steroid Scandal that Rocked Professional Sports* (2006).

75. Report to the Commissioner of Baseball supra note 20, p. SR-1.

76. *Ibid.*, p. SR-7.

77. Yvonne Dennis, "A Sports Fan's Guide to Drug Testing," *Wall Street Journal*, Nov. 12, 2009.

78. Report to the Commissioner of Baseball supra note 20, p. SR-15.

79. *Ibid.*, p. SR-26–27. Mitchell noted that Greg Anderson appeared to have "correctly predicted the dates of testing for ... at least for his client Barry Bonds." SR-25.

80. *Ibid.*, p. SR-16.

81. *Ibid.*, p. SR-31.

82. *Ibid.*, p. SR-32.

83. *Ibid.*, pp. SR-44–46.

84. *Ibid.*, p. SR-33.

85. Michael S. Schmidt, "Selig Says Steroid Era is Over," *New York Times*, Jan. 12, 2010, p. B13.

86. William C. Rhoden, "Talking, not Tears, Will Heal Baseball," *New York Times*, Jan. 13, 2010, p. B13.

87. Murray Chass, "Mitchell Report Uncovered Little," *New York Times*, Dec. 18, 2007, p. C8.

88. Mitchell Nathanson, "Major League Baseball as Enron: The True Meaning of the Mitchell Report Outside the Lines," Oct. 19, 2008; available at http://works.bepress.com/cgi/viewcontent.cgi?article=1023&context=mitchell_nathanson&sei-redir=1#search="Nathanson,+à_œMajor+League+Baseball+as+Enron."

89. Michael S. Schmidt, "At Steroid Hearing, the Hot Topic is Stimulants," *New York Times*, Jan. 16, 2008, pp. A1, A14.

90. Michael S. Schmidt, "Number of Players Given Drug Exemptions Grows Slightly," *New York Times*, Dec. 2, 2009, p. B15.

91. Major League Baseball, Joint Drug Agreement, available at http://mlbplayers.mlb.com/pa/pdf/jda.pdf.

92. Mitchell S. Schmidt, "11 Months Later, Baseball is Praised," *New York Times*, Nov. 26, 2008, pp. B10, B13.

93. John Shea, "Mitchell Stands by Report, Satisfied with its Effects," *San Francisco Chronicle*, Nov. 26, 2008, pp. D1, D6.

94. Murray Chass, "Clemens Pays Price for Reputation that is Soiled," *New York Times*, Feb. 17, 2008, p. 2.

95. "Fisk Takes Some Rips: McGwire and Clemens Targets," *Boston Globe*, Jan. 21, 2010, Sports, p. 3.

96. "Jenkins: McGwire Owes many apologies," ESPN.com: Baseball, Jan. 21, 2010, p. 1.

97. John Rocker, Major League Baseball Players Association and the Commissioner of Major League Baseball, Panel Decision No. 104 (John Rocker), (Nov. 30, 2000) (Emphasis supplied).

98. *Williams v. National Football League*, 582 F.3d 863 (8th Cir. 2009).

99. Sports Anti-Doping Programs, Hearing before the Subcommittee on Commerce, Trade, and Consumer Protection to examine the National Football Leagues (NFL), StarCaps case, focusing on whether sports' anti-doping programs are at a legal crossroads, 111th Cong. (2009) (not yet assigned) (testimony of Roger Goodell).

100. See, e.g., Barry R. Furrow, "The Problem of the Sports Doctor: Serving Two (Or Is It Three or Four?) Masters," 50 *St. Louis U. L.J.* 185 (2005); Steve P. Calandrillo, "Sports Medicine Conflicts: Team Physicians vs. Athlete-Patients," 50 *St. Louis U. L.J.* (2005); Mathew J. Mitten, *Team Physicians as Co-employees: A Prescription That Deprives Professional Athletes of an Adequate Remedy for Sports Medicine Malpractice*, 50 *St. Louis U. L.J.* 211 (2005).

101. Montville, *The Big Bam*.

102. William C. Rhoden, "Big Fish May Be Easier Targets," *New York Times*, November 19, 2007, p. D7.

103. Timothy M. Gay, "The Worst of Times? Not Bonds' Assault on History," ESPN.com, May 8, 2006. Mr. Gay also mentions a number of World Series outside of the 1919 Black Sox Scandal, including the performance of Smoky Joe Wood in the above-mentioned 1912 Red Sox–Giants finale.

104. William B. Gould IV, Op-ed, "Now Someone Needs to Penalize the Fans," *San Jose Mercury News*, Nov. 26, 2004, p. 11C.

105. In the Matter of the Arbitration between National basketball Players Assoc. and National Basketball Assoc (Ron Artest, Stephen Jackson, Anthony Johnson, Jermaine O'Neal) (Case No. 04-3) (Dec. 21, 2004) (Kaplan, arb.), p. 22.

106. *Ibid.*, p. 23.

107. *Ibid.*, p. 23–24.

108. Gould, "Now Someone Needs to Penalize the Fans," p. 11C.

109. See, e.g., "NBA, Union to Argue O'Neal Suspension Ruling," Associated Press, Dec. 22, 2004, available at http://www.usatoday.com/sports/basketball/nba/2004-12-22-arbitration-ban-reduction_x.htm.

110. In the Matter of the Arbitration between National basketball Players Assoc. and National Basketball Assoc (Ron Artest, Stephen Jackson, Anthony Johnson, Jermaine O'Neal) (Case No. 04-3) (Dec. 21, 2004) (Kaplan, arb.), pp. 16–17.

111. 2007–2011 Basic Agreement, Art. XI, § (1)(b) (Grievance Procedure), available at http://mlbplayers.mlb.com/pa/pdf/cba_english.pdf.

112. Clyde Haberman, "Throw Out the Bums ... in the Stands," *New York Times*, Oct. 11, 2005, p. A21.

113. *Ibid.*

114. Clyde Haberman, "In New Park, It's Yankees vs. the Boors," *New York Times*, April 14, 2006, p. A20.

115. Williams C. Rhoden, "Sheffield Did Right. So Should Baseball," *New York Times*, April 16, 2005, pp. B11, B13.

116. Michael S. Schmidt, "Binoculars in Bullpen? The Phillies Are Accused of Stealing Signs Illegally," *New York Times*, May 13, 2010, at B15.

117. *Ibid.*

Chapter 8

1. Jules Tygiel, *Jackie Robinson and his Legacy* (1984).

2. John Virtue, *South of the Color Barrier* (2008).

3. Larry Tye, *Satchel: The Life and Times of an American Legend* (2009).

4. *Ibid.*, p. 19.

5. Montville, *The Big Bam*.

6. Tygiel supra note 1, pp. 39–43.

7. *Ibid.*, p. 41. Some have contended that Landis was no different from anyone else in this period. See Norman L. Macht, "Does Baseball Deserve This Black Eye?," *The Baseball Research Journal* 38, No. 1 (Summer 2009): p. 26.

8. See, e.g., Lee Lowenfish, *Branch Rickey: Baseball's Ferocious Gentleman* (2007).

9. This theory was memorialized infamously in *Plessy v. Ferguson*, 163 U.S. 537, (1896).

10. 347 U.S. 483 (1954).

11. William B. Gould IV, quoting Leonard Koppett "In Memoriam, Leonard Koppett, 1923–2003," July 13, 2003; available at http://www.sportsradioservice.com/misc/misc-071303.html (Last visited September 14, 2010.

12. John Klima, "Not ready for Willie Mays: Yankees ignored black players; Giants had their eyes open," *New York Times*, Sept. 13, 2009, p. 3.

13. *Ibid.*

14. Steve Treder, "The Persistent Color Line: Specific Instances of Racial Preference in Major League Player Evaluation Decisions after 1947," *Nine* 10, no. 1 (2001).

15. Some of what follows on Pumpsie Green will appear as a chapter in a book about him later in 2011 or 2012.

16. "It's So Long Abdul-Jabbar, Hello Cowens," *Boston Globe*, October 17, 1973, p. 53.

17. Will McDonough. "Sox Racist? Says Who? Harper Case No Proof," *Boston Globe*, Apr. 17, 1986.

18. *Ibid.*

19. An extended discussion of claims that could be asserted against MLB is found in N. Jeremi Duru, "Exploring Jethroe's Injustice," 76 *University of Cincinnati L. Rev.* 793 (2008).

20. 447 F.3d 748 (9th Cir. 2006).

21. *Ibid.*

22. *Ibid.* p. 754–55.

23. *Ibid.* p. 757.

22. *Ibid.*

25. Harvey Araton, "Deflating Season, but Proof of Progress," *New York Times*, Nov. 29, 2008, pp. B9, B10.

26. However, according to 2009 data, "the percentage of black pitchers rose to 5 percent from 3 percent and the percentage of black infielders went up to 9 percent from 7 percent": Mike Fitzpatrick, "Percentage of black players in MLB rises," Associated Press, Apr. 15, 2009.

27. Fitzpatrick, "Percentage of black players in MLB rises." A more extended discussion is contained in Richard Lapchick, "The 2009 Racial and Gender Report Card: Major League Baseball," Apr. 15, 2009, located at: http://web.bus.ucf.edu/documents/sport/2009_rgrcmlb.pdf.

28. Lapchick, "The 2010 Racial and Gender Report

Card: Major League Baseball," April 29, 2010.

29. John Shea, "Big Leagues a black hole for African Americans," *San Francisco Chronicle*, April 18, 2004, p. C7.

30. Tom Verducci, "Blackout, the African-American Baseball Player is Vanishing. Does He Have a Future?," *Sports Illustrated*, July 7, 2003, p. 56.

31. Ben Walker, "Relatively Small Number of Blacks in Game Concerns Joe Morgan: Diversity in Baseball," *San Francisco Chronicle*, October 26, 2005, p. D4.

32. Again, however, as noted above, there are some signs of improvement: see William C. Rhoden, "The Rays Show the Way for African-American Players," *New York Times*, Oct. 17, 2008, p. B15.

33. Murray Chass, "Fewer Blacks Are Turning to Baseball," *New York Times*, April 19, 2004, p. D5.

34. Senior thesis of Darren Lewis, May 11, 2009 at University of San Francisco: "The Globalization of Baseball: The Rise and Fall of the Black Player in Major League History."

35. James Wagner, "Baseball's Other Racial Barrier: Latino Players Forge a Big-League Presence, but Are a Rarity on College Rosters," *Wall Street Journal*, June 24, 2008, p. A14.

36. Jeff Schultz, "Sheffield Nonsense Not Easy to Handle," *Atlanta Journal-Constitution*, Jun. 5, 2007, p. 1C.

37. Harvey Araton, "Sheffield Bares Truth on Culture of Yankees," *New York Times*, August 17, 2007, p. C11.

38. Jeff Passan, "Even perceived slights can harm Robinson's legacy," April 15, 2010, Yahoo! Sports.

39. Pat Borzi, "Black Players Often Stand Alone in College Baseball," *New York Times*, June 25, 2005.

40. *Ibid.*

41. William B. Gould IV, "Time for Affirmative Action: Baseball urged to seek out, train Blacks as managers and executives," *San Francisco Chronicle*, Jul. 6, 1986, p. C-8.

42. See generally Joe Kay, "Reds' Part Owner: Hiring of Baker is 'Historic,'" *San Francisco Chronicle*, Oct. 17, 2007, p. D7; John Shea, "For Baker, Cincy is the Place to Be," San Francisco Chronicle, Oct. 16, 2007, p. C5; "Baker Likes New Look with Reds," *New York Times*, Oct. 16, 2007, p. C19.

43. Murray Chass, "Selig Allows Dodgers to Bypass Hiring Rules," *New York Times*, Nov. 1, 2007.

44. Murray Chass, "In Hunt for Managers, Interviews Often Become A Formality," *New York Times*, November 14, 2004, p. 7: "Commissioner Bud Selig has ordered clubs to include minority candidates in their interviewing process but often clubs go through the motions with no intention of hiring them. "Before he was named the manager of the Mets earlier this month, Willie Randolph was interviewed for a dozen managing jobs, and many of them turned out to be sham interviews. On the day he was supposed to be interviewed for the Colorado job, the Rockies announced that they had hired Buddy Bell, making the announcement because word had leaked to the news media. 'Mr. O'Dowd,' Randolph recalled, referring to Dan O'Dowd, the Rockies' general manager, 'called me and said, "Can we do this on the phone?"' This is not the kind of interview Selig had in mind when he issued his directive in 1999. On the other hand, Selig said he was satisfied that the Mariners had met their obligation."

45. Michael S. Schmidt and Andrew Keh, "Baseball's Praised Diversity Is Stranded At First Base," *New York Times*, Aug. 11, 2010.

46. "The 2009 Racial and Gender Report Card: Major League Baseball."

47. "Selig Rebuffs Calls to Move 2011 All-Star Game," *New York Times*, May 14, 2010, p. B13.

48. See generally *International B'hood of Teamsters v. U.S.*, 431 U.S. 324 (1977).

Chapter 9

1. See generally Echevarria, *The Pride of Havana*; Jason S. Weiss, "The Changing Face of Baseball: In an Age of Globalization, Is Baseball Still as American as Apple Pie and Chevrolet?," 8 *U. Miami Int'l & Comp. L. Rev.* 123 (1999–2000); Scott M. Cwiertny, "The Need for a Worldwide Draft: Major League Baseball and Its Relationship with the Cuban Embargo and United States Foreign Policy," 20 *Loy. L.A. Ent. L. Rev.* 391 (2000).

2. See William C. Rhoden, "Nonstars All, Americans Dethrone Cuba," *New York* Times, Sept. 28, 2000, p. S1.

3. See Frederick C. Klein, "On the Game: The Italians' Spicy Brand of Baseball," *Wall Street* Journal, Sept. 21, 2000, p. A8. Less improbable countries are involved. See Henri E. Cauvin, "Baseball Gets Serious in a New South Africa," *New York Times*, June 27, 2000, pp. A25, A28, where it may be assumed that baseball was passed on through the U.S. military in World War II.

4. Tom Verducci, "Inside Baseball," *Sports Illustrated*, March 27, 2006, p. 70.

5. Jens Erik Gould, "Venezuela Eyes Moment in the Sun at the Classic," *New York Times*, March 1, 2006, p. C17.

6. See Steven Krasner, "Red Sox Go East For Help: Asian Pitchers Form Big Part of Future," *San Jose Mercury News*, June 5, 1999, p. 1D; Tony Massorotti, "Korean Pipeline," *Baseball America*, Mar. 15–28, 1999, p. 25. See also "Red Sox dive into Taiwan market," *Baseball America*, Nov. 13–26, 2000, p. 4. With regard to other teams, such as the Chicago Cubs, see Bruce Rives, "South Korean Connection," *Baseball America*, January 10–23, 2000, at 33.

7. See Murray Chass, "Scouts Search Globe for Talent," *New York Times*, Apr. 8, 1998, p. C3. Professor Andrew Zimbalist has noted the talent compression fueled by Jackie Robinson in 1947, the black and Latin players who came in his wake, and the reversal of that phenomenon through "decompression" of talent that has facilitated an environment in which today McGwires, Sosas, Rodriguezes, Martinezes and Wells can more easily excel. Equally important, when the better players can more reliably outperform the others, it becomes easier to buy a winning team. It is one thing for the Yankees to generate $176 million in local revenue while the Expos generate $12 million. If Steinbrenner and Cashman spend their budget on underperforming, overpriced players, then the Yankees will squander their revenue advantage. Yet, the more individual players consistently stand out, the more difficult it is for inept management to squander a revenue advantage: State of Competition in Major League Baseball, Hearing before the Subcommittee on Antitrust, Business Rights, and Competition, of the Senate Committee on the Judiciary, 106th Cong., p. 7 (2000) (testimony of Andrew Zimbalist) [hereinafter Zimbalist Testimony] [on file with author]. The recruitment of foreign players may compress talent and, thus, facilitate a more competitive balance. Contra, Jonathan Mahler, "Why A-Rod's Contract is Good for Baseball," *New York* Times, Dec. 17, 2000, P. 6; Bob Ryan, "Economic Inequality A Reality of Baseball," *San Francisco Chronicle*, Dec. 16, 2000, p. E10 (emphasizing the historic baseball inequalities involving the Washington Senators, Philadel-

phia Athletics, and St. Louis Browns, and the preeminence of the New York Yankees). Cf. Murray Chass, "One Man's Journey From Earning Thousands to Spending Millions," *New York Times* (Sports), Dec. 17, 2000, p. 48; John Feinstein, "Can Baseball Survive the $250 Million Man?," *Wall Street* Journal, Dec. 15, 2000, p. A16; Jack Curry, "By Adding Ramirez, Red Sox Spice Up Baseball's Best Rivalry," *New York Times*, Dec. 13, 2000, p. C21; Murray Chass, "Rodriguez Strikes It Rich In Texas," *New York Times*, Dec. 12, 2000, p. C27; Murray Chass and Tyler Kepner, "Rockies to Show Hampton How High Is Up," *New York Times*, Dec. 9, 2000, p. B19; "Baseball's Unfair Economics," *New York Times*, Dec. 5, 2000, p. C30; Buster Olney and Jack Curry, "The Yankees Draw Their Fourth Ace," *New York Times*, Dec. 1, 2000, p. C17. It is interesting to note that the celebrated Rodriguez contract will be paid by the Rangers' new television contract. See Richard Sandomir, "How Can Rangers Afford So Much T.V.?," *New York Times*, Dec. 12, 2000, p. C29. "We do know that Fox Sports Net supplied the cash with which the Rangers could make the Rodriguez deal; last year, FSN bought the rights to the Rangers and Dallas Stars hockey broadcasts for $250 million over 10 years — do these numbers sound familiar? — and there may be clauses for re-negotiating in case of higher ratings": Allen Barra, "An Overpaid A-Rod?," *Wall Street* Journal, Dec. 15, 2000, p. W4.

8. See Masaru Ikei, "Baseball, Besuboru, Yakyu: Comparing the American and Japanese Games," 8 *Ind. J. Global Legal Stud.* 73, 79 (2000).

9. James C. McKinley Jr., "Cuban Players Defect, but Often With a Cost," *New York Times*, April 25, 1999, § 1, p. 3; cf. Murray Chass, "Cubans Freed From Pact After Dodgers Break Rule," *New York Times*, June 29, 1999, p. C30.

10. Indeed, the Korean players have attempted — apparently without success — to establish their own union in Korea. Thomas St. John, "Korean Players Start Union, Lose Their Jobs," *Baseball America*, Feb. 21— Mar. 5, 2000, p. 5.

11. See Zimbalist Testimony supra note 6, p. 7, which takes note of "the emergence of new franchise owners who also own international communications networks or are attempting to build regional sports channels. These owners value their ballplayers not only by the value they produce on the field, but they produce for their networks. When Rupert Murdock signed 33-year-old Kevin Brown to a seven-year deal worth an average $15 million annually, he was thinking about the News Corp's emerging influence via satellite television in the huge Asian market."

12. See Michael Martinez, "Game's Global Appeal Gathers Momentum," *San Jose Mercury News*, Mar. 30, 2000, available at LEXIS, News Group, All. In 1997, the number of foreign born players was 19 percent. The percentage of foreign first year contracts is 40 percent. See the Report of the Independent Members of the Commissioner's Blue Ribbon Panel on Baseball Economics, at 41, July 2000 (R. Levin, G. Mitchell, P. Volcker, G. Will) [hereinafter Blue Ribbon Panel] (on file with the author).

13. http://mlb.mlb.com/news/press_releases/press_rel ease.jsp?ymd=20070403&content_id=1877328&vkey=pr _mlb&fext=.jsp&c_id=mlb.

14. Szymanski and Andrew, *National Pastime*, p. 49.

15. Szymanski and Zimbalist, pp. 52–53, 83.

16. Szymanski and Zimbalist, pp. 63–64.

17. David Halberstam, *Summer of '49*, pp. 237, 250.

18. Ray Glier, "In draft, school of thought shifting toward prep players," *USA Today*, Aug. 12, 2010, p. 2C.

19. Ken Belson, "In N.F.L, a Team's Wealth Says Little About Its Record," *New York Times*, Dec. 25, 2010, p. B8.

20. Belatedly, the MLB seems to be paying some attention to this problem. Jeff Passan, "Alderson addresses Dominican corruption," Yahoo! Sports, April 22, 2010.

21. Arturo J. Marcano and David P. Fidler, "Global Baseball: Latin America," in Leonard Cassuto, ed., *The Cambridge Companion to Baseball* (2011).

22. "New rules aimed at curtailing steroid use and age fraud among baseball prospects in the Dominican Republic, have reduced the number of elite Dominican teenage players being signed to contracts by Major League Baseball teams and the size of their signing bonuses": Michael S. Schmidt, "Crackdown Dampens Dominican's Prospects," *New York Times*, Oct. 10, 2010, pp. 1, 8.

23. Blue Ribbon Panel, supra note 12, p. 41.

24. However, the small-market teams like the Cincinnati Reds and the Oakland A's appear to have moved into a vacuum vacated by the Red Sox and the Yankees with regard to foreign players on whom a club would have to take a great chance. See Tyler Kepner, "Reds Win Bidding for a Potential Ace from Cuba," *New York Times*, Jan. 12, 2010.

25. Shawn Hoffman, "Make the World Go 'Round: The Sketchy Economics of an International Draft," *Baseball Prospectus*, Mar. 12, 2009.

26. *Ibid.*, p. 2.

27. Hoffman, "Make the World Go 'Round," p. 2.

28. Keith Reid, "Sox Have Dice-K But Rivals Reaping Add Dollars," *Boston Globe*, April 25, 2007.

29. Ken Belson, "The Bases Have Been Circled," *New York Times*, Sept. 16, 2003, pp. C15, C19.

30. Masaru Ikei, "The Ichiro Effect," *New York Times*, July 9, 2001, p. A19.

31. William C. Rhoden, "Japan Can Learn From Fate of Negro Leagues," *New York Times*, August 18, 2001, pp. B15, B16.

32. David Pinto, "The Big Picture: Raiding or Raising the East," *Baseball Prospectus*, September 5, 2007.

33. William B. Gould IV, "Baseball and Globalization: The Game Played and Heard and Watched 'Round the World (With Apologies to Soccer and Bobby Thompson)," 8 *Ind. J. Global Legal Studies* 85 (2000).

34. "The World Champs Go Global," *New York Times*, Feb. 19, 2001, p. A20.

35. Gregory Zuckerman and David Enrich, "Red Sox Chief's Bid for Liverpool Triggers British Boardroom Brawl," *Wall Street Journal*, Oct. 6, 2010, p. 31; John Authers, "The Trader Who Saw Red," Financial Times (London), Oct. 9, 2010, p. 7.

36. Tom O'Sullivan, "NFL agrees link with Barcelona," *Financial Times*, Jan. 31, 2002, p. 17.

37. See Murray Chass, "High Priced Orioles Humiliated by Cubans," *New York Times*, May 5, 1999, p. D5; James C. McKinley Jr., with Mireya Navarro, "Fans in Cuba Walking Tall Despite Loss," *New York Times*, Mar. 29, 1999, p. A1; Murray Chass, "Cubans Match Big Leaguers Pitch for Pitch, but Lose in 11," *New York Times*, Mar. 29, 1999, p. D1; Mireya Navarro, "Old Enemies Puncture Baseball Détente in Cuba," *New York Times*, Mar. 28, 1999, § 1, p. 6; Tim Wendel, "A Chance for Cubans to See Major Leaguers," *New York Times*, Mar. 14, 1999, § 8, p. 2; Tina Rosenberg, "Beating the Yanquis at Their Game: How the Politics of Beisbol Serve the Revolution," *New York Times*, Jan. 11, 1999, p. A1. For a discussion of Cuban defections to the U.S., see Murray Chass, "Cuban Players Scorn Those Who Defected," *New York Times*, Mar. 29, 1999, p. D5; James C. McKinley Jr., "Cuban Players Defect, but Often With a Cost,"

supra note 9.

38. See Michael Gee, "The Sydney Games; Cuba? No Cigar—It's USA—Sheets Keys 4–0 Stunner on Diamond," *Boston Herald*, Sept. 28, 2000, p. 86.

39. See "Angelos Trying to Bring Baseball to Greece," *New York Times*, Sept. 8, 1999, p. A27; Theodora Tongas, "An Olympian Task: Pitching Baseball to Greece," *Chicago Tribune*, Jan. 6, 2000, p. C8.

40. See Sam Dillon, "Beisbol, Si! But Can U.S. Players Drink the Water?," *New York Times*, Mar. 31, 1999, p. A3.

41. But this event was met with some player and public protest or dissent and may well highlight the unlikelihood of an international franchise relocation expansion. Murray Chass, "Some Can't Warm Up to the Global Outlook," *New York Times*, Sept. 27, 2000, p. 30; Murray Chass, "McGwire Criticizes the Opener in Japan and Cites Greed," *New York Times*, Mar. 3, 2000, p. A25; Nicholas Dawdioff, "The International Pastime," *New York Times*, Mar. 3, 2000, p. A31. Cf. Tyler Kepner, "Traveling to Japan Can Raise the Psyche," *New York Times*, Mar. 25, 2000, p. B16. Of course, a Japanese franchise in MLB, aside from problems of cultural imperialism and national sensibilities discussed below, would present formidable time zone problems for players and the public. And the other discussed possibility, Mexico City, contains problems of its own. Indeed, rather than potential expansion on relocation to other countries, there are now rumblings about major league contraction of franchises in North America. See Murray Chass, "The Whispers Turn to Talk of Eliminating Teams," *New York Times*, Dec. 10, 2000, p. 46. Cf. *First National Maintenance Corp v. NLRB*, 452 U.S. 666 (1981); William B. Gould IV, "The Supreme Court's Labor and Employment Docket in the October 1980 Term; Justice Brennan's Term," 53 *U. Colo. L. Rev.* 1, 3–18 (1981).

42. John Vinocur, "Continental Divide," *New York Times*, July 19, 2003, p. B18.

43. *Ibid.*

44. Henri E. Cauvin, "Baseball Gets Serious in a New South Africa," *New York Times*, June 27, 2000, pp. A25, A28.

45. *Ibid.*

46. Brian Murphy, "The Crack of the Bat in Iran," *International Herald Tribune*, June 25, 2001, pp. 1, 4.

47. Kirk Semple, "Baseball in Iraq: As Pastimes Go, It's Anything But," *New York Times*, September 7, 2005, pp. A1, A10.

48. See *American League Baseball Club of New York, Inc. v. Pasquel*, 187 Misc. 230, 63 N.Y.S. 2d 537 (May 20, 1946); *American League Baseball Club of New York, Inc. v. Pasquel*, 188 Misc. 102, 66 N.Y.S. 2d 743 (Nov. 25, 1946); *Brooklyn Nat'l League Baseball Club Inc. v. Pasquel*, 66 F. Supp. 117 (E.D. Missouri) (1946). The emergence of the American League at the turn of the previous century, *Philadelphia v. Lajoie*, 202 Pa. 210, 51 Atl. 973; the Federal League, *American Baseball Club of Chicago v. Chase*, 86 Misc. 441, 149 N.Y.S. 6 (July 21, 1914) and spawned earlier controversy. The Mexican League produced litigation by American players who were blacklisted in this country more directly implicating antitrust law. *Gardella v. Chandler*, 172 F. 2d 402 (2nd Cir. 1949); *Martin v. National League Baseball Club*, 174 F. 2d 917 (2nd Cir. 1949).

49. *Boston Celtics, LP v. Brian Shaw*, 908 F. 2d 1041 (1st Cir. 1990). See Winnipeg *Rugby Club v. Freeman*, 140 F. Supp. 365 (N.D. Ohio 1995), where the court enjoined players from playing with the Cleveland Browns of the NFL in breach of contracts with a Canadian Football

League (CFL) team on the grounds that the players were more valuable to the CFL team because of the relatively inferior play in that league. This reasoning could be applicable to Japanese, Korean, Australian, Cuban or other Latin players who are sued for breaching their contracts when they come to the United States. Cf. *Mid-South Grizzlies v. NFL*, 720 F. 2d 772 (3rd Cir. 1983).

50. *Jugoplastika Basketball Club v. Boston Celtics Ltd. P'ship*, Civil Action No. 89-1889-WD (Nov. 21, 1989). See Peter May, "Radja 'Allowed' to Play in Italy," *Boston Globe*, Aug. 3, 1990, p. 43.

51. *Van Exel v. USA Basketball*, H-98-4306 (S.D. Texas 1998). For discussion of similar problems in soccer, see Edward Mathias, "Big League Perestroika? The Implications of *Fraser v. Major League Soccer*," 148 *U. Pa. L. Rev.* 203 (1999); Lee Goldman, "Sports, Antitrust, and the Single Entity Theory," 63 *Tul. L. Rev.* 751 (1989).

52. Murray Chass, "Padres Strike Deal With Team in Japan," *New York Times*, Jan. 16, 1997, p. B13.

53. Murray Chass, "Irabu of Japan Inching Nearer to the Yankees," *New York Times*, Mar. 13, 1997, at B13.

54. 809 F.2d 954 (2nd Cir. 1987).

55. *Ibid.*, p. 956.

56. *Ibid.*, p. 959.

57. The leading hiring-hall case relating to the question of whether the hiring hall is a mandatory subject of bargaining within the meaning of the Act is Houston Chapter, Associated General Contractors (Houston AGC), 143 NLRB 409 (1963), enf'd 349 F. 2d 449 (5th Cir. 1965).

58. *Ibid.*, p. 960.

59. *Ibid.*, p. 960.

60. *Phelps Dodge Corp. v. NLRB*, 313 U.S. 177 (1941).

61. 295 NLRB 543 (1989).

62. The NLRB distinguished the facts of *Star Tribune* from those cases, such as *Westinghouse Electric Corp.*, 239 NLRB 106 (1978), enforced as modified sub nom. *Electrical Workers* IUE v. NLRB, 648 F. 2d 18 (D.C. Cir. 1980), and *East Dayton tool and Die Co.*, 239 NLRB 141 (1978), which affirmed an employer's obligation to bargain with the union over nondiscrimination policies with respected to applicants based in part on Congress's expression that antidiscrimination is an important goal of national collective bargaining policy, notwithstanding its concurrent embodiment in Title VII. The NLRB in *Star Tribune* too recognized the national policy goals in support of nondiscrimination and the compelling interest of unions in keeping discrimination out of the workplace. *Star Tribune*, 295 NLRB at 548–49. However, there the NLRB found a "significant difference" between a union's ability to address its concern over a work environment free of drug use, which might be accomplished through post-hire physical exams, and its inability to address discrimination concerns beyond the applicancy phase. *Ibid.* at 549.

63. See *Johnson-Bateman Co.*, 295 NLRB 180 (1989).

64. *Hertz Corporation*, 319 NLRB 597 (1995) enforcement denied 105 F. 3d 868 (3d Cir. 1997); cf. *NLRB v. U.S. Postal Service*, 18 F. 3d 1089 (3rd Cir. 1994).

65. 67 F. 3d 1054 (2d Cir. 1995).

66. *Ibid.*, pp. 1061–62.

67. 369 F. 3d 124 (2d Cir. 2004).

68. *Ibid.*, p. 134.

69. Major League Baseball Players Association and the twenty-eight major league clubs (Amateur draft) (Aug. 19, 1992).

70. *Ibid.*, pp. 15–16.

71. Major League Baseball Players Association and the twenty-eight major league clubs (Amateur draft) (June 10, 1993).

72. Major League Baseball Players Association and the thirty major league clubs (May 18, 1998).

73. *Ibid.*, p. 27.

74. Klein, "On the Game: The Italians' Spicy Brand of Baseball," supra note 3.

75. Calvin Sims, "Japanese Leagues Fret About Being Overshadowed," *New York Times*, Mar. 30, 2000.

76. But the bidding mechanism appears to be gaining in its use, perhaps affecting players who are about to be eligible for free agency when the leverage of the Japanese team may be enhanced, because the player is contractually obliged to play in Japan. See Murray Chass, "Majors are Scrambling for Japanese Outfielder: Suzuki Would Cross Divide as Position Player," *New York Times*, Nov. 2, 2000, p. C25. The Seattle Mariners recently won the bidding war for the coveted Japanese player Ichiro Suzuki, with an offer of over $13 million. See Murray Chass, "Mariners Gain Rights to Sign Suzuki, Outbidding Mets and 2 Others," *New York Times*, Nov. 10, 2000, p. C21. Soon thereafter, the Mariners signed him. "In a First, Mariners Sign Japan's Suzuki, An Outfielder," *New York Times*, Nov. 19, 2000, p. 41.

77. On these abuses, see Arturo J. Marcano Guevara and David P. Fidler, *Stealing Lives: The Globalization of Baseball and the Tragic Story of Alexis Quiroz* (2002); Samuel O. Regalado, "'Latin Players on the Cheap:' Professional Baseball Recruitment in Latin America and the Neocolonialist Tradition," 8 *Ind. J. Global Legal Stud.* 9, pp. 11–19 (2000): Angel Vargas, "The Globalization of Baseball: A Latin American Perspective," 8 *Ind. J. Global Legal Stud.* 21, pp. 29–33 (2000); Arturo J. Marcano and David P. Fidler, "The Globalization of Baseball: Major League Baseball and the Mistreatment of Latin American Baseball Talent," 6 *Ind. J. Global Legal Stud.* 511 (1999).

78. See Sports Digest, *San Francisco Chronicle*, Jan. 12, 2000, p. E6 ("Nobuaki Yoshida, an 18-year-old Japanese left-hander, agreed to a minor-league contract with the San Diego Padres and will report to extended spring training in April following his graduation from high school").

79. Alan Schwarz and Brad Lefton, "Japanese Are Irked by U.S. Interest in Pitcher," *New York Times*, Nov. 20, 2008, pp. B12, B14.

80. "Kyodo News, NTB, Players to Revise Free-Agency System," *Japan Times*, June 26, 2008, available at http://search.japantimes.co.jp/cgi-bin/sb20080626j1.html.

81. To date Borchard has not realized his promise shown at Stanford, not making it with the White Sox and moving on waivers to the Seattle Mariners and Florida Marlins.

82. *Ibid.*, p. 3.

83. See 15 U.S.C. § 27a. Many baseball experts have called for an international draft in the past.

84. However, this view is inconsistent with *Mackey v. NFL*, 543 F.2d 606 (8th Cir. 1976) and its progeny.

85. This statement was made by Gene Orza in my Stanford Law School seminar in 2008.

86. *North American Soccer League* 236 NLRB 1317 (1978).

87. *Silverman v. Major League Baseball Player Relations Comm., Inc.*, 880 F. Supp. 246 (S.D.N.Y. 1995), aff'd, 67 F. 3d 1054 (2d Cir. 1995).

88. *National Basketball Association*, No. 2-RD 1354 (July 26, 1995).

89. See Richard Sandomir, "Union Umps Make Call on Replacements," *New York Times*, Apr. 27, 1995, p. B12.

90. See Clifton Brown, "NBA Refs Get New Offer," *New York Times*, Nov. 17, 1995, p. B18.

91. British Columbia Labour Relations Board, BCLRB No. B172/2007, Jul. 31, 2007. The author was an expert witness for the National Hockey League in this Vancouver, British Columbia, proceeding.

92. *Williams v. National Football League*, 582 F. 3d 863 (8th Cir. 2009).

93. William B. Gould IV, "Baseball Classic Mirrors World Events," *San Jose Mercury News*, Mar. 20, 2006, p. 13A.

94. William C. Rhoden, "Selig Looks to Classic to Cement His Legacy," *New York Times*, Mar. 23, 2009, p. D5.

95. Alan Schwarz, "Scouts See Works of Art in Asian team's Workouts," *New York Times*, Mar. 19, 2009, p. D17.

96. Paul White, "WBC Seeks Tweaks for 2013 Tournament," *USA Today*, Mar. 25, 2009, p. 10C.

97. *Ibid.*

Conclusion

1. It was President Taft, after all, who made the classic comment which lives with us today: "Any man who would choose a day's work over a day of baseball is a fool not worthy of friendship." Vaccaro, *The First Fall Classic*, p. 158.

2. For a good explanation of the history and rationale for the new defensive statistics see Joe Posnanski, Defensive Numbers, joeposnanski.com, posted on Aug. 11, 2010.

3. Professional Baseball Umpire Corporation (PBUC) Case 12-CA-26612 (July 30, 2010). The Board's General Counsel concluded that the employer could implement and enforce a background policy without bargaining with the union inasmuch as the union had clearly and unmistakably waived its right to bargain over both the policy itself as well as its effects.

4. "George Mitchell Denies Paul Byrd Leak About HGH," Associated Press, Oct. 23, 2007, available at http://www.nydailynews.com/sports/baseball/2007/10/23/2007-10-23_george_mitchell_denies_paul_byrd_leak_ab-1.html

5. Jack McCallum, "Game-Fixing and Dogfighting Rock Pro Sports (AND BARRY BONDS MARCHES ON)," *Sports Illustrated*, Jul. 30, 2007, p. 34.

6. Here he seems to have tapped into what many believe: "[I]n most other places losers transform to winners almost overnight, and every new opening day brings indomitable new hope." Michael Medved, "What the

Bibliography

Abrams, Roger I. *Constructing Baseball: Boston and the First World Series* (2002).

_____. *The Dark Side of the Diamond: Gambling, Violence, Drugs and Alcoholism in the National Pastime* (2007).

_____. *The First World Series and the Baseball Fanatics of 1903* (2003).

_____. *Legal Bases: Baseball and the Law* (1998).

_____. *Sports Justice: The Law & the Business of Sports* (2010).

Adler, David A., et al. *Satchel Paige: Don't Look Back* (2010).

Alexander, Charles C. *Breaking the Slump: Baseball in the Depression Era* (2002).

Angell, Roger. *Late Innings: A Baseball Companion* (1982).

Asinof, Eliot. *Eight Men Out: The Black Sox and the 1919 World Series* (1963).

_____. *Man on Spikes* (1955).

Balliett, Will, and Thomas Dyja, eds. *The Hard Way: Writing by the Rebels Who Changed Sports* (1999).

Barnes, John. *The Law of Hockey* (2010).

Barra, Allen. *Brushbacks and Knockdowns: The Greatest Baseball Debates of Two Centuries* (2005).

Barthel, Thomas. *Baseball Barnstorming and Exhibition Games, 1901–1962: A History of Off-Season Major League Play* (2007).

Benson, Robert. *The Game: One Man, Nine Innings, a Love Affair with Baseball* (2001).

Berri, David, et al. *The Wages of Wins: Taking Measure of the Many Myths in Modern Sport* (2007).

Berry, Robert C., William B. Gould IV, et al. *Labor Relations in Professional Sports* (1986).

Bissinger, Buzz, et al. *Three Nights in August: Strategy, Heartbreak, and Joy Inside the Mind of a Manager* (2005).

Boswell, Thomas. *The Heart of the Order* (1989).

_____. *How Life Imitates the World Series: Featuring the New Statistic, Total Average* (1982).

Bourg, Jean-Francois, and Jean-Jacques Gouguet. *The Political Economy of Professional Sport* (2010).

Bouton, Jim, and Len Shecter, ed. *Ball Four* (1970).

Bowman, Larry G. *Before the World Series: Pride, Profits, and Baseball's First Championships* (2003).

Bradbury, Mark. *The Baseball Economist: The Real Game Exposed* (2007).

Breslin, Jimmy. *Branch Rickey* (2011).

Bryant, Howard. *Juicing the Game: Drugs, Power, and the Fight for the Soul of Major League Baseball* (2005).

_____. *The Last Hero: A Life of Henry Aaron* (2010).

_____. *Shut Out: A Story of Race and Baseball in Boston* (2002).

Burgos, Adrian, Jr. *Cuban Star* (2011).

Burk, Robert F. *Never Just a Game: Players, Owners, and American Baseball to 1920* (1994).

_____. *Much More Than a Game: Players, Owners, and American Baseball Since 1921* (2001).

Carroll, Will. *Juice: The Real Story of Baseball's Drug Problems* (2005).

Carter, David M. *Money Games: Profiting from the Convergence of Sports and Entertainment* (2010).

Cassuto, Leonard, ed. *The Cambridge Companion to Baseball* (2011).

Castiglione, Joe, and Douglas B. Lyons. *Broadcast Rites and Sites: I Saw It on the Radio with the Boston Red Sox* (2004).

Cataneo, David. *Baseball: Legends and Lore* (1995).

Chafets, Zev. *Cooperstown Confidential: Heroes, Rogues, and the Inside Story of the Baseball Hall of Fame* (2009).

Clark, Dick, and Larry Lester, eds. *The Negro Leagues Book* (1994).

Clemens, Roger, with Peter Gammons. *Rocket Man: The Roger Clemens Story* (1987).

Coleman, Ken, and Dan Valenti. *The Impossible Dream Remembered: The 1967 Red Sox* (1987).

Costas, Bob. *Fair Ball: A Fan's Case for Baseball* (2000).

303

Creamer, Roger W. *Babe: The Legend Comes to Life* (1992).

_____. *Baseball in '41: A Celebration of the "Best Baseball Season Ever"—In the Year America Went to War* (1991).

_____. *Stengel: His Life and Times* (1996).

cummings, andré douglas pond, and Anne Marie Lofaso, eds. *Reversing Field: Examining Commercialization, Labor, Gender, and Race in 21st Century Sports Law* (2010).

D'Antonio, Michael. *Forever Blue* (2009).

Davis, Timothy, Alfred D. Mathewson, and Kenneth L. Shropshire, ed. *Sports and the Law: A Modern Anthology* (1999).

Delaney, Kevin J., and Rick Eckstein. *Public Dollars, Private Stadiums: The Battle Over Building Sports Stadiums* (2003).

DeMause, Neil, and Joanna Cagan. *Field of Schemes: How the Great Stadium Swindle Turns Public Money into Private Profit* (2008).

Deveney, Sean. *The Original Curse: Did the Cubs Throw the 1918 World Series to Babe Ruth's Red Sox and Incite the Black Sox Scandal?* (2009).

DiMaggio, Dom, with Gill Gilbert. *Real Grass, Real Heroes* (1990).

Durso, Joseph. *Baseball and the American Dream* (1986).

Echevarria, Roberto Gonzalez. *The Pride of Havana: A History of Cuban Baseball* (1999).

Eig, Jonathan. *Opening Day: The Story of Jackie Robinson's First Season* (2007).

Einstein, Charles, ed. *The Fireside Book of Baseball* (1956).

_____. *The Second Fireside Book of Baseball* (1958).

Elias, Robert. *The Empire Strikes Out: How Baseball Sold U.S. Foreign Policy and Promoted the American Way Abroad* (2010).

Fainaru, Steve, and Ray Sanchez. *The Duke of Havana: Baseball, Cuba, and the Search for the American Dream* (2001).

Fainaru-Wada, Mark, and Lance Williams. *A Game of Shadows: Barry Bonds and the Steroid Scandal That Rocked Professional Sports* (2006).

Feinstein, John. *Play Ball: The Life and Troubled Times of Major League Baseball* (1993).

Felber, Bill. *The Book on the Book: A Landmark Inquiry into Which Strategies in the Modern Game Actually Work* (2005).

Fetter, Henry D. *Taking on the Yankees: Winning and Losing in the Business of Baseball, 1903–2003* (2003).

Frommer, Harvey. *Baseball's Greatest Rivalry: New York Yankees/Boston Red Sox* (1982).

_____. *Rickey & Robinson: The Men Who Broke Baseball's Color Barrier* (1982).

Fussman, Cal. *After Jackie: Pride, Prejudice, and Baseball's Forgotten Heroes: An Oral History* (2007).

Gammons, Peter. *Beyond the Sixth Game* (1986).

Gay, Timothy M. *Satch, Dizzy & Rapid Robert: The Wild Saga of Interracial Baseball Before Jackie Robinson* (2010).

Glanville, Doug. *The Game from Where I Stand: A Ballplayer's Inside View* (2010).

Gmelch, George. *Baseball Without Borders: The International Pastime* (2006).

Goldstein, Warren. *Playing for Keeps: A History of Early Baseball* (1989).

Golenbock, Peter. *Dynasty: The New York Yankees, 1949–1964* (1975).

_____. *Fenway: An Unexpurgated History of the Boston Red Sox* (1992).

Golenbock, Peter, with Sparky Lyle. *The Bronx Zoo* (1979).

Gould, Harold. *He Came from Gouldtown ... to Become a Philadelphia Star of the Negro Baseball Leagues* (2009).

Gould, Stephen J. *Triumph and Tragedy in Mudville: A Lifelong Passion for Baseball* (2003).

Gould, William B., IV. *Labored Relations: Law, Politics, and the NLRB—A Memoir* (2000).

_____. *A Primer on American Labor Law* (1982, 1986, 1993, 2004).

Grant, Jim "Mudcat." *The Black Aces: Baseball's Only African-American Twenty-Game Winners* (2007).

Greenwald, Hank. *This Copyrighted Broadcast* (1999).

Guevara, Arturo J. Marcano, and David P. Fidler. *Stealing Lives: The Globalization of Baseball and the Tragic Story of Alexis Quiroz* (2002).

Gutman, Dan. *Baseball's Greatest Games* (1994).

_____. *It Ain't Cheatin' If You Don't Get Caught: Scuffing, Corking, Spitting, Gunking, Razzing, and Other Fundamentals of Our National Pastime* (1990).

Halberstam, David. *October 1964* (1994).

_____. *Sports on the New York Radio* (1999).

_____. *Summer of '49* (1989).

_____. *The Teammates: A Portrait of Friendship* (2004).

Hall, Donald. *Fathers Playing Catch with Sons* (1985).

Helyar, John. *The Lords of the Realm: The Real History of Baseball* (1994).

Higgins, George V. *The Progress of the Seasons: Forty Years of Baseball in Our Town* (1989).

Hirsch, James S. *Willie Mays: The Life, the Legend* (2010).

Hirshberg, Al. *The Jackie Jensen Story* (1960).

_____. *What's the Matter with the Red Sox?* (1973).

Hogan, Lawrence D. *Shades of Glory: The Negro Leagues and the Story of African-American Baseball* (2006).

Holtzman, Jerome, ed. *Fielder's Choice: An Anthology of Baseball Fiction* (1991).

Honig, Donald. *Baseball When the Grass Was Real: Baseball from the Twenties to the Forties Told by the Men Who Played It* (1993).

James, Bill. *How Bill James Changed Our View of Baseball: By Colleagues, Critics, Competitors and Just Plain Fans* (2007).

_____. *The New Bill James Historical Baseball Abstract* (2001).

_____. *The Politics of Glory: How Baseball's Hall of Fame Really Works* (1994).

Johnson, Lloyd, and Miles Wolff. *The Encyclopedia of Minor League Baseball* (1997).

Kahn, Roger. *The Boys of Summer* (1972).

_____. *Good Enough to Dream* (1985).

_____. *The Head Game: Baseball Seen from the Pitcher's Mound* (2000).

_____. *Memories of Summer: When Baseball Was an Art, and Writing about It a Game* (1997).

_____. *October Men: Reggie Jackson, George Steinbrenner, Billy Martin, and the Yankees' Miraculous Finish in 1978* (2003).

_____. *A Season in the Sun* (1972).

Kinsella, W.P. *The Iowa Baseball Confederacy* (1986).

_____. *Shoeless Joe* (1982).

_____. *The Thrill of the Grass* (1984).

Klein, Alan. *Growing the Game: The Globalization of Major League Baseball* (2006).

Knoll, Roger G., and Andrew Zimbalist, ed. *Sports, Jobs & Taxes: The Economic Impact of Sports Teams and Stadiums* (1997).

Koppett, Leonard. *All About Baseball* (1967).

_____. *Koppett's Concise History of Major League Baseball* (1998).

_____. *The Man in the Dugout: Baseball's Top Managers and How They Got That Way* (expanded edition 2000).

_____. *The Rise and Fall of the Press Box* (2003).

_____. *Sports Illusion, Sports Reality: A Reporter's View of Sports, Journalism, and Society* (1981).

_____. *The Thinking Fan's Guide to Baseball* (2001, revised and updated).

Korr, Charles P. *The End of Baseball as We Knew It: The Players Union 1960–81* (2002).

Kuhn, Bowie. *Hardball: The Education of a Baseball Commissioner* (1988).

Kurkjian, Tim. *Is This a Great Game, or What?: From A-Rod's Heart to Zim's Head—My 25 Years in Baseball* (2007).

Kurlansky, Mark. *The Eastern Stars: How Baseball Changed the Dominican Town of San Pedro de Macoris* (2010).

Kurlantzick, Lewis, ed. *Legal Issues in Professional Baseball* (2006).

Lamb, David. *Stolen Season: A Journey Through America and Baseball's Minor Leagues* (1991).

Lamster, Mark. *Spaulding's World Tour* (2006).

Lanctot, Neil. *Negro League Baseball: The Rise and Ruin of a Black Institution* (2004).

Lautier, Jack. *Fenway Voices: From Smoky Joe to Rocket Roger* (1990).

Leavy, Jane. *The Last Boy: Mickey Mantle and the End of America's Childhood* (2010).

_____. *Sandy Koufax: A Lefty's Legacy* (2002).

Lehmann-Haupt, Christopher. *Me and DiMaggio: A Baseball Fan Goes in Search of His Gods* (1986).

Lewis, Michael. *Moneyball: The Art of Winning an Unfair Game* (2003).

Lieb, Frederick G. *The Boston Red Sox* (1947).

Linn, Ed. *The Great Rivalry: The Yankees and the Red Sox 1901–1990* (1991).

_____. *Hitter: The Life and Turmoils of Ted Williams* (1993).

Lowenfish, Lee. *Branch Rickey: Baseball's Ferocious Gentleman* (2007).

Lowenfish, Lee, and Tony Lupien. *The Imperfect Diamond: The Story of Baseball's Reserve System and the Men Who Fought to Change It* (1980).

Lowry, Philip J. *Green Cathedrals: The Ultimate Celebration of All Major League and Negro League Ballparks* (2006).

Malamud, Bernard. *The Natural* (1971).

Mandelbaum, Michael. *The Meaning of Sports: Why Americans Watch Baseball, Football and Basketball and What They See When They Do* (2004).

Marshall, William. *Baseball's Pivotal Era: 1945–1951* (1999).

Mathewson, Christy. *Pitching in a Pinch: Baseball from the Inside* (1912).

McKelvey, G. Richard. *Mexican Raiders in the Major Leagues: The Pasquel Brothers vs. Organized Baseball 1946* (2006).

Miller, Jon, et al. *Confessions of a Baseball Purist: What's Right and Wrong with Baseball as Seen from the Best Seat in the House* (1990).

Miller, Marvin. *A Whole Different Ballgame: The Sport and Business of Baseball* (1991).

Mitten, Matthew, et al. *Sports Law and Regulation* (2009).

Mnookin, Seth. *Feeding the Monster: How Money,*

Smarts, and Nerve Took a Team to the Top (2006).

Moffi, Larry. *The Conscience of the Game: Baseball's Commissioners from Landis to Selig* (2006).

_____. *This Side of Cooperstown: An Oral History of Major League Baseball in the 1950s* (1996).

Moffi, Larry, and Jonathan Konstadt. *Crossing the Line: Black Major Leaguers 1947–1959* (1994).

Montville, Leigh. *The Big Bam: The Life and Times of Babe Ruth* (2006).

_____. *Ted Williams: The Biography of an American Hero* (2004).

_____. *Why Not Us?: The 86-Year Journey of the Boston Red Sox Fans from Unparalleled Suffering to the Promised Land of the 2004 World Series* (2004).

Obojski, Robert. *The Rise of Japanese Baseball Power* (1975).

Okrent, Daniel. *Nine Innings: The Anatomy of a Baseball Game* (1985).

Panek, Richard. *Waterloo Diamonds* (1995).

Pesky, Johnny, et al. *Diary of a Red Sox Season* (2007).

Peterson, Robert. *Only the Ball was White* (1970).

Pollock, Alan J. *Barnstorming to Heaven: Syd Pollock and His Great Black Teams* (2006).

Quirk, James, and Rodney Fort. *Hard Ball: The Abuse of Power in Pro-Team Sports* (2000).

Rampersad, Arnold. *Jackie Robinson: A Biography* (1998).

Reaves, Joseph A. *Taking in a Game: A History of Baseball in Asia* (2004).

Riley, Dan, ed. *The Red Sox Reader: 30 Years of Musings on Baseball's Most Amusing Team* (1987).

Ritter, Lawrence S. *The Glory of Their Times: The Story of the Early Days of Baseball Told by the Men who Played It* (1966).

Roberts, Robin, and C. Paul Rogers III. *The Whiz Kids and the 1950 Pennant* (1996).

Roberts, Selina. *A-Rod: The Many Lives of Alex Rodriguez* (2009).

Robinson, Jackie, as told to Alfred Duckett. *I Never Had It Made* (1972).

Robinson, Rachel. *Jackie Robinson: An Intimate Portrait* (1996).

Rogosin, Donn, *Invisible Men: Life in Baseball's Negro Leagues* (1995).

Rose, Pete, and Roger Kahn. *Pete Rose: My Story* (1989).

Rosentraub, Mark S. *Major League Losers: The Real Cost of Sports and Who's Paying for It* (1997).

Rust, Art, with Edna Rust. *Recollections of a Baseball Junkie* (1985).

Sands, Jack, and Peter Gammons. *Coming Apart at the Seams* (1993).

Schell, Michael. *Baseball's All-Time Best Sluggers: Adjusted Batting Performance from Strikeouts to Home Runs* (2005).

Schwarz, Allan. *The Numbers Game: Baseball's Lifelong Fascination with Statistics* (2004).

Seidel, Michael. *Ted Williams: A Baseball Life* (2000).

Seymour, Harold. *Baseball: The Early Years* (1960).

_____. *Baseball: The Golden Age* (1971).

_____. *Baseball: The People's Game* (1990).

Shapiro, Michael. *Bottom of the Ninth* (2009).

Shaughnessy, Dan. *The Curse of the Bambino* (1990).

Shropshire, Kenneth L. *In Black and White: Race and Sports in America* (1996).

Shropshire, Kenneth L., and Timothy Davis. *The Business of Sports Agents* (2003).

Simon, Scott. *Jackie Robinson and the Integration of Baseball* (2002).

Simon, Tom, ed. *Deadball Stars of the National League* (2004).

Smith, Curt. *Voices of the Game: The First Full-Scale Overview of Baseball Broadcasting, 1921 to the Present* (1987).

Smith, Robert. *Baseball in the Afternoon: Tales from a Bygone Era* (1993).

Snyder, Brad. *A Well-Paid Slave: Curt Flood's Fight for Free Agency in Professional Sports* (2006).

Solomon, Burt. *Where They Ain't* (1999).

Sommers, Paul. *Diamonds Are Forever: The Business of Baseball* (1992).

Starr, Bill. *Clearing the Bases: Baseball Then & Now* (1989).

Staten, Vince. *Why Is the Foul Pole Fair?: Answers to 101 of the Most Perplexing Baseball Questions* (2004).

Stott, Jon C. *Leagues of Their Own: Independent Professional Baseball, 1993–2000* (2001).

_____. *Minor Leagues, Major Boom: Local Professional Baseball Revitalized* (2004).

Stout, Glenn, and Richard A. Johnson. *Red Sox Century: One Hundred Years of Red Sox Baseball* (2000).

Sullivan, Neil J. *The Diamond Revolution: The Prospects for Baseball After the Collapse of Its Ruling Class* (1992).

_____. *The Dodgers Move West* (1987).

_____. *The Minors: The Struggles and the Triumph of Baseball's Poor Relation from 1876 to the Present* (1990).

Svrluga, Barry. *National Pastime: Sports, Politics, and the Return of Baseball to Washington, D.C.* (2006).

Szymanski, Stefan, and Andrew Zimbalist. *Na-*

tional Pastime: How Americans Play Baseball and the Rest of the World Plays Soccer* (2005).

Thiel, Art. *Out of Left Field: How the Mariners Made Baseball Fly in Seattle* (2003).

Thompson, Teri, et al. *American Icon: The Fall of Roger Clemens and the Rise of Steroids in America's Pastime* (2009).

Thorn, John. *Baseball in the Garden of Eden* (2011).

Tiant, Luis, and Joe Fitzgerald. *El Tiante: The Luis Tiant Story* (1976).

Tofel, Richard J. *A Legend in the Making: The New York Yankees in 1939* (2002).

Tolan, Sandy. *Me and Hank: A Boy and His Hero, Twenty-Five Years Later* (2000).

Torre, Joe, and Tom Verducci. *The Yankee Years* (2009).

Turbow, Jason, and Michael Duca. *The Baseball Codes: Beanballs, Sign Stealing, and Bench-Clearing Brawls: The Unwritten Rules of America's Pastime* (2010).

Turner, Frederick. *When the Boys Came Back: Baseball and 1946* (1996).

Tye, Larry. *Satchel: The Life and Times of an American Legend* (2009).

Tygiel, Jules. *Extra Bases: Reflections on Jackie Robinson, Race & Baseball History* (2002).

_____. *Jackie Robinson and His Legacy* (1984).

_____. *Past Time: Baseball as History* (2000).

Vaccaro, Mike. *The First Fall Classic: The Red Sox, the Giants, and the Cast of Players, Pugs and Politics Who Reinvented the World Series* (2009).

Vecsey, George. *Baseball: A History of America's Favorite Game* (2008).

_____. *Stan Musial: An American Life* (2011).

Verducci, Tom. *Inside Baseball: The Best of Tom Verducci* (2006).

Vincent, Fay. *It's What's Inside the Lines That Counts: Baseball Stars of the 1970s and 1980s Talk About the Game They Loved* (The Baseball Oral History Project, 2010).

_____. *The Last Commissioner: A Baseball Valentine* (2007).

_____. *The Only Game in Town: Baseball Stars of the 1930s and 1940s Talk About the Game They Loved* (The Baseball Oral History Project, 2007).

_____. *We Would Have Played for Nothing: Baseball Stars of the 1950s and 1960s Talk About the Game They Loved* (The Baseball Oral History Project, reprint edition, 2009).

Virtue, John. *South of the Color Barrier* (2008).

Waller, Spencer Weber, et al., eds. *Baseball and the American Legal Mind* (1995).

Weber, Bruce. *As They See 'Em: A Fan's Travels in the Land of Umpires* (2009).

Weiler, Paul C. *Leveling the Playing Field: How the Law Can Make Sports Better for Fans* (2000).

Weiler, Paul C., and Gary Roberts. *Sports and the Law* (2004).

Wendel, Tim. *The New Face of Baseball: The One-Hundred-Year Rise and Triumph of Latinos in America's Favorite Sport* (2003).

Werber, Bill, with C. Paul Rogers III. *Memories of a Ballplayer* (2001).

White, G. Edward. *Creating the National Pastime: Baseball Transforms Itself, 1903–1953* (1996).

Whitford, David. *Playing Hardball: The High Stakes Battle for Baseball's New Franchises* (1993).

Whiting, Robert. *The Chrysanthemum and the Bat: The Game Japanese Play* (1977).

_____. *The Meaning of Ichiro: The New Wave from Japan and the Transformation of Our National Pastime* (2004).

_____. *You Gotta Have Wa* (1989).

Will, George F. *Men at Work: The Craft of Baseball* (1990).

Williams, Ted, with John Underwood. *My Turn at Bat: The Story of My Life* (1969).

Winfield, Dave. *Dropping the Ball: Baseball's Troubles and How We Can and Must Solve Them* (2007).

Winfield, Dave, with Tom Parker. *Winfield: A Player's Life* (1988).

Wollett, Don. *Getting on Base: Unionism in Baseball* (2008).

Wright. Craig R., and Tom House. *The Diamond Appraised: A World Class Theorist & a Major-League Coach Square Off on Timeless Topics in the Game of Baseball* (1989).

Yastrzemski, Carl, with Al Hirshberg. *YAZ* (1968).

Zimbalist, Andrew. *Baseball and Billions: A Probing Look Inside the Big Business of Our National Pastime* (1992).

_____. *In the Best Interest of Baseball? The Revolutionary Reign of Bud Selig* (2006).

_____. *May the Best Team Win: Baseball Economics and Public Policy* (1984, 2003).

Index

Numbers in **bold italics** indicate pages with photographs.